MYTHS
OF
MIDDLE INDIA

MYTHS OF MIDDLE INDIA

VERRIER ELWIN

GYAN

Published by

Gyan Publishing House
5, Ansari Road
Daryaganj, New Delhi-110002
Phone: 011-47034999, 9811692060
E-mail: books@gyanbooks.com

Distribution Network
gyanbooks.com
India, USA, Canada, UK, Australia

ISBN: 978-93-6433-282-8 (PB)
First Published, 1949

2nd Impression 2024

Printed at: Gyan Press, Delhi.

MYTHS OF MIDDLE INDIA
AUTHOR:VERRIER ELWIN

MYTHS OF MIDDLE INDIA

SPECIMENS OF
THE ORAL LITERATURE OF MIDDLE INDIA

MYTHS OF MIDDLE INDIA

VERRIER ELWIN
M.A., D.Sc. (Oxon)
Fellow of the Royal Asiatic Society of Bengal
Fellow of the National Institute of Sciences of India
Hon. Member of the Ecole Française d'Extrême-Orient

INDIAN BRANCH
GEOFFREY CUMBERLEGE
OXFORD UNIVERSITY PRESS

TO

JOE

In all our investigations into the origins of customs we are standing on holy ground—we are standing at the Gate of the Primitive History of Mankind—at the psychological source of all that is highest and noblest in man.

—WINTERNITZ

CONTENTS

PART ONE: MAN AND THE UNIVERSE

	Introduction	vi
I.	The Creation of the World and Mankind	3
II.	Sun, Moon and Stars	51
III.	Air and Water	78
IV.	Fire	106

PART TWO: THE NATURAL WORLD

V.	Metals and Minerals	119
VI.	Grass, Flowers and Trees	129
VII.	Arthropods	147
VIII.	Reptiles	163
IX.	Fish	174
X.	Birds	181
XI.	Mammals	200

PART THREE: HUMAN LIFE

XII.	The Human Body	235
XIII.	The Invention of Implements	300
XIV.	Food	312
XV.	Tobacco	323
XVI.	Mahua Spirit	335
XVII.	Disease	344
XVIII.	Psycho-Pathology: The Vagina Dentata Legend	354
XIX.	The Coming of Death	410

PART FOUR: HUMAN INSTITUTIONS

XX.	Some Aspects of Religion	431
XXI.	Witchcraft and Magic	443
XXII.	Custom and Taboo	469
XXIII.	Festival, Dance and Song	479

Appendixes :—

Glossary of Tribes and Castes	495
Book-List	499
Motif Index	505
General Index	530

INTRODUCTION

THIS book assembles specimens of myths of origin from widely diverse localities in Middle India. As the main title of the series suggests, it attempts nothing more than to present samples and specimens of an oral literature whose variety and extent is still largely unsuspected by scholars. No one individual could cover the whole area or investigate the ideas of so many million people diversified into so many castes and tribes. But the samples given here, which are taken from a very large area, will give at least an impression of how these people think and live.

There are no formal geographical boundaries of Middle India. In the text I have confined myself to myths from the Central Provinces, the Chhattisgarh and Orissa States[1] and western Orissa. This is a compact block of territory in which I have toured widely, though not, of course, exhaustively. All the numbered texts have been recorded by me in the course of my ordinary field-work and nearly all are new; in a few cases where, for the sake of completeness I have reproduced passages from my other books, I have indicated the fact immediately below the heading.

But this territory is not the whole of Middle India and in the introduction to each chapter I have included such additional myths as have been recorded by other writers. I have drawn these from the adjacent areas of Bihar, Central India, Mirzapur, Rajputana and neighbouring Districts. In a few cases I have drawn parallels, where these have seemed relevant, from the Punjab, Bombay, Southern India and Assam.[2] There has been a considerable amount of diffusion throughout India. Even Assam has now begun to have its influence on the Middle Indian tribesmen, for many of them go for shorter or longer periods to work in the Tea Gardens and there come in contact with their fellows from different parts of India.

Not only have the tribes reacted on each other, but they have borrowed from the common sub-Puranic and Epic tradition that

[1] This book was completed in 1945, long before the administrative changes that have redrawn the map of India. The States of Bastar, Bonai, Keonjhar and Pal Lahara are now (1949) merged in the neighbouring Provinces.

[2] But I have only permitted myself the luxury of drawing parallels with mythological traditions outside India in the chapters on the Human Body and the Vagina Dentata. I have taken this latitude because of the rarity of these legends in our records and because in the field of psycho-pathology such comparisons may be of some practical value.

pervades the whole of village India. For in India the situation is a little different from that in the ethnographic provinces of savagery. Behind the pre-literate peoples there is the vast mass of Hindu literature, much of which has now itself become an oral literature, travelling from place to place not in book form but on the lips of wandering sadhus, singers of ballads, or travelling merchants.

The propriety of combining the myths of so many different tribes in a single volume may be questioned. All over Middle India we have primitive civilizations in a state of decay. Individual endogamous units still preserve their identity, but most tribal customs have been smoothed and flattened out into a life and way of thinking that is in the main common to all.

It is with this common life of custom and religion (interrupted, of course, at every turn by personal idiosyncrasy) that this collection deals. Wherever a legend has a special functional importance for a particular tribe the fact has been noted and explained. But in general, legends that bear on customs peculiar to a tribe have been omitted for record elsewhere. For example, it was obviously better that the Muria legend that vitalizes the ghotul dormitory-club should be in my book on that subject and not in this; but I have reproduced the Muria myths of Sun and Moon and the coming of death because there is nothing specifically *Muria* about the tribe's ideas on these subjects and they show interesting parallels and contrasts to the stories of other peoples. So too the Juang myth of the leaf-dress, the Agaria myths of iron, the Bondo stories about nudity and shaven heads, the Kond myths of human sacrifice, the Pardhan account of the origin of ritual beggary are so intimately connected with customs peculiar to these tribes alone that I have not printed them here, for they would have demanded disproportionate space for their explanation and could not be properly understood except in the whole tribal setting.

But there are a score of subjects on which all the tribesmen are agreed. Ideas about the Creation of the World have been largely standardized under sub-Puranic influence. Myths of fire and death receive fresh and original treatment from different tribes, but beliefs and customs are generally similar throughout the area. There is no variation in the part that rice or millet plays in the life of a Gond, a Juang, a Gadaba or a Muria. Right across the *Bassia latifolia* area the myths about this useful tree are strikingly similar in general character and atmosphere, though there are equally significant contrasts and differences. My collection, therefore, may be found of value not only for the light it throws on the mentality and customs of the great mass of aboriginals throughout

Middle India, but it will also provide material for the study of the diffusion of legends and will indicate how far the influence of the all-pervading Hindu tradition has proceeded.

The book may, in fact, be regarded as a sort of Aboriginal Purana. Like a Purana, it abounds in fantastic stories, unreal and unusual names and far-fetched analogies. Like a Purana, it reveals without embarrassment or self-consciousness theories of the origin of life and the sexual function. This means that this volume is the least 'popular' of the series in which it appears. I have thought it my duty to record the myths exactly as they were given to me without amendment. This has necessitated printing some unsavoury and many curious passages. But these are probably the most important in the book, for they reveal psychological conflicts and stresses that have hitherto not been noticed for the Indian aboriginal, although they have been largely explored among the tribes of North America.

Our ideas about the importance and function of mythology have been considerably revised in the last few decades. It is probably safe to say that no one now seriously believes that a myth is a piece of bad history written in symbolical language. Equally out of date is the once popular theory that the myth is a speculative symbolization of natural phenomena. Few people today would endorse the view, which seems to have been held by S. C. Roy, that myths are merely a form of recreation. Roy believed that the Birhor myth, for example, was 'one of the very few recreations in the strenuous life of these unfortunate people'[1] and speaking of the Kharia he says, 'Old men, in their moments of leisure, impart their traditional knowledge and ideas in the form of folk-tales and myths.'[2]

Malinowski was one of the first to deride the view that myths were an attempt to explain or make intelligible abstract ideas. 'As to any explanatory function of the myths there is no problem which they cover, no curiosity which they satisfy, no theory which they contain'.[3] Lord Raglan also uses to the full his armoury of wit to mock and ridicule those who believe that a myth is anything other than a narrative linked to a rite.

A great deal of this cathartic mockery was necessary and has had an admirable effect. It has established the myth, not as a relic of the past, but as a living reality vitalizing and to some extent controlling the present. 'Myth as it exists in a savage community, that is, in its living primitive form, is not merely a story told but a

[1] Roy, *The Birhors*, 398.
[2] Roy, *The Kharias*, 414.
[3] B. Malinowski, *Myth in Primitive Psychology* (London, 1926), 79.

reality lived. It is not of the nature of fiction, such as we read today in a novel, but it is a living reality, believed to have once happened in primeval times, and continuing ever since to influence the world and human destinies. This myth is to the savage what, to a fully believing Christian, is the Biblical story of Creation, of the Fall, of the Redemption '.[1] I have developed this theme at considerable length in *The Baiga*, pointing out how ' myth does far more than explain the Baiga's institutions ; it is their motive power and their authorization. When a Baiga is summoned to control a man-eating tiger, he faces this dangerous task with the more courage because he knows that the duty has been his from the beginning. When he comes to perform magic to Dharti Mata, and Thakur Deo on behalf of Gond or fellow-Baiga cultivators, he recites the myth of the creation of the world and reminds his hearers of the unique share that his tribe had in it. When he is overwhelmed by his own poverty, he comforts himself and his family by reminding them that to be poor and to live close to the earth was the voluntary choice of his great ancestors, their glory and not their shame. The driving of the nail, the offering of animal sacrifice, the cutting of *bewar*, the worship of Thakur Deo, the cure of disease, the war against witchcraft, the embarrassments of menstruation, the shame of barrenness, all trace their origin or maintain their credit in what are believed to be historic events which established them as part of the social order. . . . These myths are not just interesting stories tacked on to the fringe of Baiga life. They are alive: every one of them is continually being put into action. Why does the Baiga eat with the Gond and no one else ? He remembers that it was only the Gond who at the beginning of the world would eat with him. Why does the Baiga, the orthodox Baiga, wear so little, why does he not ride on a horse, or touch cowdung, why did he never practise human sacrifice, why does Narayan Deo live on the threshold of the house ? All these matters are not so much explained in the myth, as constituted a part of the social and religious order. The myth breathes life into ancient custom ; it makes the unintelligible real. The modern Baiga feels that Nanga Baiga and Nanga Baigin are his friends, he knows them so intimately. The myth makes everything contemporary '.[2]

Frazer has emphasized the connexion between myth and magic. ' We shall probably not err in assuming that many myths, which we now know only as myths, had once their counterpart in magic ; in other words, that they used to be acted as a means of producing

[1] ibid., 21.
[2] *The Baiga*, 305 f.

in fact the events which they describe in figurative language. Ceremonies often die out while myths survive, and thus we are left to infer the dead ceremony from the living myth '.[1] Nowadays few of the myths of Middle India are linked with any surviving ritual. The stories about Karam Raja are, it is true, recited (if anyone is sober enough to remember them) during the Karam Festival; the stories of the origin of Narayan Deo may be repeated during the sacrifice of the Laru Kaj; many of the myths and legends of the Baiga are mentioned during their ceremonies; the Bison-horn Maria recite stories about the origin of the sago palm when, before tapping, they sacrifice crabs and fish. But the full stories are seldom recited in detail. They are rather referred to in intimate and almost casual fashion in the course of spell or prayer. I remember sitting by a Baiga priest during a ceremony to increase the crop of millet in a Gond village, and noticing how he continually referred to Bara Bathi Bengala in his recitation of spells. Later he told me that the references to this mysterious country, where the best and strongest liquor was to be had in abundance, were intended to ensure that the millet grew with the same abundance as the liquor there was distilled. This is a good example of the way the myth is part of the everyday life of the people and how even a passing reference to it may have magical potency. The personages in the myths, who seem so fantastic to us, are part of the ordinary routine of village civilization and are often more readily remembered than a man's own ancestors. The Pardhans of Patangarh are vague about their own genealogies, but they can give every detail of the lineage of Hirakhan and Mara Kshattri.

I think that Malinowski and Raglan go too far in their insistence that a myth is never intended to explain anything. Halliday, on the contrary, has said that ' myths represent the answers given by the human imagination to the problem of how things came to be. How were Earth and Sky created or how did evil enter the world? '[2] Of this Lord Raglan says, ' This picture is an utterly false one. The savage is interested in nothing which does not impinge upon his senses, and never has a new idea even about the most familiar things. In this he is like our own illiterates. At the elementary schools some knowledge of more remote subjects is impressed upon them with the aid of books, but as soon as their school days are over the majority relapse into the mental state in which savages remain permanently. It has been held that the curiosity which is displayed in some degree by all human beings is evidence of ability to

[1] J. G. Frazer, *The Golden Bough*, (London, 1911-15), ix, 374.
[2] Halliday, *Indo-European Folk-tales and Greek Legend*, 5.

speculate; is the interest which a herd of cattle displays in a strange dog evidence of ability to speculate? Professor Halliday's myth-makers are filled with curiosity about the origin of the universe and of evil in it, but such curiosity is not merely unknown among savages, it is extremely rare among the civilized. How many of us have tried seriously to understand the theory of Relativity and the doctrine of the Atonement? I wonder whether Professor Halliday can explain why the grass is green, and whether Professor Rose has reflected imaginatively upon the causes of volcanic activity. Anyhow, the savage attempts nothing of the kind'.[1]

I can only suppose that Lord Raglan's knowledge of savages is similar to that which a strange dog would have of a herd of cattle. My own experience of savages is that they are not nearly so bovine as they appear at first sight and, far from having no curiosity about the origin of things, some of them seem to spend a lot of their time in the most extraordinary speculations. It is quite possible that Professor Halliday could not explain why the grass is green. I too have never thought about it. But there is no mystery about it in the mind of Dani the Pardhan or of the Bondo who describe how grass began to grow as a result of a woman's violent attempt to avoid incest with her brother. Lord Raglan has fallen into the error of supposing that because modern man has largely specialized his knowledge, the savage must have done the same. Professor Halliday may not know why the grass is green, but he could give us a very good explanation of matters that lay within his own province. Einstein might not be able to explain the doctrine of the Atonement, but he could tell us all about Relativity. The 'savages' known to me, however, are able to tell me not only all about some primitive equivalent of the Atonement and Relativity and why the grass is green, but they have the most detailed, even if totally erroneous, information on a score of matters of which I have been largely ignorant all my life. The aboriginals of Middle India are consumed with curiosity about everything in the world and the reader of this book will receive from them many and sometimes rather pathetic attempts to explain what is the truth behind things.

The fact is that we must not try to tie mythology down too much. Some myths are associated with magic and ritual. Some are simply explanations and attempts at a sort of science. Some are frankly 'scientific romances' and may be intended for little more than amusement. Others again are serious and vital realities that dominate the life of a tribe.

[1] Raglan, 127.

An interesting question is raised by the great variety of names in these myths. Where do they come from and what are we to make of them? Some of course are taken direct from the old Hindu records. Rama, Lakshman, Mahadeo, Parvati, Bhimsen are conventional Hindu names that often cover much older and more primitive personages. Other names echo those of characters, such as Guru Gorakhnath, who are famous throughout village India. There are many others whose source I cannot trace. Some of them are the result of puns; others are echo-words. Others again, in the words of Andrew Lang, 'uprise from a mood of playful and erratic fancy'. The story of Kach-Mach Raja illustrates a very common tendency in name-making. The name is supposed to be derived from a word (*kach*) meaning tortoise combined with a word (*mach*) meaning fish, for the Raja was born as a result of the union of a tortoise and a fish and it is not impossible that the story grew up out of the word rather than the word from the story. For since the fish and the tortoise are united in a name the story-teller would have us believe that they were once united in fact and that the Raja was the fruit.

Throughout, references to literature are made in the simplest way possible. Except in a few cases, where only one reference to a work is made and where it is then described in full, all other quotations should be traced to the Bibliography. The author's name alone followed by the page number is sufficient for most references; where, as in the case of S. C. Roy, a number of books by the same author are quoted, I give in each case his name and short title; I refer to my own books by the title only. The Bibliography is not a list of all works dealing with Indian mythology; it is a working list of books mentioned in the text and is provided simply for the reader's convenience. At the end of Chapter XVIII, however, I give a detailed and, I hope, fairly complete Bibliography of works where references may be found to the Vagina Dentata Legend.

I had originally intended to include in this volume the myths collected in Orissa, and to end it with a discoursive catalogue of names and places mentioned in the text. But the book outgrew itself twice over, and I was forced to put most of the Orissa myths into a separate volume, *Tribal Myths of Orissa*, which will be the fifth of the series. But in order that the readers of this book may have comparative material conveniently at hand, I have allowed to remain here all the myths I have, including those from Orissa, on the Creation of the World, the Coming of Death, the Human Body and the Vagina Dentata. On the other hand the myths centering round the sago palm will go into the Orissa volume, for they are more suitable there. In a few cases, I have retained an Orissa myth which showed obvious affinities to stories from the Central Provinces.

The sixth volume of this series, which I plan to call *Aboriginal Purana*, will be a Discoursive Catalogue (the expression is Grierson's) of the mythological names and places occurring in the sub-Puranic oral literature of Middle India. This book will also be an Index to its predecessors, both those in this series and my other monographs, and will attempt to give exhaustive references to all the literature on each topic with which it deals.

I must express my gratitude to the Warden and Fellows of Merton College for financial assistance which enabled me to undertake the work of collection and translation. The book has been many years now in the making. Sundarlal and Gulabdas have had, as always, a big share in it, but two new assistants—Chain Singh and Saunu, the one a Dhulia, the other a Pardhan—gave me very valuable help. Chain Singh especially adventured far into unknown territory—the wilds of Matin and Uprora, the highlands of Drug, the unfamiliar hills of Ganjam. My interpreters, Sampat Singh for Gondi, Gandarbo for Saora and Dinabhandu for Kui, were faithful, accurate and painstaking. To Shamrao Hivale I owe the discovery of a number of good tales. To these friends and companions of my travels I tender my sincerest thanks.

VERRIER ELWIN

PATANGARH
MANDLA DISTRICT
INDIA
1 JULY 1946

PART ONE: MAN AND THE UNIVERSE

CHAPTER ONE

THE CREATION OF THE WORLD AND MANKIND

ALL the schools of philosophy, the great epic, every *Purana*[1] bear witness to the fascination which the problem of creation has had for the speculative Indian mind. The *Vedas* gave the world the sublime Hymn of Creation—

> Non-being then existed not nor being;
> There was no air, nor sky that is beyond it.
> What was concealed? Wherein? In whose protection?
> And was there deep unfathomable water?[2]

This stress on water—'without distinctive marks, this all was water'—is repeated in the *Upanishads*. Prominent in their teaching, says Hume, is a cosmogenic theory 'which was advanced among the early Greeks by Thales and which was also a widely prevailing Semitic idea, namely, that the original stuff of the world was water. Thus in the *Brihad-Aranyaka Upanishad* (5. 5) we find it stated that "in the beginning this world was just Water". "It is just Water solidified that is this earth, that is the atmosphere, that is the sky, that is gods and men, that is animals and birds, grass and trees, beasts, together with worms, flies and ants; all these are just Water solidified" (*Chandogya Upanishad*, 7. 10. 1)... In the later *Katha* a more philosophic theory of the world-ground was added on to this older theory that water was the primal entity: "Atman was born of old from the waters." Somewhat similar combinations of the earlier and later theories are made in the *Aitareya Upanishad* (1. 1. 3) where Atman, after creating the waters, "from the waters drew forth and shaped a person", from whose members the different parts of the world and of man emanated.'[3]

There is no room here to trace this conception down through history to the modern aboriginal, but we may briefly note, in view of parallels to be drawn later, that—according to the *Ramayana*—in the beginning all was water and the earth was formed beneath it. Then arose Brahma and becoming a boar raised up the earth. The doctrine of the four Yugas, however, somewhat complicates

[1] 'All the *Puranas* are required to have a special section devoted to the treatment of creation and dissolution.'—Dasgupta, 496.

[2] Macdonell, *Hymns*, 19.

[3] Hume, 10. In my quotations from Macdonell, Estlin Carpenter, Hume and other Sanskritists I have modified the spelling of words in accordance with the use adopted for these volumes.

this picture of the primal waters. The universe becomes subject to a ceaseless rhythm of creation and dissolution. Each of the Yugas ends with a general conflagration which is quenched by rain and flood. The world then dissolves again into a vast ocean. The Supreme Universal Soul, says the *Vishnu Purana*, which existed alone at the beginning, now reposes on his mighty serpent couch in the midst of the deep. After a time he awakes and becomes Brahma, the active author of creation, who springs from a lotus growing out of Vishnu's navel.

The aboriginal myths[1] reflect both the earlier and the later traditions. In some of them the world develops from the primal ocean directly and there is no hint of a previous world that has been destroyed. But in others, the starting-point is the submergence of the old world beneath the waters and the need of creating a new earth to be the habitation of mankind. Let us examine the older tradition first.

The opening of the Baiga legend is almost classical in tone :

> In the beginning there was nothing but water, water, water. There was no voice of god, no voice of ghost, no wind, no rocks, no paths, no jungle. As the sky is now, so was water then. On a great lotus-leaf, that drifted here and there on the waters, sat Bhagavan. There was no fruit or flower to his life : he was alone.[2]

The Bhuiya story begins :

> In the beginning there existed only God or *Dharma* whose visible representation was the Sun with the Moon. Then there appeared an ocean of water of the depth of seven times the height of a man with upraised hands.[3]

The Birhor :

> In the beginning all was water. A lotus plant stood with its head above the waters. Singbonga or the Supreme Spirit was then in the nether regions. He came up to the surface of the waters through the hollow of the stem of the lotus plant. He took his seat upon the lotus flower.[4]

The Chero :

> In the beginning there was all water with a lotus flower blooming over it. One day Bhagwan who was then living in the Under World came up to the surface on the back of the tortoise.[5]

[1] It is remarkable that the Chenchu and Vedda both seem to lack myths of the Creation of the world.—Fürer-Haimendorf, 201; Seligmann, 322.

[2] *The Baiga*, 308.

[3] Roy, *The Hill Bhuiyas*, 262.

[4] Roy, *The Birhors*, 397.

[5] Agarwal, 205.

The Gond:

In the midst of the water, in the ocean, the Singamali birds, male and female, lived, and there upon the water they spread their nest, and there they laid two eggs. One egg was a full cubit and the other egg was one-and-a-quarter cubits long.[1]

The Munda:

In the beginning of Time, the face of the Earth was covered over with water. Singbonga, the Sun-god, brooded over the waters.[2]

The Santal:

In the beginning was Thakur Jiu. There was no land visible, all was covered with water.[3]

A similar picture of the origin of things is given in many of the stories in the text: this almost universal agreement suggests wide-spread epic or puranic influence.

Out of this primal ocean, the Creator proceeds to make the world. The reason for creation is not always clear. In the Baiga story, Bhagavan says, 'I am lonely: I want to make a world.' The Bhuiya and Juang legends imply that the earth was made so that there might be somewhere for mankind to live, and this—for all the stories are strongly anthropocentric—seems to be the general idea. Man is often found existing before the world, which has to be created for his sake.

There appear to be three main traditions of how the earth was made. In the first, it is supposed that some earth has been stolen and the Creator sends messengers to find it; when he has it, he spreads it out on the face of the waters. In the second, which resembles a very ancient Vedic conception, the earth comes into being through sacrifice. In the third, the world forms of its own accord, 'setting' like a pot of curds.

There are examples of all three traditions in the text: I will give here some additional instances which have been recorded elsewhere. The Baiga legend may be taken as typical. It is paralleled by Agaria and Gond stories. Bhagavan makes a crow and sends it to find earth. It falls on the back of Kakramal Kshattri, the great crab,[4] who takes it to the bottom of the ocean to force earth from Gichna Raja who has swallowed it.[5] They force it to vomit and it

[1] Trench, ii, 1. [2] Roy, *The Mundas*, App. v.

[3] Campbell, ii, 15.

[4] Wrongly called a tortoise in *The Baiga*, 309.

[5] This might be taken as implying a previous world which had been destroyed, but I think the Baiga idea is that just as there is mud at the bottom of a pond, so there must have been earth at the bottom of the primal ocean, and Gichna Raja the earthworm had swallowed this.

brings up twenty-one little balls of different kinds of earth. The crow takes these back to Bhagavan. Then Bhagavan undoes the earth from the crow's neck and puts it in his lap. Then he calls a young virgin. She makes a pot out of leaves, and puts the earth in it, and she churns it. For eight days and nine nights she churns till all is ready. Then Bhagavan rolls the earth out like a great thin *chapāti*, and spreads it on the face of the waters. There it begins to grow till it has covered all the waters.

Another Baiga legend, however, says that Bhagavan gave the earth back to the crow and told her to sow it like seed upon the face of the ocean. 'She flew here and there, she dropped the bits of earth in every part of the sea. After a few days the earth began to grow. There was some here and some there.'

A Bhil story, recorded by Koppers, is on similar lines, but includes the interesting motif that the Creator's own blood had to be added to the earth to make it spread and retain its firmness.

The Lord Bhagwan was the first to be born in a statue. Then Bhagwan thought within himself that in the world there was neither Earth nor Man. Then the Earth appeared to him in a dream and he went out in all directions to seek earth, and in so seeking he came to Gujarat. There he found two handfuls of earth and took them with him. Opening his hands on the way he saw that the earth had been melted into water. Then Bhagwan went once more on his way. In a dream the Earth said to him: 'Bhagwan, thou shalt not take two handfuls! Take rather seven pinches.' Then Bhagwan cut his little finger and applied blood to the seven pinches, and took them with him. Having come to an open place, he laid them down. From that spot the earth spread itself out in all four directions. Then Bhagwan made the five Pandaws, all the trees, water, day and night, moon and sun, animals and lastly man.[1]

The Birhor:

He then commanded the tortoise to bring up some clay. 'Go thou', said he, 'and bring up some clay from underneath the waters.' The tortoise inquired, 'Where shall I leave my house?' Singbonga ordered, 'Take your house with you.' The tortoise dived into the waters. It took up some clay and placed it on its back. In coming up, the clay was washed off the shell. And thus the tortoise failed. Singbonga now summoned the crab. The crab appeared. Singbonga told it, 'Go thou underneath the waters, and bring up some clay.' The crab dived down to the bottom of the waters, took up some clay in its legs. And so the crab too failed. Then Singbonga summoned the leech. The leech appeared. Singbonga told it, 'Go thou and bring me some clay from

[1] Koppers, 276. Koppers emphasizes that this story 'bears the stamp of Hindu thought' and that it 'in no way covers all that is believed by the Bhils on this subject.'

beneath the waters'. The leech dived down to the bottom of the ocean and devoured its fill of clay. It then came up to Singbonga and vomited out the clay from its stomach in the hand of Singbonga.

Singbonga pressed this clay between his hands just as diviners press rice between their hands for purposes of prognostication. Then Singbonga threw a bit of this clay in each of the four directions of the compass. And forthwith there arose on the surface of the waters a four-sided land mass. And thus was formed this earth of ours. The waters that receded to the four sides of this land mass became the seas. The earth was moist and uneven. Singbonga began to level the earth with an iron leveller. In the process of levelling the surface of the land with the leveller earth came to be heaped up at places, and these heaps became the hills and mountains, and the level lands the valleys and plains. Now Singbonga had with him all kinds of seeds. He scattered them around, and trees sprang up all over the earth.[1]

The Chero:

Bhagwan, having come to the surface of the ocean on the back of a tortoise, commanded the tortoise to bring some clay from the Under World, himself resting on the lotus flower in the meanwhile. The tortoise went to bring the clay and started with a heap on its back. But all the clay was washed off by the water in the course of the journey, so much so that by the time it came to the surface it had nothing left to offer to God. Thereupon God commanded the rat to get some clay, but it too failed in its duty. God being annoyed at the fruitless efforts of two of his servants asked his personal servant Garur to fly somewhere and get clay. The vulture flew and brought some clay in its mouth from heaven which it delivered to God. God pressed it in his hand and threw a portion of it in each of the four directions. And forthwith there arose on the surface of the water a four-sided land mass. And thus was formed this earth of ours.[2]

The Garhwali:

In the beginning there was neither earth, nor sky, nor water. Nirankar, the Guru, alone existed. The Guru rubbed his right side and from the sweat thereof a female vulture was born. The Guru rubbed his left side and from the sweat thereof a male vulture was produced. Thus the female was placed over the male. The name of the female vulture was Soni Garuri and of the male Brahma Garur. The male came to marry Soni Garuri. But Soni Garuri objected, saying that as they had been created by the same Guru they were brother and sister and could not marry. This she follows with taunting remarks about his ugly shape. Brahma Garur begins to weep. Soni Garuri repents and picks up the tear drops which fall from his eyes. The tears penetrate her womb and she becomes pregnant. Thereupon she flies to the abode of Brahma Garur and begs him to build a nest

[1] Roy, *The Birhors*, 397.

[2] Agarwal, 205.

for her to lay her eggs in. Garur now retorts with taunts as to her chastity and ends with: 'You are very ugly, I cannot accept you as my wife.' Soni in her turn begins to weep. Brahma Garur is moved to pity and says, 'There is neither earth nor water. Where can I build a nest for you? Come and lay your eggs on my wings.' Soni replies, 'You are the vehicle of Vishnu and would be polluted by my laying on your body.' The egg thereupon drops down and is divided into two. The lower half becomes the earth and the upper half the sky. The fluid inside the egg becomes the sea and the fleshy part the earth. Thus did Nirankar create the world.[1]

The Santal:

The Santal legend is also based on the idea of the solid earthen floor to the ocean, but here the world is not created as a result of bringing up samples of this earth, for the entire floor is raised. It is notable that human beings were created first and the earth was raised up so that they could have some place on which to rest.

Living in the water were Sole Hao (Sole Fish), Katkom (Crab), Lendet Kuar (Prince Earthworm), and Lendom Kuar. Thakur Jiu having called them ordered them to raise the earth above the water. Sole Hao said, 'I will raise the earth above the water,' but after repeated trials he was obliged to own his inability to do so. Then Katkom came, and said, 'I will do it,' but he also failed. He put his head under the water, and swallowed earth which passing through him fell upon the surface of the water, but immediately sank to the bottom again. Then Lendom Kuar said, 'Within the water resides Kachim Kuar (Prince Tortoise); if we fasten him at the four corners with chains, and then raise the earth on his back it will remain, and not fall into the water again.' Having secured Kachim Kuar with chains, Lendet Kuar raised the earth on his back, and in a short time there was an island in the middle of the waters. Thakur Jiu then caused a karam tree to spring up, and at the foot of the karam tree he caused sirom grass to grow. He then caused *dhobi* grass to spring up, after which he covered the earth with all kinds of trees and herbs. In this manner the earth became firm and stable.[2]

Not unlike this tradition is another which allows the world to come more or less of its own accord. A Raj-Nengi Pardhan myth describes the earth as 'forming, setting like curds on the face of the water. When the wind blew from the east, the world began to form towards the west. Then the wind changed and it formed to the east.' In a Gadaba story from Orissa, a stream of saliva trickles from the mouth of the primal potter. It spreads on the surface of the water and slowly sets and hardens till it has formed a

[1] Gariola, 39 f.

[2] Campbell, ii, 16 ff.

crust upon it. The Bhuiya describe how 'out of the depths of the ocean up came a mass of mud to a height of fourteen times the height of a man with upraised hands.'[1]

The most remarkable of the cosmogenic traditions of Middle India is a conception of creation by sacrifice or the transformation of some great personage into the world, an idea which—however crudely imagined and expressed—links the modern tribal mythologist with the author of the famous *Purusha-Sukta* in the *Rigveda*.[2] 'Far, far back out of the recesses of the Vedic cultus the figure of Maha-Purusha emerges as the symbol of creation by sacrifice. A vast cosmic Man, human in person but divine in nature, submits to be offered up by the gods. . . The Purusha has a thousand heads, a thousand eyes, a thousand feet, expressive of omniscience and omnipresence. He envelops the earth and transcends it; he is identical with the whole universe; he is the sum of all existence: he includes all that is and all that shall be. From this exalted Person spring all the objects and beings of the world. It is a strange haphazard catalogue. First came curds and butter, the adjuncts of the sacrifice itself; then animals, both wild and tame. The verses of the *Rigveda* followed, with their metres and sacrificial formulae. Horses came next, and all animals with two rows of teeth. From the divine mouth sprang the Brahmins, from the feet the Sudras; and last of all appeared the visible scene, moon and sun, Indra and Agni, air, sky, earth. Here is the first expression of the idea that creation is the self-limitation of a transcendent Person, who manifests himself in the realm of our experience, and thereby surrenders other modes of action, pledging himself to one fixed order for his creatures' good.'[3]

This was the beginning, and the macrocosmic idea of the world as a vast personage transformed is frequently repeated. The *Atharva-Veda* (10. 7. 32-34) describes the earth as the base of the highest Brahma, the air is his belly, the sky his head, the sun and moon his eyes, fire his mouth, the wind his breathing.[4] In the *Brihad-Aranyaka Upanishad* (1. 2) the demiurge Death dismembers himself. 'The eastern direction is his head. Yonder one and yonder one are the fore quarters. Likewise the western direction is his tail. Yonder one and yonder one are the hind quarters. South and north are the flanks. The sky is the back. The atmosphere is the belly. This (earth) is the chest. He stands firm in the waters.' The magnificent and mysterious opening of the

[1] Roy, *The Hill Bhuiyas*, 262.
[2] *Rigveda*, x. 90.
[3] Carpenter, 43.
[4] Hume, 23.

Aitareya Upanishad (1. 1) describes how fire comes from the mouth of the world person, 'from his nostrils the wind, from his eyes the sun, from his ears the quarters of heaven, from his skin plants and trees, from his heart the moon, from his navel death, from his male generative organ water.'[1] A later Upanishad—the *Mundaka*—describes 'the issue of all kinds of beings from the Imperishable, like sparks from a fire. From him, as he became personalized in creation, were born breath, and all organs of sense, ether, air, light, water, earth. Fire is his head; the sun and moon his eyes; the wind his breath; his heart the universe. From him come the devas, men, cattle, birds, the up and down breathings.'[2]

Modern tribal mythology reproduces this ancient and highly philosophic conception in two forms. In one the body of a person (who may be taken to represent the Maha-Purusha) is turned into the world; in the other, the world is established, or made firm, by the blood of a human sacrifice. We have come a long way, perhaps, from Vedic cosmogony, but we are in the same world: children are now playing with the stupendous speculations of the philosophers, but both children and philosophers belong to the same household.

Most of these stories occur in the text, and need only be indicated here. The Bhuiya myth (p. 28) gives a vivid account of the sacrifice of Parihar. 'The gods picked up his body and swung it round and round. His blood spurted out and wherever it fell into the water the earth was formed. His bones flew away and became the seven rocks. His hair turned into the seven trees.' And again, 'The boy's blood fell on the ground and it became solid. His legs turned into great trees, his arms into small trees, his fingers into shrubs, his hair into grass, his bones into rocks and stones. His head became the sun, his chest the moon, and his blood coloured the red earth.' An earlier Bhuiya legend, recorded by Roy, is a variant on our text.

Out of the depths of the ocean up came a mass of mud to a height of fourteen times the height of a man with upraised hands. Then Dharma on this mud-bank created a man and a woman known as Parihar Burha and Baramani Burhi. The mud-bank (earth) began to shake and tremble. God saw from heaven that such an earth was not fit for human habitation. Then he made clay figures of a tiger and tigress (*Rai Bagh* and *Rai Baghini*), infused life into them, and ordered them: 'Go, kill the human couple, and put their blood and flesh on the four corners of the Earth so as to make it firm.' The blood and flesh of the original human couple settled down in the four corners of the earth as iron-pillars supporting the

[1] Hume, 24.

[2] Carpenter, 187.

earth; and the earth became hardened like stone. Then God created another couple who became, in due time, parents of seven sons and seven daughters. From these seven couples descended the different peoples of the earth.[1]

The Juang live next-door to the Bhuiya and are often influenced by them. Sometimes they repeat the Parihar legend, but some of them shrink from the implications of an original human sacrifice, and say that the world was steadied by the blood of a sacrificed cow.

A Gond myth from Bilaspur (p. 39) describes in detail how 'the bodies of Mother Earth and Nandsur Dano turned into the world and everything we can see.' The Kuruk repeat the myth in a curiously degenerate form, as do their neighbours, the Raja Muria of the country round Chitrakot (pp. 47 f.). Mahapurub loses his temper with the first boy and girl and kills them. As they die, their flesh turns to earth, their bones to stone, their blood to water, their hair to grass.

The Madiga of southern India say that 'Jambava Rishi was created by Adi Sakti, primeval force, six months before the Earth, and when the latter was still in a fluid state, he was floating on its surface. By the command of the Creator he killed his younger son, and mixed his blood with liquid earth, whereupon it curdled into a solid mass. The name given to his younger son is Heppumuni (*Heppu* meaning curdle). The boy however was revived by the grace of Paramesvara and Parvati, and gave rise to the caste of Dakkaloru, who are regarded as the inferior progeny of the Madiga.'[2]

On this general pattern, there are the usual variants and exceptions. A curious Agaria tale describes how a Rakshasin's daughter Hiraman kept as a pet a mud parrot in a golden cage. Rama conquered the girl's mother and when he touched the parrot, 'it turned at once into the great world.' The Baiga do not seem to have the tradition of creation by sacrifice—indeed their myths expressly rule out any idea of human or superhuman sacrifice—but in one tale, Nanga Baiga cuts off his own finger and drives it into the ground as a nail to make the world free from earthquake. A Gadaba story likewise describes how the first man cut off an arm and a leg for use as nails to keep the earth in place.

Once the world was created, a good many legends go on to tell us how it was made firm and steady. The need of emphasizing this probably derives from the belief that the world was built on or out of water, and from the existence of earthquakes. If earthquakes

[1] Roy, *The Hill Bhuiyas*, 262.

[2] Nanjundayya and Iyer, iv. 128.

can occur today, the aboriginal argues, after so long a period of comparative stability, what must it have been like at the beginning?

The Baiga give an elaborate account of this stabilizing. The Wind, Pawan Dasseri, and Bhimsen are sent by Bhagavan, for the newly-created world 'was not firm; whenever they tried to stand on it, it ran away; it was slippery as mud in the rains.' The Wind did his best, but he is blind and his work was not perfect. 'The earth was hard, but when they stood on one side, the other side tipped up.' Bhimsen then took a hand. 'Where it was thin he put a mountain, where it was too heavy he made a valley. Where it slipped about he put trees to hold it together. But even then it was not firm and steady. It still wobbled. It was as scattered and uneven as a broken spider's web.' [1] Bhagavan had to turn to Nanga Baiga for help. He sent for him, and after much delay and a long journey, he and his wife came at last to the shores of the world. 'There was a tall akawan tree growing there. At its foot Nanga Baiga sacrificed a sow to Dharti Mata, a pig to Bageshur Pat, a goat to the Banaspati, and a white cock to Thakur Deo. Dharti Mata was rocking to and fro, but when the blood of the offering fell on her, she stood still. She looked up and said to Nanga Baiga, "When I am angry and will listen to no one in the world, I will listen to you."

'From the Agaria, who was born on the same day as the Baiga, they got four great nails. Nanga Baigin made herself naked, and drove the nails into the four corners of the world. It was very hard, but all the while Gichnaraja was spitting drops of water to make the earth easier. At last the world was steady. Then the two Baiga, being weary, lay down, the man in one corner of the world, his girl in the other. Their feet met in the middle.'[2]

The Agaria say that Nanga Baiga first cut off his own little finger to use as a nail, but it was not sufficient: the Agaria had to make twelve pillars of magic iron and set them at the four corners of the world. A Gond legend describes how Bhimsen rolled about on the newly-formed earth, thus making the mountains. The Raja Muria tell how Mahapurub pulled out nine hairs from his right leg and drove them into the nine corners of the world, whereupon it became steady. The Dhanwar, however, say that it was only when Mother Earth took two legs apiece from innumerable birds (who were then four-legged) and placed them under the earth like pillars of a house that it became steady.

[1] *The Baiga*, 311 f.

[2] ibid., 315 f.

Blood, even without nails, was enough to stabilize the world. The cow-sacrifice of the Juang, the human sacrifice of the Bhuiya immediately stopped the quivering and shaking of the earth. Yet earthquakes continue, and everywhere the magicians concern themselves with some means of keeping the earth steady. The Baiga consider this to be their particular duty, for it was by their magic nails that the world was first established.

The traditional Hindu view of earthquake is that Varaha, the boar incarnation of Vishnu who supports the earth, is changing the burden of the world from one tusk to another. Another tradition changes the boar into a great bull or elephant.[1] In Sylhet the Hindus say that below the earth there is a tortoise; upon this is a serpent and upon this an elephant. Should any one of the three creatures move its limbs there is an earthquake. The ordinary Mussalman of the same area is said to believe that the earth rests on the horns of a bull which has a mosquito at its side. Whenever the bull tries to shake its head the earth quakes, but the mosquito stings it by way of warning and the bull keeps quiet again.[2] The Kannikar also believe that the earth rests on one of the horns of an ox and an earthquake occurs when he shifts the weight.[3]

Another view, from the Punjab, is that earthquakes are 'due to a fever in the earth's interior, causing ague. This is said to be a doctrine of the Yunani school of medicine. Wells act as safety-valves for the trembling, however, so earthquakes are common in Persia and Kashmir, where wells are scarce, and rare in Punjab.'[4]

Among the aboriginals, the Birhor believe that an earthquake occurs when the giant who sleeps in the bowels of the earth turns over.[5] The Bhuiya say it is when the tortoise which supports the earth grows weary and turns from side to side.[6]

The Uraon have a similar notion. The earth 'rests on the back of a tortoise which is caught very firmly between the long legs of a crab. When the tortoise gets tired and wants to change her position an earthquake takes place, but the crab is always there attentive to her duty and saves the world from a catastrophe. She catches the tortoise very firmly with her claws and never allows her to move too much.'[7]

[1] Crooke, i, 35. See, for the Muthuvan tradition, Iyer, ii, 35. Cf. also *N. I. Notes and Queries*, iv, 198; Rose, i, 134.

[2] Bhattacharjee, 122.

[3] Iyer, i, 54.

[4] Rose, i, 134.

[5] Roy, *The Birhors*, 498.

[6] Roy, *The Hill Bhuiyas*, 280.

[7] Dehon, 168.

Some Lakher say that an earthquake is due to sexual intercourse between the earth and the sky. Others say that when a chief dies, his spirit flies through the cords by which the earth is attached to the sky and as it passes it cuts through one of the cords with its dao thus causing an earthquake. The Ao Naga say that the sky is supported by a post at the end of the world, which is held in position by a being called Ningtangr. Sometimes he feels hungry and lets go for a moment to pluck and eat leaves. The post shakes and there is an earthquake.[1]

In addition to these popular and unmoral ideas there is a more pious view that earthquakes are due to sin. The Baiga consider that they are caused by incest which loosens the nails which Nanga Baiga drove into the earth to keep it steady at the beginning of the world. A similar notion apparently became popular after the great earthquake of June 1897 when it was said that the 'inhabitants of this planet had become so sinful that even the motherly and patient earth could bear their iniquities no longer and was trying to shake them off her surface '.[2]

At the time of the great Bihar earthquake Mahatma Gandhi gave expression to a similar notion, saying that the disaster was due to the sin of untouchability.[3]

In Golaghat (Assam) three different views seem to be held. The earth rests on a cobra's head and when men become 'disobedient, sinful and wicked', it grows heavy and the cobra shakes its head in an attempt to throw it off. Alternatively, the world is hung by ropes from the four corners. Sometimes squirrels playing on the ropes bite them through, thus causing earthquake. Or again, the earth is on the back of an elephant. When a mouse comes near, it moves quickly. Here too the idea is moralized. 'Only the wicked die in an earthquake.'[4]

The creation of mankind sometimes follows, and sometimes precedes, that of the world. Many varied traditions have been recorded.

The Andaman Islanders:

> The first man was Jutpu (the word seems to mean 'alone'). He was born inside the joint of a big bamboo, just like a bird in an egg. The bamboo split and he came out. He was a little child . . . He was lonely, living all by himself. He took some clay from a nest of the white-ants

[1] *Census of India*, 1931, 128 and Mills, *The Ao Nagas*, 298.

[2] Bhattacharjee, 122.

[3] It is a very common idea. See also *N. I. Notes and Queries*, i, 16, and Rose, i, 134.

[4] Lewison, 365 f.

and moulded it into the shape of a woman. She became alive and became his wife . . . Afterwards Jutpu made other people out of clay.[1]

A Toda legend also suggests—though here there is possibly a trace of missionary influence—that the man emerged first and the woman was made later. Behind the buffaloes of On (who created them) 'there came out of the earth a man, holding the tail of the last buffalo, and this was the first Toda. On took one of the man's ribs from the right side of his body and made a woman.'[2]

The Baiga:

Baba Vasistha Muni was Bhagavan's guru. For thirteen years he passed urine into a gourd. In the thirteenth year the gourd broke and Nanga Baiga came out weeping. When the Baba saw him he was angry, and picked the child up and threw him into the jungle. A black she-cobra caught him as he fell, and gave him two-and-a-half drops of her milk. Then she hid him safely in an ant-hill. After that the black cobra gave birth to Nanga Baigin. There were two parts of the ant-hill. The boy lived in one, the girl in the other.[3]

But in Baihar I was told that Nanga Baiga's mother was Basmoti Kaniya, the bamboo-girl, who fed him with her milk, and gave him a golden axe. These stories, of course, show traces of the Hindu influence which has been slowly penetrating into the Baiga Chak and among the Binjhwar Baiga of Baihar. A much more primitive stratum of myth exists elsewhere. Thus in Pandaria, the Baiga describe how 'the first gods, being hungry, went to Nangapahar, to dig for roots. They dug up some of them, and out of that hole came a little man and woman, naked, and they all laughed and said, "These are Naga Baiga and Naga Baigin." But afterwards their name was changed to Nanga Baiga and Nanga Baigin.'

In Niwas I heard a very similar account of the parents of mankind.

In the *madhuban*, the sweet forest, under a clump of bamboos, were born two children who were to be the lords of the earth. They were Nanga Baiga and Nanga Baigin. They used to play in any pit from which roots had been dug.

Many Baiga say, simply, that their great ancestors were born from the womb of Mother Earth.' We may safely dismiss

[1] Brown, 192. Another tradition says the first man cohabited with an ant's nest and thus obtained a large number of children. We may compare the Juang legend of the emergence of Rusi from an ant-hill. Nanga Baiga and Nanga Baigin originally lived in an ant-hill.

[2] Rivers, 184.

[3] *The Baiga*, 312 f.

Baba Vasishtha Muni as an accretion. The genuine Baiga story is invariably concerned with earth, roots, jungle and bamboo.

The Birhor:

Singbonga created the winged Horse known as Pankhraj. He next proceeded to create mankind. He made a clay figure of a man in the day-time and left it to dry. But at night, the Pankhraj Horse came and trampled it under its feet and spoilt it. The Horse did this as it was afraid that if Man was created, he would subjugate the horse and ride it. Next morning Singbonga found the clay figure of man thus damaged. He then made a clay figure of a dog, and a fresh one of a man. He laid them out to dry, with their faces turned in the direction from which the wind was blowing. By evening, the clay figure of the dog dried up and the wind entered its nostrils, and it became endowed with life. But the figure of the man was not yet dry, and so Singbonga set the dog to guard it. At night, the horse sought to approach the human figure but the dog kept barking at the horse; and the horse could not approach the image and damage it. When it dried up, Singbonga endowed it with life. But now it was discovered that the joints of this First Man were inconveniently stiff, and he could neither sit down nor walk properly. Then Singbonga took back life from this uncouth physical frame, and re-made it by making its joints more supple. Then he gave it life again. Such is the origin of the present race of men.[1]

The Gond:

The following is the Betul legend.

After laying their eggs on the face of the ocean, the Singamali bird began to brood upon those eggs, and nine months and nine days she brooded. Then, from these eggs a boy and a girl were born. When the girl and the boy were born, then they were left in the nest on the water. The Singamali birds, after feeding in the forest, came to their children, and seeing the girl and the boy, they began to say, 'Here we ought not to stay. These have been born like this. Some day or other they will eat us both up'. From that day the Singamali birds never went there at all. They abandoned the children.

Then, the children, with the help of God, began to live there upon the water. As they grew up, they began to talk. One day they both said to the Ocean-Mother, 'Consider! Here you are our protector, convey us hence outside this place'.

Ocean-Mother heard their word, and in a trice she sent a wave, and the children, nest and all, were borne outside and fell there. Then, they wandered in the forest and day by day they grew stronger.[2]

An earlier tradition was taken down in the seventies of the last century by Hislop from a Pardhan priest at Nagpur.

[1] Roy, *The Birhors*, 398. There is a curious variant on this in a tale told to L. Grierson by her ayah.—*N. I. Notes and Queries*, iii, 18.

[2] Trench, ii, 1.

In the midst of twelve hills, in the glens of seven hills, is Lingawangad,

In that mount is a flower tree named Dati; thence for twelve *kos* there is no dwelling—

Caw saying there is no crow, chirp saying there is no bird, roar saying there is no tiger.

Then, what happened? God spread betel nut, and called Nalliyado-rishi.

When an order to the servant Narayan was made, he heard it, and went running

To Kurtao Subal to ask him. He said there are sixteen threshing-floors of Teloogoo gods,

Eighteen threshing-floors of Brahmin gods, twelve threshing-floors of Gond gods. Thus he was asking for gods.

So many gods! Where are they? Their tidings I seek.

What did he begin to say? He said thus:

There the god Mahadewa was ruling from the upper sea to the lower sea.

What was that Mahadewa doing? He was swimming like a roller stone: he had no hands, no feet:

He remained like the trunk of tree.

Gowara Parwatee his wife, having stood, began to ask Narayan—

Who art thou? He said, I am Bhagawan's Subadar.

She said, Why hast thou come so far? I came to see Mahadewa.

Gowara Parwatee came. Narayan having gone to the banks of the Narbadda, stood there.

The Raja Mahadewa was swimming and came up.

Then Parwatee, with joined hands, stood, and so did Narayan.

Then said Mahadewa, For what hast thou come? Where are the gods of the twelve threshing-floors of the Gonds?

What did he say, Kurtao Subal? what did he say to Mahadewa?

Perform devotion for twelve months, and then you will come to know the names of them.

Five and six months passed; at the end of it, the devotion was finished.

Then came Bhagawan and stood close to Mahadewa, and called to him—

Thy devotion is finished, emerge out of the water. He said, how shall I

Emerge? I have no hands, no feet, no eyes.

Then Mahadewa received man's form.

Thus man's form complete was made in the luminous world.

He raised his eyes and saw Bhagawan ; but Bhagawan immediately disappeared.

Mahadewa said, It is not well that God should not be seen. Hear, O God, my story.

My devotion is fruitless ; I received a man's form, which is not well.

Then he began to establish a devotion.

At the end of nine months and nine days his boil moved and burst—

Kalia Adao was born. Then Mahadewa, what did he say ?

Said Mahadewa to him, Establish a devotion.

Kalia Adao began a devotion ; one month, two months passed, when a boil arose in his hand.

The boil burst and sixteen daughters were born out of it. Then said he,

What ! why are these daughters born ?

I shall have cause to cast my head down. Whence shall I bring husbands for them ?

He took hold of them and threw them in the water. After the throwing

The water was dried up, and sixteen sorts of earth were produced.

He said, I shall perform devotion, and then I shall be at peace.

He then established a devotion, and a boil arose in his hand.

Twelve threshing-floors of Gondi gods were born.

Hither and thither all the Gonds were scattered in the jungle ;

Places, hills and valleys were filled with these Gonds.[1]

In 1840 Tickell published a version of the Kol history of the creation of the world. He says that at the beginning Ote Boram and Sirma Thakoor, who is the same as the Sun, were self-created. After them the Moon was self-created.

Ote Boram and Sirma Thakoor then made the earth ; after that they clothed it with grass, trees, rocks, and water ; they then made cattle, which were first born in 'Bogo Bochee' ; after them all wild animals. They then made a little boy and a little girl, at the bottom of an immense ravine, and as they have no houses to live in, the gods told them to inhabit a huge crab's cave. They grew adult, and Singbonga came to see them every day, and called them his grandchildren ; but at length, seeing no hopes of any progeny, from their extreme simplicity, he taught them the art of making rice-beer, the use of which caused them those sensations which were in due time the means of peopling the world.[2]

[1] Hislop, 4. Sir R. Temple was responsible for the free English version which is based on Hislop's verbal translation.

[2] Tickell, 797.

The Munda story closely resembles that told by the Birhor.

Singbonga first fashioned two clay figures, one meant to represent a man and the other a woman. But before he could endow the figures with life, the horse, apprehensive of future trouble from them, trampled them under its hoofs. In those days the horse had wings and could move about much faster than now. When Singbonga found that the horse had destroyed his earthen figures of men, he first created a spider and then fashioned two more clay figures like those destroyed by the horse. He then ordered the spider to guard the figures against the horse. The spider wove its net round the two clay figures in such a way that the horse could not destroy them again. Then Singbonga imparted life to the two figures which thus became the first human beings.[1]

The Santal legend again is in the same tradition.

In the beginning was Thakur Jiu. There was no land visible, all was covered with water. Then Thakur Jiu's servants said to him, 'How shall we create human beings?' He replied, 'If it be so desired, we can create them'. They then said, 'If you give us a blessing, we shall be able to do so'. Thakur Jiu then said, 'Go, call Malin Budhi. She is to be found in a rock cave under the water'. When she came, she received the order to form two human beings. Some say she made them of a kind of froth, which proceeded from a supernatural being who had his residence at the bottom of the sea, but others that she made them of a stiff clay. Thakur Jiu was a spectator of what was being done. At length Malin Budhi made the bodies of two human beings, and laid them out to dry. In the meantime Singh Sadom (Day-horse) passed that way and, trampling them under foot, destroyed them. After an interval Thakur Jiu demanded of Malin Budhi if she had prepared them. She replied, 'I made them, but I have many enemies'. Thakur Jiu enquired who they were, and she replied, 'Who, but Singh Sadom?' Thakur Jiu then said, 'Kick the pieces into the Sora Nai and the Samud Nai'. Thakur Jiu then said to Malin Budhi, 'I again give you a blessing, go make two human beings'. Having prepared them she went to Thakur Jiu who said, 'Well, have you got them ready?' She replied, 'They are ready, give them the gift of life'. He said, 'Above the door frame is the life of birds, do not bring that; upon the cross-beam is the life of human beings, bring it'. So she went, but being of low stature she could not reach the cross-beam, so she brought the bird's life from above the door, and no sooner had she given it to them, than they flew up into the heavens, where they continued to course about, whether for twelve years or twelve months is doubtful. The names of the birds were Has and Hasin. At length the desire to breed came upon them, and they went to Thakur Jiu and said, 'You gave us being, but we cannot find a place on which to rest'. He replied, 'I will prepare a place for you'.

[1] Roy, *J.B.O.R.S.*, ii, 201.

Thakur Jiu then makes the world, whereon springs up a fine karam tree.

Then the birds Has and Hasin came and alighted on the karam tree, and afterwards made their nest among the grass at its foot. Here the female laid two eggs, and Raghop Buar came and ate them. Again she laid other two eggs, and again Raghop Buar came and devoured them. Then Has and Hasin went to Thakur Jiu and informed him that Raghop Buar had twice eaten their eggs. On hearing this Thakur Jiu said, 'I shall send some one to guard your eggs'. So calling Jaher-era, he committed the eggs of the birds Has and Hasin to her care. So well did she perform her task that the female was allowed to hatch her eggs from which emerged two human beings, a male and a female, whose names were Pilchu Haram and Pilchu Budhi.[1]

So far everything is straightforward. There is a clear picture of the primaeval ocean, the lonely Creator, the making of the world, the creation of man. But now the story is confused by the introduction of a legend of destruction, and the whole thing has to be done all over again. A human couple must be saved from the wreckage, the world must be re-made, and the population restored.

The old world is sometimes destroyed by flood, as in the Bondo, Kond, Maria and Saora myths; sometimes by fire, as in Kharia, Kol, Munda, Santal and Uraon tradition; once it is eaten by a Dano (Gadaba), once by a worm (Muria); occasionally it turns right over, precipitating the inhabitants into the waters below.

In the Kol-Munda-Santal cycle there is a reason for this disaster. The wickedness of men has so provoked the deity that he determines to punish them. The moralization of the old mythology is a common feature of this group of tribes which, it may be noted, has been more influenced by missionary teaching than any other. But the old tradition of a deluge as a punishment for sin may not be peculiar to missionary teaching. Koppers quotes the Hindu Deluge myth from the *Mahabharata* and considers (with Winternitz) that 'punishment as the motive of the Deluge would appear to be indicated by the use of the expression "time of cleansing"'[2] which indicates the moment of its occurrence. No such idea, however, is to be found either in the Bhil myths recorded by Koppers, or in those given in the text. Indeed, the naturalness and inevitability of the way the earth sinks below the waters suggests that the tribal mythologists are not echoing the story of a Deluge but are reproducing, in very simple form, the ancient Hindu

[1] Campbell, 15 ff. A rather 'improved' version of this story is given by F. B. Bradley-Birt, *The Story of an Indian Upland* (London, 1905), 134 ff.

[2] Koppers, 286. There is no hint, however, of the penal character of the Deluge in the *Satapatha Brahmana* version.

tradition of the Yugas. Each of these four great Ages of the world ends in the dissolution of the world and the re-emergence of the all-pervading ocean. During these periods of temporary annihilation, Vishnu slumbers on the back of the great serpent Sesh Nag and floats peacefully on the waters. When the new Yuga begins, the creative process is again initiated. Several passages in the text sound remarkably like this—but there is one exception: in nearly all of them, a male and a female human being are preserved in a gourd or basket to carry on the race. Here undoubtedly there is a greater likeness to the Hindu Deluge myth.

This myth first appears in the *Satapatha Brahmana*: it is found again in the *Mahabharata* and is reproduced in varying forms in the *Agni*, *Bhagavata* and *Matsya Puranas*. The story in the *Satapatha Brahmana* tells how a fish warns Manu that 'A flood will carry away all living beings: I will save you from that'. Manu preserves the fish with great care: it grows rapidly and presently bids its friend to make a ship. Manu does so and, when the flood comes, embarks in it and fastens its cable to the fish's horn. Led by the fish, Manu and his ship pass over the Himalayas and in due time the fish tells him to fasten the ship to a tree where it will settle as the waters subside. When Manu comes out of the ship, he finds that all living creatures have been drowned, and he alone is left. He devotes himself to austerities and sacrifice and a girl is produced who declares herself his daughter. He lives with her and she bears him children.

The *Mahabharata* version is similar, though embroidered with allegory and metaphysics. Manu takes the seven Rishis and a quantity of seed with him in his ship. It is remarkable that it is not thought necessary to take some suitable woman in the boat to ensure the continuity of the race.

Koppers records a Bhil deluge myth, in which a fish gives warning of the coming danger.

> Bhagwan had created out of earth two washermen, male and female. From this brother and sister the human race had its birth. They lived happily and were very charitable. It fell to the girl's lot to draw water and when going to the river she would take rice with her to feed the fish. This went on for a long time.
>
> Then one day the fish Ro asked her: 'Maiden, what reward do you desire? Have you thought of any definite thing?' She answered: 'I know of nothing'. Then the fish said: 'Through water the earth will be turned upside down. Take pumpkin seeds with you and make a cage. Then do you and your brother step into the cage, taking seed and water with you. And do not forget to bring a cock also'

The rains began to fall, slowly at first, then in ever greater torrents. It was as if earth and heaven had merged into one. Then God spoke: 'Thus have I turned the world upside down. But has not someone survived? The crowing of the cock informs me of it'.

Then Bhagwan himself went to find out more about the matter. He came to where the cage was and asked: 'Is anyone inside?' Then the girl answered: 'We are two inside, my brother and I'. And Bhagwan found within the cage two young people in the full prime and strength of life. Then God spoke: 'I have destroyed the whole world. Who warned you and gave you the advice to make such a cage? You must explain this mystery to me. For my plan was hidden from men'. Then the girl replied: 'It was the fish who instructed me'. Bhagwan then called the fish and asked: 'Was it you who brought this knowledge to these two?' The fish answered: 'O no, Lord Father, it was not I who did so'. Then God beat the fish and it became disposed to confess: 'Yes, Lord Father, I did really do it'. Then God spoke: 'Had you at once told the truth, nothing would have happened to you'. And God cut out the fish's tongue and threw it away. From this tongue leeches took their origin. But the fish has remained without tongue from that time till now.

God turned the girl with her face to the West and the young man with his face to the East. When he had made them turn again so as to face each other, he asked the man: 'Who is this?' and he answered: 'She is my wife'. Then Bhagwan asked the girl: 'Who is this?' and she answered: 'He is my husband'. Then God made them man and wife. In this way they became the progenitors of the human race. Generation followed generation and the different languages came into being.[1]

There are several accounts in the text of the dissolution of the old world by water. 'There was a great rain', say the Bison-horn Maria, 'and the first world was drowned'. The Bondo describe the continual rain which flooded the world: the Kond story tells how the earth turned over into the water or sank down below it; according to the Lanjhia Saora, the Creator's rat burrowed below the mountains and water surged up from below and the earth was submerged. The Muria say Mahapurub turned the world topsy-turvey and it was eaten by a worm.

In every case, a human couple survive: the Bison-horn Maria put a brother and sister in a gourd which at last grounds on a rock. The Bondo put them in a gourd or a covered basket, from which Mahapurub rescues them. The first Kond boy is warned by a deer (just as Manu is warned by a fish) and prepares a boat for his

[1] Koppers, 282 f. Koppers suggests that the undoubtedly curious figures of the two washermen have entered the legend 'because such would necessarily live near water and so have a natural connection with the fish living in this element'.

sister and himself: in due time the sun dries up the water and the boat settles on land. The Lanjhia Saora and Muria survive in a gourd.

New mechanisms now have to be employed to recreate the earth and establish the human couple in a position to increase and multiply. Some of the stories largely repeat the incidents at the original creation. Whether the earth had always been there on the floor of the ocean, or whether it had but recently sunk down, the problem was the same—how to get it up again.

The Bison-horn Maria use the device of a boar which manages to get some earth on its back: it shakes itself and the earth flies in all directions and the world is made again. The Bondo say that the earth was in charge of Kermo Deota in the Under World. Mahaprabhu sent the wild boar to steal it: it smeared the mud on its body and shook itself—'and the earth flew over the ocean and the world was made. Some of the boar's bristles came out and turned into grass.' The Gadaba story, which says that the world was swallowed by a Dano, reverses the process by making Mahaprabhu squeeze the thief's body so violently that not a bone remained unbroken and the earth was all excreted. A Lanjhia Saora story pictures a rat going down below, bringing the earth to the Creator who spreads it on the surface of the water.

Some tribes solve the problem simply enough by saying that the waters covering the earth dried up. The Kond say the heat of the sun effected this. The Lanjhia Saora say that Bhimo relieved himself on Ramo's head, and when the excreta was thrown into the water it dried up at once and the earth appeared again. In two of the Kond stories human sacrifice was necessary to dry the waters and prepare the new world.

Several tribes, however, believe that the original world was destroyed not by flood but by fire. There are a number of legends of this type current among the Agaria who believe that it was the war with the Sun which caused the destruction of the ancient world.[1] The Santal describe how fire from heaven destroyed the race of men; some say this happened almost immediately after their creation, others that it occurred at a later period. Some say that the fire was a punishment for the sins of the people, others that it was due to a quarrel within the tribe. All the accounts, however, agree that a man and a woman escaped the burning rain of fire by hiding in a cave or in a house of stone.[2]

[1] *The Agaria*, 97 ff. [2] Campbell, 23.

The Munda also describe how:

Once upon a time, Singbonga rained down fire whereby the earth was devastated. The ebony tree was only partially burnt and thus, although blackened, it did not die. Since then the colour of the tree has become blackish. All human beings were destroyed, except that Singbonga's sister Nage-Era managed to conceal two persons, brother and sister to each other, in a spring which was her own seat. Now that all men were gone, Singbonga was in great straits. As no offerings were any longer made to him, his tanks of milk, curds and blood began all to dry up. His wife upbraided him for his indiscretion, saying, 'I warned you then, but you heed me not. And so we suffer for your folly.' Singbonga now despatched his bird-messengers to the earth to see if perchance any human being might have survived. The sparrow, the woodpecker and other messengers searched about all over the earth in vain. At length the crow, who was Singbonga's steward, came upon a leaf-hut near a spring, and inferred the existence of some human beings in the vicinity. So the bird sat down on the branches of a tree and soon found out that two persons lived with Nage-Era. He then told her that he had been sent to take to Singbonga the two persons that were with her. Nage-Era refused to give them up and said, 'Singbonga destroys men. Who knows whether he will not destroy these, too?' The crow went back and reported this to his master. Thereupon Singbonga had to come down to Nage-Era's place to induce her to part with her proteges.

After much persuasion she agreed to give them up on Singbonga promising that he would not destroy mankind again and that Nage-Era would thenceforth have a share of the human race. Singbonga assigned to his sister's share of mankind all persons who might have leprous sores or marks on their bodies. This satisfied Nage-Era.[1]

A Kol tradition declares that after the world was peopled, Sirma Thakoor destroyed it once, with the exception of sixteen people, because people became incestuous, and unmindful of God, or their superiors. Some say he destroyed it with water, some say with fire.[2]

The Kharia tradition is of the same general kind. Ponomosor, the Supreme Being, created the world, by what method is not known. He then made two clay images, one male and one female, and put them in the hollow of a banyan tree. The milky juice dropped into their mouths and the images became alive. They multiplied and soon there was a scarcity of food and they prayed to Ponomosor to give them more. He sent a great storm and blew the leaves of trees into the air where they were turned into birds.

Men annoyed Ponomosor by cutting down fruit-bearing trees and he sent a flood to destroy them. The majority of mankind

[1] Roy, *J.B.O.R.S.*, ii, 207 f. [2] Tickell, 797.

died, but a few escaped to the hill-tops. After eight days the water subsided and the land appeared again. But once more men displeased Ponomosor and this time he sent a rain of fire to destroy them and all men died except one brother and sister. Ponomosor repented of his action and sent his bird-messengers to see if there were any human beings still living. The crow discovered where the brother and sister were hiding and used to eat the skin of the fruit on which they were living and so got very fat. Ponomosor, noticing the crow's fatness, forced it to confess where it had found the human beings. He went to them and established them again on earth, where they lived and multiplied.[1]

The Uraon also have a tradition of the rain of fire, though here the universal destruction seems to have been largely accidental. The story, as recorded by Roy in 1915, is confused, but the main outline seems to be as follows:

There appears to have been a previous creation upon which Dharmes, the Supreme Being, desired to shower down a rain of fire. Parvati (who here appears as the wife of Dharmes) told him to throw down the fire from a small bow but he rained it down out of a large brass dish with the result that every country and all the vegetation in the world was destroyed. Parvati, however, hid a brother and a sister in a crab's hole. She gave them half a grain of masur pulse and they lived on this for seven days and nights. Then Dharmes came saying he was hungry and looking for men who would raise rice for him and feed him. He sent his dogs to find any survivors of the great conflagration and they searched until they came to the crab's hole. Then Dharmes brought out the two human beings and served them. Presently they asked him to show them some means of livelihood and he taught them how to embank fields and to raise crops. He divided time into weeks of seven days and nights and taught men to make rice-beer.[2]

An interesting parallel to these legends of destruction is afforded by the Lakher story of the Great Darkness. Here too the tale is moralized and it is a brother and sister who survive for the renewal of the human race.

Originally all men were immortal, but they increased too much and fought among themselves and were wicked, till one day Khazangpa got angry, and said, 'Let all the men in the world die.' He caused a dog to swallow the sun and the whole world became

[1] Roy, *The Kharias*, 414 ff.

[2] Roy, *The Oraons*, 463 ff. There is another version of the Uraon creation legend in Dehon, 127 f.

dark . . . Some men were changed into stars and some into monkeys . . . All the fires went out. Those men who were able to keep their eyes open survived, but as hardly any one was able to keep his eyes open for seven days, all the men in the world died except one brother and sister, who turned a pig's trough upside down and hid under it so that the wild beasts could not find them and eat them. After some time the dog evacuated and the sun came out again, light returned to the world, and the brother and sister came out from under the pig's trough and, there being no other human beings left alive, married and became the ancestors of human race.[1]

But after this there came a great flood and its waters only subsided when a girl was thrown to them as a sacrifice. This flood, however, did not cover the mountains and men and animals were able to escape.

The stories now recorded for the first time in the text follow in their broad outlines the conventional pattern. But there are many details of interest, and a few of the stories stand outside the main tradition. Such is the Lanjhia Saora myth (p. 43) of the part played by the Dead in the creative process. Another strange legend is the Gadaba account of the potter swimming round and round until the saliva trickling from his mouth set and hardened to form a crust on the water, which he had to hold in place by his own amputated arm and leg.

These stories indicate a general belief in a Supreme Being, imagined in personal terms, who is active in creation and generally needs the assistance of his creatures. There seem to be parallel, and inconsistent, traditions about the presence of pre-existent matter out of which the world was fashioned. Some undoubtedly suggest a *creatio ex nihilo* [2]; others seem to imply that nothing can be made unless there is something already there.

[1] Parry, 488 f.

[2] Koppers has an interesting discussion on this problem. He is insistent that 'the idea of a personal god creating the world out of nothing is one which runs counter to almost every system evolved by Hindu mentality' (275), and quotes Monier-Williams as saying that all Hindu sects 'believe in some material cause (*upădana*)—some eternal substance out of which the universe is evolved'.—Monier-Williams, 119. But the Upanishadic conception of space as the ultimate ground of the world or Non-being (*a-sad*) as its source suggests some modification of this position. See Hume, 10 ff. Held warns us against considering the Indian idea of creation in the light of western philosophy 'thereby laying undue stress upon the act of creation as generation out of nothing instead of on the arranging, the ordering of primordial matter. . . The Indian conception of the act of creation is the classificatory arranging of things according to certain norms.' Held, 118.

I

AGARIA

Kareli, Mandla District

(From *The Agaria,* 88 f.)

Bhagavan first made the world by laying a great lotus leaf on the face of the water. But the sun arose and withered that leaf with its heat.

Then Bhagavan made the world of lac. But when he climbed on it, it broke into a thousand pieces.

At last, from the dirt of his breast Bhagavan made a crow, and allowed it to suck his milk two-and-a-half times, saying, 'Now you've drunk my milk, you'll never hunger nor thirst; you and I will search for the earth together'.

So away, away, away went that crow, till it grew weary and thought, 'My father is my enemy: he created me only to kill me'. So thinking. it fell on the body of Kakramal Kshattri, the great crab. Kakramal Kshattri went down below the water and found Nal Raja and Nal Rani sleeping. They had slept for twelve years. He shook them awake, Nal Raja said, 'Nizam Raja has the earth, not me'. But Kakramal Kshattri squeezed his throat till he vomited up the earth in little balls. So the crow took the earth back to its father, and Bhagavan made the world.

Five years passed, then Nanga Baiga and Nanga Baigin were born out of a crack in the ground. Nanga Baiga said to Mother Earth, 'Mother, where is my fiddle?' She said, 'Child you are yet but a navel and a cord; what need is there of a fiddle?' So said Mother Earth. But on that day Basin Kaniya (the Bamboo Maiden) was born, and Nanga Baiga went to cut the bamboo, in one breath, above and below. And he made his fiddle with his own hair for strings, and played it, and Bhagavan's seat shook with the sound. Then Bhagavan knew that the Baiga were born, and sent to call them. But his messenger found Nanga Baiga asleep in a winnowing-fan. Mother Earth said, 'Don't go, my son', but Nanga Baiga took his fiddle and went. Bhagavan said to him, 'Drive your nails into the earth to make it steady'. But Nanga Baiga had no nails, so he cut off the little finger of his right hand and drove that into the ground. But Bhagavan was not satisfied. 'I want strong pillars', he said.

So Nanga Baiga called Agyasur and worshipped him, and Agyasur flamed up with great flames, and from the fire an Agaria was born. Since we Agaria were born from fire, we never fear it, and can beat the slag from the glowing iron with our hands. Then that Agaria made twelve pillars of virgin iron and set them at the four corners of the world, and it became steady, and Bhagavan sowed seeds everywhere.

2

BHUIYA

Uskuda, Bonai State

There was nothing but water. Baski Mata was born on a lotus leaf. The gods looked down and saw her tossed to and fro by the waves. They wondered what to do. Baski Mata cried, ' Boram Burha's son is Parihar. Kill him and from his blood and bones the world will be born.' The gods went to Dharam Deota and told him what she had said. He replied, ' Boram Burha is my son ; what can I do about it ? Go yourselves to him and ask him.' They went and said that they needed a gourd. He said he would give it to them. For he did not realize that they wanted his son. But when they had him they did not know how to kill him. They had no weapons and no tool of iron to cut him. They went again to Dharam Deota and now he took dirt from his body and made a tiger, colouring it red. He said, ' Go brother tiger and eat Parihar as he goes for water.' The tiger hid by the water. Parihar heard of it and called the Lohar to make him an iron bow and iron arrows. With these he went to kill the tiger. He grew weary, and went to drink in a stream. For a moment he put down his weapons and the tiger caught him. He shouted and the gods ran to see what was happening. The tiger let him go, but after he had run a few paces the boy fell dead.

Then the gods picked up the body of Parihar and swung it round and round. His blood spurted out and wherever it fell into the water the earth was formed. His bones flew away and became the seven rocks. His hair turned into the seven trees. The gods looked to see if the earth was solid or no ; they called for rain and a great storm came. Some of the water fell in the hollows, the rest dried up. The gods went round the world. Their feet got dirty with the mud, and when they scraped it off it piled up as hills and mountains.

Then Baski Mata went down to the bottom of the ocean and stood on her head. Her head rested on the lotus flower and she let the earth rest on her feet. When she is tired and shifts the earth from one foot to another, there is an earthquake in the Middle World.

3

BHUIYA

Champajor, Keonjhar State

Fourteen parts were water, seven parts were mud. It was all mixed up together. Dharam Deota came out of the water. From the dirt of his right side he made a she-doll, from the dirt of his left a he-doll. He put life into them and they became Boram and his wife. They were brother and sister, but they went apart and Dharam Deota disguised them with small-pox : they did not recognize each other and they married. They had a son called Parihar.

The gods saw that the world was half mud, half water. They said they wanted to eat a gourd to make the world solid. But what they meant was that they wanted a boy. They made a tiger and sent it to catch Parihar. The boy was out hunting with his sword and iron bow and arrow. He was tired and slept below a mango tree. The tiger came, put ash on its paw and laid it on Parihar's chest ; but it was so frightened that it ran away without doing more than that. It ran to a stream, drank water and slept. When Parihar awoke, he saw the sign on his chest and said, 'I have been saved ; now I must kill the tiger'. But when he saw it, even though it was asleep, he too was frightened. He laid his sword on its chest and ran away. When the tiger awoke, it saw the sign and said, 'I have been saved'.

The gods said, 'What can we do ? These two are frightened of each other'. They said to the tiger, 'Wait till this boy goes to bathe : he will have no weapons then, and you can kill him easily'. The tiger waited and one day, as Parihar was sitting on a stone to bathe, the tiger leapt on him and killed him. The boy's blood fell on the ground and it became solid. His legs turned into great trees, his arms into small trees, his fingers into shrubs, his hair into grass, his bones into rocks and stones. His head became the sun, his chest the moon (with the mark of the tiger's paw upon it), and his blood coloured the red earth. From this red earth came the Matisar Bhuiya.

Boram wept for his son, but Dharam Deota said, 'Do not weep: for one I will give you a family'. Then Uiyi and a girl Juyi were born. Their children were Gandhi and Nidhi. Their children were seven sons and seven daughters. They were the Bhuiya and their names were Matisar, Satori, Rautari, Konti, Batori, Rajori and Saunti.

4

BISON-HORN MARIA

Rewali, Bastar State

There was a great rain and the first world was drowned. But Gajabhimul[1] put a brother and a sister—their names were Kawachi and Kuhrami—in a gourd called Dadha Burka Kawachi. This gourd drifted to and fro until at last it ran aground on a great rock. Mahapurub sent out a crow to search for men. The crow flew and flew and flew: what did it see? It saw water and a gourd on a great rock. It tried to sit on the rock, but the stone was too hot. Mahapurub sent the crow back to see if there was any living creature inside the gourd. In the meantime a banyan plant had sprung up near the gourd: the crow perched on it and pecked it open.

From the gourd Kawachi and Kuhrami came out. The rock was so hot that they climbed up into the tree. They were hungry and began to drink the sap of the tree. The crow flew away. The sap was soon finished and the two children began to cry. When Mahapurub heard the noise he was angry as a sahib and sent to the crow to stop it. But the crow was greedy and wanted the children to die so that it could feed on their bodies: it returned to Mahapurub and told him that all was well. But again the cries of the hungry children disturbed Mahapurub and this time he sent an eagle. But the eagle too was greedy and wanted the children to die so that it could feed on their bodies: it too returned to Mahapurub and told him that all was well. But again the cries of the hungry children disturbed Mahapurub and this time he sent a tiger. But the tiger too was greedy and wanted the children to die so that it could feed on their bodies: it too returned to Mahapurub and told him that all was well. But when there was no end to the children's cries, Mahapurub sent at last a monkey. The monkey sat on the rock and

[1] In some villages he is called Iru Sirma.

asked the children what was the matter. The rock was so hot that the monkey's buttocks were burnt, so were its hands and feet. It touched its face with its burning hands and its face turned black.

The monkey jumped into the tree. 'We have nowhere to go,' said the children. 'There is no food.' The monkey returned to Mahapurub.

Mahapurub sent a boar. 'Near the rock is a tortoise', he said. 'It has made itself a home of mud and clay. Remove the mud and spread it over the rock'. 'But how am I to live without food?' said the boar. 'These children will sow seed', said Mahapurub. 'There will be a harvest on the rock, and you will be the first to eat it.' That is why the wild boars always ravage the crops before men can reap them.

The boar found the tortoise and rolled itself in the mud on its back. It came to the rock and shook itself violently and the mud flew in all directions and there was the world again.

The children sowed seed and reaped their harvest. Gaja Bhimul wondered how to get living creatures in the world. He asked the two children to marry, but they refused. Were they not brother and sister? He called Budi Matal. She gave them small-pox and sent them wandering round the world. One day they met and did not recognize each other, so they were married. First twelve boys were born at one time, and then twelve girls. The names of the boys were Kawachi, Marvi, Oyami, Kartami, Kunjami, Poriami, Kalmumi, Nendi Markami, Kuhrami, Barse, Vetti and Karti.

5

BISON-HORN MARIA

Gadapal, Bastar State

As above, with the following variants :—

The boars (there were two of them) came from Warangal, where there was some earth. The earth was sticking to their bristles. They shook themselves and the world came into being. A cow drank some of the water and this turned into milk. Before this the cow had no milk.

There were no hills at first. The boy and girl yoked a bear and a tiger to their harrow and some of the earth that was thrown up turned into hills.

6

BISON-HORN MARIA

Killepal, Bastar State

As in No. 4 with the following variants :—

The children were put into the gourd by the gods Ardalkosa, Patraj, Pirusi, and Tuldokari. But Mahapurub wanted to destroy the children : he tried to cut the gourd open and let them drown. But the gods got hold of the gourd in time and threw it into the water. First it floated to the east ; then the current took it to the west.

Two wild boars escaped the deluge. They lived on a very high mountain. As they dug for roots the earth was caught in their bristles, and when they shook themselves it flew all over the sea and settled down to make the earth again. The earth is held in place by wild roots which the boars still eat.

There was no jungle then. The villagers made stacks of grass and this grew into trees of its own accord.

7

BISON-HORN MARIA

Gogonda, Bastar State

As in No. 4 with the following variants :—

The gods Iru Sirma and Marka Raj were living in little huts made of leaves. By watching them the two children learnt how to make houses.

The boars got earth, not from the tortoise, but from the Karngakike Kanyang (the dandai fish), the Lugekike Kanyang (the turi fish) and the Yerepuri Kanyang which had kept some earth in their bellies.

8

BONDO

Kadamguda, Koraput District

A Raja had a son and a daughter and the two used to play together. One day the girl got a gourd seed and threw it away on the rubbish heap. It grew and a great flower came from it and then a mighty gourd. The boy made a hole in the gourd and hollowed it out inside. He said, 'If ever it rains too much we can hide in this gourd.' One day the rain fell and the brother and sister went to play inside their gourd. As they were playing several days passed, but the rain never stopped and the whole world was flooded with water. The gourd floated on the surface and the children grew hungry and began to cry. Mahaprabhu heard them and came to see what was the matter. 'Who are you?' he asked. 'We are brother and sister and we are very hungry.' Mahaprabhu went to the wild boar and told it what had happened. The boar went to the Under World to Kermo Deota and stole earth from him. With the earth he stole seven kinds of trees—the mango, tamarind, mahua, sago palm, the dumar and pipal figs and the banyan.

The boar smeared the mud on its body and bathed. When it came out of the water, it shook itself and the earth flew over the ocean and the world was made. Some of the boar's bristles came out and turned into grass. The seeds of the seven trees were also scattered across the world and from them has come the jungle.

Then Mahaprabhu took the brother and sister out of the gourd and changed their appearance by smallpox so that they did not know each other. They married and mankind has come from their union.

9

BONDO

Mundlipada, Koraput District

The earth was covered by the waters and Mahaprabhu could see no one. He rubbed some dirt from his arm and made a crow. The crow said, 'Where shall I sit?' and Mahaprabhu let it sit on his shoulder. As it flew over the water it got very tired and said again, 'Where shall I sit?' Mahaprabhu pulled a hair out from under his armpit and made a cotton tree for it to sit on. As it flew about it saw a big covered basket floating on the water. Inside the basket were a brother and sister. The crow flew back to Mahaprabhu and told him what it had seen and Mahaprabhu sent it back again to find some earth. It caught an earthworm and took it to Mahaprabhu.

Mahaprabhu scratched the worm with his nails and brought out some earth. He threw it in all directions and the world came into being.

He opened the basket and found the brother and sister. He said to them, 'Why do you not marry?' They replied, 'We are brother and sister, so how can we come together?' Mahaprabhu sent them away in different directions and the girl became squint-eyed and the boy turned into a leper. When they next met they did not recognize one another and so they married.

They had twelve sons and twelve daughters and their race was the Remo.[1] From them all the people of the world were born.

10

DHANWAR

Barbhata, Uprora Zamindari

When the world would not remain steady, Mother Earth caused birds to be born. The first birds had four legs. But after they were born Mother Earth took two legs from each and set them below the earth like the pillars of a house. Resting on the legs of crores of birds the world became steady.

11

DHOBA

Silpuri, Mandla District

When Bhagavan first made the earth, Bhimsen drove four nails of virgin iron into the four corners with his club to make it steady. The corners of the world were strong enough but in the middle it still shook. So they made the old woman Grilya Burhin stand below the world in the middle supporting it on her head.

Every two years or so Girin Burha, her husband, remembers her and feels lonely. He comes to see her and catches hold of her. She cries, 'Don't brother, you smell horrid.' But he lies with her and as he does so the earth quakes but since the corners of the earth are held by the nails, even though it quakes it cannot fall down to the Under World.

[1] Remo is the name by which the Bondo refer to themselves.

12

GADABA

Onumal, Koraput District

Before this world was made there was born in the midst of the waters a potter. He came to the surface and tried to find somewhere to live. He swam round and round, visiting all the four quarters of the world until he was very tired. He was so tired that a stream of saliva trickled from his mouth. This spread on the surface of the water and slowly set and hardened until it had formed a crust over the ocean. The potter climbed onto it, but it sank under his feet. He cut off his left hand and his left foot, cutting each in half so that there were four pieces. He drove them as nails into the four corners of the earth's crust and thus made it firm.

13

GADABA

Kajriput, Koraput District

At first, before there were any other people in the world, a brother and sister lived together in a gourd. They had nothing but a cow and a little cloth. One day the sister died. Soon after her death, the man had a dream and his seed fell from him. He removed the soiled cloth and put it on the roof of the house to dry. Presently the cow returned from the jungle, pulled the cloth from the roof and ate it. The cow conceived and in due course a boy and a girl were born from its belly. The first man was astonished, but he kept the children very carefully. They grew up and then the first man died. One day, brother and sister went for wood to the jungle and on the way home bathed together in a mountain stream. They were naked and among the waters became man and woman to each other. From the girl was born the race of Gadaba. Because we came from the belly of the cow, we do not milk her.

14

GADABA

Alsidusra, Koraput District

When the earth went down beneath the waters, a Gadaba called Janglu and his mother hid in a hollow cotton tree. It had no branches or leaves and floated like a boat. It drifted along to Murimatikona and grounded there. The mother and son got out and made a camp but for a long while they had no food. The mother said to her son, 'Son, do something or other to make a world.' Janglu took four fingers of skin from his left side and wrote a letter. From the dirt at the corners of his eyes, he made a maina and tying the letter round its neck sent it to Kesu Raja in the Under World. The bird flew and flew and reached the place in eight days and nine nights. The Raja read the letter and at once sent seven women with water pots and seven carts to carry water. The women were able to get along the road to the world, but there was no room for the carts. The Raja therefore went to Bhim and told him. Bhim pulled out his own tongue and stretched it out and out until it was a road fit for carts to travel stretching from the Under World to the sky.

The carts and the women carried the water that had drowned the earth up to Bhim. When it was all dried up and there was only mud left at the bottom, Janglu chopped up the wood of the cotton tree and spread it everywhere. In Murimatikona there was red gravel; he dug it up and scattered it about. In this way the world was prepared.

When the world was ready Janglu's mother's appearance changed. She had been old; now she became young and beautiful. Bhim and Kesu Raja wondered how men were to be born. 'Let us make these two man and wife,' they thought. They said to Janglu, 'Is this woman your wife?' 'No, she is my mother.' And they said to the woman, 'Is this man your husband?' 'No, he is my son.' They took them to seven bazaars and asked them the same questions, but they always gave the same answers. At last Bhim and Kesu Raja filled the mother's mind with sin and then the two married and went to live at Murimatikona. Their children were the first Gadaba.

15

GADABA

Gunaipada, Koraput District

Larang the great Dano devoured the world, and nothing were left but water. But in a gourd floating on the water were a girl and boy. On Larang's tail there grew a cotton tree;[1] it grew up out of the water and spread towards the sky. Flowers blossomed on the tree. When Mahaprabhu saw nothing but water he thought and thought; at last he made a crow from the dirt of his body and sent it to find earth. That crow went flying and flying; it saw the gourd, but did not alight on it; instead it saw the red flowers of the cotton tree and, thinking that there was meat to eat, flew to the tree and sat on it. It drank the juice of the cotton flowers and found it sweet. Then it flew back to Mahaprabhu and told him everything.

Mahaprabhu went to see the tree and climbed down the trunk till he came to where Larang the Dano was. He caught hold of him and squeezed him so hard that he excreted the earth he had devoured. Then Mahaprabhu squeezed the whole of Larang's body so violently that not a bone remained unbroken and there was nothing left but flesh. He pressed his head till it became small.

From the earth that Larang excreted, the world was formed again. But it shook from side to side, so Mahaprabhu created the Kamar. The Kamar made bellows, covering them with cloth. But when he began to blow up his fire to make nails, the cloth broke. So Mahaprabhu made a black cow and the Kamar killed the cow and used the hide to cover his bellows, and soon had ready four nails which he drove into the four corners of the world. Now the earth was firm but it swelled up in the middle. The Kamar picked up his bellows and beat down the swelling. Some of it remained—and that part is the mountain. The part that went flat is the plain. But it all was due to the Kamar's bellows.

[1] In Onagelu the Gadaba said that Mahaprabhu himself made the cotton tree out of a hair taken from his armpit.

16

GOND

Patangarh, Mandla District

At the beginning there was nothing but water. On its surface floated a lotus flower on which sat Mahadeo. When he saw nothing but water, he made a crow from the dirt of his body and sent it to find earth. The crow flew and flew till it came to rest on the claw of the great crab, Kakramal Kshattri. When the crow said 'Kao,' the crab exclaimed, 'At last after many days I have got something to eat.' The crow replied, 'Uncle, my father has sent me to you.' The crab said, 'Nephew, why have you come? Tell me quickly.' The crow replied, 'My father has sent me to get earth to make the world.'

Then the two of them went to Singardip. There Nal Raja and Nal Rani had earth. After searching for a long time, the crab and the crow went to Nal Raja and Nal Rani and began calling them aunt and uncle and asked for some earth as a loan. They promised to give it and said, 'Take some food and then go your way.' Nal Rani prepared poison for the guests. When they had eaten, they became drunk and then unconscious. When they saw them safely asleep, Nal Raja and Nal Rani stole the earth and prepared to run away. But the crab awoke and caught them in its claws and squeezed the earth out of their mouths and gave it to the crow.

Then the crow took the earth to Mahadeo. Mahadeo made seven leaf-cups of lotus leaves and put a little earth in each. He stirred it up in each cup and called for Makramal Kshattri. He said to her, 'Now spin your web over the face of the sea.' The spider prepared her web and Mahadeo put the seven cups of earth upon it and fanned them with a lotus leaf. With the breeze of his fanning, the earth was carried over the web and the seven kinds of earth were prepared—the black earth, the red earth, the milk earth, the barren earth, the gravel earth, virgin earth and swampy earth.

When all was ready, Mahadeo said to Bhimsen, 'I have made the earth, but I do not know whether it is solid or no.' Bhimsen was pleased and said, 'I will come and look.' As he went, his feet sunk into the earth. But he lay down on the ground and rolled about, thus making the mountains.

17

GOND

Billhar, Bilaspur District

Nandsur Dano stood on the earth. Mother Earth said to him, 'You are a great weight on my body; you must marry me.' And so these two were married. Mother Earth gave birth to many children. From the shadow of the Dano's head was born the Brahmin; from his eyes the Sonar; from his nose the Chamar (whom they call Nakua); from his ribs the Kol (for the Kol has two-and-a-half ribs and can carry heavy loads); from his feet (*god*) was born the Gond and from his urine (*pāni*) the Panka. In this way fifty-two castes and tribes were born from the woman's body and the Dano's shadow.

The Dano caught the breasts of Earth and pulled them off and they became the Sun and Moon; her clitoris became the lightning which flashes and sparkles as the clitoris does.

The Dano pulled out his pubic hairs and threw them away; they turned into the grass that clothes the earth. He tore off his testes and they turned into great rocks, and his penis became the trees of the forest. In this way the bodies of Mother Earth and Nandsur Dano turned into the world and everything we can see.

18

JUANG

Andhari, Pal Lahara State

At first the world was unsteady; it was a sea of mud that shook and quivered. From it an ant-hill grew, and from the ant-hill came Mahesu Rusi. He lived on jungle fruit and roots. One day as he was searching for roots he came to the Keonjhar forest. There he met an Asur girl and they loved each other. The girl said, 'I am going to marry you.' Rusi said, 'No, I am afraid; even if you do not devour me, your brothers or sisters will.' But the girl said, 'Do not be afraid. I am all alone.' Thus they were married. Then said the girl, 'What do you eat?' 'I live on jungle fruit and roots. And you?' 'I eat what you eat and you eat what I eat.' 'Well, I have married you,' said Mahesur Risi, 'So I had better do what you do.' After that Rusi began to eat every kind of meat—except men, for there weren't any.

On Baora Hill lived the cow Kapila. Dharam Deota told Rusi and his wife to prepare the earth so that their children would be able to live on it. The Asur wife sent Rusi to get the cow, saying that by its blood the earth would become steady. He brought it to Gonasika and sacrificed it there. As its blood fell on the earth, all became fixed and steady.[1] From the blood came the rainbow. It stretched over the world and at either end a nail held it in place. From the cow's head flowed a great river.

At first Mahesur Risi would not eat the cow's flesh. 'But if you don't,' said the Asur wife, 'the earth will not be steady.' He ate and Dharam Deota came and made him bathe in the river Baitarani flowing from the cow's head. After he had bathed, Dharam Deota gave him a digging-stick. He gave him a belt of *kumi* bark and a dress of leaves for his wife. This is how the Patrosurni Juang began.

19

KOND

Meriahpatta, Koraput District

Formerly the hills and mountains were in the Upper World; they lived on blood and milk; men lived on bones and flesh. So even now those above drink blood and we do not drink milk. Mahaprabhu said to the hills and mountains, 'Go down to earth.' They refused. 'I will give you a cockle shell in marriage. It will give you water, and men will give you the Meriah sacrifice and you will get blood.' The hills were pleased at that and they came down. From them were born the first boy and girl. We gave them blood to drink until the British Government stopped us, and now the hills are angry and give us fever.

[1] But in another legend, the Juang tell the same story about the sacrifice of Parihar as the Bhuiya. They add, however, that the boy's ghost came to the Juang and said, 'I am your elder brother: now on my dead body you have made fields and gardens: you are living on my body, yet you do me no honour. I must have blood'. This was how cow-sacrifice began among the Juang.

20

KOND

Meriahpatta, Koraput District

The first boy in the world was one day in his field of pulse guarding the crop with his gun. A barking-deer came to steal the crop and the boy ran towards it with his gun ready to shoot. The deer was pregnant and the life in its belly spoke to the boy saying, ' Don't shoot and I will tell you something that is necessary for you to know '. It was the Sun God who was pregnant in the deer's belly. The boy lowered his gun and the life in the belly said, ' In eight days the world is going to turn over and everything will be water. Make a boat of cotton-wood, fill it with all things to eat and you and your sister sit in it.' The boy went home and when his mother saw him empty-handed, she abused him saying, ' Why have you brought no food ? ' The boy told her what had happened and his mother said, ' It is nothing but lies.'

But the boy and his sister got the boat ready and they put food and seed in it. They got into it and when the earth turned over into the water they were the only people in the world who were saved. The boat drifted along until it brushed against a great fig tree that was growing out of the water. Presently the sun began to dry up the water, for in those days there were seven suns and they were very hot. Soon the earth appeared and the boat settled on dry land but the heat of the seven suns was so great that the trees and grass dried up as well as water. So the moon pretended to eat her children and went to the sun with her mouth red, crying, ' Look, I have eaten my children ' and the sun ate his six brothers as well. But when night came the moon brought out her children the stars, and the sun was very angry since he could not bring his brothers out again.

21

KOND

Bandagaon, Koraput District

At the beginning when the world sank down under water a brother and sister hid in a hollow cotton tree. Their names were Dakpaska and

Dakadidi.[1] The tree floated on the water and at last came to rest on a hill. That brother and sister married and from them were born Gogerenga and Jagarenga.

They wept saying, 'How can we live without land to cultivate?' Mother Earth said to them, 'Give me a maiden in sacrifice.' They therefore sacrificed the daughter of Gogerenga and Jagarenga and the water dried up. But still the earth was unstable and it was not till they drove nails of a thorn-brush into the ground that it became steady.

22

KOND

Chutargaon, Koraput District

Daspajka and Dakadidi were brother and sister. They had no food and for eight days they sat weeping. Burha Pinnu and Pusrudi came to see what was the matter. They said, 'We have no food.' Burha Pinnu said, 'Give your children to Dharni Pinnu (Mother Earth).' They said, 'When we have children we will give them.' Burha Pinnu then sent the crow to Pujabutur the Tortoise which had swallowed earth and got a little. He scattered it on the water. Daspajka and Dakadidi sacrificed their son and daughter and the earth was made. Burha Pinnu and Pusrudi sat on the crow's back and it took them to live in the sky.

23

KURUK

Chitrakot, Bastar State

Before the world was made there was nothing but a great ocean. In the midst of the ocean was a lotus. On this Mahapurub lived, and from his belly a boy and a girl were born. These two played in the lotus. When they grew up they quarrelled. Mahapurub called them and said, 'You are disturbing me with your quarrels.' He picked them

[1] There is much confusion over the names of the first human couple: they are called in different villages—Dakpaska and Dakadidi, Daspajka and Dakadidi, Dakpajia and Sujamajia.

up and killed them. As they died their flesh turned into earth, their bones to stone, their blood to water, their hair to grass. In this way the world was made.

After the world was made, Mahapurub thought and again from his belly a boy and a girl were born. They shut their eyes, for they thought it would be sin for them to look at each other. Mahapurub hit them with his fist, and they opened their eyes, but they refused to marry. Mahapurub banished them in opposite directions and they wandered for twelve years. When they met again they did not recognize each other and married. Mahapurub gave them the world for their kingdom.

24

LANJHIA SAORA

Rumrumba, Koraput District

When the waters came, the Dead put seed and earth with a boy and a girl, brother and sister, into a gourd and let it float. When they came out the brother and sister lay together. The sun darkened itself at the sight. The crab brought earth to the Dead and they made the earth and levelled it. Then they showed those two how to make clearings in the forest and how to burn them and sow seed in the ashes. As the Dead taught us, so we still do. The Saora were the first made of all mankind; we were all one, without caste or clans to divide us.[1]

25

LANJHIA SAORA

Munisingi, Ganjam District

At first there was a world above the waters of the Under World. But Kittung's rat burrowed below the mountains and water surged up from below and the earth was submerged. But Kittung and Kittungboi lived in a gourd. In the sky the great Kittung made a crow and sent it to

[1] In some villages the Saora say that it was the Sun which dried up the first great waters, so that the hills and mountains appeared and the world came into being.

see what was happening. It found the gourd and flew back to Kittung to tell him where it was.

From Kittung and Kittungboi in the gourd, Rama and Bhimo were born. One day Bhimo wanted to relieve himself. 'I want to relieve myself,' said Bhimo. Rama said, 'Do it on my head' and when it was over he threw the cast into the water. The water dried up at once and the earth appeared again. They found that where the rat had heaped up the soil there were mountains, and the hollows it had made became rivers. But Rama and Bhimo thought, 'How are we to know if this is all right?' They were afraid to tread on the new world. First they made a hen and sent it; the earth bore its weight. Then they made a pig and sent it; the earth bore its weight. Then they made a buffalo and sent it; the earth bore its weight. In this way they discovered that the world was fit for use.

Soon after this Bhimo wanted to piss. 'I want to piss,' said Bhimo. Rama thought, 'If he pisses the world will be drowned again.' He said 'Piss in my ear.' Bhimo pissed in Rama's left ear and at once from the right ear two girls were born.

Rama said, 'One of these girls will be my wife and one will be yours.' The four lived together. One day as they were going somewhere, Bhimo got hold of a horse and climbed on its back. Rama thought, 'This fellow will be more important than me.' So he climbed on the back of a mountain and lived there. He found a blacksmith and got him to make him an axe. One day he met Kittung who showed him how to cut the forest and make a clearing for his crops. The Saora are the children of Rama and cut the jungle. The sons of Bhimo are the Rajas and Bissoyi chieftains.

26

LANJHIA SAORA

Olleida, Ganjam District

There was a gourd big as a small hill. When the earth sank down below the waters, a Saora boy and his sister made a hole in the side of the gourd and hid there. The gourd floated on the face of the waters. After a while, Kittung Mahaprabhu made a kite from the dirt of his body and sent it to find out if there were any men in the world. The kite flew round and round until at last it reached the gourd, and perched on it. It heard the brother and sister talking inside. It flew back to Kittung and said, 'There is a thing like a hill and a noise inside. There must be some living creature there.' Mahaprabhu made a fly and an ant and sent them into the gourd. The boy was sleeping on a cot and the girl on the floor. The fly buzzed in the girl's ears and the ant bit her and she cried, 'Brother, I can't get to sleep.' He said, 'Then come and sleep with me on the cot.' In this way they became man and wife. In due time the sister became pregnant. When Kittung heard of it, he sent the water down again and the gourd broke open. The youth and his wife came out and the broken bits of gourd turned into the earth. Many children were born and soon the world was peopled.

27

LANJHIA SAORA

Parisal, Ganjam District

Kittung Mahaprabhu lived with his sister on the Mahendra Mountain. When the earth sank down and the waters rose above it, the two, brother and sister, went into a gourd which floated on the surface. Presently *dupi* grass grew out of the water and a rat climbed up and down the stalk. The rat dug deep into the earth and filled its belly, then made its way to Kittung. Kittung took the earth from the rat's belly and spread it on the water round the *dupi* grass; the water sank down and there was the earth again above it. From the gourd brother and sister climbed out onto dry land. There they used to sleep with the rat, all three together. Gradually love grew between the girl and the rat, and one day she found herself pregnant. Kittung felt ashamed, thinking that the world would laugh at him if they knew that his sister had lain with a rat, and he said, 'Take my name and you and I will become husband and wife.' Thus brother and sister married and the child was the first Saora.

28

LOHAR

Partarpur (Seoni Tahsil), Chhindwara District

At the beginning of the world Guru Mahadeo and Gutiya Dewar prepared the earth. They sought everywhere, but they could find no one who could bear its weight. They went therefore to Dudh Nang, the Milk Cobra. She had a son whose name was Raja Girdil whose wife's name was Girdoli. When Mahadeo had told the Milk Cobra what he wanted she sent for her son and daughter-in-law. Mahadeo said to them, 'We will make you Raja and Rani of the Under World, for there are none so strong as you.' The Dewar said to them, 'The Rani must carry the world on her head. The Raja must go round and round the world and pick up all the old torn rotten rags that he can find and make them into a pad on which his Rani can balance the world.' Then the Rani went to Gutiya Dewar's wife and said to her, 'My husband and I have become the Raja and Rani of the Under World and I have to carry the Middle World on my head, but how am I and my husband to love one another?' Gutiya Dewarin said to her, 'After twelve years, when the thirteenth year has begun, give the burden of the world to your husband to hold. Lie down with him and holding it up with your hands you can then love one another.' The Rani went back to the Under World and told her husband. She held the world steady for twelve years and on the first day of the thirteenth year she went to lie with her husband and there was an earthquake.

29

MURIA

Kokori, Bastar State

(From *The Muria and their Ghotul*, 257 *f*.)

In the old days there was an earth. At the time when Lingo and his brothers were born, Mahapurub turned the world topsy-turvy and it was eaten by the earth-worm, so the Middle World became nought but water. There were two young children on the earth. God put life into their bodies by poking them in the back: the marks of his fingers still remain. They hid inside a gourd which grew up out of the water as a great creeper and reached the heavens.

Presently the worm excreted the earth and some of it fell on a siari leaf. That earth began to weep, 'Who is there to serve me, for all mankind are drowned?' When Lingo heard that weeping he went to see what was the matter. Meanwhile Mahapurub had plucked the gourd growing from the great creeper in the heavens and found inside the two small children. 'Where can these children live?' So thinking he sent his crow to search for the earth. The crow flew and flew over the ocean until at last it saw Lingo and his brothers driving their harrow across the sea. Wherever the harrow went there was land, where it went crooked or missed a place there was water and a river, where the earth was piled up at the side, there was a mountain. When the crow saw this it flew back and told Mahapurub that the earth was made again, and the two children were sent to live there.

30

RAJA MURIA

Chitrakot, Bastar State

This is a matter of long ago. In those days everything was water. The earth was in the belly of a pregnant Dano. Her name was Kaitab. She sat on the water. So twelve years passed.

Mahapurub created men. He thought, 'Here is water, here in Kaitab's belly is earth.' How was he to get the earth from her? From the dirt on his forehead, Mahapurub made a man. For twelve years he held him on his lap and the man grew. Then said Mahapurub, 'I made you, and I have nursed you for twelve years. Now do something for me. Kill this Kaitab and I will make you lord of the earth.'

So the man went to fight Kaitab and killed her. When she died her flesh turned into earth and her bones to rocks. Soon the earth was ready but it still shook and quivered. Mahapurub pulled out nine hairs from his right leg and drove them into the nine corners of the world and it became steady. Mahapurub made the man lord of the world and he was able to pick it up with his little finger. Then men were born everywhere.

After this a boy and a girl were born from Mahapurub's belly. When they grew up these two, brother and sister, married. In due time they had seven sons and seven daughters. The gods wondered how to make separate castes and tribes. They made the eldest brother a Raja, the second brother a Brahmin to worship the gods, the third a Dhakad to fight for the Raja, the fourth a Rawat to care for his cattle, the fifth a Muria to carry his loads, the sixth a Kuruk to catch his fish and the seventh a Maria to see to his hunting. These were the seven castes of Bastar. From seven they have grown to thirty-six.

31

RAJA MURIA

Ratenga, Bastar State

When there was nothing but water in the world, a brother and sister lived in a gourd that floated to and fro. Slowly the gourd moved, then it stayed in one place for twelve years. It was blown by the wind against an adan[1] tree. It shook the tree and Mahapurub too was shaken. He thought in his mind, 'I have done penance for twelve years; what is this?' He was angry and went to the tree and killed that brother and sister. Directly he killed them the earth was made from their bodies.

The gourd broke in half. Each half lay face downwards on the ground. Mahapurub kicked them aside and they turned over. There was a new boy in one and a new girl in the other. Mahapurub took them home, and when they were grown up, he married them and from them all mankind has come.

32

RAJNENGI PARDHAN

Madhopur, Mandla District

While the world was forming, setting like curds on the face of the water, the wind blew from the east and the world began to form towards the west. Then the wind changed and it formed to the east.

[1] *Terminalia tomentosa*, W. & A.

Then Mahadeo was born. He sowed seven kinds of herb seed in seven seed-beds. The first was the sweet herb; the second was the herb that stays hunger; the third was the herb that makes one happy; the fourth was the herb that brings one all the news; the fifth was a herb that if one eats it and then rubs a little dirt from one's body and makes something, that thing will live; the sixth was a sorrow-giving herb and the seventh herb gave children.

After the herbs had been sown, the earth was still quaking and trembling. Mahadeo said to Parvati, 'I am going to drive nails into the earth. You can eat all the herbs except the seventh; don't eat that.' He took a gold adze with a silver handle and went to Kajliban Pahar. There he cut a sandalwood tree, made nails of the wood and fixed the earth in place.

But Parvati thought and thought. 'Why did he tell me not to eat the herbs in the seventh seed-bed?' At last she could not resist it and cooked and ate. She was pregnant at once and was very frightened. She ate the herb that brought news, and at once she saw Mahadeo in Kajliban driving nails of sandalwood into the earth. She wanted to call him, but could not. She ate the fifth kind of herb, made a tiger from the dirt of her body, and told it, 'From today you are king of the jungle. Go to Mahadeo; hide behind the trees and frighten him home.'

The tiger went to Mahadeo and he threw some of the shavings of his nails at it. They turned into wild dogs and drove it away. But Mahadeo went home to see what was the matter. When he saw Parvati was pregnant he went to Bhagavan and said, 'Why did you let her become pregnant?' Bhagavan said, 'Unless she is pregnant how will we people the world?'

In time Parvati gave birth to many boys and girls. She felt ashamed to be bearing so many at once and buried the babies under different trees. The best of the boys she kept; Mahadeo saw him and was pleased. But he said, 'What have you done with the others?' So Parvati brought the others out. Mahadeo gave them names and divided them into tribes and clans, and arranged their marriages.

At the time of the Rama-Rawan war, a Gond and Gondin lived together in the thick jungle. In Lanka there were two Gond with Rawan. Mahadeo cursed those Gond and said, 'Until Rama comes to Lanka and you wash his feet and drink the water, you will have no children.'

So when Rama went to Lanka, he met that Gond and Gondin and they washed his feet and drank the water. He gave them this blessing:

'You will be Rawanbansi Gond and you will have three sons whose names will be Alko, Talko and Korcho.' Then Rāma killed all Rawan's followers save the Gond who went over to Rama's side. When Rama returned from Lanka he brought these Gond to the Gond who were living in the thick jungle. These were Surajbansi Raj Gond and they had five sons, Parteti, Markam, Maravi, Durwa and Bhagadiya. The Rawanbansi and the Surajbansi lived together as brothers.

Rawan had lost his glory and his honour; he turned into Bara Deo. To Parteti he gave a dream. 'Bara Deo will be born for both Rawanbansi and Surajbansi. Make a platform of mud and erect a pillar for him.' Parteti told the others his dream and they made a pillar. Then Bara Deo was born.

They all agreed that the youngest brother should have a *bāna* and should worship Bara Deo, while the eldest should sit on the throne as Raja. Such was the order of Bara Deo. When the youngest boy, Bhagadiya, danced and played before Bara Deo, Parteti gave him many presents—cattle, gold and silver. He said to him, 'From today you will be our Pathari. We will give you Sukdan and when any of us die you will have your share.'

33

YERNGA KOL

Phuljhar, Bonai State

At the beginning all was water. Above were the Sun and Moon. These were Singbonga and Chando. These were man and wife. These were the greatest gods. They looked down and saw nothing but water. 'What shall we do?' They both rubbed dirt off their bodies and Chando made a girl and Singbonga made a boy. They put life into them and threw them into the water. The boy and girl met in the water and copulated. Singbonga was angry at the sight and rained down fire to kill them. But Nagera, the Water Goddess, hid the pair and saved them. By this fire, the water was dried up and the earth appeared, and the boy and girl came out onto dry land.

Singbonga thought, 'These two did no sin. What they did was good, or they would have died.' So he made every kind of tree and shrub and grass to keep them alive.

From these two all mankind has come.

CHAPTER TWO

SUN, MOON AND STARS

I

The Sun and Moon

In the classical Hindu tradition, Surya the Sun and Soma the Moon are both male and are unrelated. Surya is described in widely varying terms, but always splendidly. He is the source of light, the son of the mighty sky-god Dyaus. His wife is Ushas the Dawn. He moves across the sky in a golden chariot drawn by seven horses.

He is addressed in a number of hymns in the *Rigveda* where he is described as 'all-seeing, the spy of the whole world, beholding the good and bad deeds of mortals. . . . The Dawn reveals or produces Surya; like a lover he follows the radiant goddess. He arouses men to activity; he is the soul of all that moves or stands. He is the son of Heaven (Dyaus). Surya is variously described as a bird traversing space; as a mottled bull or a brilliant steed; as a gem of the sky, or a variegated stone set in the midst of heaven; as a brilliant weapon; or as a wheel . . . He dispels the darkness, which he casts off like a skin. He measures the days and prolongs life.'[1]

Soma in Puranic legend is often called the son of Atri the Rishi and his wife Anasuya. He rides across the sky in a three-wheeled chariot drawn by ten jasmine-white horses. He is very much a man and the *Matsya Purana* gives a vivid account of his seduction of Tara, the wife of Brihaspati, which earned him the anger of the gods. He married the twenty-seven daughters of Daksha (who represent the twenty-seven Lunar asterisms) but he was so fond of Rohini the fourth wife that the others were jealous. They went to their father and persuaded him to curse the Moon with consumption and sterility, which he did. But when the wives saw his pitiable state, they went to their father and got him to make the curse periodical instead of permanent; this is why the Moon waxes and wanes.

Crooke gives two other legends about the Moon. In one, of which there is a trace in the *Rigveda*, the gods, by drinking up the nectar, caused the waning of the moon. Another curious expla-

[1] Macdonell, *Hymns*, 29.

nation was current in Bombay. One evening Ganesa fell off his steed, the rat, and the Moon could not help laughing at his misfortune. To punish him the angry god vowed that no one should ever see him again. He prayed for forgiveness, and Ganesa agreed that he should be disgraced only on his birthday, the Ganesa Chaturthi. On this night the wild hogs hide themselves that they may not see the Moon, and the Kunbis hunt them down and kill them.[1]

About the sex of the Sun and Moon there is much confusion. In Assam the Sun is generally regarded as feminine and the Moon as masculine. This view is held by the Angami and Sema Naga and by the Khasi, Dafla and Lakher. On the other hand, the Abhor, Miri and Mishmi seem to make the Sun a man and the Moon a woman.[2] This is the most common belief in Middle India, though here too there is a certain amount of disagreement. The Santal say that Sing Chando the Sun is a man and the Moon is his wife[3] and the Sauria in the neighbouring hills agree with them.[4] The Bhuiya, however, who also identify the Sun with the Supreme Being, appear to regard the Moon not as his wife but as his younger brother. In this case both are male. The stars, however, are the Moon's daughters, presumably by some unknown consort.[5] The Kharia say the Sun and Moon are husband and wife and the stars are their children.[6] The Birhor say the Sun and Moon are related as brother and sister.[7]

Among the legends of origin, perhaps the most common of the extra-Puranic tales is that which suggests that the Sun or Moon was originally too hot. There is a hint of this in the *Ramayana* where Surya is described as being of so overpowering a brightness that his wife Sanjna gave him Chhaya (shade) for a handmaid, and retired into the forest to devote herself to religion. 'While thus engaged in the form of a mare, the Sun saw her and approached her in the form of a horse. Hence sprang the two Aswins and Revanta. Surya brought back his wife Sanjna to his home, and her father, the sage Viswakarma, placed the luminary on his lathe and cut away an eighth of his effulgence, trimming him in every part except the feet. The fragments that were cut off fell blazing to the earth, and from them Viswakarma formed the discus of Vishnu, the trident of Siva, the weapon of Kuvera, the lance of Karttikeya, and the weapons of the other gods'.[8]

[1] Crooke, i, 13.
[2] Mills, *The Ao Nagas*, 227.
[3] Bompas, 402.
[4] *Census of India*, 1931, 113.
[5] Roy, *The Hill Bhuiyas*, 279.
[6] Roy, *The Kharias*, 431.
[7] Roy, *The Birhors*, 486.
[8] Dowson, 311.

A good example of this tradition, which is reflected in our stories, is seen in the Uraon version.

Formerly there were seven brothers as Suns. Complaints went to the Moon that the whole world was melting from the heat of the Suns, unless she took measures to stop it. The Moon began to eat a bel fruit in presence of the Sun. The Sun asked his sister what it was that she found to be such good taste, as he also wanted to eat it. The Moon replied it was nothing but one of her own children the stars, and suggested to the Sun to boil the flesh of his own brothers, and to use them in this way which would give a similar taste. The Sun killed his brothers accordingly but when he began to eat them it gave a different taste and smelt differently. The Sun thinking that he was cheated by his sister rushed towards her with open sword to make away with her. The Moon instantaneously concealed herself in the hollow of a banyan tree and thus escaped death but had a slice of her body cut off by the Sun. Since that time there is only one Sun. The Moon gets an eclipse twice a year and has a black spot which represents the hollow of the banyan tree.[1]

The Santal have a similar tradition but in this case, the Sun, who seems to be identified with the Supreme Being, having decided to destroy mankind on account of its wickedness, blazed with such a fierce heat that man and beast writhed beneath its torment.[2] The Lakher say that formerly the Moon was bright and hot like the Sun, 'but his light was so fierce that one night it killed a widow's child which was sleeping on the platform in front of her house. The widow got very angry at this, killed the Moon's child with a spear and threw the refuse out of her beer-pot into the Moon's face that thus making it dirty and reducing its light'.[3] The Khasi say that when the Moon desired to marry his sister the Sun, she threw a handful of hot ashes in his face. 'Ever since then the light of the Moon has been pale, marred by dark shadows, and that is the reason he does not show his face in the day-time.'[4] The Lhota Naga legend combines with the notion of excessive heat the further widely-spread tradition of the exchange of the functions of Sun and Moon, whereby the hotter orb is turned into the cooler one.

At the beginning of time what is now the Sun was the Moon, and what is now the Moon was the Sun. In those days when what is now the Moon was the Sun it was very hot, so that all the leaves and the trees in the jungle shrivelled up and died, and men suffered torments from the heat. Then what is now the Sun said to the Moon (which was the Sun in those days), 'Why do you shine so

[1] *Census of India*, 1931, 116.
[2] Bompas, 402.
[3] *Census of India*, 1931, 127.
[4] Rafy, 90 f.

fiercely that you make all the leaves and trees in the jungle shrivel up and die, and cause men to suffer torments from the heat? You by being the Sun are making men and leaves to die from heat and the world will be destroyed. Therefore from today I will let you be the sun'. With these words he smeared the face of what is now the Moon with cow-dung, and what is now the Sun became the Sun. Therefore men say that the dark marks on the Moon are where the Sun smeared cow-dung on its face.[1]

The Lepcha have a tradition that the world suffered greatly in the days when there were two brothers who kept it always hot and light. One day the toad shot the elder brother with an arrow from the red cockscomb plant. The younger brother covered himself with a black cloth and the world became dark and many died. At last the bat cried through its nose as it hung upside down from a bow. The Sun looked down and smiled and it grew light again. Of the same order is the Ao Nago myth that the Sun grew angry because men complained of its heat and a cock had to trick it into shining again.[2]

The Agaria are so impressed with the heat of the Sun even now that they have developed an extensive mythology of the ancient war between the Sun and mankind.[3]

Another tradition, from North India, describes how the Moon was a dutiful daughter, who gave water to her mother when she was thirsty. The Sun was an undutiful son and would give nothing to his mother; so he has been doomed to burn ever since.[4]

A similar tradition was recorded by Russell in the Central Provinces.

A myth of the Sun and Moon is that the Sun and Moon were a brother and sister who were asked to a wedding. Their mother told them to bring back something from the feast for her. The Sun was greedy and ate everything that he got, keeping nothing for his mother. But the Moon remembered her and took back something from the feast. When they got home and their mother found that the Sun had brought nothing, she cursed him and said that as he had neglected to satisfy the soul of his mother, he should always burn; but as the moon had satisfied her, she should always remain cool.[5]

Another cycle of legends is less interested in how the Sun and Moon got cooler than in how they perform their regular daily task of crossing the heavens. Since many tribes regard the two great

[1] Mills, *The Lhota Nagas*, 196. [2] Stocks, 363 ff.
[3] There is a full account of these legends in *The Agaria*, 97 ff.
[4] *N.I. Notes and Queries*, iv, 198. [5] *Census of India*, 1901, 94.

luminaries as man and wife it has to be explained how they are always separated. The obvious explanation is that there has been a quarrel and this is often connected with the trick whereby the Moon made the Sun destroy his children, the stars, which used to shine by day. Thus the Santal describe how the Moon deprived the Sun of his power to burn up the earth by persuading him to eat up his children.

But when that night Ninda Chando (the Moon) let out her own children from under the basket she warned them to beware of the wrath of their father when he found out the trick that had been played him. When Sing Chando (the Sun) saw Ninda Chando's children still alive he flew to her in passion and the children at the sight of him scattered in all directions and that is why the stars are now spread all over the sky; at first they were all in one place. Although the stars escaped Sing Chando could not restrain his wrath and cut Ninda Chando in two and that is why the Moon waxes and wanes; at first she was always full like the sun.[1]

Hutton gives a story about the Naga of Patkoi State, 'that the Sun and Moon were originally sister and brother respectively. They quarrelled, and the Moon in a fit of temper burnt up everything on earth. A tree fell on him and he died, after which the Sun died of grief for her brother and eventually they were reborn with their sexes reversed.'[2]

The Buna account for the spots in the Moon by the following story. Sun and Moon are brother and sister. 'The Moon was once brighter than the Sun. One day they quarrelled and as a result the Sun took some mud and flung it at his sister's face. The Moon did not wash her face and the Moon became less powerful than the Sun, and the spots that are found in the Moon are due to the scattered patches of mud.'[3]

Stories about the marks on the Moon are suggested by some of its Sanskrit names, Sasi, 'marked like a hare', or Mriganka, 'marked like a deer'. The legends accounting for these marks are endless. There is an interesting Khasi story which tells how the Sun and Moon were sister and brother.

The Moon was a wicked young man, for he began to make love to his elder sister, Ka Singi. In the beginning the Moon was as bright as the Sun. When the Sun became aware of his bad intentions, she was very angry. She took some ashes in her hand and said to him, 'Do you harbour such an incestuous and wicked intention against me,

[1] Bompas, 403.

[2] Mills, *The Ao Nagas*, 299.

[3] Basu, 87.

your elder sister, who has taken care of you and held you in her arms, and carried you on her back like a mother does; now I will cover your brow with ashes, you wicked and shameless one; begone from the house'. Then the Moon felt very much ashamed, and from that time he gave out a white light because the Sun had covered him with ashes. What we see like a cloud on the Moon when it is full, are the ashes which adhered from the time the Sun covered him with them.[1]

In the Sylhet District, 'besides the stories that are given in the Puranas regarding the Moon's black spots, there is a popular belief among the Hindus that an old woman resides in the Moon who is busy with her spindle and the dark spots are nothing but that creature. The thread-like substances that are wafted by the wind on a fine day in the autumn season generally, are called the "old woman's threads". According to some Mussalmans, the dark spots are nothing but rows of palm trees, and according to others the spots represent a woman threshing corn with a dog by her side.'[2]

A curious Buna legend accounts for the difference in the length of the days during the course of the year.

In ancient times the days were very short. The people were busy and could not find sufficient time for work during the day. One day they met in a council and discussed how to make the day longer. There was one person who could bear heat, and he said that if they could manage to bind the Sun so that the Sun might not go fast, the days would be longer. All paid attention to this remark and agreed to this proposal. Then one morning some young men climbed a tree and tried to tie the Sun with a rope, but there was a slight mistake in tying for which the Sun for a few months in the year goes fast and for the rest of the year goes slow. So we find longer days in Summer and shorter days in Winter.[3]

I

BHUIYA

Champajor, Keonjhar State

The Moon was eating a roasted bel fruit and the Sun asked her, 'What is that you are eating?' The Moon replied, 'My children.' 'Then give me a little.' The Sun ate the fruit and found it sweet. Pleased with this the Sun ate all his own children, except one which ran away like the lightning. The Sun was angry and cursed the Moon saying,

[1] Gurdon, 172. [2] Bhattacharjee, 118. [3] Basu, 86.

'You will always have to be living and dying.' The Moon cursed the Sun in return and one of the Sun's eyes broke; that is why it has only one eye. For eight months of the year it does not wash its eye, then it wipes away the dirt and pus and gets very hot.

2

BISON-HORN MARIA

Tikanpal, Bastar State

When Kawachi and Kuhrami, the first boy and girl in the world, were married, they went to fish in a stream. They caught a turu fish and as they were cutting it up, a voice from inside its belly said, 'Cut me open carefully'. Inside, the children found the Sun and the Moon. For a time they kept them in their house. Then they had them married and asked them to go and live in the sky, for there was no room for them and their babies in their little leaf-house. The Sun and Moon did as they were bidden and the sky is now full of their children.

3

BISON-HORN MARIA

Dugeli, Bastar State

A man of the Kuhrami clan made the Sun and Moon out of an irpu[1] tree. He used to send the Sun up into the sky every morning and in the evening he would bring it down and send up the Moon instead. But the light of the Sun was so great that in a few days the man became blind, and could no longer control the Sun and Moon. Seeing this they went up and down of their own accord.

Formerly the Sun used to visit the earth disguised as a black bull. Once a Maria caught it wandering in his field and tied it up. This is why there is darkness in the world for half the day. After that, whenever the Sun wishes to visit the Middle World, it comes in the form of a dark man.

[1] *Bassia latifolia,* from the corollae of which ardent spirits are distilled.

4

DEWAR

Newari, Dondi-Lohara Zamindari

In the Binjpahar hills there was a village called Nirbanjpur and here lived Astangi Devi. Twelve years passed and she had not looked on the face of a man. One day came Pawan Dasseri the wind and blew in her ear and she found herself pregnant. When her time came she gave birth to twins, a girl and a boy. The girl's name was Chanda (Moon) and the boy's was Suraj (Sun). On the Chhatti day, when it was time to give the children some food, Astangi Devi wondered what she could give them, for in those days people lived on roots and fruit. She went to another village to try to find something more suitable for them to eat.

As she went along she met a very poor man whose name was Anusur Moru. He said, 'O Devi, where are you going so fast?' She said, 'I can't feed my children on those roots and so I am going to find some other kind of food.' The man said, 'I have heard that in Jinjhigarh there is some grain in the keeping of Basin Kaniya. I myself was going to her, but who knows if she will give anything to a poor old man like me.' So Astangi Devi said, 'Very well, I will go instead. You go to my house and look after the children till I return.'

Astangi Devi came to Jinjhigarh and found Basin Kaniya in the midst of a clump of bamboos. She begged for grain, but Basin Kaniya said, 'If you want it for yourself, I will not give it; but if you want it for the world, I will give it.' She gave Astangi Mata the seven grain sisters and the Mata brought out her milk and fed them at her breasts. Basin Kaniya said, 'Make seven fields and sow one grain in each field. From each grain there will be a cart-load at harvest time and the whole world will feast with pleasure.'

So Astangi Devi returned home and said to Anusur Moru, 'Stay with me and make seven fields.' He went to Basuladongri, to the place where the Churelin lived and there made seven fields. On the first day of Asarh he sowed the grain, one seed in each of the seven fields. In Sawan, Astangi Mata went to see the fields and found them covered with growing plants—rice, kodon, kutki, kang, sawa, mandia, urda. When the crop was ready Anusur Maro went to cut it and brought the sheaves to the threshing-floor. The piles of sheaves went eighty *jojan* high—there was only the width of an adze between the top of the pile and the sky.

But when Anusur Maro went home he said, 'There is only a small crop; the piles of sheaves are only three cubits high.' When she heard that, Astangi Mata said, 'How can we divide so small a crop among so many people; it will be better to burn it and then there will be no quarrels.' She sent her son Suraj to the place and said, 'If there are ten or twelve measures keep it; but if there is less burn it.' When Suraj saw the great harvest he wanted to return to tell his mother, but Anusur Maro threatened that he would kill him. Suraj was only a little boy and he too told his mother that there was a small crop.

Then Suraj set fire to the crop. The smoke was so great that it covered the world and no one could see anything. Since then there has been mist in the world. The sparks went up to heaven and set fire to the clouds. The clouds had bodies covered with skin and when the skin was burnt, the bones and flesh appeared and that is why the sky is blue. When Astangi Mata saw the smoke she ran to put out the fire and threw water on it and scattered it. With a long pole she pushed the great pile of sheaves over. Great balls of blazing straw and chaff blew up into the sky and stuck there. They are the stars.

When the fire was out and everything was cool, Astangi Mata took the grain to her house. This is bagri rice, it still is black and looks burnt, and sitahi kutki which looks the same, and urda. She turned Anusur Maro into an ill-omened star. But she blessed her son Suraj and made him Raja of the sky and earth. 'But because you set fire to the grain,' she said, 'Your body will always be fire.'

Astangi Mata married her daughter Chanda to Megh Raja's son Megh Kuar, and said, 'Daughter, your life will be happy. Go cool and come cool. All mankind will long for your light and will love you for it. Your beauty will be always changing and always new.'

As her daughter was going away her mother patted her on the shoulder. The mark of her hand is still to be seen.

5

GOGIA PARDHAN

Jhanki, Mandla District

Bhagavan wanted to piss. There was nowhere for him to do it, for there was danger that he would drown the earth. But when he could wait no longer, he got a great bamboo, cut the top and bottom, hollowed it out and pissed into it. In the Under World there was a lake called Kalipatpar: Bhagavan closed the bamboo and put it there.

In that place, where the bamboo full of Bhagavan's urine was put, Rawan, Maharawan and Madodri were born.

The spangle from Bhagavan's forehead fell into that urine and turned into the Sun and Moon. Before that the only light in the world was that from the sandal on Bhagavan's forehead.

Raja Vishesha lived in Amarpur. In that kingdom nothing ever died. Bhagavan thought, 'This man is greater than me.' So he sent Agindeo and Mahadeo there to take away the souls. When they reached the place the Raja asked, 'What will you eat?' Mahadeo replied, 'A measure of raw meat.' The Raja thought in his mind, 'How can I sin in killing one of my own subjects?' So he cut off his own foot and went to weigh it. It did not come to a full measure, so he cut off his leg and an arm, and gradually his whole body. Mahadeo said, 'You are a true Raja: is there any greater than you?' 'Yes, Jagat Raja.'

Guru Mahadeo returned to Bhagavan and told him what he had seen. Bhagavan set out to visit Jagat Raja, but on the way he met Rawan, Maharawan and Madodri, and Bhagavan, who is Rama, killed them. Then he caught the Sun and Moon and took them into his control.

From that time people in Amarpur began to die and their souls went to Bhagavan. Then Bhagavan married Sun and Moon and blessed them: 'Sun, you are master of the day: Moon, you are mistress of the night.' Sometimes Sun and Moon have intercourse in the east, sometimes in the west.

6

GOND

Bohi, Pandaria Zamindari

Megh Raja and Megh Rani had two daughters, one was the Sun and the other the Moon. The Sun was the elder and bigger. The Moon was very beautiful and so Lakshman went to serve for her as Lamsena. Then the Sun was jealous. 'I am the elder, but she is so beautiful that she has got a husband immediately.' One day as the two girls were playing together, Lakshman was sitting in a little hut playing his fiddle. When they heard him the Sun said to the Moon, 'Lend me your ornaments and let us go to listen to this sweet music.' The Sun put on the Moon's ornaments and by a trick cut off her head. But she was afraid that the head would join itself onto the body again. So she cut it into several pieces and sat on her flying chariot and flew away. Because she wears the Moon's ornaments she shines more brightly. The Moon is always in pieces and the stars are drops of her blood.

When Lakshman saw his bride cut to pieces, he quarrelled with her parents and her sister the Sun. 'I have worked for twelve years as Lamsena: either give me wages for those twelve years or else celebrate my marriage.' Megh Raja and Megh Rani were frightened and did not know what to say. After some time Megh Rani gave birth to another daughter whose name was Bijaldeo Kanya. Then the father said to Lakshman, 'Live and work here for another twelve years and we will give you this girl in marriage.' So he worked for another twelve years. But the parents said to themselves, 'If we marry our daughter to this man, her name will be famous and there will be war on her account.' So they put the maiden inside a hollow bamboo and said to Lakshman, 'We give you our daughter. Take her home but do not open the bamboo until you are inside your house.' Lakshman said, 'You have not arranged my marriage, and now you are giving me a bit of bamboo. I won't take it.' Then the parents made a little booth, anointed Lakshman with haldi oil; they dressed up the hollow bamboo in a girl's cloth and carried it with Lakshman round the pole. They said to him, 'This is our daughter. Take her home, but do not look at her on the way.' But as he was going along, Lakshman could not resist opening the bamboo to see his bride. She slipped out and disappeared as lightning in the sky. He made a bow and arrow of grass, and the thunder is the noise of his endless pursuit.

7

GOND

Sunpuri, Mandla District

There was a Lohar who had a very beautiful daughter. The Sun seeing her beauty fell in love with her. One day the father caught them together. Full of rage he dug a pit deep as twelve men with arms outstretched and shut the sun up in it. Everything was dark, there was no wind or rain or anything. Men came to the Lohar for help. There was a creeper near his house; they beat it to get wind out of it. Wind was in the creeper and his bones began to ache from the beating; soon he was whirling round and round and rising out of the creeper. From the wind were born two goddesses, Piri Baiha Mata and Piri Mata. The wind blew so strongly that the iron lid that the Lohar had fixed over the pit came off and the Sun escaped.

The Moon was very angry with the Sun over his love for the Lohar girl. 'I won't have a co-wife in the house,' said she. But the Lohar said, 'A woman should allow her husband to make seven mistakes and should forgive him every time.' So the Sun and Moon began to live together again.

8

MURIA

Ulera, Bastar State

(From *The Muria and their Ghotul*, 259)

When this world was first made there was neither Sun nor Moon and the clouds and the earth were like husband and wife, they lay so close together. Men were very small and had to move between them. They ploughed with rats and to pick brinjals they had to reach up as though they were getting mangoes from a tree. As they walked to and fro they used to knock their heads against the clouds.

Then Lingo and his brothers raised the clouds into the sky and there was room for men on earth, but there was no Sun or Moon and everything was dark. There was a tree called Huppe Piyer. When this tree blossomed it was day, when it dried up it was night. The twelve Lingo brothers and the thirteen Bhimul brothers thought and thought how they could bring more light to the world. 'Where can we find something which will make light and darkness ?' So thinking they came to the tree Huppe Piyer. 'This is what we want,' they said and began to cut it down. It was so big that the twelve Lingo brothers and the thirteen Bhimul brothers could cook their food and sleep in the space cut by their axes. When it was nearly cut through, it still did not fall, for on the top of the tree sat the bird called Gara-surial-pite holding it up. Said Lingo to his brother, 'We must kill this bird,' and Kosa Kana took his axe and killed it. Then the tree fell to the ground.

When the tree came down it fell on the thirteen Bhimul brothers and they shouted with fear. Lingo picked it up with one hand and threw it aside. Now this tree stood in the kingdom of twelve Rajas, and when these heard the noise they sent their police to see if the tree was safe. The police reported that someone or other had cut it down and the Rajas sent their soldiers to arrest the culprits. Lingo said to the soldiers, 'We have come to make two lanterns so that there may be light by day and light by night. We have done no evil.' So said Lingo. But the soldiers took no heed of what he said and attacked the brothers with their spears and swords. Lingo took the blows in his own body and saved his brothers. Then he himself took his sword and fought and killed all the soldiers. With their blood the tree became red, for its roots drank it. Then the brothers stripped off the bark and cut the wood into two great rings.

They made the lower ring into the Sun and the upper ring into the Moon. The Sun was as big as the kingdoms of the twelve Rajas, but the Moon was smaller. When they were ready, the brothers wondered how to put into them a living soul. Mahapurub had a son. 'Only by killing Mahapurub's son and giving his blood to the Sun and Moon to drink will they become alive and be man and woman.' So said Lingo. The brothers thought and thought how to catch Mahapurub's son, but at last Lingo said, 'I will catch him,' and went to the Upper World.

Mahapurub was working in his fields. His wife put the child in a swing and went for water. Lingo stole the child and brought him down to earth. There he sacrificed him and offered his blood to the Sun and

Moon. The Sun, who is a man, drank a lot of the blood and that is why he is always red. The Moon, who is a woman, only drank a little and is always pale.

When Mahapurub's wife returned and could not find her son, she ran to tell her husband and they were full of sorrow. But next morning when the Sun rose red into the sky, Mahapurub cried to his wife, 'Look, there's your baby in the sky; don't weep, for you will always be able to look at him.'

9

RAJA MURIA

Chitrakot, Bastar State

After Mahapurub had finished making the earth, he made two mirrors, one for himself and one for his wife. They looked in the mirrors and saw the whole world: it appeared like fire. Mahapurub thought and he gave life to the mirrors so that they could go about of their own accord. He married his own male-mirror to his wife's female-mirror, making his male-mirror the Sun and his wife the Moon.

These two had many children. The Sun's children were like him; the Moon's took after her. As they grew up, their heat was so great that the grass withered and the rocks cracked and men died everywhere. Mahapurub thought, 'What shall I do? All living things are dying and there will be too many in the Upper World.' He dug a pit and pushed the Moon into it and covered her with earth. Mahapurub also hid in the pit.

The Sun went searching for his wife and came to the pit. He called to the Moon, 'Come out.' But the Moon's mouth was full of earth and Mahapurub, taking the Moon's voice, replied, 'Your children and my children are giving me a lot of trouble: let us both devour our children.'

'Very well,' said the Sun, and Mahapurub let the Moon out of the pit. They began to devour their children. The Sun ate all his, but the Moon stuffed hers into her cheeks like a monkey. Then Mahapurub appeared. 'What is going on here?' he asked. They told him and he said, 'You are very foolish: bring your children out of your bellies.' The Sun tried and tried but could not bring out a single child, but the Moon at once brought out hers. Mahapurub was again anxious. 'Now there will be many children and more trouble. I must stop these two ever coming together again.' So he gave them separate kingdoms and after that each wandered in his own domain.

For fifteen days Sun and Moon live apart; for fifteen days they are together. But all the time they are together the Moon is in her period and looks defiled and ugly. So the Sun never approaches her and goes off quickly to his own work. But sometimes he searches for his wife and then the Moon hides in the clouds.

10

RAJNENGI PARDHAN

Sanhrwachhapar, Mandla District

The Sun and Moon are the eyes of Rama. After Lakshmanjati's death, Rama went in anger to the jungle and tore out his eyes. These became the Sun and Moon.

11

RAJNENGI PARDHAN

Patangarh, Mandla District

One night while Sita and Rama were lying together, Sita discussed Lakshman very affectionately. She said, 'There he is sleeping alone. What is it that keeps him away from woman? Why doesn't he want to marry?' This roused suspicion in Rama's mind. Sita slept soundly, but Rama kept awake the whole night imagining things. Early next morning he sent for Lakshman from his lonely palace and asked him suddenly, 'Do you love Sita?' Lakshman was taken aback and could hardly look at his brother. He stared at the ground for a long time and was full of shame.

Without saying anything Lakshman went to the mountains with his axe and cut down a forest of twelve hills and brought the wood to a place near the palace. Seeing the great heap of wood the people of the town came to discover what was the matter. Among them was a little child who was screaming. Lakshman took him in his arms and climbed on the heap of wood. Then he shouted, 'Set fire to this wood and if I am pure and innocent I will not be burnt.' The people set fire to the wood and it began to blaze, but Lakshman stood there with the crying child; to keep him quiet he began to play on his fiddle. When the fire burnt down, the villagers, and Rama and Sita too, were standing anxiously to see if Lakshman and the baby had been burnt or no. But there they were standing free and not even singed.[1]

After this test, Lakshman left his brother and said he would never visit his palace again. Rama tried his best to persuade him, but Lakshman would not listen to any persuasion. Sita, however, considered how she might win him round. As her *dewar* was going rapidly through the jungle he saw a vixen leave a little newly-born cub on the road and run away. The poor cub was blind and could not get any milk and Lakshman chased the vixen with the cub in his hand. At last he was able to catch the vixen and with one hand he caught one of its udders and put it in the cub's mouth. Suddenly there was Sita, instead of the vixen, with Sita's breast in Lakshman's hand. Lakshman was very embarrassed and immediately removed his hand, but Sita said, 'For truth and purity, you ran away from your brother only to touch my breast. Now I know how virtuous you are.' Lakshman was very annoyed by this taunt and ran away again, but Sita went forward and now became a fig tree.

Lakshman was hungry and when he saw a beautiful fig tree in the way, he caught a ripe fig in his hand—and there was Sita standing there instead of the fig tree and he was holding her breast in his hands.

Then Lakshman ran away again but Sita could not leave him. She turned her pubic cloth into a tobacco plant growing by the path. Lakshman was very tired and seeing the beautiful tobacco desired to have it, but as he caught it in his hand he found he was holding his *bhauji's* cloth. Sita again appeared saying, 'Why are you trying to pull off my cloth?'[2]

But Lakshman now was weary of the world and stamped so violently that he made a hole in the ground and he walked down and reached the Under World. There he found Ses Nag sitting in his palace with the Sun and Moon as two lamps. With him were his three unmarried daughters. When the three girls, Raimandi, Phulmandi and Bijloki saw the young man they begged their father to keep him as a Lamsena in their house. Lakshman was very sad and he agreed. The Nag was not very pleased with the boy and tested him harshly.

[1] Compare the ordeal of Lingo: Lingo also plays instruments of music while in the fire.—*The Muria and their Ghotul*, 236,242.

[2] Another version of this story is given in Hivale, 99 ff.

The first trial given to Lakshman was to plough twelve *kos* of land which had never been ploughed before, with a share made of brittle cotton wood. But by his merit Lakshman was able to plough it.

Then twelve measures of sesamum were given to sow in it, but when he had sown the seed the Nag sent for Lakshman and said, 'I don't want sesamum to be sown, so remove all the grains, for I am going to sow rice instead.' Lakshman went to the field and sat weeping. A wood pigeon heard him and was very sorry. She went and brought her friends and they soon picked up all the seeds and Lakshman was able to take all the twelve measures back to the Nag. That is why the wild pigeon always sings '*Thil puris, thil puris*?' (Is the sesamum enough to fill all the measures?).

There were many other tests and Lakshman could hardly ever eat his food. For misery and anxiety he used to throw his food away and it turned into great mountains.

After three years of labour, however, Lakshman was married to the three girls, but he insisted that they should be married not to him but to his sword. The Nag put the three girls in three baskets and took them round the sacred pole with the sword. At the time of giving the girls his offering all the three demanded that the Moon and Sun should be given as their wedding-present. The Nag gave them these two gifts on one condition, that the Sun and Moon would only remain half the time in the Upper World and half the time in the Under World.

When the party started back to the World, as they were going alone Lakshman wanted to open the baskets and look at the girls. The youngest girl Bijloki suddenly turned into the lightning, and even today Lakshman is madly trying to hit her with his arrow but has never been able to possess her.

The two other girls were stolen by a Dano. They appear in the world every ninth year as the mohati and amhera flowers. When these flowers blossom, the world has all the honey that it desires, because the bees love them.[1] The Nag had put food for the girls in the baskets, and when Lakshman in his rage and disappointment saw it, he kicked it away and it turned into snakes and all the poisonous creatures that are in the world today.

[1] The Baiga celebrate a Honey Festival at this time. See my article, 'A Honey Festival', *Man in India*, xxiv, 85 ff.

II

Eclipses

The traditional Puranic account of the eclipse is that Rahu the Asura, whose name means 'the looser' or 'the seizer', disguising himself as a god at the Churning of the Ocean, obtained a little of the *amrita* and drank it. The Sun and Moon discovered what he was doing and told Vishnu, who cut off his head with his discus. The *amrita* which he had drunk made him immortal and his head and tail went to the sphere of the Moon where the head still takes vengeance on the Sun and Moon by swallowing them from time to time.[1]

Penzer has pointed out that the origin of this myth appears to be unknown. The story is not early Buddhist nor even ancient Hindu. It occurs in the *Mahabharata* but it is not found in the *Vishnu Purana.*[2] The idea, however, of an animal or demon trying to devour the Sun and the Moon is one that would naturally occur to untutored minds and is widely distributed throughout the world. In India it is, of course, common everywhere among village Hindus and to some extent among the aboriginals. The Buna believe that there is a Rakshasa of great power, but with a hole in his throat. During an eclipse he swallows the Sun or the Moon and brings darkness on the earth, but soon the Sun or Moon comes out through the hole and light returns.[3] The Muthuvan say that a solar eclipse is caused when a serpent coils round the sun.[4] The Toda say that during an eclipse of the Moon a snake is devouring the hare that lives on its surface and they fast until the eclipse is over and shout to frighten away the snake.[5] Emeneau has recorded among the Kota a detailed account of this incident. Hunters were chasing a hare, and an enormous snake was chasing them. The hare went for refuge behind the moon, who 'having had pity, put it on his own lap under the cloak' and the snake 'whose belly had become hungry, swallowed the hare with the moon'.[6]

A more romantic version of the 'devouring' motif was recorded from Gilgit in the last century. The eclipse is 'a giant and a lover of the moon whom he seizes . . . when she is in her full beauty leaving untouched only the part which contains a fig tree.' The eclipse, personified as Grahn 'also becomes angry at the sun

[1] Crooke, i, 19.
[2] Penzer, ii, 80.
[3] Basu, 86.
[4] Iyer, ii, 35.
[5] Penzer, ii, 82.
[6] Emeneau, i, 68 f.

whenever a good king dies or is banished his country and he then darkens the whole or a part of the sun's face '.[1]

But there is another tradition that competes in popularity with this type of legend. Over a very wide area it is believed that an eclipse is due to the fact that the Sun and Moon are either in debt themselves or have stood surety for a debt to a money-lender, who duns them and thus causes the darkness by shutting them up somewhere. The Ghasia of Mirzapur, for example, say that the Sun and Moon once borrowed money from a Dom and did not pay it back. Now in revenge the Dom occasionally devours them and then vomits them out, thus bringing the eclipse to an end.[2]

Among certain Telugus, eclipses are regarded as being caused when the moon, interfering to protect a money-lender from a client who is about to strike him, is partly obscured by the assailant's body. Another Telugu version says a sweeper is about to strike his son with a broom, but the moon intervenes and is obscured.[3]

The Santal say ' that once upon a time the Sun or the Moon or both together stood security for humanity, when they had to borrow food from the Dusad, a certain godling. As men are unable to pay back, the Dusad now and again catches hold of the Sun or the Moon to get its dues; this happens during an eclipse and the Santals call out and beat their kettle-drums to make the Dusad let go his hold.'[4]

The Birhor theory is very similar. The Sun and Moon once stood security for the debts of poor men. The creditors now and again send bailiffs to arrest the Sun and Moon and at this time there is an eclipse.[5] The Chero say that the Sun and Moon stood security for the debts of the Chero and when they failed to repay the money their creditors send their agents to arrest the Sun and Moon and there is a fight, but sometimes the sureties are overshadowed and the result is an eclipse.[6]

Sweepers of the Central Provinces collect alms during an eclipse, for the Sun and Moon are in Rahu's debt and he goes and duns them; the alms given to the sweepers are a means of paying the debt.[7] Of the Teli also the story is recorded that ' the Sun is indebted to a sweeper. The sweeper has gone to collect the debt and the Sun has refused to pay. The sweeper is in need of the money and is sitting *dharna* at the Sun's door; you can see his

[1] *Rose*, i, 127. [2] Crooke, i, 21. [3] Venkataswami, 176.
[4] *Census of India*, 1931, 102. [5] Roy, *The Birhors*, 495. [6] *Agarwal*, 216.
[7] Russell and Hiralal, iv, 232.

shadow across the Sun's threshold. Presently the debt will be paid and the sweeper will go away.'[1]

It will be noticed throughout these stories that there is a certain suggestion of defilement; there is a curiously persistent association with the impure castes of Doms or sweepers. A similar idea is found in a somewhat different legend recorded by J. J. Modi in Bombay.

Rama, on his return from the defeat of Rawan in Lanka, gave a feast to his victorious army. Mahadeo and Parvati were serving the food. Presently Mahadeo drew the attention of Parvati to the presence of a low-caste Mang boy (a caste who act as village musicians and castrate bullocks, the women serving as midwives) in the assembly and asked her to be careful, and to serve him the food from a distance. But as soon as Rama saw the Mang he slew him for daring to mar the sacredness of the feast by his impure presence. The mother of the slain boy took up the head, placed it in a basket and tried in vain to resuscitate it with fresh water. With the basket containing the head of her son, she went to the gods and goddesses begging for food. In turn she still goes to the Sun and Moon, threatening to touch them, thus desecrating their sacred character if her request is not granted. It is the shadow of her basket that causes the eclipse, and so it is to remove this Mang woman, this importunate creditor, that people are asked to give offerings to the luminaries and alms to the Mang caste.[2]

The Kanikkar legend is a variant on the debt motif. The serpent is the parent of the Moon, which one day angered its parent by refusing to give it betel. The result is that the serpent occasionally shrouds the Moon with its hood.[3]

A Khasi story is of a different order. It is associated with a legend of the 'Skin Dress' type. The Giant Toad attempts to devour the Sun because she destroyed the skin concealing a lovely maid who married her son.[4] And another theory of a totally different character is revealed by a Ho legend that an eclipse is the result of sexual intercourse between Singbonga the Sun and Chandobonga the Moon who are believed to be man and wife.[5]

[1] Russell and Hiralal, iv, 550.

[2] J. J. Modi, 'A few Ancient Beliefs about the Eclipse', *J. Anth. S. Bom.*, iii (1894), 346 ff.

[3] Iyer, i, 55.

[4] Rafy, 1 ff.

[5] D. N. Majumdar, 'Some Ethnographic Notes on the Hos of Kolhan', *Man in India*, v, 185. The Ho believe that fishing-nets made during an eclipse will draw fish into them, for there will be an eclipse-like darkness in the water and the fishwill not see their danger.

12

BAIGA

Rewa State

(From *The Baiga*, 334)

Once at the beginning of the world the gods found they had nothing to eat and they grew very hungry. They went to a Basor to beg for food. The Basor said, 'I will give you what you want, but you must eat from my hands first.' What could the gods do? They had to agree. Now the Basor had a great bin full of grain and he told the gods to remove the grain through the hole at the bottom of the bin. When they had taken it out, the Basor took enough for their meal and made it ready.

But the gods sent Bhimsen secretly to fetch Pawan Daseri the Wind. When he came they told him that when they sat down to eat, he must come and blow the food away, for how could they eat from the hands of a Basor?

And so it happened. The Basor put the food before the gods and went away. Then the wind came in a great gust and carried it away, and when the Basor returned and saw the plates were empty he supposed they had eaten their food. But when the gods were removing the grain, the Basor said, 'Who is going to repay me?' 'O the Sun and Moon will do that,' they answered. The Basor said, 'Well, they must fill the bin through the hole in the bottom, not from the top. That is my rule.' Then the gods went away.

After some time the Basor sent for the Sun and Moon and they came and tried to fill the grain-bin from the bottom upwards. But they couldn't do it. So the Basor caught hold of the Sun and Moon and kept them in his house till the gods came and set them free.

Again, after a time, the Sun came, and at another time the Moon came, each bringing sacks of grain and tried to fill the bin. Each time the Basor caught them and kept them in his house until the gods came and released them.

And so it continues for ever, and that is why the Sun and Moon sometimes go dark with the shadow that is cast on them by the walls of the Basor's house. Nor can the debt ever be repaid, for who could fill a grain-bin through the hole in the bottom?

13

BHUIYA

Ronta, Bonai State

The Sun and Moon were great Zamindars. One day the gods came to take a loan from them but the Sun and Moon said, 'We have not enough; go to the money-lender instead.' The gods prepared to go. Hearing they were coming, the money-lender cooked twelve measures of rice, twelve troughs of vegetables and brought twelve troughs of water. When the gods arrived, they said, 'Give us a loan.' But Bhimsen said, 'First give me something to eat and then your loan.' The merchant said, 'Go, the food is ready.' Bhimsen went and in two great mouthfuls finished the whole feast.

When the money-lender saw that his careful preparations were useless he was very angry and said, 'I will give you nothing.' Bhimsen too lost his temper and they quarrelled. The money-lender showed him two great grain-bins and said, 'If you can lift these, you can take them away.' Bhimsen tried but even he could not lift them up, so he broke them and took as much grain as he could carry and cried, 'The Sun and Moon are my sureties for this loan.'

After Bhimsen had gone away the money-lender came and when he saw the broken bins he was very angry. He sent his servants to find Bhimsen, but they were unable to catch him, for he had crossed a great river. So the money-lender sent his servants to catch the Sun and Moon. He is always doing this and, whenever his servants catch them, there is an eclipse.

14

BONDO

Gokurupada, Koraput District

Arke the Moon and Singi the Sun were two friends. In the great ocean the three Lakmi sisters were born, but because they were afraid of men they hid in a hollow bamboo.

A Chandal saw the bamboo and pulled it up by the roots and took it home. When he put it down in the court the three sisters came out and he took them into his house. The bamboo he turned upside down. The three sisters came out and again went into the bamboo.

Men could not get grain to eat. Mahaprabhu went to find it for them. As he was searching across the hills, he came to the Chandal's house. There he found two or three grains had fallen out of the bamboo and were lying on the ground. Mahaprabhu asked for the seed on loan. The Chandal said, 'Only if you can get someone to stand surety for you.' Mahaprabhu brought Singi the Sun. The Chandal said, 'Here is a length of bamboo; the grain is in it. I will bring out the grain without cutting the bamboo open. If I can do that, then you must fill a length of bamboo without cutting it open.' 'Very well,' said Mahaprabhu. But the Chandal secretly called the culm-borers and they made holes in his bamboo and the grain came out. Then Mahaprabhu tried to fill his bamboo, but he could not. The Chandal took a stick and went to the house of Singi and sat in the door, saying, 'Fulfil your bargain and I will let you into the house.' This is an eclipse.

Mahaprabhu took the grain and gave it to mankind. But when the harvest was ready and they wanted to eat it, they had no plates. They wanted to make leaf-platters but they had no bamboo pins to stitch the leaves together. Again Mahaprabhu went to the Chandal and this time he took Arke the Moon as his surety. The Chandal said, 'I will give you a green bamboo, but you must return it exactly as I give it to you.' He pulled a bamboo clump up by the roots and gave it to Arke to take away. But the Moon found he could not carry it through the jungle and had to cut off the top and bottom. When the time came for repaying the debt there were no bamboos ready. So the Chandal went also to Arke's house and refused to let him in. And this too is an eclipse.

15

GADABA

lu, Koraput District

Sun and Moon borrowed a lot of little bamboo pins to stitch leaf-plates, but they were unable to repay the loan and the bear and the scorpion catch them from time to time and demand repayment. It is lucky when the bear catches them; there will be good crops and many children born, but when the scorpion catches them it means there will be smallpox. If a pregnant woman goes out of the house during an eclipse her child will be born with a hare-lip.

III

The Stars

The most common account of the origin of the stars among the aboriginals of Middle India is the legend, of which variants are given in the text, that the Sun and Moon devoured their own children, the Sun in reality, but the Moon only by a trick. Thus the Baiga give an account of how the Sun and Moon quarrelled about the ownership of their children and had a test to see which would be able to eat them. The Sun swallowed his children but the Moon kept hers in the pouch of her cheeks like a monkey. She was able to bring them out and that is why there are many stars at night, but only two by day.

The Santal say that after the great heat of the original Sun had been lessened, 'the Moon feared that the Sun would again get angry with the new race and destroy it; so she made a plan to trick him. She covered up all her children with a large basket and smeared her mouth and lips with red and going to Sing Chando told him that she had eaten up every one of her children and proposed that he should now eat up his. At first Sing Chando declined to believe her, but she pointed to her lips and said that they were red with the blood of the children; so Sing Chando was convinced and agreed to eat up his children except two whom he would keep to play with. So he devoured all but two and the two that were saved are the morning and evening stars.'[1]

The Turi have a similar tradition.

The principal deity of the caste is Singbonga, the Sun, and according to one of their stories the Sun is female. They say that the Sun and Moon were two sisters, both of whom had children, but when the Sun gave out great heat the Moon was afraid that her children would be burnt up, so she hid them in an earthen pot. When the Sun missed her sister's children she asked her where they were, and the Moon replied that she had eaten them up; on which the Sun also ate up her own children. But when night came the Moon took her children out of the earthen pot and they spread out in the sky and became the stars. And when the Sun saw this she was greatly angered and vowed that she would never look on the Moon's face again. And it is on this account that the Moon is not seen in the day time, and as the Sun ate up all her children there are no stars during the day.[2]

[1] Bompas, 403. [2] Russell and Hiralal, iv, 591.

The Birhor also describe how the Sun ate up his children.

The Sun and Moon are related to each other as brother and sister. Of the stars the more brilliant are the children of the Sun and the rest are the children of the Moon. The great heat that emanated from the Sun and his children troubled all creation. One day the Sun asked her sister for some vegetable curry. She gave him a dish of curry made of the lotus flower. The curry tasted exceedingly sweet. And so the Sun asked his sister what it was made of. The Moon, with a view to save creation from being scorched by the cumulative heat emanating from the Sun and his children, cunningly replied, 'This curry is made of the flesh of my children, the stars.' And the Moon soon afterwards took care to keep her own children in hiding. The Sun began to eat up his own children, and thus one by one the brilliant stars were eaten up—all except one who had gone to a distant place for dancing. This was Bhurka or the Morning Star.[1]

The Kharwar of southern Mirzapur say that the Sun and Moon are the shadow of Paramesar and the stars are their children.[2] Crooke says that women in Mirzapur were fond of telling their children that the stars were kine and the Moon their shepherd—a survival of the Vedic idea that the stars are the cattle of the Sun and led through the clouds by the Moon.[3] The Warli believe that the stars were made of mud left over from the making of the world, which was thrown up into the sky.[4]

Shooting-stars are often described as star-excrement. Both the Hill and Bison-Horn Maria say that the stars are the children of the Sun and Moon and that falling stars are their excrement.[5] The Santal use the same expression; so do the Kuki of Assam.[6] The Uraon say that shooting-stars were back-biters in this world and after death go to hear the talk of Rishis at Indra's darbar and are punished with fire.[7] The Baiga sometimes call a shooting-star 'excrement' and sometimes 'a spirit coming down to earth to make a woman pregnant', 'a spirit of a sinner burning', or 'a star that comes down to graze'.[8]

[1] Roy, *The Birhors*, 486 f.
[2] *N. I. Notes and Queries*, i, 141.
[3] ibid., iv, 125.
[4] Sawe, 162.
[5] Grigson, 230.
[6] *Census of India*, 1931, 101.
[7] ibid., 117.
[8] *The Baiga*, 336.

16

AHIR

Rusa, Mandla District

Twenty-one brothers of the Singhwar tribe and twelve brothers of the Dhoba tribe lived together as one family, and learnt magic from the same Guru. The eldest Singhwar brother had two wives; the younger of the two was very beautiful and the youngest of the Dhoba brothers fell in love with her. One day the Singhwar husband came home suddenly and found them together. There was a row that lasted a full month; the magic of the Dhoba was stronger and they attacked the Singhwar brothers and killed them all. When they saw the corpses lying in the village street, the Dhoba were frightened and went to their mother to ask what to do. She said, 'If we throw them in a stream or leave them in the jungle, the police will find them sooner or later and we will be in trouble. It will be better to throw them into the sky by your magic.' So at midnight the twelve brothers went naked to the dead bodies and muttered charms above them and blew upon them, thus driving them up into the sky. When they reached the clouds their heads began to shine. Four days later the young wife and her Dhoba lover also went into the sky and became the Lagnahi Sukua stars. The elder Singhwar brother soon followed them and became the Machhamar Sukua star. His elder wife became the Pahati Sukua star. In this way stars came into the sky.

17

OJHA

Nipaniya, Raipur District

Lanjha Guru and Lanjha Guruain lived in the jungle with their children. Lanjha Guru thought in his mind, 'There is nothing to eat or drink here.' He went to a god and asked for something. The god and his wife were pleased and said, 'Ask for anything you want.' Lanjha Guru said, 'Give me anything you like, but it must be something that does not exist on earth.' The god said, 'What is there I can give you?' But when Lanjha Guru continued to ask, the god got angry and cut off his own penis and gave it to him. His wife cut off her breasts and gave them to him.

Lanjha Guru took these things home, and showed them to his wife. She said, 'What can we do with such dirty things? Throw them away.' The Guru took them into the garden and planted them carefully. Soon from the breasts a coconut palm sprang up and from the penis a stalk of maize.

When the maize was ripe, they picked it and hung it up in the house. One day Lanjha Guru and his wife had a quarrel. The wife went off somewhere in a temper, and the little children cried. Lanjha Guru prepared the maize to please them. He put it in a winnowing-fan and was amusing the children. He shook the fan up and down singing, 'Break, break maize, your mother is very quarrelsome.' But as he shook the fan the grains of maize went *ragrag-ragrag* up into the sky. They turned into stars and are still there.

CHAPTER THREE

AIR AND WATER

I

AIR: SKY AND CLOUD

THE aboriginals are not very interested in the sky; even aeroplanes do not greatly impress them. There are, it is true, a few divine or semi-divine beings like Indal, Megh Raja and Bhimsen who are located in the heavens. The Saora name for a class of Supreme Beings is Kittung, the sky. The Upper World, where Bhagavan or Mahapurub has his place, is vaguely imagined as 'above'. But in dealing with the sky-gods the aboriginal theologian's chief concern is to bring them down to earth. The Saora Kittung wanders among the Parlakimidi Hills; Bhimsen is a familiar figure in the Bastar forests; even Indal comes to this world and busies himself in its affairs. It is earth, not heaven, whence the tribesmen sprang and to which they offer devotion and sacrifice.

Perhaps as a result of this, some of the legends about the sky and clouds are rather silly. A Gadaba story describes how the first cloud came of a cowhide that was thrown into the air during a ribald drinking-party. According to an Agaria tale it was a plate tossed into the sky during a Laru Kaj. The Lanjhia Saora tradition is that a weary Saora, exasperated because his supper was late, threw a chapati at the sky: it stuck there and became a cloud.

But there are two traditions represented in the text of this book, both common today in aboriginal India, which stretch back into the remote antiquity of Vedic times. The first is the widely distributed tradition that at the beginning earth and sky lay close together. 'Heaven and earth,' says the *Aitareya Brahmana*, 'were once joined. Subsequently they separated. After their separation there fell neither rain, nor was there sunshine. The five classes of beings then did not keep peace with one another. Thereupon the gods brought about a reconciliation of both these worlds. Both contracted with one another a marriage according to the rites observed by the gods.' [1]

Aboriginal tradition describes the union and separation of heaven and earth and their subsequent re-union in marriage. A Gond tale tells how the sky lay so close to the earth that one day when an old woman was sweeping, she knocked her head against it.

[1] *Aitareya Brahmana*, iv, 27. From Muir, v, 23.

She lost her temper and with her broom pushed it up into its present position.[1] The Birhor tell the same story, but with an old woman husking rice, and she does not hit the sky in a temper, but by accident, with her pestle.[2] The Warli of Western India, who say the sky was so close that it touched the water-pots on women's heads, agree with the Birhor. A woman's pestle pierced the sky and it went up.[3] The Andaman Islanders say that originally 'the sun was low down near the earth, only just above the tops of the trees'. A giant made a bow and lifted it. The top struck the sky and raised it to its present position. This was apparently an accident.[4] But the Buna make the pushing of the sky deliberate: an old woman is sweeping her yard and beats the sky with her broomstick.[5] And a version of the same story from Golaghat in Assam says that a old hunchback woman bumped against the sky and struck it with her broom.[6]

A Khasi legend is a little different.

> In olden days when the earth was very young, heaven and earth were very near to one another, because the navel-string of heaven drew the earth very close to it. . . . But the string was cut by men and it became short. As soon as it shortened, heaven then ascended high.[7]

As so often, the Santal version of the story is moralized, and the separation of the sky is due to the bad habits of mankind.

> In the old days the sky was quite close to the earth and Thakur Baba used to come and visit men in their houses. But one day a woman after finishing her meal threw the used leaf-plate out of the door, and a gust of wind carried it up to the sky; this displeased Thakur Baba and he resolved no longer to dwell in the neighbourhood of men, as they were so ill-mannered as to throw their dirty leaf-plates at him and so he lifted the sky to its present height above the earth.[8]

We have already seen how the *Aitareya Brahmana* overcomes the difficulty of the separation between earth and sky by reconciling them through marriage. This is a widely-spread notion in classical Hinduism where Dyaus (who with Varuna is the great sky-god

[1] *Census of India*, 1901, xiii, 94.
[2] Roy, *The Birhors*, 436.
[3] Sawe, 162.
[4] Brown, 199 f.
[5] Basu, 85.
[6] Lewison, 344.
[7] Gurdon, 173.
[8] Bompas, 402 f. Frazer quotes similar legends from Africa. The Kassma say that the sky was once so close to the ground that it was in the way of an old woman who was about to cook. In a rage she cut off a slice and made it into soup: the sky in turn withdrew to its present place. The Ashanti say it was an old woman constantly hitting it with a pestle that caused the sky to retire, a story that is also known in Liberia. The Ewe-speaking people of West Africa believed that once the sky was so near the earth that men could touch it with their hands, but their fires and dirt annoyed it and it withdrew out of the way. J. G. Frazer, *The Worship of Nature* (London, 1926), 96 and 109, where references are given.

of Vedic mythology) is so commonly associated with his wife Prithivi the Earth that their names are united in the dual compound *dyava-prithivi.*[1] They are the most frequently named pair in the *Rigveda*, so closely associated that Dyaus, the Sky, is never addressed alone, though they are involved together in six of the ancient hymns.

> Devoutly I the two seats wide and lofty,
> The parents of the gods, invoke with fervour,
> Who, fair of aspect, grant us life immortal.
> O Heaven and Earth, from dreadful darkness save us.[2]

From this sublime conception of Heaven and Earth as the Father and Mother of all things, there is a sudden descent to the fantastic stories in the text. The trouble with the primitive mythologist is that he cannot maintain for any length of time a level of high seriousness. Cheerfulness is always breaking in. He must have his little joke. And so here he finds it impossible to contemplate the marriage of sky and earth without going on to consider the technical and material difficulties likely to be created by the consummation of their union. Between the upper and lower elements of this mighty conjugation all things are likely to be ground to dust, all creation will be destroyed.

The tribal mythologist has heard of this marriage. He cannot get away from it. He has got to fit it into his scheme. But the technical difficulties are so great that after he has told us all about it and described every detail of the wedding, at the last moment he calls it off and there is no match at all.

I

AGARIA

Umaria, Mandla District

At first the sky had no clouds. One day a Binjhwar Baiga dedicated a Laru pig. In that village lived an Agaria. When they killed the Laru, the Baiga invited the Agaria to the feast. They drank a lot of liquor and got drunk as two kings. The Baiga's wife brought rice on a plate of mohlain leaves and put it before the Agaria. There was a quarrel. The Baiga and the Agaria shouted abuse at each other. The Agaria lost his temper, and picked up his plate of food and threw it into the air. It went up and up into the sky: the plate turned into a cloud and the grains of rice became the stars.

[1] Macdonell, *Vedic Mythology*, 21 f. [2] Macdonell, *Hymns*, 66 ff.

2

AHIR

Barbaspur, Mandla District

When the world was water and nothing but water, the gods sat on a lotus leaf floating on the surface and wondered how to make the world. The world they made easily, but they were worried about the means whereby they could stretch above it a roof of clouds. Jam Raja and his Rani Jikoranbai were dissatisfied with their house in the Under World. They called the gods and said, 'Make us a palace in the clouds.' But the gods did not know what to do and the Rani was very annoyed. This Rani had between her breasts a black mole.

Then Raja Bijay let his seed fall to the ground and a spider was born of it. It came out of the ground crying, 'I'll make the clouds and sky. Come and help, all of you.' But there was no way up into the sky so the spider spun thread from its own body, threw it into the air and climbed up. There it broke off one of its legs, fixed it as a peg and tied a rope to it. The others climbed up and taking the black mole from the Rani's breast stretched it out across the sky as if it were a cloth. Then the spider made a great web and they hung this under the black skin. On top the gods made their homes.

3

BAIGA

Pandpur, Mandla District

The world was made, but it was unsteady. Bhagavan sent for Bhimsen and asked him to fix it in place. Bhimsen said, 'Let me first smoke a pipe, and then I'll see what I can do.' He puffed away and clouds of smoke went floating up into the air and turned into clouds. Sparks from the burning tobacco flew up and became stars.

4

BHARIA

Rewa State

Todiyamal Dano went to Nanga Bhairat and told the people there that they must give him every day a cartload of bread cooked with oil, sweets, rice and pulse. They arranged to provide it turn by turn. When the cart with its driver reached Koeli-Kachhar, Todiyamal Dano ate the food and cleaned his teeth with the body of the man.

Then Bhimsen came, like a small boy with a fat belly. The villagers said, 'Don't come here: the Dano will eat you.' But Bhimsen said, 'I am not afraid' and he remained there. Then he said, 'Today it is my turn. I will take the cart.' He filled a cart with food and took it to Koeli-Kachhar. As he went he ate all the food himself. The Dano was hungry and when he saw the cart empty he tried to kill Bhimsen. But Bhimsen, like a fearful mountain, picked him up with one hand and killed him. Then he set fire to his palace and stables and the store-houses. The blue smoke went up and that is why the sky is blue.

5

GOND

Mangwani, Mandla District

Originally the sky was very near the earth. There was an old woman. Every day she used to clean her courtyard. One day the sky knocked against her back as she bent down to sweep. She was annoyed and pushed the sky up a bit with her broom. But the sky went right up up up to where it now is.

II

AIR: THE WIND

The Wind is usually personified as the blind god Pawan Dasseri or Dessahi. He is specially honoured in the little village of Chirai-dongri in Mandla District where a strong wind blows continually from a neighbouring hill and drives away every disease. The Baiga tradition is that the Wind was created from the breath of the mouth of Bhagavan and was the first to attempt to make the newly-created world firm and steady. 'He blew on the earth, he drove some of it up into the air, he mixed it all up, he blew till it began to be hard and firm. But the Wind is blind: that is why he is knocking things over and banging up against people: so the work was not perfect. The earth was hard, but when they stood on one side the other side tipped up'.[1] It needed the help of Bhimsen and Nanga Baiga to complete the Wind's work.

A story about Pawan Raja comes from Bhandara in the Central Provinces.

King Pawan (the Wind) is said to have reigned as far as Amraoti in Berar and Bhandak in Chanda; and there is a fable that it was his daily custom to bathe at Pauni, to break his fast at Bhandak, and sleep at Amraoti. His wife also had miraculous powers. She is stated to have had the power of walking over the tanks as on dry land, and of drawing water in unbaked pots by means of a string that had never been twined. Both she and Pawan himself, though they possessed wealth untold, wore simple white garments and laboured with their own hands. One account says that they were content with the possession of the philosopher's stone, so that they could, if they so wished, turn their subjects' tribute of iron ore and such like things into silver and gold. But there came a day when Pawan's wife, known as Kamalpati, 'queen of the water lily,' saw the rest of the women going out to celebrate the Pola festival, clad in garments of many colours and with ornaments of gold and silver about their persons. She, too, must own such things, and before the next Pola feast came round, by constant importunity she had induced her lord to let her dress and adorn herself as other women did. She joined the festival no longer distinguished by the simplicity of her apparel; her eyes were now opened, and she found that her virtue was departed from her. No longer would her untwined string and unbaked pot perform their office; no longer would the leaf of the lotus support her steps. The end of it was an earthquake which overthrew the town of Pauni.[2]

6

BAIGA

Lalpur, Mandla District

In the days when there was no wind, a Baiga went to sow rice in his forest clearing. When the crop was ready the Baiga threshed it with his feet. But how could he winnow it without wind? He brought

[1] *The Baiga*, 311.

[2] *Bhandara Settlement Report*, 47 ff. There are similar stories in Temple i, 39 and S. M. Moen, *Bareilly Settlement Report*, 20.

twelve cartloads of sarai incense to offer to Pawan Dessahi. Then came his old woman with a pot of gruel on her head. The Baiga said, '*Sur-sur pawan chale : bhur-bhur ras badhai*—May the wind come *sur-sur*, may the grain grow *bhur-bhur*.' As he said that the old woman undid the cloth between her legs and farted. The wind came out with such force that there was a storm all over the world and the Baiga's grain was winnowed.

Since that time there has been wind, and Baiga women do not tie the *kanch*[1] between their legs.

7

BINJHWAR

Dhaurabhata, Raipur District

In Duganigarh the wife of Sukla Dewar was pregnant. When in due time a daughter was born, the Dewar was pleased and said to himself, 'Now I have a daughter. I will at least get a little liquor when they come to ask for her in marriage.' But the baby would not take her mother's milk, nor would she take cow's milk or any food. Sukla Dewar examined his measuring-sticks and through them the child said, 'I am not a human life, my name is Pawan Dessahi. Sukni Mai has sent me to the world because there is no wind and people die of heat.'

As the child said this, she began to tremble like a reed on the banks of a stream. She cried, '*Bharr-bharr*' and flew up into the air and disappeared. In this way Wind came into the world.

8

DHANWAR

Barbhata, Uprora Zamindari

A potter and his wife lived in Bursidongri. There was no wind and no cloud in those days. All the wind in the world was in the navel of the potter's wife. One day the potter said to himself, 'It is very hot. We must have some clouds to shade us from the sun.' He rubbed dirt from his body and made a crow. But the bird sat silent and still before him, for without the wind how could it fly? The wife came by and laughed at her husband saying, 'Why have you made that bird

[1] For the *kanch*, see *The Baiga*, 12.

just to sit still? Why not let it fly?' He explained the difficulty to her and said, 'I want the crow to go up and make the clouds, but how can it fly without wind?' His wife said, 'The wind is in my navel. I will lie down and if you will lie with me you will be able to drive it out.'

They went into the house and the potter took his wife so vigorously that the wind came out through her navel and drove the crow up into the sky. There it made the clouds.

9

GOND

Pharisemhar, Rewa State

Manmohan Dewar and his wife were cultivating their fields. They were rich and prosperous. Near by in the Kandrakol jungle lived Dharsingh Dano. Every now and then the Dewar's wife used to go there for leaves. One day she came to the place where the Dano was lying asleep. This Dano had love-charms in his eyes. When he heard the noise of the woman picking the leaves he awoke and raised his head. The two looked at one another and at once the Dewar's wife fell in love with the Dano; she went to him and massaged his hands and feet.

When all was over she went home and cooked gruel and wild vegetable for her husband, but made bread and sweets for the Dano. She did this every day and always took the best food into the forest for the Dano. One day the Dewar said, 'I am going to the field to build a watching-platform. Make my food quickly and bring it to me.' He went out and directly the house was empty the Dewar's wife cooked bread and sweets and took them to her lover. Then she returned and cooked her husband's gruel and wild vegetable. When she reached the field it was very late and her husband, hungry and impatient, beat her till she screamed. The next day the woman went to the Dano and told him about her beating. The Dano in a fit of rage pulled off his left testicle. He blew upon it and threw it towards the field where the Dewar was working saying, 'Turn into a storm and spoil his crop.'

The thing flew through the air and as it went turned into a storm of hail which fell upon the field and ruined the wheat. The Dewar was unable to take shelter and the storm killed him. His widow went to live with her lover.

10

GOND

Bilhar, Bilaspur District

Sahas Raja lived in Garhgarhpur. He made seven storeys of rooms. When he opened his mouth in the daytime, wind came from it; when he closed it at night, the wind ceased. After two or four days, Sahas Raja called all living creatures, men, deer, tigers, butterflies, birds, and shut them up in his house. He shut his mouth also and there was no wind. The living creatures were frightened and for lack of wind grew so hot that they could not breathe. They cried to Sahas Raja, 'We will soon die; let us go and send the wind again.' So he let them go and opened his mouth and the wind came.

Then a Dhur Gond came to Sahas Raja. He put a lock on the room where Sahas Raja was and shut him in so that he could not any longer draw in his breath and steal the wind shutting his mouth upon it. Since then there has been wind all over the world.

11

KOL

Jubbulpore District

Pawan Dessahi the Wind was born from the mouth of Mahadeo. One day Mahadeo put ganja, opium and datura leaves in his pipe and as he exhaled the smoke Pawan Dessahi was born. When Mahadeo saw him he was frightened and said in his mind, 'This child will bring trouble to all the world. I must marry him to someone.' He caught him and put him back into his mouth.

Bhagavan offered Kari Anjani as his wife. They were married and Pawan Dessahi went to her through her ear. Kari Anjani was angry at losing her virginity and tore out one of her husband's eyes.

When the great Asur had caught the Sun and was trying to eat it, Pawan Dessahi went to the rescue and the Asur kicked him in the other eye. So now the Wind is blind and wanders through the world. He can go everywhere, but he never knows where he is going.

12

PANKA

Sanhrwachhapar, Mandla District

A Baiga lived with his Baigin. His name was God-duar and her name was Dubbulchhak. They were arranging the marriage of their son. But there was no wind and the booth dried and withered with the heat. Many of the guests fell fainting on the parched ground. They sent for Binjhwar Baiga and when he looked in his broom-sticks he saw that in Jalhalpur there was the fish Manbod, which had wind.

Binjhwar Baiga said to God-duar, 'Go and get a fresh bamboo.' God-duar went to Kattakban and cut a fresh bamboo. He brought it home and Binjhwar made a trap from it. Binjhwar went with his fish-trap to Jalhalpur. He set the trap in the river and the fish was caught. But when he tried to take the fish out of the trap he could not move it. He folded his hands and told the fish the story of the marriage and the failure of the wind that had withered the marriage-booth. And now when he tried to lift the trap he found he could, and he returned bringing the fish Manbod with him.

The fish opened its mouth and wind came to the world. The withered marriage-booth revived and the fainting guests sat up. When men saw the violence of the wind they were afraid and breathed deeply. Since that time men have begun to breathe.

13

RAJNENGI PARDHAN

Upri, Rewa State

Raja Logundi made plates of iron for twice twelve miles round his city Loharipur. When the earth and the sky were going to be married the Raja said in his mind, 'How are we to live when these two come together? We will be crushed to death between them.' Many gods assembled for the marriage. Logundi Raja said secretly to his servants, 'Go and blow the bellows.' They ran to the forge and stamped on the bellows with dancing feet till the plates round the city grew very hot and Dhahu Dhukan Deo was born. A great fire blazed up and the gods were frightened. They went to Guru Mahadeo and asked him for help. Mahadeo whispered a seed-charm in the ear of Desphiri Mata and she became pregnant. From her belly Pawan Dasseri the Wind was born. He asked his mother where his father was and she told him to go and find him.

Pawan Dasseri went to find his father and on the way he met Bhimsen. 'Where you are going, boy?' said the giant. 'I am going to find my father.' 'But I am your father.' Pawan Dasseri was angry and they quarrelled. In the struggle Bhimsen broke the boy's eyes and went away.

Since then Pawan Dasseri has gone *bhatak-bhatak*, blindly searching for his father through the world.

III

Thunder and Lightning

The tradition of popular Hinduism about thunder and lightning is that lightning was one of the weapons of the Maruts and the thunderbolt wielded by Parajaniya. It is often said that the soul of the first man came to earth in the form of lightning. The first man born of a thunderbolt was Yama, who first trod the path of death and became regent of the dead.[1] Another popular Puranic tradition recorded in the Sylhet District is that forty-nine Vayu (winds) were born together in the womb of Indra's mother Aditi. Indra, fearing the loss of his kingdom, divided them into forty-nine pieces inside his mother's womb. After their birth, whenever they tried to unite together their father hurled his thunder at them. This caused so much trouble that at last the gods arranged that the winds were never to try to unite unless the heavens were cloudy and Indra was not to hurl his thunder unless they actually united.[2]

In the *Mahabharata*, thunder is described as originating from the bones of the saint Dadhichi. Yet another ancient Hindu belief is that lightning is the breath of Sesa Naga, king of the snakes. As fire consumes wood, so lightning consumes water. It strikes those who have been guilty of *vidyuta pap*, or 'lightning sin'—incest or killing a Brahmin in cold blood.[3]

Enthoven records a large variety of beliefs current in Western India. The thunder is now Indra's angry voice, now his loud

[1] Crooke, i, 33.
[2] Bhattacharjee, 122.
[3] R. G. Chaube, *N. I. Notes & Queries*, iv, 129.

laughter. It is the noise he makes when playing tip-cat or football with the clouds. He is getting married, at war, shooting his arrow to bring rain, beating the clouds with his whip. Sometimes the thunder is made by the chariot of Bhagavan rushing across the sky or it is the kettle-drum beaten by the gods in delight at the coming of the rain or the noise of an old hag grinding or rolling stones across the sky.[1]

The Muthuvan say thunder is caused by Devas rolling a stone across the sky[2], the Kanikkar believe it to be caused by a demon who has a stone wrapped in a cloth and makes a loud noise by striking it against a tree.[3]

Lightning is the girl whom Kansa tried to dash against stones but who escaped into the sky, the sister of Megh Raja who announces his approach, or the flashing of the fireworks at Indra's marriage.[4]

The Chero say that the lightning is the sword of Indra which he strikes against the clouds that hinder his torrents from falling on the ground.[5] The Khasi say that lightning is the stolen silver sword of U Kui the lynx which U Pyrthat the thunder giant brandishes in the sky.[6] The Thadon Kuki, like certain Hindu Castes, moralize their belief. They explain thunder and lightning as 'an exhibition of the powers and anger of Pathen [the ruler of the universe] who visits those with whom he is displeased by striking them with lightning. Thunder is to remind them that Pathen is still very much alive as the Thadon admit they are very careless and forgetful.'[7]

Among the aboriginals of Middle India the lightning, as in the stories in the text, is connected with Lakshman. The Birhor, for example, say that 'Ram-Lakshman have an old grudge against the species of yellowish frog known as *chokey* which leaps about from tree to tree and croaks at night in the rainy season. Whenever Ram-Lakshman see one of these frogs, they shoot their arrows at it with their mighty bow from above and the roaring sound of the huge bow is what men call thunder, and the arrow-heads come down as thunder-bolts'.[8]

[1] Enthoven, 76 f. [2] Iyer, ii, 35. [3] ibid., i, 55.

[4] ibid., 77. It is dangerous, according to an old tradition recorded from the Punjab, for an uncle and his sister's son to sit together during a storm. For 'the lightning was once born as the daughter of Devki, niece of Kansa, and was struck by her uncle, who cast her to the ground against a stone. She flew up to heaven, but has ever since borne enmity to all maternal uncles.'—Rose, i. 129.

[5] Agarwal, 215. [6] Rafy, 98 f. [7] Shaw, 71 f.

[8] Roy, *The Birhors*, 498.

The Santal also know the story of Rama shooting his arrow, but Bodding says, 'I have the impression that the Santal deem this only a story—some Santal may try to guard themselves against the lightning by keeping an arrow on the bowstring in aim against the threatening clouds.'[1]

The Gond of Mandla, according to Ikramullah, say that 'when the clouds are full of water they contain waves. The thunder is merely the noise of those waves.'[2]

14

BAIGA

Bohi, Pandaria Zamindari

(From *The Baiga*, 336 f.)

The Pandava wanted to know what was underneath the earth, and they fell at the feet of Bhimsen and begged him to go down and see. So they tied him to a little seat and let him down by a rope. He went down down down for eight nights and nine days. Then the Pandava out of mischief let the rope go and he fell to the bottom. He began to weep, wondering how he was to get back. But the old cobra who lives there gave him the horse of lightning and he sat on it, and before he knew what had happened he was back home. He has never ceased wondering at his wonderful ride.

Now Bhagavan keeps Bhimsen as his servant, and when he wants to give the world water he sends Bhimsen to give it. Bhimsen drags it along in the skin of a rat and as the skin rubs along over the air, it makes the roaring noise of thunder. Bhimsen rides all over the four corners of the world on his horse of lightning, dragging his rat-skin behind him.

[1] *Census of India*, 1931, 102.

[2] ibid., 77. For further comparative material, see Mitra, 'The Thunder-Myths of the Primitive Races', *J. Anth. Soc. Bom.*, ix, 454-71.

15

BAIGA

Bauna, Mandla District

Hemasiri Mata had a daughter. Her name was Bijaldai Kaniya. She was lovely as a mirror with which a boy reflects the sunlight. Her father's name was Jallandar. He kept Lakshman in his house as a Lamsena, for he had no son, and the boy worked hard for twelve years. Then Jallandar took dirt from his body and made it into a little pot. He cut his leg and filled the pot with the blood. He said to Lakshman, 'Take this as your reward, but do not open it. Go to your house, go inside and shut the door, then open it.' Lakshman took the pot to his house, shut the door, shut everything and opened the pot. Bijaldai Kaniya sprang out and leapt upwards so violently that she burst through the roof and flashed into the sky. Lakshman took his bow and arrow and chased her : the thunder is the noise of his arrow crashing through the sky.

16

DEWAR

Dondi-Lohara Zamindari

In Garh Lohari Mata Kankalin's daughter, Beti Bidyarsin, was living alone. She had no husband. So twelve years and thirteen ages passed. One day she went to bathe in the river. Higher up the stream Raja Bijay was also bathing. He saw the maid from afar and rubbing himself during the bath, presently his seed came from him and fell into the water and was carried down to the girl. She had just put her head under the water and the seed fell upon it and she conceived.

After nine months she gave birth to a daughter. It was midnight but the darkness of all the Three Worlds was illuminated by the brightness of the child. The girl, trailing her cord and placenta behind her, flashed round and round the house. But they caught her and shut her up in a hollow bamboo, closing it at either end.

On the Naming Day, Kharaki Guru came to the house. He gave the child the name of Bijaldai Kaniya and said, 'This child will marry Bel Kuar. She was born of a virgin and will be a Sati.' So saying he went away.

The girl grew tall with the wind and strong in the sun. When she was twelve years old her mother and grandmother began to think about her marriage. At this time Raja Bijra of Barahangarh came with his son Bel Kuar to hunt. The boy was thirsty and came to the house to ask for water. When Bijaldai's mother and grandmother saw him they were pleased and said to each other, 'If this boy is willing, he is just the sort of husband we want for our daughter.' They said to the boy, 'O Raja's son, where are you going? Where have you come from? Whose Raja's son are you?' But the poor boy was so thirsty that he could not answer. At last he was able to say, 'I am Raja Birja's son and my name is Bel Kuar.' They said to him, 'Will you agree to whatever we say? If you will, good; but if not, we will give you no water to drink.' The boy said, 'First tell me what this is all about?' They replied, 'We wish to marry our daughter to you. Marry her quickly and take her home with you. We do not want any bride-price.' The boy was pleased at this and said he would marry the girl. Then at last they gave him water to drink. He took the bridle from his horse and tethered it to a tree.

At once the women sent invitations to everyone in the village for the wedding on the following day. The people went to cut wood for the booth and prepared haldi and oil.

But on the next day, when the marriage began and Bijaldai Kaniya was brought for the Lagin, Bel Kuar saw that he was being married to a bit of bamboo. He thought in his mind, 'I am being fooled by these people.' So he said, 'If you are going to put haldi on a bit of bamboo, bring my bow and arrow and put haldi on that instead of on me.' They agreed to this and took Bijaldai Kaniya inside the bamboo and Bel Kuar's bow and arrow together seven times round the pole.

When the wedding was over the women gave Bel Kuar the bamboo and said to him, 'Take her to your home. But, look, do not open it on the way. When you get home, go into an inner room; shut the door and windows; wait till night and then open the bamboo to see your bride.'

But as he was nearing his home Bel Kuar thought that his father would laugh at him. 'I must see what is inside this bamboo,' he thought and opened it under a bija tree. At once Bijaldai Kaniya sprang out of the bamboo and leapt into a hollow in the tree. Bel Kuar, full of anger, seized his bow and arrow and fired at her. His wife leapt from the hollow into a clump of bamboos and entered into one of them. Bel Kuar ran to the place and cut down the bamboos and broke them into pieces. But the lightning slipped from knot to knot and from bamboo to bamboo and escaped him. At last she sprang into the sky. Bel Kuar fired at her again. Then he said, ' Whenever I see her face I will shoot at her ' and went home.

Thus came knots in the bamboo, and the bija tree often struck by lightning, and no lightning without thunder, and Bijaldai Kaniya is still a Sati who has never been to her husband.

17

DHANWAR

Senha, Uprora Zamindari

The lightning was born in Bijagarh. Here a great river flowed. In the midst of the water lived Panbijiya Rani. She was as fat as a great ricebin and her arms and legs were as thick as the cross-beam of a house. She had never been to a man. One night Pawan Dasseri came to her in a dream and enjoyed her. Soon she was pregnant ; the eight months passed ; when the shadow of the ninth fell a girl was born. She was Bijaldai Kaniya. Her body was like a shower of sparks from the Holi fire or the full moon rising red. Because of her heat the water began to burn and its colour changed. Panbijiya Rani's body was shrivelled and became as it is today, small and black. She became Panbichiya, the leaf-scorpion, and lives among the saraí leaves. She put the girl in her hole, but Bijaldai would not stay there ; she broke through the ground and jumped into the sky like the wind, her father.

18

DHURWA

Netanar, Bastar State

There was water all round the world. The water was full of little fish. During the months of rain they came out to play, up and down, to and fro, so they played. Their play was the lightning.

At this time, at the height of the rains, the childless dead gather together and pull a chariot of iron things—arrow-heads, plough-shares, knives, sickles, harrows—over the sky. This is the thunder. Sometimes these things fall down from the sky and the earth is impregnated and bears rich fruit.

19

GOGIA PARDHAN

Jhanki, Mandla District

From the blood of the dead giant Rawan, a girl was born. She went to Lakshmanjati and begged him to marry her. He refused and fell asleep. She broke her bangles and left them in his bed. When he awoke he was very angry and tried to kill her. But she fled into the sky as the lightning and hid in a black cloud.

20

KURUK

Temra, Bastar State

There is a great ocean all round the Middle World. In its waters lives a great fish. In the Upper World Mahapurub has an iron cart. To it he harnesses two barren women; when he pricks their buttocks with his iron goad, they drag the cart very fast across the sky. When the fish hears the noise, it says in its mind, 'Now after many days I am going to get something to eat.' In its excitement it swims here and there, beating the water with its tail, and flies into the sky using its fins as wings. The flashing of the fins is what men call the lightning.

21

MURIA

Kokori, Bastar State

(From *The Muria and their Ghotul*, 260)

Bhimul is man; Earth is woman. When Bhimul is on heat, he tries to approach Earth. But there is no road or path, and he rushes about trying to find the way, he hurls rocks and mountains to and fro—and this makes the thunder. At last he can contain his seed no longer: it spurts out—and a thunderbolt falls. From this seed man gets his food. Unless Bhimul gets on heat there is no rain or harvest.

IV

Water

There are scores of local legends about the origin of rivers and springs, but they are too elaborate and varied to be given here.

The curious Bhuiya legend (No. 22), which finds a parallel in a Baiga story about Bara Bathi Bengala is based on a very ancient and apparently widespread tradition that two women can come together to produce a boneless child.

Havelock Ellis quotes a *Short History of Aryan Medical Science* that 'the Hindoo medical works mention the possibility of a woman uniting with another woman in sexual embraces and begetting a boneless foetus.'[1] As so often, there are parallels with the North American material. A Fox legend describes the intercourse of two girls. 'She who was lying on top had her clitoris standing out: it had a queer shape: it was like a turtle's penis. . . It is said that afterward one of the maidens became big with child. In the course of time, she gave birth, and the child was like a soft-shell turtle.'[2] Lowie has a similar legend from the Assiniboine of Canada and Montana: a woman fell in love with her husband's sister and ran away with her; there was a child from their union, but it was boneless.[3]

In Garo myth, water originated when a jet of water came from the womb of the mother of the human race, and became the source of all rivers.[4]

An interesting Toda story has been recorded by Emeneau. In ancient times two persons made toy buffalo-horns of hill-guava twigs; they ate the ripe fruit and spat the seeds on the horns. 'On account of their spitting, the chewed skins became the mist on the hills. The spray of the spit became the monsoon-rain. On account of their blowing when they spat, wind arose.' One of the ancients made a home for the monsoon, and controlled its incidence.[5]

[1] H. Ellis, *Sexual Inversion* (New York, 1936), 208.
[2] W. Jones, 'Fox Texts', *Publ. of the Amer. Ethn. Soc.* (Leyden, 1907), i, 151.
[3] G. H. Lowie, 'The Assiniboine', *Anthropological Papers of the Amer. Mus. of Nat. Hist.* (New York, 1909), xiv, 223.
[4] Bonnerjea, 122.
[5] Emeneau, 165 f. Compare Rivers, 165.

22

BHUIYA

Raisua, Bonai State

Kumba Karana Rusi was doing penance. Two Kaniya (maidens) defeated him. He married them both and sat underneath a bod tree between his two wives. When the gods came in search of the maidens and saw what had happened, they were very angry and said to Karana Rusi, 'You have done great evil.' They cursed him and he was turned into ashes.

But the two girls would not leave the place. When the bod tree flowered, many bees came to get the honey. When the girls saw the bees they said, 'If only there was a man here, he would sip our juice like that.' They were filled with passion and went to one another. The younger was below and she conceived.

In due time a son was born, but since he was begotten by woman, there were no bones in his body. There was only flesh : he could neither sit nor stand. His body flowed about like water. Then came Mahapurub. 'Where is Karana Rusi ?' 'The gods cursed him and turned him into ashes.' 'But how have you got a son ?' They were very ashamed. 'I know what happened,' said Mahapurub. 'Where is the boy ?' They carried him to Mahapurub's feet and he spread over the ground like water. 'If you really loved one another, he would have bones.' 'We really loved ; we did no sin.' At that bones grew in the child's body and he sat up crying, 'Where is my father ? I am going to find him. I will soon bring him back to life.'

Mahapurub said, 'Ganga has indeed been born, but it has gone to the Lower World. Go and bring some of its water in a siari leaf-cup and you can bring back life to your father.'

After twelve years the boy found Ganga wandering through the Lower World. There was nothing but water on every side. The boy filled his cup and set out for home. He came to a great mountain which he could not cross. And the cup of water had grown and grown till it was large and heavy as a lake. On this hill dwelt a goddess. She sent her elephant to cut a way through the hill. At that time elephants had four tusks, but in cutting through the hill two of them were broken off. Then through the gap the water poured in a great stream up to the bod tree—the boy and the elephant swam with it—and when it reached the ashes that had been Karana Rusi, he sat up alive. Karana Rusi called the boy Baghrati. Karana Rusi went with his two wives to the Upper World, but the elephant stayed with men on earth.

Ganga flowed on and became the seven great oceans, whose names are Rage, Fire, Water, Salt, Milk, Grain, Wealth. When Bhimsen picked up the water and threw it over the world, there was rain.

Wind and water are man and wife. Water is a woman.

23

GOND

Barratola, Mandla District

A Gond Raja, Raja Singmar, went to hunt in the jungle. As he went he came to a place where the young daughter of a Dano was living. Her name was Manmohanibai. He went to her house and said, 'Give me a little fire to light my pipe.' The girl asked him to go inside. He went inside and sat down. When he had finished his smoke the girl said to him, 'Marry me'. The Gond Raja agreed and they were married at once.

Inside the house there was a deep well from which flowed seven streams and in the well there was a ring. When the Raja was going to take his wife back to his house the girl found the ring and put it on her finger. Then as she went towards the Raja's home, the seven streams followed her and water spread out all over the world where there had been no water before.

24

GOND

Dumgarh, Rewa State

Dhursur Dewar used to go daily to collect mahua flowers in the jungle near Hardinagar. In the mahua tree below which he gathered them, there was born Tipkasur Mai. One day Dhursur Dewar was very thirsty and asked her for water, for in those days there was no water in the world. She told him to bring a gourd. He did so and she pissed into it and filled it. But as the Dewar was taking it home it fell to the ground and Tipkasur Mai's urine spilt out and flowed *khar-khar-khar* across the world in the form of streams and rivers.

25

RAJNENGI PARDHAN

Patangarh, Mandla District

Shriyal Jango lived in the jungle. She made a seven-storyed house. A Raja's son went to hunt. As he went he came to her house and she caught hold of him. She said, 'I am going to sacrifice you.' The boy was very much afraid. Then Shriyal Jango said, 'If you will marry me, I will not kill you.' 'Very well,' he said.

She made him a dish of boiled maize and pulse of wild urda and gave him his supper. As he ate, the Nau Singhi went into his belly and pressed him from inside so hard that his eyes came out of his head. But Shriyal Jango roused him and laughed at him.

Now before this people never used to feel thirsty. They used to eat all they wanted but did not trouble about drinking. But since the Nau Singhi went into his belly and frightened him, the boy began to feel very thirsty and said, 'Give me some water to drink.'

Shriyal Jango took some water from her own belly, put it in a golden pot and gave it to him. He drank water from her golden mouth and the next day they were married.

V

WATER: THE RAIN

The origin of rain is associated even by the remotest aboriginals with the Hindu deity Indra. This god has had varying fortunes. In the Vedas he stands in the first rank among the gods. 'He rides in a bright golden car, drawn by two tawny or ruddy horses with flowing manes and tails. His weapon is the thunderbolt, which he carries in his right hand; he also uses arrows, a great hook, and a net, in which he is said to entangle his foes. The soma juice is his especial delight; he takes enormous draughts of it, and, stimulated by its exhilarating qualities, he goes forth to war against his foes, and to perform his other duties. As deity of the atmosphere, he governs the weather and dispenses the rain; he sends forth his lightnings and thunder, and he is continually at war with Vritra or Ahi, the demon of drought and inclement weather, whom he overcomes with his thunderbolts, and compels to pour down the rain. Strabo describes the Indians as worshipping Jupiter Pluvius, no doubt meaning Indra, and he has also been compared to Jupiter Tonans.'[1]

In the later mythology Indra is inferior to the ultimate triad, but he is the chief of all the other gods. He reigns over the sky. He sends the lightning and hurls the thunderbolt, and the rainbow is his bow. But he is continually drunk and his sensuality develops into an almost exaggerated lasciviousness. In the *Puranas* Indra appears especially as the rival of Krishna. He had been an object of worship among the pastoral people of Vraja, but their attention was diverted by the new and splendidly youthful god. Full of rage Indra sent a deluge of rain to overwhelm them, but Krishna sheltered his admirers with the mountain Govardhana.

Among the aboriginals, however, I have not found Indra regarded as either drunken or lascivious. He has a wonderful court in the sky and his seven daughters, like the seven daughters of Bhagavan or Mahapurub, sometimes come down to earth to bathe or dance. He is generally the Rain God, a function which he shares with Bhimsen. The Chero say that Indar has a great store of water near his palace. Whenever his devotees beg for water he fills a jar from his tanks and pours it down through a sieve so that it falls to the earth in the form of rain.[2] The Bhuiya say that Indra brings rain and cloud as a loan from the Ocean. He lives on the loan for six months in the year, from the middle of June to the middle of December, just as many Bhuiya have to live on loans of rice during that period. For the next six months the debt is repaid by Indra to the Ocean God just as the Bhuiya debtors pay their creditors.[3] The Buna say that at the beginning of the world there was no rain and this meant that it was difficult to change one season to another, for rain was necessary to wash the old season and welcome the new one coming in. One day a Buna went to Singbonga and asked him to provide the world with rain. He did so and since then rain has fallen at every change of season.[4]

A story from the Central Provinces describes how 'clouds are Indra's messengers sent to bring rain. They go to the sea and take up the water, and returning, discharge it over the earth. During their journey they rest on the hilltops and refresh themselves by eating the leaves of the forest.'[5]

For some reason, probably because he is the son of Vayu the Wind, Bhimsen is regarded by the Gond, Muria and many other

[1] Dowson, 124.
[2] Agarwal, 214.
[3] Roy, *The Hill Bhuiyas*, 280.
[4] Basu, 86.
[5] *Census of India*, 1901, 94.

tribes as a god of rain. The Urali of Travancore 'believe that thunder, lightning and rain are caused by the duels among the Bhima in heaven. The duel takes place on a plank laid on the ground. One Bhima stands at each end of the plank, and in measured steps they approach towards the centre and attempt to strike each other with their swords. The rubbing of the swords causes lightning; the sound of treading on the plank is the thunder; and the sweat of the duellers trickles down as rain'.[1] The Baiga believe Bhimsen is sent by Bhagavan to give water to the world: the rainbow is his horse. The Muria expect both Lingo and Bhimul to provide them with rain in due season. If there is a drought, Bhimul's stone is covered with cowdung with the idea that he will quickly send rain to wash himself clean. Hislop describes a festival held in Bhimsen's honour at the end of the rains: two poles some twenty feet high and five feet apart are set up with a rope attached to the top, by which the village boys climb up and slide down.[2]

It is interesting that the discovery of mahua liquor, commonly ascribed to Bhimsen, is connected with rain—for it was the rain falling on the mahua flowers that caused them to ferment and thus attract the birds which in turn attracted Bhimsen.

The Birhor account for the origin of frost and hail-storms by saying that the climate of their country was formerly much colder than it is now and frost used to fall from above every night. But nowadays the climate is much warmer than it used to be and so there is less frost and only for a short time. The result is that the frost goes on accumulating in the sky and falls down from time to time as hail-stones.[3]

26

BAIGA

Kasaikund, Kawardha State

Megh Raja and Megh Rani lived in the Darbar of Bhagavan. Bhagavan asked them to give him three gourds of water and told Bhimsen to scatter it as rain all over the earth. Bhimsen took the gourds and went away. As he was passing through the jungle, night fell and he lay down and slept. As he was sleeping Durha Dano came and stole one of the

[1] *Census of India*, 1931, 236. [2] Hislop, 18. [3] Roy, *The Birhors*, 497.

gourds. The next morning when Bhimsen saw that one had been stolen he said, 'How can I scatter this water all through the year? I wanted to throw one gourd in each month—Asadh, Sawan, Bhadon, but now what can I do with only two?' So he divided his two gourds into four and scattered them during the four months, but Durha Dano throws the water from his gourd in the other eight.

27

GOND

Kawardha State

Jhursu Baiga lived in Bandichor. There he cut clearings in the forest and sowed mandia seed. There was no rain and the crop withered. The Baiga went to Singhbhawani and asked her to give rain to the earth.

Singhbhawani's son was Kakramal Kshattri the Crab, which lived in the Under World. She went to her son to ask for his help. The Crab said, 'As you are my mother I will help you.' It pulled off one of its claws and a bit of its back and threw them up into the sky and the rain came down like a pestle crashing into its mortar.

28

GOND

Pharisemhar, Rewa State

Bijay Karan Raja's kingdom extended for twice eighty miles around. Every caste and tribe lived there but there were more Baiga than any other. The Baiga made their clearings and sowed mandia. There was no rain in the world in those days and the crop always died.

The Baiga went to the Raja and told him what had happened. He was very sorry for them and went to get help from Jadrat Dano. This Dano had a gourd with twelve divisions. Four of them were full of dust, four of water and four of frost. Inside in the dust-rooms lived a hare and its wife. The Raja took the gourd back to his palace and set it up on a pole in the middle of his court.

So long as the hare remained in the four rooms of dust, the weather was hot and a dry dusty wind blew round the world. After four months the hare and its wife moved into the water-rooms and turned into prawns. Then the rain fell. Then again after four months the prawns moved on to the frost-rooms. Then they turned into chhaka-chhaki birds and the world became icy cold. Then after four months in the frost-rooms the birds became hares again and so went round and round the gourd.

VI

Water: The Rainbow

Beliefs about the rainbow are varied and perhaps not very serious. Sometimes it is a bow, sometimes a snake. A common tradition associates it with the bow of Rama. The Hindus of Sylhet believe it to be the very bow he broke on the occasion of his marriage.[1] Others associate it, as might be expected, with Indra the Rain God. It is to be seen 'when Indra draws his bow to release the rains from demons; or when successful in bringing down rain Indra manifests his glory by drawing a bow; or when, in the struggle for supremacy between the hot weather and the rainy season, Indra draws his bow to defeat the hot weather.'[2] The Chero say that it is the bow of a Rain God who comes out of his celestial home to see the fruits of his rain on the earth below.[3] The Bison-horn Maria call it the bow of Bhimul.[4] The Muria say it is Lingo's *aginban*, or magic arrow of fire.[5] The Muthuvan say it is the bow of Arjuna. The red hue is the string and the blue the stave.[6]

A number of traditions connect the rainbow with a snake. The rainbow is connected with the snake, being the fume of a gigantic serpent blown up from underground. In Persia, it was called the 'celestial serpent'.[7] The aboriginals of Betul call the rainbow *dhaman-gota*, or a bow of variegated colours. It is believed to shoot forth from a snake's hole. Two of these holes simultaneously throw out balls which meet in the sky and form a bow. The snake-holes are believed to contain a hidden gourd which is like the seed of the lotus and can be of great value for the treatment of *bathar-rog* or 'cloud disease' with which children are often affected.[8]

[1] Bhattacharjee, 120. 'To Hindus of the Punjab the rainbow is Ram Chandra's bow: to Muhammedans that of Baba Adam. But in the Punjab it is generally called *pigh*, the swing or the old woman's swing... In Marwat it is called the bowl.'—Rose, i, 133.

[2] Enthoven, 74.

[3] Agarwal, 215.

[4] Grigson, 230.

[5] *The Muria and their Ghotul*, 260.

[6] Iyer, ii, 35.

[7] Crooke, ii, 144.

[8] Hiralal, 'The Rainbow', *Man in India*, iii, 97.

The Pardhan of Mandla say it is the raised head of Basuk, the cobra that supports the world. The Baiga also say that the rainbow comes out of an ant-hill which is, of course, the traditional home of snakes. 'At the bottom of the ant-hill is a tiny gourd. The rainbow goes up into the air and across the sky searching for another ant-hill and when it sees one descends into it. Only a great Gunia can find the gourd but if he can find it and give it to a barren woman she will have a child.' The Birhor say the rainbow is 'formed by water which the *bandelele* snake gurgles out of its mouth.'[1] The Hill Maria call the rainbow the earth-serpent and say that it crawls out of a great ant-hill and throws its light across the sky as a sign of no more rain.[2] Another Muria tradition calls it the great snake Bhumtaras that rises from its ant-hill to stop the rain.[3] The Kol describe the rainbow as Lurbeng the serpent.[4]

An Uraon tradition is that the two ends of the rainbow which appear to touch the earth collect scorpions.[5]

In eastern India there is a remarkable story current among the Chak which associates the rainbow with incest.

> Once there was no water in the locality anywhere except in the house of a blacksmith. A brother and a sister being very thirsty went there to drink water. When they asked for some, the blacksmith told them that if they could live like husband and wife he could give them water. In order to quench their thirst they were compelled to live as husband and wife and then drank water and died soon afterwards. After their death they became rainbows and appear in the sky occasionally. Still now two rainbows are seen at the same time. The bright one is the sister and the faint one is the brother.[6]

The Lakher say that the rainbow is the tail of a red cock that comes down from heaven after rain to catch crabs in the streams. Its tail spreads out over the sky and forms the rainbow.[7] The Naga do not seem to have very definite ideas about the rainbow. The Ao Naga regard it as in some way symbolical of wealth. The Angami say it is the path used by a god. The Thado call it a spirit rope.[8] The Andamanese too say that it is a bridge by which the spirits visit their friends on earth. They generally regard it as an evil omen, believing it to be a precursor of sickness.[9]

1 Roy, *The Birhors*, 497.
2 Grigson, 230.
3 *The Muria and their Ghotul*, 260.
4 Dalton, 177.
5 *Census of India*, 1931, 116.
6 ibid., 124.
7 Mills, *The Ao Nagas*, 304.
8 ibid., 304.
9 Brown, 145.

There is a very great variety of beliefs. The Kanikkar, for example, say the rainbow is the bone of a Rakshasa;[1] some Pangia Kond of Orissa say it is the umbilical cord of an ancient Lohar stretched over the sky in promise of decreasing rain; the Gond of Mandla often associate it, as in the text, with a horse.

29

AHIR

Barbaspur, Mandla District

Galmancha Kachia and his wife made a beautiful garden in the Rameli-Kachhar. They had every kind of flowering shrub and tree, and kept their beautiful young daughter Raibhedan to look after it. One day Mainkuar, the son of Raja Indra, came that way hunting. He was thirsty and approached the maiden for a drink of water. They chatted and laughed together, love came to them and they lay together. Mainkuar went away, but next morning he returned and came again and again. At last they asked their parents to let them marry. They agreed, and Raja Indra came with the wedding-party from the Upper World. After the marriage, as they were taking the girl home, the curved roof of the litter broke and Indra Raja wrenched it off and threw it by the wayside. But it flew up into the air, away and away into the sky. 'Very well,' said Indra Raja. 'Cover the world as the roof covers a litter of lovers. As you are bright with haldi and vermilion, so shine that all the world will see you and will remember my name.'

30

GOND

Kawardha State

Indra Raja was born of the goddess Kamlapati in Lohagarh. He did not come by the ordinary way, he broke out through her ribs. When he was born he said to her, 'Now have a bow made for me.' She said, 'You have got to rule your kingdom. How can you go hunting?'

[1] Iyer, i, 55.

But she took from her body two handsful of entrails and said to her son, 'Go and rule over the sky. These entrails will stretch across it as a horse and when the people see it they will know whether it will be dry or wet.'

31

GOND

Upri, Rewa State

When the earth and the sky were to be married, the earth's Suasin was the maiden Singal Karo. The sky called all the gods to the wedding. But when it was time for the sky's marriage-party to start there was nothing for the bridegroom to ride on. The gods sent Bhimsen to find a horse.

In Pampapur, Ahiwan Dano had a mare called Kabutri which had just given birth to a foal. The foal's name was Jaitkaran. Bhimsen stole Jaitkaran and the gods tied to every hair sparkling diamonds, rubies and pearls.

But Bhimsen said in his mind, 'If earth and sky are married, how can men survive when the two lie together?' He rubbed some dirt from his body and made a cock and on the eve of the marriage the cock crowed crying, 'The Kali Yug has begun.' The gods at once declared, 'Earth and sky cannot be married in the Age of Darkness.' They went away and the marriage was stopped.

The earth was standing lovely in her ornaments, watching the road for the marriage-party of her future husband. From afar the sky saw her beauty and his seed fell from him to the earth. From his seed were born fish and insects. The gods put Jaitkaran the horse, every hair gay with a precious stone, into the sky as the rainbow.

CHAPTER FOUR

FIRE

FRAZER has studied the myths of the origin of fire in great detail, but he was not able to call many Indian witnesses, for few of these had hitherto recorded their statements. He has an important and interesting passage which throws some light on stories in the text which suggest that fire came from the vagina and was possessed by woman before man discovered it.

The notion that fire was elicited from a woman's body, and particularly from her genital organ, finds a ready explanation in the analogy which, as we have seen, many savages trace between the working of the fire-drill on the one hand and the intercourse of the sexes on the other. In all such cases the horizontal stick, which the drill perforates, is regarded as female, while the upright stick or drill proper is considered as male; so that on this analogy fire elicited by the fire-drill may be said to be produced from the body of a woman, and particularly from her genital organ, which in the fire-drill is represented by the hollow in which the drill revolves. This analogy is clearly recognized, and carried out practically in the ritual by which to this day the Brahman fire-priest (*Agnihotra*) and his wife between them kindle the sacred fire by means of the fire-drill. On the night before fire is made, the plunger or upper part of the fire-drill (*arani*) is put in charge of the priest and the lower part is put in charge of his wife, and husband and wife sleep with these parts at night, 'the process of fire-making symbolizing coition'. Next morning they together kindle the sacred fire; the man holds the plunger firmly so that the point cannot leave the hole in the base-board, while his wife causes it to revolve by pulling the cord wound about it until fire is produced and communicated to the tinder. Both husband and wife are subject to special taboos while they are engaged in the performance of this sacred duty.

The same analogy may possibly also explain why in the myths women are sometimes represented as in possession of fire before men. For the fire which is extracted from the board by the revolution of the drill is naturally interpreted by the savage as existing in the board before its extraction by the drill, or, in mythical language, as inherent in the female before it is drawn out by the male; just as the savage imagines fire to be stored up in all the trees from whose wood he elicits it by friction. Thus to primitive thought it might seem natural to conclude that fire was owned by women before it came into the possession of men.[1]

[1] Frazer, *Myths*. 220 f. See also on this, Held, 140 f.

I

AGARIA

Bahapur, Mandla District

(From *The Agaria*, 115 f.)

A sadhu did penance for twelve years without food or water, meditating on Fire. He had no fire. Save for the fires in the sky he had never seen fire nor felt its warmth. At last Fire in the form of a Virgin stood before him and said, 'I am very cold: make a fire for me.' The sadhu said, 'I have nothing, I have never made a fire.' The Virgin said, 'Bring a bit of cow-dung and some wood, and put them into a small pit in the ground.' So saying, she disappeared.

The sadhu dug a hole in the ground, and put the cow-dung and wood as the girl had said. The dry dung and the wood burst into flames of their own accord. When he saw the fire, the sadhu's nature changed; he gave up his penance and went to the nearest village. There was no fire there: the villagers ate raw meat and uncooked rice. The sadhu went back to the forest to fetch fire for the people, but he found that it had once more taken the form of a Virgin and run away.

Bhagavan was going to kill a great Dano. He saw the Fire Virgin and said to her, 'Come and help.' She said, 'Certainly I'll help, but what will you give me?' He said, 'I'll give you an offering of *ghī* and *gur*.' Bhagavan went to Sabar Sai and said, 'I am going to kill the Dano, come and help me.' Sabar Sai said, 'I have this great kingdom, and no fire. How can I come with you?' When Bhagavan promised to give fire to the Agaria, Sabar Sai went to the battle.

During the great fight, Sabar Sai was killed and with him his son Logundi Raja. Logundi's son, Kariya Kuar, escaped. He went home and wanted to work in his smithy, but he had no fire. He went to the iron-pit, and killed a black cow there in the name of Lohasur. As he did so, all the implements and tools of iron rose out of the pit and came to him. Logundi Raja also returned to life and said, 'My father's name was Sabar Sai, and Bhagavan promised fire as a reward for his help.' Thus said Logundi Raja and returned to the pit.

So Kariya Kuar made his smithy and prepared his furnace in the Kajliban hills. There were many bamboos there. As the dry bamboos rubbed against one another in the wind, they caught fire. Kariya Kuar found a blazing bamboo and brought it home. This was the Virgin Fire, and from this the first charcoal was made. So fire began in the world.

2

BAIGA

Bohi, Pandaria Zamindari

In the days before there was any fire in the world, the cat and the bear were married. All the animals in the world went in the husband's—the cat's—marriage-party. The cat was the tiger's mother's sister's son. The animals said, 'We're not going to eat this raw meat. We want something tasty. Let us get fire.'

The panther said, 'You go and fetch it.' The hyena said, 'No, you get it.' The leopard said, 'No, someone else should get it.' At last the tiger said, 'Very well, I'll get it.' And it went off to find fire.

Now the firefly had collected all the fire in the world and was sitting on it. The tiger came and began to fight, but the firefly turned the tiger into a leaf and summoned the wind to blow it into the air. The leaf called on the name of Jhinjha Guru and became a tiger again.

The tiger returned to the fight and now the firefly turned it into dust and the wind blew it about. The tiger called on the name of Binjha Guru and became a tiger again.

The tiger returned to the fight, and this time when he was conquering the firefly she said, 'Let me go and I will give you fire.' The tiger let her go and she cut her little finger and let a drop of blood fall on a leaf. The tiger took the blood and went away. It made a bundle of spear grass and let the blood fall on it, whereupon it burst into flames.

The marriage-party cooked their food with the fire. One day the cat went out and came to a village. It saw a house and wondered what it was. It went in and there was a pot of milk. It drank some but did not like the taste. 'It ought to be cooked as at home,' it thought. It went back, got a bit of fire in a stick, tied it round its neck, and lit a fire and so boiled the milk. But the people came home and the cat ran away. They drank the boiled milk and liked it and since then men have cooked their food.

3

BAIGA

Jalda, Mandla District

In the days when men ate their food raw, a ghost (*bhut*) found himself in trouble with a sick child. He went to a village and, finding a man eating his food, seized him and carried him away to his house. There the man, who was a Gunia, looked in his winnowing-fan, discovered the reason of the child's sickness and cured him.

The ghost was pleased and asked the man what reward he would take. 'I have everything I need,' said the man. 'There is plenty to drink and I have two wives and there are many children. But there is one thing that bothers us—we have to eat our food raw and it twists our bellies.' The ghost gave him two small earthen pots and an iron bangle. 'Take these,' he said, 'and when you get home make a pile of wood, put the bangle in the middle of it and the pots on top, and you will find you have a meal ready cooked, good hot rice and pulse.'

The man returned home and gathered wood together. He put the iron bangle in the middle of it and the two pots on top. Fire came of its own accord from the bangle and soon there was a meal of hot rice and pulse. Since then no one has eaten raw food.

4

BINJHWAR

Raipur District

Agnisur Dano lived in a cave in the depth of the forest. One day a Baiga woman went to get leaves. When she saw the Dano, she fell in love with him and began to live in his cave, for he was very beautiful and light came from all parts of his body. The woman thought, 'Now that I sleep daily with the Dano, I must get fire from his mouth and give it to the world,' so she said to him, 'I have been with you a long time; yet you have never opened your mouth. Now open it and show me what is inside.' The Dano said, 'Go and wash yourself and then I will show you.' She went to the river and bathed and came back wet and glistening. As she came she passed under a cotton tree and bits of cotton stuck to her body and covered her. When the Dano opened his mouth, fire came out and the cotton sticking to her body caught fire. She threw the bits away and the jungle blazed up and thus fire came into the world.

5

BISON-HORN MARIA

Tikanpal, Bastar State

There was no fire in the world at first. There were six Kanyang who belonged to the Halavetti, Pulavetti, Utvetti, Godrevetti, Gatvetti and Parendvetti clans. Each went in turn to search for fire and failed to find it. At last Pulavetti said she would try again. She wandered across the world alone. On the way she found a mesh of siari cords. She untied the knot and inside discovered fire.

6

BISON-HORN MARIA

Borgum, Bastar State

One said fire was discovered in a stone; another that it was found in a bamboo.

7

BISON-HORN MARIA

Bara Harmamunda, Bastar State

Dadaburka was the first man in the world. He went out to search for fire and found it first in a stone, then in a bamboo, then in the *girtonda* plant, and last in the *jiwlatonda* plant.

8

DHANWAR

Putwa, Matin Zamindari

Gutia Dewar's daughter-in-law said to him, 'Where can I get fire and water so that I can cook your food?' The Dewar said, 'There is fire in the hand and water in the ant-hill; get it from there.' The girl took two sticks in her hand and made fire, and went to get water. But she forgot where the Dewar had told her to go. When she could not find any water she returned to her father-in-law and asked him, 'I have fire, but where can I get water so that I can cook your food?' 'Since you have forgotten what I said, you must search for water in streams and hollows.' So she went through the forest looking for water and at last found a stream. She drew water and brought it back and cooked the Dewar's food. From that day there has been fire in the world but the water that was in the ant-hill sank down into the earth.

9

DHOBA

Sajatola, Kawardha State

When men were first born they did not know how to cook or how to bathe or how to wear clothes. Their nails grew very long, for they did not know how to cut them. They had no houses or villages but five or ten people would gather together and live under trees or in caves.

One year the bamboo disease came and the bamboos withered directly they had flowered. It was the very hot weather just before the rains. The wind blew the dry bamboos to and fro. They rubbed together and fire came from them. The whole jungle was nothing but dry wood and it was soon in flames. When the fire died down the long-nailed men came to the jungle and found many animals lying roasted in the ashes. One of them said, 'What is this?' He touched the roasted body with his nail and it went into the hot flesh and was burnt. The man quickly removed his hand and put it in his mouth to cool it. He noticed a pleasant taste and smell and said to himself,

'This is worth eating,' and he called his friends and they had a great feast on the roasted bodies of the animals.

The next day they went to hunt and killed a hare. Now they no longer would tolerate raw flesh and they tried to roast the creature. They tied it with a bark-rope and made a tripod to hang it over the fire. But when the fire blazed up the rope was burnt and the hare fell into the flames. Only the hair was burnt off but the flesh was not cooked. However they were hungry and ate it.

Next day the long-nailed men killed a sambhar. First they skinned it, then they cut up the flesh into little pieces, wrapped them in the skin and put it into the fire to cook. This time the meat was well cooked and everyone was pleased.

But still the long-nailed men had no vessels to cook in and they could not boil things in water. As they went to and fro during the rains they noticed how the mud stuck to their feet and filled up the gaps between their toes and that when they came home and sat by the fire to warm themselves, the mud hardened. One day a man thought, 'If the earth hardens like this, why not make a pot.' He made a pot and dried it in the sun. He put water and meat into it and set it above a hearth of three stones. But when he lit the fire the pot broke and the water poured out and extinguished the fire. Then he saw that the heat of the sun was not sufficient. 'If we are to cook on fire, we must make the pot with fire.' So this time he dried the pot in fire, and when he cooked the pot did not break. Since then men have made pots and have used fire to cook their food.

10

GOND

Pendra Zamindari

At first men ate their food raw. It pricked their bellies like an ox-goad. The Gond were living in the jungle. Todiyamal Dano was living in Binjhpahar Bursigarh. One day the men living on raw food saw the Dano's fire and sent one to see what it was. He found the great Dano, like a hill shaggy with hair, sitting by his fire. The Dano cried, 'Today food has come to me of its own accord.' But the man said, 'No, I did not come to be eaten. I came for fire, for we have to eat our food raw.' 'No, no, I am going to eat you; how can I give you fire?' 'But there are many men waiting for me.' 'How many?' 'Who knows? But very many.' Hearing this the Dano felt still more hungry and told the man to take fire in one hand and oil-seed in the other. He put the fire in a semur pod.

The man went home and as he went the seed fell from his hand along the path. Now the Dano had made the man stand before him holding the semur pod. The Dano had all the fire in the world inside his body. He blew it out of his mouth and it went into the cotton. The man told this story to his friends. Presently the Dano came following the trail of oil-seed. But the men took their bows and arrows and killed him. They cut open his body and took out the fire, and since then fire has belonged to men.

II

KOL

Jubbulpore District

In Lankapur lived Bhuleri Baiga with his son Lohi. In Kolargaon lived Bartaniya Baiga with his daughter. Bhuleri married his son to Bartaniya's daughter. There was no fire in those days and men lived on raw roots and leaves.

After they were married the girl and boy did not know what to do. Neither of them had ever cleaned their parts, and the boy's was covered with slime and the girl's with a green scum. One day the girl said to the boy, 'Why did we ever get married?' The boy said, 'I have heard that people are married so that they can be called husband and wife, but what "husband" and "wife" means I have no idea.' The girl said, 'Once long ago I saw my brother lying with his wife and I think that must be what it means.' The boy said, 'But I have never done it.' The girl said, 'Nor have I.' The boy said, 'Lie down and I will try what I can do.' The girl said, 'No, I cannot do it here. Let us go to the jungle and there I will teach you.'

They went to the jungle to a place where there was a great black rock. Living in that rock was Dedhkulhia Mata who had only one-and-a-half buttocks. Nearby the boy and girl made a bed of dry leaves and they lay down together and the girl taught the boy what to do. But when the slime and the scum came together it grew so hot that a fire broke out and the bed of leaves caught fire.

Dedhkulhia Mata heard the *pat-pat-pat* noise of the burning leaves and was annoyed. She cursed the boy and girl and said, 'Go away and may fire burn your organs.' The girl's organ burnt so fiercely that it has ever since been black; her hairs too were burnt and since then woman's hair has not been long. From the girl's organ fire spread to the whole jungle and then went throughout the world.

12

JUANG

Korba, Keonjhar State

Rusi lived in an ant-hill. From time to time he would come out for air and drum on a grindstone. As he drummed twelve years went by, and at the end of that time fire came from the grindstone and the stone itself and the hills and trees began to burn. The gods saw it and were afraid; they thought, 'No one will be able to put this out; we will be burnt to ashes.' They came to the fire and with folded hands addressed it: 'You are the greatest of us all. You will be honoured first, and we will only be remembered afterwards.' The fire said, 'Very well, but you must show me a place to live.' The gods said, 'Live in wood and stone.' Since that day fire has been in wood and stone. That is why we always first offer incense to fire and then to the other gods. The grindstone on which Rusi drummed became the sun which is full of fire, and the grinder became the moon which brings the fire out of the sun. As Rusi beat his stone little chips used to fly off and these became the stars.

13

MURIA

Kanhargaon, Bastar State

(From *The Muria and their Ghotul*, 262)

At the beginning of the world, when the earth sank beneath the great waters, there were no men left but the seven Koroho-Lingo brothers. When the water went down again, they set out to find fire to warm themselves and cook their food. Presently they saw a Maharin whose name was Parajunge; she had a fire. They made their camp near her house and went to get fire from her. The girl gave the eldest brother some fire in a bundle of grass but it went out. Then the next brother went, and the next, but every time the fire went out. At last Lingo himself went. When she offered him fire in the grass he hit her twice and picked up a burning log from her fire and took it to his camp.

The brothers went away, but the girl soon found that she was pregnant from the two blows which Lingo had struck.

14

PANKA

Sanhrwachhapar, Mandla District

At first people ate their food raw. There was a very poor man. He had three sons, who got a little work in the houses of the neighbours. The eldest was married. One day his wife said to her parents-in-law and the brothers, 'Look, everyone works according to his own wish, but there is no leader to say what is to be done.' They considered and at last decided that they would make the girl the head of the house. She said, 'Well, I will be the head of the house. But whatever I say you must follow and observe.' They promised to do whatever she said.

Her first order was: 'Make a new house.' When it was ready she said, 'Now when you return from your master's fields, bring whatever you may find on the road—it may be a bit of bamboo, or rope, or fruit, whatever it is—and put it inside the house.' This they did; one brought cow-dung, one a bit of bamboo, one some leaves; they put everything into the building and went to the master's house to get their food.

One day the youngest brother came tired and failed to bring anything home. But he was afraid that his elder brother's wife would be angry and he got up and ran back along the road to see if he could find anything. He found a dead snake and threw it into the new house. As it fell on the ground fire came from its mouth. The girl saw this and came running with cotton from the semur tree; she caught hold of the snake's mouth and let the fire catch the cotton. She cooked food for the family and fed them, and they were all pleased.

The girl put that dead snake up in the roof.

PART TWO: THE NATURAL WORLD

CHAPTER FIVE

METALS AND MINERALS

THE stories in this Chapter illustrate very simple mechanisms of association. It is at weddings that ornaments are displayed, so the origin of gold and silver must be associated with a wedding. The precious metals, bright and shining, are naturally connected with the gleaming bodies of fishes or snakes. The notion that salt comes from a dead body, or from the bones of a corpse, may be due to its power of checking decay or perhaps ultimately to the custom of some classes of Hindu ascetics who bury their dead in salt. Very interesting is the tradition that menstrual blood can turn stone to gold and human urine can transform rocks to iron.

I

AGARIA

Umaria, Mandla District

In Pampapur lived a Raja with seven wives. Each of them had one son. The Raja married a new young wife and from her was born a son with a face of a mongoose. The Raja was very angry and made the girl dress in tattered clothes and sent her to the fields to drive away the crows.

One night the Raja had a dream of a silver pillar covered with golden flowers. He called his seven sons and sent them to find it. The mongoose boy also went with them, but they beat him and drove him away. But he followed them, riding on his horse Hansraj. When they came to a cross-roads the seven brothers went to the left and the youngest boy to the right.

When he reached the Madhuban forest he came to the spot where Koeli Nag used to come up from the Under World for food. The mongoose boy killed the snake and turning Hansraj into a stone left it above while he himself went down by the cobra's passage to Jhalalpur in the Under World. Here lived, each in a separate palace, the three daughters of Koeli Nag—Mainabai, Karanbai, Salhobai. The mongoose boy enchanted each of them in turn with his love-charms and married them.

One day the three girls gave the boy a sword and a stick and then they danced before him naked as cows. When they were tired the boy killed them. From the dirt of his body he made two sparrows and sent them to drink the blood. As their beaks touched the blood the girls' bones turned into a silver pillar and their livers turned into golden flowers. The boy touched the pillar with his stick and the girls appeared again.

Then the boy went up the passage with his three wives and a great army. He brought Hansraj back to life and made a fine palace near Pampapur. His father came and took him home. They sent for the poor mother who was driving away the crows in the field and the boy made his three wives dance naked in the darbar. He killed them with his sword and again made the birds drink their blood. The bones turned once more into a silver pillar and the livers into golden flowers and a great shower of gold and silver filled the palace. The Raja gathered as much as he needed and then the boy touched the pillar with his stick and the girls appeared again. The boy ruled with his three wives in Pampapur and since that date there has been gold and silver in the world.

2

BAIGA

Gotai, Mandla District

Bhagavan had a black fish and a black snake. There was no earth then. Bhagavan thought and said to his fish, 'If I ask you for something, will you give it to me?' 'Yes,' said the fish. Bhagavan said to his fish, 'Then give me your eyes.' The fish gave its eyes to Bhagavan and he made a pot of them. He made his snake into a churn. With the snake's belly he made a cord. He filled the pot with water and churned it, and from this there came the thirty-two kinds of earth.

From the roe of his fish Bhagavan made gold, from its liver he made iron, from its scales silver, and from its skin copper.

3

BAIGA

Kasaikund, Kawardha State

A Raja had a daughter beautiful as a parrot. When she grew up, the Raja sent the news to every country and many princes came wishing to marry her. A poor boy called Chandra-Uriya came to the palace with a basket of roots and fruit to sell. The princes sat in a row but the Raja's daughter went to the poor boy and put the garland of her choice on him. The people said, ' She must be mad ; make her do it again.' She did it a second time and a third, but each time she put the garland on Chandra-Uriya. The Raja was very angry. He called to his servants to throw dung on his daughter and her husband and had them driven out of the palace.

Chandra-Uriya and his bride went together into the forest and built a little hut. The girl cleaned the place and tied leaves and flowers everywhere until it looked like a palace. She found coloured stones and earth of various tints. One day as she was cooking, a red stone fell from the wall of the hut into the fire and when she took it out it was glowing beautifully. In this way she learnt how to put stones in the fire and thus make them more beautiful. She and her husband made string from bark and they threaded the stones upon it until they were shining and beautiful as garlands of flowers. In this way the girl made diamonds, rubies, gold and silver ornaments and the boy used to take them into the city and sell them, until soon they were richer than the Raja himself.

4

BHARIA

Mandla District

There was a Dewar called Sidha. In the same village lived a Dewarin called Dubulchak. This village was in Koeligarh. One day Sidha Dewar went to the Dewarin to ask for her daughter in marriage to his son. She was agreeable and one Sunday the betrothal was fixed and on the Monday was the building of the marriage-booth. But when the marriage began Dubulchak's daughter said, ' Unless he gives me golden ornaments (*tarki*) I will not go with him round the pole.' When

Sidha Dewar heard this he took mandia bread wrapped in leaves and went to search for gold. He reached the Madhuban forest and began to feel very thirsty. He found a pond and went to get water. In this pond lived Sohagi Dano. After drinking water the Dewar sat down on the bank and wept and the Dano heard him. She came to him and asked what was the matter and he told her how the marriage of his son could not go forward because he had no gold. The Dano said, 'Eat the food you have brought and then I will tell you where to go in order to get what you want.'

When the Dewar finished eating, the Dano went three times round the pond and then brought out from its depths a stone that looked like someone's liver. She said to him, 'Take this to the goldsmith and he will get gold out of it.' The Dewar took the stone to a goldsmith's house and asked him to make it into ornaments. The goldsmith put the stone into the fire and when it was heated it turned black. The goldsmith's wife was in her monthly period. Her husband called her and when she saw what was happening, she was angry and threw a few drops of her blood upon the stone. Directly the stone was touched by the blood it turned into gold.

The goldsmith made ornaments from the gold and the Dewar took them to the wedding with great joy and his son was married.

5

BINJHWAR

Dhaurabhata, Raipur District

Surti Dano and Jitho Dano lived as neighbours. Surti wanted to marry his son to Jitho's daughter. But Jitho said, 'Unless you bring me a lot of ornaments, I will not give you my daughter.' Surti was very upset at this and went to the jungle to see if he could find any ornaments.

By and by night fell and Surti lay down under a teak tree to sleep. At midnight, a krait came to him in a dream, 'Do not be afraid. I will give you my bones for ornaments and my eyes as a spangle and my tongue for a nose-ring.' When Surti awoke the krait gave him its bones and eyes and tongue and Surti Dano went to the Katak Mountains to find the twelve Agaria brothers, the thirteen Tamesur brothers and the fourteen Lohasur brothers.

When he found them he asked them to make the snake's bones into ornaments. They said they would do so if he would pay them by finding them iron. He said, 'Get a pile of stones together.' The Dano pissed on the stones and they turned into iron. The Agaria were very pleased and at once made the snake's bones into ornaments. Surti Dano took them home and when he gave them to Jitho, the marriage was arranged for the following week.

6

DHANWAR

Barbhata, Uprora Zamindari

A man and his wife had no child for many years. At last by the help of Susri Mai a son was born to them. But after his birth the child refused to drink his mother's milk or to take any food and soon he got thin as a rope. The mother said to her husband, 'Bhagavan has given us a child but he won't eat and soon must die.' That night they both, husband and wife, had a dream. One said to them, 'You eat your food without salt and so the milk is tasteless as water and the boy will not drink it.'

The next day the husband went to find salt but it was nowhere in the world. At last he came to Kandalpur where Namakatri Devi was ruling. He pleased her in some way and she took out her liver and said, 'Cut it up into little bits and find a place where there are white stones and throw the bits upon them. Wait for a night and the next day take the stones home and eat them with your food.' The man did as she told him and the stones turned into salt. After the mother had eaten salt, her son was always clamouring for her milk.

7

DHOBA

Mohgaon, Kawardha State

In Bijagarh there wsa a lake called Mallaj. Here lived a great fish which ate everyone who went to bathe there. It had a large fin that stuck out of the water. Sometimes a crow would sit on it. The fish then would knock the crow off and eat it.

At this time the five Pandava brothers who were then in exile made their camp in Bijagarh. The people told them about the fish and begged them to kill it. Bhimsen went to kill it, but the fish caught him instead. But Bhimsen got hold of the fin and hurled the fish into the air. It fell on the bank and burst into a thousand pieces, as an earthen pot breaks when it is thrown somewhere. The bones flew in all directions.

These bones turned into white marble; the ribs were driven deep into the ground and turned into silver.

8

GOND

Barratola, Mandla District

In Kotgarh lived Raja Darwai and Raja Durbansai. They were Gond Rajas. Raja Darwai was great and wealthy, but Durbansai was poor. Raja Darwai had a daughter whose name was Satwantin. This girl used to give her father a pot of water and a tooth-twig early in the morning and for the rest of the day she did nothing else except worship Burha Nang.

After some time Durbansai went to Darwai to ask for Satwantin in marriage to his son. Raja Darwai said, 'You are so poor that you cook in earthen pots and drink from wooden pots. I can't give you my daughter.' Durbansai was for returning home but Satwantin said to her father, 'Father, whether he is poor or rich, I want to marry this boy. Otherwise I will marry no one. Your wealth will one day turn into a ghost.' Her father was angry but he said, 'Well, you may marry this boy, but you are not to come again to my house till he is as rich as I am.'

So the marriage was arranged. The booth was erected and Satwantin and her husband went together round the pole. They sat for greeting and relatives and guests came and saluted them. But when it was Burha Nang's turn to greet them, Satwantin covered her head with her cloth. Burha Nang said, 'Do not hide your face, my daughter. Let me greet you and whenever you are in trouble, remember me and I will come to help you.' At this Satwantin uncovered her head and Burha Nang put five grains of rice on her forehead.

When Satwantin went to her husband's house he wanted to embrace her, but she said, 'This is the time when I must do my worship. When I am finished, I will myself call you and you can embrace me.' Then every day Satwantin used to give a pot of water and a tooth-twig to her father-in-law and the rest of the time, night and day, she spent in the worship of Burha Nang.

One night when all were asleep, Satwantin collected the earthen pots and wooden vessels and put them in front of her ; then she sat down and wept *feh-feh* like a she-jackal. Burha Nang heard her and at once came to see what was the matter. Satwantin said, 'What a sad fate is mine ! Here am I the daughter of a great Raja and yet I must fetch water in an earthen pot and cook in an wooden vessel.' Burha Nang said, 'Bring a lamp in my honour.' Satwantin lit a lamp and waved it before him, whereupon Burha Nang struck the earthen and wooden vessels with its tail and the wooden vessels turned to silver and the earthen pots to brass.

Then at last Satwantin called her husband and allowed him to embrace her. From that day, they became rich, and their eight parts laughed with pleasure. Soon Raja Darwai heard of it and let his daughter come again to his house.

9

GOND

Jubbulpore District

In Sumelidongar Nattul Dano was bitten by a spider and died. As he was about to die he said to his son, Waisur, 'Dig a pit as deep as five men with arms outstretched and bury me there, but keep round me an empty place one cubit wide. After three years my flesh will liquify and a squirrel will burrow down and will lick it up. It will take it into the world and men will call it *non* (salt) and will eat it.'

Waisur did as his father asked and after three years the squirrels began to bring salt out of the pit. When men tasted it they were very pleased and once they had found it they could not live without it.

10

GOND

Koelari, Rewa State

When Mahadeo and Ñanga Baiga had made the world many men were born. Nanga Baiga rubbed some dirt from his body and made an Agaria and his wife. He taught them how to make bellows and to build a kiln. In this kiln was born Dauha Marra Deo. After he was born, iron came out of the kiln.

The Agaria made the iron into an axe and a sickle. In due time the Agaria and his wife had twelve sons, and they were married. The Agaria made for them twelve axes, twelve digging-sticks and twelve sickles. When he had finished he did not know how to spend his time. He went to Nanga Baiga and asked him what to do. Nanga Baiga taught him how to make many different instruments of iron. When they were ready he put them on a carrying-pole and took them to Jhinjhigarh. Here Dhummasur Mai was living. She fell upon the Agaria and possessed him. When Nanga Baiga gave food-sacrifice, she said, 'Take these things to Garh Parsaoli. There lives a Dhoba Raja who will buy them and distribute them to the whole world.'

When Nanga Baiga and the Agaria reached Garh Parsaoli they found the Dhoba Raja and his Rani swinging in a golden swing. Underneath it were heaped up twelve measures of haldi. When the Dhoba Raja saw Nanga Baiga he got down from the swing and greeted him and made him sit beside him. The Agaria showed his iron instruments and the Dhoba was very pleased and bought them. Now that he had iron he began to plough and the rest he distributed to his subjects.

11

KHUNTIA CHOKH

Pondi, Lapha Zamindari

Kaitabsur Dano stole all the salt in the world and there was none left for anyone else. He went to Hahuban and sat down spreading his testes like two great hills before him. One day Bhimsen came to that forest to dig roots. When the Dano saw him he said, 'Before you dig here you will have to fight with me. If you win you can dig, otherwise I will devour you.' They fought and in the end Bhimsen killed the Dano and buried him in a great pit.

Down in the pit the belly of the corpse broke open and the salt turned into water and came up above the earth. Many deer came to drink the water and when they found it salty, animals came from every side. Their feet dug up the earth and the place became a muddy swamp.

In Bittalgarh was the blind Juna Bhoi with his wife and twelve sons. One day the sons went to hunt in the Hahuban. The youngest brother was thirsty and went to the salt-lick, but he was caught in the mud and drowned. After some days the other brothers found the corpse, but there was nothing left but bones. They found the water was salty and all round the earth was white. When they tasted it they discovered that this too was salt. They said to themselves, 'In place of our brother we have found salt.' Each took as many of the crystals as they could back to their palace. They spread them out in front of the old blind people saying, 'This is *Nān*' ('Little', meaning the youngest brother). Juna and his wife fondled and patted the salt saying, '*Nān Nān Nān*'. Now people call salt *non* in memory of the youngest brother who was drowned at the salt-lick.

12

KOL

Bilaspur District

There was a Kol woman who had no one to care for her. She was dying of hunger and wandered from place to place begging a little food: sometimes she made chutney of wild figs and ate them. One night she had a dream. One said to her, 'Biskarma Deo is at the cross-roads.' The woman went and found Biskarma Deo living there and told him about her miserable state.

Biskarma Deo pulled a hair out of his head. As he gave it to the woman, it turned into a sickle. With this she went and began to work. She found that with the sickle she could cut as much as twelve other women who had to use their hands. Gradually she got very rich and earned the name of Bara-Bhutiharin. After a few years she made a golden palace and a golden cock. When the cock called, the gods assembled and Bara-Bhutiharin asked them to give mankind the sickle that brings gold to the world.

13

RAJNENGI PARDHAN

Kawardha State

Bansmar Marahi Mata lived with her daughter in Jhalalpur. A Baiga and a Baigin were in Duganigarh and one day the Baiga rode on a tiger to see the Mata.

Bansmar Marahi Mata used to distil liquor from the bodies of house-flies. When the Baiga arrived, she washed his feet and tethered the tiger to a tree. She gave him a cot, woven with the webs of spiders, and asked him, 'Why have you come?' 'For the marriage of my son and your daughter.' The Mata gave the Baiga food.

The Mata kept salt in her belly and as she was cooking she bent over the pot and let a little of the salt fall in. When the Baiga ate the food he was very pleased and said to himself, 'I will get salt at the greeting time at my son's marriage.'

At the time of the marriage, the Baiga told the bride to cover her head and not to undo her cloth until her mother gave her salt as a present. She did so and the Mata had to agree. She bent over the dish and bits of salt fell into it. The Baiga took them and gave them to the world.

14

RAJNENGI PARDHAN

Upri, Rewa State

A squirrel stole salt from the Under World and brought it to the Jhalpaghat forest. Not far away in Kukripani lived the Baiga Gonga Dewar. He cut his clearing in the forest and sowed a crop of cucumbers. Every day the squirrel used to eat a cucumber. When Gonga discovered that his crop was being destroyed he hunted for the squirrel. He found its hole and all round it were bits of salt shining like silver. He picked up a bit and touched it with his tongue and liked the taste. 'If what this creature throws away is so tasty, how good its flesh must be! I will kill and eat it.' So the Baiga put a trap outside the hole and soon caught the squirrel. He roasted and ate it and found the flesh savoury and good.

But the children of this squirrel ran in every direction and wherever they went they brought salt up from the Under World and men found it and ate it.

At the very place where Gonga Dewar killed the first squirrel, Rai Linga Deo was born. He gave a dream to Gonga saying, 'I sent the squirrel to give salt to the world and you have killed it. From now onwards, therefore, if you stay in this forest your race will be destroyed.' Having cursed him, Rai Linga Deo went to the south and travelled on until he came to Bastar Rai and ruled there. Gonga Dewar thought, 'I may die, but let me take as much salt as I can first.' He gathered a lot of salt and went away to live elsewhere. Now no Baiga ever goes to Jhalpaghat, for if he does, a tiger will kill and eat him.

CHAPTER SIX

GRASS, FLOWERS AND TREES

I WAS surprised at the difficulty in getting from people who spend all their lives in the forest any account of how trees came into being or acquired their different characteristics. Some tribes trace the colour or shape of trees to contact with a tribal hero. The Birhor, for example, look back to the wanderings of Rama and Lakshman in the jungle. The date-palm's leaves are now long and narrow, though formerly they were broad, because Lakshman shot at them and split them into narrow strips.[1] The *zizyphus jujuba* is hardy because when Rama and Lakshman were searching for Sita, they gave it their blessing.

They came to a plum tree. . . They asked the tree, 'Well, friend, did you see Sita being carried off by Rawan Raja ?' The tree answered, 'Yes, I caught hold of her cloth, and here is a bit of it'; and the tree pointed to a rag entangled in its thorns. At this Rama blessed the tree, saying, 'Well done, friend, henceforth you will not die, however much you may be hacked at and mangled. Even if a single root is left, you will spring up afresh from that root.' And since then the plum tree has become one of the hardiest of plants.[2]

The ebony tree is black because when Hanuman jumped from burning Lanka into safety he wiped his blackened hands upon it.[3] The Munda, however, say that the ebony tree turned black because it was partly burnt in the great rain of fire sent by Singbonga upon mankind.[4]

The Korava believe that the *terminalia calappa* is lucky because Rama made a bower beneath it as he was wandering through the forest of Dandaka.[5]

The Muria, however, attribute these things to Lingo. As he sprang from the ordeal of fire in which his virtue had been tested, his foot struck the tinsa tree[6] and the bark has ever since looked dry and dead on one side. The white ash from his body flew over the saja tree[7]—and it became white and holy. He rubbed his body, black with oil and smoke, against the ebony tree,[8] and ever since its bark has been black.[9]

[1] Roy, *The Birhors*, 411.
[2] ibid., 415.
[3] ibid., 421.
[4] Roy, *J. B. O. R. S.*, ii, 207.
[5] Thurston, iii, 268.
[6] *Ougenia dalbergioides*, Benth.
[7] *Terminalia tomentosa*, W. & A.
[8] *Diospyros melanoxylon*, Roxb.
[9] *The Muria and their Ghotul*, 243.

The Santal story is on rather similar lines. Once, it is said, a woman was found to be with child by her own brother and the two had to fly the country. On their way they found a date-palm and got very drunk on the juice. 'At nightfall they rested at the foot of a bael tree and fell into a drunken sleep from the date-juice they had drunk.

'As the woman lay senseless her child was born to her and no sooner was the child born than a bael fruit fell on to its head and split it into four pieces which flew apart and became four hills. From falling on the new-born child the bael fruit has ever since had a sticky juice and the tree is covered with thorns which are the hair of the child. In the morning the man and woman went on and came to a forest of tarop trees and the woman wiped her bloody hands on the tarop trees and so the tarop tree ever since exudes a red juice like blood.

'Next morning they went on and came to a spring and drank of its water and afterwards the woman bathed in it and the blood-stained water flowed over all the country and so we see stagnant water covered with a red scum. Going on from there they reached a low-lying flat and halted ; almost at once they saw a thunderstorm coming up from the South and West, and the lightning came and slew them both '.[1]

The Munda have a story to account for the fact that the leaves of the tamarind tree are so small. Barnda and Singbonga were two brothers. 'They were great hunters and always carried about with them a fierce hawk, a golden club and a golden basket. One day after they had proceeded some distance from their house with their hawk, they were overtaken on the road by a heavy shower of rain. To protect themselves against the rain, they took shelter under a wide-spreading tamarind tree. In those days tamarind trees had large leaves ; but yet this tree could not afford them complete protection. At this the two brothers were highly chagrined and struck at the tamarind leaves till the leaves were split into numerous minute divisions. Thenceforth tamarind leaves have been as small as we see them now '.[2]

The Birhor story is almost the opposite of this. Rama, Lakshman and Sita go to the forest and make leaf-huts under a large tamarind tree 'which protected their huts from rain water, for in those days the tamarind tree had large leaves. But Rama told Lakshman, "We have been exiled to the forest to bear hardship and privations, but these leaves shelter us from the rain. Shoot

[1] Bompas, 413f.

[2] Roy, *J. B. O. R. S.*, ii, 202.

at the leaves with your bow and arrow ". Lakshman obeyed and the leaves of the tamarind tree were split asunder into innumerable tiny bits and admitted water into their huts. And since then the leaves of the tamarind tree have remained so small '.[1]

There are two trees, unrepresented in the text, about which legends are current in other parts of India. The kadam tree (*Anthocephalus cadamba*) is well-known for its association with Krishna, and its flowers are offered in honour of the god who delighted in swinging from its branches with the milkmaids of Brindaban.[2] The asoka tree (*Saraca indica*, Linn.) is also famous. The beauty of its bright orange flowers slowly turning red is celebrated in the classical literature and it was regarded as one of the five love-arrows of Kama, the God of Love. Rawan put Sita in the Asokavana pleasure-garden, but all its beauty did was to turn her thoughts to Rama.[3] The bark of this tree, which is said ' to keep away sorrow ', is sometimes used for menorrhagia and as an astringent. It is the symbol of love, a charm to preserve chastity and is used in temple worship.[4]

It is remarkable that the aboriginal story-teller, who loves flowers, should declare that flowers were not created for their beauty or scent or to adorn a lover : they came into being so that men should have something to offer to the gods. A Hindu legend describes how Vishnu was fascinated with the beauty of Vrinda, the wife of Jalandhara, to redeem him from whose enthralment, the gods applied to Lakshmi, Gauri and Swadha. Each gave them seed to sow where Vishnu was enchanted. The seeds given by the deities sprang up as the *dhatri* (*Emblica myrobalan*), the jasmine and the basil, and appearing in female form they attracted the admiration of the deity and saved him from the wiles of Vrinda.[5]

The Saora of Orissa believe that fowls and goats were not created to be a valuable form of food, but were made to be offered to the gods in sacrifice. Dancing too originated, not as recreation, but as a ceremonial rite connected with marriage.

The origin of sabai grass,[6] a grass which is economically of some importance in Bihar, is described in Ho and Birhor stories.

[1] Roy, *The Birhors*, 410.
[2] S. C. Mitra, ' Studies in Plant Myths ', *Q. J. M. S.*, xxvii, 412ff.
[3] Venkatesan, 133.
[4] S. C. Mitra, ' On a Few Myths and Legends about the Asoka Tree ', *Q. J. M. S.*, xxviii, 40ff.
[5] Crooke, ii, 110.

It is connected with the relations between a sister and her brothers. The brothers murder their sister but in the end she comes to life and forgives them. But they are so ashamed that they beg the earth to swallow them up, which it does, engulfing them. Their sister vainly tries to save them by catching the tufts of their hair. The tufts remain above the ground and are turned into sabai grass.[1] A Gadaba story (and there are similar Bondo stories), it is interesting to note, which accounts for the origin of grass, is also linked with the brother-sister motif, though here it is apparently the fear of incest and not an act of murder which causes the tragedy, and it is the girl and not her brother who goes into the earth and whose hair turned to grass.

Creepers

I

DHULIA

Karondi, Mandla District

The wife of Mirchamal Dano, Buchki Rakasin, was a strange woman. She never bore a child; she did not even have a monthly period. The Dano got her a lot of medicine and called many medicine-men, but it was no use. One day the Dano went to visit his father-in-law and on his way home picked up a dead crab. He gave it to his wife and said, 'Your father has sent you this for supper.' Buchki roasted and ate it, and that very night she began to menstruate. In a week she washed her head, that night lay with her husband, and conceived. In due time a child was born. He was Bakrenda Dano. Mirchamal Dano took the placenta and cord to Tehardongri jungle and there made a peacock trap with it. Next day there were three peacocks caught in the trap. But when the Dano went to see what had happened the following morning, he found that the trap had turned into a camel's-foot creeper; the cord was the stem and the placenta had turned into great broad leaves.

[1] For a further account, see *Folk-Tales of Mahakoshal*, 367ff. and an article by W. G. Archer, 'Sabai Cultivation in the Rajmahal Hills', *Man in India*, xxvi, 12ff.

Flowers

2

BAIGA

Boira, Mandla District

There was a very tall hill. The trees grew straight upwards and if you tried to look to the top your turban would fall off down your back. The trees were so thick that no one could pass through them. A great river flowed from the place and the water was always up to the waist throughout the year. None could cross it on foot. One day the Raja's servant went at dawn to relieve himself on the bank. When he had finished he went to wash in the river. There was a flower floating down the stream and the servant caught it in his hand and found it had a beautiful smell. He went back to the palace and gave it to the Raja and the scent filled the room.

The Raja asked him where he had found it and his servant told him. After that the Raja sent men daily to find the flower, but without success. Then he heard that the flower could only be found at midnight.

The Raja himself had a boat made, he put food in it and took three men with him. They went up the stream for eight days and nine nights until they came to a temple in a beautiful and lonely place where many ascetics were living. Some sat in the midst of fires, some raised their hands above their heads, some stood on one leg, some sat on spikes. Two of them were hanging from trees by their legs and the blood was slowly dripping from their heads. From the blood of the first sprang up a thorny tree, from the blood of the second came sweet-smelling roses. The other ascetics used to offer the flowers to the gods. The Raja stole the rose-tree, pulling it up with its roots while the ascetics were worshipping in the temple. He planted it in his own garden and since that time the world has been full of roses.

3

DHANWAR

Rawa, Uprora Zamindari

An Ahir and his wife were out in the jungle grazing their cattle. It was two days before Diwali and the leader of the cows talked to the rest of the herd, ' In two days' time there will be the great festival of the year. How are we to decorate ourselves for it ? In my belly live Gondarani and Tiraiyarani, the flowers. But who will make them into garlands ? ' The Ahir heard what it was saying and begged the leader of the cows to give him the flowers promising that he would make them into garlands. So the cow vomited every kind of flower. They fell to the ground and at once took root and sprang up. The Ahir made the flowers into garlands and put them on the cows.

The cow-Rani was pleased and blessed the Ahir saying, ' From today you will always care for us and the world will be full of flowers.'

4

DHOBA

Silpuri, Mandla District

Men were always working. They could not shut their eyes ; they did not know how to sleep. Even after there was a sun and moon and it was sometimes dark, they went on working. Nanga Baiga considered how to give them rest. He found aconite flowers and sprinkled poison on them. The wind blew and carried the poison into men's eyes and they began to sleep. But there was not enough poison in the aconite flowers and so the Baiga made sleep come from a different flower every month.

In Jeth sleep comes from the poison of the unseen flower of the wild fig ; in Asadh it comes from the sarai flowers ; in Sawan from the kirsair flowers ; in Kuar from the flowers of sesamum ; in Kartik from the saja flowers ; in Aghan from the dhawar flowers ; in Pus from the tinsa flowers ; in Magh from the sargi flowers ; in Phag from the dehawan flowers ; in Chait from the mango flowers ; in Baisakh from the jamun flowers.

5

GOND

Koelari, Rewa State

In Hirdenagar Darputi Mata lost her temper and devoured many of the inhabitants. The people went to find a Gunia who could save them. There was a famous Dewar named Juna living with his wife in Duganigarh and the people went to find him. Juna Dewar said to his wife, 'I am going to hide, tell them that you don't know where I am.' But when the people saw that the Dewar was not there they wept loudly and Juna sprang laughing out of his hiding-place and asked them, 'What is the matter?' When they told him, he consulted his measuring-sticks and Darputi Mata said through him, 'Give me a garland of flowers and I will give no more trouble.'

But there were no flowers in the world and the people did not know what to do. So Juna Dewar went down to the Under World and there on the head of Ses Nang was a marigold and below it were all the other flowers. When it saw Juna Dewar the cobra killed him. But his Singhi Tumi brought life-water and threw it on his body and he recovered. The old cobra laughed at him and Juna Dewar told his story. The cobra took the flowers and seeds from its head and gave them to him. As Juna Dewar went back to his village he dropped the seeds all along the way behind him and when he looked back he could see the flowers blossoming for many miles. The people then took the flowers and made them into a garland for the goddess and after that Darputi Mata gave no more trouble.

6

RAJNENGI PARDHAN

Kanchanpur, Mandla District

Bandasur Deo[1] was doing penance. Bhagavan was pleased with him and came to him and blessed him. He threw flowers over him. Bandasur picked up the flowers and preserved them. He dried them and got the seeds and planted them. From these flowers came the marigold.

[1] Bandasur Deo was a Raksa, so called because 'he was circumcised like a Mussalman'. He figures sometimes in the erotic dreams of women.

Grass

7

BAIGA

Sajatola, Kawardha State

When Mother Earth put the garland of victory round the neck of Nanga Baiga all the gods who were present threw cowdung and dirt at it to make it dirty. Then Nanga Baiga took Mother Earth with him to his house. When they had gone half-way home, Mother Earth said, 'It is true that I put the garland round your neck, but you have not taken me round the pole.' By the road-side was a sal tree.[1] Nanga Baiga caught hold of his bride's plait and she caught hold of his scalp-lock and gripping each other like this they went round and round the tree. Seven times they went faster and faster and when they stopped, each fell violently in a different direction. So violently did they fall that Mother Earth's plait came out of her head and Nanga Baiga's hair was torn out. Each was in pain and annoyed with the other. Mother Earth threw away her husband's hair and Nanga Baiga threw away his wife's hair. Nanga Baiga's hair turned into spear-grass[2] and Mother Earth's hair turned into thatching-grass. The Baiga puts spear-grass in the thatch of his roof and for this reason does not allow women to climb on the roof, for this grass is the hair of Nanga Baiga.

The Banyan[3]

8

PARDHAN

Khairtola, Seoni Tahsil, Chhindwara District

In Mirgulagarh lived Guru Jalranda. He had five sons and they were all married. But the youngest had not brought his wife to his house. After a time he went for his bride. At the time of greeting

[1] *Shorea robusta*, Gaertn. The branches of this tree are used for marriage booths by some tribes in Bengal, and it is interesting to find the tree associated with marriage here, for this is not usual in Middle India.

[2] *Andropagon contortus*.

[3] *Ficus bengalensis*, Linn. This great and famous tree is honoured throughout India. See Crooke, ii, 98f. and S. C. Mitra, 'On the Cult of the Banyan and the Pipal Trees', *Q. J. M. S.*, xxx, 446ff.

between the two fathers-in-law, the bone of a pig ran into the Guru's foot. The wound swelled up and became full of pus ; after a time the Guru died in pain.

The five sons carried their father's body to a place where there were many parsa trees[1] and buried it there. Every day in the evening they went to light a fire above the grave to frighten away wild animals. Inside the grave the pig's bone slowly went through the body from the foot up to the head and then came out of the grave in the form of a banyan tree. When the boys saw the tree they no longer lit a fire. The eldest son had a dream and one said to him, 'This is a banyan tree. It has grown from your father's bone and brains. Therefore serve it well.'

That is why the roots of the banyan tree hang down like a Guru's long and matted hair.

THE GUAVA

9

DHULIA

Medhakhar, Mandla District

In Baligarh Sukali Panka lived with his wife ; they were fond of each other but they had no children. When she was old, the wife fell ill and after six months, in spite of all the efforts of the medicine-men, she died. Sukali carried her body to Garlaiyya-Kachhar and buried her there. Three months afterwards from her two breasts sprang two trees ; from the left breast grew a guava, from the right a plum (jamun). His wife came to Sukali in a dream and said, 'Go to my grave and you will find two fruit trees.' He went to the place and when he saw them he dug up the trees and planted them in his garden.

[1] *Butea frondosa*, Roxb. The Flame of the Forest, sacred among Hindus, for its large trifoliate leaves symbolize the trident or the Trinity of Brahma, Vishnu and Siva. The wood is also used to produce the sacred fire.

The Mango

10

GOND

Koelari, Rewa State

When the world was first made Mahadeo created out of the dirt of his body a carpenter whose name was Chiula. He pulled out three of his hairs and threw them on the ground and they turned into three trees, the kassi,[1] the teak and the mango. The carpenter made a plough from the teakwood and gave it to Mahadeo saying, 'There are only three trees here and I will soon finish the wood. Then what will there be left for me to do?'

Mahadeo took some ashes and charmed them and sent the carpenter to throw them over the trees. When he did so they blossomed and gave fruit and seed and so all other trees came into being.

11

OJHA

Kakarwani, Chhindwara District

Many Baiga lived in Pauri village. Asru Dewar's son was Gathu. He was very learned in magic, so learned that you could see the gods living in his house. He was married to the daughter of Sarmandal, the girl Lendwari, in Bijagarh. One day in Bhadon at the time of the First Fruits Festival Gathu went to his father-in-law's house in Bijagarh to fetch his wife. On the way he passed through the Burbusidongri forest in the midst of which was the shrine of Nakti Pat. Any man who came to this place was filled with lust and sought for any one he could find, even an old man or woman. Gathu did not escape. Filled with passion he sat on a rock exclaiming, 'If only my wife was here how nice it would be!' His seed fell to the ground and he said, 'I must not waste it, but I must make something precious with it.'

[1] *Bridelia retusa*, Spreng. A common deciduous tree with a durable wood used for carts, the pillars of houses and agricultural implements.

Now Gathu was so great a magician that he could wither a green tree and he could make a dry tree green. With his seed he created the first mango tree and said, 'Go, be a mango and all men will delight in your fruit.' Then he said to the tree again, 'O my son, live here. I am going to fetch your mother. Next year I will perform your marriage.'

Gathu brought his wife home and next year they went to Nakti Pat and married their son, the mango tree, to a tamarind.

THE PIPAL FIG [1]

12

BAIGA

Dhanwahi, Kawardha State

In Bhengarh lived a Bhoi called Gulla; he was rich with a great store of grain of every kind. He had nine sheds of goats, ten sheds of cows, eleven sheds of buffaloes and three sheds of horses. You could not see the house for the grain-bins that surrounded it on every side. But with all this Gulla was very mean; he would eat ghee with his head covered with a patchwork quilt; he never gave food to the starving or alms to beggars; he never asked anyone to sit in his house; he never lent money to anyone; yet all his bins were full of grain.

Gulla ate only rice; he did not eat wheat or kodon[2]; he would not even touch kodon. The kodon in his bins, left alone for such a long time and growing more powerful all the time, full of gods and ghosts, said in her heart, 'This man never even touches me; he has grown very proud; in his pride he recognizes neither great nor small; he does not eat himself and he does not give to others.' So thinking kodon felt very sad and her breast broke for sorrow.

Then from the gall-bladder of kodon, the pipal tree was born. This is why the seed of the pipal looks like kodon and because it was

[1] *Ficus religiosa*, Linn. One of the most sacred trees, honoured even by the aboriginals. Its slender petiole causes its leaves to tremble readily in a breeze. For a curious tale of a pipal tree which turned into a cock to save a Raja's daughter, see O'Malley, 94. Such transformation tales are not uncommon; among many others, there is an Angami Naga story, current also among the Lhota and Sema Naga, of a girl turned into an orange tree which bore a single fruit, and the Thado Kuki legend of Ashijaul who was transformed into a fruit.—See Hutton, *The Angami Nagas*, 286ff. and Shah, 106f.

[2] The small millet, *paspalum scrobiculatum*.

born from grain people consider the tree holy and worship it. Kodon turned into a tree so that in its different form at least someone might eat it.

After this Gulla Bhoi became very poor and since Kodon Dai was angry with him he soon found he had no friends. After his death his money turned into an evil spirit which tormented his children and grandchildren.

13

PANKA

Jangwai, Matin Zamindari

In Madhuban Koelikachhar there was a pipal fig tree, and on it dwelt a green parrot; it used to live on the figs growing on the tree. One day it went to a village where there was a Panka. This Panka had in front of his house a clean and tidy courtyard and there was a parsa tree. The parrot settled there and daily let its droppings fall down into a hollow at the bottom of the tree. Some of the fig seeds that it had not digested fell there too and in time these came alive and sprouted. The Panka said, ' What tree is this ? ' He took a bit of wood, dug out the seedlings and planted them in his field, fencing them round with bamboo stakes to keep away the goats. When the trees had grown large that Panka died. In the wind the leaves of the fig tree sounded *pat-pat-pat-pat*, and the villagers were afraid and said, ' This is a bad tree. For just as a Panka goes round the village talking *pat-pat-pat-pat*, so do the leaves of this tree sound. We should not keep such trees in our village. Let us cut them down and throw them away and so we will stop their noise.' So they cut down the fig trees and threw them away. But when new shoots sprung again from the roots the people said, ' What can we do ? We had better let the trees be.' But they began to use the wood for fuel. They do not hold the tree sacred; it is a tree born from another's belly.

THE SAJA[1]

14

GOND

Kotmarra, Matin Zamindari

A blind man and a hunchback lived together. The hunchback planted a saja tree and the blind man planted a mahua.[2] When the saja tree grew up, it was crooked as a hunchback; when the mahua grew up, its buds did not open and the corollae did not fall from the fruit.

One day the blind man and the hunchback went together to see the hunchback's son and daughter-in-law. As the hunchback went along pulling the blind man by a stick behind him, he thought, 'I will die if I have to go on doing this much longer.' They rested in the middle of the day, and the hunchback went to get wood for a fire. He found a dead snake and thought he would cook it and so poison the blind man. He brought it back and said, 'I have got some fish.' He cooked the snake, but the blind man picked up a bit of the flesh and sniffed at it. The smell went into his nostrils and there was medicine in it; his eyes were opened. When he saw that the hunchback had cooked snake-meat he was very angry. He beat the hunchback so hard that the crooked body was made straight. Then they went home.

When they got home they saw that the saja tree was now growing straight and that the buds of the mahua had opened and that the flowers were falling.

The saja gave flowers and fruit. The fruit was ripe and filled with sweet juice. The hunchback picked it and ate. He found it sweet, so he sucked out all the juice and squeezed it with his fingers. So today you can still see the marks of five fingers on the fruit of the saja and it has no juice and no one ever eats it.

[1] *Terminalia tomentosa*, W. & A. The tree is especially sacred to the Gond, for it is the traditional home of Bara Deo.

[2] *Bassia latifolia*, Roxb., which 'so admirably combines beauty with utility, is one of the main sources whence the jungle tribes derive their food and intoxicants.'—Crooke, ii, 102.

THE SALAI [1]

15

GOND

Koelari, Rewa State

In Sawatpur lived a Gond. One day the villagers went to cut bamboo and when the others climbed the hill to get it the Gond stayed below with his brother-in-law (*sāla*). As they were cutting bamboo the brother-in-law's axe slipped and cut his thigh. When the other saw the blood, he felt very sorry. He thought, 'My brother is unmarried and has never been to a girl; that is why the blood is flowing.' In his pouch he had some husked rohilla gram. He mixed a little of this with the blood and said, 'If my *sāla* has been truly virtuous, let there grow from this blood a salai tree. When he is married I will cut the branches and make his marriage-booth with them.'

The brother-in-law was a virtuous youth and a tree sprung up from his blood. The salai tree has fruit that looks like gram and the Gond use its branches in their marriage-booths.

THE TAMARIND [2]

16

BAIGA

Baona, Mandla District

Mata Kankalin had a daughter Bidarsinh. She grew up and her mother was worried about her marriage. Parasu's son was Moharsai. Kankalin Mata sent invitations to the whole world to come for her daughter. They all came, kings, princes, Baiga, Dewar, Gond. When

[1] *Boswellia serrata*, Roxb. A fairly large deciduous tree, with a white resinous wood: the resin is used for incense by the aboriginals.

[2] *Tamarindus indica*, Linn. A large evergreen tree; the leaves to which such frequent reference is made in the text are pinnate, each with ten to twenty pairs of small half-inch leaflets attached. The Gond generally regard it as rather unlucky, saying that the man who plants a tamarind will ruin his own family, but the Uraon revere the tree and bury its dead under its shade.—Cp. Dalton, 189. It is perhaps in line with the Gond tradition that the Pulaya of southern India use tamarind branches to beat a woman taken in adultery.—Iyer, i, 122.

they had assembled, Mata Kankalin proclaimed the conditions for winning her daughter. 'He who would marry my daughter must first, standing on an iron plate filled with boiling ghee upon a fire, shoot down with a single arrow the mango tree that grows in the sky. Then by a single glance he must tell the number of grains of rice in a great cooking-pot. Thirdly he must guess the number of leaves on a tamarind tree.'

Moharsai was supported by Mata Hinglajin. By her aid he was able to stand in the boiling ghee and bring down with a single arrow the mango tree in the sky. When he tried to count the number of grains of rice in the cooking-pot, Mata Kankalin clapped her hands and they increased tenfold. But Mata Hinglajin was stronger and Moharsai told the number correctly. When he turned to the tamarind tree, which in those days had large leaves, Mata Kankalin again clapped her hands and every leaf divided into a dozen pieces. But Mata Hinglajin was still stronger and by her aid Moharsai was able to guess the number. He fulfilled the tests and took Bidarsinh as his bride.

17

DHANWAR

Rawa, Uprora Zamindari

In the old days tamarind leaves were big as plantain leaves. When Rama, Lakshman and Sita were living in exile in the jungle they used to sleep out under the open sky in the dry season. But in the rains they had to find shelter and they went to live under the great leaves of the tamarind tree.

But half-way through Sawan (July-August) rain fell night and day and a great wind blew the leaves about so that the water poured in and put out the fire on which Sita was cooking. Rama and Lakshman were very angry and wrote a letter to Indra saying, 'Put Megh Raja and Megh Rani back into the hole whence they were born.' Lakshman tied the letter to an arrow and fired it into the sky. As it went, it tore the leaves of the tamarind to shreds and ever since the leaves of this tree have been small.

8

GOND

Barratola, Mandla District

Formerly the leaves of the tamarind tree were large and its fruit was sweet. There was a Baiga and his wife. One day the Baiga got ready to go to the Marhai bazaar and he said to his wife, ' Quickly stitch some leaf-cups and put my food in them and I will eat it on the way as I go along.' The Baigin stitched cups of tamarind leaves and put the food in them, but the leaves broke. When the Baiga saw this he was very annoyed and said, ' The Marhai bazaar comes only once a year and I shall miss it. May fire burn your leaves and leaf-cups.' The Baiga beat his wife and she wept, crying, ' May fire burn the Marhai '.

That Baiga woman was a witch. Directly her husband left for the bazaar she tore up the tamarind leaves in a temper and said, ' From now onwards, you will always be small.' She spat on the tamarind fruit and since that day it has been sour.

Trees and Flowers

19

DHULIA

Karondi, Mandla District

Mangola Marar and his wife Suhatiya had a white cow which, although it had never calved, gave them abundant milk. The Marar used to milk it every day and take the milk to sell to Raja Jalosi. One day as the cow was grazing it ate a poisonous insect and its belly swelled up. When it came home to be milked it wept and said to Mangola, ' Tomorrow I must die. Cut up my bones and flesh and scatter them round the house. Kill a monkey, and make the skin into a drum. Go round the house seven times drumming.' And next day the cow did die and Mangola did as it had bade him. As he completed the seventh circuit of the house, there sprang up from the cow's flesh and bones every kind of flower, tree, shrub and creeper. From the belly came the camel's-foot creeper, from the two eyes an aonra tree, from the front feet a sal tree and from the hind legs a banyan.

20

PARDHAN

Batama, Seoni Tahsil, Chhindwara District

In Gulbansagarh lived Mohasingh Raja and his two wives. The younger wife had one son and one daughter. This was the kingdom of the Baiga and one day they went to the Raja and asked him to give them jungle where they could cut *bewar*. The Raja said, 'Go to such and such corner of the jungle and cut.' They made their clearing and sowed sugarcane, cucumbers, beans, roots, maize and wild rice. When the crop was ready there came Koha Dano and devoured the crop. The Baiga tried to kill him but failed and they went to the Raja for help. The Raja, riding on the mare Champi, took his soldiers armed with guns. He made his men surround the clearing and said, 'I will kill this Dano wherever he tries to escape.' But the Dano put his feet on the Raja's shoulders, jumped over his head and escaped. The men shouted, 'The Raja is killed,' but he was angry and said, 'No, what you should say is, "The Raja has killed".' Then he said, 'You all go home, but I am going to follow this Dano and I will not return until I have killed him.'

The Dano hid under a stone. The Raja followed his footsteps and tried to pull him out from under the stone but without success. He put his sword and gun at the entrance to the cave, tied Champi his mare to a tree and lay down to sleep. Presently the Dano came out and asked the sword, 'Who are you and what are you doing?' 'I am a sword and when the Raja wakes up, he will take me in his hand and cut you into pieces.' Then the Dano said to the spear, 'Who are you and what do you want?' The spear replied, 'I am a spear and when the Raja wakes up he will take me in his hand and cut you into pieces.' When he heard this the Dano went to the Raja and killed him. He took out both his eyes, dressed himself in the Raja's clothes, picked up the sword and spear and rode back on the mare to the city. The people thought it was their own Raja who had come victorious and welcomed him home.

That night the Dano slept with the Raja's wife but the children of the younger wife lived in the upper palace and the Dano did not see them. After a time he grew hungry for human flesh and began to eat his own subjects and many left the kingdom in fear.

The Raja's son thought that he must go and find out from Champi the mare what had really happened, for he could not believe that the Dano was really his father. When the boy came to the stable the mare wept and told him what had really happened. She said, 'The Dano will kill everybody. Come with your sister, bringing food to last twelve years and I and the elephant will take you away to safety.' They brought food and clothes and rode on the mare and the elephant away to Nagar Pahar.

After a time Champi said, 'I am going to die. Bury my head separately and from it there will come a palace. Bury my eyes and from them will grow aonra[1] and jamun[2] trees. Put my blood in a pot and it will turn into a lake. Tie my entrails round the pot and there will be a garden around the lake. My liver will become a hibiscus flower which you can offer to the gods. My kidneys will turn into sunflowers.' The boy did what the mare told him and everything happened as she had said. Then the elephant prepared to die and told the boy to bury its head in one place and it turned into a temple and its testes in another and from them there grew a bel tree.

The brother and sister stayed on in the palace and the boy used to go hunting daily to search for food. One day he got nothing but he found a monkey which became his friend and used to bring animals for him to eat. After a time, the monkey went to Lohagarh and had a great axe made. He told the boy that he and his sister should come with him back to their kingdom. When they reached the city they found it deserted by every one, for the Dano had eaten all the people. The Dano had to graze his own cows and make his own curds and ghee. The monkey climbed on to the roof of the palace and shouted abuse at the Dano, who became very angry and so swelled with rage that his head almost touched the clouds. The monkey made itself very small and the Dano also made himself small in order to catch it. Then suddenly the monkey made itself big and picked up the axe and killed him.

Then the boy and the girl with the money cleaned the city and called the inhabitants back again and ruled over it in great content. They brought the seeds of the hibiscus and the sunflower in the jungle and planted them in the palace, and made a grove of jamun and aonra trees in memory of Champi the mare and the faithful elephant.

[1] *Emblica officinalis*, Gaertn. A tree sacred to the Hindus and credited with magical properties by the tribesmen.

[2] *Eugenia jambolana*, Lam. The black plum.

CHAPTER SEVEN

ARTHROPODS

IN this Chapter I group stories about all those animals which are classified by zoologists as arthropods, the crustaceans, insects, spiders and so on.

There is a considerable body of folklore about these creatures, but not many stories of origin have been recorded. I give a few of them here.

A Birhor tale describes how Parvati made a swarm of mosquitoes from the 'dirty excretion off her neck' and sent them to frighten Mahadeo home. He turned wood-shavings into *dulu* insects which eat mosquitoes.[1] An Uraon variant says it was Chando who neglected his wife and she made mosquitoes 'to worry him and drive him home. But Chando made some dragon-flies and they ate up the mosquitoes and he went on with his work'.[2] The Kol say that Sankara, who was the greatest of all ascetics, covered his body with ashes, and when the dirt of his body fell to the earth it became alive and turned into insects, snakes, scorpions and wasps.[3]

The Warli describe how, after the wife of the first farmer had given birth to a child:

On the fifth day the Sati deity was worshipped. She wrote something on the forehead of the babe that night. The rats and cats should not be beaten that night, since Sati comes, in any form. An image of Sati was drawn with vari corn. The midwife threw some rice grains in the hollow of the tree. The rice became honey-bees; hence the bee-hive has an appearance of bread. The tube of oil became the serpent; and the hair-comb thrown in air became a bird. Out of the dirty clothes thrown on the slope of the hill was born a lizard. The menstrual fluid was thrown on the teak tree; therefore the tender leaves of the tree are reddish. It was also thrown on the fruit of Karavandi; that is how its fruit is red.[4]

[1] Roy, *The Birhors*, 404.
[2] Bompas, 404.
[3] Griffiths, 206.
[4] Sawe, 176.

The Ant

I

RAJNENGI PARDHAN

Patangarh, Mandla District

In Aranban there lived the elephant Bankasur. It used to eat and destroy everything in the world.

Jithu Baiga cut his clearing, but the elephant came and ate his beans and cucumbers.

Jithu Baiga examined his measuring-sticks. 'How can I destroy this elephant?'

From his ear he removed a little dirt and wax and made it into an ant. He sent this ant to attack the elephant and the ant drove it away.

The elephant ran away to the Surguja jungle where there were many of its caste-fellows living. It said to the other elephants, 'Save me.' They said, 'You come from another kingdom. Take out everything that is in your belly and throw it away in front of us.'

The elephant Bankasur farted with a great trumpeting noise *barr-barr*. Out came grasshoppers, butterflies, lizards, rats, parrots and flew away to their own country. As Bankasur was doing this the ant arrived and bit the end of its trunk.

The elephant Bankasur died.

Since that day the elephant has always blown on the ground as it goes along, for fear that its trunk will be bitten by an ant.

The Bee

2

BAIGA

Mandla District

(From *The Baiga*, 482)

Once the bees, which were born from a bull's ears, went and sat on the food of a great Dewar. In that food was poison. The Dewar said, 'As there is poison in my food, so will there be poison in your teeth. And for troubling me, you will have to live, seven hundred thousand of you, in one house. And you will eat your own children.' So from that day, bees eat their own children, and those who are left survive.

3

GOND

Sunpuri, Mandla District

Hema Kalar lived in Garh Bengal. He had an affair with Naita Dhobnin and when Hema Kalarin discovered it she made herself very unpleasant to them both. After a time Naita Dhobnin found herself pregnant but her enemy struck the child in the womb by her magic and it was still-born. Naita Dhobnin put it in a new pot and buried it behind the house. At night she went to the place and by her magic turned the bones of the head into bees and sent them swarming to sting Hema Kalarin to death. At night they dug their way into the house and were about to kill the woman when she said, ' Don't sting me and I will give you a blessing. Go to the forest and you will have a golden palace of honey to live in. Go and live in a banyan tree in Madhuban.' The bees were pleased with her saying and flew away to the Madhuban and made there in a banyan tree their home of gold.

4

GOND

Barratola, Mandla District

Mahadeo made a garden of champa, jasmine, and keonra flowers in Korbasera's enclosure. When the flowers blossomed they began to talk to each other, ' What lovely flowers we are, yet no one comes to play with us or marry us and we have to live here ignored by men.' Then they said again, ' Let us go and put our grievance before the person who made us.' They asked the jasmine, who is the Raja of the flowers, to go to Mahadeo on their behalf.

The jasmine went to Mahadeo and served him for twelve years and when he was pleased and asked her what she desired, she told him the sad state of the flowers he had made. Mahadeo took a little dirt from his body and a little dirt from his testes and rubbed it into a ball between his hands. Then from the fire he took some ash and blew it over the ball of dirt. He threw it into the air and it became a bee.

The bee flew away to the garden of flowers and lived with them as their husband. Soon the flowers gave birth to children and these are fruits.

THE BUTTERFLY

5

DHULIA

Medhakhar, Mandla District

One day Mano Dhimar went to fish in the Biloran River and got a fine catch. He cut the fish up on the bank and threw the scales away by the waterside. A few days later Komod Guru went to bathe there and, removing his clothes, put them down on a stone. The desire for easement came upon him and he went down stream and relieved himself. On the way he passed the place where the Dhimar had thrown away the fish-scales. Although when he relieved himself he passed no urine, as he came back he felt his bladder full and pissed all over the scales lying by the waterside. Immediately life came into them and they flew into the air. This is why butterflies haunt the place where people urinate.

6

GOND

Tikaitola, Rewa State

Bhukhansur Deota was living in Garh Kailas. He thought in his mind, 'How can I be famous?' He went to Koelagarh and married Koelasur Mai. Even while they were both yellow with haldi they slept together and on that very day Koelasur Mai conceived. In due time—it was in the passing of the month of Jeth into Asarh—Phiphlisur Mai the Butterfly was born. She sucked two-and-a-half times at her mother's breasts and said, 'Let me go into the world, I do not want to stay here at your breasts.' So saying, the butterfly flew away.

Caterpillars and Grasshoppers

7

GOND

Manjhwani, Kenda Zamindari

There was a Kumbharin, a potter's wife. One day she had a dream 'You are to create three kinds of living creatures—caterpillars, grasshoppers, and the green Kumbharin caterpillars.[1] Make three pots of three different kinds of earth and in each put some of your menstrual blood and place them on the hearth. Then from each, one of the three kinds of life will come.' The Kumbharin awoke and did as she was told, and that was how the caterpillar, the grasshopper and the Kumbharin caterpillar came into being.

The Cockroach

8

DHANWAR

Barbhata, Uprora Zamindari

In the Kajli-Bindraban Binjhpahar lived the Surahi cows. There was no one to look after them. They would go to graze and then gather under their trees to rest. Giving dung daily daily, there grew a great pile. At the bottom were born the scorpion and cockroach. Black scorpion, white scorpion, crab scorpion, queen scorpion—these were born. And of the cockroach these castes—Asaraha, Kartikaha, Jeth-Masiha—were born in the months from which they were named. When the rain fell heavily in Asarh the dung liquified and flowed away under stones and trees. The scorpions and cockroaches went with it, and that is why they now live in those places.

[1] The Kumbharin or Potter Woman's caterpillar is a small green larva commonly caught by hornets and immured by them in little mud nests that look not unlike earthen pots. The caterpillar gets its name because it is supposed to be shut up in a pot.

9

GOND

Upri, Rewa State

Patranji Dewar used to worship Jhangi Devi. One day he asked her for a gift. 'We Baiga are only stupid jungle-dwellers. We never know when it is going to rain. Give us someone who will warn us of the coming of the rain. The Hindus have the Brahmins who look at their books and tell them. Give us Brahmins to help us.'

Jhangi Devi was in her menstrual period. As the blood ran down her leg she wiped it off with a little bit of reed and threw it away saying, 'In Jeth when these begin to cry you will know that the rain is coming and that it is time to sow your seed.' The reed turned into a cockroach and ever since has warned the Baiga that the rain is coming.

10

KOL

Jubbulpore District

In Jhinjhigarh lived a great Dewar. He made a clearing in the forest and sowed it with the kutki that has long ears. One day an old woman went through the clearing and broke some of the plants with her feet. When the Dewar saw it he abused her and she was annoyed. 'For so little he abused me so much.'

Now that old woman was a witch. She stole some of the ears of kutki and turned them into cockroaches. She made hundreds and hundreds of cockroaches and sent them to the field where they devoured every grain of kutki. Since that time cockroaches have spread throughout the world.

The Crab

11

DEWAR

Tendubhata, Raipur District

The crab is the grandson of Bhagavan. For twelve ages it did penance and at last Bhagavan gave it a blessing: 'What I write you can read, but no others. You are the Raja of the waters.' In the old days, therefore, when there was nothing in the world but water the crab lived in the ocean. It killed everything that fell into the water. Bhagavan thought, 'If I give my blessing to the crab, then when I am in trouble it will help me.' And when Bhagavan wanted to make the earth he could get no one to help him but the crab. When at last the earth was ready Bhimsen was sent to level it, but the crab thought he was stealing it and ran to fight him. Across the path the spider had made its web. The crab was very angry. 'Are you trying to trap me?' it shouted. And it put its foot on the spider. The spider cursed the crab. 'You have trodden on me. Henceforth you will live under the earth. Unless you hide in your hole, you will die.'

The crab is the master of the earth and sees that no one steals it. When the earth was ready, Bhagavan gave Bhimsen the kingdom of water and the crab the kingdom of dry land. When no rain falls, the crab weeps and makes a humming noise. Bhimsen's ears stand like those of a frightened horse at the sound and rain begins to fall.

12

DHANWAR

Rawa, Uprora Zamindari

There was a great spring and all around the earth was moist. There were black rocks. Andha Guru, the Blind Guru, drove a nail into the ground and cursed the place that if anyone went there he would melt like salt. Kakramal Kuar the crab came from the Lower World, breaking its way up through the rocks. It broke them with its claws and pulled up the Blind Guru's nail. After that men could go there safely. For this reason a crab's children are born from above, breaking out through the chest.

13

GOND

Taurbahara, Bindra-Nawagarh Zamindari

Formerly the crab had a trunk like an elephant. But when Mahadeo cut off the head of Ganesh and Parvati was very angry, he cut off the crab's trunk and put it on Ganesh instead. But this killed the crab. Parvati got angry again. 'You are not content with ruining Ganesh: you must destroy the poor crab as well.' So Mahadeo said, 'Crab, O brother crab, get up and live even without a head.' Up got the crab and in compensation Mahadeo made its back very strong. You can still see the marks of Mahadeo's sword on the place where its head should be.

14

GOND

Barratola, Mandla District

In former times the crab had no claws. One day a Baigin went to the river to fish. Under a large stone she found a crab and caught it. As she was about to kill it the crab folded its hands and said, 'Mother, don't kill me; keep me in your house and I will make all arrangements for you.'

The woman took the crab home. A few days afterwards the Raja sent his servants to call the villagers to come to his fields to cut the crop. When they came to the Baigin's house, she had neither husband nor son to send to the fields. But the crab said, 'Don't be afraid, mother, I will go instead.' She went to the Agaria's smithy and got him to make two small knives of iron. She fixed the knives in front of the crab's body and by her magic ensured that it would be able to cut anything it desired.

The crab went to the Raja's fields and cut a whole field by itself and piled up the grain. It returned to the Baigin's house and she was pleased and sent it back to live in the river.

Lice

15

DHULIA

Karonḍi, Mandla District

An old man and his old woman lived in Suharingarh. The old man was blind of one eye, the old woman deaf in both ears. They had seven daughters, Hiro, Jiro, Sekhi, Maniya, Daniya, Runiya, and Budmati. They were unmarried, but mature. In those days lice big as frogs lived in their hair and they spent most of their time catching and killing them. They were so busy at this that in the evenings there was only one grain of rice for each person in the house. The old parents did all the work outside the house; they never let the girls go out. One day an old Malin laughed at the parents. 'While you are out,' she said, 'these girls call boys to the house and have a grand time with them.' The parents were very disturbed at this and next day the old mother hid in a grain-bin to see how the daughters spent their time while she was away. She saw them sit down and proceed to spend the whole day catching the frog-lice and killing them. 'This will never do,' thought the old woman. 'It doesn't matter here, but when they go to their husbands' houses they won't be able to waste their time like this.' So she got seven wooden measures and filled them with sesamum seed. She placed one of these on the head of each girl and husked the sesamum then and there. As a result the frog-lice became very small and the girls were no longer troubled. Thereafter there was plenty to eat in the house.

16

JUANG

Kantara, Pal Lahara State

There never used to be lice in people's hair. Rusi and Rusiain had a daughter. Rusiain was searching her daughter's head for leeches which in those days hid in the hair. She tried to pull them out, but they stuck fast and the girl cried.

Just then Ishwaro and Parvati came by and Parvati heard the girl crying. 'Some creature is in distress,' she said. Ishwaro said, 'Never mind; let them be.' But Parvati went to Rusiain and when she looked at the girl's hair she found a very long leech stuck there. Parvati thought in her mind, 'If everyone gets leeches like this in their hair, they will die.' She said to Ishwaro, 'Get it out somehow or other.'

Ishwaro said, 'Take her to the river and dip her head in the water and the leech will come out.' Rusiain took the girl to the river, dipped her head in the water, and the leech went into the water and has lived there ever since.

Instead of the leech, Ishwaro put two oil-seeds in the girl's hair and these presently turned into lice. So leeches live in water and lice in hair.

Maggots

17

GOND

Dhameri, Rewa State

A sadhu lived for twelve years in Binjpahar. One day a Baiga and his wife came to the place to cut bewar. When they had finished they went to the sadhu and sat with him. The Baiga lit his pipe and smoked. But when the sadhu saw the Baigin he was enchanted by her and wondered how to get her. Every night she danced in his eyes.

One day when the Baiga was working in his bewar the sadhu went down the path along which the Baigin would have to come bringing her husband's mid-day food. When she arrived he caught her and enjoyed her. Then the Baigin went on to her husband. He was angry because she was so late and he suspected that she had betrayed him with some other man.

The Baiga went to Lohagarh and got a great iron dish that four-and-twenty men could hardly carry. He fetched oil from the Teli and made a great fire under the dish and heated the oil. Then he said to his wife, 'Swear on this boiling oil that you have not been to a man.' But she was afraid and confessed that the sadhu had her by force. As she spoke the earth quaked.

The Baiga said, 'We are the Raja and Rani of the earth and this sadhu has robbed us of our virtue and so the earth is quaking.' Filled with anger he cursed the sadhu and said, 'May maggots devour your body.'

That very day the sadhu fell ill and maggots swarmed on his body and devoured him. Before this there were no maggots in the world but since then they have spread everywhere and troubled men and cattle.

18

GOND

Upri, Rewa State

Kirjhisur Mai lived in the water of the Under World. There was every kind of worm and maggot in her belly. One day a cow went to drink the water and by accident put its foot on Kirjhisur Mai. Her belly broke open and the maggots came out and climbed on to the cow. Kirjhisur Mai in her pain cursed the cow saying, 'These maggots now will drink your blood and from your body they will spread throughout the world.'

THE MANTIS

19

AHIR

Chiriyamatta, Mandla District

The wife of Pandru Ahir used to graze the cattle of Sonhara village. One day when she was out in the forest one of the cows died and she sent for the Chamar to come and skin it. He was a fine youth and when he had finished the work of cutting up the carcass, he began to flirt with the Ahirin. Soon they became friends and began to meet regularly in the forest. This went on for three months, and then the woman ran away to the Chamar's house and began to live with him as his wife. But after a day or two the husband fetched her home and after giving a feast for her had her readmitted into caste.

Now above this woman's vulva was a long hair that had been growing since her babyhood. It divided in two at the end and was thick and strong. On the night after her feast, she cut off the hair and by her magic turned it into a mantis with long claws. She sent it to the Chamar's house and told it to hide in his bed. That night the Chamar lay with his wife and when it was over the mantis cut off his organ and the Ahirin was avenged.

The Mosquito

20

GOND

Banjar, Mandla District

Formerly in the month of Asarh, when rain fell, the earth talked with her living creatures, flies, crabs, frogs, insects; they talked '*Sai-sai-sai-sai.*'

Earth and Night are husband and wife; they went to one another and Night too said '*Sai-sai*', and his seed fell on the earth. From his seed was born the mosquito.

The mosquito said, 'What shall I eat?' Earth said, '*Sai-sai*, go and drink men's blood.'

Since then the mosquito has enjoyed the blood of men.

21

GOND

Tikaitola, Rewa State

Ghokhchand Raja and his wife had no child. On the bank of the Sayr River lived a sadhu. The Raja and his wife went to serve him and when the sadhu was pleased they asked for the blessing of a child. The sadhu gave the Raja a stick and said, 'Go to such and such a mango tree and throw the stick into the branches. Pick up the first mango that falls and give it to your wife, whereupon she will conceive.'

But when the Raja went to the mango tree he found it surrounded by witches. When they saw him they turned themselves into bees and swarmed about him to sting him. The Raja ran for his life and escaped to the sadhu's hut. The sadhu took ash from his hearth and blew upon it. The ash turned into thousands of mosquitoes and they attacked the witches. They sat in their eyes and bit their bodies. While the witches were engaged in driving away the mosquitoes the Raja went to the tree and got the mango which he gave to his wife and she conceived.

The Scorpion

22

GOND

Thewa, Mandla District

There was a fat and conceited Gond. One day he kicked an image of Mahadeo in a Hindu temple near his village. Mahadeo was angry at this. He made a scorpion and sent it to bite that Gond. He made a stone in the shape of a scorpion ; he touched it and it came alive. From this scorpion many others were born and spread through the world.

23

GOND

Pakhri, Mandla District

When Parvati was mature her father was worried how to find her a husband. She said, ' Father, there is no mate for me on earth. But above there is Mahadeo.' In those days Mahadeo lived in the deep forest. They sent a man for him. Parvati's father made great preparations, but Mahadeo hid all his marriage-party in a bundle of cloth and came with only Bhimsen to escort him. When Parvati's father saw this he was angry. ' I have prepared such a great feast, and this man comes with only one companion for the marriage.' Bhimsen said, ' I at least am hungry.' He sat down and ate the whole of that mighty feast. Then Mahadeo opened his bundle and there was a great marriage-party. Parvati's father fell at Mahadeo's feet, ' Forgive me, son-in-law.'

Then said Parvati, ' What ornaments has he brought for me ?' Mahadeo had gathered all the poisonous things in the world and made ornaments from them. He had toe-rings of little snakes, he had made armlets of snakes from the dirt off his thighs, he made a nose-stud of a hornet from the dirt of his chest, he took the dirt from his eyes and made scorpions to serve as ear-rings, he took the dirt from his penis and made a toad to serve as spangle in the middle of the bride's forehead. Thus adorning Parvati in things of poison, he took her home to the Madhuban.

24

LANJHIA SAORA

Maneba, Ganjam District

Manjur Saora had a daughter named Kunti whom he married to one Mardu. The boy took his bride home but did not sleep with her for a single night. The girl would go to lie beside him but he would jump up and run away to another house. The girl loved him but he would do nothing. She tried to get another boy to sleep with her but no one was willing. Not a single man would touch her, and at last old and a virgin she died. She went to Kittung and told him what had happened. He asked her, 'Tell me what you want and I'll give it to you.' She said, 'I do not want to go to earth again. But this I do want: that as I wept for men, so I may be the cause whereby men may weep for me.' Kittung said, 'Go and be a scorpion?' The girl came back to earth as a scorpion and now men weep for her as formerly she wept for them.

The Spider

25

GOND

Batama, Seoni Tahsil, Chhindwara District

In Kajliban there was a great forest called Daunagiri. That forest was full of monkeys. One day, a monkey, attempting to take its wife, let its seed fall to the ground and a lizard ate it and became pregnant. After nine months the lizard gave birth to a child which they called Makramal Kshattri. It had nine legs. When it had grown up it said to its mother, 'How can I live with you? Tell me some place where I can go to live.' The mother said, 'My son, go to live in the Under World; that is the proper place for you. There is no warrior that can conquer you. You will bring thread out of your belly and with that thread you will bind the world. With your thread you can make a palace for yourself and live there. When the time comes for the marriage of Mahadeo and Parvati, they will come to you for thread to tie round the marriage-booth. Give it to them and they will give you a blessing.'

Makramal Spider then went down to the Under World and made its home there. When the time came for Parvati's marriage, Mahadeo sent a Baiga to get some thread. The Baiga got thread from the spider but he was not able to climb up to the Middle World again. So the spider itself threw a thread into the sky and the Baiga climbed up it. After the Baiga had gone up the spider followed him and since that day it has lived in the Middle World.

Mahadeo gave it this blessing: 'The store of thread in your belly will never be exhausted.'

26

GOND

Patangarh, Mandla District

There never used to be any marriages. Buchkibai's son was Abujh Deota. One day Buchkibai said to her son, 'Work hard and well, and I'll get you a lovely girl to be with you.' The boy worked hard, he spun thread and wove a cloth and took it to the bazaar to sell. The people said, 'How much is it?' He said, 'One pice above and one pice below.' A man came and put one pice above and one pice below, and took the cloth away.

The boy took the two pice and bought a gourd. As he was taking it home he met a friend who said, 'What's that you've got?' The boy said, 'It is an elephant's egg.' But as he went along he tripped and fell, breaking the gourd.

The water of the gourd turned into spiders, its handle became a frog, and the seeds became maggots and the three creatures went away.

The boy went home to his mother and she said, 'What have you brought?' He said, 'I bought an elephant's egg in the bazaar but I broke it on the way and the spider and frog and maggots went away.' The loving mother said, 'Son, it was by your virtue that they were created. So do not mind.'

White Ants

27

DHULIA

Karondi, Mandla District

One day Mahadeo far away on Kailasgarh felt thirsty and bored. He called Dilarsai and his wife from Kachnarigarh and said to them, 'You are Kalar; make me five bottles of fully distilled liquor. When it is ready call me to your shop.' The Kalarin went to Bairangdongar and brought twelve sacks of mahua. She prepared seven hundred great earthen pots, filled them with mahua and began to distill it. As a result she got five bottles of the fully distilled, so strong that it burst into flame even when it saw a fire far off. Dilarsai went to tell Mahadeo that his drink was ready. But Mahadeo said, 'If I come to your house, where am I to sit? There is no room for me in your shop. Go, make me a house of earth without using water.'

Dilarsai did not know what to do, but his wife was a clever woman and a witch. At that time she was in her period. She called the nine hundred Singi Tumi and the sixteen hundred Chhittawar, and by her magic turned the mahua waste into white ants, and in no time they built a palace of earth without the use of water. The Kalarin blessed the ants saying, 'Go and live in the Under World, and make your home without water.'

CHAPTER EIGHT

REPTILES

Snakes

THE literature of ophiolatry is enormous and I cannot even indicate it here. There are some interesting new stories in the text, but one of them (No. 2) is a variant on a very old theme, of which Crooke gives the following account:

> Pipa, the Brahman, is a deity in Rajputana. He was in the habit of giving milk to a serpent whose retreat was on the banks of the Sampu, or Snake Lake. The serpent used in return to present him daily with two pieces of gold. Being obliged to go away on business, he gave instructions to his son to continue the offering; but the youth, deeming it a good opportunity of becoming master of the treasure, took a stick with him, and when the serpent came forth for its expected food, he struck it violently. But the snake managed to retreat into its hole. On his return, the young Brahman related his adventures to his mother. She was horrified at the account, and forthwith made arrangements for sending her son away out of danger. But in the morning when she went to call him she found to her horror that her son was dead, and a huge snake lay coiled up beside his body. Pipa on his return was inconsolable, but, stifling his thoughts of revenge, he propitiated the monster with copious libations of milk. The serpent was appeased, and revealed to Pipa the treasures which it guarded, commanding him to erect a monument which should transmit the knowledge of the event to future ages. Hence Pipa has become a sort of snake godling, and the town of Pipar and the Sampu Lake still by their names commemorate the legend.[1]

Snakes which can destroy human beings merely by looking at them are as old as the *Secretum Secretorum* and the Sanskrit name *drigvasa* or *dristivasa*, 'poisonous of aspect', seems to be ancient. There is a story that Alexander the Great came to a valley on the Indo-Persian frontier which was guarded by deadly serpents whose mere glance was fatal. He erected mirrors in which the snakes might stare themselves to death.

The Saora believe in, and go to some pains to appease, two serpent deities, Ajhorasum and Jayondenusum, who are specially troublesome to young children.

There is an account of a deadly *dristivasa* snake from Matin in the text. Forsyth was given a tale by the Thakur of Lapha about a 'loathly worm' that haunted the forests of the neighbouring

[1] Crooke, ii, 133.

Uprora. It was 'slimy and horrid like a great caterpillar, a cubit and a half in thickness, and dull grey in colour, with a scarlet head, to look upon which was death. Many had seen it, but none had lived to tell the tale.' Once the Thakur of Uprora himself was travelling, with an attendant behind him, when at the crossing of a stream the latter called out, 'What is that great slimy caterpillar-like monster with a scarlet head?' on which his master warned him not to look at it, and did not do so himself. He was too late, however, for the servant was dead in a few moments.[1]

The Maria of Bastar, also, 'speak with fear of a water-witch in the form of a great serpent, known as Tondetaras, haunting river rapids and waterfalls, the mere sight of whom is fatal.'[2]

1

AGARIA

Daldal, Mandla District

The deadly chaparra snake comes from Matin. It lives in water and has the colour of ground turmeric. It is one-and-a-half cubits long. Any man who sees this snake at once gets cholera and dies in a day or two. When a man dies of seeing the snake no one should go near to touch his body before they have offered a goat to the stream where the snake was living. Once near Kabir Chabutra four young men who were working on the road went to get water. They saw the snake in the stream and two of them at once died of cholera.

2

AHIR

Nawagaon, Dondi-Lohara Zamindari

Once long ago an Ahir made his grazing-place in the Binjhiban forest. Nearby was a black ant-hill, and in it lived a great python. The man and the snake soon became friends. The Ahir used to give the python a pot of milk every day and in return the python brought out much treasure from its ant-hill for the Ahir. But the Ahir's son came to know of this

[1] Forsyth, 418.

[2] Grigson, 206 f.

friendship and decided to kill the python and steal the hidden treasure. So thinking the boy took a stout stick and a pot of milk and went to the ant-hill. He called to the python, 'Come out friend and drink your milk.' But directly the snake put its head out of the ant-hill the boy struck it heavily with his stick. But the snake was only wounded, and full of fury it attacked the boy and bit him. The boy died at once.

In its anger the snake declared, 'Men are very treacherous. We must always bite them and kill as many as we can.' Then it went back into its hole.

When the boy failed to return home, his father got anxious and went to find him. When he reached the ant-hill there was his son lying dead. The Ahir returned home and got a pot of milk and returned, for he thought, 'My friend was angry, but if I talk to him he will surely save my son.' He poured the milk into the ant-hill and the snake came out and cried, 'You too get away from here. You are no friend of mine. You are all my enemies.' The Ahir tried to persuade it, but the snake pointed to the wound in its head and said, 'No. Men and snakes can never be friends. Go away quickly or I will bite you also.'

3

BAIGA

Banghor, Kawardha State

There was an Ahir called Lachhi. He used to graze his cattle on Ghaili-kachhar and wandered through the forests with the cows, playing on his bamboo flute. One day as he was going along, he trod by accident on a cobra and it bit him. The poison spread through his body and he died. He was standing against a tree and fell back against it and his body remained there upright. Nearby was an ebony tree. The man's flute fell from his lifeless fingers against the ebony tree and it lay with its mouth towards the wind and when the wind came its music went on playing.

When the snake heard the music, it said to itself, 'Here I have wasted my poison on this man, for I cannot kill him and he goes on playing his flute.' It went to the foot of the ebony tree and dropped its poison there. There was so much fire in this poison that the tree was burnt and it has been black ever since. In those days only the cobra had poison and other snakes were free of it. But now hearing what had happened they came and licked up the poison at the foot of the tree. This is why most snakes have poison nowadays. A few snakes were unable to get to the tree in time and they too are free of poison.

4

BAIGA

Gotai, Mandla District

There was a potter living with his wife. In their kiln was a hornet. It made its nest there by the hands of many servants. One day when the potter's wife went to see if there was fire in the kiln, the hornet flew out and bit her. She was very annoyed at this, and picked up some ash and threw it with a spell over the hornet. From the ash were born snakes, scorpions, toads and centipedes. She threw some colouring water from her pot over them, and it turned into poison as it went into their mouths. They ran away, some into holes, some under stones, some into a stream. The snake went into an ant-hill.

One day an Ahir was grazing his cattle and passed by the ant-hill. He sat on the hill and began to play his flute. The snake's poison left its body and entered into the flute. Krishna came to listen, but the poisoned breath of the flute passed over him and turned his body blue. That is why Krishna and the Ahir are brothers.

The snake, now deprived of its poison, returned to the potter's kiln and told the hornet what had happened. The hornet gave it its own poison. The snake went back to the ant-hill and bit the Ahir and killed him.

5

DHANWAR

Barbhata, Uprora Zamindari

In Latagarh village lived Asaru Baiga, the great Dewar. His daughter was Bhuja Chamkawan Kula Matkawan Dant Gijoran Muski Dharaiya Bane Bane Turanke Laimithai Khawaiya Naktehar Turi Mahamai

Gango.[1] This was her name. It was a very long time before she ever had a dirty head. She had sucked the juice of twenty boys before then. When the blood trickled down, she could not understand it. Her mother said, 'Don't worry. Tie up some ash in a cloth and put it between your legs.' For in those days a great deal of blood used to flow and it went on for eight days. On the ninth day she washed her clothes, putting ash with them in a pot, and boiled them on a separate hearth outside the house. Then she took the clothes to Katora River. She washed them and spread them to dry. She herself bathed in the river and cleaned her head with mud. She rinsed the hair and combed it with a bamboo comb.

Some of the hairs fell into the river and were carried away; they turned into the snakes that always live in the water. Her black lice became ducks and the white ticks turned into small ducks. She sat down to clean the comb and when she threw away the hairs, they became black snakes. Some of the hairs were grey and these became grey snakes. Some were white and these became white snakes. At last the woman took the pot to wash in the river; some bits of coal were sticking to the bottom; these fell off and became fish.

6

DHOBA

Mohgaon, Kawardha State

One day Sita went to bathe in a river. She took a handful of clay to clean her head. The clay smelt like sandalwood. Sita went into the river, dipped her head in the water, rubbed her hair hard and when she combed it, seven hairs came out.

Sita thought, 'If I throw these away and any one treads on them I will get a headache. If I throw them on the ground it will rot.' So she made her seven hairs into snakes. There was a little clay on the hairs and its marks still remain on the snakes' bodies. Since these snakes were made of the hair from Sita's head they never bite and they are called the Seven Sisters.

[1] Her shoulders sway as she walks, her buttocks undulate, she shows her teeth (in her grins), she is always smiling, she takes sweets from well-to-do boys, she is free with everyone, she is Gango the great mother.

7

GOND

Bilhar, Bilaspur District

At first men and snakes lived together ; they used to eat from the same kitchen and would visit each other's houses for festivals and marriages. The snakes never bit men and men never killed the snakes.

One of the cobras had a beautiful young daughter. This daughter went down one day to bathe in the lake. At that time Minmiddasur the Dano had gone with a party of men to hunt in the forest by the lake. The Dano and the young girl cobra talked together and the Dano said, 'Come home with me and I will keep you happily.' He took the girl and she went with him willingly.

But when her mother heard of it she was angry and called all the snakes and they followed the Dano. She shouted, 'Why are you stealing my daughter ?' Minmiddasur Dano killed one of the snakes with his axe. At that the snake headman cursed men saying, 'From now on snakes will bite you and there will be poison in their teeth.'

8

GOND

Chakmi, Mandla District

The *manhair* snake was at one time to be found in many places but it is never seen now. It was bright red in colour and twenty-five cubits long. It lived in the hills and so strong was its poison that all the grass and trees round its hole were burnt. If it looked at any one it killed him at once, for its poison flew through the air. No bird or animal could go near it and only the biggest trees could resist the poison.

One day a potter heard that the snake had come to a certain place. He made some pots and carried them out still damp and unfired and put them down a little distance away from where the snake was. Then he went a full half mile away and played on his flute. The snake heard the music and came out and looked at the pots. Its poison flew through the air and covered the pots which were immediately made ready as if they had been heated in the furnace. When the snake went back to its hole the potter very quietly rescued his pots and showed them to the other villagers.

9

KAHAR

Khuria, Bilaspur District

A Gond and Gondin lived in the jungle. From the Gondin's belly were born a snake, a tiger and a human child. The woman used to feed the snake at her breast and put it to sleep in the empty hearth. Near the hearth she kept some chilly and garlic. The son was married and the daughter-in-law came to the house. The snake used to play with the chilly and garlic, putting it in his mouth. One day the daughter-in-law, not knowing the custom of the house, made a fire in the hearth. When the snake was half burnt, it said, 'Do you think because you are my bhauji you can frighten me' and it bit her. The chilly and garlic that was in its mouth turned into poison. But when the girl was about to die, the snake called for its father and said, 'Now there is poison in my mouth. You must become a Gunia and learn how to cure anyone I may bite.' It taught him what to do and the Gond was able to save his daughter-in-law in time.

The tiger went to a Chamar's house. It used to go there daily. The Chamar thought, 'This is a very big dog.' He was so frightened that his hair bristled like a pig's. One day a cow died and the Chamar was curing the skin; some of the flesh was in a pot near by. The Chamar thought, 'I must make friends with this dog.' He beckoned to it and threw it one of the cow's bones. The tiger ate it. Since that day tigers have eaten flesh.

10

RAJNENGI PARDHAN

Kanchanpur, Mandla District

There were nine Gond brothers ploughing in a field near a river. A snake bit the youngest. The boy said nothing about it to his brothers but unyoked his bullocks and, leaving the plough in the field, ran weeping home.

When the boy got home and his parents heard what had happened, they called the villagers and held a Jagar.[1] There was a Baiga boy

[1] See *Folk-Songs of the Maikal Hills*, 347 ff., for an account of this ceremonial treatment of snake-bite.

present and Thakurdeo came upon him. The bystanders began to take the names of all the different snakes in turn and when they reached the name of the *domi* snake the Baiga boy fell senseless to the ground. Then the people knew that it was the *domi* snake that had bitten the Gond boy, and they were able to cure him.

Afterwards the snakes gathered together and held a council. They said, 'Just because one or two snakes bite men the names of all of us are taken and we all suffer very much from the bad reputation of one or two. We must excommunicate those snakes that bite human beings.' Then said some of the snakes, 'How are we to distinguish which bite human beings and which do not?' They could not think of any way of doing this and so they went to consult Mahadeo.

Mahadeo heard their story and said, 'Those snakes that bite men will hereafter have their tails docked.' Since that day, those snakes which have bitten men have had blunt tails and have been excommunicated by the other snakes.

The Crocodile

II

BHUIYA

Ronta, Bonai State

A crocodile lived in the Baitarani River. It used to ferry men across, but when it took two men it would eat one of them for its pay. One day Bhimsen wanted to go over: he was all alone, with a great load of grain. The crocodile said, 'I will take you over the river, but I will have to eat you.' Bhimsen replied, 'At least carry my grain across; you can eat me afterwards.' The crocodile took the grain, returned and put Bhimsen in its belly. But Bhimsen had a knife with him and he began slashing at the crocodile's entrails and liver. The crocodile roared with pain and tried to expel Bhimsen through its vent. But Bhimsen was too fat to come out that way, so in the end the crocodile brought him up in a mighty vomit. As he came up, he pulled out the crocodile's tongue. That is why the crocodile has no tongue.

12

GOND

Koelari, Rewa State

A Sahis had a pretty wife who was always running away from him like a cow seeking fresh green grass, and this troubled him greatly. At last he went to Aswarigarh where lived a Bhima, who was a very great magician, and asked him what he should do. The Bhima said, 'Go to the river where there are many black rocks and there sacrifice a speckled fowl and a coconut and rice.' The Bhima made the fowl eat the rice ; he then cut off its head, broke the coconut and threw everything into the river saying, 'If this girl tries to run away again, catch her as she passes by.'

The head of the fowl turned into a crocodile. After two or four days the girl ran away again but as she passed by the place the crocodile caught her by the leg and kept her in the river. After a few days her husband came and took her home and she ran away no more.

13

PARDHAN

Khairtola, Chhindwara District

Rama Naik lived with his wife in Chodnagar. But though they lay together three times a day they got no child. When the month of Kartik came at the end of the rains and it was time to go trading the Naik brought hemp to make rope and sacks. He took it to the Kalori River to wash it. It got very late in the afternoon and his wife grew anxious. She thought that her husband the Naik must be enjoying himself with some other woman. So she took some dust from her left foot and a pinch of ash from the hearth and a few of her pubic hairs and blew the charm towards the river saying, 'Go, Singhi Chhittawar and take from the Naik's hand the stick with which he is beating the hemp and throw it in the river. Let it turn into a crocodile and run towards him with open mouth and frighten him home.'

Away by the river Rama Naik was washing the hemp and beating it with his stick. Suddenly it flew out of his hand and turned into a great crocodile which came towards him with open mouth. The Naik ran for his life and soon reached home. In great excitement he told his wife what a narrow escape he had had and she wept a little to please him. But the next day when she went to the river for water she cursed the crocodile saying, 'From today always live in the water. How dare you frighten my Naik? But you will be the strongest of all the creatures in the water and no one will be able to kill you.'

The Tortoise

14

GOND

Barbaspur, Mandla District

Naulu Gond and his wife had no children but they had a pet dog. They belonged to the Naitam clan. One day the Gond got very drunk and staggering home embraced his wife. The dog stood by watching them, and the Gond got angry and killed it. He took the body to the bank of the river and threw it down there. Kites and vultures soon ate the flesh, but the head remained. Six months later Kacheran Deo was walking by the river when his foot knocked against the skull and he picked it up and said, 'What cruel man could have killed you and thrown you here?' He took the skull down to the water and put it in saying, 'Go and be Raja of the water. And one day you will trick the man who killed you and be able to drown him.' The skull turned into a tortoise and used to carry people across the river. One day Naulu came there and the river was in flood. He sat on the tortoise's back and began the crossing. Half way over the tortoise said, 'It was you who killed me; now I am going to drown you.' But the Gond promised to regard it as a god and worship it, so the tortoise relented and took him across. Since then the Naitam[1] clan has honoured the tortoise as a god.

[1] The word 'Naitam' is derived from the Gondi *nei*, a dog, which seems to have been the original totem. This story accounts in an interesting manner for the possible change of devotion from the dog to the tortoise, which is the totem nowadays.

15

PARDHAN

Nodora, Chhindwara District

In Lohagarh lived the twelve Agaria brothers and the thirteen Tamesur brothers. They in honour of Narayan Deo dedicated Singho and Surja cocks and a Laru pig.[1] When twelve years had gone by they invited their relatives and neighbours for the celebration of the Laru Kaj. They took the Singho and Surja outside and killed them. They roasted them there and ate them. From the feathers of the Surja cock, *mowa* grass came into being and from the comb of the Singho cock there was born the red *tiraya* flower. When the brothers had killed the two cocks they proceeded to sacrifice the pig and place the head in the *phulera*. On the second day they carried it out to the Raisur Lake and threw it in. When they had done this they returned to their homes and took their food.

In that village there was an old Agaria woman who was expert in magic. She found the thread by which the *phulera* had been tied and turned it into a white cobra. The lamp that had burnt below the *phulera* she turned into a tortoise. The cobra went to live in an ant-hill and from its belly every kind of snake was born. The tortoise lived in the Raisur Lake. Its head was like the wick of the lamp out of which it was made and could be pushed in and out as men push a wick in and out. The old woman put her magic into the tortoise's belly and said, 'Go, because of this magic you will not die easily. It is only if anyone can hit you in the belly that they will be able to kill you.'

[1] For an elucidation of the ceremonial terms used in this story, see Hivale, *The Pardhans*, 125 ff.

CHAPTER NINE

FISH

FISH often appear as the counsellors and guides of human, and even divine, beings. It was a fish which, in the Hindu story of the deluge as given in the *Satapatha Brahmana* and the *Mahabharata*, warned Manu of the coming flood and guided the sage's boat by a cable attached to its horn. In the Bhil legends, a fish warns a maiden—or a dhobi—of the danger of flood.[1] In an Asur Agaria legend, the father of mankind was born from the belly of the Fish Raghuman. A Chokh Agaria story shows this same fish, Raghuman, advising Bhagavan where to get earth for the creation of the world.

In other cosmogenic myths, it is the crab Kakramal Kshattri rather than a fish which assists the Creator in his work; indeed the fish's place is taken now by a spider, now by a wild boar, even by a rat.

Many songs about fish, and some elaborate comment, will be found in *Songs of the Forest*, *Folk-Songs of the Maikal Hills* and *Folk-Songs of Chhattisgarh*.[2]

There is a Lepcha fable about the origin of fish-eating. In a river lived a devil which was partly a fish and partly a woman; it had long hair and breasts and a vulva. It used to bite pieces out of the other fish, so it was decided to kill the devil. A fisherman made a trap and, when he had caught it, cut it up and cooked it as a punishment. When he took it from the oven, its body was very hot and some fat got on his thumb. He shook it off and put his scalded thumb into his mouth. Since then everybody can eat the flesh of fishes.[3]

I add to this chapter a few stories about the amphibia and annelida since they were not sufficient to merit a chapter to themselves.[4]

[1] Koppers, 282; C. S. Venkatachar, 'An Ethnographic Account of the Bhils of Central India', *Census of India*, 1931, xx, 239.

[2] There is an interesting account of fish by T. C. Das in his article 'The Cultural Significance of Fish in Bengal', *Man in India*, xi, 280 ff. and xii, 97 ff. I have studied the folk-lore of crabs in *Folk-Tales of Mahakoshal*, 133 ff.

[3] Gorer, 490 (abbreviated).

[4] There is some account of the folk-lore of frogs by S. T. Moses, 'Frog Folk-Lore', *Q. J. M. S.*, xxx (1939-40), 13 ff.

BAIGA

I

Rewa State

A Baiga and his wife went to the jungle to dig for roots. As they were digging they grew thirsty as a new pot. They found a small spring near by. The Baiga dug in this with his digging-stick and presently found water. He sat down with his Baigin and they ate raw roots and drank the water. The Baigin said to her husband, 'This is fresh and beautiful water. How nice it would look if you could make some creatures to live in it.'

The Baiga picked up some of the sand and mud and uttered a spell: 'The companion of water is Jalahin; the companion of Jalahin is Sawat Guru. The Guru's companion is the bod fish. Let not the earth rise up; let not the sky come down. Who makes the charm? I make it. My Guru, Sawati Guru, makes it.' Then three times the Dewar went round the spring and threw the sand and mud into the water, and it turned into fish.

At that time the Baigin was in her period. She said to the Dewar, 'Well, you have made fish. Now I will make a leech.' She took off her blood-stained cloth and washed it in the spring and from the blood was born a leech.

2

DHULIA

Medhakhar, Mandla District

Abujh Raja and his Rani ruled over the Aranban. After four hundred years they had one son; his name was Bisori. Before the boy was married the Rani died. After her death the royal family became very poor. One day the boy went to the forest for wood and on his way home found a nectar fruit. He took it home and put it above the door, and went out to see someone in the village. The Raja came home and ate the fruit. Immediately his body was transformed and he became a young man. When Bisori saw him, he thought, 'I must get my father a wife' and he went to find a girl for him. It was difficult and for a long time he could find no one. At last in Gorkagarh, he saw a very beautiful girl; she was the daughter of one Mahatu Dhimar. The father was fishing by the Janwar River, and Bisori went to him and asked for his daughter. The Dhimar refused. 'No, for if she has children, you will quarrel with them.' Bisori promised that he wouldn't. 'Then if you have children, they will quarrel with her.' Bisori lost his temper at that and said, 'Then I'll never have any children.' He pulled out his penis, cut it off and threw it into the river where it turned into a fish which began to play in the water. When the Dhimar saw this he was pleased and gave his daughter to Abujh Raja. From this fish came all the castes of fish throughout the world.

3

GOND

Dhaurabhata, Raipur District

The seven daughters of Bhagavan begged their father to allow them to go to bathe in the Raisur Lake. They took off their clothes and left them on the bank. While they were bathing naked, Manna Deo came from Handigarh and hearing the laughter and cries of the girls took the form of a dirty little boy with swollen belly and running nose. He hid the clothes and sat on the bank. The girls came fom the water and asked the child where their clothes had gone. 'What will you give me if I tell you?' They offered him fruit, ornaments, money. 'No, give me the youngest girl.' But they said, 'Well, play hide and seek with us: if you can catch her, you can have her.' At once the seven sisters jumped into the lake and Manna Deo after them. This happened three times. When it was his turn to hide, he turned himself into an eel. They could not catch him and had to give up. The second time he became a lotus. Again they could not find him and had to give up. The third time he turned into a fly and sat on the post in the middle of the tank. He flew away to Hema Kalar's out-still for a drink of liquor and returned. When the sisters could not find him, they admitted they were beaten and gave him the girl. To escape him she took the form of a gadni fish. When he could not find her, he was very angry and cursed the other sisters and turned them into fish. But the youngest fish he caught and went to her as a fish, and from them the seven Samduria sisters were born and then from them all the other gods. So the gadni fish is the mother of the gods.

4

GOND

Banjar, Mandla District

Jalsingha Devi lived under the water in Jalhalpur. The bod fish used to serve her. After it had worked for a long time, it asked for a reward. 'Take me with you and let me see the world.'

Jalsingha Devi took some dirt from her ears and from under the nails of her feet and made a Dhimar fisherman. With moss from the river she made a net and hung it round his neck. She said, 'Take this net, throw it in the river and catch this bod fish.' The Dhimar did so and brought the bod fish to her. The Devi sent the Dhimar to show the bod fish the world, and since then there have been fish in the rivers and Dhimar on the banks.

5

PANKA

Pakhri, Mandla District

The ganda fish is the Kotwar[1] of all the fish in the river. When men were born, the ganda fish brought the Panka out of its belly in the water. Then said that fish, 'For seven ages your name will be Ganda and you will be a Kotwar among men.' But one day the spider spun its web down by the river. No one knew what it was. But at last the Ganda came and recognized it. His name was changed to Panka and since then he has lived by weaving like the spider.

Ahir ke mantar jattar kattar,
Gond ke mantar gānd bhitar,
Panka ke mantar mangtha bhitar,
Bania ke mantar thaili bhitar.

The Ahir's living is in wandering about,
The Gond's wealth is in his privates,
The Panka's living is in his loom,
The Bania's money is in his bag.

[1] Many Panka are also known as Ganda. Members of this tribe are often appointed Kotwars or village watchmen.

The Frog

6

BINJHWAR

Dhaurabhata, Raipur District

Beyond the seven seas and the sixteen rivers there lived the goddess Jallandhari. Her husband belonged to the Panduldul caste. One day she conceived and after twelve months gave birth to a frog. Her child had four legs and a tail.

He grew tall with the wind and strong in the sun and when he was grown up, he went and served Jalso Devi. When he had served and pleased her, she said to him, 'What do you desire? Tell me and I will give it to you.' 'May my tail be removed and my tribe increase from one to twenty-one.' Jalso Devi said, 'It shall be as you desire, but at your birth, every member of your tribe will have a tail. In your youth it will disappear so that you will remember me and by your crying the rain will come.'

7

GOND

Pakhri, Mandla District

A Gond Raja and his Rani ruled over their kingdom but they had no children. Since he had no son the Raja made a great tank to preserve his memory. The tank gradually filled with water but it gave a dream to the Raja that until he honoured it with a proper sacrifice his wife would not be able to draw water from it.

But when the tank was full of pure clean water and the Rani saw it, she was filled with desire for it and said in her mind, 'I will fetch a pot of this clear water and will make it hot and bathe.' Although she was in her period, she went to the tank and brought a pot of the clear water home and set it on the fire to warm. But when she looked back at the tank, she saw that the water had turned red like blood. She looked into the pot and this water too was red and although there was no living creature in it, it began to cry *tar-tar-tar*.

The Raja came home and the Rani told him what had happened. They were both too frightened to go near the pot of water. So the Raja sent for Latti Dewar.

Latti Dewar came and by his magic saw that the cause of the trouble was the god of the tank. He offered suitable sacrifices and the water became clear again. Then he said to the Rani, 'Put on clean clothes and take the pot from the hearth down to the tank and throw it down.' The Rani did as he said and when she threw the pot down, the drops of water in the pot turned into tadpoles and the bits of the broken pot turned into frogs. The tadpole is the younger brother and the frog is the big brother.

8

GOND

Nodora (Seoni Tahsil), Chhindwara District

In Bijagarh lived Gutia Dewar and his wife Gutiain. They had five sons. The name of the eldest was Asru Dewar for he was born in the month of Asarh. He knew every kind of magic. One day the five brothers went to hunt in the Chhandongarh forest. As they were hunting they killed a porcupine. They decided to roast it on the spot and go on with their hunting after they had eaten it. They carried the porcupine to Ghaila-Kachhar to the spring called Chhapa. They removed the quills and roasted the flesh. Then the four brothers said to the eldest, 'Now tell us by your magic whether we will get any more animals in our hunt or not. If you tell us rightly we will know that you are really a great magician.' There was no reed or grass, so the Dewar took the porcupine's quills to measure them for his divination. From the quills he learned that in Bandi Kachhar they would find two sambhar and would kill them. Then being pleased with the quills he planted them in the ground and they turned green in colour and became chir grass. When the other brothers saw this they were very pleased. The eldest brother said, 'This grass will always be used by magicians and it will serve mankind in many ways.'

Then the four brothers said, 'You are truly a great magician. Now if you can turn this creature's rectum into something, we will really believe in you and you can have all the flesh to eat yourself.' Hearing this Asru Dewar was annoyed. He called for his nine hundred Singhi, his sixteen hundred Chhittawar, his fifty-two lakhs of Chandi. He took the porcupine's rectum in his hands and laid his charm upon it saying,

> At Guru, Mat Guru, Takesur Beta!
> The bazaar has gone false.
> Come Dasma Guru and Dasma Guruain with your Vidya.
> As I order you to be, so do you become.
> As the porcupine sheds its quills
> So do you spread throughout the world.

With this spell he threw the rectum into the water of the spring and it turned into a frog and began to cry *tar-tar*. The Dewar said, 'Go, you will be the Rani of the water and your children will spread through the world.'

THE EARTH-WORM

9

GOND

Rusa, Mandla District

Phulmotin was the daughter of Raja Joda and Rani Kamolin of Sambalgarh. One day she found herself pregnant though she was unmarried. The Raja was very ashamed about this and would not let the girl out of the palace. He tried hard to get an abortion, but it was no use and at last the child was born. The Raja took him with placenta and cord to Pondrimatta and buried him alive. Some time afterwards there came from the child's head eighty thousand earth-worms.

Aghori Guru was going along when he found himself surrounded by these worms and unable to move. He was very alarmed and did not know what to do. They said, 'Give us a blessing and we'll let you go.' The Guru said, 'You are born of earth. Now live in the earth and the earth will be your food and drink. When you die you will live again. Now go through the world and till the soil for men.'

CHAPTER TEN

BIRDS

THE tradition is that formerly birds had no wings. One story says that they began to fly as a result of a competition between two sets of magicians—and indeed it is common for magicians to turn people into flying creatures and keep them well out of the way up in the sky. Other tales regard flying and being wild in the woods as a curse or punishment; yet another story suggests that it was necessary for birds to have wings in order that they could get at the fruit on trees. The Kharia say that when men prayed to Ponomosor to provide them with food, he sent a great storm which blew the leaves of the trees high into the air where they were transformed into birds.[1]

'At first all birds were white. But when, after the rain of fire by which Ponomosor attempted to destroy mankind, he sent the birds to find any traces of survivors, the *dhechua* sat on a burnt tree and became black, the *kuhu* sat sometimes on trees and sometimes on the ground and became brownish-black, and the *lipi* sat on the ground and became brown.'[2]

There is a widespread idea that birds are organized in a sort of kingdom. One of them is Raja, another the Inspector of Police, a third is the watchman. There are very popular Holi and Dadara songs based on this. There is no agreement about it, but the general belief is that the peacock is the Raja of the bird kingdom.

There are naturally many and varied stories about the origin of different birds. The crane was first a dwarf and it got its long neck and legs by being pulled about by Mahadeo. Another story suggests that it was the child of the unnatural union of a parrot and a snake.

[1] Roy, *The Kharias*, 415. Compare the Garo story of the bhimraj and the rat. 'Once upon a time, the bhimraj and the rat used to comb each other's hair and feathers. The rat did his work very well. For this reason the bhimraj has to this day two beautiful feathers in his tail. But the bhimraj, after his own tail had been dressed by the rat, was lazy, and rolled the rat's tail between his hands and rubbed it. For this reason, the rat's tail is round and without any hair. The rat now wishes to bite off the tail of the bhimraj. For this reason, the bird will never sleep often in the same place, and at night flits to another perch every time it wakes up, for fear of the rat.'—Playfair, 136.

[2] ibid., 416. For the change of colour in birds, see S. C. Mitra, 'On a Sema Naga Aetiological Myth about the Black Colour of the Jungle-Crow, the Red Colour of the Scarlet Minivet and the Red Chin of the Ruby Throat,' *Q. J. M. S.*, xxi, 69 ff.

The Birhor have a legend to account for the long neck of the stork. When Rama and Lakshman were going through the forest searching for Sita, they asked the stork if it had seen her.

'No,' said the stork, 'What do I care for your Sita or Fita? I am engrossed with the thought of my own belly.' Annoyed at such a rude reply, Rama told Lakshman,' Seize hold of the bird.' Lakshman caught the stork and pulled it by the neck, and since then the stork has had a long neck.[1]

Parrots are often made by human beings: Sukra Chamarin cut off her breasts and used her pubic hairs for wings. A Baiga made a parrot of *odhar* leaves with lotus leaves as wings. Another woman, a Chamar, made it, as so commonly, to be a messenger to her lover. Two girls in a Gond tale made the bird of the leaves of the Gold Mohur and used its bright red flowers for its beak.

There are various stories about the owl, always ominous in India. It is born in a grave: it is the ghost of a woman who suffered a miserable death in a tree; it is born from a half-burnt bit of wood off a pyre.[2] The owl, according to a Rajput fable recorded by Fitzpatrick in Kangra, 'was once naked, hungry and poverty-stricken and it went round and borrowed a feather from each bird. From that day the owl has never shown his face to his creditors, to whom he had promised repayment, and he skulks till nightfall invisible, his voice being that of a ventriloquist.'[3]

The peacock, as I have said, is often regarded as the Raja of the bird kingdom. There is always stress on its beauty and a belief that it reproduces itself by letting its seed fall from its mouth during the dance. This, according to the Kota tradition, is the result of a curse, a punishment on the birds for failing to prevent a certain couple from having intercourse. 'I have put a curse upon your privates. They will certainly not rise up. Instead of that,—when those black monsoon clouds come covering the land, to you two joyfulness will come. At that time, your wife must be thinking about you : I want him to join with me, and suffering toil and suffering extreme fatigue and going around you. Instead of you for your part joining with her and going through the movements of sexual intercourse, when you are dancing beautifully on

[1] Roy, *The Birhors*, 416.

[2] In Bengal if a screech-owl hoots on the roof of a room where a pregnant woman or a woman in childbirth is living, the woman may exclaim, 'O ghost, go away or I will cut off your nose with a fish-knife'. The owl is here regarded as a messenger of death.—S. C. Mitra, 'Studies in Bird-Myths,' *Q. J. M. S.*, xxvii (1936-37), 411.

[3] Fitzpatrick, 563. See further J. J. Modi,' The Owl in Folklore,' *J. A. S. B.*, xix (N.S., 1923), 51-60.

that mountain with the tail which I have given to you, because of the fatigue of your dancing, the seeds which are in your penis will not come through there but will come through your mouth. At that time, when you dance with sweat covering your face, that seed will without fail come by itself from your mouth with a cough. At that time, your wife must come with desire and eat the seed which you coughed out. From that day she also will without fail become pregnant.' [1]

The peacock's feathers are valuable as a demon-scarer; it was created to please a goddess; its tail is used both for decoration and in worship. Mrs Rafy has a charming tale to account for the peacock's feathers. The sun was in love with it, and the spots on the tail are the tears of the sun whom it deserted.[2] Less attractive is the Kangra legend. The peacock, when first created, had the legs of the myna, and asked for a change. He was granted his request and when dissatisfied with the result was not allowed to re-take his own legs. The result is that to this day when dancing before his mate he sees his ugly feet and screams through agony. . . . He weeps and the lady bird catches his tear-drops and generates eggs.[3]

How Birds Began to Fly

I

BAIGA

Baghmara, Kawardha State

When Bhagavan first made the world the trees were very tall and reached up into the clouds. For this reason men and animals could not get fruit to eat. So one day Mahadeo said to Bhagavan, 'There is all this fruit up in the sky, but no one can climb the trees to get it. Make some winged creatures who can bring it down.'

Bhagavan first made the peacock and after that the sarus-crane. The crane was jealous of the peacock's beauty and went to Mahadeo and said, 'Look at me, I am small and dwarfish and look, how beautiful the peacock is.' Mahadeo caught hold of it and pulled its neck in one direction and its legs in another so that it became tall and graceful. Bhagavan made the peacock the Raja of the birds and the crane his Diwan. After this Bhagavan made all the birds pair by pair and they flew up and brought down fruit to men.

[1] Emeneau, i, 115. [2] Rafy, 10 ff. [3] Fitzpatrick, 562.

2

BHAINA

Kenda Zamindari

At first birds could not fly; they used to walk or hop about. One day there was a Raja's wedding. Everyone was invited. Among the guests was a Baiga Guru and a Bhaina Gunia. They tried to prove which was the greater magician. First the Baiga turned the guests into horses and asses. But the Bhaina turned some into water, and some into fire. When they had been turned back again into men, they came to the angry magicians and fell at their feet saying, 'Trouble us no more; we have seen what great power you have.'

The Baiga was going home. He saw many birds who had been invited to the wedding following him. Across the path he set bird-lime. A bird was caught in it and began to weep. The Bhaina saw it and by his magic gave the bird wings. It flew into the air and escaped the Baiga, who was very angry. But since that day birds have been able to fly.

3

GOND

Bhendi, Raipur District

Raja Risal and his Rani lived in Siliguri. One day, as they were walking in the garden, they saw some birds talking to each other in a tree. The Rani said, 'What are those birds?' 'They are eagles,' replied the Raja. 'No,' said the Rani. 'They are geese.' They began to quarrel and at last they made this bargain: the Raja said, 'If those birds are not eagles, I will collect scraps of cloth from twelve villages and make myself a cloak and will go to wander outside my kingdom.' The Rani said, 'Well, if those birds are not geese, I will collect the pubic cloths from the women of twelve villages and stitch them into a sari and will go to wander outside my kingdom.'

The next day they sent four chaprassis; two for the Raja and two for the Rani, to examine the tree and report what birds they really were. The chaprassis went and said, 'Brothers, what bird-caste do you belong to?' The birds replied, 'We are geese.' So the Rani's chaprassis were very pleased and they began to return home. But on the way, the Rani's chaprassis felt very hungry and their food was finished. They asked the Raja's chaprassis to give them something to eat, but they said, 'We will only give if you promise that when you get back you will say that the birds were eagles.' The men were so hungry that they agreed, and when they returned all the four chaprassis declared that the birds were eagles. The Raja had won his bargain and he proclaimed the banishment of the Rani. She collected the pubic cloths from the women of twelve villages and stitched them into a sari and went to wander outside her kingdom.

The Rani was pregnant and after a time a son was born to her in the jungle. There came to that place a hunter. He was very thirsty and approached the Rani for water to drink. She told him to go and ask her son. The boy said, 'If you will take us home and look after us, I will give you some.' The hunter, who was a rich landlord, agreed. Then the boy cried very loudly and beat the ground with his foot and at once water sprung up. They drank and bathed in the stream and the hunter took the mother and child home. The villagers said, 'Our landlord has brought a jungle maid as wife,' and they greeted her with great honour.

But presently the Rani fell ill and as she was about to die she cursed the birds saying, 'As you caused me to be turned out of my home and made me wander from place to place, so now you will have to fly in the air and you will never live in houses, but will always be going restlessly from place to place.'

Since then birds have begun to fly and are never able to get proper rest.

4

HALBA

Khaira, Dondi-Lohara Zamindari

Once in the city of Sasarawar there was a Raja and his Rani who kept many birds. Their Raja was the hawk; the parrot was the post-runner who carried the letters; the koel was the Diwan; the king-crow was the liquor-contractor; the peacock was the Superintendent of Police; the crow was the sweeper.

Every day the Rani used to feed the birds; she used to make them sit in a line and so fed them. But the hawk used to come late and got his food last of all. This made him very angry for he was the Raja of the birds and one day he lost his temper and as the Rani was serving the food onto his platter he scratched her cheek with his claw.

The Rani was very angry and went home to a small room of the palace and lay down with her face to the wall. When the Raja returned from his court he talked to the Rani and promised her that he would have the hawk killed. He had his food and called the hawk into his presence. 'Brother, why did you scratch the Rani's cheek; today I am going to have you killed.' Hearing this the hawk was terrified and said, 'I will not do it again.'

Since then people have not kept birds in their houses except in cages. The Raja and Rani let their birds go and since then they have been wild and lived in trees.

The Crane

5

BAIGA

Baona, Mandla District

Nanga Baiga and Nanga Baigin lived in the jungle. One day a Kol and a Gond came there. Nanga Baigin said, 'If you go to that cotton tree over there, you'll get something or other.' They went and found a maina and a parrot. The Gond took them home and kept them in his house.

One day when the maina was out somewhere, the parrot flew away to the jungle. There it met a snake; the two copulated and the parrot became pregnant. When it got home the maina beat it asking, 'Where have you been?' 'I only went to get something to eat,' said the parrot. In due time the parrot gave birth to a child; it had thin legs and a long neck like a snake. When the maina saw it, it was angry and said, 'This child was not born from my seed. How did you get it? My child is taller than I am.' The Gond tried to make peace and said to the maina, 'Don't be angry; your wife may have made a mistake, but forgive her and take the child as yours.' But the maina refused and flew away. The Gond gave the child the name of *sarus* (crane). Since then the parrot and the maina have been enemies.

6

GOND

Pakhri, Mandla District

Hukum Dano was out grazing his cattle. Gachka Dano's wife was Satibai. Each of the Dano had an organ three-and-a-half hands long. One day when Hukum Dano brought the cattle home he went with them into Satibai's cowshed. Satibai was there and he shut the door and enjoyed her among the cows.

After a time Gachka Dano discovered what was going on. One day he made sure that Hukum Dano had come, and that Satibai was preparing to meet him. Then he got a log from the fire and, making his wife stand against the wall, thrust it into her. A large swelling appeared on her parts. Presently Hukum Dano crying '*Hukurdum*' came to meet his lover. The woman said, '*Aijao tum*'.

When they were together the woman kept on stretching her head up to see if her husband would come back again. Her swelling broke and out came a crane; its neck is long like the woman's when she looked up to see if her husband was coming. She cursed Hukum Dano and turned him into an owl which cries '*Gugju-gugju*'. Her own husband she cursed into a hawk for taking a burning log and thrusting it into her. She cursed the organs of men and they became only eight fingers long.

The Crow

7

GOND

Rewa State

On the Nanga Parsaoli mountain lived Narsingh Deo and Rahabedni Mai. Narsingh Deo had a son, Rahabedni Mai had a daughter, and Narsingh Deo wanted to marry his son to Rahabedni Mai's daughter. But he was very poor and did not know how to pay the bride-price. One day Rahabedni Mai said, 'If you can finish the whole marriage in one day and one night I will give you my daughter, but not otherwise.' By his magic Narsingh Deo turned three days and nights into one day and night and in that day and night he completed everything except the procession round the pole. When the time for this came, Rahabedni Mai thought in her mind, 'This wretched beggar is going to take my daughter, for he will certainly finish the marriage before dawn.' So she took some dirt from her body and made a crow. She put a seed-charm (*bij-mantra*) into it and it became alive. Crying '*Kao-kao*' it flew up into the air and Rahabedni Mai cried, 'Listen, the dawn has come. You have failed to finish the marriage and I will not give you my daughter.'

Ever since the crow has been a bird of ill-omen in the world.

8

PANKA

Bhotidi, Raipur District

In Mamchipur there lived twelve Baiga brothers and thirteen Dhanwar brothers together in this one village. One day they felt a longing for meat and discussed among themselves how to get it. They decided to go hunting. They took with them a great net fit to catch a tiger and a smaller net fit to catch a deer, a one-pointed spear and a two-pointed spear, axes, and bows and arrows.

When they reached Bhursidongri, the twelve Baiga brothers spread the nets and the thirteen Dhanwar brothers went to drive the game towards them. They drove once and got nothing. They drove twice and got nothing. The third time they put up a great sow and it was caught in the net. They speared and killed it. Then in triumph they carried it to a stream underneath a jamun tree and roasted it. As it was roasting, they cut bits off the body and ate them, they were so excited and hungry.

From a distance Guru Danatar behind a tree was watching what was going on. Smelling the roasted pork he himself began to feel hungry. He found one of the hoofs of the sow and by his magic turned it into a crow and said, 'Go and frighten them away so that not one of them will have any meat in his hand and then eat what you can.' The crow flew towards the party of hunters and flapped its wings in their faces crying, '*Kao-kao*'. They got annoyed and tried to kill it and while they were chasing it, Guru Danatar went to the place and removed the meat.

Nearby there was living a Dano whose name was Bhaska Pitar. When he heard the cawing of the crow he came out to eat it. He opened his great mouth which was large enough to take a bullock and the crow went down his throat into his stomach. The twelve Baiga brothers and thirteen Dhanwar brothers returned and found their meat gone and no crow anywhere. The Dano said that he had not seen either crow or meat.

Meanwhile the crow was pecking at the intestines and liver of the Dano, whose stomach soon began to ache. He thought that he must be suffering from indigestion as a result of eating the crow. Taking some leaves he went aside to relieve himself, and all of a sudden he burst open with a great noise '*bhang bhangle*' and the crow came out. It flew away with the end of the Dano's intestines in its mouth and the poor Dano had to run after it trying to pull back his intestines into his body, but after he had run some way he died.

The crow flew away to Koeli-Kachhar and lives there eating excrement, for it is born from the hoof of a creature that lives on filth.

Fowls

9

PARDHAN

Batama (Seoni Tahsil), Chhindwara District

In Damhidadar lived Dudha Raksa and Dudhi Raksin. One day in the middle of the morning they were lying together in their courtyard. A hawk came flying by and perched on the Raksa's back. It caught hold of his backside and the Raksin's waist. The Raksin's backside was as big as a very large basket. As a result of the hawk's touch the woman became pregnant and in due time gave birth to two eggs. When the eggs broke there came out a cock and a hen. The Raksin was distressed at this and when presently a sadhu came to her house she asked him what to do. He said, 'Do not worry, for this cock and hen will save your life when you are in danger.' The Raksa and his wife kept the birds carefully in the house and in time the hen laid eggs and had chickens.

About this time a ghost came from Kachotidongar and caught hold of the Raksa. When he was about to die, he said, 'Do not kill me and I will give you as many of my children as you want.' The ghost asked for two of the chickens and the Raksa agreed to offer them.

That is how cocks and hens came into the world and that is why men now offer them to the gods.

The Koel

10

GOND

Kakarwani (Seoni Tahsil), Chhindwara District

A Panka and his wife lived in Chingainagar. They had no children. One day the Panka said in despair, 'Daily I do what I can, yet nothing comes of it,' and he said to his wife, 'Let us go to the jungle.' They went to Chechandongri and there the Panka went to his wife, jumping, jumping until she said, 'How well you have done today! Surely there will be a child,' and indeed at once she felt the weight in her belly.

So she was pregnant and in due time a child was born, but it was formed only on one side, with only one arm and one leg and one eye. In a short time it died and they took the body to Koeli-Kachhar and buried it. As the Pankin was going away, she said, 'O my child, I never had a child till now and you died. I got you in the jungle and I leave you in the jungle. Live here as a bird and make sweet music.'

In the child's grave the body turned into a bird. There was a stone above the grave and a crow came and sat upon it and cried '*Kaha-kaha*'. The bird from the grave replied, '*Kuki-kuki*', as one pleases a baby to make it eat. The shadow of the crow fell on the bird and that is why the koel has black feathers. Its cry was so sweet that the earth broke and it flew out and perched on a mango branch.

So the koel was born and since it is the child of a Pankin its voice is sweet like a Pankin's and it talks swaying its head to and fro. When men hear it they are filled with love, just as love comes to them when they listen to a Pankin. The koel has no mate, but as the crow sat above it in the grave so now it flies above it and impregnates it. The koel lays its eggs in the crow's nest and the crow looks after them.

The Maina

11

BINJHWAR

Dhaurabhata, Raipur District

In Haldinagar lived Lasku and his wife. They were potters. They had no children. Lasku's wife was a very loose woman. Not a single handsome boy in the village was safe from her. One day when the potter was making his pots, his wife went inside the kiln with a Dhobi boy. The potter discovered what was going on and interrupted the affair so that the Dhobi boy's seed fell to the ground. As it fell to the ground, a spider was born with nine legs. It got up and began to quarrel with the potter. It brought a thread out of its belly and spun a net round the unfortunate man. The Dhobi boy, however, made his escape. The potter, unable to chase the boy as he was caught in the net, picked up a broken bit of red earthenware and said to it, 'I have no child; you are my son. Go and find the Dhobi.' He threw it into the air crying '*Kurul-kurul*' and it turned into a maina. It flew after the Dhobi boy and sat on his head. With its beak, it pecked violently and broke the boy's head open. But so hard were the bones of the skull that the maina's beak split in two and has remained so ever since. Its body was splashed with the blood and that is why the maina's colour is blood-red.

The potter gave the maina this blessing: 'Your race will increase, but as you were born of earth, so in Sawan, when the earth is wet with rain, you will fall sick. But those who survive will increase greatly.'

The Owl

12

BAIGA

Dhanwahi, Kawardha State

In Karwargarh lived Raja Karwati; he had a son called Kaila Kuar. One day the boy went with the villagers to dance the Saila in Dingagarh. There lived Dingwai Raja; his daughter's name was Phulchuhuki Bai. She was married to Balbadri, but when she saw Kaila Kuar with his party of dancers, gay and adorned with peacock's feathers, she fell in love with him.

When the dancers returned home Phulchuhuki Bai slipped out of her house and ran away to Karwargarh and there she entered Kaila Kuar's house as a Paithu wife. He put bangles on her and kept her as his wife. Many days passed. Then one day small-pox came to the village and Kaila Kuar died of it. The people put his body in a great pot and buried it in the ground. The flesh rotted and liquified, until only the pupils of his eyes and the skull were left.

Every day a Dano used to come to the place where the boy's body was buried. Phulchuhuki Bai too, because of her great love for him, used to go often to the grave and weep there. One day the Dano came when the girl was weeping above the grave and when she saw him she ran home for fear. The Dano was very angry at this. He walked round the grave three times and clapped his hands three times. As he did so there was created out of the pupils of the boy's eyes a chui bird which flew up into the air. The Dano again walked round the grave three times and clapped his hands seven times, and from the boy's skull was created an owl, and it began to hoot inside the buried pot.

Next time the girl came to the place and heard the owl hooting inside the grave she was very frightened and never visited the place again.

13

LOHAR

Bharatpur, Raipur District

In Telinagar lived a Teli and his wife. They had no children and when the Teli died his body was burnt near the stream Baharanar. On the tenth day the people celebrated his obsequies and all was done in order.

But the next Asarh there was a great storm and rain and every river and stream was flooded. On the Teli's pyre remained a small bit of wood unburnt and this was carried away by the flood. But as it floated along it suddenly turned into an owl. It flew up into the air and went to settle in a convenient hole on the bank of the river. Next morning it flew to Telinagar and its hooting greatly alarmed the people who had never seen such a creature. They turned it out of the village.

Since the owl is born of a bit of wood from a pyre the owl's speech is of bad omen. The Teli was a bad man and everything to do with him was bad. When an owl hoots near a village there follows a death or disaster. Its appearance reminds people of a Massan. This is also why no one likes to meet a Teli early in the morning.

The Papiha

14

GOND

Rewa State

Bigla Dewar and his wife lived in a golden house. They used to worship Mother Earth and she was pleased with them. They were full of Sat (virtue), for when they went to relieve themselves they did it like cows and did not wash themselves with water. This pleased Mother Earth greatly.

But one day Bigla Dewar went to drive nails into the trees around a village to keep away tigers that were destroying the cattle. He went to relieve himself, but there were two or four men there and being shy of them the Dewar washed himself. Mother Earth was very angry and turned into a tigress and devoured him. Bigla Dewar's wife went up and down the hill searching for her husband and crying '*Mor piha*, my love, my love'. So saying she died and turned into the papiha bird.

The Parrot

15

BAIGA

Rabda, Kawardha State

The old cobra took the Grain Maiden to the Under World. Many men wanted to go to rescue her, but they were afraid. They could see nothing but fire below and they thought they would be destroyed if they went there. The Baiga made a parrot to be the messenger of men. He made its body of odhar leaves and its wings of lotus leaves. He put a little of his semen into its ear and it lived. He sent it to bring the Grain Maiden back to the Middle World.

When the parrot reached the place, it found the old cobra sleeping. It sat on its head. The cobra spat and some of its poison touched the parrot's beak and it turned black.

Then the parrot and the crab picked up the Grain Maiden and brought her back to the Middle World.

16

GOND

Mangwani, Mandla District

There was a Dano called Gaj Singh; his first son was Hachka, his younger son Gachka. Duni Raksahin Dano had two daughters—Panbai and Kaniyabai. The four children were great friends and were always playing together. But when Gaj Singh knew about it he was very annoyed and shut Hachka and Gachka up in his house. When the girls saw that the boys did not come to play with them as usual, they got some leaves from the flame of the forest tree and made them into a bird. With the flowers they gave it a red beak. They wrote a letter and tied it round its neck. There was a hollow cotton tree and the girls put the bird into the hole. They brought a dog, put a lighted lamp on its head and led it round the tree seven times clockwise. When the seventh round was complete the bird flew into the air crying *karan*.

The parrot flew to the imprisoned boys, and the boys broke out of the house. They joined the girls and ran away with them to another country.

17

LOHAR

Semra, Raipur District

Sukra Chamar and his wife lived in Burla. They had three daughters and two sons. They married their children and one day, long afterwards, Sukri Chamarin went to her mother's house and stayed there for fifteen days. On her way home, she stopped to bathe in a river. As she bathed and looked upon her beautiful body, she said to herself, 'If I die, what will remain of my youth and beauty? I must make something with my hands that will last after me.'

Now this Chamarin was a witch. She cut off her two breasts, stole the livers from the bodies of dead men and with them turned her two breasts into living parrots. With her pubic hairs she made them wings.

In Madhuban Koeli-Kachhar there was a hollow saja tree and the two parrots went to live there. She said to them, 'Your name is Karan Sua and you must stay here for one-and-twenty days. When your wings have grown strong, you may fly away to the forest and eat fruit and flowers.' That is why the parrot's feathers do not grow quickly, and as the areola of the breast is black so there is a black ring round the parrot's throat. The witch said to the birds, 'As men love the breasts of women, so they will love you and keep you in their houses and teach you wisdom.'

18

RAJNENGI PARDHAN

Sunpuri, Mandla District

There was a Gond Raja. He had an affair with a Chamar girl. He went one day to visit her in her house. There was the great pot where the skin was cured. The Raja and the girl went into this together.

In the pot was a sambhar skin that the Chamar had found in the jungle and put there for curing. That day he thought, 'The sambhar skin has been curing a long time; I will take it out.' But when he came to the place he saw his wife in the Raja's arms. The woman jumped up and ran away, but the Raja was caught. The Chamar by his magic cut up his curing-bag and made it into a seven-storeyed house. In this he imprisoned the Raja. He shut the door with a lock made from the bones of a horse. The key was made of the bones of a jungle buffalo. Then he proclaimed in every direction that he had hanged the Raja.

The Chamarin wept for her lover. From the dirt of her arm she made a parrot; she threw on it some of the water from the curing-bag and it came alive. She sprinkled it with harra juice and coloured it. She wrote a letter to the Raja saying, 'For seven births you will be my true husband.' She tied the letter round the parrot's neck and said, 'Go, Karan Sua, and take this to my beloved.' The parrot flew to the prison and picked the lock with its beak. When the Raja saw the letter and the open door, he took the parrot with him and made his escape. That is how the first parrot was made.

The Peacock

19

BAIGA

Bohi, Pandaria Zamindari

Sanaha Dano was born of a hemp plant (*san*). His son's name was Kohalohi. His younger son's name was Kilko. Manjhu Dano was born in the middle of a house. He had two daughters—Tengo and Badbadhi. Sanaha Dano came one day and danced with the daughters of Manjhu Dano. As he danced saliva fell from his mouth to the ground, and Badbadhi ate it. She conceived, and when the child was born Sanaha Dano considered what to do with it. He broke off a lot of hemp stalks and stuck them into the child's body and a bunch of them in his hair. He sprinkled the hemp with magic water and the stalks turned into feathers. Then the child crying '*Tengo-tengo*' flew into the air with his wings flapping *bad-bad bad-bad*. This was the first peacock.

20

BINJHWAR

Dhaurabhata, Raipur District

In Surjalpur village lived a carpenter called Musraha. In those days there was no rice-husker, no plough, no grindstone. The people used to turn over the soil with a hoe. They used to get the rice out of the husks with their nails. One day the carpenter took his tools to the Chhandongri forest. When he reached the heart of the forest he met Banda Dano and the carpenter saluted him saying, '*Rām-rām*, uncle.' The Dano said, 'Well, today you've become my son-in-law, otherwise I would have eaten you.' The carpenter said, 'It is to see you that I have come. Your daughter told me to go and see her father and beg him for something to husk grain with, and something to plough our fields. Your daughter's nails are torn and broken from cleaning the rice and my hands are covered with blisters from using the hoe to turn over the earth in my field. Father-in-law, show us some means of freedom from this trouble.'

The Dano took the carpenter to a harra tree. He cut a crooked branch and made it into a plough. He went to a khair tree and cut a straight bit of wood and made it into a rice-husker. He called Kunur Tamesur and got him to make a copper ferrule for it. As he was working a blue jay flew by and cried '*Kach-kuch*'. The carpenter was annoyed and threw some shavings at it. '*Dekho-dekho*', he cried. When the shavings touched it, the jay turned into a peacock and flew into the air trying to say '*Dekho*', but all it could manage was '*Tegho-tegho*'. Presently it returned and sat by the carpenter.

Musraha said, 'You were made by my hands and you belong to me, so your name is Mor (mine, or peacock). Your beauty will be wonderful and all men will love you.'

21

DHIMAR

Lalkati, Mandla District

On Garhparbat there lived a very old Gond and a Baiga; they were great friends. They said to themselves, 'If we can make something to please Mother Earth, she will help us in this wild place.' The Baiga measured his sticks. He tried offerings of pigs, fowls, coconuts, flowers—nothing pleased Mother Earth.

In the Under World, in Jalalpur, lived Logundi Raja's wife; she had a peacock in her belly. The Baiga took a gourd full of aconite and his pellet-bow and went to the Under World, riding on a horned tiger. When he got to Jalalpur he fought against the people there. He caught Logundi's Rani and cut the peacock out of her belly. The bird came crying '*Kehu-kehu*'. The Baiga pulled out some of its feathers and offered them to Mother Earth and she was pleased.

22

GOND

Baihar, Balaghat District

In Hyderabad, Durupti Mata was trembling with anger. She devoured some of the people and made the rest poor and miserable; she sent disease to the crops and cattle, and there was weeping everywhere.

In the jungle lived Nanga Baiga and Nanga Baigin. The Nizam sent for them and said, 'Durupti Mata is troubling everybody; come and stop her.' Nanga Baiga took dirt from his body and made a peacock; he got a lot of little mirrors and coloured a great tail green and red and yellow. He made a crown for it and beautiful feathers. He gave it everything but a penis. When all was ready he took it to Durupti Mata. When she saw it she was very pleased, and made the poor people of Hyderabad rich. The houses turned to gold and the Nizam became the richest man on earth.

But the peacock, though it is beautiful, gets no pleasure. When it dances, its seed falls from its mouth and the peahens run to eat it.

The Vulture

23

BAIGA

Lalpur, Mandla District

When Juna Dewar died, his wife Jitho remembered him and wept loudly. 'What trouble I took to prepare his body and make him fat. For years I fed him and now no one will eat this rich body, but it will rot and stink.' She went round the body the wrong way (that is, she went clockwise) with a lamp and worshipped it. As she did so the vulture Rangidh came flying. When she saw it the Dewarin said, 'Eat my husband's body.' 'No, I cannot,' said the vulture. 'I will only eat it if you make my name famous and give me a blessing so that I will have beautiful ornaments on my body.'

Then the Dewarin gave the vultures names. She called one Jappa, and another Koroliha and a third Dhorkawaha. She said, 'Every day you will get fresh meat and you will send all living creatures to the Under World.' So Rangidh went to Juna Dewar's body and ate it. Afterwards it went to the tank and washed its beak. It sent Juna's soul to the Under World.

24

GOND

Karanjia, Mandla District

At first men and animals used to live together and in the same way. Then one day Niranjani and Nirankali thought to themselves, 'We must teach these people what sort of things they should eat.' So they called the whole world; to the Hindu they gave *khir* and *puri*, to the Gond *pej* and vegetables, to the Baiga roots and rats, to the Chamar beef, to the pig excreta, to the tiger meat of every kind, to the horse and cow grass, to the bear fruit. To birds they gave grain—kodon and kutki—and fruit, but they sent the vulture, the stork and the goose to a little stream to find pearls among the mud; the stork and the goose ate them, but the vulture was sick. The birds came home to tell Niranjani and Nirankali about this. But on the way they passed a Chamar who was cooking beef, and he threw a bit of raw meat out of the house. The vulture saw this red thing on the ground and ate it. It tasted good and since that day it gave up eating pearls and has lived on carrion instead.

CHAPTER ELEVEN

MAMMALS

THERE are naturally innumerable legends and stories about the larger mammals and their folklore has been studied by Crooke, Enthoven and others. Stories of the 'How the Leopard got his Spots' type are common, but actual myths of origin are less easy to discover. Those in the text do not seem to me to be of any special significance. In two stories the origin of animals is traced to an atrocious pun—the camel from a play on *uth* and *unt*, the hyena from a similar play on *rehr-behr* and *rehra*.

There is a famous episode recounted by many different tribes wherein a Wood God is making a plough in the forest and his neglected wife tries to frighten him home by creating animals and birds. The Juang ascribe this incident to Rusi, the Munda to Singbonga, the Santal to Chando, the Birhor and Baiga to Mahadeo and Parvati. The Birhor describe how Parvati first makes mosquitoes, then a tiger and then snakes, but Mahadeo is a match for her: he creates *dulu* which eats mosquitoes, dogs to chase the tiger and a vulture to destroy the snakes.[1] In the Munda variant Singbonga's elder wife throws a bit of firewood at her husband and it is transformed into a bird which flaps its wings noisely and frightens Singbonga home.[2] The Santal say that Chando's wife first sent mosquitoes, then various animals and finally a tiger. But Chando made dragon-flies and wild dogs and destroyed everything his wife could send.[3] The Baiga tale is associated with the creation of the tiger and its pact with members of the tribe.

In the text there is a Bhaina story which describes the creation of tigers, bears and hyenas in order to protect a man and woman who were threatened by a Dano. A variant of the Baiga story describes how after the tiger had been chased away by the wild dogs of Mahadeo it returned to Parvati and hung on to her breast. At that moment she was cleaning an old blackened earthen pot and her hands were dirty. She stroked the frightened tiger in order to soothe it and the black lines of her fingers are the tiger's stripes.

[1] Roy, *The Birhors*, 403.
[2] Roy, *J. B. O. R. S.*, ii, 205.
[3] Bompas, 404. See also Griffiths, 215, for a similar Kol story about Mahadeo and Parvati. The Uraon story, in Dehon's version, is curiously different. Mahadeo and Parvati were 'one day burning the jungle to prepare a spot for cultivation. A strong wind arose and drove some smoke and ashes into Mahadeo's eyes. Taking them out he cursed them and sent them into the world. They are still flying about and are the direct cause of all sore eyes.'—Dehon, 179.

These stripes are, of course, a great temptation to any story-teller. The Chiru of the Manipur Valley, for example, trace them back to a race run by a tiger and a snail. The tiger is defeated and all the snails gather together to express their joy and crawl about over its carcase leaving stripes upon its skin.[1]

A rather charming Kol story about cats has been recorded by Griffiths.

Once Mahadeo sent a cat to spy upon a certain home. He wanted to know whether there was a fire in there at that particular time. This cat had stayed with Mahadeo for a long time and obeying his commands, she went to the house where she found the fire burning and milk nicely warmed beside it. There was also some freshly prepared butter on the floor. The cat tasted the butter and found it so delicious that she ate it all. Next she drank the milk, and feeling very comfortable, she curled up to sleep beside the cosy fire. She never more left the house, for she preferred it with its warmth, and butter and milk to the treatment and food she had with Mahadeo. Since that time the cat has become a household animal, and it is a great sin to kill one, as it came directly from Mahadeo.[2]

Upreti gives the following accont of folk-lore of cats and dogs current in Kumaun and Garhwal.

The dog is considered a grateful animal and auspicious, while the cat is regarded as ungrateful and unlucky. The cat is supposed to be the maternal aunt of the leopard, whom she has taught all the evil he knows, except the trick of climbing a tree, according to the saying that 'One thing should be reserved from a pupil.' The leopard formerly used to feed on dead cattle, but the cat instructed him to kill live cattle, so that she also might have a share; since that time the leopard has preyed on live animals. This is quoted as a reproach to the cat.

The dog is supposed to have remarkable powers of hearing, and the cat of sight. Once a king set a dog and a cat to watch his horse. At night the dog began to bark, hearing some sound. The cat reproved him for making such a noise, saying that she had seen (in the dark) only a hair falling from the horse.

Evil spirits are supposed to appear often in the form of a cat, but never of a dog.[3]

In addition to the stories in the text a legend of how the monkey got its tail and why the Birhor began to catch and eat it was recorded by S. C. Roy.

Ravan Raja abducted Sita to his kingdom in Lanka. Ram, Lakshman and Hanuman went there to rescue her. The Birhors were then living

[1] *The Linguistic Survey of India*, vol. iii, Part III, 226ff.
[2] Griffiths, 215.
[3] Upreti, 398.

in those parts. When Hanuman first appeared within the fort of Ravan, his men sought to catch Hanuman but failed. At length Ravan ordered them to call some Birhors as they lived in the jungles and might be more skilful in catching the Hanuman. An old Birhor couple were brought. But all their efforts were unsuccessful. Then Hanuman took pity on them and taught the old man how to make suitable nets. 'Make your nets,' said he, 'with interstices thrice the breadth of a human finger. And then you will be able to catch me.' And so they did; and Hanuman was caught in the net, but then Hanuman told the Birhor, 'Why should you kill me? I shall kill myself. Just do what I tell you. Wind up all available cloths in the shape of a tail and attach it as a terminal appendage here (pointing to the extremity of the vertebral column); smear the "tail" profusely with oil and ghee and set fire to it'. And the Birhors did as they were instructed. And Hanuman with his tail all aflame leaped from house to house all over the town of Lanka, and thus all the houses in the town were burnt down. Then Hanuman caught hold of his own "tail" with his hands, and thus the palms of his hands turned black. And then he caught hold of a keond tree with his hands and it too became black; and then he sought to clean his hands by rubbing them against his own face and his face too turned black. Ever since then the colour of the keond tree and of the face and the inner part of the hands of the race of Hanumans (baboons) have remained black.

Finally, Hanuman plunged into the sea to wash himself clean. Then he asked Ram, who was his maternal uncle, 'Who will dispose of my body when I am dead?' Ram replied, 'Those who entrapped you—the Birhors—and their progeny will eat you and your race.' And since then the Birhors have taken to eating the flesh of different sorts of monkeys and baboons.[1]

The Juang account of how men were turned into monkeys finds a curious parallel in a Lhota Naga legend.

Once upon a time a man called Kimongthang called his sisters' husbands' relations together and gave them rice-beer to drink and said to them, 'I have cut a chentung tree ready for a sacrificial post. Go and drag it in for me, but do not let a single leaf fall to the ground.' So they went and began to drag the tree, but the leaves were half withered and they kept letting them fall. Then, determined not to let the leaves fall, they tied them onto the twigs and set to work to drag the tree again. In spite of this all the leaves fell off. Then they were ashamed to go back to the village and meet Kimongthang. So they fled away into the jungle, and the men became mynas and called '*Kyon-kyon*'. But the women ground up rice-flour to make rice-beer and smeared it on their foreheads and called out, '*Woka-woka*', and became gibbons. That is why the gibbon now has a white forehead.[2]

[1] Roy, *The Birhors*, 425. The Khasi say the monkey's hair is grey because it was burnt during Rama's assault on Ceylon.—Rafy, 106f.

[2] Mills, *The Lhota Nagas*, 184f.

In India the elephant has always been regarded as lucky and sacred. It brings victory to kings, it is the mount of gods. The elephant-headed Ganesh is the giver of perfection. Indra, lord of the sky, mounts the white elephant Airavata. In the Jataka literature Buddha himself is represented as a white elephant. In ancient India the elephant was so sacred that Kautilya prescribes the death sentence for anyone who kills it. On the other hand, if a man is killed by an elephant his relatives must pay compensation to Government for such an auspicious death.

The very early *Hastyayurveda* gives some interesting details about the origin of elephants. Formerly they could fly. But one day a flock of elephants came flying to a sage's hermitage and sat on the branch of a tree near by. Unable to bear the weight, the branch broke and the sage cursed elephants to be henceforth the mounts of men. The elephants went to Brahma who was powerless to reverse the degree but promised to create an elephant-doctor who would help them. As the elephants, morose, unhappy, earth-bound, wandered across the world, they entered another sage's hermitage. During the night he got up and passed urine: one of the she-elephants drank it; she was impregnated and in time gave birth to a beautiful child who grew up as Palakapya, the first doctor of elephants. The Raja of Anga later captured the whole herd and took them to Champa, whither they were followed by Palakapya who cared for them.[1]

There is an excellent story about flying elephants and a foolish weaver recorded from Tilauriya Bansi, Basti District.

There was once a weaver whose field used to be grazed every night by an elephant of Raja Indra, who used to come down from Indrasan. He asked the other weavers what animal could be injuring his field. 'Perhaps it is the village grindstones that do it,' they said. So he had every grindstone in the village tied up, but the damage went on as before. He again consulted his friends and they said, 'Perchance it is the village rice-pounders that do it.' So he had all the rice-pounders tied up, but the damage continued as before.

Then he went one night and lay in wait in the field. He saw the elephant fly down and graze the crop, and as it was flying away again he caught hold of its tail and flew away with it to Indrasan. There he sat for the night in the darbar of Raja Indra and saw the fairies dance and heard them sing. Next night, when the elephant was flying back to earth, he held on by his tail and came home.

When he arrived he told his friends all the wonders he had seen and said: 'What is the use of living in this wretched place? Let us all go to

[1] These details are from an article by V. Bhattacharyya and G. K. Shrigondekar, 'Sanskrit Works on Elephants', *J. B. O. R. S.*, x, 317ff.

Indrasan.' They agreed, and when the elephant was flying back after his nightly meal, first the weaver clung on to his tail, his wife held on to his legs, and so all his kinsfolk held on too. The elephant flew away with them through the air. When they had got ever so high the weaver began to think to himself: 'What a fool I was not to bring my loom with me!' And with this he let go his hold and they all came tumbling down to earth again. This is why a weaver has never succeeded in getting to heaven since.[1]

The belief that the elephant once could fly may derive from its traditional association with Indra, the Sky God. Theobald, discussing the occurrence of elephant-designs on ancient punch-marked coins says that,

> In India the elephant is symbolical of Indra and the animal is probably intended for 'Airavatas', the elephant of Indra. The symbol is an animal personation or embodiment of those huge banks of dark clouds, which during the rainy season traverse the vault of heaven, and in India form so striking an object. Especially welcome to the parched earth is then the advance of Indra's elephant ('*Nimbus*' of meteorology) and it has given rise to the pretty metaphor in the Meghaduta which Griffith thus renders:
>
> When on a day in June, he upward cast
> The aching eyes, lo! on the mountain lay
> A glorious cloud embracing it, so vast
> As some huge elephant, that stoops in play
> To trample down the bank, that bars his onward way.[2]

The elephant, indeed, figures constantly in Indian poetry for, as Andrews points out, the Eastern poet finds in this splendid animal 'his synonyms for the superlative of strength, grace and symmetry. The soft and graceful gait of an Indian woman is likened to that of an elephant; and in the East where a woman's garments permit freedom of movement and sympathetic co-operation of the muscular system this is an apt comparison. In

[1] *N. I. Notes and Queries*, iv, 193.

[2] W. Theobald, 'Notes on some of the symbols found on the punch-marked coins of Hindustan,' *J. A. S. B.*, lix (1890), 246. The literature of elephant lore is considerable. The Gajashastra was a common subject of study and the title Ibhavidyadavah—one possessing a knowledge of elephants—highly coveted. There exist many treatises such as Palakapya's *Hastyayurveda*, already quoted, Nilakantha's *Matanga-Lila* and Hamsadeva's *Mriga-Paksi-Shastri*. The first deals with the medical treatment of elephants' diseases, the second (which has been translated by Edgerton) describes the sport of elephants and divides them into four castes according to their colours and twelve classes according to their age, the third classifies thirteen kinds of elephant. See F. Edgerton, *The Elephant Lore of the Hindus* (Yale, 1931): C. Minakshi, 'Elephant Lore in Pallava History,' *Q. J. M. S.*, xxviii (1937-8), 290ff.

the west the natural swing of the hips, only possible in conjunction with the free, lithe play of the muscles of the foot and torso, is restricted and becomes jerky. The divinely exquisite Sita (surely one of the sweetest characters in any literature, over whose abduction by the lord of Lanka such fearful carnage ensued) possessed "thighs like the trunks of elephants". And the lord himself, the Rakshasa god Ravana, although an evil person addicted to wine and very quarelsome, was still godlike in the majesty of his form, and he had "fingers like the trunks of elephants".'[1]

There is an exceptionally interesting note by the late Rai Bahadur Hiralal on 'Untouchables amongst Animals and Plants'. He points out that the sociological rules of Hinduism have been extended to animals and plants. 'A bullock is a Brahmin; a lion, a tiger or a horse is a Kshattriya; a fox is a Bania; an ass, a pig, a lizard, and a vulture are Sudras.' Indeed these Sudras are untouchables, for their touch pollutes a Hindu. Similarly in the vegetable kingdom, the pipal and the banyan trees are Brahmins. 'They are invested with the sacred thread. People of all classes prostrate themselves before them. They dare not uproot them or cut their branches. They are extremely afraid of their displeasure. They propitiate them with offerings as they would do in the case of a live Brahmin.' But the hiwar (reongha) tree is a Mahar; the mehndi (hina) is a Chamarin. These are untouchable trees. No one would use twigs to clean the teeth for they would pollute the mouth. Nor can the wood be used in a kitchen, for food cooked with it would be made impure.[2]

In a hunting song recorded in *Folk-Songs of Chhattisgarh*, deer are advised to fly before the hunter. They refuse, for if they do—they say—'we shall betray our Kshattri birth'. In the same book, a long and complicated Kewat song allots every conceivable kind of fish to different castes. It will be noticed that the crab and the spider are always called Kakramal Kshattri and Makramal Kshattri.

[1] Andrews, 52.

[2] Hiralal, 'Untouchables amongst Animals and Plants,' *Man in India*, vii (1927), 277f.

I

Why Men and Animals no Longer Talk Together[1]

AHIR

Panderwa, Bilaspur District

In the old days all the animals, cows, tigers, dogs, bears, goats, jackals used to graze together and talk with the Rawat who took them to the forest. For at that time men and animals could talk together freely.

On the Dumketi Kachhar hills, Kawar Rawat used to graze his herd of animals and daily he talked and laughed with them. One day when his wife was pregnant he wanted to go home early. He asked the cow, 'Is your belly full yet? If it is, we will go home; if not, we will go further in the jungle.' The cow said, 'No, my belly is not full; I still am hungry.' At home the Rawat's wife began to feel her pains and she sent a boy to call her husband.

'Come, your wife is in pain; there will be a child.' The Rawat said to the herd, 'Come, brothers, let us go home. There will be a child.' But they said, 'Our bellies are not full. We won't go yet.' Kawar Rawat took his stick and beat the cow so hard that still on one side of her body there is a hollow place and only one side is full. To the tigers and bears he said, 'Go away into the jungle; I will graze you no more.' To all the animals he said, 'From today you will be dumb. I don't want to hear you talk again.' He drove the bears and tigers into the jungle and took the cows home quickly, and that day there was a child in the house.[2]

[1] But even now rats are said to understand human speech. It was a custom in the Punjab that when people made rat-poison they declared they were cooking food for the neighbours, for if they overheard the talk the rats were supposed to understand the word poison.—*N. I. Notes and Queries*, i, 100.

[2] The hollow behind the cow's ribs is similarly explained by the Khasi. The ox was sent by god with a message to mankind but was persuaded by the crow to alter it. God being angry hit the ox on the mouth, knocking out the upper teeth and behind the ribs making a hollow that can never be filled up, no matter how much it eats.—Rafy, 134ff.

THE BEAR[1]

2

BAIGA

Rabda, Kawardha State

When the Earth and the Cloud were born the gods held a panchayat and they said, 'Earth is a virgin. Where shall we find her husband?' They said again, 'The Cloud is a virgin. Let her marry him.'

Bhagavan sent his messengers everywhere and invited the gods and every living creature. When they came Bhagavan said, 'Has everybody come?' They answered, 'Chachhundarmal Raja who lives in Chipligarh has not come.' Bhagavan said, 'Go and bring him.' When the Raja came he said, 'Before anything else, I must say something, whether you be angry or not.' They answered, 'Brother, say whatever is in your mind.' He said, 'When these two, Earth and Cloud, go round the pole like two parts of the grind-stone, where are we to sit? We will be ground to bits between them.'

The gods cried, 'Chachhundarmal Raja has spoken well.' They were pleased with him and went to kiss him on the cheek. There were so many of them rubbing his cheeks on either side that his face grew pointed like a bear's.

The gods wondered then how they were to get their food. Bhagavan told them to make their own arrangements but they did not know what to do. In his fish-basket, Mahadeo had a Kari Bhulin, the ghost that makes a man forget his way in the jungle. Mahadeo picked her out and rubbed her in his palm as one rubs a quid of tobacco. He made her into a bear and married Earth to her instead of to Cloud. It is because Earth is the bear's wife that it fondles and plays with ant-hills for these are her breasts.

[1] According to a Dard tradition, the first bears were the offspring of a man who was driven mad by his inability to pay his debts and took to the hills in order to avoid his creditors.—Leitner, 90.

DHOBA

3

Mukam, Kawardha State

One day Mahadeo and Parvati were wandering in their garden. Suddenly they came to a clearing where an Agaria was making charcoal. All the trees round about had been cut and were lying on the ground, many of them half-burnt. When they saw this, Mahadeo and Parvati were very angry. 'These Agaria are afraid of nothing. They burn our trees and make charcoal and ruin our garden.' Parvati said, 'If you make some animals, then the Agaria will be frightened and will not come into our garden.' Mahadeo said, 'What you say is right.' He picked up a half-burnt and blackened stick and turned it into a bear. Ever since the bear has chased the Agaria when he goes to make charcoal.

The Bear and the Panther

GOND

4

Baridih, Kenda Zamindari

Cheri Dano and his wife Chachrangi used to make a living by grazing goats and sheep. One day when the Dano's wife went to bathe in the river on the last day of her period, a Sadhu came along wearing a hair blanket; the blanket was black and the hairs were long. His shadow fell on the Dano's wife as she came from her bath and she soon found that she was pregnant. Before she had gone many steps, her pains began and a child was born. It had long hair and at once began to crawl about on its hands and knees. When the Dano saw it he said, 'What is this? It is Bhalu (bear).' He beat his wife and when he had finished they found that the child had crawled away into the jungle.

Now in the Dano's herd there was a fine he-goat, black, brown and white in colour, which was regarded as the leader of the herd. It was very handsome and one day when they were in the jungle Chachrangi lay with it and in due time she conceived and bore a child. After the child was born she put it in a tree and let it swing to and fro, while she went into the jungle for something. She said to the goat, 'You look after it.' Presently the child said, 'I'm hungry.' The goat said, 'What shall I get you to eat?' The child said, 'I'll eat you.' The goat was frightened and ran to Chachrangi. She returned to the child and when it said, 'I'm hungry; what can I eat?', she said, 'Here is this goat; you may eat that.' The child sprang on the goat and ate its father and since that day panthers have always eaten goats.

The Boar

5

BAIGA

Bursipakri, Kawardha State

In Ghaila-Kachhar lived the Rawanbansi Gond. They always had a great deal of grain, for every harvest was so good that one crop was sufficient for two years. These Gond lived at home proud and arrogant and drunken and they beat and robbed everyone who went by.

But when Ghughus Raja saw their pride he made a boar out of earth and sent it to graze in their fields. This was the first boar and after it had robbed the Gond of half their crop, they found they had to cultivate every year and even then did not get enough.

The Buffalo

6

GOND

Rewa State

In Parsaoligarh Hinglajin Mata was born. There was a Gond Raja there and she caught him by the throat so that he could neither eat nor drink. He sent for the Gunia to find out what was the matter and Latti Dewar came. Through him Hinglajin Mata said, 'Sacrifice a buffalo to me and I will make you well.' But there were no buffaloes in the world. They sought everywhere and at last Latti Dewar went to Bhainsasur Mata for help. She took dirt from her body and made a buffalo and a she-buffalo. As the Gond Raja was taking them home the she-buffalo calved on the roadside. The Raja offered the calf to Hinglajin Mata and he recovered. In this way buffaloes came into the world and buffalo sacrifice began.

The Camel

7

KAMAR

Bindra-Nawagarh Zamindari

There was a Gond and his wife. The Gond's name was Kuber and his wife's name was Kuberin. They had no children, though the Gond tried very hard indeed to give his wife a child. One day Kuber went to his fields and was late in returning. His wife exclaimed, 'You are *kubera* (late) in coming; when will you do your work?' The husband was angry at this and said, 'I'll wear you out today, but not here. There are too many people,' and he took his wife outside the village. He found a place called Utpatang Hudududu—it was uneven and full of rocks. He took his wife there and continued for a very long time. When the woman was exhausted she said to her husband, 'Now get up.' As he got up a child was born. Its head was long, it had a tail and four legs, and it came out quickly. The woman said to her husband, 'Because it was born as you got up (*uth gaya*) so its name will be camel (*unt*).' The camel was born in an uneven place and that is why its back is like that.

One day the Bhoi of the village was marrying his daughter to someone and he sent the people to get him wood and leaves. Kuber Gond sent his son. The others brought small bundles but Kuber's son carried an enormous load of wood and leaves on its back. Since that day people have learnt to load and to use it for carrying burdens.

Cats and Rats

8

BAIGA

Baghmara, Kawardha State

After their marriage Parvati went to live in Mahadeo's house. But Mahadeo was never to be found at home. He was always away on some business or other in the jungle. Twelve years and thirteen ages passed while Parvati remained lonely in the house. Then from the dirt of her body she made a tiger and sent it to frighten Mahadeo home. Mahadeo was making a plough and he threw the shavings of the wood at the tiger.

They turned into wild dogs and chased it away. The tiger ran back, its tail tucked into its arse, and since it had been made of the dirt from Parvati's chest, it sprung on to her chest and hung there. At that time Parvati was cleaning an old blackened earthen pot and her hands were dirty. The dogs came chasing the tiger and tried to catch it. Parvati pushed them away with her hands and that is why the wild dog's face is black. To soothe the frightened tiger Parvati stroked its face with her fingers and the black lines can still be seen.

Mahadeo got hungry and at last came home for a meal. When the tiger saw him it again jumped on to Parvati's chest. Mahadeo picked up a long wooden spoon, put the handle into the fire and drew lines all over the tiger's body to punish it for coming to frighten him. Sometimes he put the bowl of the spoon into the fire and made round marks instead.

Then to punish Parvati for what she had done, Mahadeo took dirt from his body and made a rat and told it to eat the food in the house and even tear Parvati's own cloth. Having done this he went back to the jungle and continued making his plough.

When the rat began to be a great nuisance in the house, Parvati rubbed her thigh and from the dirt made a cat. That is why the cat's body is round like a woman's thigh and its head like a knee, and now directly a rat comes out a cat attacks it immediately.

GOND

9

Sukua, Chhindwara District

In Narwagarh lived an Ahir and his wife. The Ahirin was a disciple of Naita Dhobnin and fell in love with a man of the Dhoba caste. When the man's wife knew about it she started a fierce quarrel with the Ahirin and the Ahirin thought to herself, 'If only this Dhoba woman were dead, how very good it would be.'

Accordingly on a Tuesday night when her husband was sound asleep she removed his soul (*jiv*), tied it to her waist, stripped off her clothes and fell into a trance. She removed her pubic cloth and tied it up in the form of a cat. She caught two fireflies and stuck them on for eyes. She tied her own waist-band as a tail. She pulled out a few of her pubic hairs and fixed them as the cat's whiskers. Then she called for her nine hundred Singhi, her seven hundred Chittawar, her fifty-two thousand Chandi and her thousand Bir Baital and made them sit on the cat. She threw black and yellow rice and life came to it and it said, '*Mai-ao mai-ao.*'

Then said the Ahirin to the cat, 'Since you have been made of my cloth you are my daughter and you must do everything I tell you. Go to this Dhoba's wife and rob her of her life and liver and bring them back to me.' The cat managed to get into the Dhoba's house through a crack in the door and found the woman and her husband sleeping together on one bed. When it got inside it said, '*Mai-ao mai-ao*'. The Dhoba's wife woke up and, wondering what this creature was, took a stick and chased it. Directly the stick touched the cat it turned into a snake and bit the woman She fell down and died whereupon the cat removed her liver and took it back to the Ahirin. The Ahirin made *chila*-bread with the liver. She called her spirit-helpers into the bread and ate it herself.

The Ahirin again spoke to her cat. 'From now onwards you will live in this world and if anyone desiring to learn magic eats your liver, he will learn it very quickly. You have been born in an Ahir's house and as I go from house to house begging my wages for the work I do for the village, so you will go from house to house to get your food.'

Deer

10

BINJHWAR

Dhaurabhata, Raipur District

Bhangarh Deo was always ailing; he went one day to Sisu Deo for medicine and advice from her winnowing-fan. Sisu Deo said, 'You must sacrifice an antelope in my name and then you will recover; otherwise you will die.' Bhangarh Deo said, 'And where will I get an antelope? I have never heard of such a creature.' Sisu Deo said, 'If you will pay me enough I will make one for you.' Sisu Deo said, 'Come after two days and I will have the antelope ready and you can take it away.'

There was a harra tree and at its foot a little ash. Sisu Deo took the ash in his hand and muttered a charm—'By this charm let

Dhodhi[1] give birth and let it come leaping and go to the back of the Baba's house.' He got a keu root and made horns; he fixed a leaf for a tail and coloured it with harra juice and there was the antelope ready. He tied it by his house. After two days Bhangarh Deo came with money and bought the antelope and sacrificed it, and recovered.

11

DHANWAR

Barbhata, Uprora Zamindari

A god (*deo*) was doing *puja* for Bhagavan; he was sacrificing a fowl with sandal water and fire. A black buck came by, leaping and dancing, and jumped right onto the sandal water, putting out the fire and kicking the fowl away. The *puja* was spoiled and the god was angry. There were a few drops of the sandal water left. He threw these and some of the fire over the black buck. On its body the water left marks and the fire burnt other marks, and thus the black buck turned into a chital.

12

GOND

Nodora, Chhindwara District

In Samalgarh lived Raja Durpan and his wife Bilaro. They had two daughters, Bai Samlaihin and Bai Hiroli. One day thinking of their fate and virtue they went on a pilgrimage to Putlu Guru of Kanjhigarh. He was such a Guru that he could tell the number of stars in the sky, the number of grains of rice in a field, the number of seeds in a pumpkin and the sex of the child hidden in the mother's womb. When the visitors asked what was in store for them, he said, 'Bai Samlaihin will marry Raja Damau of Kontigarh. From her belly will be born a child with four feet. Bai Hiroli will marry Raja Chainta of Guriagarh. She will give birth to seven sons and from the place where they bury the

[1] Dhodhi was Sisu Deo's wife. They had quarrelled and she had gone down to her mother's house in the Lower World. But Sisu Deo still had power over her womb by his magic, and forced her to give birth to the antelope.

placenta there will spring an antelope. When the antelope runs away the eldest son will chase it and will follow it into the jungle where he will become a Pardhi.'

So saying the Guru hit each girl on the forehead with his organ which was one-and-a-quarter cubits long. The girls returned home and in the month of Magh they were married. Their father sent invitations to the neighbouring forts and among other visitors he called Guru Koelasur of Koelagarh. The Guru thought in his mind, 'These Rajas will go on elephants and horses, but how am I to go?' In a cotton tree there was a great hive of bees. He broke the hive and with the wax made an elephant. He mounted it and rode to the wedding.

One day some time after the marriage Bai Samlaihin went to the cow-shed to get cowdung and went inside. In the shed was tied a young bull. When it saw the girl it broke its cord and mounted her and the girl conceived. In due time she gave birth to a four-legged creature. It was a sambhar and she fed it with her milk for ten months and then it ran away into the jungle. The girl was angry and cursed it saying, 'One will kill you, but a hundred will eat you.'

When Bai Hiroli gave birth to her seven sons they buried the placenta in one pit. For twelve years nothing happened and then when the eldest boy was old enough to go with the plough it so happened that he drove the bullocks over the very place where the placenta had been buried. The plough went into the pit and there sprung out a four-legged antelope. It ran away into the jungle and the boy pursued it. Now Bai Hiroli cursed her son, 'Go and as you kill the creature, so you will eat it.' This boy was the first Pardhi.

The Dog

13

BHAINA

Kenda Zamindari

The dog is the Kotwar (watchman) of Mother Earth and Thakur Deo. If disease approaches a village, the dog can see it and it barks, 'Drive in the nail and protect the land.'

Parsusinghi is the Guru of the dogs. Once he was living in the form of a sadhu on Banbrindan. The dogs gathered round and tried to serve him. After twelve years he opened his eyes and there was a dog sitting by. In those days the dog had no tongue and could not bark. Parsusinghi was pleased when he saw it and said, 'Now you will be Kotwar. Go and inspect the gods and goddesses everywhere, find out who they are and where they came from, piss on them like a proper Kotwar and bark like a Kotwar.'

Since then the dog has been the Kotwar of the gods; it pisses where it will and barks to warn people of the arrival of a stranger.[1]

14

BISON-HORN MARIA

Lakhopal, Bastar State

Long ago, before the Rebellion, when a man died, and the soul (*jiwa*) left the body, it was chased by the village dogs. In those days Maria could understand dog-language, and the dogs would inform the people, barking, 'It has gone to Mahapurub; we watched it go.' Then the people would not bury the body. After a while the soul would come down to earth to see what had happened to its body, and the dogs would bark, 'The soul has come: it has gone into the corpse.' The relatives would rush to the corpse and catch the soul and the dead would return to life. In this way Mahapurub lost all the souls from his kingdom and he was very worried, for there were not enough people to live in the Upper World. Mahapurub cursed the dogs and said, 'From today when you bark no one will understand your language.'

Yet even now when a dog barks we know why: it sees a dead man's soul going about the world. Once Mahapurub had many souls in his kingdom, he turned them into Duma and these live in their old homes and help their descendants. Should the Duma get angry and leave the house, many disasters follow.

[1] According to the Khasi the dog came to live with man because it was badly treated by the other animals at the great Animal Bazaar.—Rafy, 68ff. The dog was kept as a pet as long ago as the Mohenjo-daro period.—Marshall, i, 348.

15

GOND

Sikosa, Dondi-Lohara Zamindari

In Ranjher village lived an old man called Kurtali and his wife. They had one daughter whose name was Bai Birhuliya. She was a girl of whom the people said that she was '*Sat ke āgar bur ke sāgar*', that though her parts were as large as the sea yet her virtue was still greater. She never looked at a man, never laughed or flirted.

The parents had a pet dog, called Mangumna-jabbu. In those days dogs did not bark. One day when the villagers were going to the jungle to get fencing-branches, Bai Birhuliya went too. Arrived in the jungle the people scattered to cut the branches. With Bai Birhuliya was an Ahir boy called Koltu; he was like a mad dog for the girl. He said to her, 'You are beautiful as the ripples made by the wind on a stream.' She laughed with pleasure and he said, 'Girl, tonight I am going to come to you.' She said, 'Brother, why do you want to come to me tonight?' The boy said, 'Girl, you are grown up now and yet you have never known pleasure. If you do not know this, what other pleasure will you have in the world?' He talked very sweetly and played on his flute till the girl's heart was charmed and she consented to receive him. She said, 'I do not know how to get this pleasure, but if you will teach me I can learn.' The boy said, 'Certainly I will teach you.' Then they cut their wood and carried it home by evening.

Night fell and the girl ate her supper and lay down to sleep. When everyone was quietly sleeping the boy approached the house. The dog Mangumna-jabbu was sitting in the courtyard. The girl too was awake for she kept on thinking, 'What is the pleasure that he will teach me? What time will he come?' When the boy reached the gate, suddenly there came to the dog the power of barking. It barked loudly and the noise woke the old man and his wife. They ran out to see what was the matter and the boy had to run away. The girl felt very disappointed, and cursed the dog: 'Because you ruined our pleasure with your barking, you shall now bark all your life, and you will be well beaten for it. But on the day a leopard comes for you, it will catch you unawares.'

16

GOND

Sunpuri, Mandla District

A man went to the jungle; he met in the way the puppy of a jungle dog. He picked up the dog and took it home, tamed and fed it, and when it grew up the dog became so fond of the man that it did everything like its master. When the man coughed, the dog coughed. One day a jackal howled outside and the dog tried to imitate it, but it could not get the noise right. So the next time the jackal howled *Hu-u-u*, the man howled *Bhu-u-u* and the dog did what the man did and howled *Bhu-u-u*. Since then dogs have barked and howled.[1]

17

RAJNENGI PARDHAN

Kanchanpur, Mandla District

Early in the morning the dog gets up and goes round its village. Outside it pisses in twelve places and then comes into the village and pisses in another twelve. At night if any animal approaches the village and puts its foot on to the place where the dog's stale has fallen, the dog knows about it and begins to bark. In this way the dog is able to protect its village from tigers and panthers. In the same way, if a thief comes to the village and treads on the stale the dog begins to bark.

[1] The Vedda tradition is exactly the reverse of this. It was the dog which started man talking. 'There were men before Wasawatiya but they could not talk; otherwise they were as ourselves. Wasawatiya made and sent the first dog to those people, and the dog barked at them; so that those people feared greatly and stammering and stuttering began to talk, and the first words were *ballakai ballakai*—dog will bite'.—Seligmann, 322.

The Elephant

18

AGARIA

Daldal, Mandla District

In a former age elephants used to fly. They had great wings. One day an elephant flew down to a lake and went in to drink water. There was a crocodile in the lake and when it heard the elephant splashing about, it wondered what this great creature was. It swam through the water and caught it by the leg.

The elephant tried to fly away but could not because of the crocodile which dragged it into deep water. They struggled together for twelve years and thirteen ages until the elephant called on Bhagavan for help.

Bhagavan came and saw that the crocodile had torn the wings of the elephant and that the great creature was worn out and ready to die. Its whole body had sunk under the water except for its nose and ears. Bhagavan pulled the nose and it became very long; he took it by the ears and they became very broad. Then he cut off what was left of the wings, for the elephants were always coming down from the sky and crashing on houses and cowsheds and ruining them. So Bhagavan said, 'From now onwards elephants should not fly'.

19

DHANWAR

Barbhata, Uprora Zamindari

There was a Dano and his wife; she was a field which killed every seed, so they had no children and people called them Banjha Banjhlin. One day a sadhu came to their house and they gave him food. He was pleased and told them to ask him for a boon. The Dano wife said, 'There is only one thing; give us a son.' The sadhu said, 'Yes, I can do that, but there is one thing: first of all I must examine your parts.' Now this Dano's wife was a good woman, very faithful, and was frightened. She said, 'I don't want to do that, for in my vagina are two long teeth.' But the sadhu said, 'No, if you want a child you must show me.' She opened her clothes and the sadhu said, 'First show me your clitoris.' She showed him. At that moment from her clitoris (*tita*) was born the lapwing (*titihi*). It cried '*Tiu-tiu*' and flew away. Then she showed the rest to the sadhu and there were two great long teeth.

The sadhu disappointed said, 'When your child is born, he will have two tails, one in front and one behind.' So saying he went away. In due time the woman conceived, and when the days were complete, it happened that the Dano was away somewhere. The child was born and it had a tail in front and a tail behind. The mother saw it clearly and then the child flew up into the sky and was gone. But the teeth that had been in the mother's vagina stuck in the child's head and he carried them away with him.

When the Dano came home, he asked his wife where the child was. She said, 'He had two tails and two great ears and has gone into the sky.' He broke the waist-band and went to hunt for the child. He caught him and brought him home. He broke off his wings and the child began to weep. But the Dano consoled him saying, 'In the world they will worship you and consider you a god.'

20

LOHAR

Partarpur, Chhindwara District

Jalpat Baiga lived in Sirhori. His son's name was Birju. He arranged a marriage for his son with the daughter of Tobra of Chikorapur. When the marriage-party went to the village they took an elephant with them and Lahtu, who was Birju's paternal uncle, rode upon it. This Baiga was strong and a bully. When they reached the village the bride tied her cloth as a *kanch* between her legs and demanded a present in Neng before she would undo it again. Lahtu refused to give the present and began a quarrel and thus made himself so unpleasant that some members of the marriage-party went away. Then Tobra's son Pikla got annoyed; he sat on a peacock with a great spreading tail and began to fight against Lahtu. As they fought, the peacock flew into the air and the elephant followed it. Pikla drew his sword and cut off both the wings of the elephant. The elephant's wings fell into a lake and the elephant fell with them. Lahtu was killed but the elephant's wings turned into lotus leaves and its blood turned into prawns. Many leeches clung to the elephant's body and drank its blood. That is why today there are many white marks all over its skin and since that time elephants have not been able to fly.

The Fox

21

GOND

Mangwani, Mandla District

An old man and his wife had seven daughters. Whenever the old man and woman cooked anything nice for supper, the girls used to eat it all and the parents got nothing. One day the old man and his wife decided that they would get up in the middle of the night and make a feast just for themselves. But one of the girls overheard them talking and quietly told the others.

The old man and woman got up at midnight and the old man whispered to his wife, 'Old woman, where is the *dauri* basket ?' One of the girls, who was only pretending to be asleep, said loudly, 'Here is the *dauri*', and got up. The old man said, 'Don't make such a noise, child. Lie down and go to sleep and don't wake the others.' The girl lay down, and presently the old man whispered to his wife, 'Where is the grindstone?' This time another of the girls jumped up and said, 'Here is the grindstone.' The old man said, 'Don't make such a noise, child. Lie down and go to sleep and don't wake the others.' In this way each of the girls got up and offered to find something or other for her parents.

The next morning the old man and woman, hungry and sleepy, decided that the only thing to do was to send their daughters out into the jungle. They sent the girls to get wood. The girls went off and presently found themselves in the house of a fox. The fox had gone to graze its cows and milk was cooking in a pot over the fire. The girls took the milk, made it into *khir* and ate it with great enjoyment. In the evening the fox came home with its cows and the girls seeing it coming hid behind the grain-bin. The fox tied up its cows and came to sit by the hearth. As it sat down some of the hot *khir* stuck to its backside. It jumped up crying, 'The mouth has eaten chaff and straw, the arse has eaten *khir*. Now I'm going to burn you.' It got a pot of ghee, put it on the fire to boil, and walked round and round shouting, 'The mouth has eaten chaff and straw, the arse has eaten *khir*.' When the ghee was boiling it dipped its tail and arse into it, and then went round again. But one of the girls jumped out of her hiding-place and pushed the fox right into the pot of boiling ghee and it was burnt to death.

After that, foxes—who previously lived like human beings in houses—gave up their houses and lived in holes in the ground.

THE GOAT

22

GOND

Banjar, Mandla District

Daugun Guru married Lohakat Loharin. The twelve Mata sisters went on tour searching for witches, magicians and wizards of every kind. One day they came to Lohakat Loharin, and said to her, 'Sow the Jawara quickly.' She got bamboo and made baskets, filled them with earth and sowed the grain for Jawara. After eight days it was time for Atwahi. On the day that they took the baskets to the river the Mata began to tremble with anger. 'You must make sacrifice to me,' she cried.

Lohakat said to her husband, 'You make a goat and I will make a young she-goat.' She cut off her tongue and made Daugun do the same, and with their tongues they made the goats, and sacrificed them to the Mata. The Mata was pleased and said, 'Now you may go all over the world and devour human beings, for you have pleased me by making these goats.'

Since then there have been goats in the world for the protection of human beings against witches and gods. For whoever offers a goat to the gods is safe.

THE HORSE

23

GOND

Jubbulpore District

There was a Sahis. He had no work and his entrails were cracking with hunger. His belly sank down to the Under World. He was half a corpse already. One day he went to Gormuhi Mai and, promising her a black goat, begged her to give him some work to do. She was pleased with the Sahis and called a tiger from the jungle and lay with it. She conceived and from her belly was born the horse Hansraj. Its face was white and its tail was bushy.

Gormuhi Mai gave Hansraj to the Sahis and said, 'Your work will be to look after this horse. You may ride on it and when you go anywhere riding on its back, people will be afraid of you and will give you anything you ask.'

24

GOND

Pakhri, Mandla District

In Kuteligarh, the squirrels had a marriage. The squirrels of Chirpani were to take the wedding party, and they grumbled a lot about the long journey and how tired they would get on the way. 'Let's make horses so we can ride there,' said someone. So the groom's father and mother went to Kosiari Pat in the Panbajja Forest and asked him for horses. He took some dirt from his chest and made a horse, then with the dirt of his left eye he made a mare. The squirrels led them home in triumph. It was night now, but in the light of the fire the squirrels gathered round and at last one, greatly daring, jumped on the mare's back. But it sagged under the weight. They were very upset by this, for they said, 'If its back bends under one squirrel, how will it carry us all to the wedding?' As they chattered the sun rose. Directly the rays touched the horses' backs they became strong, and all the squirrels clambered on and rode away to the wedding.

When they got back home again, one of the squirrels was tying up the horses outside to a tree, when a great storm of wind and rain swept through the forest and the squirrels ran for shelter in their holes. The horses terrified bolted and galloped away until they were caught by a Sahis. After that they lived with men and served them.

THE HYENA

25

GOND

Sunpuri, Mandla District

A goat and a bear were friends. They lived very happily together for a long time, but at last the bear began to want to eat the goat. 'How can I eat this creature?' it thought.

The bear said to its friend, 'Come to my house. There is worship in my house.' As they went along together, they came to a great tank. The bear said to the goat, 'Let us see which is greater. The one who can go right round this tank excreting all the way will be the husband. The one who fails will be the wife. And the husband may kill and eat the wife.' The goat started ; it went right round excreting all the way. The bear then tried ; it was able to excrete once, and then twice, but the third time it found it could do no more. The bear was frightened and tried to run away, but the goat caught it. In the place where it caught it there was a pile of cow's bones. The bear smelt the bones and cried, 'O nephew, up and save me.' The cow's bones at once turned into a hyena and drove the goat away. The bear went off home and the hyena ran to call a leopard to eat the goat.

26

GOND

Bursipakri, Kawardha State

There was a very poor Badi whose name was Ojha. His wife was two months pregnant. One day seeing they had nothing to eat in the house, he said to his wife, 'Let us go somewhere to dance ; they may at least give us bits of dirt from the rice to eat and somehow we will keep alive.' He took his *kinnari* fiddle and they went to dance. Ojha played and his wife danced. They danced at one house, they danced at two houses ; when they got to the third house, the wife's belly began to pain her. Ojha thought, 'My wife is only pretending', and said to her, 'You have eaten bad food *rerh-berh* and so your stomach is aching and the food you have eaten is shaking about inside. Are you a bitch that your child should be quickened within two months ?' Hearing these words, the wife began to dance again.

But when after nine months the son was born he looked like a dog, because Ojha had called his mother a bitch and he grew up into a hyena (*rerha*) because Ojha had said she had eaten *rerh-berh*.

The Jackal

27

BINJHWAR

Dhaurabhata, Raipur District

Kohasur Dano lived always in the thick jungle. His wife said to him, 'You never bother about me. Here I am with the children, and I have to feed them and myself on bhoir fruit and white ants, while you enjoy yourself in the jungle.'

One day when Kohasur Dano came in from the jungle he said, 'Give me something to eat, for I must go quickly.' But she said, 'Lie with me first and then I will let you go.' The Dano took his wife out into a dry river bed where there was a bhoir tree growing. Under the tree he lay with her. The shadow of the bhoir tree fell upon them and presently the Dano's wife found herself pregnant and in due time she bore a child.

Soon after the child was born there was a marriage in a neighbouring village and the Dano's wife was going to it with the child. When she reached the boundary of the village, the dogs there began to bark violently when they saw the child in her arms. Now that child was red in colour and had a tail, and the mother hid it under her cloth. But when the dogs barked, it jumped from her arms and ran away, for it was afraid that it might be eaten. As they saw it go the villagers cried, 'Aha there goes Koliya Diwan'. That was how the jackal came into being.

28

GOND

Banjar, Mandla District

There were two Dano. One of them got on his horse and went somewhere. The other Dano took a bullock with him. In the jungle they met and night fell. One tied his horse on one side, the other tied his bullock on the other. During the night the horse gave birth to a foal. It wandered off and sat down behind the bullock.

In the morning the Dano saw it and said, 'Oho my bullock has given birth to a foal.' But the other Dano said, 'Impossible. The foal was born from my horse and it is mine.' So they quarrelled.

To settle the dispute they went to the tiger. But the tiger said, 'Brothers, I know nothing about these matters. Everybody goes to the bear nowadays. Go to him.'

They went to the bear, but the bear said, 'Brothers, I cannot settle these matters. Go and see the jackal.'

When they reached the house of Jackal Diwan, they found it sleeping. They said, 'Diwan Saheb, please settle our dispute.' The jackal was angry. 'How can I find time for your affairs? The water in my well has caught fire and I must go and put it out.' The Dano said, 'How can water in a well catch fire?' The jackal said, 'And how can a bullock give birth to a foal?' The Dano who owned the horse was pleased and took possession of his foal.[1]

The Raja of that country was Ghamarra Dano. He called all the inhabitants of his kingdom, the tigers, bears, jackals, everyone. He gave the jackal a chair to sit on. Its tail hung down onto the ground. Ghamarra was angry when he saw that. 'I have made you a Raja because of your wisdom and you let your tail trail on the ground.' He cursed it and the jackal's tail became short.

The Monkey

29

GOND

Rewa State

One day a man mounted a tiger in mistake for his horse. The tiger, full of terror, ran into the jungle, for it thought that the man was going to eat it. The man too was frightened out of his wits, but as the tiger passed under a tree he caught hold of an overhanging branch and swung himself up. That tree was hollow and the man hid inside.

The tiger went on and presently met a monkey and told it what had happened. 'This creature man is greater even than I am, for he was not afraid to get on my back.' The monkey said, 'Where is this creature, for I would like to see him?' The tiger took the monkey to the tree and the monkey climbed up and let its tail down into the hollow. The man caught hold of it and pulled it violently. The monkey caught

[1] For an account of this widely-distributed 'Impossibilities' motif, see *Folk-Tales of Mahakoshal*, 228ff.

hold of a branch and the man pulled and in the struggle the monkey's buttocks rubbed against the tree and became red. Ever since the monkey's buttocks have been red.

30

JUANG

Pitanari, Keonjhar State

Formerly monkeys were men. One day they went to the jungle and cut down trees for a cultivation clearing. They brought fire to light the wood, but it would not catch. They piled wood on wood; they brought fire from the Darbar (village dormitory), from the house of the headman, from the house of the priest, from the house of the magician, from the house of the village watchman. But the wood would not catch fire. Their hands were sore, their faces running with sweat. Their pubic hairs were burnt, but their clearing was not burnt. They said to each other, 'Surely our wives will abuse us.' So they stuck bits of wood in their arses and started to jump about shouting, '*Hoop-hoop hoop-hoop*' to amuse their wives. But the bits of wood turned into tails and the dirt and sweat into hair. Now they were monkeys and they went to live on fruit in the jungle.

31

RAJNENGI PARDHAN

Patangarh, Mandla District

Raja Bijra, lord of the buffaloes, lived with Rani Bijri, queen of the she-buffaloes, on Garhparbat. From a young shoot of green bamboo was born Bado Karelin Kanna. She lay in the jungle crying. Rani Bijri heard it and said to her old buffalo, 'Some god has been born in the jungle. We must take care or it will destroy our buffalo army.' Raja Bijra went to see; as he went along he dug up the ground with his horns; at last he found the Kanna. He lifted the child up with his horns and put her on his back.

The buffaloes cared for the girl and in twelve years she was grown up. Katsungha Raja came to marry her. He started a great battle with

Raja Bijra and killed him. He married Bado Karelin Kanna. Presently she said to him, 'You have killed my parents, but there is one fit to fight with you. He is Logundi Raja and he lives in Kankalpur.' Katsungha Raja went to Kankalpur and began to fight against Logundi Raja and killed him also. Mata Kankalin, Logundi's mother, was sleeping in her house. She took a lamp; it was made of the head of a dog, and a cat's tail was the wick; the oil was black marking-nut juice. When she saw Katsungha Raja she ran to devour him. At that moment from the belly of Mother Earth was born a monkey.

Katsungha Raja cried to Mother Earth, 'Save me'. She took him into her house and fed him on rice and pulse. When he had done, she gave him betel to eat and his teeth and lips were red with it. He said, 'Show me your baby.' Mother Earth brought out the monkey baby, and Katsungha Raja was so pleased that he kissed its bottom with his betel-stained lips. Since that day the bottoms of monkeys have been red. When it grew up the monkey drove Kankalin Mata away and Katsungha Raja returned home.

The Pig and the Fly

32

GOND

Bilhar, Bilaspur District

A sadhu lived in the jungle. He used to eat fruit and roots. He went to relieve himself. He thought, 'By eating fruit and roots I have passed delicious excreta, but who is there to eat it?' He rubbed his hands together and brought three balls of dirt from them. He said to one ball, 'You become a horse-fly; wander round men's houses as a watchman, and when the cow-mother comes home tired from ploughing sit on her and drink a little of her blood and she will feel fresh and strong again.' To the second ball he said, 'You become a house-fly. Wherever there is good food, you may live.' To the third ball he said, 'You become a pig. Every day I will make you delicious excreta of fruit and roots; you must live on that.'

Sheep

33

GOND

Mangwani, Mandla District

A man was doing penance. Many years passed but nothing happened. He did not get his way. So he began to curse and abuse Mahadeo, and Mahadeo was annoyed. He turned that man into a sheep and said, 'Now if anyone ties a shoe to your ear, you will have to lie down like a dead man on the ground.' From that day there have been sheep in the world and if anyone ties a shoe to a sheep's ear it will lie down and sleep.

The Tiger

34

BAIGA

Gotai, Mandla District

The tiger did not know how to catch animals or men. If it found someone's corpse it would eat it, but that was all. It was stupid as a cow then: it could not brush away its own flies. The tiger used to watch men walking along swinging their arms. 'Those arms will break in time', it thought in its mind. 'They will fall off and I will be able to eat them.'

The tiger and the wagtail became friends. The bird got plenty to eat, but there was little for the tiger, and the bird thought how to help its friend. The bird said, 'Let us go to play hide and seek.' First the bird hid and the tiger could not find it. The bird came out and laughed at the tiger and said, 'Now you hide and I'll try to find you.' Now the tiger was very honest; it had no idea how to conceal anything. It stood in the middle. There was a monkey there. The bird came and caught hold of its friend violently round the waist; the mark is still there. The tiger was frightened and jumped into the air and landed on top of the monkey. It had the monkey now and ate it. After that it knew how to jump on people and eat them.

35

BAIGA

Pandpur, Mandla District

(From *The Baiga*, 326)

Mahadeo and Parvati made birds and animals out of mud and they gave life to them. Nanga Baiga and his wife gave them their names. They all decided that the Baiga should not eat tigers, jackals or hyenas. They also made the clans which are to stop brothers and sisters living together.

After a time Parvati became pregnant, and went away to her own house. For twelve years Mahadeo lived alone in the jungle and worked as a carpenter. Parvati felt very lonely : every day she used to ask, 'When will he come ?' At last she made a tiger from the dirt she rubbed from her breasts and sent it to frighten Mahadeo, hoping that he would then run home to her. When he heard the tiger roaring, Mahadeo said, 'For twelve years not even a bird has dared to twitter near me and now what is this ?' He threw wood-shavings all over the tiger, and turned it into a jungle-dog. The tiger-dog ran home and sat in Parvati's lap. She put fire in a stick and thrust it into its mouth, and it ran back to Mahadeo, turning into a tiger again as he went.

Then Mahadeo called Nanga Baiga and Nanga Baiga said, 'What's the matter now, Mahadeo ?' Mahadeo fell at his feet and said, 'Do go and kill this tiger for me.' Nanga Baiga picked up his axe, he went into the jungle, and threw his axe at the tiger and killed it.

There was a banyan tree twenty-four kos long. Nanga Baiga buried the tiger under the tree. But as he was digging, he cut one of the roots, and the tiger drank milk from the root and returned to life. It went again to trouble Mahadeo. Mahadeo called Nanga Baiga and was very angry. They had a quarrel. Nanga Baiga at last went back to the jungle to kill the tiger a second time. He raised his axe to hit it, but the tiger lifted up its paw, and said, 'Wait, listen to my story.' So Nanga Baiga sat down on the stump of a tree and began to smoke his pipe.

The tiger said, 'Whenever I catch men, goats, cattle, chickens in a village, all the people will call on you to help them. You won't get gold or silver—that is for the Hindus. But wherever you do your magic in a village or forest, there I will never come, and the people will trust you and will give you enough for your livelihood.'

When Nanga Baiga heard this, he thought, 'What has this Mahadeo done for me? If I make a pact with the tiger I will always have enough to drink at least. For food I can get roots. I will do what the tiger desires.' So he let it go.

36

BHAINA

Kenda Zamindari

A man and woman were in the jungle. There were no others. Asur Dano stopped them copulating. Many days passed and the woman thought in her mind, 'What shall we do? This Asur has stopped all the joy in our life.' She cut a branch from an ebony tree and cut off a lot of little bits. She threw them at the Asur and they turned into bears and chased him. She threw shavings of the harwa tree at him and they turned into hyenas. She threw shavings of the saleh tree at him and they turned into tigers. She said to them, 'Go and guard our camp. Do not let the Asur come near us.' The bears, hyenas and tigers prowled round and round, keeping the Asur far away. The man and woman copulated and there was seed and fruit.

37

GOND

Banjar, Mandla District

In Kankalpur Logundi Raja was getting married. His Rani was Hachka Bai. He invited the gods to his wedding. He also called Singbhawani Mata. She thought, 'How am I to travel there?' She took dirt from her two ears and from it made Sing-bagh, the greatest of all tigers. Logundi Raja also invited Baba Jalandar. He cut off his penis, which in those days was very long and turned it into a cobra and hung it round his neck. He gave the old cobra seven sisters—Kariya, Asariya, Jaddu, Dandakarail, Hardariya, Sua and Sat Bahini. Singbhawani Mata and Baba Jalandar then sat on the two tigers and followed by the snakes set out for the wedding.

The tigers turned into horses on the way. When they reached Logundi Raja's palace the servants tied them up and gave them grass, but they would not eat it. There was a pig there for the entertainment of the guests. The horses broke their tethering-ropes and devoured the pig. Since then there have been tigers and they have lived on flesh.

38

RAJNENGI PARDHAN

Kanchanpur, Mandla District

In Dhutiadongri lived a Baiga whose name was Latia. His wife was pregnant. One day the Baiga and his wife went to the jungle to dig roots. The Baiga dug in one place and his wife in another. As she was digging the Baigin's pains began and she shouted to her husband, 'O Dewar, my belly is hurting me.' As she said this, a god came upon the Baiga and he cried, '*Ochha-ochha*', and presently he said to his wife, 'O Dewarin, if a boy is born do not bring it to me, but only bring it if it is a girl'. As the poor woman was weeping in her pain, she called out to the Baiga, 'But why should I not bring the child if it is a boy?' The Baiga answered, 'If it is a boy, I will have to go to someone else's house to get him a bride and I will have to touch another's feet, but if it is a girl people will come to my house and they will fall at my feet'.

As they were talking the child was born and it was a boy. When the Baiga heard it he grew red with anger and with his digging-stick he knocked off some chips from a saja tree and holding them in his hand, uttered a spell and turned the chips into a tiger and tigress that should devour the child.

When the mother saw them, she left the child on the ground and ran away. But when the tiger and tigress found the child, they said to each other, 'What is the use of such a little creature? We cannot fill our bellies with this,' and they took the boy home and cared for him.

When the boy grew up, he looked after the tiger and tigress who had grown very thin because of the scarcity of food. He used to hunt for them with his bow and arrow and cared for them in every way until they died.

This is why the tiger and the Baiga are friends. The tiger was created by the Baiga, and the Baiga boy was brought up and cared for by the tiger.

PART THREE: HUMAN LIFE

CHAPTER TWELVE

THE HUMAN BODY

THE fastidious reader will do well to skip this and Chapter XVIII. The human body may be regarded from the standpoint either of the doctor or of the poet. Other volumes in this series reveal the aboriginal poet's attitude to the warm and breathing loveliness of human flesh. But here we have very much the medical, almost the psychiatric, point of view. To the aboriginal—let us be frank—the most important thing about the body is its sexual apparatus; it is this on which he lavishes his most tender fancies; it is this which excites his most eager interest in narration.

In aboriginal theory the chief difference between modern and primæval man is the displacement of the sexual organs and their present meagre appearance and capacity as compared with the gigantic trunks or cavities of former times. It is interesting to find here some parallel to the displacement up or down that so often occurs in the dreams of civilized persons.

There are hardly any parallels to be found in Indian ethnographic literature and throughout this chapter therefore my comment will necessarily be brief.

I

ASSEMBLING THE BODY

I

KAHAR

Khuria, Bilaspur District

At first men had nothing inside them; when they ate any food it went straight down—*bhang*—onto the ground. Sankasur and his wife Sirbhang called mankind to a feast, but they found that however much food they provided it went straight out of their bodies. Sankasur thought in his mind, 'What can we do about this?' He said to his wife, 'Give me the cord round your waist.' When he got it he wound it round and round and round and stuffed it into a man's belly. For a liver he took the seven leaves of the *karowan-sok* tree. For kidneys he got leaves of the *takla* tree, and with its flowers he made teeth. With a stick he made a hollow in the middle of man's chest and fixed the ribs in place and made the backbone. He put everything right; all men and all animals were repaired—except the camel and the tortoise. To this day the tortoise has no liver or teeth and the camel's back is not straight.

A man breathes because of the trembling of his liver.

Sirbhang took a bell in her hand and worshipped. But Sankasur troubled his wife. He took the bell from her and stopped her worshipping. But she made him open his mouth and tied the bell inside his throat. When the bell rings we say that a man is coughing.

2

GOND

Jubbulpore District

In Jalhalpur lived Nal Raja and Nal Rani with Hukum Raja and Hukum Rani. These four had no hands or feet and no eyes or noses. They lived by eating earth. From their excreta Jalhali Mata was born. She too had no hands or feet and no eyes or nose. But there was a lump of clotted blood in her. She lived in a lotus. One day she cried, 'My mother and father have given me birth, but they have not given me hands or feet.' As she cursed them, she turned into a bee. As the bee flew over the lotus flower its seed fell upon the flower and Machhandar Kaniya was born. She too had no hands or feet.

Nal Raja and Hukum Raja with their wives made hands and feet out of mud for Machhandar Kaniya. They made her a mud nose and poked holes in it. They made her eyes with water and foam gathered from a torrent. They made her skull of fish-bones and her teeth of shells. From her were born the gods and then all mankind.

II

The Origin Of Hair

The aboriginals admire hair, especially when it is carefully dressed, and regard it as one of the chief means of erotic attraction. The comb is a token of intimacy between lovers; its gift is a pledge of fidelity in marriage.

The pubic hair, references to which occur with regrettable frequency both in formal myth and casual conversation, is removed, at least by women, in most of the tribes, though not by the Juang and

Bondo, perhaps on account of their very scanty traditional clothing. Generally for a woman to retain her body-hair suggests that there is something wrong with her. She may be a witch and indeed it is one of the marks of a Rakshasin to have very long pubic hair. Those of a Birhor ogress were so long that she was able to use them as a trap to catch shrimps in a river.[1] To refer to the pubic hairs in a quarrel is regarded as grossly insulting and more than one murder in Bastar has followed as a result.[2] If a Bondo pulls out a few hairs and throws them at an adversary, a passionate feud is almost bound to follow.

The belief that woman formerly had the sexual characters of the male is widely diffused and connects with the common notion that in the old world the functions of things and people were the opposite of what they are today. Thus formerly it was the Moon that was hot and the Sun cold. It was the man who menstruated, the woman who had a beard. According to one tradition, certain women even had a kind of penis in the form of a gigantic umbilical stump which had the power of erection and of impregnating other women. These traditions probably are to be associated with the transvestite perversion—a large and fascinating subject as yet inadequately explored in primitive civilizations.

3

BAIGA

Baona, Mandla District

Before men had hair on their bodies, the crops in their fields were very poor. Nothing would grow properly. Mother Earth gave a Baiga Dewar a dream. She said, 'Go and serve Mahadeo for twelve years and when he is pleased, ask him for something to make the crops grow.'

[1] Roy, *The Birhors*, 457. There is a remarkable instance of a she-devil using her pubic hairs for divination in a Lepcha story recorded by Gorer. Her son runs away and she follows him. Failing to find him she sits on the edge of a pit where he is hiding and consults her oracle. 'She undid her sash and bared her parts; the hair hung right over her vulva. She looked fixedly at it and then made the invocation, at which the long pubic hair erected at once and then pointed straight down to show that the boy was underground.. But this seemed nonsensical.. and she kept on qustioning it, getting angrier and angrier till in the end she cried, "My bush is telling me lies!" And with that she pulled it out with the skin and returned home'. Gorer, 487.

[2] *Maria Murder and Suicide*, 66, 147, 154. For a fuller account of Indian ideas about hair, see *Folk-Songs of Chhattisgarh*.

The Baiga went to Mahadeo and served him for twelve years. When Mahadeo asked him what reward he wanted, the Baiga said, 'At least give me some hair.' The god pulled out a few of his pubic hairs and gave them to him. When the Baiga got home he put some of Mahadeo's hairs on his head, some under his armpit, some under his nose, some on his chin, some round his privates. Then he went out and sacrificed to Mother Earth. That year there was a great crop of kutki.

4

DHOBA

Mukam, Kawardha State

Long ago women had beards and moustaches. In those days the tiger was the Raja of the jungle. It had a son, and when it grew up, the tiger went everywhere looking for a daughter-in-law but it could not find any-one pretty enough. The tiger said to the people of the jungle, 'I will marry my son to any pretty girl you can find.' When the animals heard this they thought, 'If only my daughter could be the daughter-in-law of the tiger and be called Rani of the jungle!'

There was a woman who had a she-goat. When this creature heard the tiger's proclamation it said to its mistress, 'Give me your ornaments and then I will look so pretty that the tiger will give its son to me and after two or four days I will come back and return everything to you.' The woman removed her beard and moustache and put it on the she-goat. But it went away to the jungle and never returned and since then the faces of women have been free of hair.

5

GOND

Upri, Rewa State

Women used to have beards and moustaches. One day a woman was going to a bazaar with a basket of kodon on her head. She came to a ban-yan tree where merchants had been camping; they had gone leaving the ashes of their fire behind. The woman said to the ashes, 'Take my kodon', but how could the ashes answer her? So she went and danced on the ashes. As she danced she found a golden rolling-pin. She took it and went home.

In a neighbour's house there was a marriage. When she heard the drums sounding she danced in her own courtyard. Dancing and dancing she took the golden rolling-pin to the Dhulia's house. She gave him the golden rolling-pin and took his drum instead.

Her husband was out with the cattle in the forest. The woman hung the drum from her shoulder, put a pot of gruel on her head and went to take him his food. When her husband saw her coming along with the pot on her head and dancing and beating the drum he was annoyed. He ran to beat her, but she climbed a tree to escape him.

Four thieves came below the tree. They lit a fire and the flames leapt up and burnt the woman's beard and moustache. In pain she jumped down with the drum. Three of the thieves ran away in fright, but the fourth—a one-eyed man—remained. The woman said, 'I will marry you.' 'Very well,' said the man. 'But I must test you,' said the woman. She put her finger in his eye and made him put his finger in her mouth. She broke his eye and bit off his finger. She left him weeping and ran away.

Since that time women have not had beards or moustaches.

6

GOND

Pakhri, Mandla District

At first women had beards. One day a Gunia was searching for a lost goat with the help of his gourd and winnowing-fan,[1] but the god took no notice of him and refused to come. The Gunia lost his temper and cried, 'Let there be hair round my wife's sex and growing from her tongue; let horns sprout on horse and ass, if it does not come.' But nothing happened, except that his wife lost her beard and the hair grew instead round her sex.

[1] That is, he was 'divining' in the usual manner of a village magician.

7

HALBA

Kumhalori, Dondi-Lohara Zamindari

Long ago in the Basuladongri forest there was a village called Kachnari. There the women had beards and moustaches, and the men had inside their bodies a small shell-like thing containing a living creature that every month caused them to discharge blood. Their wives had no flow of blood, but every month men had to stop cutting wood, or working in the fields—for if they did so—at the time of blood, tigers ate them immediately.

One day there was a marriage in Kachnari and everyone got ready to go with the marriage-party. A young wife said to her husband, 'You take my beard and moustache and give me your little shell; I want to see what it feels like to have blood flowing from me.' So they exchanged; the girl stuck her beard and moustache on her husband's face and she fitted into herself his shell with the living creature. They went to the wedding and afterwards when they tried to return the things they had exchanged, they found that the hair had stuck to the man's face and that they could not remove the shell from the girl. 'It is a good thing,' said the girl. 'I can now get plenty of cloth, for I must have seven layers to cover my parts, and my husband looks very handsome with that beard.'

She went out and directly the other woman touched her, they too began to have a monthly period.

8

JUANG

Kirtanpur, Dhenkanal State

At first, a woman had no bush round the vulva, but a beard grew on her chin. One day when she was out in the forest grazing her goat, she saw the fine hair growing round its privates and was filled with desire for it. She gave her beard to the goat and the goat gave her its bush.

Since that day we have not cut the hair. Even if it gets dirty it is cleansed of its own accord when a child is born. Until a child passes through, it is known as 'virgin hair'.

9

KAHAR

Khuria, Bilaspur District

At first everybody had a beard. Men and women, girls and boys, all had them, beards and moustaches. Mahadeo invited mankind to a feast. When they came he could not distinguish which were men and which were women. He called Basmasur Dano and told him to separate the company. But the Dano could not distinguish them either. He went to Anjan Devi and told her the trouble. She held her breath and tore off a bit of her cloth, four fingers wide. Basmasur Dano took it back to Mahadeo. Of its own accord it burst into flames. The Dano went from person to person. Whenever it was a women the flames burnt the beard and moustaches, whenever it was a man it left them alone. Since that day, as a result of Anjan Devi's curse, women have never had hair on their faces.

10

KOL

Bilaspur Distrct

In the Age of Truth, women had beards and moustaches. But when they slept with their husbands at night, and kissed them, the men found their faces were tickled by the hair and were sometimes sore.

The men cursed their wives saying, 'If we must live with such wantons, let there be pubic hairs growing on their tongues.'

At once women found hair growing on their tongues. But when they ate their food the hair was scraped off and passed down the throat, through the belly, and down until it pushed out and grew as a bush round the vulva.

11

KOND

Kardi, Koraput District

Sukera Kond and his younger brother Budra lived on the hill called Nikulkonda. Sukra was married, but Budra was still free. In a place not far away, at Kanaipad, there was a big marriage: Ringu Kond's son was being married; the two brothers were invited and they both, with

Sukra's wife, accepted. In those days men had no hair on their bodies. Budra said to Sukra's wife, 'I'm not going, for my body looks so bare and naked.' She said, 'Go to Nelahuru Hill and you will find a python. Exchange skins with it?' Budra took a fowl and a pot of milk: the python took the gifts and agreed to lend Budra its skin for three days. When he put it on, he found he had hair everywhere: there was a good moustache, hair on his chest, under his arms, on his legs and a fine bush round his privates. When Sukra's wife saw him, she was enchanted and lay with him on the way to the marriage. They thoroughly enjoyed the ceremony, but their host's daughters-in-law also fell in love with Budra and followed him home. Now he had two women, but he had to return the skin. When the python saw his skin, however, he knew it had been used sinfully and refused to take it. So Budra had to keep it, and his two women were pleased, but ever since hair has grown on men's bodies.

12

KOND

Kerma, Koraput District

Formerly the pubic hairs were twelve cubits long. One day as a woman was cooking, her hairs caught fire and she was burnt to death in the flames. Since then the hairs have been short as they are now.

13

RAJNENGI PARDHAN

Madhopur, Mandla District

Barjhusur Dano was living in a clearing of the forest with his young wife. One day a man passed by. He was very thirsty and came to the house to ask for water. The Dano was away doing something and when the wife saw the visitor she was tethered by love to him. She gave him water and he gave her water in return. But when he was satisfied he wanted to go away and leave her. Her angry eyes started out like tigers and she spat on him. By her spittle his whole body became covered with hair. That is why men even now have hair all over their bodies.

III

The Origin of Sweat

The origin of sweat is often associated, very naturally, with that of salt. The Uppara of Mysore have a tale that 'Parvati finding food tasteless, complained to her lord, who created a man from a drop of his sweat, and commissioned him to manufacture salt out of earth; and as he pleased his divine patrons, he was blessed with a large progeny, who were directed to have salt-making as their profession.'[1]

The *Vishnu Purana* describes how Marisha was born from the pores of the skin of Pramlocha her mother, in the drops of perspiration excited by the anger of the sage Kandu. Pramlocha fled from him, rubbing the sweat from her body with leaves of trees and the trees received the drops and the wind collected them and the child grew. Of a similar character is the Toda legend that Kambataraya, perspiring profusely, wiped from his forehead three drops of sweat, from which he formed the Toda, Kurumba and Kota.[2]

14

BAIGA

Kasaikund, Kawardha State

It was when men first ate salt that they began to sweat. Previously people could not distinguish between sweet and sour and they never ate salt with their food. But when they discovered salt and it first went into the belly, it turned into water, just as we can see it turn into water during the rains, and it came out through the skin. We know this is so, for the sweat still tastes salt.

15

KAHAR

Khuria, Bilaspur District

There was a sadhu. He lived in the forest. His wife was with him. For some reason he was cross with her and did not go to her. The woman thought, 'If only some other man would come here, I would enjoy myself with him.'

[1] Nanjundayya and Iyer, iv, 641. [2] Rivers, 640.

One day an Ahir grazing his cattle came wandering by. He came to the sadhu's house and asked for fire to light his pipe. But the sadhu had gone out; only the wife was there. She said, 'Come in and sit down, and I'll give you fire in a moment.' But when he went in, she caught hold of him and forced him to it. But her organ was so hot that he could not do it properly, and while they were together the sadhu returned.

He took water and threw it over them, cursing his wife: 'All women will get their pleasure slowly.' When the water touched the Ahir his whole body broke out in sweat and his water left him. He broke away from the woman, leaving her unsatisfied, and ran away. Since then men have sweated and women have been hard to satisfy.

16

LANJHIA SAORA

Kerba, Koraput District

The seven sons of Rajno Saora lived on Reli Hill and each cut his own clearing and sowed his seed. But when the harvest was ripe two pigs came and ate it. One day while the pigs were sleeping after their food the brothers found them. They tied them up with rope and began to beat them. But they beat so hard that the rope tying the sow broke and it escaped. But the brothers tied the other pig to a pole by its four feet and roasted it over a fire. Hearing its screams the sow came back and watched from afar. When the male pig died, the sow came weeping and cursed the seven brothers. 'From now onwards, just as my pig's fat ran down while it was being roasted and its life went out *talap-talap*, so when you are roasted by the sun, your fat will run out as sweat and you will tremble with the heat.'

17

RAJNENGI PARDHAN

Patangarh, Mandla District

Bigra, Phirangi and Khursa Dewar were three brothers and they lived together. They made a clearing and sowed maize, mandia and kutki. There was a good crop; they reaped it and gathered it on the threshing-floor.

At night Chor Dewar Matiya and Marra Deo, with their carrying poles, came to steal the crop. They filled their baskets with the grain and made off. The three brothers awoke, discovered the theft and chased the thieves. When they found they could not catch them, they threw black and yellow rice and charcoal after them with charms.

Suddenly Chor Dewar Matiya and Marra Deo found there was a fire burning in their bodies. In those days bodies were always cool; they never got hot in the sun and they never sweated. But now from every part of the bodies of the two gods there poured out sweat because of the heat of the fire inside. The sweat filled their eyes and blinded them; it made them slip on the path; they could go no further and they sat down. The three brothers came up and beat them. They took the grain back and let the thieves go without further punishment. But since then people have sweated.

IV

The Origin of Tickling

Tickling has been called the most intellectual mode of touch sensation, the psychic factor in it being indicated by the impossibility of tickling oneself. Tickling, says Havelock Ellis, who as so often has the last word on the subject, is 'a kind of sensation, founded on reflexes developing even before birth, which is very closely related to sexual phenomena. It is, as it were, a play of tumescence, on which laughter supervenes as a play of detumescence. It leads on to the more serious phenomena of tumescence, and it tends to die out after adolescence, at the period during which sexual relationships normally begin.'[1] It is, however, curious that the stories in the text suggest that tickling was invented, not for the stimulation of young people, but to reconcile husbands and wives. Its sexual character is clearly implied, for its aim is to enable offended couples to resume normal matrimonial relationships.

It has generally been assumed that the cutaneous reflexes, which are the basis of the ticklishness of the body, 'greatly diminish after sexual relationships have been established.' In fact, it has been reported that in Iceland, the susceptibility to tickling was taken as a test of chastity. If a girl could not be tickled, it suggested that she was not a virgin.

I am very doubtful how far this view can be maintained. The Pardhan, who may be regarded as the erotic experts of aboriginal

[1] Havelock Ellis, i, iii, 41 f. [2] ibid., 17 f.

India, describe tickling as 'an introduction to the shy, a pacifier of offended partners, and a delight for lovers.' It is, in fact, part of the normal technique both of married couples and of lovers who are well practised in sexual technique. When I was studying the Muria ghotul-dormitory, I was struck by the fact that the girl and boy members, some of whom had certainly been accustomed to sexual relationships for years, were very susceptible to tickling, and it was part of the daily routine for a girl to titillate with a comb the skin of her lover before she slept with him.

18

BHAINA-BAIGA

Amadob, Bilaspur District

There was a Dano; his name was Bakrenda. One day he came in tired and spoke sweetly to his wife. 'Give me my dinner quickly,' he said. 'or otherwise let me lie with you.' Then he used to talk like this every day. One day when the Dano came in, his wife was cooking gruel. As usual he asked for his food. She was busy cooking and did not answer, so he told her she would have to lie with him. Again she made no reply. The Dano was angry—it was as if blood came from his eyes—and he lay down alone. When the food was ready the wife wondered how to please her angry husband. She wandered about till she found a cast snake-skin. She slipped bits of it onto her hands and went to her husband. She caught hold of him on each side of his body under the ribs and began to tickle him with the snake-skin. The Dano's skin grew glossy with the rubbing and his wife gradually went on rubbing until she reached his armpits, when he began to laugh. Desire came to him and he embraced his wife. After that he ate his food happily. That was how tickling began.

19

GOND

Baratola, Mandla District

Mahadeo and Parvati were living in the Binjpahar hills. Mahadeo took a gourd and went to beg food from a village. When he returned Parvati cooked what he had got and they ate it. After this Mahadeo went away somewhere and Parvati thinking that he would not return, went to the house of a Dano and stayed there. But Mahadeo returned suddenly and found his house shut up and a lock on the door. He lost his temper and kicked the door open, went in, spread his bed and lay down to sleep.

Presently Parvati returned. When she saw Mahadeo sleeping there she woke him up, but he was so angry that he would not speak to her. Six months passed and Mahadeo neither ate nor spoke. In despair Parvati went from house to house seeking advice as to what she should do. Somewhere in the village lived an old Panka woman. When this woman heard what had happened, she gave Parvati an oil extracted from the body of a caterpillar and obtained a blessing for her from Kutlisingh Mata. She said, 'Put this oil *kut-kut-kut-kut* on his body beginning from the legs upwards'. Parvati took the oil and went home.

Parvati put the oil on Mahadeo's legs and gradually rubbed it up his body. He felt more and more ticklish and began to laugh. Soon he was talking again to Parvati and had a good meal. He gave mankind this blessing, 'Whenever anyone is in a bad temper his wife should tickle him and all will be well'.

20

LANJHIA SAORA

Arangulu, Koraput District

A Saora ran away with a girl to Angridongar and the two made their home on the hillside. Soon a son was born. That man and woman loved each other very much. One day the Saora returned from the bazaar and the wife had not got his food ready. The Saora was angry and the woman quickly prepared something, but he would not eat. For eight days he refused to eat. At midnight the woman got up and went to Kittung and wept on his verandah. Kittung heard the noise and got up to see what the matter was. The woman fell at the god's feet and said, 'My husband won't look on my face nor will he eat anything; what am I to do?' Kittung took a little dirt from his left eye and said, 'When he lies down, rub a little of this under each armpit and on his ribs. Then he will begin to laugh and everything will be all right.' The woman went home and as she rubbed the armpits and ribs, her husband began to laugh and soon forgot his anger. In this way tickling came to the world.

21

RAJNENGI PARDHAN

Patangarh, Mandla District

Mahadeo was a god, Parvati a human creature. Mahadeo wanted to approach the beautiful Parvati, but he did not know how to do it, for she was terrified of his divine power. So he created in her the sensation of tickling so that he could easily make her laugh. When as a result he won her, Mahadeo was pleased and gave the blessing of it to the world. Now it is an introduction to the shy, a pacifier of offended partners, and a delight for lovers.

V

THE DANGER OF SNEEZING

Throughout the world there are special customs and traditions connected with sneezing. When 'the twitching or itching of various parts of the body is regarded as ominous, how much more would such a violent and sudden thing as a sneeze be looked upon as caused by some unknown power, or as an omen to be most carefully regarded.'[1] An Orissa myth describes how:

Yama, the God of Death, once took away the soul of a beautiful boy. The spirit of the boy had a strong longing for its home and requested Yama's mother to send it back. Yama's mother knew well that this was not at all possible, so she resorted to a stratagem. When Yama was taking his meal, his mother had the spirit of the boy near about and asked it to sneeze. It did as it was bid; and Yama's mother affecting that her own son had sneezed, uttered the the usual blessing. When it was found out that the spirit had sneezed and not Yama, his mother took her stand on the blessing of a goddess and requested her son to send the spirit back to its earthly home. In these circumstances Yama had to send the spirit back to life most reluctantly. Mothers to this day remembering this incident deems it a good omen if their sons sneeze over their plate of rice and give them an additional handful to ensure a long life.[2]

1 Penzer, iii, 303 f.

2 S. N. Roy, 'Some Popular Superstitions of Orissa', *Man in India*, v (1925), 222. There is a full discussion of sneezing superstitions in Penzer, iii, 303ff.

22

BAIGA

Jalda, Mandla District

In the days of Nanga Baiga and Nanga Baigin, people did not even know what a sneeze was. One year Nanga Baiga had a very fine crop of kodon. He prepared sacks out of rat-skins and made ready to fill them with the grain and load them on the monkeys that he used for bullocks. But just as he thought the crop was ready for reaping, a koel and a kiddari bird sneezed near the clearing and at once the stalks decreased by half.

Nanga Baiga sat down and examined his measuring-sticks to discover what was the matter. When the god made his eyes clear he saw that it was because the koel and kiddari had sneezed. Then Nanga Baiga told the whole world what a dangerous thing it was to sneeze.

VI

Why Men Blink

23

GOND

Bursipakri, Kawardha State

In former times men used to look staring *bit-bit-bit-bit*. They did not know how to blink. Raktahin Mata was a maiden twelve years old. She went to Baura Raja who lived on Sumringarh in Matin Zamindari.

When he saw her the Raja went to catch her, for he desired to marry her. But when she saw him coming she ran away. After she had gone some distance she returned. She was a witch. In her hand was a sword, on her head a bit of a broken pot, and she threw at him this charm:

Let there be the noise of *gutum-gatam* in your mouth
May your nose sound *sarak-suruk*
May your ears listen to everything
May your staring eyes begin to blink.

So saying she ran away. The Raja's eyes began to blink.

24

KAHAR

Khuria, Bilaspur District

Formerly men had four eyes. Two of the eyes were in their present position and the other two were above them where eyebrows now are. There was a Gond called Baitmal. He ate nothing but meat. He could not bear to touch grain or vegetables; he ate only meat. But when he went to hunt in the jungle and the animals saw his four eyes they ran away in terror and he got nothing. He grew more and more hungry, and wandered like a famished cow staggering down a path in search of grass.

Then came Mahadeo. Baitmal said, 'You have given me four eyes. But what is the good of filling my eyes with sight if I cannot fill my belly with food?' Mahadeo then gave him a boon. He turned the two upper eyes into eyebrows as we have them today.

After this Baitmal went about staring. He never blinked. And when the animals saw him staring *bat-bat-bat* they ran away more than ever. Baitmal was still hungry, dry as a withered fruit. Then came Mahadeo. Baitmal said, 'What is the use of giving me eyebrows, for the animals still run away when they see me staring at them.'

Mahadeo grasped the poor man's head between his fingers—the marks are still there on either side of the head—and pulled Baitmal's eyelids down and set them moving. Baitmal was so frightened that he started to blink and has never stopped.

VII

THE ORIGIN OF TEARS

25

GOND

Sukua, Chhindwara District

Churhur Raja lived in Chutanagar. His Rani's name was Kaja and she had no child. Her sister laughed at her saying, 'A barren cow is ready to receive five bulls.' Near by on Chitridongri hill lived a sadhu named Balkhandhi. When the Raja and Rani found that they could not get a child they went together and served the sadhu for seven years and three months. When the sadhu at length was pleased he said to them, 'Ask for whatever gift you wish'. The Raja replied, 'There is nothing we want except that you should give us a child'. The sadhu said, 'Very well, I have granted your desire', but after a little while he added, 'First let me see the Rani's belly'. When he saw it he said, 'It is true that I have given you the gift of a child but in your belly there is no flower to cause its birth. What shall we do?'

The sadhu went to Bhuta-dongri and caught a hare and removed the liver. When he returned he said to the Rani, 'Shut your eyes and open your mouth. Whatever I put into it you must swallow immediately'. The Rani shut her eyes and opened her mouth. The sadhu popped the liver in and she swallowed it. It went right down into her womb and remained there. From this liver there came the child's placenta. The Raja took the Rani home and after a few days she conceived and after ten months gave birth to twin daughters. The name of the first girl was Sleep and the name of the second was Tears.

When the two girls grew up Tears went to her mother and said, 'I have no place to live; tell me where I should go'. Her mother replied, 'You are to live in the throats of men'. Sleep too asked her mother, 'Tell me where I should go', and the mother replied, 'You are to live in the eyelids of men'. For this reason Tears have lived in the throat and, when a man is sad he sobs and sends the water up into his eyes.

26

RAJNENGI PARDHAN

Sunpuri, Mandla District

There never used to be tears. When Sahadeo, the father of Mahadeo, went to his wife he was able to continue for six months without rest. As a result Sahadeo's wife conceived; when it was time for the child to be born, the feet were presented first. For two months the feet remained sticking out; then half the body came—that took six months; and from the eyes of the poor woman fire began to flash. She cried, 'O husband, fire is flashing from my eyes. I am bound to die. Save me somehow or other.' Sahadeo had magic water with him in a gourd. He muttered a charm over it and threw it on his wife's eyes. Her eyes cooled and water began to flow from them. At once the child was born. The child was Mahadeo. After that people began to cry.

VIII

The Origin of Laughter

27

GOND

Pakhri, Mandla District

Formerly men could not laugh. There was a Ganda called Manghia. He had a son and a daughter. In his courtyard was a hollow bel tree in which lived a spirit called Hasni Mai. This spirit one day caught hold of the mouth of Manghia's daughter and it swelled up. Manghia gave the girl a lot of medicine but it had no effect.

Then Manghia had a dream. 'In Duganigarh lives a man of the Bhima tribe on whom there rides the god Aswari Pat. If you can bring him here your daughter will be cured'. Manghia went at once and brought the Bhima. Directly he saw the girl Aswari Pat came upon him. The god demanded rice and chickens and when these were offered and he was pleased, the swelling of the girl's face subsided and she began to laugh. Aswari Pat said to Hasni Mai, 'Always live happily like this'. The result is that Hasni Mai now makes people laugh everywhere in the world.

28

GADABA

Puttapad, Koraput District

Of old when the earth was made and men and women were born, among the first were Janni Gadaba and his wife, whose name we forget and does not matter. They lived in Kasagarh. In those days men neither laughed nor wept. This Gadaba and his wife had no children. One day the Gadaba went to bring *nul* branches for his wife to make yarn from the bark. He found Jhoka Deota sitting with his eyes shut under a pipal tree. When the Gadaba saw him, he thought, 'He must have some important business here : I'll sit down also and see what it is.' He sat down, and seven years passed. Then Jhoka Deota opened his eyes. The first thing he saw was Janni Gadaba and he said. 'What do you want ?' 'I want a son', said Janni. The Deota blessed him and said, 'Go and you will get a child.' Janni went home and his wife soon conceived and in due time bore a son. Janni went to tell Jhoka Deota about it and said, 'What ought I to do now'. The Deota said, 'Now you must be happy, for you have a son. You must laugh.' Janni went home laughing: he reached the village and shouted with laughter. He went from house to house; no one had heard such a noise before, but they joined him, and soon everyone was laughing.

After seven years the child died, and Janni went giggling, chuckling and laughing to tell Jhoka Deota about it. But the Deota rebuked him. 'You've got to be sad now. Stop laughing and weep instead.' So Janni went home weeping: he reached the village and shouted with sorrow, and they all joined in his tears.

IX

The Penis

'Of all the sexual organs', says Havelock Ellis in a justly famous passage, 'the penis is without doubt that which has most powerfully impressed the human imagination. It is the very emblem of generation, and everywhere men have contemplated it with a mixture of reverence and shuddering awe that has sometimes, even among civilized peoples, amounted to horror and disgust. Its image is worn as an amulet to ward off evil and invoked as a charm to call forth blessing. The sexual organs were once the most sacred object on which a man could place his hands to swear an inviolate oath, just as now he takes up the Testament. Even in the traditions of the great classic civilization which we inherit the penis is *fascinus*, the symbol of all fascination. In the history of human culture it has had far more than a merely human significance; it has been the symbol of all the generative force of Nature, the embodiment of creative energy in the animal and vegetable worlds alike, an image to be held aloft for worship, the sign of all unconscious ecstasy. As a symbol, the sacred phallus, it has been woven in and out of all the highest and deepest human conceptions, so intimately that it is possible to see it everywhere, that it is possible to fail to see it anywhere.'[1]

In India particularly, the phallus, in the form of the linga of Siva or Mahadeo, has received due honour, an honour only possible in a country which, at its best, is singularly free of sexual inhibitions and hypocrisy. Phallic-worship in India is of great antiquity, though

[1] Havelock Ellis, ii, i, 121.

the passages referring to it in the *Mahabharata* are comparatively recent interpolations.[1] Siva and Parvati die in the embrace of love and are reborn as Linga and Yoni. Siva tears off his organ and throws it away: it drives into the earth and sticks there. Meyer summarizes the account in the great epic: 'Siva's member is always stiff, and this because of his unbroken chastity; therefore it is worshipped by the world. It is always kept standing fixedly up; he has a great, upstanding, pleasing linga; he is head warden of the phallus, and appears in the penis, as being his origin; the all-shaped god is in the linga, and through all the ages of the world he has been worshiped by the other gods, by the spirits, and the seers, in the linga; the phallus-worshipper wins the highest happiness and Siva's full approval.'[2]

So too Lingo, the cult-hero of the Muria, is so named because his *ling* stands up strong and straight before him, and thus is a symbol of his chastity, for he is the purest of all the heroes of Middle India—a great contrast to the amorous Bhimsen and the lustful Nanga Baiga.

The aboriginals of Middle India tell us that ancient man had a great penis, as mighty and even longer than an elephant's trunk: it was the symbol of the miraculous sexual energy that is often attributed to the traditional heroes and elders of a tribe. In modern times man has lost many of his former powers. Interference with old tribal custom has caused the Baiga penis to shrink. Woman has brought down the splendid organ of antiquity, cutting off all but a fraction that a man can hold in his two hands.

The tradition of the long penis is probably widely distributed and is certainly old. Thus Ktesias describes the swarthy hairy pigmies living in the middle of India as having 'thick privates, so large that they depend even to their ankles'.[3] The motif is known to the Santal of the Damin-i-koh, who have stories similar to those in the text; one describes how a girl struck at a boy's penis which was finally gnawed to its proper length by mice; another, of a more ribald character, shows the organ being used to knock down berries from a tree and as a bridge to take people over a river.[4] The Eastern Rengma Naga describe the sex-hero Zosheto as having 'a sexual organ so long that he was able to wind it round his waist'. He had

[1] See J.R.A.S., 1907, 337 ff. [2] Meyer, ii, 339. [3] McCrindle, 300.

[4] Private communication from Mr W. G. Archer. For a similar tradition elsewhere, see M. Mead, *The Mountain Arapesh* (*Anth. Papers, A. M. N. H.*, xxxvii, 1940, Part 11, 360).

a secret intrigue with a woman, but there was no need for him to enter her house to love her. Instead he made a hole in the wall opposite her bed and standing outside the house he used to have connection with her through it.[1]

'The most peculiar feature of the (Lepcha) stories dealing with anthropomorphic characters', says Gorer, 'is the preponderating role played by the genitalia, which are almost endowed with independent life; various semi-heroic humans and supernaturals possess genitalia of peculiar formation and characteristics, and the adventures of these organs together with the bodies to which they are attached are told in a number of tales'.[2]

The motif of the exchange of the private parts, either between a man and woman, or a human being and an animal, is found in the classical literature. The Sthūnakarna episode in the *Mahabharata*, where a Yaksa takes pity on a princess and lends her his sex, is echoed in a tale in the *Arabian Nights*.[3] A closer paralled to the tribal legends, however, occurs in the *Ramayana*. As Indra is leaving Ahalya after seducing her, he is caught by the mighty sage Gautama who curses him with the loss of his testes. Indra goes to the assembly of gods headed by Agni and begs them to restore his virility. The gods approach the heavenly Manes who remove the testes of a ram and graft them on the body of Indra.[4] In this case, however, the ram is not compensated, as it would have been in an aboriginal story, by the gift of human parts in exchange.

29

BAIGA

Silpuri, Mandla District

Every Baiga used to have a very long penis, like an elephant's trunk, and we took its help in making jungle clearings. But since Government has stopped our *bewar* (shifting cultivation) and robbed us of our hills, the Baiga penis has shrunk to a little thing that a man can hold in his hand.

[1] Mills, *The Rengma Nagas*, 260 f. [2] Gorer, 226.

[3] *The Thousand Nights and One Night* (Translated by Powys Mathers from the French of J. Mardus), 573-76.

[4] *Srimad-Valmiki Ramayana*. Edited by T. R. Krishnacharya and T. R. Vyasacharya. Cants I, Chap. 48, 16-34 and 49, 1-10. I owe these references to Mr Saurin Roy.

30

BAIGA

Kenda Zamindari

In Bhoramgarh lived Bhoram Deo and his wife Mata Shodhar. In her old age the woman conceived and bore a son. On the day he was born the boy's organ was one-and-a-quarter cubits long, and his parents called him Linga. As he grew older the organ grew until it was two-and-a-half cubits. Linga was very embarrassed by it and left his parents to go and live alone on Suranpahar. There he lived the life of a saint and never looked into the face of woman. Nearby on Naksar Hill lived Bai Bidyarsin's daughter, Bai Dulaurin, a young girl, only twelve years old and not mature. One day the girl met Linga in the forest and he liked her and forgot his saintliness. He tried to take her by force, but she ran away. He chased her for twice twelve miles and when he caught her she pulled out her knife and cut two cubits off his organ. Full of rage and pain Linga cut off half the girl's nose and she turned into Nakti Devi. The hill where this happened became known as Nakti Dongar. Linga's organ turned into a stone, and those who have no children go there to offer sacrifice.

31

BHUIYA

Raisua, Bonai State

At first Boram Burha had an enormously long penis. His wife had no breasts, no vulva, nothing. But Boram Burha had a hole in his own calf. Boram Burha's penis used to get very hungry—for it could not get its proper food and at night it used to crawl out of the house and eat beans growing on a tree in the garden. Buram Burha's wife said one day. 'Who knows what creature is eating up all our beans!' and she hid behind the tree with her axe. As the penis began to pick the beans and eat them, she struck at it: Boram Burha grasped it with both his hands, and that much was saved. The rest was cut off. Boram Burha went to Dharam Deota and asked, 'What am I to do for children? This woman has no vulva to bear them, no breasts to feed them.' Dharam Deota cut out the hole from Boram Burha's own calf and put it on the woman. At that time women had beards. Dharam Deota cut off this woman's beard and gave it to a goat to wear. Since then children have been born in the world.

32

DHANWAR

Dhawaitikri, Uprora Zamindari

On Naktidongar Hill was Nakti Pat. Nearby was Bardorkonha village. In this village lived elephants, she-elephants, men and women. One day there was to be a marriage in another elephant-village. The elephants of Bardorkonha prepared to escort their girl with a wedding-party. Now in those days man's organ was big as a pestle and woman's was wide as a mortar, but the elephant's was very small. The elephants said to the men in their village, 'We are going to a marriage; lend us your organs and we will leave ours with you as security.' The she-elephants also said to the women in their villages, 'We are going to a marriage; lend us your organs and we will leave ours with you as security.' So they exchanged and the elephants stuck the human organs on, and found they could take them off and fit them in again at will, and everyone was pleased and amused. When the wedding-party went away, the men and women stood on Naktidongar Hill and waved and shouted to it.

When they came back the men went to the elephants and the women went to the she-elephants and asked for their organs. 'Here are yours,' they said, 'and see how carefully we have used them.' But the elephants had gone to it with such vigour that the pestles were stuck in firmly and they could not remove them. And the she-elephants had been husked so hard that the mortars now were part of their bodies and they could not remove them. That is why today men and women have such small organs, and the elephants and she-elephants have large ones.

33

GADABA

Kujambo, Koraput District

In former days the penis was very long and we used to wind it round the waist. Where the clitoris is now there used to hang a tail that was a cubit and a quarter long. So long was the penis that it quickly wore women out and they lived only for a few years after they were mature.

One day after a wife had died of exhaustion as usual the husband took a new wife in her place, and she was sitting cutting up mangoes with her knife. The husband drank a great deal of rice-beer and came drunk to his wife to lie with her. That woman had a son and he was sitting by his mother. The woman was angry and said, 'When the child is sitting here, how can you do such a thing?' She picked up the knife with which she was cutting the mangoes and chopped off her husband's penis. The man seized his organ to save it and only that much was preserved.

Afterwards when the man went to his wife he found that now his organ was so small that the woman's tail interfered with his pleasure. One night he distracted her attention and cut it off.

34

GOND

Pakhri, Mandla District

In former times, the penis grew from a man's forehead: it was three hands long and hung down in front like an elephant's trunk. Woman's vulva was in the middle of her chest. But one day Bhairopal went in a marriage-party to a certain village. He was chasing the girls with his long trunk, shaking it at them as if he would beat them. The Manjhi's wife was angry at this and came out with a knife to cut it off. He grasped it in his hands but he could only save four fingers' breadth. The Manjhi's wife cut off the rest and threw it away. But now the stump sticking out from the forehead did not look nice, and men went to Mahadeo and begged him to put it somewhere else. He placed it between the thighs. Then Parvati went to him and said, 'It is not good that men should have their thing so low down and women should have it so high up.' Mahadeo kicked her between the thighs and made a hole there.

35

GOND

Bilhar, Bilaspur District

When the first child was born, his mother sprinkled his penis with hot and cold water. When the boy went for the first time to a girl, he found fire inside her. Because of the fire, the skin of his penis shrank. That is why the prepuce can be pulled back.

36

JHORIA

Lamda, Koraput District

Long ago a Gadaba and his wife lived on Jarahodongar. Their parents were dead, and there were very few people then in the world. Woman had only a tiny hole for urine between her legs, and the man's stick was very thin and slender. The Gadaba and his wife lived together for many years but they had no child. One night, after a lot of rice-beer and a heavy meal, they lay down together and fell asleep, and a rat began to burrow into the woman between her legs. She was so sound asleep that she felt nothing, even when the rat enlarged the hole and got right into her.

There was a cat in the house, and while the rat was busy on the woman, it bit off the man's penis and ran off to the goatshed, and said to the goat, 'Lend me your organ for an hour or two, and fix this one on instead for the time being.' The goat was agreeable and the cat put the goat's organ on the man.

When morning came, the cat woke the woman and told her the rat was inside her. The woman screamed with fright, but the cat only laughed. When the rat came out it jumped to and fro, from thigh to thigh, the woman trying vainly to catch it; until at last it ran up over her belly and escaped. The marks it made with its claws as it jumped about in fright can still be seen on any woman's thighs and belly.

When the goat asked the cat to return its organ, the cat only laughed. That is how the male and female organs got their present size.

37

KOND

Meriahpatta, Koraput District

The penis used to be very long and men had to wind it round and round their waists. Pusrudi was afraid that the unmarried girls in the dormitories would be killed and one day when she was with Burha Pinnu she cut off his organ with a wooden spoon and reduced it to its present length.

38

KOYA

Akarpalli, Koraput District

One day a woman was engaged in roasting rice. A man went by on his way to plough in his fields and asked her for fire. She was sitting with her legs stretched out and he saw her thing and liked it. He thought, 'If I ask for it, she will never give it to me.' So he went behind her and sent out his long penis : it went circling and curving round, and at last went in. The woman lifted up her rice-husker and brought it down with a bang on the penis, cutting it in two. The seed came out : she planted it in an anthill and a mushroom grew from it : that is why the mushroom is always slimy. For this reason too woman wears a pubic cloth, so that men may not see her thing.

39

KOYA

Siarimal, Koraput District

The same story as above, with the variations that the woman was parching gram-pulse, the boy made a hole in a fence, and the woman cut off the penis with a sickle.

40

LANJHIA SAORA

Munisingi, Ganjam District

Kornja Saora and his wife were old. They had nothing but their only daughter and a cock and hen. So to keep their home together they brought a Kinnarsing boy for their daughter. This boy and the cock became great friends. So many days passed. Then one evening the boys assembled with their drums and trumpets to go to dance in another village. In those days man's penis was very small but the cock's was big. The Kinnarsing, forseeing that he might have need of strength, said to the cock, 'Friend, lend me your organ and I'll give you mine as security. When I come back from the dance we can exchange again.'

But the boys danced and danced till the sun rose upon them, and with its light the cock's organ stuck to the boy and when he met the cock he found his penis also was stuck. From that day the cock has been dumb and men have had the size and strength of a cock's organ.

41

OJHA

Nipaniya, Raipur District

Ghughus Raja and Ghughus Rani had a son called Alakhniranjan. Nal Raja and Nal Rani had a daughter called Dharti Kaniya. Ghughus Raja and his family lived up above, but not right in the sky; they were in between, not on earth nor yet in the sky. While they were wondering what to do about this, and how to find good earth to live on, Dharti Kaniya as a beautiful maiden of twelve years flew into the air and approached Alakhniranjan. When he saw her he wanted to devour her. For he had no penis and he could only find pleasure in swallowing. But Dharti Kaniya thought, 'If he swallows me there will never be earth for people to live on.' At that moment five gods were born and they came to save her. Among them was Mahadeo. He went to Dharti Kaniya and between her legs with his nails he made an oval opening. He cut off his thumb and stuck it onto Alakhniranjan's body. On Mahadeo's ears were two swellings. He cut these off and gave them to the boy as testicles. Then Alakhniranjan went to Dharti Kaniya and the world was saved.

42

PANKA

Sanhrwachhapar, Mandla District

Woman used to have a round vulva; it was fifteen hands wide. The penis was sixteen hands long. Men used to approach their wives like animals, taking them from behind. A woman was stirring pulse on the hearth with a wooden spoon. A man came running and cried '*Hohn honh honh*' like a horse with his great penis uncoiled. That woman was faithful to her husband, a good woman. She was angry and struck at the thing with her wooden spoon. The man grasped it with his hands, but all he could save was ten fingers' breadth. The rest she cut off with her spoon. It fell on the ground and the woman picked it up and threw it on the fire.

That woman cursed men and said, 'From now onwards you will have to do it lying on the ground'. Then the vulva too changed its shape, it became small and long and was no more round. When the man first went to his woman with the cut penis, the skin which was cut round slipped back and that was the origin of the prepuce.

43

PARDHAN

Kolwakero, Mandla District

A Pardhan and a Gond girl were in love with one another. One day the Pardhan went to the girl's house when she was putting rice in a pot to cook. He said to her, 'Come soon.'. 'I'll come after a little while when I've finished this rice.'

The Pardhan went behind the house and waited there for a while. But he was full of desire and grew more and more impatient. Inside the house, near where he was standing outside, the girl was cooking. There was a hole in the wall. Into the hole the impatient Pardhan put his penis, which in those days was fifteen hands long, and it sought his love. The girl was annoyed. 'I told him to wait till I had finished,' she said. She threw the boiling water over it and hit it so hard with her spoon that she cut it off. She took the piece and gave it to her horse; that is why the horse's member is now so long.

X

THE VULVA

Although the yoni is joined with the linga as an object of veneration in India, the female organ has rarely been able to compete with the male in the feelings of awe and fascination that it excites. By comparison with the penis, the vulva is insignificant, negative, even though aesthetically it is so much more beautiful. The grace and beauty of the vulva was recognized by Indian writers of antiquity. The *Ramayana* describes, though through the mouth of Rawan, 'the secret parts of woman spread wide and firmly swelling, the thighs as elephant's trunks'. The secret parts of Rambha are pictured as 'like a golden wheel, decked with a gold band; they are embodied heaven '.[1] In the *Mahabharata* a woman is said to have ' lovely secret parts, rising like a river island.'[2] Traditional Hindu erotics classifies the vulva as the Padmani or lotus-scented, the Chitrini or bright-coloured, the Shankhini or snail, and the Hastini or elephant. Vatsyana describes the vulva of the Padmini type as resembling the lotus bud just opened, and its love-seed perfumed like the lily that has newly burst.

The aboriginals of Middle India indulge in similar classifications, though the standard of measurement is not beauty but value in intercourse. The *kokma*, with its prominent labia, is considered ' very good ', so is the *sutei*, 'like a shell from the river bed '. The *chepti* is small and boney and is believed to give little pleasure. The *chena* of a multipara, which the tribesmen describe by words which may be translated ' untidy ' or ' slipshod ', is too large and broad. There are other, coarser, definitions which I need not give here ; those I have mentioned are sufficient to indicate the utilitarian rather than the aesthetic interests of the aboriginals.

The myths describing the origin of the vulva are of considerable variety. Some resemble those about the penis : the vulva, like the penis, was formerly in another part of the body—on the forehead or in the calf.[3] A woman exchanged her organ with that of an elephant (the traditional Hastini vulva ?), just as her husband did with his. An enormous vulva grows small just as the great penis shrinks. Probably the most common—and rather obvious—idea is that woman originally had no aperture for intromission. It was made when Mahadeo kicked it open between the thighs or scratched a hole with his nails, when Mahesur Risi pulled the skin away, when a snake bit or a rat burrowed below the Mons Veneris. In one story a semi-divine being has a hole in his calf: he cuts it out and gives it to his wife so that he can enjoy her sexually.[4]

[1] Meyer, iii, 432 f. [2] iv. 14, 18 f.

[3] A Santal tale, sent to me by Mr W. G. Archer, gives the original location of the vulva as in the armpit.

[4] *Woman* assembles a few legends about the origin of the female organs. The Southern Slavs declare that St. Elias clove the first woman through the middle. The Bakongo negroes say that when the Creator sewed up woman to suit his fancy, his thread was too short, so a piece remains open to this day. A Samoan legend tells how a man cleft open the first woman with a shark's tooth. The Queenslanders say that the Great Spirit made little children of clay and before putting them in their mother's bodies, opened them on a wooden fork. Australian aboriginals on the Prosperpine River declare that woman was cleft open with a slice of pandanus root, so that she could be distinguished from man — *Woman*, i, 281 f. The Kiwai Papuans have a myth that at first woman had no vulva, but the mythical hero Marunogere bored an opening with a bone dagger and poured pig's blood into the hole.—Landtmann, *The Kiwai Papuans*, 114.

44

BAIGA

Kapripani, Mandla District

Of old, woman had no vulva. There was an old man who gave his whole life to the search for pleasure. But since there was no such thing as a vulva how could he find it? One year he sowed a field of channa-pulse and had a very good crop. Many women used to go to steal it. He thought he would frighten them. He lay down in the field, his body flat, his pole upright. Presently a woman came to steal. When she saw the man, she was very angry. She put two big lumps of earth on either side of his body and squatted down on them, intending to excrete all over him. But the earth broke and she fell violently on the pole, which pierced her body. At last there was a vulva, and the old man succeeded in his search.

45

BISON-HORN MARIA

Gadapal, Bastar State

Once the vulva lived below the knee of the left leg, in the soft part. One day a chicken pecked at it and it jumped up between the thighs and has lived there ever since.

46

BISON-HORN MARIA

Phulpar, Bastar State

Once the woman's thing was in the calf of her left leg. A cock pecked at it until it bled, and it ran up the woman's leg to hide in the hair between her thighs.

47

BISON-HORN MARIA

Dugeli, Bastar State

Originally Maria women did not have a vulva. One of them went to relieve herself near an ant-hill. A snake came out and bit her between the thighs so deeply that there came an opening in the flesh.

48

JUANG

Kajuria, Keonjhar State

At the beginning of the world, woman had a vulva but there was no opening to it. Mahesur Risi pulled the flesh away and threw it into a stream where it turned into a leech.

49

KAMAR

Bindra-Nawagarh Zamindari

A Gond peasant had a son. He was married, while still a child, to a motiari. When the father went to bring the girl to her husband, he taught her as you might teach a parrot. 'Daughter-in-law, never put your foot in the marks of a cow's hoofs, where the earth rises up around the hoof-print.'

One day the girl was taking food to her father-in-law who was ploughing in the big field. It was the time of rain and the chief farmers had sown most of the rice. Both the high and the level lands were covered with water. As the girl went, she thought, 'Why has he told me not to put my foot in a hoof-print?' So thinking she put her foot in just such a hoof-print and the mud splashed up, all over her vulva.

The girl ran *chechak-pechak*, waddling to and fro, to her father-in-law. When he saw her, he said, 'Why don't you run straight? You come as if you were drunk.' 'The mud splashed from the hoof-print all over my thing,' said the girl. 'Go to the stream and wash it,' said the old man. The girl sat in the water to wash.

In those days the vulva hung down outside, like a bag, swinging like a gourd at the end of a pole. Men and women used to stand for intercourse. The girl's bag swung to and fro in the stream. A crab saw it and caught it in its claws. The girl screamed and the father-in-law ran to the place, lifting his ox-goad to kill the crab. When the crab saw this, it pulled the bag away from the girl's body and took it into its hole. Since that day the vulva has been flat with the body and a girl must lie down for intercourse.

50

KOND

Meriahpatta, Koraput District

The vulva used to be in the calf of the right leg, but a hen pecked at it and it jumped for safety to the hollow between the thighs.

51

KOYA

Akarpalli, Koraput District

Once the vulva was in the middle of the forehead, but people thought it did not look nice there, so it went to the arm-pit. But it was difficult to do the work there, so it went to the navel. Thence it went to the soft hollow behind the knee. But one day a hen pecked at it and it jumped up to hide between the thighs.

Because it was once in the forehead, women part their hair and put a red mark on the forehead ; because it was once in the arm-pit, hair grows there ; because it was once in the navel, there is still a sort of hole there ; because it was once in the soft hollow behind the knee, you can still see it if you bend your leg.[1]

XI

The Clitoris

This highly sensitive and excitable organ, richly endowed with erectile roots and nerves, has been called by Havelock Ellis ' the key to the genital apparatus in woman from the psychic point of view.' Yet its appearance is so insignificant that its full importance has been recognized only in modern times—indeed Realdus Columbus claimed that he had discovered it. Here he was wrong for, as Havelock

[1] With this compare a ribald Gond story from Motinala, Mandla District. 'An Ahir boy was married, but he was angry with his parents, for he did not know what to do with a girl. One day his grandmother came and said, "At least do something with her." "But what can I do ?" "Lie with her." "But where ?" " Where it looks red." So that night, when the boy saw the red mark on his wife's forehead, he took her there, and she was very angry. The next day the old woman said to the boy, " Where there is hair," and that night the boy took her in the arm-pit. The next day the old woman said to the boy, " Where there is a hole ", and that night the boy took her in the navel. Finally the old woman said, " Where you find all three ", and that night the wife was satisfied.'

Ellis says again, 'the Arabs appear to have been very familiar with it and, from the various names they gave it, clearly understood the important part it plays in generating voluptuous emotion. But it was known in classic antiquity; the Greeks called it μύρτον the myrtle-berry; Galen and Soranus called it νύμφη because it is covered as a bride is veiled, while the old Latin name was *tentigo*, from its power of entering into erection, and *columella*, the little pillar, from its shape. The modern term, which is Greek, refers to the sensitiveness of the part to voluptuous titillation'.[1]

By the aboriginals of Middle India the role of the clitoris (*tita*) is fairly well understood. It is usually displayed in carvings and drawings of the vulva. 'It is red like the tongue of a bird: its work is to bring out the woman's water (orgasm)'. 'It looks like a nose: its task is to excite.' 'The clitoris goes out to meet the penis, and in their meeting is delight.' It is believed that if the clitoris is 'bent', or if its 'nose is blunt', a woman will be barren.

In the stories recorded here, however, the clitoris is regarded as either an ornament or a joke. Mahadeo makes it with one of his finger-nails, to be the watchman and chaprasi of the vulva. It is a nail which an angry blacksmith drove into his wife's vulva to shut its mouth. It is a bit of stuff which Mahapurub had left over after making man and woman and which he stuck on the vulva as an ornament. It is the claw of a crab which caught a woman's vulva while she was fishing.

52

BAIGA

Jalda, Mandla District

One day, before women had a clitoris, a woman went to fish in a stream by throwing water out of a pool. As she squatted in the water feeling with her hands for the fish, a crab caught her vulva with one of its claws and she screamed with pain. Machhandar Mata heard her and told her to pull the crab's claw off and that it would stay where it had bitten her and in future give her as much pleasure as it had then given her pain.

The woman broke the claw from the crab's body and returned to the village with the claw hanging in front of her. When the people saw it they laughed at her, but she told them of Machhandar Mata's blessing and as she spoke every woman in the village found she had a claw growing in her vulva.

[1] Havelock Ellis, ii, i, 130.

53

BISON-HORN MARIA

Bara Harmamunda, Bastar State

Mahapurub was making mankind out of some stuff or other. He completed the arms, legs, head, body and privates. He looked in his hand and saw that only a small bit of stuff was left. 'What shall I do with this?' So pondered Mahapurub in his mind. He looked at the woman's body: the vulva was bare and naked, without decoration. 'It must have some ornament', said Mahapurub, and he fixed the bit of stuff on the top of the vulva.

54

GADABA

Thal Duralu, Koraput District

There was a Kamar. He was sitting in his forge making iron nails. The Dissari wanted nails to drive into a tree at the boundary, for a tiger was destroying the cattle. While the Kamar made nails, his wife went out to piss. She went behind the forge. When she pissed, the noise she made was *chher-chher-chher*. Now that Kamar's name was Chheram. When he heard the noise, he went out and said, 'Who is that calling me?' There was no one there but his wife pissing and he said, 'Was it you who called me?' 'No, I was only pissing.' 'Then who called Chheram, Chheram?' 'That was my vulva: it always says that when I piss.'

When he heard that, the Kamar was furious with his wife's vulva for taking his name. He had a nail in his hand. He threw the woman on the ground and drove the nail into the vulva to shut its mouth. There it is: it is the clitoris now; and now when women piss the noise they make is *sir-sir-sir*.

55

GOND

Pakhri, Mandla District

When Mahadeo kicked the vulva open, he put a nail from one of his fingers at the top. This is the clitoris. It is the watchman and chaprasi of the vulva.

56

MURIA

Berma, Bastar State

There was a marriage and the Belosa was very busy setting the girls to work, cooking, cleaning, making plates and cups of leaves. Suddenly she found she had lost her clitoris (*tita*). She went hunting everywhere and presently met the titur bird and borrowed a clitoris from her. She promised to return it, but never did, and now the bird is always crying, '*Tita de*; give me my clitoris'.[1]

57

RAJNENGI PARDHAN

Patangarh, Mandla District

In the beginning each part of the body went where it would and of its own accord. One day the breasts picked a quarrel with the vulva and drove every vulva in the world away to the hills. That night there was dismay in the homes of gods and men, and next morning they all set out to the hills to bring their wives' vulvas back. But it was a long task, for the vulva is a thing not quickly caught, and only with great difficulty could they bring them back and put them into place. And by the time they returned home, some old women had already died, and there were too many vulvas. Men cut them into small pieces and stuck them onto the top of the vulvas of the other women. In this way the clitoris was made.

XII

The Origin of Menstruation

Very few accounts of the origin of menstruation have been recorded, though this does not mean, of course, that such accounts do not exist. The Agasa washerman of Mysore traces the origin of his caste to an incident connected with menstruation and it is

[1] This story is known to the Baiga, Gond and Pardhan of the Central Provinces. The bird is probably the Red-wattled Lapwing.

interesting that, as in the stories in the text, menstruation is associated with the Hindu goddesses. Five goddesses, so the Agasa legend runs, Sarasvati, Lakshmi, Parvati, Sachi and Chaya found it very difficult to get anyone to wash their clothes for them during the period of their monthly defilement. One day they saw a woman coming towards them with a boy and they asked her to do the work, promising to pay her anything she wanted.

The woman took the clothes to the sea in a bundle, and finding no slab to wash the clothes on, cut off the head of her son, used his blood as colouring matter, eyes as indigo, the flesh as fuller's earth, the back as a slab, legs as fuel, forearms as ironing rods, and the abdomen as the pot. She obtained fire by praying to Agni, the god of fire, and having thus cleaned the clothes, took them back to the Divine consorts. They were naturally gratified at the result, but not finding the boy with her, they questioned the woman, who reluctantly informed them of the use she had made of his mortal frame. Highly touched by his fate, they asked her to call him by name, and when she did so the boy stood smiling before her. The gods were pleased on hearing this, promised her a further boon as she desired, which was formulated as knee-deep water for washing, ankle-deep food as wages, and a monopoly for washing clothes.[1]

A Lepcha account of the origin of menstruation which is not unlike some of the stories in the text is given by Gorer.

'Originally women had their vulvas on the top of their heads. Then the menstrual blood used to flow all over their faces and it looked so unpleasant that the gods transferred the blood to men's knees; but then, when they went hunting and travelled about the country the blood used to drip everywhere, and Narzong-nyou saw this and was displeased thereat. Moreover the gods still did not like the vulvas on the top of the heads, so they called for volunteers to move this unpleasant thing. Different birds essayed the task and at last one of them pecked and pecked and eventually moved the vulva to the forehead; there it stuck and then after a time moved slowly to the nose, the upper lip and the chin; at the chin it stuck a year, then travelled slowly down sticking five years at the navel; eventually it got to its proper place where it now is and where it is hidden. Seeing this hidden place Narzong-nyou who had invented menstruation so that people could tell when babies were going to be born retransferred the blood thither.'[2]

In Middle India myths about menstruation are of three main types: those that regard it in the light of a Fall due to the eating of a forbidden fruit or vegetable or to some other act of dis-

[1] Nanjundayya and Iyer, ii, 2.

[2] Gorer, 226 f.

obedience to the male, those that say it was instituted to protect women against enemies who would dishonour them and those that attribute its origin to the bite of a snake or animal. There are several examples of the first type in the text. Of the second there are more examples in the folk-tales. It is a very common folktale motif for a heroine captured by some ogre or other enemy to say that she has taken a vow not to yield to a man for twelve years or that she has been cursed with perpetual menstruation for a similar period. Thus the Hinduized Agaria and many Gond and Pardhan in Mandla say that when Rawan carried off Sita, she menstruated for twelve years as a protection. The Pando of Uprora also tell a long and involved tale of Draupadi who was attacked by Kichakmal, 'in whose kingdom was a rule that whenever anyone was married, the girl must go first to the Raja,' an interesting echo of the *jus primae noctis*. When Kichakmal approached Draupadi, 'blood flowed from her and the monster was afraid'. She said she would be ready after eight days, but Bhimsen disguised himself in her clothes and when the ravisher came, tore him to pieces. 'From this began the flowering of women, and they are unclean for eight days in memory of the deliverance from Kichakmal'.

58

BAIGA

Bohi, Pandaria Zamindari

(From *Essays in Anthropology presented to S. C. Roy*, 145)

Amardevi wanted to put a flower in Parvati's belly. As she slept the goddess put a lotus in her mouth. At once blood came from her. Whenever a drop of blood fell on the ground, there was a lotus. The lotus lived three days and died. This went on for three months. Then Mahadeo picked all the flowers and burnt them. But he dreamt that without flowers there could be no fruit. The next day he saw a fruit in the midst of the lotus.

59

BAIGA

Silpiri, Mandla District

(From ibid., 146)

In the beginning, blood used to flow from Nanga Baiga's left knee for five days in every month. One day he was summoned to the court of the Raja. His sister said, 'If they see this, we'll be dishonoured, they'll laugh at us. Give the blood to me.' Nanga Baiga said, 'Then you'll be dishonoured.' She said, 'We will manage somehow.' So he gave the blood from his knee to her, and she found blood flowing from her vulva. She tied a cloth between her legs and stopped it flowing down.

60

BAIGA

Pandpur, Mandla District

(From *The Baiga*, 209)

Nanga Baiga and Nanga Baigin lived in the Nanga Pahar near a deep well hidden in the jungle. Nanga Baigin always had to go to a pond for water, it was a long way off. She wanted to go to the well, but Nanga Baiga wouldn't let her. But one morning, when Nanga Baiga had gone to cut his clearing, she took a broom and went to clean the well. For a long time, she couldn't find the way, but after wandering here and there she discovered it, and at last reached the well.

In those days no blood flowed from women during their period, but it was then that they had greatest pleasure : the blood of all the women in the world was in the well. That blood was like the sea ; it was alive, it stirred with waves. When Nanga Baigin saw it, she laughed at the sport and at her laughter the sea of blood fell calm. Then the blood sank down, down, down to the bottom of the sea that is below the world. When the blood was shut down there in the darkness, it began to ask, 'Who has imprisoned us here ?' It was living blood : it awoke : it rushed up through the earth : it spouted up in the well. It covered Nanga Baigin's face, her nose, her arms, her belly, her legs. She began to have pain in her belly. After that every month blood flowed from her.

When this happened, Nanga Baigin fainted. When her daughter fainted, Mother Earth trembled a little. Nanga Baiga felt it in his clearing and he ran home to see what had happened to his wife. There he found a river of blood flowing, so great a flood it was that all the gods were hiding behind trees for fear of it. None dared approach her. Nanga Baiga came to within two miles. But a little of the blood touched him and he became impure.

Nanga Baiga took his axe and went away, away, away through the forest, beyond the seven seas and the sixteen rivers, till he reached the place where Guru Binjhwar and his wife were living. They were sitting on a little stone in the middle of the sea, their faces to the sun. When he heard the story, Guru Binjhwar took his fan and his wife took the gourd and they sought for the reason of the trouble. After three days the Guru said to Nanga Baiga, 'You can go now : your wife is well again.'

When Nanga Baiga reached home, he found that his wife had had a bath and was waiting for him, a pot of water in her hand. He took her into the house and said, 'Why did you go to the well ? You have spread this disease to every woman in the world.'

But Guru Binjhwar sent the blood to the moon. That is why it comes to women according to the moon.

61

BINJHWAR BAIGA

Baihar, Balaghat District

Earth was a maiden. All the gods gathered to seek her in marriage. They were dressed in their best clothes and covered with ornaments. For a joke they called the Baiga, for they thought, 'She will certainly put the garland of her choice on one of us, and not on that dirty fellow.' The Baiga, dressed in mohlain leaves, came there, and sat on the edge of the crowd.

The Earth Maiden walked round looking at every one. Last of all she saw the Baiga hiding himself. When she saw him she put the garland round his neck. The Baiga took her to his house.

He made a wedding-booth of saleh and dumar branches; he made cloth of bark and clothed the girl with it. He made the feast with the grains of spear grass and called the bears and tigers for the marriage-party.

He made a paste of saja flowers instead of haldi. The tiger's wife led the Baiga and the Earth Maiden round the pole.

The Baiga made a long trough and filled it with gruel for the tigers. He put two-and-a-half seeds of spear grass into a great pot, filled it with water and by his magic it was filled with rice. Then at night they slept.

When the Baiga first went to the Earth Maiden, blood came from her. She said, 'Today blood has flowed from me. Now for fifteen days my head will be unclean.' Then this happened to all women.

62

BONDO

Mundlipada, Koraput District

When the earth was first made, no one used to die. But one day a snake bit a man, and he died. His wife wept continuously and abused Goigekko Raja, lord of death who had stolen her husband.

Goigekko Raja was angry when he heard the woman and cursed her. As abuse has come from your mouth, so blood will come from your vulva. As you have lost a man now, so men will avoid you then.' Since that day women have had a period of blood-flowing every month.

63

DHANWAR

Dhawapur, Matin Zamindari

In Bindraban Koeli-Kachhar lived Bulbusur Gond and his Gondin. He had a son. He married that son to an orphan girl when they both were babies. They did not know that they were married, but they grew up together thinking that they were brother and sister. Bulbusur and his Gondin died and told them nothing. The two lived in the jungle, they lived and ate, saying, 'We are brother and sister'. They never looked at each other or touched anything. One day each had a dream. Bulbusur and his Gondin came to them and said, 'You are husband-wife; we told you nothing. You were married in the cradle. Now do the work of husband-wife and live and eat.' When they woke, each thought, 'What shall we do?' and so talking and talking they spent the night. In the morning they decided to do what the dreams said. The boy began to desire the girl and his cart-pole was lifted up. They began the husband-wife work. But they did not know what to do. The boy made her lean forward, her head to the ground, and he took her from behind like a horse.

In those days, man's organ had a spike like a bamboo shoot growing from the tip and all down the sides were side-shoots like a bamboo. So when he went into her, her vagina was torn.

When he had done, he pulled out his pole and the blood began to flow. He was very frightened. 'What is the matter? How can I save her?' He went to find a Gunia.

The boy wandered through the jungle, until he came to Binjhiban Chirpatamber where there was a small hut. He went to it. A Gunia called Aughat was living there. The boy said, 'I have suffered a great disaster and so I have come to you.' He told him what had happened. 'Twelve years and thirteen ages ago we were married, but our parents died and never told us. Then they came in a dream and we enjoyed the act of love and after that came blood.' The Gunia went with the boy to his hut in the jungle. He found the girl lying with blood flowing from her. She had tied leaves between her legs, but the flow did not stop. The Gunia took ash in his hands and seven times blew it with charms over the girl. 'Be cured,' he said. 'Do not be afraid. Every month you must live outside. For eight days the blood will flow. Then it will stop. You must then wash your clothes and your body and you may go inside. On that day go to your husband but to no other man. In this way the flowing of blood will pass to all the women in the world.'

64

GOGIA PARDHAN

Jhanki, Mandla District

(From *Essays in Anthropology presented to S. C. Roy*, 144)

Parvati and Mahadeo lived together on the Naked Mountain. One day, Mahadeo made seven garden-plots and sowed vegetables in each. In the seventh, where he used to bathe and piss, he put red spinach and recited a 'seed-charm' over it. There was no fence round the other plots, but only round this one. Presently, Mahadeo said, 'I am going away to the jungle; you look after the garden; you may eat everything except the red spinach.' He went to that garden and cursed it, saying, 'Whoever eats you will have a period twelve years long.' Then away he went to the jungle to work as a carpenter.

Every day Parvati used to eat vegetable from the gardens, and as she ate she was very happy and forgot her husband. But when she had finished she remembered him and wondered when he would come back. 'If I eat from the seventh garden,' she thought, 'he will have to come.' So she went and ate some of the red spinach there.

At once her fire flowed and she lay down for twelve years. Then she felt hungry and went back to the seventh garden. There was a fruit growing there now, and she ate it, and at once became pregnant. After a few days a child was born, and Parvati thought, 'What is this thing?' and buried it under a tree. But when Mahadeo came home, it leapt out and sat on his shoulder.

All the world came to receive gifts. Mahadeo said, 'You are tired, we will feed you.' He gave them curry with little bits of the vegetable and fruit from his garden, and when they had eaten it, menstruation and child-bearing began throughout the world.

65

GOND

Lamni, Bilaspur District

Dharti Mata took the form of a woman and went to a place where many people had gathered. They said to Bibi Mata, a young man, 'Marry her.' He caught her by the hand. 'But you are my father. You mustn't do such a thing.' But he took no notice and was dragging her away. There she said, 'Don't touch me. My head is unclean for twelve years.' He left her, but since then blood has flowed from women every month.

66

GOND

Mukam, Kawardha State

Raja Indal had seven daughters. One day they said, 'Father, we want to see the Middle World.' 'Don't go, my daughters,' said Raja Indal. But they took no notice of him and began to discuss how they were to get down. Makramal Kshattri the spider was hanging in his web: four feet reached to the sky, four feet rested on the ground. Raja Indal got caught in the web. The spider was angry and cried, 'Who has disturbed my twelve years' penance?'

Raja Indal said, 'It is Raja Indal, master, please forgive me.' The spider said, 'What is the matter? Have you some business with me?' Raja Indal said, 'I have seven daughters; please take them down to the Middle World.' The spider agreed and told him to send the girls. When they came, the spider spun his web round them; they went down and he went up. Now this thread of the spiders' came out of its organ and with the thread came blood. The blood left the spider's body and went into the girls' mouths. That is why the spider has no blood in its body now.

The girls reached the Middle World. There was a beautiful tank. They took off their clothes and jumped in and swam about. The blood went right through their bodies. Presently the youngest girl said, 'My belly feels very heavy: I can't swim any longer.' The eldest girl rubbed dirt from her breasts and made a doll. She hit it with a bel stick and sprinkled life-water on it; it lived and she put it into her own belly.

Inside the belly the doll struggled and bit her, and the girl got frightened. 'My name will be ruined,' she thought. She went to the Baiga. 'My belly is hurting me,' she said. He said, 'Bring sihar seeds and a copper coin'. She brought the seeds and a coin, and the Baiga said, 'Come, let us go to your house.' There he looked in his winnowing-fan, and discovered the names of the seven sisters. To the first he gave the name of Garabmar (Pregnancy Girl), to the second Tankibai (Gonhorroea Girl), to the third Sujagbai (Gleet Girl), to the fourth Garmahinbai (Syphilis Girl), to the fifth Parmahinbai, to the sixth Banasmarbai and to the seventh Phulmarbai.

Bak-bak-bak like water in a river, *bak-bak-bak-bak* flowed the blood from the vulva. The Baiga said to the seven sisters, 'Every month blood will flow like this for a week. During that time you will have different names.' And he called the first Achrahibai, the second Murmailibai, the third Phulahibai, the fourth Chhekhahibai, the fifth Asudahibai, and the names of the sixth and seventh are forgotten. Since that day women have had blood every month.

67

HALBA

Kartuli, Dondi-Lohara Zamindari

Ganitmal Dano lived in Uritpur in the deep jungle. His wife's name was Ganitnithi. The night after their marriage Ganitmal said to his wife, 'Come and lie with me.' At that moment Ganitmal's penis sprouted all over with a number of little branches. There were seven-and-a-half such branches. When Ganitnithi lay down and prepared for her husband, she saw the seven-and-a-half branches and was afraid. She had never been to her husband before, and cried, 'I am not ready for it; how can I bear the force of all these branches?' The Dano tried again and again to persuade her, but she still refused. At last he lost his temper and attempted to take her by force and the seven and-a-half branches helped him. But she escaped them and ran away, he and the branches following.

She came to the Burli River. She jumped into the stream and made her way across. Now on this river there was this curse. 'That if any Dano's wife crosses it, the river will divide into seven streams and from that wife's vulva there will flow seven streams of blood.' So when Ganitnithi, was half way across, a stream of blood began to flow from her. When she reached the bank she took off her cloth to look at it. Ganitmal saw the blood-stained cloth and thinking that his wife had got some dangerous disease returned home and let her be.

She ran on and went to the Marria Sandugarh Mountains where Burlisar Devi lived. She served her for seven-and-a-quarter years and when the Devi was pleased she begged to be freed of the disease that was tormenting her. The Devi caught some of the blood in her hand and letting a few drops first fall by her sacred place, made a mark with it on the woman's forehead. She said, 'This is no disease, but will be every month for all women and from this children will be born.'

68

JUANG

Tambur, Pal Lahara State

At first women had no periods. The seven Kaniya Sisters and the Seven Bhendia Brothers were born in a great lake. They used to play together in the water. One day some girls were bathing naked in the lake. When the Kaniya saw them, they said to the Bhendia, 'Tonight go and enjoy them.' That night the boys enjoyed them and after that blood came from girls every month.

Nowadays, it is only when a girl dreams that the seven Bhendia Brothers are enjoying her, that she has her first period.

Little boys have no seed. Seed is made when a youth dreams that he is having the Seven Kaniya Sisters.

69

JUANG

Kajuria, Keonjhar State

When Mahesur Risi pulled the skin away from the soft part between a girl's thighs, blood came from the wound. This was how menstruation began.

70

JUANG

Balipal, Keonjhar State

Women had no vulva at first. Man did his work with his long umbilical stump and the woman's navel was his mortar. Children were conceived in this way.[1]

A certain man had a rat, Birkatri Mussa was its name. One day as he was sleeping with his wife, the rat came and bit the woman between her legs, and blood came out. When the man saw the new cavity in his wife's body he entered it just as the blood was flowing and his eyes burst open.

He wandered about blind for a time, then at last Mahapurub gave him a dream. 'Why did you go in as the blood came out?' The rat brought medicine to cure the man's eyes and he saw again.

But since then we never approach our wives during their periods, and we never eat this rat—it stinks, for it is covered with old blood.

71

JUANG

Kirtanpur, Dhenkanal State

Once when a man was lying with his wife, a snake bit her between the thighs. Since then blood has come from the wound every month. If a woman can eat a lotus, the flow of blood will stop.

[1] The old Buddhist and Hindu tradition was that ascetics, who did not want to break their rule of celibacy yet desired to bring a son into the world, achieved this end by touching a woman's navel. Thus, in the *Mahabarata* story, the Sun-god, taking a magic body, joins himself with Kunti and touches her on the navel, impregnating but not dishonouring her. See Meyer, i, 33 f.

72

KHUNTIA CHOKH

Pondi, Lapha Zamindari

(From *Essays in Anthropology presented to S.C.Roy*, 143)

At the beginning of the world, Ashtangi Mata was approached by her husband, but she was in her period. She said, ' If this blood falls on the ground, it will be a very bad thing ', so she made an earthen lamp and put all the blood that came from her in two-and-a-half days into it and buried it in the earth. Soon afterwards a tree grew up from the lamp and was called a binj tree. Ashtangi Mata was afraid that if anyone ate its fruit they too would suffer as she did. So she ordered that no one should eat it. ' Whoever does will be " out " for five days.'

But then Bhagavan called all the world to his court to allot every man his work and duties. While the men were sitting with Bhagavan, the girls gathered round the tree. They were hungry, they ate, and from that day they have been ' out '.

73

KORKU

Patbakera, Betul District

After her marriage with Mula, one day Mulai found blood falling from her body to the ground. Mula thought it was very bad that it should go into the ground and he made an earthen pot and caught the blood in that. One day he said to himself, ' What is the purpose of this blood ? '

At this time Mahadeo was making models of men out of mud. But the trees in the forest said to one another, ' These models will come to life and cut us down '. So when Mahadeo went home, the trees came and destroyed the mud models. Mahadeo was very angry and turned the trees upside down, burying the branches in the ground and letting the roots be in the wind. He made many new models and now he took a little of Mulai's blood out of the pot and sprinkled it on them and they became men.

Because of this blood, men are clothed in skin ; otherwise they would only be flesh.

Mula buried the pot in the ground and a tree sprung up from it. At first it gave beautiful flowers, and then good fruit. Mulai thought, 'How can I eat this fruit? It is born of blood.' He gave it to the new men and women made by Mahadeo, and from that day women have been unclean with blood every month.

74

KURUK

Temra, Bastar State

The Moon is woman and for half a month she lives outside her house of light, dark and unclean. Her shadow fell on the women of the world and their homes too were dark for fifteen days. Mahapurub took the form of a magician and looked in his winnowing-fan. He went to a poor man's house and asked for food. The man replied, 'My wife is not touching the pots and I cannot leave the house'. 'How many days are you troubled like this?' 'For fifteen days.' 'What will you give me if I make the period less?' 'I am a poor man. What can I give you? But at least I will always take your name.' At that Mahapurub took a handful of the mud-plaster by the door and made three little balls, which he gave to the man for his wife. Then he went from house to house, giving some seven balls, some five, some three, and went away. The women ate and their periods lasted for as many days as they had eaten balls of earth.

75

LANJHIA SAORA

Gailunga, Koraput District

Biklu Saora was married as a child. After that both his parents died. It was in Almatigarh. In those days there were no menses; men and women went to it without interruption. One day Biklu drank a great deal of palm wine and went drunk to his wife. Now in her vagina was a little thread and Biklu did it with such fury that the thread broke and blood came out. When he saw it the man felt very sorry and sobered. They went together, man and wife, to Galbesum and asked what they should do. He gave them two-and-a-half grains of rice and said, 'Eat this and the blood will stop. But now it will always be like this. During the month the thread will be whole, then it will break and blood will flow for two-and-a-half days.'

76

RAJNENGI PARDHAN

Patangarh, Mandla District

There was a brother and his sister. The brother made two bathing-places, one for himself and one for his sister. He was attacked by a demon, a host of demons. He killed them all and the blood went into his own body. Then as he bathed, the water that touched him turned into blood.

He cursed that blood, did the girl's brother, crying, 'If any woman touches this, blood will flow from her for two-and-a-half days.' And he said to his sister, 'Never go to my bathing-place.' Then from the blood a beautiful red flower blossomed.

The sister saw it, she could not contain her longing, she ran to pick it. From that day blood flowed from her, and people said, 'Today is the flower, tomorrow will be the fruit.'

XIII

The Origin of Sexual Intimacy

In the earliest Upanishad, the *Brihad-Aranyaka*, there is a myth of the origin of copulation and procreation so rough and simple that it might have come from modern tribal India. Atman is shown lonely and without delight. He desired a second. He bifurcated into husband and wife. 'He copulated with her. Therefrom human beings were produced. And she then bethought herself: "How now does he copulate with me after he has produced me just from himself? Come, let me hide myself." She became a cow. He became a bull. With her he did indeed copulate. Then cattle were born. She became a mare, he a stallion. She became a female ass, he a male ass; with her he copulated. Thence were born solid-hoofed animals. She became a she-goat, he a he-goat; she a ewe, he a ram. With her he did verily copulate. Therefrom were born goats and sheep. Thus indeed he created all, whatever pairs there are, even down to the ants.'[1]

But later, in the same Upanishad, there is a discussion of the art of procreation which is as splendid and dignified as anything in the

[1] *Brihad-Aranyaka Upanishad*, 1·4. 3-4 (Hume's translation).

literature of the world. It links the origin of human copulation with the creative power of all things and pictures woman as the sacrificial altar on which man lays the libation of his strength.

'Verily, of created things here earth is the essence; of earth, water; of water, plants; of plants, flowers; of flowers, fruits; of fruits, man; of man, semen.

'Prajapati bethought himself: "Come, let me provide him a firm basis." So he created woman. When he had created her, he revered her below. Therefore one should revere woman below. He stretched out for himself that stone which projects. With that he impregnated her.

'Her lap is a sacrificial altar; her hairs, the sacrificial grass; her skin, the soma-press. The two labia of the vulva are the fire in the middle. Verily, indeed, as great as is the world of him who sacrifices with the Vajapeya ("strength-libation") sacrifice, so great is the world of him who practises sexual intercourse, knowing this'.[1]

There is a rather obscure passage in the *Mahabharata* (xii, 207. 40) which Meyer regards as descriptive of the origin of copulation and marriage. 'The passage might be translated: In the Dvapara Age it was that the usage of copulation arose among creatures; then in the Kali Age mankind came to pairing.'[2] That is to say, formerly there was simply sexual union, it was only in our evil age that mankind took to marriage.

To the minds of the tribal mythologists there were apparently three things which prevented human beings taking to sexual intercourse.

The first, and probably the most important, was the fact that the first man and woman were brother and sister and shrank from an incestuous relationship. The second was early man's innocence of desire, and the third his ignorance of erotic technique. The legends describe how these obstacles were overcome.

First of all then, the parents of mankind were brother and sister. This fact did not trouble Nanga Baiga.

> They were brother and sister. What were they to do? 'What is the harm in it?' asked Nanga Baiga. When they were old enough they desired each other. 'What need of marriage?' asked Nanga Baiga. They were both naked. Nanga Baiga used to go and bathe in a pond and his sister went to watch him. He came to her on the bank and said, 'If you're ready, let's do it.' She answered, 'If you have a mind to it, I'm ready'. So they became mated among the trees on the bank of the pond.[3]

[1] ibid. 6. 4.1-3. [2] Meyer, ii, 554. [3] *The Baiga*, 313 f.

The Lanjhia Saora also represent Kittung and his sister as needing little encouragement. The two are shut up in a gourd which is floating on the face of the ocean. The boy is sleeping on a cot, the girl on the floor. Mahaprabhu sends a fly and an ant into the gourd. The fly buzzes in the girl's ears, the ant bites her and she cries, 'Brother, I can't get to sleep.' He replies, 'Then come and sleep with me on the cot'. And in this way they become man and wife.

But other tribes take the problem more seriously, and represent brother and sister as refusing to mate with one another. The convention, shared by the Bison-horn Maria, the Bondo, the Kuruk, and several other tribes, is to separate the pair for twelve years so that when they meet again they do not recognize each other and marry. Sometimes recognition is made more difficult by giving them both smallpox: the Bondo say that Mahaprabhu made the girl squint and the boy a leper—social rather than biological considerations being the more important. In the Bhil legend, the Creator arranged the matter very simply. 'He turned the girl with her face to the west and the young man with his face to the east. When he had made them turn again so as to face each other, he asked the man, "Who is this?" and he answered, "She is my wife". Then Bhagwan asked the girl, "Who is this?" and she answered, "He is my husband." Then God made them man and wife.'[1]

Koppers rightly points out that although 'it was unavoidable that the children of the original parents of the human race should intermarry, that only a brother and sister should have survived the flood appears somewhat illogical. To say the least of it, it is a very unpractical arrangement.'

A curious variant of this tradition suggests an abhorrence of mother-son incest. The Banjara of Mysore derive mankind from the union of a girl with her own son.

> Out of the seed of the Creator shot into space, was born a beautiful damsel, who in turn created a boy out of the sweat of her body. She desired to consort with him, but her offer was rejected. A second boy was created for a similar purpose, and he also proved equally obdurate. But at last her attempt succeeded, and the two were the progenitors of the human race.[2]

The socio-psychological taboos overcome, there is another obstacle to the establishment of sexual intercourse, the absence of desire. This was noticed by the Kol. When Singbonga's 'grandchildren' grew up, he had great expectations from them, 'but at length, seeing no hopes of any progeny, from their extreme simplicity, he taught them the art of making rice-beer, the use of which

[1] Koppers, 284. [2] Nanjundayya and Iyer, ii, 137.

caused them those sensations which were in due time the means of peopling the world.'[1] Marang Buru, the Santal deity, also showed the first brother and sister how to make rice-beer. 'He then left them, and they, finding the liquor to their taste, drank deeply, and becoming intoxicated forgot they were brother and sister. They confessed to Marang Buru when he visited them next day, but he assured them they had been guilty of no offence'.[2]

The Hill Maria of the Abujhmar Mountains and the Muria of their immediate neighbourhood attribute the origin of desire to the benevolent influence of the sago palm.

At the beginning of the world, Tallur Muttai came with Kadrengal [whom some call her brother and some her husband], to the forest of Bastar. Kadrengal was innocent of sexual desire, and so Tallur Muttai created sago palms with the hope that their juice would excite him. When Kadrengal first went to tap the trees, he tied a thread from the cut peduncle down to a hole which he dug below, but the wind blew it to and fro and the juice was scattered. Then Tallur Muttai taught him how to tie a gourd to catch the juice and place a leaf to guide it safely. Kadrengal drank a great quantity; desire came to him; and he went to Tallur Muttai.

The final difficulty was an ignorance of erotic technique: a number of stories in the text reveal how this trouble was overcome.

77

BAIGA

Gotai, Mandla District

Formerly men did not know how to achieve sexual intercourse. An old man and woman had a son. He was born though his parents had never copulated. The old man arranged the boy's marriage, but the boy's wife continued to live at her mother's house. One day the old man went to fetch his daughter-in-law. As they were coming home they were caught by night in the jungle. They slept where they were under a tree. They slept apart from each other. But during the night a panther growled, '*Hirko hirko.*' The girl said to the old man, 'Father-in-law, what is it saying?' 'It is saying *Hirko hirko.*' The girl said, '*Hirak ao*, come near.' The old man came and slept with his daughter-in-law. After a little while a wood-pigeon cried, '*Dar dudu dar dudu*'. The girl said to the old man,

[1] Tickell, 797. [2] Campbell, 21.

'Father-in-law, what is it saying ?' 'It is saying *Dar dudu dar dudu.*' The girl said, 'Then *dar dudu*, catch hold of my breasts.' So the old man caught his daughter-in-law's breasts.

They slept like that for a time and then a kappe bird called '*Kapkeh kapkeh.*' The girl said, 'Father-in-law, what is it saying ?' The old man replied, '*Kapkeh Kapkeh.*' The girl said, 'Then *Kapak jao*, sleep face downwards.' And the old man embraced her and lay upon her face downwards. So they lay for a time and then the kussera bird cried, '*Karkas Karkas.*' The girl said, 'Father-in-law, what is it saying ?' 'It is saying '*Karkas Karkas.*' So the girl said, 'Then *Kassao*, put it in.' And the old man put it in and beat it *karkas karkas*. They both liked it very much.

Next day they went home and the old man gave his daughter-in-law to her husband. That night he did not know what to do, but the girl told him what she had learnt—part of it—in the jungle. From that day mankind has known how to copulate.

78

BISON-HORN MARIA

Muskel, Bastar State

The first man and woman did not know how to come together. Bhimsen gave them a bear's organ to eat. Power came to them, and they embraced each other. From them has come the whole human race. The woman ate more and that is why women have more power and more pleasure in copulation.

79

BONDO

Dumiripada, Koraput District

Originally men used to be present when a child was born. But one day when a father saw his child come from the womb, he was afraid. 'If I go into such a great hole, my wife will swallow me ; I will go right inside and be destroyed.' He ran away and afterwards refused to go to his wife. When he told her why, she said, 'Come with me to my mother's house.' On the way they passed an ant-hill. The woman kicked a great hole in it and they went on their way.

As they returned, they passed the same ant-hill and saw that the hole had now become quite small again. 'Look at the ant-hill', said the woman. 'That is not the one you kicked: it is a different one.' 'No, it is the same one. So with women, what is large becomes small again.' The man lost his fear, and once more went to his wife.

80

GOND

Bhanpur, Mandla District

A man desired a woman but she refused him. He sought relief by visiting the place where she urinated and ridding himself of his drunkenness there. One day the woman said to him, 'Come to the bank of the river with me.' They went together there. She showed him a broom and a spear. She said, 'This spear is man, the broom is woman. Dip these things in the water.' The man did so and the woman said, 'How many drops fell from the point of the spear?' The man said, 'Two or three.' And she said, 'How many fell from the broom?' The man said, 'So many that I couldn't count them.' She said, 'For you it is nothing, the work of a few drops, but for us women it is a flood.' He was ashamed and left her alone.

81

JUANG

Tambur, Pal Lahara State

When the first brother and sister were made and had matured, a horsefly settled on the girl's breast as she was sleeping. The boy struck at the fly and it turned into a nipple. The girl jumped up, thinking that her brother had been fondling her breast and that the nipple had grown as a result. Desire grew between them and they married, and from these two came all mankind.

82

KOND

Gangaguda, Koraput District

Before the world was made a great rock fell from above into water. On the rock milk-shrubs were growing. Out of the rock came a boy and a girl. They drank the milk of the shrubs and kept themselves alive. At first this milk was sweet but when Burha Pinnu saw that men would drink the milk and live for ever he made it bitter.

Now this boy and girl were brother and sister. How could they marry? So they separated and went to see if there was any other people in the world. As they went both got smallpox and later when they met again they did not recognize each other. Each thought he had discovered another human being; so they married and from them all human beings have come.

83

KORKU

Pathakera, Betul District

The first man was Mula, the first woman was Mulai. They were brother and sister and grew up together in the jungle: they ate raw roots. As they grew older each desired a yoke-fellow, but they were too shy to tell each other so. One day, when Mula was out getting roots, he sat down by the path and wondered how to get a wife. Mulai took the form of a young she-ass and was eating green dub grass on the bank of a stream. Mula desired the she-ass; he caught it with a golden rope and enjoyed it. Afterwards the ass kicked violently and ran away with the golden rope still round its neck.

Mulai took her own form and returned home, but she still had the golden rope, and she hung it from the roof. Presently Mula returned home and when he went into the house he saw the rope and at once came out again. Mulai hid for shame behind the house. Then came Mahadeo and said, 'Shame on you, Mula! How did you go to your own sister in the form of a she-ass? You must now be married'. So saying Mahadeo married Mula and Mulai and they lived together as man and wife.

84

LANJHIA SAORA

Maneba, Ganjam District

Pidal Saora and his wife lived in Patmukhgarh. They grew old with their only son caring for them. They arranged his marriage and died. The youth and his wife set up house together, but they were young and did not know how to come together. There were no people in the world at that time; there was no one to teach them. The boy did all he could; he made the girl kneel on her hands and knees and tried to take her in the rump; he bruised her badly by his efforts. So many days passed fruitlessly. His dead parents seeing this, said in their minds, 'If we allow this to go on, our race will die out.' So they came to the house and the mother gave a dream to the girl, saying 'O daughter-in-law you do not know what to do; don't be afraid, we will show you.' And in the dream the old father-in-law went to his wife before the girl to show her what to do. The girl watched and understood. The father went to the boy in a dream at the same time. He said, 'O boy, between a woman's legs is a place for urine; that is where you must go.' When the dreams were over, the dead parents went away, and boy and girl awoke and told each other what they had seen. The boy lit a lamp and searched for the place. He put his wife on a cot and separated her legs and saw it. Then he sat for the work, and since then everybody in the world has known what to do.

85

MURIA

Kokori, Bastar State

(From *The Muria and their Ghotul*)

Mahapurub told the boy and girl that they should marry each other but they refused saying, 'We are brother and sister'. So the smallpox goddess came and separated them and each got smallpox. Afterwards when they met they did not know who they were, for their faces were covered with the marks of disease, and they got married. Now these two, man and woman, had no knowledge of sex. They lived together working in their fields, but the man never went to his wife. Presently Mahapurub sent Lingo to see how they were getting on. 'They know nothing of love or copulation, they are living as brother and sister', so said Lingo. This made Mahapurub anxious about the peopling of the world. So he gave Lingo two pills filled with his love-charms.

When Lingo reached the house, he found the man had gone to hunt but the woman was bathing. He gave her the two pills and told her to eat one of them after the bath and to give the other to her husband when he returned. Having done this, Lingo went away. The woman ate one pill but was so pleased with it that she ate the second also, leaving nothing for her husband. Directly she swallowed the pills she was filled with excitement and passion and ran into the forest to seek her man.

At last when he returned from hunting, instead of giving him his food, she took him into the house and pulled him down to the ground beside her. But for all her caresses there was no desire in him and he did nothing. He ate a heavy meal but she could not eat. All night she tried to rouse him, but without success. Then once again Lingo came to see how they were. He peeped through the door and saw the woman trying to rouse her husband. So he brought two more pills and this time gave them one each. Now at last the husband's desire was awakened and he went to his wife again and again, but since the woman had a greater number of pills she was much the more passionate. That is why the Muria say women remain more passionate than men unto this day.

So strong was their passion that the very next morning a child was born. After this children were born throughout the world and men and women increased in number.

xiv

Conception and Birth

According to a popular tradition, conception, like menstruation, came to the world through breach of a taboo. A Baiga legend describes how Mahadeo sowed *bij-bhāji* (herbs that had had a 'seed-charm' recited over them) in his garden. He told Parvati not to go there, but she disobeyed him. At her first visit, she began to menstruate; at her second, she ate the herbs that contained birth-magic and became pregnant.

A similar story was recorded by Trench from the Gond of Betul. The first boy and girl have reached dry land from their original ocean home.

One day Sukma-devi-velar the girl says to Addi-rawan-pariol the boy, her brother, 'Dada, how many days are you and I to stay in this forest? Accordingly, it would be a good thing if you were to build a house'.

Then Addi-rawan-pariol listened to his sister's word, and took cross-bars of jay's feathers and rafters of peacock's feathers, such a house did that elder brother build. There both persons began to dwell, eating yams of the forest and fruits of the jungle. Thereafter, in a little while, both became of marriageable age.

Where both used to wash, in the washing-place the green herb called *pokra* had sprung up. The girl says to her elder brother, 'Dada, very tasty salad has sprung up. If we were to eat it it would be a good thing'.

The boy says to the girl, 'Sister, one ought not to eat salad which grows in a nasty place'.

Says she, 'Brother, my soul yearns to eat it'.

Her honoured brother doubted in his mind, thinking, 'Some day or other the girl will eat it, and then what will happen ?'

Therefore, he fenced that green herb with thorns ; then he remained free from care.

One day, the girl says to herself, 'Why does my brother not let me eat this salad ? One day I will eat it'. Whereupon, so saying, she evaded his notice, picked the salad, boiled it, and ate it. From that day she conceived and became pregnant.[1]

86

BAIGA

Jaldar, Mandla District

In Bandaogarh lived Rama and Lakshman. They had a sister called Anjini. There were seven houses. The two brothers used to go to piss in the seventh house.

They told Anjini that she must never go there. One day they went out hunting. Presently their sister became curious, she went to the door, she opened it; she looked inside, she saw red spinach growing. How she longed for it ! She went in and picked some, put it in the fold of her sari; she went home and cooked it quickly and ate. Next day she was pregnant, she could not eat her food. The brothers came back, they were puzzled. There was no man in that place, how could this have happened to our sister ? At last she told them. They were very angry and took her out into the jungle and left her there. In nine months the baby was born.

[1]Trench, ii, 2 f.

87

BAIGA

Baona, Mandla District

A Gond and his wife were living on Koeli-Kachhar. There were no children, for women never became pregnant then. But the Gond woman longed for a child. She went to Mahadeo and served his *lingam* for twelve years. When the thirteenth year began he was pleased and said, 'Daughter, what do you desire?' She told him, and he bade her come to him during her next monthly period. This she did and went to him when her head was defiled. He gave her two mangoes and when she had eaten them he lay with her. She conceived and bore a son and a daughter. Mahadeo was pleased and sent this through the world.

88

BAIGA

Randpur, Mandla District

When Parvati was pregnant the child's soul within her longed for earth. The ground was white in the place where Mahadeo went to urinate. Parvati visited the place, and ate the earth, for she liked the white colour, and it was salt and tasty. From that day all the women in the world have suffered from these cravings.

89

BHAINA

Penda Zamindari

From the placenta a Malin was born. She took the placenta and kept it with her. A barren woman came to see her. She said, 'Look, I have no child. Give me some medicine so that I may be fruitful.' The Malin said, 'Take this flower and eat it. There will be a child in your belly. When it is ready to come out, eat some bitter seeds of a gourd. Then after the child is born, the flower also will come out. But before the child is born, it will desire to eat all strange foods, beef and earth and the flesh of monkeys'. So it happened. There was a child in the woman's belly. It craved for earth.[1] The mother was wise and did not deny its desires. It was born happy and strong.

90

CHOKH AGARIA

Thanakar, Bilaspur District

From the head of the fish Raghuman bloomed a lotus and bore two fruits. One day they broke open and from one came Mahadeo, from the other Parvati. When Mahadeo grew up, he could not control his desire for his sister, so he turned his back on her and refused to see her face. But when Parvati too became mature, she also was filled with desire and begged her brother to look at her. At last he turned round and as he did so his seed sprang from him. Parvati caught it in her hand and held it in her clenched hand. Soon she was pregnant and after that children were born in the world.

91

DHOBA

Silpuri, Mandla District

When Parvati became pregnant she cried, 'Let this spread to every woman in the world!' So Mahadeo came and blew in the ears of men and put his seed into them through the ears, he blew also in the ears of the women and put Parvati's water into them. After that day women began to be pregnant and to bear children. And still today those Dhoba who are childless declare that in a former birth they were not disciples of Mahadeo.

[1] Geophagy during pregnancy is known all over the world. The women of the Torres Straits eat a red earth which they think will make the child light-skinned, in New Guinea a grey marine clay. In Africa the custom is recorded of Mayombe and Wakissi women and in Batanga. Women of Bengal are reported as fancying a light ochreous-coloured specimen with a distinctive odour which is made into thin cups: Kalidasa has a queen who eats it to make her breath fragrant. Before giving birth to Raghu the Rani of Ayodhya hankered for baked clay. Lasch was of the opinion that pregnant women eat earth and clay to make them vomit and thus facilitate delivery by causing contractions of the uterus, but Laufer has questioned this. It appears to be a genuine 'craving'. See B. Laufer, *Geophagy* (Field Museum of Natural History, Chicago, 1930); R. Lasch, *Uber Geophagie* (Wien, 1892); M. Bloomfield, 'The *Dohada*, or Craving of Pregnant Women: a *Motif* of Hindu Fiction', *J.A.O.S.*, xl (1920), 1-24; D. Hooper and H. H. Mann, 'Earth-Eating and the Earth-Eating Habit in India', *Mem. A, S. Beng.* (Calcutta, 1906).

92

GOND

Barratola, Mandla District

There was a Kurmi cultivator. He sowed every kind of seed in his fields, but when the grain had sprouted the rain failed and it began to wither. The Kurmi went to Sumringarh to consult a Baiga Dewar. The Dewar examined his measuring-sticks and declared that, 'It is because you have failed to offer sacrifice to Mother Earth that your crop has withered. Go home and sprinkle cowdung water over the Ahir, then take him to the river and throw him in.'

The Kurmi went home and finding the Ahir milking his cows, sprinkled cowdung water over him, then dragged him down to the river and threw him in. Directly the Ahir fell into the water the clouds began to thunder and soon there was a great storm and rain.

When it began to thunder mushrooms came out of the earth. The Baiga Dewar picked one of them and took it home to his wife. His wife was barren and he gave her the mushroom uncooked and raw to eat. When she ate it the mushroom turned into a placenta and the woman conceived and in due time bore a son. That was how mushrooms and the placenta came into the world.

93

KOND

Kerma, Koraput District

Originally human children came from the womb like worms, very small and many of them together. Most died but the rest grew big afterwards.

94

KOND

Jangroda, Koraput District

There was a Gadaba, Patali, whose wife Mangli did not bear him a single child. But indeed in those days there were no children, for women did not know how to bear them. One day Patali set out to find some charm or medicine that would enable women to conceive: he wandered across the world for six months, but found nothing and at last turned his steps homeward. On the way back he passed under the hill called Maimanjal, where Bandosiri Deota had his home. The two met and Patali told the Deota about his fruitless search. Bandosiri Deota took some wax from his ear and gave it to him. ' On the day your wife bathes at the end of her period ', he said, ' take her to a river and spend the night together on the bank. Put this medicine into a little water and give it to your wife three times '. Patali went home and did all that the Deota had told him. His wife conceived and after ten months gave birth to a son. In this way, a son was born every year for twelve years. After the first child was born, Patali's wife washed her dirty clothes in the river. All the women who used the water also conceived and in this way childbirth spread throughout the world.

95

PANKA

Sanhrwachhapar, Mandla District

There was no discharge of any kind from a woman's vagina in the old days. Only men had the discharge. The result was that children were not born and women had no pleasure in intercourse. Women used to look at the offspring of cows, buffaloes, she-goats, birds and wonder why they too did not have children.

There was an unmarried girl. She had a dream. ' In Binjban there is a faithful woman ; she is doing penance ; she has water with her.' That girl told the other women and they said, 'Look, you have no husband ; go and get this water for us.' She went to Binjban to ask for the water. For twelve years she served that holy woman. At the beginning of the thirteenth year, the holy woman was pleased and said to the girl, ' Ask for anything you want and I will give it to you.' The girl said, ' Spit '. The holy woman spat. The girl then said, ' Lick it up or else give me water.' The holy woman hung her head in shame on hearing this, and said, ' Ask for some good thing.' ' No, that is all I want, ' said the girl. The holy woman then took water from her vagina with her left hand and put it in the girl's cloth from behind, not looking at her. The girl went at once back to her village and divided the water to the women. She herself married that very day. After that women had water and children were born to them.

96

RAJNENGI PARDHAN

Patangarh, Mandla District

There was a Baigin; she was in her period. When it was over she went down to the river to bathe her head. A Sadhu came by and his shadow fell on her. She conceived, and when the life came to the child in her belly it thought, 'If I am born from the vagina, she will call me son; if I am born from the mouth, she will call me leavings; so I will break the belly and thus be born.' So the child broke through the mother's belly and was born. His name was Bodraha Baiga. Ever since he was born there has been a mark on women's bodies in the middle of the belly.

XV

URINE AND EXCRETA

There is a fairly extensive folklore of this not very pleasant subject. In Salsette, it was believed that if a man who had been badly beaten drank his own urine, he would recover. If little children drank their own urine, they would grow fierce. A certain root got medicinal value if it was buried for six months in a stable and a black cow urinated over it.[1] Among the Chingannivetan group of Malavetan, it is reported that after the birth of a child 'a decoction of medicinal herbs and charcoal powder is made in the husband's urine' and is given to the mother.[2]

Both in Salsette and over a wide area, it is believed that sore eyes can be cured if they are washed with the first urine passed in the morning: urine on a cut stops it bleeding: if an insect gets into the ear it can be killed if someone urinates into it; swelling of the feet can be cured by urinating over them. The Angami Naga apply earth made muddy with urine to burns.[3]

In Mandla there is an idea that if a youth urinates on the burning Holi fire, he will become 'as potent as fire', a fire which will only be quenched by a woman's water. The medicinal and magical value of cow's urine is widely held by the Hindus. The Pardhan of Mandla have some curious notions of the attitude of the hare. 'To

[1] G. F. D. Penha, 'Superstitions and Customs in Salsette', *The Indian Antiquary*, xviii, 115.

[2] Krishna Iyer. i, 148.

[3] Hutton, *The Angami Nagas*, 100.

the hare, cow's urine is liquor. When a hare hears the music of a cow's hoof, it comes out in joy and drinks its urine and dances as it drinks. If it cannot get fresh urine, it licks the ground.''[1]

97

GADABA

Pottapad, Koraput District

Long ago Budra Bodo Gadaba and his wife had twelve sons, but there was no grain to eat, nothing but fruit and roots. Men had no place for urine and excreta; they vomited their dirt up through their mouths. One day the twelve brothers made a field and brought seed from Dumri Kaniya in Sukaligarh and sowed it there. But directly they began to eat rice and pulse, their bellies swelled, for they were unable to relieve themselves. They ran to Ilad Kaniya and she heated an iron bar and bored holes in the men and women and their dirt poured out. With handfuls of ash she healed the wounds and after that men were able to urinate and excrete.

98

GOND

Tikaitola, Rewa State

In the old days men neither excreted nor urinated. In Binjpaḥar, Basmasur Dano used to swing himself on a banyan tree. One day a man went there to fetch wood and cut down the swing and took it home as firewood. When Basmasur Dano saw what was done he was angry and cursed the man saying, 'What he fills in at one end, let him empty out at the other'. Directly the man reached home he began to pass stools.

This is why men are always hungry. Formerly when men ate their food it lasted them for weeks, but now because it passes through their bodies so quickly they are hungry again in a few hours.

[1] There is not yet sufficient material for a discussion of the interesting question of Undinism among Indian aboriginals.

99

GOND

Pakhri, Mandla District

In former days man used to eat and excrete through his mouth. One day Mahadeo made a trident. He thrust it up through man's backside and made a hole there for his excreta. Since that day men have had two buttocks. He also made a hole in front for urine.

100

LANJHIA SAORA

Munisingi, Ganjam District

The seven Bhima Brothers lived on the Salsar Mountain. In their day men did not excrete; the only vent they had was for urine. Once when the brothers had gone to the forest to hunt, they killed a sambhar. They cut it up and roasted it and ate it all, at once on the spot, there in the forest. They filled their bellies to overflowing and soon a dreadful pain seized them. One rolled on the ground; another danced in agony; a third wept loudly; all were in misery. So loud were their cries that Jamosum heard it and came from the Under World to see what was the matter. The brothers said, 'Our bellies are stuffed so full that we are bound to die.' But Jamosum took an awl and made each of the brothers in turn bend down in front of him. With the awl he made a hole between each pair of buttocks. Then he picked up some dust and gave it to the brothers to eat. Directly they swallowed the dust, the food they had eaten poured out of the vent between their buttocks. Thus the Bhima brothers who send rain on the earth taught mankind to excrete.

101

RAJNENGI PARDHAN

Patangarh, Mandla District

In the old days men and women used to eat and drink through their mouths and excrete through their mouths and piss through their mouths.

At that time the twelve Agaria brothers and the thirteen Tamesur brothers smelted cow's bones in the forge and made them into bracelets and armlets. When the bones were smelted they appeared like silver.

Nanga Baiga and Nanga Baigin were living in the jungle. Burhi Mata was born from the earth, breaking out of it. She gave them a dream. There was a trident stuck in the ground where she was living. She said, 'When the Agaria's wife next has her period, call the twelve Agaria brothers and the thirteen Tamesur brothers.' Then Barasin Mata was born from a hollow bombax tree. She said, 'Make a broom out of my pubic hairs and prepare the ground for worship.'

Nanga Baiga and Nanga Baigin made a broom of her pubic hairs and swept the ground in front of Burhi Mata's shrine. The twelve Agaria brothers lifted up the trident and heated it in their fire. They smeared a little of the Agaria's wife's menstrual blood on it, and made holes in Nanga Baiga and Nanga Baigin; each had one hole for urine and one for excrement. This was the beginning of excreta and urine in the world.[1]

[1] Boas records an Eskimo legend of a people without anus. They stuck pegs in the ground and sat down vigorously upon them, thus opening themselves. See F. Boas, *The Eskimo of Boffin Land and Hudson Bay*, 170. Cf. also W. Bogoras, *Tales of Eastern Siberia*, 89, for the origin of the anus and urethra among a people who had neither.

Ktesias speaks of one race of Indians, among whom 'children are born with the anus closed up and the contents of the bowels are therefore voided, it is said, as urine, this being something like curds.'—McCrindle, 302.

CHAPTER THIRTEEN

THE INVENTION OF IMPLEMENTS

THERE is a general belief among most of the tribesmen that the implements of husbandry and the processes of agriculture were invented by the gods and taught by them to mankind. The practice of shifting cultivation is everywhere regarded as having been inaugurated by the original tribal hero: Lingo taught it to the Muria, Nanga Baiga to the Baiga, Rusi to the Juang, Boram Burha to the Bhuiya.

The Kota hero, Kiturpayk, was the first to make fire and invented pottery and agriculture. 'He took black clay and made an unbaked pot and baked that and made a pot. In this pot he boiled flesh and made them eat it. . . He took stones from the jungle and put them into the fire and heated them and made smelted iron. From that iron he made arrows, bows, knives, axes, everything, and made them to cut. . . . He caught jungle buffaloes and jungle cows and tamed them. He ploughed tne fields with the bullock. He milked the female buffalo.'[1]

In Garhwal tradition, it was the Guru Nirankar who initiated men into the art of agriculture.

> The Guru asked the lion to plough, and then all other animals, but all refused till the bullock came. 'The Guru was much pleased with him and blessed him. . . . Then the Guru called Melu the ploughman and asked, 'Of what wilt thou make the plough?' Melu named all the metals from gold to iron. But Nirankar said, 'The poor cannot afford to make their ploughs of precious metals. Make the plough of wood and the ploughshare of iron' . . . Then the Guru called the bullock and put silver caps on his horns. He also created butter to rub his neck with, so that the yoke should not hurt it. He then ordered the pig to rub the butter on the bullock's neck with his snout. The pig ate part of the butter himself and rubbed only a little on the bullock's neck. Hence the neck of the bullock has remained soft and is hurt by the yoke.[2]

The yoke and plough and the use of plough-cattle are often, naturally enough, associated with the Hindu deities, especially Mahadeo, for it was probably the Hindus who taught the aboriginals a reverence for the cow and the use of improved implements. Mahadeo also showed the Agaria how to make tongs and a hammer.[3]

[1] Emeneau, 39. [2] Gariola, 40 f. [3] *The Agaria*, 104 ff.

The widely-distributed story (which is discussed at page 200 of this book) of the creation of the tiger is also associated with the first plough and is told by the Munda in a peculiarly attractive way.

When the Old One had put a soul in the clay-figure of man, he started making a plough for this man to plough with.

Taking a large tree he carved out of it the plough with its shaft, grip and handle all in one piece.

This kind of work took him a very long time.

So his wife sent a mosquito to call him; the mosquito went and buzzed around his ears.

Even so the Old One remained absorbed in his work of making the plough.

Then his wife sent a tiger.

The tiger to attract his attention and make him forget the plough, rustled the leaves around him, but the Old One taking a chip threw it at the tiger, saying 'Begone, wild dog.'

At once the chip became a wild dog and chased the tiger.

That is why even to this day tigers are afraid of wild dogs.

When after a very long time the Old One had finished his plough he took it home.

His wife seeing it said: 'What a poor plough thou hast made and what a time it has taken thee!

'In making such ploughs the children of men will lose their time, they will not be able to find trees big enough, and such a plough will not last.

'Come, throw the plough on the ground and we shall see how it fares.'

Then the Old One threw it on the ground and pieces broke off.

Then the Old One said: 'My plough is spoiled, with what shall the sons of men plough?'

Then the wife said: 'I shall make another kind of plough.

'See, it will be made quickly, will not need a big tree and will not break even when thrown on the ground.'

Her husband consenting, she applied herself to the making of the plough.

She made the plough, the shaft, the handle and the grip in separate pieces and having cut holes in the plough, she joined the pieces together; this work took but a short time.

When the plough was ready she made her husband throw it on the ground and they saw that nothing was broken.

Then the Old One said: 'Thou hast beaten me, who am a man, in making the plough; therefore I say: From to-day I free all women from the hardship of making ploughs.

'The men shall make them and let the women not even touch them.'

Thus spoke the Old One and therefore to this day women are forbidden to touch the plough.[1]

I

BAIGA

Gotai, Mandla District

There was a Parteti and a Markam. The Markam's sister was unmarried, and no one wanted to marry her. The Markam thought, 'If my sister grows old unmarried, it will be bad.' So he made rice of spear grass and filled a sack and took it to sell in the bazaar. He shouted in the bazaar. 'If anyone can tell me what is in this sack I'll give him my sister, free of cost, in marriage.' But no one could guess what was there until at last a Parteti came. That Parteti's wife had just given birth to a child; he had smeared the blood on his moustache and was twisting it with pleasure; he had shoes of rat-skin on his feet. He stood on the sack. One of the spears of grass ran into his shoe and pricked him. He went away a little and examined the spear of grass and declared, 'This sack is full of the grain of spear grass.' So he got the Markam girl in marriage.

When they got home the Parteti gave his wife grain to prepare for supper. She tried to husk it with the stone roller, but she could not do it properly, and her husband abused her: 'May your ashes fly in the air.' The Markam girl prayed to Mother Earth, 'Give me something to husk the rice and I'll offer you my first child in sacrifice.'

That night Mother Earth gave her a pestle—it was of khair wood, its tip was of copper, it had rings round the top. She gave the woman a dream and said, 'Make a hole in the ground, and pound the rice in that.'

The woman awoke and seeing the pestle felt happy as a bird wheeling in the smoke above a bonfire. She began to husk the grain and it was soon ready. But when her first child was born she had to sacrifice it.

[1] Hoffmann and Emelen, xiii, 3984 ff.

2

BHAINA

Kenda Zamindari

The Bhumia were born from the earth (*bhum*), but when they came into being they had no tools and no means of getting food. So they went to Bansmar Marra Deo who was living in Koelasur Garh and asked him what they should do. He created the twelve Agaria brothers and they made tools for mankind.

3

BHUIYA

Champajor, Keonjhar State

The first Bhuiya were very good to their children. They made seven kinds of musical instruments. They built a dormitory to house them and here at first boys and girls slept together. They used to play all day until at last Gundhi-Nidhi got angry and said, 'Now if you want to eat, you will have to work.' But the boys said, 'What can we do ?' 'You are Matisar Bhuiya : break the earth and eat.' So saying Gundhi-Nidhi fell down, buttock to buttock, his legs on Nidhi's breast, her legs round Gundhi's body. He caught her breasts : they were buttock to buttock. When the boys saw the father's penis enter their mother's vagina, they understood how to make a plough. 'We will make an iron share to be penis and the wood will be vagina.' They made the parts of the plough from the lips of the vagina. When they saw him catch their mother's breasts they learnt how to make the yoke. When they saw him put his feet between her breasts they learnt how to fix the nail and tie the rope.

Thus they made a plough. They put a girl on one side, a boy on the other. The two together dragged the plough. That is why today we yoke a cow with a bullock.

4

BINJHWAR BAIGA

Baihar, Balaghat District

Gulbhakaoli Kaniya (the Maid of the Gold Mohur Tree) had a snake in her belly. The day came for the marriage of the earth and the clouds. But there was no flour for the marriage feast. Bondu Baiga and Mukhi Agaria caught Gulbhakaoli Kaniya and took her to Kari Patpar and brought the snake out of her belly by their magic.

They made a great pile of wood and burnt the snake. Its ribs and bones remained. They powdered them up with a heavy hammer carried by twenty-four men and a light hammer carried by twenty-six men. They made the powder into a grindstone. The pin of the stone was of dhawa wood, its handle was of tinsa. In the grindstone they put sihar seeds and made them into flour.

Bondu Baiga brought oil-seed from the jungle. He made a seed-basket and an oil-press and a cord of mohlain creeper. He ground the oil-seed with a stone and put it in the press and the oil came out. He then made the flour into cakes and cooked them in the oil. Thus there was food at the wedding and he gave the cakes to the earth and the clouds to eat. They were pleased and blessed him saying, 'In your next birth you will be a Bharotia.'[1]

5

DHOBA

Silpuri, Mandla District

Machhandar Kanna lived in Garh Kalsapurima. Near by was the city of bears and monkeys. Over eighty kos spread the city and was in two parts, one for bears and one for monkeys. There lived Machhandar Kanna. One day there was a great monkey wedding. One day Lakshman went for Machhandar Kanna; he took with him nine hundred and eighty lakhs of Singhi Tumi. On Kari Patpar he made a great shelter of the branches of a fig tree and slept, while the Singhi Tumi watched.

[1]A group of Baiga specially renowned for their magical powers.

When the Singhi Tumi saw the monkey-marriage they were frightened and said, 'Let us go back to our own country.' But Surtamal Singhi threw charmed rice at the monkeys. One grain hit the monkey's wedding-booth and it withered. Another grain hit the bride and bride-groom and they fell senseless. A third grain hit them and their pulses grew feeble. Tiblu the monkey was their Gunia. He made a winnowing-fan of sarai leaves and a gourd of mohlain leaves; he used sihar seeds for rice and sought the omens.

The god came upon him and he learnt what had happened. In turn he threw magic rice at the Singhi Tumi and now they fell senseless.

Sukli Chamarin was a mighty witch. She made a lamp of a human skull; she held it back to front with a hole in the neck. Her menstrual blood was the oil, her menstrual cloth the wick. She went to the Singhi Tumi and waved the lamp over them. They stood up and went to where Machhandar Kanna was swinging in her attic. Machhandar Kanna was afraid that they would carry her off and ruin her caste, so she ran away and hid in the belly of a bod fish. The Singhi Tumi tried to catch it but the fish escaped to Jalahalpuri. At the boundary of the village the fish made seven lines of flour and cried, 'Let no one step across this.' But Gursaman Singhi pulled hairs out of his arm and tied them to a saja branch. With this broom he swept the flour away and they were able to go into the village and catch the bod fish and bring Machhandar Kanna to Lakshman as his bride.

This was the first broom and since then there have been brooms in the world.

6

GOND

Banjar, Mandla District

Nindhan Guru married Sukri Chamarin, and they enjoyed it, but they had no grain to eat. So Sukri made maize and with cowhide fashioned a grindstone four fingers broad, and ground the grain and cooked it.

Her old mother, Rana the witch, gave her a dream. 'What are you doing that for? Why don't you make a bullock?' So Nindhan Guru and his wife urinated on the ground and he formed the wet earth into a bullock and she formed it into a cow.

They searched for some *murmaili* ground, ground defiled by menstrual blood, and there they drove the first plough. Three kinds of grain sprang up—kodon, kutki and mandia. When it was ready, Sukri Chamarin took the leather grindstone and cursed it saying, 'Go into the Middle World and be of use to people everywhere.' And as it went into the Middle World the leather turned into stone by the witch's knowledge and soon everyone was using it.

7

GOND

Daonjara, Pendra Zamindari

Jitho Gondin lived with her husband in Narhapur. She used to grind the rice in an ordinary rolling-mill. One day a Pankin came to see her and found her very tired of this work. 'I cannot go on, my waist hurts all the time.'

The husband of Jitho was a Gunia. He had a dream. 'In Bauragarh there is a tree with silver leaves. There is Chandi Devi.[1] Worship him with a cock whose feathers are reversed and he will give you his penis as a pestle.'

Jitho's husband took the cock and went to Bauragarh to offer it to Chandi Devi. The god said, 'Hold out your cloth in front of you. Go over there in front of me and stand on one leg.' Chandi Devi took off his penis and threw it at the Gunia. It hit him on the left shoulder and fell into the cloth. Chandi Devi said, 'Next full moon erect it by offering rice to it. Take it to the Agaria and he will fit an iron band round the glans. You must first husk kodon brought from your clearing.'

The Gunia took Chandi Devi's penis home. His wife came out with a lamp on her head to greet him and bring him into the house. She cowdunged the court and they put the penis there on a little platform and offered it fire and sarai resin. On the full moon day they offered a black chick and a coconut; they threw rice at it and it was aroused. They brought virgin kodon, millet that grows in a forest clearing that has not been penetrated by the plough. Jitho caught hold of the strong hard penis and husked the kodon with it. Then said Chandi Devi in a dream, 'For seven ages you will make the pestle of khairkuta wood, which never bends.'

[1] This is an example of the not uncommon convention whereby goddesses can be regarded as male or gods as female.

8

GOND

Tikaitola, Rewa State

In Koeli-Kachhar was born a Gond named Korbasera. He had many children but no food. One day Bairasin Mata came to him and from her body pulled out two sets of entrails. She gave them to Korbasera and told him to make an adze with one of them and a ploughshare with the other. 'Go to the Madhuban and find a daura tree. Cut it down and bring the wood'.

The Gond found the wood and with the Mata's entrails made a plough. With a piece of bamboo he made an ox-goad.

9

KAHAR

Khuria, Bilaspur District

In the old days men did not eat grain, but only the fruit and roots of the jungle. In the jungle lived the Dano Banhahu; he used to eat grain. But though he had a store of rice he had no idea how to husk it and used to eat it as it was, unhusked. With the unhusked grain he used to eat one man every day. One day he failed to get a grown man; all he had was a small boy. He thought, 'I will never fill my belly with a child like this; what is the good of eating him,' and so he kept the boy in his house and ate grain in his presence.

The next day when the Dano was out searching for food, the boy began to play with the grain. He took a stick and beat it and presently the rice began to come out of the husks. The Dano came back and when he ate the husked rice he was very pleased. He said to the boy, 'Make me food like this every day and I will never eat you.'

Every day the boy used to beat the grain with his stick. When it was ready he would get a mohlain leaf, cook it and give it to the Dano to eat. But presently the grain was almost finished and now when the boy beat it, it scattered and the husks were not separated. So he got a stone and shaped it into the form of a pestle and made a little hole in the ground and so husked the rice. Basmotin Kaniya came to the boy in a dream and said, 'Marry me and I will show you the best way to husk rice.' The boy promised and the Kaniya was born from inside a bamboo. She gave the boy a winnowing-fan. After that the boy used to take the grain every day to his wife for husking. The Dano never found out.

10

KAMAR

Bindra-Nawagarh Zamindari

In the great Binjhiban jungle lived a Basor called Bichhua. He lived below a great rock in a cave, and ate roots and fruit and leaves. One day he said to himself, 'Let me get some work, so that I and my sons may live better.' So thinking, he made an hatchet of lac and a blade of wax and went to Ghaila-Kachhar. There were growing fine bamboos and tall chir-grass. When he reached the place he cut three bamboos and cut off the top and bottom sections; the bits he kept were as long as his two arms outstretched. He then wondered how to cut chir-grass for making brooms, for he could not cut it with his blade of wax. He took a little dirt from his hand and lifted up a pebble with the toes of his left foot. With these things he made a black crab and gave it eight legs and two claws. He blessed the crab saying, 'Go, my son, your home will be below the earth and your name will be Kakramal Kshattri.' He said again, 'Son, there is something for you to do. Cut me a load of chir-grass and I will be able to go home.'

The crab at once cut a load of chir-grass with its claws and the Basor took it home. He cut the bamboo and dried it in the sun. With the grass he made a broom. For a winnowing-fan he chose the finest bamboo. With what was left he made baskets. When everything was ready he went to Surjalpur village and sold the things he had made. He got a lot of money and grain. Indeed the women of the village were soon quarrelling over his baskets, for each of them wanted one.

11

KEWAT

Andarisama, Dondi-Lohara Zamindari

A Kewat and his wife lived in the city of Jalhalpur. One day the Kewat went to the jungle and made a great net from the fibres of the odhar tree, tying it with cords made of chanahur creepers. He weighted the net with stones. One day after taking his supper he went to Raktahi River, to the rapids called Jhumardar, to fish. There he threw his great net into the water. He caught many fish in it, and at last even the Raja of the fish, Raja Saur Paharua. The net was so heavy that he could not draw it out of the water. The Raja was as large as a stout grain-bin.

The Kewat tied the net to a tree and went home to get a pair of plough-buffaloes. He attached the buffaloes to the net and made them pull it out.

But as he was about to kill the fish, Raja Saur Paharua said, 'O Kewat, wait a moment. Listen to my word and then you may kill me.' The Kewat said, 'Well, tell me quickly what you have to say.' Raja Saur Paharua said, 'In my head there is a stone. Take it out and you can use it as a grindstone for grinding wheat and rice.' The Kewat killed the great fish and when he had opened the head, he found a stone and took it home.

The Kewat cut up the flesh of the fish and took it round the village to sell. With the money he got a chisel of virgin iron and a hammer of virgin iron from the Agaria. He broke the stone into two pieces and prepared a grindstone with the hammer and chisel. From the bits of stone that he chiselled off, other grindstones were made and spread through the world. Even now there is a little stone in the head of the saur fish. It should not be eaten, for it causes stone in the kidney.

12

KUNTIA CHOKH

Pondi, Lapha Zamindari

At first people used to husk grain with a roller and stone. They had no mortar and pestle. The Lamana were carrying red earth on their pack-bullocks. At that time lived Toro Naik and Parsu Lamana. There were no cooking-pots then, no *handi* or *tilai.* Toro and Parsu put the bells of twelve bullocks and the trappings of thirteen bullocks on the leader of the herd, on whom the god would ride. The Lamanin made flour by grinding aonra fruit; she moulded the flour into a pot and hardened it in the sun. Toro and Parsu left the Lamanin and went to trade. She grew weary of husking grain with roller and stone and went to the Agaria.

She found the twelve Agaria brothers, the thirteen Tamesur brothers, the fourteen Kalesur brothers, but when they saw her coloured dress they ran away for fear. But Sabal Sai said, 'It's only a Lamanin; don't be afraid.' And he asked her, 'What do you want?' She said, 'Make me a sounding pestle, with iron rings that will make music like a bed.' Sabal Sai made her the pestle of khair wood and put iron rings on it. He said, 'When you sit to husk, sit with one leg outstretched and with the heel of the other leg pressing against your thing. You are always without your husband for he wanders with his pack-bullocks, but as you husk with the heel pressed against you, you will get pleasure and your waters will flow.'

Then the Lamanin went to the Basor and got from him twelve winnowing-fans and twelve *churki* baskets. She took them home and thus the work of the fan and the pestle began in the world.

13

LANJHIA SAORA

Taraba, Ganjam District

Kanjam Saora and his wife grew old. They had seven daughters: they were all unmarried. They went to an old Saora witch, Kabri, to learn magic. For seven years they stayed and when they had learnt everything from her they returned to their parents. The people of their village were frightened and got one of their women taught magic also. One day the seven sisters, followed by the village woman, went to the forest for wood. When it was cut and ready tied in bundles, a Raja came hunting. The eldest sister was very beautiful and the Raja caught her and enjoyed her. Then he leapt up and was going away, but the women struck him with their magic and he fell from his horse and died. The sisters took out his brains and liver and started for home. On the way was a river and they halted on the bank, considering how they might cook and eat. They had wood, and there was water, but there was no hearth. So the eldest sister took out her vagina and put it on the ground. The others put wood in it and fire and cooked the liver and brains. Thus these women learnt how to make a hearth and when they got home they made a hearth of baked earth. It was in the shape of a vagina and at the top was a small tip like the tip of the clitoris.

14

PAṄKA

Sanhrwachhapar, Mandla District

There was a marriage between earth and sky. These two were going round the pole when they fell down together, slipping on moss that had grown in the court. A god came on Nanga Baiga and said, 'Go to the gotaiya shrub; below it you will find chir-grass. Go and bring it and make a broom.' Someone went and brought the grass and Nanga Baiga made a broom and cleaned the courtyard very carefully with it. Then earth and sky went again round the pole.

15

TAKALA SAORA

Jirango, Ganjam District

The daughter of Raja Sambher was a great magician. The Raja made a separate palace for her and she lived there with her parrot. One day Raja Marhar rode by on his camel. He saw the shady garden in front of the palace and rested there. The parrot saw him and flew back to tell the girl. When she saw him, she enchanted him with her magic and took him to her house. She kept him with her for many days, but at last the memory of his home came to him. He went to his camel and said, 'I want to go home: how can we escape?' The camel said, 'First kill the parrot and then while the girl is sleeping get up quietly and come to me.' The Raja killed the parrot and that night, when the girl went to sleep, he escaped from the palace and rode away on the camel. But the girl awoke and followed them. She caught them up just as they had reached the river at the boundary of her kingdom. The camel went into the water but the girl caught it by the tail. The camel said to the Raja, 'Cut off my tail'. The Raja did so and they escaped across the river. The girl in rage threw the tail onto the bank. From it sprang up the chir-grass. The girl cut the grass and made a broom. She kept it in her palace in memory of her lover and since then there have been brooms in the world.[1]

[1] This is a curious echo of the famous Chhattisgarh tale of Prince Dhola. See *Folk-Songs of Chhattisgarh*, 371 ff.

CHAPTER FOURTEEN

FOOD

I

The Discovery of Grain

In Chota Nagpur the Uraon and the Kharia attribute the origin of grain to the Supreme Being. According to the Uraon story taken down by Roy, after the first human beings had made an embankment for their field, Dharmes gave them one seed of the bottle-gourd. This they planted and it grew, it trailed, it put forth flowers and bore fruit, and the fruit ripened. Dharmes had a threshing-floor prepared and cleaned. Then he pointed out a stretch of low-lying land where the peasants could dig and plough. Paddy began to come out; grain came out, wheat came out. And indeed all the different kinds of grain, pulse, and oilseed began to grow. Then Dharmes showed the first parents of mankind how to reap the rice crop with a sickle and pile the sheaves on the threshing-floor and taught them how to thresh and winnow. From that day man has ploughed and sowed paddy.[1]

The Kharia story is similar, though the names are different. Here it is Ponomosor who teaches the first human couple saved from the universal fire that destroyed the world. According to his advice they cut down trees and burnt them. In the clearing they sowed a pumpkin seed, given by Ponomosor, and it germinated and the plant grew up. It bore three fruits. Of these, the first fruit was found to grow slowly while the second developed rapidly and ripened first. Ponomosoṛ told the man and woman to pick it and offer its head in his name. When they opened it they found that it was full of the grain *panicum miliare*, but being ignorant of the art of cooking they only powdered it and ate it raw. Even now, Roy says, the Kharia eat this grain in powdered form before they take it boiled and at a feast they offer a little of the powdered grain to Ponomosor before drinking rice-beer.

There was enough grain in the gourd to last till the third gourd ripened. The man and woman again offered its head to Ponomosor and this time when they opened it they found it full of upland rice. The first and largest gourd ripened last of all. Before opening

[1] Roy, *The Oraons*, 468.

it the man and woman offered a special sacrifice to Ponomosor and now they found the gourd full of lowland rice. To this day the Kharia offer a cock to Ponomosor in their rice-fields before they cut the crop and they recall that it was this deity who taught them how and when to sow rice.[1]

The Warli tradition is different. The earth was bare and no seeds could be found. Naran Barambha went to an ant-hill where an ant had stored the various kinds of seed. The gods forced it to give them some of them, but they were not sufficient. They then went to the squirrel, where they got fruit-seed, and to the parrot, but the store was still inadequate. At last they got what they wanted from the king Lakhpati.

The seed then had to be sown. Naran Deo asked Isar Deo to help him. Isar Deo and his consort, Gauri, separated the different kinds of seed and stored them in bags. 'What road will you take?' asked Gauri. 'I will go by the road of bullocks,' answered her husband. 'And what road will you take?' 'I will go by the road of cows. And how will you sow the seeds?' she asked. 'I will sow the seeds of the palm and the date palm very sparingly,' he said. 'We may take twelve years to sow them all, and we may forget each other in such a long time,' she replied. So Isar Deo gave her his wedding kerchief.

The couple sowed seed in handfuls on the earth. At the same time they called for the rains, so that there should be no delay. After twelve years they met again and at first did not recognise each other. Hungry and thirsty they wept. Isar Deo planted a palm and Gauri planted a date palm. When they grew, Isar Deo dug for water at their roots and they drank and became intoxicated.[2]

I have recorded four different accounts of the origin of seed and the birth of Annadai or Kutkidai, who is the goddess of food, in *The Baiga*,[3] but they are too lengthy to reproduce here.

[1] Roy, *The Kharias*, ii, 424 f. [2] See Sawe, 163 ff. [3] *The Baiga*, 318 ff.

1

AGARIA

Koelari, Rewa State

Mahadeo first made Nanga Baiga, a Gond and an Ahir. When children were born they went to Mahadeo and said, 'We have no food, no water and nothing to make houses. How are we to live ?' Mahadeo took a ring from his finger, some hairs from his beard and a few of his eye-lashes and gave them to Nanga Baiga saying, 'Throw these where you will and you will have all you need '.

Nanga Baiga went away and first he threw down the ring and there came into being the seven seas and the sixteen streams. He threw the hairs from the beard and soon the earth was covered with grass which people cut and used to thatch their houses. He threw the eye-lashes on to the side of a hill and soon there was a crop of kodon and kutki which men used for food.

2

BHAINA

Kenda Zamindari

At the beginning there was no grain in the world, and men sought for it everywhere. At last they heard that it might be found in the raised hood of the great Cobra of the Under World. Bhimsen sent the parrot to the Under World to get it. The parrot flew down, cut the Cobra's hood and found a grain of kodon. It took the grain in its beak and flew away. As it was flying over a thick bamboo jungle, the grain fell from its beak.

A Basor was passing through that jungle. As he was cutting some bamboos the grain fell with a crash to the ground. He was about to pick it up when the grain said, 'Don't take me now, but first go to your house and prepare store-bins ready for me.' The Basor went home and made many great store-bins. He returned to the jungle and when he brought the grain home and put it in the bins, it at once grew of its own accord into a vast quantity of kodon and filled every bin to overflowing.

The news went through the world and many people came to the Basor to ask for grain. He said, 'Well, I will give it, but first you must eat at my house, and Bhimsen must marry my daughter.' 'Very well,' said Bhimsen. 'Get the food ready.' They got a great feast ready, and when it was laid out on leaf-plates and the guests were about to sit down, Bhimsen clapped his hands and at once a storm of rain and wind swept down, carrying away the plates and food into the air. Bhimsen said, 'Look, we agreed to your conditions. Now you must do as you promised and give us grain.' So they brought their sacks and bullocks and the Basor distributed grain to the whole world.

3

BONDO

Gokurupada, Koraput District

In the great ocean the five Bhima brothers were bathing and playing about, throwing the water to and fro and making a lot of noise. The seven Singraj-surang sisters were born from the contact of the Bhima brothers with the water. The three Lakmi sisters were also born; their names were Kerong (Rice), Rikdar (Sawa) and Game (Mandia).

The ten sisters met and played in the water. Gradually as they wandered dancing and playing, they came to the Middle World. But when they saw men the Singraj-surang sisters hid below the water, but the Lakmi sisters could find nowhere to hide and tried to run away.

On the way the five Phoga (tobacco) sisters were born. Sitya-Mahalakmi was in her period and a drop of the blood fell to the ground and from it these Phoga sisters were born. The Phoga sisters said to the Lakmi sisters, 'Why are you running away. Don't be afraid. They will only eat you twice in the day, but us they will eat all day long.'

So the three Lakmi sisters and the five Phoga sisters came to the Middle World and lived there.

4

DHANWAR

Rawa, Uprora Zamindari

Jhinjhigarh was a great mountain. There no crow cawed, no bird chirped. There lived Bhakku the Basor, in that jungle. One day he went with his axe, which had a handle of silver and a head of gold, to cut bamboo for a winnowing-fan. When he found a clump he walked round and round it; in the middle he saw a bamboo he liked; he cut it and took it home. When he began to cut it up there, twenty-one kinds of grain came from the hollow. Bhakku put it in his house—there were seven grains of each of the twenty-one grains. Then he split up the bamboo into slats to make his winnowing-fan. When he cut through one of the knots, out came a spider. Thus was the spider born. Grain and the spider are sister and brother. 'Wherever you live,' said the spider, 'I will live with you and will spread my web above you.'

The Basor thought in his mind how he could increase the grain and so make a profit. He cleared a field and cut the grass and when the time came he prepared to plough it. He caught two tigers to serve as bullocks. He tied them up with snakes for rope. On the end of his goad he fixed a scorpion. He made the ploughshare of a krait, the handle of a viper, the yoke was a python. With this plough he ploughed five hands deep. At harvest time the spider went to call men to help in the reaping. But there was no one to be found, so he spread his web across the trees and caught many parrots, twenty hundred green parrots. 'Come and cut the rice and kodon, or I'll kill you all.' So said the spider. He took them with him and in two days they had reaped the crop. They took it grain by grain in their beaks to the threshing-floor, and when it was done flew back to the forest.

But there was no room for all the grain in the Basor's house, so he called the neighbours and people from other villages. Each village got one measure of seed and thus grain was spread through the world.

5

GADABA

Onumal, Koraput District

Bengan Raja and his Rani lived in Kalaput. In those days there was no grain in the world and the Raja and Rani lived on roots and wild berries. The Raja had seven daughters. When they were grown up, they said to their father, 'We are not going to spend our lives eating roots and wild berries. Go and find grain for us.' The Raja wandered over the world, but he could find nothing and was returning disappointed when he met the seven Jalkamni Sisters. He told them his trouble, and the youngest of the sisters said to him, 'Cut off the bun of my hair, and you will find seed-grain inside. Take it home and when your field is ready, shake the bun of hair over it.' The Raja did as she told him, and when he shook the bun seed fell over the field, and when the rains came down every kind of grain sprang up. After the harvest the neighbours came to the Raja for seed.

6

GOND

Pakhri, Mandla District

Kanwa Lawa the Quail was the Raj Panda of winged creatures, birds, flying ants, butterflies and every insect. He had only one eye and could see everything when the god rode upon him. He was a great Gunia and in his court he settled every quarrel and imposed fines on all winged creatures who broke the law.

The twelve Gond brothers went to Sumringarh Pahar, but there was no good land there for cultivation. Their leader was Gorsa; he said, 'What are we to do in a place like this?' He looked at the jungle and saw the bamboos rubbing against one another and the sparks flying up. He cut two bamboos and made a fire-drill, rubbing a stick between his hands. He tore off a bit of his cloth and set fire to it, and with it fired the jungle so that the people would be able to make fields.

Then the god came upon Kanwa Lawa and he saw what was to happen. He called the winged caste and said, 'Now the Gond army has come, and soon they will eat every one of you for food. All of you leave this place at once. I will give you another home.' Hearing this they flew away from that place.

The Gond brothers had no cattle, but they dug the ground with their digging-sticks and sowed the kodon they had got from the Basor. From that day the Gond began to turn the jungle into fields.

7

GOND

Bohi, Pandaria Zamindari

Shriyal Jhango was born from the left side of Parvati, Angarmoti from the right. Each had twelve sons and twelve daughters. The Gond were born from Shryial Jhango; the first Gond's name was Dharticharan. From Angarmoti were born the Hindus, the Mussalmans and the English. To feed them Mahadeo at first gave the seeds of the bamboo and sarai. But they refused to eat such poor food, and he had to give them proper grain.

8

JUANG

Bali, Keonjhar State

One day when Rusi and his wife were living in the jungle and Rusi had to be away a great deal leaving his wife alone, he made two wooden dolls and covered them with earth to make them look nice.

Ishwaro and Parvati were wandering through the jungle and when Parvati saw the dolls she was pleased and said to Ishwaro, 'Look, what pretty things those are. Do give them the gift of life.' Ishwaro said, 'Very well, go away and I will make them alive and then you may follow me.'

Parvati went away and Ishwaro made the two dolls alive. When Parvati went to see them she found them playing together. Then she said, 'But what can they eat?' Ishwaro said, 'Go away again and I will give them food.' He took two sticks and put them in their mouths. When Parvati came the next time to see them, she saw the sticks in their mouths and said, 'How can they eat this wood? Do give them some grain.' But Ishwaro said, 'No, that is their proper food. Where can I get grain?' Parvati said, 'Let us go and find some.'

By the sea the twelve Lakmi sisters were living and of these the greatest was Rice. The sisters always lived in the water but they got very tired of this and one day they said to Rice, 'Sister, how boring it is in this water. Let us go on earth and wander about.' Rice said, 'If I go to the dry land they will eat me.' The others said, 'Very well then, you come last. We will go ahead and if they want to eat anything they can eat us.' So the twelve sisters came on to dry land and as they went Parvati saw them. She told Ishwaro and he begged them to go and live with the two living dolls. They did so and from that day men have eaten grain, but because of the two sticks that Ishwaro first put in their mouths they have always cleaned their teeth with tooth-twigs.

9

RAJNENGI PARDHAN

Kanchanpur, Mandla District

In Deogarh lived the gods. In Garha lived a Gond. The Gond went to Deogarh and climbed a little hill near the place when the gods saw him. They said to him, 'Brother, who are you and what do you want?' The Gond replied, 'I have come from Garha, but my real home is Titihidongri.' The gods said, 'What is your name and your clan?' The Gond said, 'My name is Mahasingh and my clan is Parteti.' The Gond said again, 'Brothers, I have come a very long way and I am hungry. Give me something to eat; even a few roots will do.' The gods replied, 'Do not eat roots, brother. Here is spear-grass. We will show you how to take the grain from it and cook it.'

Mahasingh went and cut a lot of spear-grass; he piled it up and removed the grain and when it was ready he took it to the gods and they tied it up in a bundle with mohlain leaves. Mahasingh took the bundle home and when he opened it he found that it was full of kodon. This is how kodon came into the world.

II

The Omnivorous Tradition

There are a few legends to account for, and to support, the aboriginals' freedom in their use of food. One of the earliest occurs in the Lingo legend recorded by Hislop.

How did the Gonds conduct themselves ?
Whatever came across them they must needs kill and eat it ;
They made no distinction. If they saw a jackal they killed
And ate it ; no distinction was observed :
They respected not antelope, sambhar, and the like.
They made no distinction in eating a sow, a quail, a pigeon,
A crow, a kite, an adjutant, a vulture,
A lizard, a frog, a beetle, a cow, a calf, a he-and she-buffalo,
Rats, bandicoots, squirrels—all these they killed and ate.
So began the Gonds to do. They devoured raw and ripe things ;
They did not bathe for six months together ;
They did not wash their faces properly, even on dung hills they would fall down and remain.
Such were the Gonds born in the beginning. A smell was spread over the jungle.[1]

10

BISON-HORN MARIA

Lakhopal, Bastar State

Gajabhimul and Pallebhimul had two daughters, Ilo and Palo. Both girls wanted to marry Koyabhimul. But the parents were unwilling and tried to get rid of the boy. They hid a great snake called Permadighuse by the path along which he used to go to fetch sago-palm wine. But the girls warned him and told him to call on their father by name as he went along. 'Then the snake will do you no harm.' When he reached the house safely, Gajabhimul was angry and tried to kill him in some other way. But the girls again warned him and he escaped. Then Gajabhimul took him to offer sacrifice. He asked the boy to feed the chicken with rice, planning to kill him as he was engrossed in this.

[1] Hislop, 4. See also, for myths about beef-eating, *The Agaria*, 125 ff.; Roy, *The Hill Bhuiyas*, 31 ; Russell and Hiralal, iii, 508 ; Nanjundayya and Iyer. iv, 128 f. ; *Folk-Tales of Mahakoshal*, 477 ff.

But the boy said, 'I do not know how to do it; show me first.' Gajabhimul bent down to give rice to the chicken and Koyabhimul took a knife and cut off his head. When the time came for the boy's marriage with Ilo and Palo, Mahapurub found there was no curry for the guests. He told Koyabhimul to go and relieve himself behind the house. From his excreta two pigs were born. The boy caught the pigs and killed them and the marriage-party enjoyed the pork. Since that time we have eaten pigs.

11

JUANG

Phanasnasa, Keonjhar State

One day Dharam Deota sent two sepoys to call Sadhan Burha. But Sadhan Burha made a tiger and it devoured them. Then Dharam Deota sent four sepoys, and Sadhan Burha said, 'Let them die' and they died. Dharam Deota said to Sadhan Burha, 'I called you; why didn't you come?' Sadhan Burha said, 'I had fever; how could I come?' 'Where are my six sepoys?' 'How should I know?' 'Open your mouth and I will see.' Sadhan Burha opened his mouth and there was a hair growing from his tongue. Dharam Deota tried to remove the hair, but it would not come out. He gave Sadhan Burha frogs to eat, but the hair would not come out. He gave him fish, snakes, crabs, frogs, tigers, everything and anything in the world to eat, but the hair would not come out. Finally he gave a hairy caterpillar and out came the hair. Then said Dharam Deota, 'Since you have already eaten everything and anything, now you may always eat what you will.'

12

RAJNENGI PARDHAN

Kanchanpur, Mandla District

When cows were first born in the world there was a great forest all over the land and many wild men lived there and ate much meat. If on any day they were not able to get deer or wild goats or hares they used to catch the cows and eat them. So eating eating the cows they grew very fat and presently turned into Dano.

But the race of cows began to disappear. When this happened the Kapila cow was born out of the ground. She was white as an egg, everything about her was white, her ears, horns, feet, tail all were white. She went to the jungle called Jhalsura and there prayed to Kalpadi Deo, 'I have been born to give milk to the world and to care for men.' Kalpadi Deo said, 'Go without fear and I will protect you. Anyone who now eats a cow and swallows the liver will find fire in his belly and he will die.' This happened and many Dano died. Presently they gave up eating beef.

13

RAJNENGI PARDHAN

Patangarh, Mandla District

Before Mahadeo sent men to live in the world he wanted to test them. He called a Hindu, a Gond and a Baiga and put before them food made by mixing everything in the world—liquor, the blood of living creatures, the sap of bitter trees, bits of meat, the legs of frogs and red ants. When the Hindu ate the mixture he vomited and was very ill, but the Gond and Baiga swallowed it without difficulty and enjoyed it. Since then the Hindu has been very careful of what he eats but the Gond and Baiga eat anything in the world.

CHAPTER FIFTEEN

TOBACCO

TOBACCO was introduced into India by the Portuguese in the fifteenth century.[1] It is not held sacred by the Hindus, but some aboriginal tribes ascribe to it a divine origin. And there is a South Indian verse which certainly gives it a high place in human affairs. 'Once Indra asked Brahman, " What is the best thing in the world ?" And he replied by his four mouths, " *Tabaku*, *pogaku*, *hogesoppu*, and *pogele* ", or " Tobacco, tobacco, tobacco, tobacco ", in Hindusthani, Telugu, Kanarese and Tamil.'[2] With this judgement the aboriginal of Middle India would heartily agree.

There are four main traditions about the discovery of tobacco. The first is that it was found by accident: someone used the leaf as a platter and inhaled the fumes with his food; a dancer idly picked and chewed a leaf while he was relieving himself. Then tobacco is a medicine revealed by Bara Pen as a cure for sickness, by Burha Pinnu as a solace in bereavement. Tobacco, in fact, as modern sophisticated man likes to believe, is good for one; it is a necessity of life. Tobacco also has a humanitarian purpose; the gods introduced it to stop men working so hard and thus wearing out their bullocks. Fourthly, there is the motif of 'The Girl Nobody Loved' who turned into a tobacco plant and was then desired by all the world.

This last idea is probably widely distributed. I have found it among the Kond, Gadaba and Juang of Orissa, the Muria of Bastar and the Gond of Mandla.[3] Bompas gives a Santal tale with the same theme.

This is the way that the chewing of tobacco began. There was once a Brahmin girl whose relations did not give her in marriage and she died unmarried. After the body had been burned and the people had gone home, Chando thought, 'Alas, I sent this woman into the world and she found favour with no one; well, I will confer a gift on her which will make men ask for her every day'. So he sowed tobacco at the burning-place and it grew up and flourished.

[1] G. Watt, *Commercial Products of India*, art, Nicotiana.

[2] S. M. Natesa Sastri, 'A Verse on Tobacco,' *The Indian Antiquary*, xx, 297. See also Ganpat Rai, ibid., xl, 39.

[3] There is a curious variant, given at p. 160 of this book, that the girl whom nobody loved had herself turned into a scorpion so that she could revenge herself on men.

The story goes on to describe how a cowherd, suffering from toothache, found the leaves and discovered that they soothed the pain. Soon men who had no toothache also took to it and acquired a craving for it.[1]

There is a Khasi parallel to the Muria story (No. 13) given in the text. A man and wife have nothing with which to entertain a friend and kill themselves for shame. A robber takes shelter in the house, finds the corpses and kills himself for fear. When the friend hears what has happened he begs the Great God to show 'a way of keeping up the customs of hospitality without the poor having to suffer and be crushed.' God makes three trees spring from the ground where the bodies lay, *betel*, *pān* and tobacco—the three necessities of Indian hospitality.[2]

I

GADABA

Kairiput, Koraput District

A Raja had a daughter; she was cross-eyed, dwarfish, covered with sores, one arm was deformed. Yet in spite of all her face was beautiful as a parrot: her eyes shone like fireflies; she spoke sweetly as a maina. To get her married her father used to dress her in many lovely clothes and cover her body with ornaments. Yet no one would come to drink liquor for her.

The girl was very *buffu*; she longed for men; she was always thinking about lying with men and of being loved by them. She wanted to be tethered to one and feel the hurt of the peg. Yet not a single man would look at her. At last in misery she went to the jungle. As she was wandering through the trees, she met Mahaprabhu and fell at his feet saying, 'Lie with me.'

Mahaprabhu was angry and cursed the girl, 'Go, you will be no more a woman; become a tobacco plant and then all the men you want will enjoy you.' As she stood there the girl became a plant, the precious tobacco plant that men desire above their food and wives.

[1] Bompas, 407. The story is also printed in Bodding, Part III, 492 f.
[2] Rafy, 75 ff.

2

GOND

Ghatiya, Mandla District

Formerly tobacco grew wild in the jungle and the people did not know what it was. A Gond called Sonsai was famous as a Gunia. A man came to him with a very bad cough. Sonsai Gunia looked in his winnowing-fan and found nothing. But at night Bara Pen came in a dream and told him to get tobacco leaves from the jungle as medicine. Sonsai got the leaves and when the sick man had smoked them he recovered. He went home and next time someone had a cough he told him of the remedy and he too was cured.

In this way the new medicine spread through the world.

3

GOND

Dhameri, Rewa State

Nanga Baiga was cutting his clearing. When he got tired he put down his axe and made a pipe of a parsa leaf and filled it with tobacco of aonra leaves. At that very moment Gungusur Mai was born and said to Nanga Baiga, 'Why are you smoking these wretched aonra leaves? Go to the Kajliban and you will get real tobacco there'.

Nanga Baiga therefore went to the Kajliban. He sat down and examined his measuring-sticks. From them he learned that in an ant-hill to the north lived a cobra which had tobacco seeds in its head. Nanga Baiga went to the place and when the cobra saw him it was pleased and spoke in a friendly way. Nanga Baiga asked for the tobacco seeds and the cobra said, 'You may take them from my head'. Nanga Baiga struck the cobra's head with his arrow and got the seeds out. That is why arrows have poison in them, for the poison came from the cobra's head on to the arrow. That too is why tobacco makes a man drunk just as poison does.

4

GOND

Bodachapar, Khariar Zamindari

As in No. 7, except that here it is Gond who are ploughing on Koeli-Kachhar, there is no mention of Kachra-Durwa, and when the smoke first came out of a Gond's mouth the people thought he was on fire and emptied two pots of water over him.

5

JUANG

Balipal, Keonjhar State

There was no tobacco at first. Men used to dry wild ganja leaves, powder them up and smoke them in pipes made of turmeric leaves. Women dried *ranijar* leaves and made lime by mixing the powder with *bandanjar* resin : this they used to eat.

Once the twelve brothers and thirteen sisters were dancing, but because there was no tobacco their bellies swelled and they wearied. But on a pile of cow-dung a tobacco plant had sprouted. One of the twelve brothers went to piss there : he saw the plant, broke off a leaf, tasted it and called to the rest to eat it also. They all ate, their bellies were calmed and they went to the dance with new vigour.

6

JUANG

Nan Gan, Pal Lahara State

Siromati Raja had one daughter. When the girl was mature, her father took rupees in his hand and went to find her a husband. Many boys came to see her, but she was so ugly that when they saw her they lost their power of speech and ran away silent.

As she grew older the girl saw how happily all the world was living, all were in pairs, ants, rats, birds, cattle, men and women. The Raja tried and tried to find a mate for her, but not a boy was ready. When the girl saw this she was very sad. She went to her father and said, ‘ No one will marry me. I do not want to go on living, ’ and she lay down and died then and there.

The Raja decorated her body and prepared to bury it. But the neighbours said he should burn it. So he made a great pyre and burnt his daughter's ugly body and only a little of the back-bone remained.

The girl's life went to Mahapurub who was well pleased at seeing her. ‘ Ask for anything you want ’, he said. The girl replied, ‘ In my lifetime no one desired me. Now make me into something that the world cannot do without.’ ‘ Very well ’, said Mahapurub and sent the life back to the pyre and into the little bit of bone. In due time this grew up as a tobacco plant.

A goatherd passed that way and saw the plant. ‘ This looks fresh and good’, he thought. He broke off a leaf and smelt it. It was a good smell. He got the seeds and sowed them till he had many plants. He used to smell the leaves. Then one day he put the leaf in his mouth and ate it. Soon he was drunk with it. Then he began to eat it daily : he gave it to all who visited his house. They too got drunk with it. They took seeds from him, and gradually tobacco spread over the world till men now say, ‘ There is no difference between tobacco and a wife : we love them equally.’

7

KAMAR

Bilaijhor, Bindra-Nawagarh Zamindari

First made was the earth and sky, then man. Kachra-Durwa wandered on the hills seeking food. He made a plough and drove his bullocks from dawn till night. He took no rest in the day and ate only after the sun had gone down. The bullocks said in their minds, ‘ How can we live like this ? We will surely die ’. The cow-queen went to tell Mahadeo of the sorrow of its sons. When Mahadeo heard the story, he took the form of an old man and came to earth. He met Kachra-Durwa in his field. ‘ Have you any fire ? ’ ‘ No. Why ? ’ ‘ I want to smoke a pipe of tobacco ’. ‘ What's that ? ’ Mahadeo gave some to Kachra-Durwa and his servants. They were soon drunk with the smoke. Mahadeo taught them how to sow the seed, pick and dry the leaves, powder them, wrap them in a pipe of parsa leaves, put fire in the bowl. Soon every half hour Kachra-Durwa and his men were finding it necessary to rest from their ploughing so that they could sit down for a smoke. In this way the bullocks got a little rest.

8

KHUNTIA CHOKH

Dumarkachhar, Bilaspur District

Long long ago Mahadeo sat on Kailas with his tongue hanging out. Three winds came there bringing the seeds of every plant. The banyan sprang up and Mahadeo's disciples picked it and threw away the seed. As the three winds blew, the hemp, tobacco and mahua seeds took root and began to grow. Soon the hemp and the tobacco were ready and they picked the leaves and dried them, and the mahua bore flowers that fell to the ground. Mahadeo said to his disciples, 'Eat, my disciples, eat whatever you like.' Those who ate the mahua began to extract the juice, for if they only ate the flowers they did not get enough. Mahadeo showed them how to make the juice into liquor. He showed them also how to dry the hemp and make ganja and prepare tobacco leaves and put them in a pipe.

9

KOND

Sarsopadro, Koraput District

In the Under World Bhim Raja had a Paik called Kotlamta. This Paik had seven sisters whom no one would marry. They came to the Middle World in search of husbands but, although they fell in love with every man they saw, no one returned their love and they went home miserable and disappointed. When Kotlamta heard their story, he took them to Bhim Raja and said, 'What are we to do with them ? Nobody wants these girls.' Bhim Raja rubbed a little dirt from his body and gave it to the sisters ; as they took it they turned into earth. Bhim Raja waited a little, then beat a gong with both his hands. At once a row of plants sprang up; for the elder sister, a haldi root; for the next, a sago palm ; for the next, tobacco; for the next, a date palm; for the next, a rose bush ; for the next, a hemp plant; for the youngest, a mahua tree. In this way the seven sisters turned into things that all men crave for.

10

KOND

Kurutigadu, Koraput District

Sonamali Dom and Rupamali Dom were going to a bazaar to trade. They camped under a tree by a river. Near the tree was growing a plant that was born from the *tulsipokali-bogipokali* in the heart of the jungle. The Dom cooked their food and picked some of the leaves of the plant to use as plates. They put the steaming hot rice on the leaves and some of the leaves' power went into it. When the Dom and his wife ate their food they became drunk. They went to Burha Pinnu and Pusrudi and asked them what had happened. 'That is tobacco,' they said. 'Get the seeds, sow them in your gardens, and chew the leaves.'

After some time Sonamali Dom died, and his wife wept so much that she fainted. The neighbours did everything they could to revive her. They offered the gods cows, goats, chickens, everything. But it had no effect. Then her mother put a little tobacco leaf into Rupamali's mouth, and she sat up and wept no more. Since then whenever someone dies we buy tobacco from the Dom and give it to the mourners and they soon forget their sorrow.

11

LANJHIA SAORA

Gailung, Koraput District

In Palagud lived a Pano[1] and his wife. They had no children. One day the Pano bought medicine and gave it to his wife. She fell ill and died. Her soul went to Mahaprabhu and told him, 'I had no children and no one in the world to care for me. Now grant that when I return again I will be welcome in every house and all will love me.' Mahaprabhu was pleased and said, 'Go to the world again. From the bones and skin of your breast will grow tobacco and you will live in every house.'

The neighbours took the corpse to the pyre, but in spite of all their efforts the bones and skin of the breast would not burn. On the third day they found a tobacco plant growing in the burning-ground. The woman gave a dream to her father and told him to pick the leaves and smoke them in a pipe.

[1] The Pano often go from village to village selling tobacco to the Saora.

12

LANJHIA SAORA

Maneba, Ganjam District

A Saora and his wife lived together for many years. They had no children, but they had a favourite cow. Every day they let it wander out of the house, graze in the jungle and return home. One day the cow wandered very far across the hills till it came to a glade where a tobacco plant was growing. The cow ate it and came home. When it excreted, it passed tobacco seeds in its dung. The old woman spread the dung, with the seeds, in her field and in due time there were many tobacco plants there. One day the Saora's belly swelled up and hurt him. He took every kind of medicine, but it was no good. At last he picked a tobacco leaf and chewed it. He felt better; he felt drunk and soon was fast asleep. Since then the whole world has used tobacco.

13

MURIA

Berma, Bastar State

In the old days it was the custom to entertain visitors with a few grains of rice, just as it is our custom today to offer them tobacco. But Rice grew weary of having to satisfy the needs of so many people and one day when its master was absent it fled from his house.

On the way it met a tobacco plant which asked what was the matter. When it heard the story the plant said, 'Do not worry. From today, when visitors come to the house I will take the first place and you can come afterwards and be given to them as food'. When the master of the house came home he found Rice missing and was embarrassed, for he had nothing to offer to his friends. He went in search of it and presently he saw a beautiful flower growing on a plant. He picked it and stuck it in his ear. After a little while the strong scent of the flower made him feel drunk and he wondered whether the seed and the leaf would be even more powerful. He brought seed and leaf and flower to his house and Rice followed him unobserved.

He then gave his visitors the tobacco leaves which they chewed and smoked and the flower which they smelt and everyone was satisfied and pleased. When the householder went into the kitchen he found that Rice had returned and was being cooked for the visitors and he was still more satisfied. So it is today: tobacco is first given to a visitor and afterwards rice is cooked as food.

14

OJHA

Singarpur, Raipur District

A man called Baghirati and his wife lived on roots and any fruit and vegetables they could find in the jungle. Baghirati wearied of this and went to serve Mahadeo. When his service was finished at the end of twelve years, Mahadeo was pleased and said, 'Ask for anything you want.' Baghirati said, 'Give me such a thing as will give me my food and living, and which when I beat it three times and it runs away, will return of its own accord.'

Mahadeo got one grain of spear grass and one grain of the best rice and gave them to Baghirati saying, 'Take these and give them to your wife to eat.' He took them home and gave them to his wife; she ate and conceived. In due time she gave birth to a black she-calf and a brown bull.

When these grew up Baghirati's son took them to his field and ploughed with them. He never rested, but worked all day long till the cow and bull were exhausted. Mahadeo came to the place. In those days cattle had four ears. Mahadeo cut two of the ears from the cow and the bull, and threw them away. They took root and tobacco plants sprang up from them.

Mahadeo took his penis in his hand and squeezed it. The glans came off and he gave it to Baghirati's son who made it into a pipe. Ever since, when people plough they stop frequently to smoke their pipes and in this way the cattle get a little rest.

15

RAJNENGI PARDHAN

Patangarh, Mandla District

A Brahmin who lived alone without any other Brahmin neighbours lived in a village in the jungle. He had a most beautiful daughter. One day a handsome light-coloured Chamar boy came to their house and said that he was a Brahmin and desired to work for the girl as a Lamsena. The Brahmin agreed and in due time the girl and boy were married.

One day the girl prepared a very tasty curry of vegetables and without thinking the boy exclaimed, 'It tastes as sweet as the leg of a cow.' The family wanted to know what he knew of beef and after a lot of questioning it came out that the boy was really a Chamar. The shock was so great to the girl that she died of grief. When he saw his beautiful wife lying dead the boy died also.

But the father had the two bodies cremated together and from the ashes of the girl's body grew the tobacco plant and from the boy's ashes grew the hemp plant. Ever since people have smoked tobacco and ganja together.

16

THE ORIGIN OF GANJA

GOND

Tikaitola, Rewa State

Maisur Dewar lived in the Ranjhikarola jungle and made a living by spinning rope. One day when he was in the deep forest he found a black she-cobra and fell in love with her. He used to go daily to massage its hands and feet. One day he did it with such vigour that he grew weary and sighed deeply. The she-cobra thought, 'My Dewar is tired, how can I put his weariness away from him?' She scratched her head and brought out two seeds and gave them to him. 'Sow these', she said, 'and when the tree grows pick the leaves and make an earthen pipe and smoke'. But the Dewar by mistake took the leaves with water and this made him so drunk that he could neither see nor hear.

17

GOND

Barratola, Mandla District

In Jhinjhgarh lived Korwasai Dewar the Baiga and his wife Andaro. They had a daughter whose name was Suknibai. Mahadeo came to serve for her as Lamsena and worked for five years in her house. But the Dewar and his wife did not give the boy proper food to eat, with the result that he grew very thin.

When the five years' service was completed, the Dewar and his wife said to Mahadeo, 'Now go and call your relatives and we will celebrate your marriage'. Mahadeo called for tigers, bears, snakes, scorpions and brought them in his marriage-party. The Dewar had collected a great quantity of food and liquor and when he saw the animals and reptiles in Mahadeo's marriage-party he was very angry, for he said, 'Who will eat the feast that I have provided?' Then Mahadeo by his magic power caused the animals to say that they would drink the Baiga's liquor but the snakes and scorpions said, 'We must have ganja'.

The Baiga gave the pots of liquor to the bears and tigers to drink but he had no ganja and wondered how to get some. Finally he sent his wife to pick datura leaves and when she brought them to the house he rubbed and rubbed them till a drop of juice fell to the ground. From this drop was born the hemp plant. Then the Baiga got the water of twelve tanks and made a pipe as big as twelve threshing-floors. He mixed the datura leaves with the water and filled the pipe and gave it to the snakes and scorpions to drink. They soon became drunk and began to dance. As the snakes danced—in those days they went upright like men—their backs broke and ever since they have gone flat along the ground.

18

The Origin of Opium

GOND

Upri, Rewa State

The baby daughter of Mahato Dewar and his wife was always crying. The Dewarin was unable to do any work because of the child and her husband used to beat her shouting, 'You do no work and just sit about all day with your baby in your lap'. As a result of the beating the wife grew thin as a bamboo stick. One day after she had been beaten the mother got very angry with her baby and said in her mind, 'It is because of this child that I have to suffer. Let me get some poison and kill her'.

So the mother went to the jungle to find some poisonous leaves. On the way she met Basuk Nag the cobra and told him her story. Basuk Nag took out his liver and gave it to her saying, 'Cut this up into bits and mix it with water. If you then give it to your baby she will sleep quietly'. When he took out his liver a few drops of blood fell to the ground and from these sprang the opium plant. The Dewarin took the liver home and gave a little to her baby. After that the child always slept quietly and the mother was able to do her work.

CHAPTER SIXTEEN

MAHUA SPIRIT

I

DALTON says that of all trees there is none that has a greater claim on the gratitude of the aboriginal than the mahua[1] and even the missionary Bodding writes, ' It is a tree of the greatest importance to the people.'[2] The corollae are boiled, roasted or parched and used for food either alone or with other things. At the beginning of the rains and in time of famine this is often the only food of the people. The expressed oil is used for lighting or cooking and even the crushed husks are used in Bastar for massage and are everywhere given to cattle for food. The use of mahua as the basis of country liquor is by no means the most important thing about it. More important than any other tree to the Chenchu, says Fürer-Haimendorf, is the mahua, ' whose sweet corollae provide him for weeks with an excellent food, rich in sugar and vitamins '.[3] There have been deplorable attempts in various parts of India to destroy mahua trees in order to prevent the illicit distillation of liquor. This shows, on the part of the authorities or politicians who have attempted it, the supremest ignorance both of the economic needs and of the psychology of the people, for the mahua is not only of the first economic importance but it is a sacred tree and the liquor distilled from its flowers is an important part of most aboriginal ritual. A branch of the tree is placed by many tribes as the wedding post round which the bride and bridegroom must process. Liquor is offered at every ceremony and in the name of every god. So highly do the Kharia value the tree that they call the month of Chait ' Murun Lerang ' because this is the month in which the mahua comes to flower and fruit.[4]

There are not, however, a great many legends about the origin of this tree or of the discovery of liquor. The most common legend is one—I give several examples in the text—whereby liquor was discovered by a god or hero who saw birds sipping mahua juice and getting drunk on it. There is actually a widely spread belief

[1] Dalton, 281. [2] Bodding, 467.

[3] C. von Fürer-Haimendorf, ' Food from Forests', *The Hyderabad Forest Magazine*, Vol. iii (1943), 3.

[4] Roy, *The Kharias*, 433.

among the villagers that bears get intoxicated on the mahua flowers for which they have a very strong attraction.[1]

A legend about the origin of the Sondi liquor-distillers was recorded by C. Hayavadana Rao.

According to a current tradition, there was in days of old a Brahmin, who was celebrated for his magical powers. The king, his patron, asked him if he could make the water in a tank burn, and he replied in the affirmative. He was, however, in reality disconsolate because he did not know how to do it. By chance he met a distiller, who asked him why he looked so troubled and, on learning his difficulty, promised to help him on condition that he gave him his daughter in marriage. To this the Brahmin consented. The distiller gave him a quantity of liquor to pour into the tank, and told him to set it alight in the presence of the king. The Brahmin kept his word, and the Sondi are the descendants of the offspring of his daughter and the distiller.[2]

Another story traces the origin of the caste to a certain Bhaskar or Bhaskar Muni, 'who was created by Krishna's brother, Balaram, to minister to his desire for strong drink. A different version of the same legend gives the Sondi for ancestor Niranjan, a boy found by Bhaskar floating down a river in a pot full of country liquor, and brought up by him as a distiller'.[3]

The Sondi have yet another tradition, 'that Brahma created the world, and pinched up from a point between his eyebrows a little mud from which he made a figure, and endowed it with life. Thus Suka Muni was created, and authorized to distil spirit from the ippa [or mahua] flowers, which had hitherto been eaten by birds'.[4]

A Puranic legend associates liquor with the kadamba tree.

Whilst the mighty Sesha, the upholder of the globe, was engaged in wandering amidst the forests with the herdsmen, in the disguise of a mortal, Varuna, in order to provide for his recreation, said to his wife Varuni (the goddess of wine), 'Thou, Madira, art ever acceptable to the powerful Ananta: go therefore, auspicious and kind goddess, and promote his enjoyments.' Obeying these commands, Varuni went and established herself in a hollow of the kadamba tree in the woods of Vrindavana. Baladeva, roaming about, came there, and smelling the pleasant fragrance of liquor, resumed his ancient passion for strong drink. The holder of the ploughshare, observing the vinous drops distilling from the kadamba tree, was much delighted, and gathered and quaffed them along with the herdsmen and the Gopis, whilst those who were skilful with voice and lute celebrated him in

[1] 'There is a common belief that on occasions bears become intoxicated as a result of eating fermented flowers.' A. A. Dunbar Brander, *Wild Animals in Central India* (London, 1931), 7.

[2] Thurston, vi, 395. [3] ibid., 395. [4] ibid., 396.

their songs. Being inebriated with the wine, and the drops of perspiration standing like pearls upon his limbs, he called out, not knowing what he said, 'Come hither, Yamuna river, I want to bathe.' The river, disregarding the words of a drunken man, came not at his bidding: on which Rama in a rage took up his ploughshare which he plunged into her bank, and dragged her to him, calling out, 'Will you not come, you jade? Will you not come? Now go where you please, if you can.' Thus saying, he compelled the dark river to quit its ordinary course, and follow him whithersoever he wandered through the wood.[1]

I

BAIGA

Bohi, Pandaria Zamindari

Then came Bhimsen, that great giant, in one mighty stride he came, one foot was in his house, the other came to Bhagavan. But he was very tired and he told Bhagavan that he must have some food before anything else. So Bhagavan gave him twenty-five sacks of rice and twelve sacks of lentils. He ate it all and said, 'This is nothing; give me more.' Then they gave him twelve sacks of gram. When he had eaten that also, he said to Bhagavan, 'Old uncle, you've given me nothing to drink.'

'You must go and find some liquor,' said Bhagavan.

'What is that?' asked Bhimsen.

'Go and see,' said Bhagavan.

Bhimsen went into the forest and searched and searched. After a long time he came to a mahua tree. The tree was hollow and that hollow was full of liquor. All round on the branches were sitting birds who had been drinking it—green pigeon, blue pigeon, parrots, crows, maina, every kind of bird. They were all nodding their heads. Why are they nodding their heads like that? thought Bhimsen. He climbed the tree to see and there the hollow was full of liquor. Bhimsen dipped his hand in and sucked it.

'This is liquor! This is liquor!' he shouted, and began to drink. When he had had a bellyful his head began to nod also. He sat down with the birds and they all nodded their heads together.

Then he filled twelve gourds full of the liquor and brought it back for Bhagavan to drink. They sat down, Bhagavan and the wind and the crow, and they drank the liquor out of leaf-cups. Then when their heads were nodding, Bhimsen got up and walked round the earth.

[1] Dutt, 385f.

2

BONDO

Andrahal, Koraput District

Once when Mahaprabhu and his wife were wandering through the jungle, Mahaprabhu collected some mahua flowers and put them in a hollow bamboo tube. He hung this tube from the branch of a tree and went away, intending to return for it later. But rain fell heavily, and he forgot all about it. Some of the rain went into the tube and the flowers fermented of their own accord. Presently the seven brothers passed by in search of game. They rested below the tree and one of them saw the bamboo tube. He tasted the liquid in it and soon he was very drunk. Then they all drank and thus learnt how to make mahua spirit.

3

BONDO

Dumiripada, Koraput District

A Raja was giving a feast to his Bondo and Gadaba subjects. After they had finished eating they sat round with full bellies and could think of nothing to say. Mahaprabhu came there and said, 'What is the matter? Why are you so dull?' They replied, 'There is no fire in us.' Mahaprabhu then showed them how to make rice-beer and how to distil spirit from the mahua flowers, and from that day there has been laughter and dancing in the world.

4

DHANWAR

Rawa, Uprora Zamindari

Hemar Kalar and Hemar Kalarin lived in the village Garh-Bengala-Jajhnagar-Pali. Once Bara Deo went there at midnight and woke them up. When their sleep opened, they fell at his feet and said, 'Sir, who are you? Where have you come from? We do not recognize your face.' 'I am Bara Deo, and I have come for a bottle of the fully-distilled liquor. If you don't give it to me, I will kill your five sons.' Hemar Kalarin was frightened and said, 'We have never heard of this "liquor" and we do not know how to make it.' Bara Deo said, 'Do as I tell you and you will be able to make it. In Kundalgarh there is a mahua tree; bring flowers from there; put them to soak in a new pot with water for seven days and seven nights. Then take them out and put them in a still.' And he told the Kalarin, 'For the still, you must cut off your own head and use it as the pot. Your arms will be the tubes and will fit into your eye-sockets. Your husband will place your head full of mahua on a hearth which he will make out of your vagina, and your legs and bones will be burnt for firewood. Do this, or I will take your five sons.' So said Bara Deo and went away.

The next morning Hemar Kalar thought, 'Bara Deo has been here. I must lose my wife or my five sons. It had better be my wife.' He went with her to Kundalgarh and brought mahua flowers. They soaked them in water for seven days and seven nights. Then the Kalar killed his wife. He scooped out the head and made a pot. In the two eyes he fixed her arms as tubes. He took out her vagina and made a hearth and put her legs and bones into it as firewood. He filled the skull with mahua flowers and lit the fire and soon there was a bottle of fully-distilled liquor ready.

Then came Bara Deo. 'Where is the Kalarin?' he asked. 'Sir, she is dead, for I killed her to make the still.' Bara Deo said, 'Do not be troubled. Your wife will live. But give me a bottle of liquor.' The spirit was so strong that when they poured it onto a green leaf, the leaf was burnt at once, but Bara Deo drank the whole bottle at a draught. Then he restored the Kalarin to life and said to her and her husband, 'Give a bottle of this for every field and the villagers will bring you grain in return. In your shop there must be no tribe or caste. The gods, the devils, low caste and high must be able to drink there. And always give three drops to the ground in my name before you drink.'

5

JUANG

Kedahatar, Dhenkanal State

Rusi kept a Brahmin Garhjawai boy in his house to serve for his daughter, but they quarrelled and the boy took the girl to live in another part of the hills. One day the Brahmin youth was going through the jungle when night fell and he lay down to sleep below a semur tree.

Now there were three friends, a tiger, a jackal and a parrot who used regularly to meet under the tree. This night the parrot came first and when it saw the Brahmin, considered how to save him from the tiger. So when the tiger came, the parrot cried, 'O friend, look, after many days your father's friend has come to visit you. But he is very poor now and has nothing with him.' The tiger made all arrangements for his food and water. And in the morning the tiger gave many ornaments and gold from people he had killed to the Brahmin. The jackal was angry, but the Brahmin tied the treasure in his cloth and took it to his wife. She told him to go back for more. The next night, therefore, the Brahmin, this time taking his dog with him, went back to the place and again lay down below the semur tree.

But now when the parrot saw him, it said in its mind, 'This man is no friend. He has taken our gold and silver, yet he has returned through greed for more. Let him be eaten tonight.' It spoke to the jackal and when the tiger came, the jackal said, 'Yesterday the parrot told us lies. This man is no friend. Let us eat him.'

But when the tiger had killed the Brahmin and the dog, the parrot came weeping. 'What a great sin is yours! You have killed your own father.' 'What shall I do?' asked the tiger. The parrot said, 'Get a lot of wood and set fire to it. When it is well ablaze throw the Brahmin in and no sin will attach to you.' The tiger and jackal got wood and set fire to it. When it was well ablaze they threw the Brahmin in, but when the jackal saw the body burning it said to the tiger, 'Why listen to the parrot? Let's pull the man out and eat him.' The tiger went into the fire and was burnt. The parrot cried, 'Your father is burning; pull him out.' The jackal went into the flames and it too was burnt. The parrot flew away.

After a time, rain fell on the pile of ashes and presently a mahua tree grew up in the very place. One day Rusi and his wife came by and collected the flowers. The wife cooked them and they both got drunk. Since that day men have made liquor.

Because the mahua tree grew from the place where the Brahmin, his dog, the tiger and the jackal were burnt, so when a man drinks mahua spirit he first speaks cleverly and sweetly like a Brahmin; when he has a little more, he becomes a tiger, he quarrels and pulls his moustache. Next he becomes a jackal and shouts loudly. And at last like a dog he tries to bite the neighbours, barks abuse at them and like a dog goes off to sleep.

6

KAMAR

Bhalubahara, Khariar Zamindari

On the Sumher Mountain, Mahadeo fell into a trance. But there was no joy in it, for he had nothing to intoxicate him. He rubbed some dirt off his skin and made a man and a woman, Hemar Kalar and Sirma Kalarin, giving them the caste of Kalar. He sent them to the Sumher Mountain to get mahua flowers.

Hemar said, 'How am I to know mahua flowers when I see them? Give us a sign so that I can recognize them.' Mahadeo said, 'Go to the hill and say, "Which is Mahadeo's boon-giving mahua tree?" and the tree will reveal itself to you. Cut down the tree and keep it with you.' Hemar and Sirma went to the mountain and standing among the trees cried, 'Which is Mahadeo's boon-giving mahua tree?' The mahua tree at that time was laden down with flowers. It answered, 'I am Mahadeo's boon-giving mahua tree.' Hemar gathered the flowers and put them on Sirma's head; he made an earthen pot and set it over the flowers; he put a bamboo pipe from his wife's head down to another pot at her feet. Woman's body is full of fire and from the fire in Sirma's body the mahua spirit was prepared; soon the purest brandy flowed down the bamboo pipe. Hemar and Sirma took it to Mahadeo and he gave it the name of *mand*. 'From this will come every kind of talk, many quarrels and the varied ways of love.' He drank: there was a little left—and he gave it to Hemar and Sirma; even then there was a little left—and he gave it to the Bhut, Pret, Sankani, Dankani, Pisaka, Jogini. Since then when we drink we too offer liquor to the ghosts and spirits. The custom was born in the house of Mahadeo.

7

KOND

Kurutigadu, Koraput District

Pusrodi was going through the forest and saw bengrai birds drinking mahua water and getting drunk on it. She called a Sundi and taught him how to make the spirit.

Formerly the Sundi was a crab. The gongi-shell provided water and the crab-Sundi distilled the liquor. He always first supplied the gods and then men. That is why we offer a few drops to the gods before we drink ourselves.

8

LANJHIA SAORA

Taribel, Koraput District

There was a Saora Raja; he invited his subjects to a feast. After they had gone home, he sent one of his servants to listen to what they were saying about him. He overheard them grumbling, 'This Raja gives us good food, but there was no meat and nothing to give joy to the heart. Only if one has the joy-giver can one dance and be happy.'

The servant reported to the Raja what he had heard. 'What is this joy-giver?' thought the Raja. He called Bhimo and asked him. Bhimo did not know, but he went out to find someone who did. As he wandered through the forest, he saw birds drinking water that had fallen into a hollow parsa tree. Now this hollow was full of mahua flowers. The birds were drinking and dancing and singing. Bhimo also drank the water and too began to dance and sing. He gathered a lot of the mahua flowers and returned home.

On the way he met a wild buffalo. The two fought and at last Bhimo conquered the buffalo and killed it. He tied the body in his cloth and took it home. When he saw what Bhimo had got, the Raja invited his subjects again and this time he gave them roast meat and the joy-giver to drink. Soon they were all drunk and smacking their buttocks began to dance, men and women, smacking their buttocks. Since that time we drink night and day and offer buffaloes to the Dead.

9

LANJHIA SAORA

Tumulu, Ganjam District

Budra Saora and his wife were always thirsty. They lived high up on the Kinching Mountain, where there was no stream, and they could not get enough water. Seeing this, Kittung came to them and said, 'I cannot bear to see you climbing up and down this hill for water and to know you are always thirsty.' He gave them two mahua seeds and explained how they should be sown. In fifteen days there were two fine trees laden with flowers. When the flowers fell, Budra and his wife gathered them and put them in a new earthen pot. They poured in water and set it on one side. After seven days they put it into another pot and set it on the fire. They placed a hollow bamboo there and let the spirit flow down. Into this they put some bark of the siris tree. When it was ready, Kittung drank it first to see what it was like. Then he gave it to Budra and his wife, and they all got drunk together.

CHAPTER SEVENTEEN

DISEASE

THE general belief, still almost universal in tribal India, is that disease is caused by supernatural means and often by supernatural beings. A significant story about the coming of disease to the world is given in *The Baiga.*[1] A Kol story describes how, ' there were once seven sisters in heaven who were sent from there to the earth to live among men. As they left Bhagavan, they asked him for boons, for they said, unless they had power of some kind no one would respect them nor would men worship them. It happened that each was granted a boon. Khermai, called Bhagavati, chose the power of small-pox. If any one should fail to please her, she would appear *in* that person in the form of small-pox. Or, if not that, some other in the family would be with the pox, euphemistically called Mata, 'mother'. She was given the power to remain in full control of the person for two-and-a-half days, and during that time the sick person should be worshipped, for it really means the worshipping of Bhagavati, and so men must respect and honour her for her power.'[2]

Perhaps the most striking thing about these ominous and gloomy stories is their lack of any kind of moral sense. In two cases, it is true, there is some idea that disease, and particularly venereal disease, is due to 'sin'—but the sin is always to force a woman against her will : it would not, apparently, be equally wrong to approach a prostitute. But otherwise the gods and magicians are shown spreading indiscriminate and haphazard misery ; man in his turn aids the diffusion of disease by his attitude—' Let sickness go where it will, let it spread everywhere, so long as it leaves me and my family alone.'

[1] *The Baiga*, 363 ff. Cf. *Folk-Tales of Mahakoshal*, 459, 465.
[2] Griffith, 266.

I

AGARIA

Khaira, Dondi-Lohara Zamindari

In Lohagarh the twelve Agaria brothers lived with their wives. They had twelve kilns and twelve pairs of bellows. The eldest of the brothers had a daughter. Her name was Bai Tanki.

Now this girl had never seen the face of man, though she was pretty as running water. One day the boys and girls of the village went to the jungle for wood, and Bai Tanki also went for charcoal. On the way the boys said, 'This girl has always resisted us. Today let us catch her and take her by force.' When they reached the heart of the forest, therefore, the boys caught the girl and threw her on the ground. One by one they went to her, but each, directly he sat for the work, found himself impotent. His thing curled up like a centipede. He got up and when he looked at himself, he found that he was diseased. One had sores on his parts, another had itch, a third found an evil discharge, another suffered agony when he urinated.

But there was one boy who somehow or other managed to copulate with the girl. From her body a stream of blood began to flow; there was so much that it made a hollow in the ground and flowed down it like a river. Soon it joined another stream, the Janwar River. In this blood was every kind of disease, gonorrhoea, syphilis, gleet, itch, ringworm, leprosy, wounds and sores, chancres, bubos, every affliction of the skin. They all came from the Agaria girl's body and spread through the world.

2

AHIR

Chiriyamatta, Mandla District

Jakkar Lohar and his wife had two sons and both married good girls but neither had a child. The old man made every attempt with medicines and love-charms, but to no avail. Then one day Baitmal Guru came to the house and the old man told him his trouble. Baitmal said, 'Make the girls naked and bring them before me.' Jakkar called the wife of his elder son, and she was very shy. She made herself naked but covered herself with white mud, slipped into the room for a moment and ran away. Baitmal Guru did not like this and said crossly, 'She will have a child, but he will be a leper.' Then the other girl came; she was a wanton and not ashamed. She stood before the Guru naked as a cow and talked to him. After ten months both girls bore children, but the elder girl's child was the first leper.

3

BAIGA

Gotai, Mandla District

In Sumringarh, Danga Guru and Danga Gurain, Lanjha Guru and Lanjha Gurain, Juna Dewar and Juna Dewarin, Jitho Dewar and Jitho Dewarin were living. In Loharigarh lived Tabla Guru and Tabla Gurain.

The people of Sumringarh heard that Tabla Guru and Tabla Gurain were expert in all sorts of magic and went to see if they were as wise as themselves. Taking their *chāng* tambourines they went dancing and singing and camped at the boundary of Loharigarh.

Near the camp many women passed going to fetch water. The Sumringarh people turned their water-pots into snakes. The water-girls ran to Tabla Guru and told him that, 'Strangers have come and are turning the pots into snakes.' Tabla Guru and his wife threw magic in their turn and the camp of the visitors was changed into tigers. The Sumringarh people then turned Loharigarh into scorpions and these began to bite the people there. But Tabla Guru and his wife filled the Sumringarh camp with poison; some of the visitors vomited, some fainted, some died.

At this time a young beautiful girl went for water. One of the Sumringarh Guru's disciples followed her into the jungle and seduced her. She went back to Loharigarh and told Tabla Guru that the boy had taken her by force. The Guru and his wife were angry and they sent their strongest magic and the boy found he had syphilis and gonorrhoea. At the same time the Guru made two snakes; one attacks the throat and the other the stomach of man. Danga Guru, Lanjha Guru, Juna Dewar, Jitho Dewar and their wives and disciples returned to Sumringarh weary with disease; like porcupines, they were nothing but bones and quills.

4

BAIGA

Baona, Mandla District

Surti and Phirangi, two brothers, lived together in the Kajliban. They were great Dewar. They made their clearing and sowed kutki. There was a fine crop. Near by in a hollow mahua tree were born Narayan Deo and Dulha Deo. They gave the Dewar a dream saying, 'Dedicate a Laru pig for us and you will have a better crop still.' The Dewar agreed and got a pig; he cut a bit of the ear and tail and crushed its testicles; thus it was dedicated. The people cut the crop and gathered it. The next Tuesday they prepared for the Laru Kaj. They killed the pig, crushing it beneath a log of wood, and cut up the flesh. But Surti's wife stole the liver and ate it, before everyone, before they had offered anything to the gods.

Narayan Deo said to Surti Dewar, 'Since your wife has stolen my food, her body will be covered with sores.' But Surti promised, 'I will give you another Laru pig. Send the disease to the rest of the world, but keep it from my wife.' Narayan Deo was pleased and sent leprosy[1] throughout the world.

[1]Hindus generally regard leprosy as a punishment for sin, a view shared by some of the aboriginal tribes. Thus it was the sacrilege of Vasuki, king of serpents, that brought leprosy to the Punjab.—Crooke, ii, 137. Those who told lies in the Bhadanwara grove at Madura became lepers—ibid., ii, 91. Sometimes leprosy is a punishment for an offence against the Sun.—Forbes, *Ras Mala* (London, 1924), i, 59. In a Baiga folk-tale it appears as the penalty for incest.—*Folk-Tales of Mahakoshal*, 465. The Kharia call it *machhi patak*, or 'fly-sin' and have to atone for it by a tribal dinner.—Roy, *The Kharias*, 186. The Rengma Naga, on the other hand, attribute it to maggots. When they cremate the body of a leper, they hold burning brands for fear 'the mother of the maggots should fly out and attack one of them'.—Mills, *The Rengma Nagas*, 118. For further details, see my article, 'Dreams of Indian Aboriginal Lepers', *Man*, xli (1941), 55 ff.

5

BAIGA

Bohi, Pandaria Zamindari

Mahadeo and Basamkara Deo lived in Marogarh. Basamkara was in love with Mahadeo's beautiful wife Parvati and was ever trying to seduce her. One day he said to himself, 'Here I have an amulet round my neck given me by Basmasur. I'll touch Mahadeo with it and when he has turned into ashes I'll take his wife away.' Holding the amulet in his hand he went towards Mahadeo's house. But the god saw him coming and read what was in his mind and was able to escape in time. He ran and ran until he reached a cave where he hid.

When Lakshmanjati heard what was happening he took Parvati's form and came running to the place where Basamkara was standing outside the cave and smiling at him said, 'What is it you want Mahadeo for? Don't waste your time with him. Come with me.' Thus Lakshmanjati led him away and they went together to Jhunjhiban. There Basamkara prepared to fulfil his desire, but Lakshmanjati in the form of Parvati said, 'My Maharaja first dances, then he does it.' So Basamkara began to dance swinging his arms to and fro. Lakshmanjati said, 'This is poor dancing. My Maharaja tosses his arms in the air, and lays them on his head.' Basamkara tried to do better and lay his hands on his head. Directly the amulet touched it he turned to ashes. But as he was dying his seed came from him, and Lakshmanjati caught it in his hand and put it in a hollow bamboo. Then he took his own form and went home.

Some time later Mahadeo and Parvati were walking through the forest when they passed that very place and there they found that two little girls had come out of the bamboo and were sitting on the ground weeping for fright and hunger. Mahadeo recognized them and said, 'You were born of evil seed; you will be Tankibai and Garmibai. Whoever lies with you will get gonorrhoea or syphilis.' In this way these diseases came into the world.

6

BHAINA

Kenda Zamindari

Woman gives man gonorrhoea. It is when a man goes to a woman and his seed leaves him quickly, before her's comes. When her water does not come, there is evil blood in her vagina. It goes into the mouth of the penis, and after that the urine is chill and tortures the man.

A man was very strong and lustful. He desired a woman but could not find one. His seed spurted from his forehead down his body in the tube to the penis ; it came out and fell on Mother Earth. Then Earth cursed him, 'I am a virgin, and you have thrown your seed on me. There will be sores now.' From that day there has been syphilis and sores breaking out on a man's penis, that make him dry as a spider.

7

GOND

Banjar, Mandla District

Mahadeo and Parvati were living in the jungle. There were no trees there and no flowers or fruit. Parvati said to Mahadeo, 'It looks very ugly. Make trees and hang them with flowers and fruit.' Mahadeo made many beautiful trees and covered them with flowers. Their pregnancy scent went into Parvati and she conceived.

But after three months she miscarried and they threw the foetus into a stream. It turned into Banasmar Marra Deo, which is a fish.

Jalandar Guru had seven daughters. They went to bale out water for fish. When they had nearly emptied the water from the pool, and there was only a little left, they all together fell in and the water and mud was smeared over them. The eldest sister got syphilis from this and the youngest gonorrhoea ; the second sister had pains in herjoints, the third had bloody discharges, the fourth was covered with boils, the fifth with sores, the sixth did not menstruate properly. It was because of the foetus of Parvati, the fish Banasmar Marra Deo.

8

GOND

Rusa, Mandla District

Sabar Sai Raja had two wives. When the elder conceived she bore Raja Marra Deo who broke his way out of her body through the ribs. When he grew up he asked his parents to let him travel through the world. They let him go and he went first to Telinagar. On that day one Lalmaniya Teli had died. The people carried him outside the boundary and burnt him. Marra Deo was watching and by accident he tripped and fell into the fire, burning his arms and legs. Hegot up and ran to Jalandar Guru who cured him, blowing and muttering above his wounds. Then the Guru said, 'Go back to Telinagar and hide yourself there. When the men and women come on the tenth day to gather the bones and ashes, cover their bodies too with wounds like yours.' Marra Deo did as the Guru bade him, and when the men and women came on the tenth day he burnt their bodies with the patches of leprosy. So leprosy spread through the world.

9

GOND

Rusa, Mandla District

Bhola Guru, the great Guru of Binjhighar had a son called Bhukan. Bhukan had a daughter. Three days after the child's birth, she got up while all were asleep and entered the belly of Pawan the Wind. At the same moment her mother began to shiver and her whole body was full of heat. The household was roused but could not find the baby anywhere and her mother lay unconscious with fever. Bhola Guru took his divining rods and measured them until he found where the child had gone. She came to him and declared, 'I am Bhukan's daughter Dhukan Kapnibai. I cannot live in your house. I must wander round the world. Give me some present and I will trouble my mother no more.' The Guru quickly offered a coconut, a spangle and something for her hair and said, 'Go wander round the world, but do not trouble people too much. Never stay more than three days with one person. Leave him then and go to someone else.'

10

GOND

Kawardha State

A Baiga and his wife lived in Koeligarh. They had no children and the Baiga went to serve Kaindo Mai. On the day he was to receive his reward, the goddess said to him, 'Do not go to your wife until your worship is completed and you have sacrificed a white goat'.

But that night the Baiga thought, 'How will she know whether I go to my wife or not?' and he approached her as usual. The next day he took a white goat to sacrifice but Kaindo Mai said to him, 'You have been to your wife and are giving me a tainted offering. You will have a child, but he will be born a leper.' This was the first leper.

11

KAHAR

Khuria, Bilaspur District

A Gond went to the jungle. Before going he ate sweets made of mahua mixed with ramtilla. As he was cutting wood, he felt thirsty. There was a stream and many virgin rocks untrodden by men. There was a spring; here lived Raktahin Mata. The Gond went to the place and drank. The Mata went into his body and when he reached home she broke out in sores all over him. When the Gunia looked in his winnowing-fan to see the reason, Raktahin Mata said, 'This man drank my virgin water. Therefore being angry I have filled his body with syphilis and gonorrhoea.' Then Raktahin Mata said, 'Give me fowls of three different colours and the child of an unmarried girl, and I will free the man of his disease.'

In a neighbouring house was an Ahir. His daughter was very beautiful. She had a son, though she was unmarried. In his mind the Gond offered the boy to Raktahin Mata and soon the boy died of his own accord. The Gunia offered fowls of three different colours and took them to the boundary of the village and said, 'Now go and spread through the world. Go where you will, but do not come here.' Since that day syphilis and gonorrhoea have spread through the world.

12

KOL

Jubbulpore District

Patangi Dewar made Sukri Chamarin his Guru. She taught him her magic and when he had learnt it he said to her, 'You have taught me all this, but how am I to make profit from it?'

Sukri Chamarin went to Hukni Mata. The Mata was in her period. She went to bathe and wrung out her dirty clothes in the stream. The people in a neighbouring village drank the water; it gave them a tertian fever which comes to men every third day. When they were ill Sukri Chamarin sent the Dewar to cure them. She told him how he should go to a place where three streams joined and there pick the three-fold bel fruit, offer it to the gods and the people would recover. Patangi Dewar did this and earned a lot of money. After that he made his living by curing people of fever.

13

LOHAR

Barbaspur, Mandla District

In a village were five Baiga brothers. Their Raja refused to give them fields or gardens so they went to another Raja for land and made a clearing in the forest. There they sowed their crops. One night came Marra Deo in the form of a deer and ate the crop and ran away. The brothers were very angry and the next night sat up to keep watch over the clearing. When the deer came they shot it with their arrows, but it escaped. A week later it came again and this time they killed it. The five Baiga were delighted at this and ran to the body, singed off the hair, cut it up, roasted some of the flesh on the spot and then carried it home in triumph. The women ran out to greet them and they had a great feast far into the night. Then sleepy and tired they went to bed. But they had eaten Marra Deo and after a little while their bodies began to itch. They scratched till they could think of nothing but scratching and itching. That very night the eldest Baiga died of it. The four brothers went quickly to Lanjha Guru and showed him their sores. He knew what it was and told them to sacrifice a pig, a black cock and a black chick to Marra Deo on the bank of the stream near Chipligarh. They did so and their itch left them and was carried by the stream to other people.

14

PANKA

Pakhri, Mandla District

In Rameshwar, Mahadeo was born. At the same time Jagat Dhanu Panda was born. Jagat Dhanu by his magic power shut up in an iron bin many gods and goddesses—Marhi Deo, Loharjhar, Kolerai, Nirodh, Garbmar, Angmar, Jalkandevi, Tanki, Garmi, Burhi Mai, Piri Dessahi, Kaini Dessahi and Hukni Marki. He shut them up and did not let them out.

The gods gathered together and said to Jagat Dhanu Panda, 'Why have you shut us up in this fashion? Let us out; we won't do any harm to anyone. And when we have been out, we will come back again.' So Jagat Dhanu the Panda let the gods out.

The gods went wandering and roaming about the country. Kaini Dessahi and Hukni Marki said to the others, 'You stay here and we will go somewhere. If the Panda makes a fuss, soothe him down.' But when the others went back, the Panda did not notice that they were not all there and shut them up in the iron bin without saying anything.

Kaini Dessahi and Hukni Marki went to Thakur Deo, the landlord of the gods. They said, 'We are dying of hunger; give us something to eat.' Thakur Deo said, 'Go and find some man. Sit in his throat where the grasshopper hops up and down. Drink its blood.' This he said to Kaini Dessahi, and to Hukni Marki he said, 'You go right down into the man's chest and say *Huk huk huk*'. The two gods did what Thakur Deo told them and from that time men began to cough.

CHAPTER EIGHTEEN

PSYCHO-PATHOLOGY: THE VAGINA DENTATA LEGEND

'THE essential unity in the psychoses', says Seligman, 'makes it unlikely that neurotic symbolization—apart from symbols socially determined—is different in the different races. There is in fact one fear, the neurotic dread of sexual intercourse, which is symbolized in the same manner as the Vagina Dentata by many people in many countries.'[1] This curious and significant nightmare has not, however, been studied in detail, though it has been recorded in various parts of the world.

In view of the difficulty of studying this material—much of which is in periodicals and other publications difficult of access—I will assemble part of it here, as an introduction to my presentation of the evidence from Middle India. The comparative study of the legends is in this case of considerable importance and illustrates a useful point made by Lincoln.

To state, as some anthropologists do, that this widespread pattern appearing in myth, legend and dream has no psychological significance but is merely the result of diffusion, is tantamount to saying that the human mind plays no part in the formation and spread of culture. Since this sexual anxiety fantasy occurs in diffusable myths and legends, as well as in non-diffusable individual dreams, it would be more logical either to regard them all as products of the same unconscious way of thinking, or to find out whether the myths and legends may not have originated in dreams, the former being secondary elaborations and the latter the initial expression of universally similar psychic material. Some anthropologists write as if myths, legends and folklore existed in a sort of vacuum totally without relation to the human mind in spite of the fact that they are in large part of identical psychological structure.[2]

The Vagina Dentata legend has been recorded for the Ainu, in Samoa[3] and among the Naga of Manipur.[4] Landtman has noticed it as a dream among the Kiwai Papuans (who regard the sexual organs as the primary source of magic). He records a characteristic dream.

[1] C. G. Seligman, 'Anthropological Perspective and Psychological Theory', *J.R.A.I.*, lxii, 219.
[2] Lincoln, 109. Throughout this Chapter references to the special Bibliography at the end of it will be made by giving author's name and short title only.
[3] Pilsudski, 85 ff.
[4] Lincoln, 108.

The dreamer was asked by a woman to have connection with her, but did not venture to do so, for her vulva was provided with sharp teeth and opened and closed continuously like a mouth. Again and again he tried to muster up courage but shrank back every time. At last the woman got up and attacked him with a piece of wood, and he fled into the water. But he found that he could not swim, and to add to his horror a crocodile came towards him and was about to catch him when he opened his eyes.[1]

It is, however, in North America that this legend has been most frequently noticed.[2] This does not necessarily mean that it is more common there; it may simply be because our records of this area are more extensive, exact and unbowdlerized than those elsewhere. The motif frequently appears as part of the 'Test-Theme', which has been fully studied by Lowie. We often find the incident, which occurs also in the Indian stories, where the hero is able to break off the teeth of the woman and enjoy normal intercourse with her. The straightforward Vagina Dentata theme is sometimes combined, as in our stories, with symbolical representations of it, and there are the usual variations of the snake in the vagina and the amputated hand.

Boas refers to twenty-two versions of the legend among the Tsimshian Indians. A young hero must pass a number of tests; he has to swallow red-hot stones, escape from a flood, endure heat and poison, and 'in connection with these tests, we find very often the idea that the girl whom the young man marries kills all her husbands. In the most characteristic versions her vagina is set with teeth, which are then broken out by means of a wedge or stone; or, in place of teeth, a rattlesnake head is found. This form is characteristic of the Thompson versions and recalls the East European stories where a pike's mouth is introduced in its place.'[3]

Lowie has studied the motif as part of the Test-Theme in North-American Mythology[4] and has given several versions of the legend in his own collections. For example, in the Crow Indian tale of 'The Dwarf's Ward', the hero is given a rough stone, some soft wood and a cord from a buffalo's legs and sent out with a warning to have nothing to do with three pretty young girls who are tanning hides. But when he sees them, he finds them irresistible and goes to join

[1] Landtman, *Folk Tales*, No. 398.

[2] It occurs among the Arapaho, Bellabella, Bellacoola, Blackfoot, Chilcontin, Comox, Coos, Crow, Dakota, Jicarilla Apache, Koasati, Kwakiutl, Maidu, Nez Percé, Newettee, Pawnee, San Carlos Apache, Shoshone, Shuswap, Staeelis, Thompson, Tsimshian, Utamgt, Walapai and Wichita.

[3] Boas, *Tsimshian Mythology*, 809.

[4] Lowie, *The Test-Theme*, 110.

them. The youngest girl says, 'I first saw him; so I want to cook and feed him and sleep with him.' She gives him a woman's clitoris to eat, but he throws it away. Then he lies with her. 'The girl spread out her legs. The young man pulled out his member but stuck a black stone in. As it went in she began to chew it and the stone was all eaten up. He put a second stone in and the same thing happened. He put some driftwood in and it was a long time being chewed. At last he used the cord. She kept on biting it, but could not do anything to it. After a while he removed his breech-cloth and really possessed her. The two sisters asked, "Are you done?" He sat smiling. The young girl said, "He is my husband, you cannot do anything to him."' After a struggle in which the other girls and seven young men try to destroy the hero, he magically freezes them and the place is still 'there on the Little Horn, where there is a spring coming out of a rock shaped like a woman's genitalia.'[1]

Lowie gives another tale, this time from the northern Shoshone. Coyote is the hero. By the big sea he is tempted by a pretty girl who takes him to her island home. He notices that when she and her mother eat their food, the eggs slide right down their throats and he can hear them cracking in the vaginae. He goes to relieve himself and asks his anus for advice. It tells him that the mother and daughter have teeth in the vagina and that when he goes to either of them he should only pretend to insert his member and in fact thrust in his elk-horn scraper and break off the teeth. That night Coyote has a narrow escape. The mother ties up the door with a rope, but rats gnaw it through. He inserts his scraper into the girl's vagina and escapes. As he goes he can hear the crepitation of the teeth closing on the scraper. But he cannot keep away, and next day returns. The girl comes in at evening after a day in the water looking for people to kill. After eating eggs and breaking them in her vagina, the girl takes Coyote to sleep with her, but this time he succeeds in breaking off her teeth, and then performs a like office for the mother. He copulates with both women and in the morning they send him to fetch water. In his absence babies fall in great numbers out of the women's wombs; these babies are the ancestors of all the Indians of America.[2]

Another Coyote story occurs in a Nez Percé text. Here Coyote is seduced by Butterfly who takes the form of a 'lovely elaborately dressed woman, and is crushed to death in the act of coition.' Afterwards Coyote is restored to life and is told,

[1] Lowie, *Myths of the Crow Indians*, 16[illegible] f.
[2] Lowie, *The Northern Shoshone*, 237 ff.

'She is the Butterfly woman and a killer. She has killed many people in that way.' In the end Coyote takes a brushwood pole and, at next coition, pries her apart and kills her.[1]

An Arapaho hero removes the dangerous teeth with a grindstone. The story tells how a very handsome woman had husband after husband, but every one died after a night with her. At last the hero determined to discover the reason and went to her armed with a slender whetstone. The two went to bed, he very attentive, she taking the lead in the conversation. When he went to her, she welcomed him eagerly, but he inserted the grindstone without her knowledge. 'When the vagina felt it, it at once began to eat it.' But he broke off the teeth with the grindstone and after that the vagina remained innocent.[2]

In the creation myth of the San Carlos Apache, the hero Naiyenezgani is pursued by a maiden whom he first sees up a tree and who claims him as her husband. She catches him and builds a house.

> The boy was not pleased and did not touch the girl, for she was not as she should be. She was anxious to accomplish her purpose but could not. The boy knew what was the matter; the girl's vagina was provided with teeth. He got pieces of brush and stuck sand on them with pitch, making four implements. These he inserted one after the other as he lay with the girl. Three of these were chewed to pieces and the fourth one partly. The boy then took his white stone and broke the teeth off with it and cut around inside with his obsidian knife. 'This is the proper condition,' he said. 'This way it should be named. Now I will marry you.'

The girl then tries to kill the hero by removing four of her pubic hairs which she turns into bears.[3]

Wissler and Duvall state that legends of Vaginal Teeth are known to the Blackfoot Indians, though they do not record any examples.[4]

The Shuswap and Chilcotin tell how Tsakelsxenelxa of Pavilion Creek kills men with her toothed vagina. The hero breaks out the teeth with his arrow feather.[5] In the Thompson Indian version, the woman's privates are the mouth of a rattlesnake. The hero chews a leaf, spits on the privates and transforms them into those of an ordinary woman.[6] Boas says the motif is frequent in the

[1] Phinney, 53 f.
[2] Dorsey and Kroeber, *Traditions of the Arapaho*, 260.
[3] Goddard, *Myths from the San Carlos Apache*, 32 ff.
[4] Wissler and Duvall, 16.
[5] Boas, *Tsimshian Mythology*, 614.
[6] Teit, 221.

mythology of the Kwakiutl, in many cases belonging to the Test-Theme. In the Salmon myth, the tale is confined to the Bellacoola and their immediate neighbours, the Bellabella.[1] In some versions the teeth are associated with the symbols of crushing rocks or a closing door. Thus in a Jicarilla Apache tale, the hero Naiyenesgani has to lie with the woman who has become his wife.

He pounded some sumac sticks and twisted them together. Having them in his hand he went with her and when she lay down for him, he inserted the sticks first. Her vulvae were provided with teeth by means of which she killed men. She cut these sticks with her teeth and destroyed them. After that she had no such teeth. Before that, cutting the men with her teeth, she had killed them.

Immediately afterwards, as in a dream association, the story proceeds to describe how Naiyenesgani saves men from being crushed by rocks.

The reeds needed for arrows stood at the junction of two canyons. When anyone came there for arrows the rocks closed on him and killed him. Naiyenesgani came there, made as if to pass four times and then went to the reeds and broke some of them off. The rocks did not come together.[2]

Among the Bellabella also the myth is connected with the snapping door. The hero of one story has a friend. They visit a Salmon village and as they are going through it they see a house with a snapping door. The friend sees a beautiful girl inside and wants to marry her. He does so and they have a daughter.[3]

Some of the American stories show the same kind of variation that we will notice in the Middle Indian material. For example, in a myth from the West Coast of Washington the hero meets a woman whose vagina is set with teeth and when he tries to cohabit with her, she bites off his hand.[4] A Yukaghir tale describes how a woman tricks a male monster into tearing off his two testicles and thus kills him.[5] Another Yukaghir tale is about a 'pretty young cannibal girl who kills her husbands on the wedding night. Her method is to tire them out and when they fall into an exhausted sleep to kill them. The hero, warned in time, wears the girl out instead and when she is asleep finds the instruments of death—an awl and a knife—under her pillow. He thrusts the knife into her heart and

[1] Boas, op. cit., 778.
[2] Goddard, *Jicarilla Apache Texts*, 202 f.
[3] Boas, op. cit., 778.
[4] Boas, *Tsimishian Mythology*, 604.
[5] Bogoras, *Tales of Eastern Siberia*, 127.

the awl up her anus crying, 'Iron to iron.' The tools meet inside her body and she dies.[1]

With the above material and the Middle Indian texts that follow there is abundant evidence for a study of the fundamental problems of the Vagina Dentata legend. Not all the stories and dreams are about teeth, but they all testify to the widespread belief in the dangers of sexual intercourse and the primitive dread of losing any part of the body. What are we to make of this evidence? How did the legend arise? What deep-rooted human fears and nightmares does it symbolize? Even more difficult, what are we to say of the reverse of the legend, the stories of the Penis Aculeatus and the danger to the woman?

Is there, in the first place, any actual physical or medical basis for the phantasy? I gather that there is very little, though the danger of vaginal spasm and the penis captivus, though remote, is not unknown.

Oral activity plays a part in the preliminary stage of sexual intercourse (kissing), and in the female the sucking element is in unconscious phantasy transferred to the vagina. When the biting component is strong, the vulva is pictured as a biting mouth (vagina dentata) and is feared in later life as a possible instrument of injury; indeed this biting impulse may lead to vaginal spasm, which in the extreme case produces penis captivus if intercourse has begun. Reaction against 'taking in' may have two forms: the local musculature may become either flaccid (passive resistance) or spastic, causing vaginismus (active resistance). Fears due to and unconscious dread of making a destructive attack upon a prized object, the genital of the partner, play an important part in the production of impotence and frigidity.[2]

The explanation of the legend is more likely to be found in psychology than in physiology. Let us then consider in some detail various ways in which this very remarkable material may be interpreted. First to be mentioned must be that element of cruelty in sex which so has often attracted the notice of psychiatrists. Sadism is not wholly unnatural; it has its roots in normal, if rather primitive, sexuality. We may take an eloquent statement of this point of view from Briffault. 'Lions and tigers', he says, 'which furnish favourite examples of mating among carnivora, commonly kill and devour their mates.'[3] He quotes instances of this to show

[1] ibid., 97f.

[2] *The British Encyclopaedia of Medical Practice*, Vol. xi (1939). I owe the reference to Dr A. P. Pillay.

[3] R. Briffault, *The Mothers* (London, 1927), i, 118.

how the ' danger of allowing the sexes to associate is a commonplace of menageries '. ' With both the male and female, "love" or sexual attraction, is originally and pre-eminently "sadic" ; it is positively gratified by the infliction of pain ; it is as cruel as hunger. That is the direct, fundamental, and longest established sentiment connected with the sexual impulse. The male animal captures, mauls and bites the female, who in turn uses her teeth and claws freely, and the lovers issue from the sexual combat bleeding and mangled. Crustaceans usually lose a limb or two in the encounter. All mammals without exception use their teeth on these occasions. Pallas describes the mating of camels : as soon as impregnation has taken place, the female, with a vicious snarl, turns round and attacks the male with her teeth, and the latter is driven away in terror . . . . The congress of the sexes is assimilated by the impulse to hurt, to shed blood, to kill, to the encounter between a beast of prey and its victim and all distinction between the two is not infrequently lost. It would be more accurate to speak of the sexual impulse as pervading nature with a yell of cruelty than with a hymn of love. The circumspection which is exhibited by many female animals in yielding to the male, the haste which is shown by most to separate as soon as impregnation has taken place, would appear to be due in a large measure to the danger attending such relations rather than to coyness.'[1]

The danger, however, as Havelock Ellis points out, is normally to the male rather than to the female. ' It is the male spider who impregnates the female at the risk of his life and sometimes perishes in the attempt; it is the male bee who, after intercourse with the queen, falls dead from that fatal embrace, leaving her to fling aside his entrails and calmly pursue her way '.[2]

In human beings also, particularly among those who have an ambivalent attitude to sex—either because they think it is immoral or have been frustrated in their youth—it is not uncommon to find sexual phantasies of an aggressive or violent type : they imagine themselves forcibly penetrating and tearing the vagina, the partner is made to bleed and even killed. In the normal individual this aggressiveness is moderated and even becomes a type of sexual fore-pleasure.

But in the neurotic or pervert, the tendency to inflict pain becomes what we call sadism. It is generally said that while male sadists avoid, female sadists not infrequently attack the genital organs of their partners.

[1] ibid., p. 119. [2] Havelock Ellis, i, ii, 128.

Related to this impulse is the love-bite and the love-scratch, important elements in classical Indian erotics, and indeed of peoples throughout the world. The *Kama Sutra* gives eight forms of love-scratch and eight different kinds of love-bite ; a scratch made on the foreparts of a woman's breast is compared to the marks of a tiger's claw ; tooth marks on the base of the breast are compared to the 'chewing of a boar.'[1] Savage Landor was bitten all over by an Ainu girl who was in love with him.[2] Briffault refers to a report that the Migrelians of Transcaucasia regarded the betrothal of a girl as sealed only when her lover firmly bit her breast. And he says that 'among the ancient Egyptians the word that is translated by Egyptologists as 'to kiss' meant 'to eat'. He concludes that in this impulse also we can see the relation between the female licking, biting, mauling and even eating its young and the 'primal undifferentiated assimilation of every desired and beloved object with a prey to be torn, killed, devoured'.[3]

There is obviously an element of this in the Vagina Dentata legends, particularly in their references to eating. Some of the stories are very cruel and may gratify an unconscious craving for cruelty in the hearers. The love-bite and the love-scratch, though present, is not a prominent element in the erotic culture of this part of aboriginal India. The Pardhan, who have developed a high standard in the art of love, practice the love-bite : I know a Panka who some weeks after his marriage had his whole body covered with little tooth-marks : but Baiga and Gond are singularly unenterprising in everything sexual except its frequent repetition.

The tribesmen, however, practice other—they are, of course, quite different psychologically—forms of sexual cruelty. Clitoridectomy is not unknown as a punishment for an erring wife, and the cutting off the nose as a penalty for adultery is common all over India. The Gond and Baiga punish a riggish woman by putting chili and salt into her vagina. Stories in which a crab catches and sometimes excises a woman's clitoris are very popular.

For the real meaning of the Vagina Dentata, however, we must go deeper into tribal psychology. Sex is not only sometimes cruel, it is often highly dangerous. Westermarck considers that 'a very important cause of religious celibacy is the idea that sexual intercourse is defiling and in certain circumstances a mysterious cause of evil. The Syryenians maintain that it develops a peculiarly

[1] Penzer, v, 181, where an abstract of the *Kama Sutra* will be found.

[2] Savage Landor, *Alone with the Hairy Ainu* (London, 1899), 141.

[3] Briffault, op. cit., 120. See also Havelock Ellis, *Studies*, ii, 84 ff. ; and Block, *The Sexual Life of our Time*, 559 ff.

dangerous and contagious quality or substance called *pez* ; hence a man who has had intercourse with a woman must undergo a rite of purification.'[1]

Among the Kiwai Papuans, 'the female sexual organs are regarded as in high degree the source of all kinds of witchcraft'.[2] 'The sexual act is regarded as fraught with risk' and is thus taboo on many occasions. 'The female organs are as perilous as an open grave, with which they are associated'.[3] A woman given to much intercourse is not allowed to attend a sick person. To dream of the vagina before a battle is very dangerous, for it represents the arrow-wound the dreamer will receive.[4]

Other people stress the defilement rather than the dangers of sex, though of course the condition of being in a state of defilement is itself sufficiently dangerous.

Among the Hebrews both the man and the woman had to bathe themselves in water and were 'unclean until the even' (Leviticus, xv, 18). The Nandi in eastern Africa say that people are dirty when they have had sexual intercourse, hence they must purify themselves by bathing. The belief in the defiling effect of such intercourse seems to underlie the idea prevalent among various peoples that incontinence, and especially illicit love, injures the harvest.[5]

There does not, however, appear to be a very strong belief in the defilement caused by sex among the tribes from whom I have recorded these stories, though the Muria of Bastar observe chastity before important festivals and believe that a wife's adultery may ruin a man's prowess in the chase. Sexual intercourse is dangerous rather than defiling.

This idea of the dangers of intercourse finds classic expression in the figure of the Poison Maid.[6] The Vish-Kanya, Vish-Kanyaka, Vishmayi Kanya, or Vishanghana is a familiar character in ancient Indian literature. She was a beautiful maiden so charged with poison that her very look sometimes caused death. J. J. Modi suggests that the original word for poison (*vish*) seems to be Sanskrit (Avesta *tbish*), meaning, 'to harm', and the Vish-Kanya thus originally meant 'harming damsel', not necessarily a poisonous damsel.[7]

[1] E. Westermarck, *The History of Human Marriage* (London, 1925), i, 406 f.

[2] G. Landtman, *The Kiwai Papuans of British New Guinea* (London, 1927), 238.

[3] ibid., 250. [4] ibid., 278. [5] Westermarck, op. cit., i, 407.

[6] The Poison Damsel has been elaborately studied by Penzer in an Appendix to Vol. ii of his edition of *The Ocean of Story*.

[7] J. J. Modi, 'The Vish-Kanya of Ancient India', *Folk-Lore*, xxxviii, 327.

In the *Katha Sarit Sagara* such maidens are sent as dancing girls to enemy countries to do all the damage they can. In the *Mudra-Rakshasa* of Visakhadatta, written about the seventh century A.D., there is an account of an attempt on the life of King Chandragupta who is saved by his minister Chanakya who passes the girl on to another King, Parvataka, who succumbs to her fatal love. But much the most famous tradition is, of course, the attempt to murder Alexander the Great by this method. The first reference to this story, which later gained great currency in Europe, occurs in the pseudo-Aristotelian treatise *Secretum Secretorum*, which purports to contain a series of letters addressed by the aged philosopher to his famous pupil. Among the rules for 'the ordinance of the king, of his purveyance, continence and discretion', Aristotle is represented as warning Alexander against entrusting the care of his body to women and recalls a great danger which he himself was able to frustrate. 'Remember', he says, 'what happened when the king of India sent thee rich gifts, and among them that beautiful maiden whom they had fed on poison until she was of the nature of a snake, and had I not perceived it because of my fear. . . and had I not found by proof that she would be killing thee by her embrace and by her perspiration, she would surely have killed thee.'[1] Penzer gives an account of the different texts of the book and remarks that while in the Hebrew text, it was a King of India who sent the girl, 'in some of the Arabic texts it is the King's mother and in most of the later versions the Queen of India who sends the poisoned woman. Then again the contamination differs—sometimes it is caused by the kiss or bite, in other versions by the perspiration, intercourse, or even only by the look.'

Penzer gives many other references to the Poison Maid in literature, and discusses the various means by which she destroys her victims. One of the most important of these methods is sexual intercourse. Penzer suggests that 'an amorous bite on the lip, probably drawing blood', or the amorous scratch or bite, was the means by which the poison was injected. He concludes that 'the motif of the poison damsel originated in India at a very early period before the Christian era. The poison damsel herself has no existence in actual fact, but is merely the creation of the story-teller who derived the idea from what he saw around him. First of all he was acquainted with poisonous herbs and knew something of the uses to which they were put, but he was still more familiar with the ways of the snake-charmer and the methods of his gradual

[1] Quoted from Penzer, ii, 291.

inoculation. He could not help being fully aware of the fatal results of the bite of the cobra and krait, and the reverence and fear of the snake throughout India was everywhere evident. Thus there was plenty of material for the creation of the poison damsel, and in later days the knowledge of opium and other foreign drugs would merely introduce some new variant of the tale.'[1] Had Penzer been acquainted with the stories of the Vagina Dentata he might have sought a deeper meaning for the Poison Maiden. But at least this tradition indicates a widespread belief in the possible dangers of sexual intercourse; all men, not only kings, should learn the rules of 'purveyance, continence and discretion'.

Why is sexual intercourse dangerous? The first and obvious answer is that hymeneal blood has always been regarded as magically toxic and to be avoided. Have the Vagina Dentata stories arisen out of a dread of deflowering virgins? There is a very remarkable passage, quoted by both Westermarck and Penzer, in *The Voiage and Travaile of Sir John Maundevile*, which dates from the middle of the fourteenth century. Describing a far eastern island in the lordship of Prester John, he says that on the marriage night it was the custom of the people to engage some other man to have the wife's maidenhood. 'And ther ben certain men in every Town that serven of non other thing; and thei clepen hem Cadeberiz, that is to seyne, the Foles of Wanhope. For thei of the Contree holden it so gret a thing and so perilous, for to have the Maydenhode of a woman, that hem semethe that thei that haven first the Maydenhode, puttethe him in aventure of his Lif.' The woman must never again speak to the man that performs this office. The reason given for the custom is very germane to our present discussion. 'Of old tyme, men hadden ben dede for deflourynge of Maydenes that hadden Serpentes in hiré Bodyes, that stongen men upon hire Zerdes, that thei dyeden anon.'[2]

In the Indian stories recorded above, there are several in which the danger arises from a snake living in the vagina, the belly or the mouth. Penzer also remarks that 'apart from the custom of employing proxies for the first night of marriage, there has always been a curious connection between snakes and intercourse.'[3] In India the snake is often represented as encircling the *linga*. In a paper read before the Asiatic Society, J. H. Rivett-Carnac refers to certain paintings in Nagpur and says that the 'positions of the women with the snakes were of the most indecent description and left no

[1] Penzer, ii, 313. [2] Westermarck, op. cit., i, 189 f. [3] Penzer, ii, 307.

doubt that, so far as the idea represented in these sketches was concerned, the cobra was regarded as the phallus.'[1]

Are we then to suppose that the Vagina Dentata legends arose out of the fear of defloration and the hymeneal blood? There is much that is attractive in the idea. The physical distress of both man and woman might well suggest teeth in the vagina or a thorn on the penis. A Konyak Naga told C. von Furer-Haimendorf that the first intercourse with a virgin was like 'walking barefoot over sharp-pointed flints'. A girl who was being forced into premature intercourse might well so exercise the *constrictor cunni* as to burst the cavernous bodies of the invading penis. 'In the Vedic literature the blood of the bridal night is represented as a poison and a seat of danger; and a similar belief probably accounts for the old German custom of bringing new clothes to the married couple on the first morning of their wedded life. The woman, as well as the man, may be supposed to be in peril. . . . The hymeneal blood may also be regarded as dangerous to the offspring. In Andjra, in Morocco, there are bridegrooms who take care that no offspring can result from the defloration of the bride, since many people believe that the child would be diseased if the semen came into contact with the blood.'[2]

But the fear of hymeneal blood cannot account for the rise of the Vagina Dentata story among the Gond, Baiga, Agaria or Muria of India. These tribes would doubtless be afraid of the blood if they knew what it was. But it is very rare for a girl to approach her husband as a virgin. There is no word for the hymen and its very existence is unknown.

There is little discredit attached to pre-nuptial intercourse, provided both the endogamous and exogamous rules of the tribe are observed. There are no 'tests of chastity' and since girls are not expected to be virgins there is no provision for their defloration. We must therefore look elsewhere for an explanation of this cycle of stories in central India.

In a supplement to his work on marriage Westermarck has a note on 'penis-envy' which leads to that 'embitterment which many women display against men'[3] and particularly against the man who

[1] J. H. Rivett-Carnac, 'The Snake Symbol in India', *J.A.S.B.*, xlviii (1879), 17-30.

[2] Westermarck, op. cit., i, 190.

[3] Westermarck, *Three Essays on Sex and Marriage* (London, 1934), 46. We may compare with this Laubscher's interesting account of penis-envy among female Bantu schizophrenics who have fantasies of mythological snakes living in the vagina.—*Sex, Custom and Psychopathology* (London, 1937), 23 ff.

deflowers them. Hence, he suggests, the rule of the *jus primae noctis* to protect the husband against such an antagonism. A Gond girl may say to a husband or lover whose fidelity she suspects, 'I would take off your penis and keep it always with me, so that it can go to no other woman'. Dr Masani reminds me of such penis-envy in hysterical girls who have phantasies of incorporating and retaining the penis inside them so as to possess permanently the coveted organ. Penis-envy may undoubtedly play its part in what I believe is an essentially complex situation.

That it is not unrecognized is shown by the stories of the Umbilicus Elongatus (Nos. 36-41), fantasies which by showing women possessed of an umbilicus, a trunk, a penis, of enormous size and power, compensate them for the most serious physiological defect from which they suffer.

Much more plausible is the suggestion that sexual intercourse is regarded as dangerous because of the dread of menstrual blood. For a man to have intercourse with a woman during her menstrual period is regarded not only as aesthetically disgusting—'It is dirty, it is sinful, it has a bad smell', as a Baiga once told me—but also as highly dangerous for the man. 'Worms may attack his feet and he may get an acute attack of gonorrhoea.' It is of course well known that a urethritis may be excited by the toxic character of the menstrual discharges or by intercourse with a woman subject to chronic leucorrhoea. The danger is not only physical; any infringement of the menstrual taboo is visited with supernatural penalties.[1] Penzer discusses the possibility of syphilis being the origin of the poison damsel motif, but he concludes that the time the disease takes to show itself is greatly against its use in a story where the effect has to be immediate and causing practically instantaneous death.[2]

But in our stories and dreams from central India, the bite of the vagina does not always cause death and is often curable. Moreover, Penzer was thinking chiefly of syphilis which has an incubation period of some three weeks and which in any case does not resemble a bite. Gonorrhoea or some other form of urethritis more closely resembles the sharp, acute, sudden bite of a tooth or serpent's sting. But it is significant that in many of the central Indian stories there is little emphasis on the pain caused by the amputation of the penis. In Story 3 the victim makes no outcry, in Story 4 he does not even notice what has happened, in Story 5 he does not seem

[1] I have recorded many of these in *The Baiga*, 211.
[2] Penzer, ii, 310.

greatly affected, and in Story 12 he hardly realizes his fate at first. In other stories, of course, the victim shouts with pain and makes an appropriate demonstration. But I do not think that we can trace the stories to the pain caused by a urethritis, though this undoubtedly is a contributory factor to the psychological situation that produced them.

On the other hand, Dr K. Masani has pointed out to me that it is the loss of the penis as such rather than any possible pain accompanying the amputation that is the real dread of the neurotic. The neurotic attitude is more easily explicable as fear of a punishment by the removal of the penis anticipated by the patient because of his strong super ego or unconscious sense of morality. Since the act of intercourse and the use of the penis at all is regarded as immoral, the neurotic fits the punishment to the crime and imagines his penis being amputated simply because it has been used.

We may finally note that during intercourse men are supposed to be specially subject to the attack of witches. Such an attack may be symbolized by the Muria story of the rat which bit off the blacksmith's penis and carried it home to its hole—a significant detail which may well represent the witch's supposed desire to attract all the libido of the neighbourhood to herself.

Reich traces the Vagina Dentata phantasy to what he calls 'orgasm anxiety'.

> In the male, orgasm anxiety is often covered up by the sensation of ejaculation. In women, however, it appears in undisguised form. Their most frequent fear is that of soiling themselves during excitation, of passing wind or of urinating involuntarily. The more drastically vaginal excitation is inhibited, the more non-genital phantasies have taken possession of the genital, the stronger is the inhibition, and, consequently, orgasm anxiety. Orgastic excitation, if curbed, is experienced as a threat of physical destruction. Woman fear 'falling into the power of the man', being injured or exploded from within by him. Under these circumstances, the vagina becomes in phantasy a biting organ which is going to render harmless the menacing penis. Every case of vaginismus has this origin. If it appears before the act, its significance is that of refusing penetration to the penis. If it appears during the act, it reveals the unconscious desire to retain the penis or to bite it off. In the presence of strong destructive impulses, the organism is afraid of 'letting go' for fear that destructive fury might break through.[1]

We must now briefly consider a much more fundamental cause for these stories, I mean the manifest or latent fear of castration and

[1] W. Reich, *The Function of the Orgasm* (Eng. trans: New York, 1942), 137.

impotence which is said to be present in every primitive or civilized human being. Let us hear a psycho-analyst who has made a careful study of anthropology; in quoting him I do not mean to suggest that I follow him in all his conclusions. 'The one great terror in the life of primitive mankind', says Roheim, 'is the same that plays such a fundamental part in individual neurosis: the dread of castration.'[1] 'It seems', he says again, 'that the fundamental fear of savages is connected with the idea of a part being separated from the whole.'[2] This fear is not associated with some catastrophic disaster effected by an enemy, but is inherent in the very act of coitus and the loss of semen. 'Actually it is the seminal fluid which leaves the body, but there is an unconscious tendency to dread the total cutting off of the penis, i.e., castration, as the inevitable consequence of coitus. Following the recent researches of Dr Ferenczi, we may regard this as the survival of the archaic multiplication by fission, the phase of development in which the propagation of the species was also the death of the individual.'[3]

It is noticeable that in several of our stories castration is associated with death, an equation which is common throughout the world. Some of Roheim's remarks about this have some bearing on the Indian stories and I will quote him in full, in order to illustrate one line of possible interpretation.

'The hero of the folk-tale has frequently to pass through crushing rocks or smiting door and usually he does not come quite unscathed from the ordeal. The doves fly through the Symplegades to bring Zeus ambrosia, but the last is always crushed by the relentless rocks... In a folktale of the Tarantschi, a Tartar Tribe in Central Asia, we find the hero passing through the moving rocks on his way to his sister-wife. The tail of his camel is cut off.

'If we know what the moving door means we shall understand the missing tail. The motif is very frequent in the mythology of north-western America, and its unconscious meaning can be studied there with advantage. The Chilcotin and Shuswap tradition of Little Dog contains a series of episodes which evidently all have the same meaning.... Little Dog and his children come to a house with a great stone door. Inside the house sits a woman who is weaving a basket. Suddenly, while they are talking to her they notice the stone door beginning to shut and Little Dog quickly places his staff so that it holds the door open. The boys slip through and Little Dog after them, but when he pulls the magic staff out behind him his little finger is caught by the door and the end cut off. Now

[1] Roheim, 55. [2] ibid., 4. [3] ibid., 25.

they come to a woman whose vagina is full of teeth. She wants our hero to have intercourse with her, but he first inserts his magic staff into the vagina and breaks her teeth. Then he and all his boys cohabit with her.

'If the door is the vagina, the pigeon's tail or the little finger snapped off can only mean the penis... The passage of the soul is coitus, the soul itself the semen, yet at the gate of the other world we find castration. But primitive views on death are modelled on the castration anxiety, and therefore if by castration we mean death it is natural enough that this should be the preliminary to the entry into heaven.

'If there should still be any doubt our meaning is made perfectly clear by the myth of Maui, crushed between the opening and closing legs, in the vagina of his ancestress Great Mother Night.'[1]

Another significant link with castration in our tales is the notion of eating. In the act of conjugation, there is a 'narcissistically resented element of mutual eating up.' 'The result is that the dread of castration is displaced to the vagina and we see the latter as an organ with oral qualities, as the devouring beast.'[2] The primary purpose of teeth is, of course, to eat. And so we find the penis not only amputated but eaten. In Story 6 there is the curious notion that after a boy had intercourse with a girl at the navel the semen entered her mouth and a new tooth was cut as a result. In the main body of the folk-tales collected from these tribesmen, the only cannibalistic stories are associated with the murder of a sister by her brothers. There are several such tales and all end in the same way, in the boys cooking and devouring the sister's flesh. In Story 3 the flesh of the girl who had teeth in her vagina was so deadly that when it was cooked even the smell was sufficient to end the tale in an orgy of sudden death.

Whether we agree with all Roheim's suggestions or not, I do not think it can be doubted that the Vagina Dentata stories are closely related to the primitive dread of castration. In Story 28 there is a very significant account of the rivalry between a father and his sons. The fear of castration is not perhaps manifest in the consciousness of the tribesmen, but a related fear—the dread of impotence—is often present and has far-reaching effects.

The actual occurrence of *impotentia coeundi* among the Gond and Baiga is less common than the fear of it. This is what we might expect. The tribesmen live a simple, out-of-door life. Neuras-

[1] Roheim, 53. [2] ibid., 48.

thenic and morbid conditions are rare. The homosexual impulse is almost wholly absent.

On the other hand, the aboriginals are often enervated by malaria and usually undernourished. Many of them suffer from venereal disease. With few other pleasures to divert them, they indulge in sexual intercourse far too frequently. Their ordinary lives are deeply marked by fear and anxiety. They believe that witches, an accidental connection with a menstrual woman, the infection of someone with unusually weak libido, or even aesthetic repugnance may make them impotent. Such a condition holds a man up to the ridicule and scorn of society and commonly leads to divorce. It may well be that this fear finds expression in some of the dreams and stories that we are considering here[1]

So far we have approached the subject entirely from the man's point of view. Sexual congress is a danger to the male; it is the woman who is armed with teeth. But a number of interesting stories suggest that this is a one-sided way of looking at things. A man may have a double penis, or a spike on the end, or teeth on either side, or it may be artificially elongated. In all these cases the danger to the woman is very great. In Story 32 an old man with horse-hair round his penis merely tortures his victim; the same effect is caused in Story 37. But in Story 33 an elongated penis kills, unintentionally, a man's own wife. In Story 17 the hero kills three wives in succession with the teeth on either side of his penis. In Story 1 the hero kills the girl who had mutilated him with his new aculeate organ. Equally dangerous is the amputated penis. This was the real cause of the wife's death in Story 33. In Story 35 it kills both a girl and her mother by jumping down their throats and out through the vagina. In Story 28 the amputated leg of one of the heroes, which obviously represents the penis, is stuck into the girl's vagina and kills her. In the drolls 7 and 16 jealous husbands attempt to frighten their wives with stories of the disastrous effect of intercourse with youths who possess a double penis. In Story 34, the penis is not an amputated organ but a magic aboriginal *gode-miche*. When it attacked an immature girl, it caused her great pain and might have killed her. The snakes in the vagina or belly are, of course, symbols of the penis but appear to be more dangerous to a male lover than to the woman herself.

It is tempting to associate these stories with the use of instruments of the *ampallang* type common throughout Indonesia and not un-

[1] For a full account of this important, and little studied, subject, see my article 'The Attitude of Indian Aboriginals towards Sexual Impotence', *Man in India*, xxiii (1943), 127-46.

known in India. Horse-hair is specially mentioned as employed in the Argentine and in Borneo.[1] But no such custom is known in actual practice to the tribesmen of Central India. The stories of the Penis Aculeatus are probably nothing more than a symbolization, from the woman's point of view, of the dangers of sexual intercourse. Dickinson considers that these dangers have been exaggerated: the risk of vaginal rupture is very slight, and among 4100 married patients he only found 161 cases of painful intercourse, or 1 in 25. On the other hand, 'coitus with little girls may result in severe hemorrhages and an occasional perforation into the rectum', and lacerations of the upper passage may occur in older women. He quotes Rahm as having collected twelve fatal cases, generally due to excessively vigorous action and too big an organ.[2]

It is worth noting that intercourse with the Devil was described by medieval witches in Europe as both cold and painful. Murray quotes Jan Bosdean (1594) as saying, 'there appeared a great *Black Goat* with a *Candle* between his horns. He had carnal knowledge of her which was with great pain.' When the devil exercised his right of *jus primae noctis*, the woman lost 'an infinity of blood and suffered a thousand dolours'.[3]

A few minor points may be noticed. Although homosexuality is practically unknown among the tribesmen, one or two of the tales contain a homosexual motif. In Story 2 there is a demon who consorts with members of his own sex and, curiously enough, lives with a Vagina Dentata girl in the same house. In Story 36 an amputated penis enters a man's rectum as he is copulating with a girl, and in Story 34 the magic *gode-miche* drives itself into the anus of a cart-man. But these incidents may be purely ribald and without psychological significance.

The power of long pubic hairs to cause impotence is a recognized fact among these tribesmen. Very few women ever allow the hairs to grow; those who do are regarded with repulsion by the majority of men. In a story from Raipur, not unlike Story 2 of this collection, the hero has to remove a woman's pubic hairs before he can have intercourse with her. I have recorded dreams in Mandla wherein the penis is caught in these hairs as in a noose, and thus injured or amputated.[4]

[1] Havelock Ellis, *Studies*, ii, 98 ff.

[2] R. L. Dickinson, *Human Sex Anatomy* (London and Baltimore, 1933), 100.

[3] M. A. Murray, 'Witches Fertility Rites', *Man*, xix (1919), 57.

[4] Dr Masani tells me of a patient who used to feel that his wife's long hair was tied tightly round his big toe (symbolizing the penis).

It is interesting that the tales contain no reference to either clan or kin incest, the more so as these tribes, especially the Baiga, are rather prone to this. I have sometimes, but not very frequently, found in dreams references to incest. In these it is noticeable that intercourse is not consummated. The dreamer on approaching his mother or sister finds that dispareunia is so great that coitus is impossible. An Agaria of Mandla District dreamt that when he tried to have intercourse with his sister he found 'nothing but blood' and could do nothing. A Gond of the same area dreamt that he was sleeping with his sister. 'She lay naked beside me and put oil on my penis till it stood erect. But when I went to her, my penis slipped into her anus and I awoke.' An Agaria told me that when he dreamt of congress with a sister or other near relative, her vagina was either too small or too big; another Agaria said that in dreams of intercourse with his mother, his penis could never find the vaginal aperture but always slipped over it, and he awoke before consummating the act. I believe that there is a close connection between the dreams and the legends, and this fact may be one reason why the legends do not have any incestous reference. There are, of course, a number of tales about illicit relations between brothers and sisters, but these are always tales of dread and misery, and desire is rarely attained.

In conclusion, therefore, it may be said that the discovery of the Vagina Dentata dream and legend in the remoter States and districts of Middle India is of great interest as establishing parallel psychological development among people as diverse as the Baiga of India, the Chilcotin of north-western America and the Ainu of Siberia. Stories of a poisonous snake hiding in the vagina or belly link up again with the classical Indian tradition of the Poison Maid. Tales of the Penis Aculeatus witness to the woman's view of the element of cruelty in sexual relations. All the stories testify to a very widespread belief that sexual intercourse is often defiling and often dangerous. It does not appear that here this danger is due to the infection of hymeneal blood, but is the result of a complex psychological situation, in which a recognition of the toxic character of menstrual blood, the possibility of venereal contagion, the exposure of both male and female to hostile magic and witchcraft at the moment of sexual congress, the universal latent dread of castration and the fear of impotence with all its social and domestic embarrassments are contributory factors.

I

The Vagina Dentata

I

AGARIA

Rewa State

A youth was very fond of his elder brother's wife. One day when his brother was away from home he slept with her. But he was drunk and did nothing. The girl was very annoyed and the next day she gave him only gruel to eat. That night he slept with her again, and he was again drunk. The girl quietly cut off his penis with her knife and stuffed it into a hollow bamboo and stopped up the end. When the boy got up, he saw blood flowing from the place and looked for his penis, but it was not there. Instead there was a little black tip growing out of the wound.

After a time this tip grew very big, as big as a large penis, and it had a sharp point like a thorn. By now the girl had gone away, but he followed her and asked her to marry him. She refused saying, 'You're impotent; what would I do with you?' But he waited his chance and one night went to her. He pierced her with his sharp spike and she died.

2

AGARIA

Bhoira, Mandla District

There were seven brothers who set out to find the Maiden Bijnakin. But the youngest had a running nose and the others left him behind in scorn. After many days the six brothers came to a great jungle, then they crossed the seven seas and the sixteen streams and at last reached the place where Bijnakin and her sister Gajdantar lived. Gajdantar said, 'Each of you must sleep with me for a night. If you can conquer me, you can take both of us away. If not, I will turn you into girls.' Now in that girl's vagina were teeth and the opening was covered with very long hairs. When the first brother went to her, he found these hairs woven criss-cross over the opening, and he could not thrust his penis through them. So he lost power. Gajdantar laughed at him and made a hole in his nose and put a cowrie in it and bangles on his wrists and shut him up in a separate house. This was the fate of each of the six brothers, and for a long time they lived there impotent.

But the youngest brother followed them. On the way he met a fox who told him what had happened and advised him what to do. The boy got a sharp arrow-head and a pot of curds and an iron rod as thick and long as his own penis. Then he greeted Gajdantar and went in to her. First he smeared her hairs with curds and cut them off with the arrow-head. He inserted the iron rod and broke off the teeth that were in her vagina, and then enjoyed her. He had conquered and went to Bijnakin to carry her off. But she begged him to wait seven days. In that house were seven rooms; in one lived the six brothers, in one Gajdantar, in one Bijnakin, in one the youngest boy, in one food and in one a Rakshasa with thick skin and long hair who copulated with men. Bijnakin thought, 'If this boy stays here seven days he will sooner or later go into the Rakshasa's room and the Rakshasa will go to him and for shame the boy will run away.' But when the boy actually met the homosexual demon, he vanquished him by threatening to set fire to his hair. The demon saved himself by telling the boy where Bijnakin's life-index was hidden. The boy obtained this and by its means rescued his brothers, restored their potency and took the girl home.

3

AGARIA

Bhanpur, Mandla District

There were twelve sons of a Dhoba. One day they met an Agaria and his wife in the forest. The Agaria had a wound on his penis caused by the *bamni* insect which gradually devours that organ. The Dhoba boys told him to dip his penis in boiling oil; he did so and it was burnt off. Then the Dhoba boys said to the girl, 'You marry us, as your husband is no use now.' She said that if anyone of them could exhaust her, she would go with them. They sent the eldest boy first to her. As he took her, blood flowed from his penis. Ten others went and each was defeated. At last only the youngest boy remained. He opened her vagina with his fingers and looked in. As he did so, from the girl's mouth a tiny thin snake emerged and tried to bite him. Happily, the boy killed it in time. When the boy killed the snake the girl fainted, but he threw black and yellow rice over her; she recovered and he carried her off.

The other brothers were left with their wounds. Presently from every penis there grew a new little penis on one side. They went to the youngest boy and he told his wife. She said, 'I have a sister. Let them go to her, and they will recover.' After a long search in the forest they found the girl and each boy went to her. She had teeth in her vagina and cut off the penis of every boy as he went to her. When the youngest brother went there, he looked at her vagina and saw the two teeth like knives that clashed together. He pushed a stick into the place, broke off the teeth and ground them up. He put a little of the powder on the penis of each of his brothers and they grew again. The brothers killed the girl and cooked her flesh in a pot. But as it was cooking there came a voice from the girl's flesh saying, 'As I died, so you will you die.' And when the brothers lifted the lid of the pot to remove the meat, the smell went into their nostrils and they fell dead.

4

ASUR

Pathar, Chhuri Zamindari

A Rakshasa was in love with a human girl; from their congress was born a daughter who built the town of Dantinpur (the Tooth City). She declared that whoever would sleep with her for one night could marry her and be the Raja of that place. Many a prince came to visit her, but when they slept with her she cut off their organs with the two teeth in her vagina, and many a prince went home without his penis. At last came two friends, a Raja's son and an Asur boy. The young prince slept with the girl and his penis was cut off. He came out and told his friend. The Asur boy went to his smithy and made an iron penis hollow inside; this he fitted over his own organ. When he went to the girl, he pushed the instrument violently into her vagina; the teeth closed upon it and broke. He pulled them out and threw them down; they stuck in the ground and turned into *kurkutti* roots. These roots do not dry all the year round, and your teeth stick in them. They are the roots of a girl's vagina. Then the Asur boy said, 'Mend my friend's penis or I'll kill you.' She mended it and married the Asur. For the prince she got her father's brother's daughter as wife.

5

BAIGA

Pandpur, Mandla District

A girl and a hare were married and went to the jungle to earn their living. They lived in a cave under a huge rock. When the hare went to sleep with his wife, he put his paw in her vagina and scratched it till it bled. The hare sniffed at it and a little of the blood went up his nose. He sneezed and scampered away to clean himself. Then he came back and mounted the girl. But she squeezed him between her legs till he cried, 'Let go, let go, I'm dying.' But she would not spare him and squeezed and squeezed him till he died.

6

BAIGA

Silpuri, Mandla District

A Baiga girl was married to a very stupid boy. He had no idea how to perform sexual intercourse. He inserted his penis in her navel, and at his orgasm the semen went into her mouth, whereon a new tooth was born there. But the next night, he took her in the vagina, but as he withdrew she caught hold of one testicle and broke it. A snake came out and the girl ran away for fear and hid in a bear's den.

7

BAIGA

Bahapur, Mandla District

An old Baiga married a girl of only twelve years. He used to fondle her breasts and rub her cheek but that was all he could do. She consoled herself with a lover in the village. When the old man discovered this, he took her away to another place. He called a Dewar (priest) and asked him to whisper a charm in the girl's ear. He was to say, 'In this village every man has not one penis, but two, and if a girl goes to him her vagina bursts open.' The girl was very frightened at hearing this, and the old

Baiga also told the young men of the village that his wife had a tooth in her vagina which cut off the penis of anyone who went to her. So for a long time the girl lived unsatisfied. Then one day by the well, she met a very handsome Baiga youth and they sat under a tree to talk. 'I have heard', said the girl, 'that every man here has a double penis.' 'Well, I only have one', said the boy. 'No, you must have two', said the girl. 'No, I'll show you. But we all know you have a knife in your vagina and will cut off my penis if I give it to you.' Then they began to laugh and they examined each other and when they saw there was no cause for fear, they lay together. When the girl got home, the old man guessed what had happened, and he declared that they would go on to another village where, he said, 'the people copulate so violently that they kill their wives.' 'We must certainly go there', said the girl. Next day they set out. But it was very hot, and the old man died by the way. The girl went back and married the handsome Baiga youth.

8

BAIGA

Kandawani, Kawardha State

A Brahmin and his wife went to live in a Baiga's house. Every day the Brahmin went out to beg and the wife stayed at home flirting with the two fine sons of the Baiga. One day she made an appointment with both boys at the same time and they quarrelled violently. At last she called the elder boy to lie with her. In her vagina were teeth and these cut off the boy's penis, but he was so angry with his brother that he did not cry out, saying to himself, 'Let him suffer the same fate.' The woman laughed at him saying, 'You're very quiet today; go to it with more vigour.' But he had lost his penis and went away. Then the woman called the younger boy and cut off his penis also.

The boys sat by the roadside and when the Brahmin came home told him what had happened; but they did not admit that it was they whose organs had been lost. The Brahmin went to his room; he bathed and did his worship; then as he rested he desired his wife. But he was afraid of the teeth and put his hand into her vagina to feel them. But she covered them with long skin as a tiger hides his claws. But he found first one penis and then another. When he brought them out, the woman cried, 'Oho.

I have given birth to twins.' 'You lie', cried the husband. 'These are the organs of two men.' 'How can such a thing be possible?' she said. 'No, they are my babies and you have killed them. Now take them out and bury them.' The Brahmin went out very sad at the loss of his children, but still doubted the truth of his wife's story, so the next night he hid in a grain-bin to see what would happen.

That night a blind sadhu came to the house, and the woman seduced him and cut off his penis also. When he had gone weeping away, the husband entered the room and made his wife lie down. He had secretly brought a pair of tongs from the Agaria's smithy. He began to play with his wife with one hand, telling her how beautiful she was, while with the other hand he inserted the tongs and removed the teeth. Neither said a word about what was happening. But then when the teeth were gone the woman could get no pleasure, her vagina was so large. She called many men to her, but there was no joy in it. At last she went to the Brahmin's horse, but it went to her with such violence that it killed her.

9

BAIGA

Ledra Taliyapani, Mandla District

An Ahir came home one day very tired and said to his wife, 'Massage my feet, and then I'll massage you.' While she massaged him, she cut off his penis, but he did not notice what had happened. When the Ahir began to massage (that is, have congress with) his wife, he wondered why he did not get an erection. He touched the place and found nothing there. She had hidden the penis in her vagina. He was very frightened and ran to the village saying, 'My wife has teeth in her vagina and she has cut off my penis.'

The next day a stupid Sadhu came to the house, and this wife forced him to lie with her. He did not know what to do, so she put him on the ground and mounted him. But his penis was very weak and she cut it off. An old man heard what had happened, and was filled with desire for her. He tied his penis round and round with horse-hair and came to see her. She persuaded him to lie with her, but when he took her the hair tore her vagina and she got up screaming. But the old man carried her away and married her.

10

BAIGA

Daukera, Mandla District

A Brahmin and his pretty daughter came to a Baiga's house to beg. After they had been fed the Brahmin lay down to sleep, and the girl went into the garden to steal some cucumbers for their supper. The Baiga caught her in the field and had intercourse with her. But she had teeth in her vagina and with these she cut off the Baiga's penis. He began to shout with pain. His elder brother's wife, who was in love with him, had been watching to see if he would go to the Brahmin girl or no, and when she heard the noise she ran to the field and said to the girl, 'Put back the bit you have cut off, or I'll tell your father.' At that the girl was frightened and she put the penis back in its place. When it was fixed on again, they laid the girl down on the ground and the Baiga pulled out the teeth with a bit of string. The Baiga soon found himself in love with the Brahmin girl, and after a few days they ran away together.

11

BAIGA

Bohi, Pandaria Zamindari

There was a Baiga girl who looked so fierce and angry, as if there was magic in her, that for all her beauty, no one dared to marry her. But she was full of passion and longed for men. She had many lovers, but—though she did not know it—she had three teeth in her vagina, and whenever she went to a man she cut his penis into three pieces. After a time she grew so beautiful that the landlord of the village determined to marry her on condition that she allowed four of his servants to have intercourse with her first. To this she agreed, and the landlord first sent in a Brahmin to her—and he lost his penis. Then he sent a Gond, but the Gond said, 'I am only a poor man and I am too shy to do this while you are looking at me.' He covered the girl's face with a cloth. The two other servants, a Baiga and an Agaria, crept quietly into the room. The Gond held the girl down, and the Baiga thrust his flint into her vagina and knocked out one of the teeth. The Agaria inserted his tongs and pulled out the other two. The girl wept with the pain, but she was consoled when the landlord came in and said that he would now marry her immediately.

12

BHUIYA

Raisua, Bonai State

Once there were teeth in the vagina. Men were so afraid of women that they never approached them. But women grew more and more lustful, and at last they went to the jungle and found a bombax tree. Each cut off a small branch and pushed it into her vagina. The teeth stuck in the wood and may be seen on the tree to this day.

13

BISON-HORN MARIA

Tikanpal, Bastar State

In the old days, women had teeth far back in their vaginæ. The penis was then of enormous length, but it was gradually bitten away by the teeth until it became as short as it is now. Then men brought pestles and broke off the teeth. In those days also the penis was covered with thorns and stood like a bombax tree.

14

BONDO

Bodapada, Koraput District

There was a Bondo girl with teeth in her thing. She used to entice young boys and cut off their organs and send them crying home. After a time, when many had been mutilated, no one would go near her. But one night, during the Pus Parab festival, a party of boys and girls came from Andrahal to dance. There was a great hearty fellow among them, with an enormous organ over which he wore an iron sheath. He began smacking and playing with the girl and, though the other boys warned him, he took no notice. That night he went to her and she tried to cut off his organ, but all that happened was that her own teeth were broken. But she took a knife and cut off all but a little of the boy's penis.

The teeth turned into crabs, and it was from the iron sheath worn by the boy that people learnt how to make spears.

15

BONDO

Pinnajangar, Koraput District

At the time when the wind and the clouds were made, Soma Bodnaik and his two wives Sombari and Sukri were living on the Samudra Hill. In Sombari's vagina were teeth, two above and two below, thin and sharp as a rat's and one and a half fingers' joints long.

Soma Bodnaik had no notion of what to do; one day he went with his younger wife to the garden and took her as if she was a cow. Mahaprabhu saw what was going on and hurried to the spot. Soma and Sukri were ashamed and sank into the ground. But presently Soma came up again and talked to Mahaprabhu who told him not to do it like that, but properly and that then he would soon have children.

The next day Soma sent his younger wife to fetch water and in her absence went to Sombari in the manner that Mahaprabhu had explained. But her teeth caught his penis and began to bite at it. But he pressed her with such force that the teeth were broken off and pushed inside.

16

DHOBA

Kumharwar, Mandla District

There was a riggish wife. Tired of watching her, her husband took her to a new village. He told the men of that place that his wife had teeth in her vagina and that she had cut off the penis of every man in their old home and the people had driven them away. He told his wife that the men there each had a double penis. This depressed her greatly. But after a time she began to long for the Double-Penis men and, since she was beautiful, they too longed for her. One day six or eight men agreed that they would go to her. The leader told the others to tie a rope round his waist and if he felt in any danger he would shout and they could pull him away.

When the man went to the girl, she saw to her astonishment that he had only one penis. 'The other must be at the back', she thought and she put her hand round to find it. But the man thought, 'Whatever is she doing?' and gave a shout of fear, whereupon his companions hauled him out of the room, and the girl was left unsatisfied.

17

DOM

Berma, Bastar State

An old woman once forgave a monkey a beating and it became her devoted servant. After a time it brought a wife for the woman's son. This wife was the daughter of a Rakshasin and had teeth in her vagina. But the boy also had teeth sticking out on either side of the penis. After marriage the boy and his wife slept together in a corner of their hut. When the boy's penis entered his wife's vagina, the teeth bit her so that she died. But at the same time the teeth in her own vagina cut off the penis. The boy cried, ' O mother, mother ! What has happened to me ? ' and he showed his bleeding penis to his mother. The mother wept looking at the dead body of her daughter-in-law and cried, ' O monkey, monkey ! ' The monkey went to find another girl and brought her to the house.

The boy married this new girl. He thought, ' Here am I without a penis, what am I to do ? ' There were still teeth there in the place of the penis and when the boy went to his new wife she died also. Again he wept, ' O mother, mother ! What has happened to your son ? ' Once again the old woman sent the monkey to find a bride for the boy. The monkey ran hard through the jungle and quickly brought another girl and when the boy went to her, he killed her also with the teeth in the place where the penis should have been. At this the monkey grew very angry, and when it brought a fourth girl, it piled a lot of wood round the house, and the boy and his bride with his mother were burnt to death.

18

JUANG

Kantara, Pal Lahara State

In the old days there were teeth in the vagina, and if a man was bold enough to go to a woman he would lose his penis. One day there was a man grazing goats ; he had a very long penis and there was a thorn growing out of the tip. One day he desired a girl and threw her down among the ripe wheat in his field and with his thorn he broke out her teeth. He threw them away and they became bhoir trees. But the girl was angry and in pain : she caught hold of the man's penis, cut it off and buried it. In time it grew up as a bombax tree. As she cut it off, she exclaimed, 'May you turn into a Raksa'. Since then Raksa have lived in the bombax tree and always trouble any woman who goes near. If you remove bark from a bombax tree and beat it, a fluid like man's seed comes out. If a pregnant woman goes underneath a bombax tree she is in great danger. The thorns of the bhoir tree are crooked like teeth and men find them specially troublesome.

19

JUANG

Bali, Keonjhar State

In the old days, when there were teeth in the vagina, a crab used to live there. When the teeth were cut off and thrown away, they turned into stones, and that is why the crab makes its home among stones.

20

KOND

Turiya, Koraput District

There were eighty Kond houses in Siknadongar. The Naik was a Kond called Ramulu. His wife was a famous witch. In her vagina this woman had two teeth and all the villagers were afraid of her. One day she went to the jungle and by her science turned herself into a tigress. As a tigress she went to catch the cattle grazing in the jungle. She leapt on a cow from behind, but it kicked out and knocked out her teeth. The teeth rolled down the hillside to where a horse was grazing in an open space below and stuck in its mouth. The woman turned back into her ordinary shape, but now she had no teeth in her thing. She went home and told her husband. He fetched the horse and patted its back saying, 'Now you have my wife's teeth ; keep them well.'

21

KOND

Pukur, Ganjam District

At the beginning of the world, Dakapaji and Sujamajenja came out of the hollow of a bombax tree. At that time Sujamajenja's thing was as big as the door of a pigsty. At the bottom was a hand and at the top were two teeth. The teeth could only be seen at night, for then they shone brightly. Dakapaji's thing was also very big. The hand would seize it and it could see its way about by the light of the teeth. Within six months Sujamajenja had given birth to seven sons and seven daughters. During the birth of the fourteenth child, the teeth got caught in the umbilical cord and were broken off. Dakapaji buried them behind his house. Later he pulled out the hand by the roots and threw it away.

22

KUTTIA KOND

Pringeli, Ganjam District

Nirantali had a daughter and when the child grew up, she found that she had teeth in her vagina. Pijju Bibenj came to marry her, and on the way home desired to lie with her. But when he saw the great teeth like the tusks of elephants, he was frightened and ran away, leaving the girl by the wayside.

The girl returned to the mother, and she was so beautiful that she soon found another husband. But when he approached her, she cut off his penis and he died. The story got round and everyone was afraid of the girl. But there was one man with an organ twelve hands long. He married her, and when they came together, she bit off all but a hand's breadth. They both lost consciousness and lay together till the morning. Nirantali wondered why they were so late, and going in saw the teeth in her daughter's thing. She at once broke them off, and then revived the couple who henceforward lived happily.

23

KORKU

Dedhpani, Betul District

Two friends set out to find themselves wives. After they had married they met one day, and the first friend said, 'How is your wife's thing?'. 'Very deceitful', said the other. 'And how is yours?' 'Mine is very faithful', said the first man. The second friend went to the village and distributed sweets in honour of this faithful wife. But there was a man there called Thaggu. He did not believe the story and decided to put the matter to the test. He was a good-looking fellow, so he went to the house of the faithful wife and persuaded her to lie with him. Above her vagina was a saw, and with this she cut off his penis. He shouted with pain and the husband came crying, 'What's the matter?' 'Your wife's cut off my penis.' 'Of course', said the husband. 'That's why I said she was so faithful.' After that everyone in the village used to laugh at Thaggu.

24

LANJHIA SAORA

Maneba, Ganjam District

Sapung Saora had one daughter: he lived with her in Sarkigudi. In those days there were teeth in the vagina, two above and two below. One day as the girl was going for leaves in the forest, Kallu Saora caught her and tumbled her. But as he was withdrawing his organ, her teeth caught at it: he took fright and pulled hard, and broke the skin at the tip. He told his friends in the village and the girl was ashamed.

Soon after this there was a dog's marriage in a village near by, Kussalgarh. Sapung had a bitch in his house and it was invited. That bitch said to the girl, 'Lend me your thing and you can have mine'. For the dogs of Kussalgarh were very loose and the Sarkigudi bitch was frightened of what they would do. The girl gave her thing to the bitch and fitted on the bitch's instead. But during the marriage, night and day changed places, and the things were stuck fast in their new positions.

From that day the bitch became dumb. And since then women have no teeth there, but a bitch catches a dog's organ and holds it.[1]

25

LANJHIA SAORA

Taribel, Koraput District

Woman used to have teeth in her vagina, but this did no harm for man approached her through the navel. A Saora had a pet parrot. One day the Saora went somewhere. While he was away the parrot pecked its way into the woman's vagina, forcing the teeth apart. The woman cursed it saying, 'May you have teeth in your beak; may you ever dig for your food.' For woman is earth and the parrot dug in her. This is why, when we worship Mother Earth, we remember the parrot.

26

MURIA

Koelari, Bastar State

There was a Rakshasa's daughter who had teeth in her vagina. She used to live mostly as a tigress and kept ten or twelve tigers with her. When she saw a man, she would turn into a pretty girl, seduce him, cut off his penis, eat it herself and give the rest of his body to her tigers. One day she met seven brothers in the jungle and married the eldest so that she could sleep with them all. After some time she took the eldest boy to where her tigers lived, made him lie with her, cut off his penis, ate it and gave his body to the tigers. In the same way she killed six of the brothers till only the youngest was left. When his turn came, the god who helped him sent him a dream. 'If you go with the girl,' said the god, 'make an iron tube, put it into her vagina and break her teeth.' The boy did this, and when the tigers came for his body, he climbed into a mango tree and made himself very small. The tigers chased him and the girl

[1] At Tikanpal, Bastar State, I recorded a Bison-horn Maria tradition that 'in former times dogs were very potent and went to their bitches constantly, with the result that countless litters of puppies were produced. This made Mahapurub anxious, and he cursed the dogs with impotence for ten months of the year, and gave them a knot or knob on the organ, as a result of which they were caught by the bitch and so prevented from excessive intercourse.'

too became very angry. He cursed her, 'Let nothing but your face remain!' And so it was; she became a bat, which eats, excretes, urinates and copulates through one and the same aperture. One of the mangoes opened and the boy crept inside. A parrot carried off the mango to a Raja's palace. It dropped it, the fruit broke open, the boy emerged, and at last married the Raja's daughter.

27

RAJNENGI PARDHAN

Jingratola, Mandla District

There was a woman with teeth in her vagina. No man dared to approach her. She had no breasts and lived in misery. She used to weep continually, sitting on the banks of a lake.

One day an elephant came to the lake to drink water. 'Why are you crying, girl?' it asked. She said, 'Because I have teeth in my vagina and no breasts and, because of that, men are afraid of me and I have no happiness.'

In those days elephants had very beautiful breasts, round and firm, so beautiful that great Rajas fainted when they saw them. The elephant said to the woman, 'Well, give me your teeth and I'll give you my breasts.' The woman took out her teeth and fixed them on either side of the elephant's head and the elephant removed its breasts and gave them to the woman. Since that day, when men see the breasts of women, they are filled with desire.

II

The Vaginal Snakes

28

AGARIA

Umaria, Mandla District

A Raja had two sons. When his wife died, he said to his sons, 'Shall I get a wife for myself or for you?' The boys said, 'Marry her yourself and we will call her mother.' The Raja then married a very beautiful girl. But when he kissed her on the mouth as if she was a child, he died. It was as he was lying upon her, lost in love and he kissed her as if she was a child. The sons thought, 'This girl was really for us and our father took her and has died for his sin. Now which of us shall marry her?' The younger boy said, 'You marry her,' thinking that he could still enjoy her.

One day, as the elder boy slept with her, a snake small as a thread came out of the girl's mouth, then grew very big and swallowed up the boy. The younger brother was near by and saw what had happened. He cut the snake into three pieces with his sword. But in doing so he cut off one of his brother's legs. The brother was very angry and got out of the snake's body. He thrust the leg that had been cut off into the girl's vagina. She died, but the leg stuck on to the boy again. But now when he tried to pull it out of the vagina he could not. So the younger brother cut open the belly of the girl and took out the leg, and they ran away together, very sad, to find other wives.

29

GOND

Surguja State

One night the wife of Mansingh Gond went out to excrete near an ant-hill. As she sat there the ground broke and a small snake came out and entered her vagina. In her belly it grew fat. Her husband thought her pregnant. So twelve months passed. One day she went with her husband to the bazaar. As she sat in a bania's shop, the snake poked its head out from under her sari. The bania saw it and knew what danger the husband was in. He bade him get a crowing cock, tie his wife's hands and feet to four staves, open her clothes and run away. 'Tie the cock near and when it crows the snake will come out and you can save your wife and yourself.' All happened as the wise bania had said. This is a true story.

30

GOND

Mangli, Pandaria Zamindari

An old man and woman had seven sons, six of whom were married. The youngest boy had an affair with his eldest brother's wife. Unless they met each other sometime during the day, they could not eat their food. This went on for a long time until at last one day, for some reason or another, there was a quarrel between them, and the boy took a broken cot to the stable and lay down there in temper. When they found him missing in the evening, the parents looked for him and found him in the stable. They all tried to console him, but when they failed they called an old Mali woman. She brought a basket of gram, a pot of ashes, a spinning-wheel and some cotton. She sat on the ashes and began to eat the gram and spin the cotton. *Chara-chara* went the wheel, and she farted *bhara-bhara*. At last she farted so violently that the ashes flew up over the boy's face. The boy abused the woman. But she had got him talking and at last he said to her, 'If you will bring me a girl who is more beautiful than my eldest brother's wife, then I will eat my food.' But the girl was listening secretly and she cried out, 'O boy, if you get a prettier girl than me, certainly you may eat your food. Go and find such a girl. There is one called Bijinakan Kanya.' The boy went off to find the girl. Sometimes he walked; sometimes he ran.

Now Bijinakan Kanya was beautiful as the lightning and lived in her father's city. She used to swing in her golden swing every day. She never went out of the house. But one day when she was twelve years old, she went to the Raisur Lake to bathe. After bathing, the cold wind made her sleepy and she lay down to rest under a banyan tree. While she slept, her seven servants were playing hide-and-seek. Near the girl was an ant-hill. It was very hot and a snake came out of the hill to find water. As it was passing by the sleeping girl, it heard the noise of the seven servants playing their game and was frightened and entered the girl by her little vulva and hid in her belly. But the girl knew nothing of what had happened. As the days passed the girl's belly swelled. The father, thinking she had become pregnant by a lover, sent her out of the house to a place where no man ever came. They took her to a cave in the forest and left her there. The girl could hardly move for pain, and became very thin for hunger and thirst. A crow, which had its nest in the banyan tree, saw where the girl was taken.

One day the boy weary and exhausted came to the tree and embraced it crying, 'O tree, tell me where is Bijinakan Kanya'. The tree said, 'I will tell you, but first of all rest here.' Now the Raja's servants thought it was a wrong thing to banish so beautiful a girl, and they decided to marry her to someone and send her away happily. The servants took her food and went. They all planned to have intercourse with her. She refused and one of them took her by force. But the snake put its neck out of her vagina and bit the man. As he was dying, he said, 'I died because I have sinned in trying to take this girl by force'. When the others saw what had happened, they ran away.

The tree told the boy what had happened, and the crow hearing the conversation told the boy that it would take him to the girl. 'I will go flying ahead, and you look up to see where I am and follow me.' The boy came to Bijinakan Kanya and said, 'I have come to marry you.' There was nothing to eat and the boy dug up some roots and they ate them. The boy desired her, but she said, 'Until we marry, you must not touch me.' There was a sadhu living in the jungle, and one day as the boy was digging roots he found him and told him the story. The sadhu said, 'Bring the girl here and I will marry you.' But the girl could not walk. So he put her on his shoulder and carried her to the sadhu. The sadhu married them. When the girl went to sleep, the boy got up and sitting apart thought how he was to save the girl's life. As she slept, the snake came out of the girl and approached the boy to bite him. But he saw it in time and killed it. He tied the snake to a stone and put it near the girl. The girl slept all night and the next day. The boy told the sadhu everything. He threw black and yellow rice on the girl and aroused her.

31

LOHAR

Rajasevvayya, Raipur District

Lohakutti Lohar lived long ago in the deep jungle. One day while his daughter was pissing by the roadside a Brahmin passed by, and asked if that was the blacksmith's house. The girl turned round just as she was and said, 'Yes'. The Brahmin cursed her saying, 'You have shown me your thing; from to-day there will be death in your thing.' The Brahmin went to the Lohar and said, 'What are you doing, fellow?' The Lohar replied, 'I am minding my own business.' The Brahmin said, 'You will all be burnt in this smithy.'

The following day as Lohakutti and his two wives were working at their kiln, fire broke out of its own accord and burnt them to death. The girl tried to kill herself; she put her head in the mouth of the kiln, but as she did so, the fire died down. For a long while she lay like that.

From another village came five Lohar brothers and seeing the girl were filled with desire. They went to the jungle and felled a tree for charcoal. In that tree was a snake; it ran away for fear of the fire and came to the smithy and went into the girl's vagina. The girl knew nothing of it; she was lying with her head inside the furnace. Then the brothers came back.

The eldest brother took the girl's head out of the furnace. Desire entered his mind and he went to her. But when his penis entered her vagina, the snake cut it off. He ran away, ashamed of what his brothers would say. So the second, third and fourth brothers in turn approached the girl and had their virile organs removed. But when the youngest boy saw the blood in the vagina, he took a stick and poked it in. The snake bit on the stick and the boy saw what was the matter. With his tongs he pulled out the snake and was about to kill it when it said, 'Spare me and I'll stick on the penis of each of your brothers.' Then the boy took that girl home, and when the brothers saw them they were very angry. They attacked them, but the girl kicked each brother in turn, and as she did so his penis was restored. The youngest brother told the whole story and the next day he was married with great rejoicing.

III

The Penis Aculeatus

32

BAIGA

Bohi, Pandaria Zamindari

There were seven sisters, tall, with full breasts. The eldest was a witch. For fear of her no one would marry the other sisters. One day an old Baiga with his son and five other men went to work in that village. The old man's son was a fine boy, handsome and strong, just ready for a girl. The witch said that if they all seven could overcome her, she would give them her six sisters. The men thought, 'Surely seven of us will be able to wear her out.' Five of the men went to her, but they were all defeated. Then went the young boy and he suffered the same fate. Then it was the old man's turn. He cut off some hair from the tail of a horse and wound it round his penis. When he thrust this into the woman she cried, 'Stop, stop, you have defeated me. You may take away my sisters.' The men went away very pleased, but where the hair had torn the witch's vagina she was in great pain. Presently the old man died, and the witch went to the village where the six men were living with her sisters and made them impotent.

33

BAIGA

Pandpur, Mandla District

Two Baiga discovered that their wives were having an intrigue with a Brahmin beggar and decided to make a trap for him. They made nooses of hair and tied these in the organs of their wives. When the Brahmin next visited the first girl, she waited till he was fairly at it, then hastily pushed him from her. The noose tightened round his penis and cut it off. But he did not cry out, he said, ' I have dropped my medicine on the ground. Give it to your husband to eat and he will get great strength'. When the man came to supper there was fish to eat, and the girl put the penis with the fish and served it to her husband. He picked up the penis saying, ' This is a fine fish', but it jumped out of his hand on to his brother's plate. The brother swallowed it whole.

That night the penis broke through his stomach and entered his wife's vagina. He got up and went to her. But the cut-off penis stuck on to his own and made it double in length ; it was so long that it killed the girl.

34

BAIGA

Pendra Zamindari

A Baiga had a garden of cucumbers. One day a sadhu came begging, but the Baiga was angry and said, ' I've no cucumbers, I've only got a penis. You'd better eat that.' The sadhu said, ' From to-day every cucumber in your garden will turn into a penis.' The Baiga was frightened and ran to his garden to see if anything had happened. There he found growing a penis of a speckled colour. Its name was Chanduwa. The Baiga took it to the bazaar. Many abused him and some wanted to beat him, but at last he met a Brahmin woman with a little daughter. This woman was very passionate but she had no husband. She bought the penis for forty rupees and the Baiga went home well pleased. The woman went home and lying down called on the penis to come to her. It entered her vagina and worked till she was satisfied, whereupon she sent it to live under the roof. Day by day she did this and her little daughter watched her. One day when the mother was out fetching water, the little girl lay down and repeated the charm that would bring the penis from the roof. The penis jumped down and entered the child's vagina, but blood flowed from her and she began to scream. The mother came in and sent the penis back to the roof. Another day some cartmen were staying near the house, and one of their bullocks was called Chanduwa. One of the men addressed it by name, but the penis heard it and entered the cartman's fundament. At last that woman got married, but she still used the penis. At last the husband discovered it, and caught it in a trap and burnt it.

35

BHARIA

Rewa State

A youth found himself in trouble at home because he was often impotent. One day he went to catch fish, but could not even do this properly. He returned home angry and miserable. He tied up his penis in his loin-cloth into a little bundle, showed it to his wife and said, 'Here are some fish. Come and take them.' She caught his penis, pulled it off and threw it in the fire. The boy died and the penis jumped *phit-phit phit-phit* in the fire and so jumped into the girl's mouth and then out through her vagina. She too died. The penis went jumping along to where the girl's mother was cooking fish. It got into the pot and when the old woman stirred it jumped out. The mother thought it was a fish and tried to catch it. But it went into her mouth and out through the vagina and killed her too. Then came a boy and caught it in a basket. He tied it up with a bit of string and kept it in his pocket.

36

GOND

Lormi, Bilaspur District

A man went with a girl to the forest. On the way desire entered his mind through his eyes, and he bade her stand naked against a tree. He went some way off and ran at her with penis erect. But as he approached she moved aside and he dashed his penis against the tree and broke it. His seed fell on a stone under the tree. Presently two men came by. He gave them the seed. 'It's all the wealth I have', he said. They picked it up on a leaf and went off with the girl. But the penis followed them. On the way the first man took the girl aside and had congress with her. The penis entered the man's rectum. He thought, 'This girl has got both a penis and a vagina', and he quickly ran away. The same thing happened to the second man and he too ran away. Then the penis jumped up and sat on the girl's head. She returned to the tree where her first lover was sitting. He had tied a large root in front of him and cried, 'Now I have a penis big enough to kill you.' She ran for her life. He chased her. By the roadside sat a great ogre with his mouth wide-open. The girl ran down its throat and out through his rectum. But the man's big 'penis' stuck in the ogre's throat and it devoured him.[1]

37

LANJHIA SAORA

Talasingi, Ganjam District

Jammu Saora and his wife lived together in Raohalgarh. In this man's penis there was a little tongue and on the tongue were many little thorns. When he went to his wife, he used to put out the tongue and it scratched her vagina. The woman was frightened. One day Jammu got very drunk and in this state sat before his wife for intercourse. When he got up, his wife said, 'Bring a cloth and I will wipe my face'. But with the cloth she caught the tongue and pulled it out. She threw it away behind the house and a tiger ate it. That is why the tiger's tongue rasps as if it was covered with thorns.

[1] The attribution of an independent life to the genitalia is found also in North America. In the Crow tale, *Mentula Loquens*, for example, a man urinates and shakes his penis at a buffalo. He asks the penis if it can see the animal. The penis replies, 'I see it' and goes on talking, refusing to stop, it says, till it is pressed by its owner's wife's mother.—R. H. Lowie, 'Myths of the Crow Indians,' 225. There is a Trobriand story of a detachable penis which can leave its owner, wriggle through the grass like a snake, and assault unsuspecting women.—B. Malinowski, *The Sexual Life of Savages* (London, 1929), 348.

IV

The Umbilicus Elongatus

38

GOGIA PARDHAN

Jhanki, Mandla District

Bodhmancha's son was Kuhimancha, the Raja of Chandagarh. He had two daughters, Ramo the elder, and Bodrahin whose umbilical stump was seven-and-a-quarter cubits long and one-and-a-quarter cubits thick. On the end was a ferrule made of five iron harrows and at the tip projected an iron spike of twelve ox-goads joined together. In the middle of the stump was a depression large as a warming-pot, and in this sat a hen hatching a brood of eggs. In the stump lived a goddess, Kochkosur Maharani Devi. Bodrahin had six servants—the ever-chattering Chaiti, the slow-spoken Sulki, the gossip Jalkajholan, the quick-tempered Pharuachalawan, Laharlagaunin the scandal-monger, and Manusmarani the seductive.

When Bodrahin was born the Pandits said to her father, 'This girl is dangerous; don't look at her for twelve years. If you do you'll die at once.' So Raja Kuhimancha avoided his daughter for twelve years, though he heard many stories of her wonderful beauty and her embarrassing affliction.

As a little girl Bodrahin used to be swung in her golden swing by her six handmaidens. When she was twelve years old and began to soil her head, she desired men. But boys were afraid of her. Her stump was very strong and she used to penetrate her handmaidens—in fact poor Chaiti became pregnant with it.

When Kuhimancha first saw his daughter he was greatly embarrassed. 'How am I to get a husband for this girl?' he thought. 'My shame will go from land to land and the world will laugh at me.' He made plans to have her killed, but the Pandits warned him against this course, and in time he got used to the great stump and came to love the girl as a father should.

Ramo was very beautiful—and so indeed was Bodrahin. Ramo was the elder and must be married first. Kuhimancha announced that he would give her to whoever would pay a bride-price of eighty sacks of gold mohurs and who would go to Kalipatpar and standing there would take in his body twelve blows from his great spear Bairisal. Many Rajas came anxious to prove their valour and virility and camped by the Raisur Lake. Ramo asked Bodrahin to go and see which was the most handsome and report to her. Bodrahin set out for the Lake with her maidens. This girl was always playful and now she amused everybody by poking the girls with her stump, now in the breast, now in the backside, now in—and so hard did she do it that poor Chaiti was delivered of a boy prematurely by the roadside. Bodrahin picked up the baby, cord, placenta and all and put him beside the hen in the middle of the stump. She said the boy was to be called Jhathmurda.

When they reached the camp of the suitors by the lake, Raja Rassia took them into his tent and made them sit down. He gave the maids betel, but threw Bodrahin's to her from a distance. This made the girl very angry. 'Am I a Chamarin?' she shouted and threw it away. Then she went for Raja Rassia with her stump. She hit him over the head with it and split his head open. She poked him in the ribs and blood flowed over the floor. She stuck it up his backside and he excreted in front of them all; Manusmarani could not contain herself for giggling. The Raja was soon subdued. He fell at the girl's feet. 'O Babisahib, it was my fault; forgive me. Here are eighty sacks of gold mohurs; take them, but don't poke me again.'

Bodrahin was pleased at this, and picked up the sacks as an elephant picks up a log with its trunk and slung them onto her stump, and staggered home.

Raja Rassia said to the other Rajas, 'I have given the sacks; now for the rest of the test.' He went to the Raja Kuhimancha and said, 'Johar, father-in-law.' Kūhimancha laughed and said, 'If I'm your father-in-law, come along to Kalipatpar and face my blows.' He picked up his great spear Bairisal. When the suitors saw it they excreted in their dhoties. They said, 'Let's be off. We can at least save our lives. If we can't get Rani, we can still get a *kāni* (girl with a squint).' They ran away just as when a jackal comes into a village to steal the fowls and it is seen and everybody shouts at it, it runs away with its tail between its legs.

But when Birsingh Raja of Birhulgarh heard Raja Kuhimancha's terms he prepared to marry Ramo. But he said, 'I can't give eighty sacks of gold mohurs; that is absurd. But what I can do is to break twelve pairs of iron shoes in a day and I can take five spear blows on my chest, standing before my father-in-law at Kalipatpar.' Birsingh was very strong, very handsome, and he got ready. He tied iron plates over his chest, so heavy that four and twenty men could not lift them. When he reached

Chandagarh he went to the Raja's darbar and said, 'Johar, father-in-law.' 'Don't be in a hurry to say "father-in-law"; break your twelve shoes and then stand up to my five blows.' Birsingh broke the iron shoes, and the Darbaris murmured their admiration; Ramo watched from an upper window and nearly swooned for love. Then they went to Kalipatpar. Kuhimancha lifted Bairisal and cried, 'Here is my Johar' and struck the youth a mighty blow. But there was no wound. Then the Raja struck again and the spear penetrated four fingers deep into the flesh. Birsingh Raja thought, 'At the next blow I will be killed', so he fell at Kuhimancha's feet and begged that his life might be spared. Raja Kuhimancha laughed and let him stay in the palace as a Lamsena until a better man should come.

Then Katsungha Raja heard of these tests and trials, and came to betroth his son Marakhan Kshattri to the lovely Ramo. He spread tents by the lake splendid as ten cities and prepared to meet Kuhimancha on the morrow. But during the night Birsingh broke into the camp and cut off Katsungha's head while he was asleep.

The news flew to Bairagarh, where Marakhan was still a little boy. When Ramo heard what had happened she wept, 'How will I ever get a husband?' Her pet maina heard it and said, 'Do not be sorry. Your husband has been born and soon you will hear of him and see him.' 'O maina, where is he?' 'He is in Bairagarh. His name is Marakhan. Write him a letter and I will take it to him.' Ramo wrote at once and the maina took it in its beak and flew to Bairagarh and dropped it in front of Marakhan. When he read it the boy saddled his horse within the hour and was away to Chandagarh. He met Raja Khora on the way and, finding that he wanted to marry Bodrahin, took him with him. Khora had a great spear made of copper. It was seven-and-a-half cubits long and he planned to use it to cut off Bodrahin's stump and so make her fit for marriage.

The two boys reached Chandagarh and pitched their tents by the lake. Their horses danced in front of them. There were lights and flowers everywhere. The boys sat on chairs in front of their tents. The water girls saw them and were excited. They whispered to one another, 'O if Bhagavan would send us husbands like these.' They ran home and spread the story through the court. Birsingh heard it and went to fight. The two friends killed him and threw his body in the lake. Then Bodrahin sharpened her stump and with her six girls went to the camp and asked angrily, 'Who killed my Lamsena Birsingh Raja?' Khora Raja was angry at hearing this and struck her stump two or four times with his great copper spear. He cut off two cubits and the girl fell at his feet. 'O husband, forgive and marry me.'

When Kuhimancha Raja heard of this he was very angry and told the two youths that they must go to Kalipatpar for their test before they could have his daughters. But Marakhan took ten blows from Kuhimancha without flinching, and when he said, 'Now, father-in-law, take my greeting', the Raja fell at his feet and declared himself beaten.

But Bodrahin, hearing her father was defeated, came to the rescue, her broken stump high in the air. But Khora Raja caught it in his hand and pulled it out and threw it away. It turned into a hill that can still be seen near Chanda, the Bodra Hill. Once the stump was gone, the beauty of Bodrahin could not be described. Her name changed too, and after she was married she was known as Hiroli Bai.

39

GOND

Bohi, Pandaria Zamindari

There was once a king who had seven daughters. The youngest of them had an umbilical stump one cubit long. For this reason, although she was very beautiful, no one would marry her. Many a prince came to seek her, but when they saw the stump they went away in despair. Nor were the six elder sisters willing to be married so long as the youngest remained with them. For every day they used to play at Houses, and during the game the youngest daughter used to go to each of them with her stump so that they were satisfied and did not desire men.

In this way many days passed. But the youngest girl grew weary of the game, for, although her sisters were satisfied, she herself got no pleasure in it. One day she went to the bank of a lake and sat there weeping. A donkey came by and asked her what was the matter, and she told it her story. The donkey said, 'Come along and see my wife, and she will make everything right'. The donkey took the girl to its wife and told it everything, whereupon the she-donkey said, 'My child, give your stump to my donkey'. And the girl did so. This is why the donkey's organ is always so large.

Then the girl went home, and her marriage was arranged. But the other sisters had all grown old; they could not get married, and they had no other means of satisfaction.

40

KUTTIA KOND

Kalanguda, Ganjam District

At the beginning men had umbilical stumps that were seven cubits long. This was very tiresome, and when the farmers went to work they had to tie their stumps round their waists to get them out of the way.

Mangragatti had a son. He got up one morning, tied his stump round his waist and went out to play. A crow flew down and bit it off. The boy died.

Mangragatti went with the neighbours to Nirantali. 'My son has been killed. If children continue to be born with these great stumps, many others will also be killed.' Nirantali called all the people to her and cut off their stumps. Since then they have been small as they are today.

41

PANGIA KOND

Kesarguda, Ganjam District

After the creation of the world the blacksmiths Mukutera and Kanutera made the sky and raised it into its place. The gods went to live in the sky and sent their blessings down on the two brothers.

Now Kanutera had an umbilical stump twenty-two and a half cubits long. Mukutera said to the gods, 'We have made the sky for you to live in. Do something to preserve our names for ever.' Bura Pinnu said, 'I will give you anything you want.' Mukutera said, 'Take my young brother's stump and stretch it across the sky so that all the world will see it.' Bura Pinnu took the stump between the toes of his left foot and gave a tug and it came out. He stretched it across the sky as the rainbow. He said, 'When people see this during the rains they will know that on the next day the rain will not be so heavy.'

42

PARDHAN

Balaghat District

In Awadhatola there lived a Dhimrin. She was pregnant. When her time came she gave birth to a girl child. After the child's cord had been cut, the stump began to grow and became very long. When the parents saw this they were troubled, for they said, 'How will we be able to marry such a girl? And besides everyone will laugh at her and us'. They called the girl Bai Bodrahin.

When the girl grew up, she was so fat that twelve men could not embrace her with their arms outstretched. She was a hundred cubits tall and enormously strong. Round the tip of her navel stump was a ferrule made of twelve iron harrows. It was decorated with twelve cartloads of coloured ribbons. Every third year the people sacrificed a male pig to the stump. Whatever commands Bai Bodrahin gave were immediately obeyed. She fought against many Rajas and conquered them, taking their kingdoms into her control. She used to strike the enemy in the chest, using her stump as if it was a spear.

For Bai Bodrahin the people made a house two miles long. When she lay down to sleep her stump used to look up in the air through a hole in the roof. An owl used to come and perch on the tip of the stump at night and call *gugju-gugju*. When Bai Bodrahin felt amorous she used to send her stump into the neighbours' houses. It used to seek out handsome youths and tickle them.

When it was time to go to the bazaar Bai Bodrahin used to take one hundred and forty of her girl friends sitting on the stump.

Now-a-days if a pregnant woman sees Bai Bodrahin in a dream, or if she meets her ghost[1] by the wayside, her child will be born with a large stump.

[1] There is a Pardhan tradition that such a woman was in the old days honoured even by Rajas and that every third day a pig was sacrificed to the stump. In the Bellary District there is, or was, 'in the middle of the threshold of nearly all the gateways of the ruined fortifications round the villages, a roughly cylindrical or conical stone, something like a lingam. This is the Boddu-rayi, literally the navel stone, and so the middle stone. Once a year, in May, just before the sowing season begins, a ceremony takes place in connection with it. Bullocks are driven past it. The stone is worshipped, mango leaves are strung above it.'—*Bellary District Gazetteer.*

43

PARDHAN

Jubbulpore District

In Bhondin-Kachhar long ago a wild boar was born. In Hiragarh eighty lakhs of young girls took their pots to the Raisur Lake to bathe. As they were going Kamal Hiro saw them. She went to her mother Damalghaila and said, 'Mother, have a pot made for me, for I want to go with the other girls to get water and to bathe in the lake'. When her mother sent for Bardamal Pande the potter, Kamal Hiro said to him, 'I want the pot made with a golden mouth and on the side a picture of a pair of cranes'. The potter brought many kinds of earth, but he could not make the pot. The potter's wife, Bardamal Borar, was the special friend of Bodrahin, for her own navel stump was very long, though not so long as Bodrahin's. Bardamal Borar said to her friend, 'I am weary of looking for earth to make Kamal Hiro's pot. You go and get some for me'.

Bodrahin went to the jungle and came to Bhondin-Kachhar where the wild boars were rooting in the ground. She dug up some of the earth with her stump and brought it back to Hiragarh on its tip. With this the potter was able to make a decorated pot for Kamal Hiro and from that time the place has been known as Ghaila-Kachhar.

44

RAJNENGI PARDHAN

Mandla District

(An incident from 'The Song of Hirakhan Kshattri', *Folk-Songs of the Maikal Hills*, pp. 364 ff.)

Bodrahin is on her way to celebrate a Festival. She and her girls set out to bathe in a lake.

From this girl's navel projected a stump.
So large it was that the very ring round it
Contained enough iron to make twelve harrows.
The tip was long as a digging-stick.
It was tied round with twelve ribbons,

It was tied round with thirteen cords,
It was tied round with nine baskets of cord.
So Bodrahin prepared to go to the lake.
Bodrahin had six maids to carry her stump;
Each supported it on a turban tied about her head.
Even then the ox-goad at the tip projected
And was borne by a black cock which strutted in front crying *Kukure koo.*
If one of the girls stumbled, Bodrahin would poke her back
And the girl would jump *kalbal.*
As they started out, the earthen nagara sounded *dum-dum,*
The courtyard of bronze went *tan-tan,*
The rhythm of the copper drum went twelve kos all around.
The boys of Bhago Tola were playing *killi.*
When they saw all these girls on the way,
The boys ran together to turn them back.
Some of the girls they caught by the breasts,
Some they threw down and climbed upon them.
The girls shrieked and ran away.
But when Bodrahin heard it, she said to her six maidens,
'Let there be maggots in the privates of these impotent youths!'
She raised her stump straight to the sky and ran after them.
She pushed them in the back and they bled and bled.
Hardly were the boys saved, they ran home weeping;
They went to Mahangu Mahila and told him what had happened.
Mahangu Mahila got up, his pyjama was of python skin,
His coat of leopard skin, his cap of peacock feathers;
His turban was of the shining gunsi-gadian snake.
With a great red stick Mahangu Mahila came out,
And stood below the pipal in the midst of the village.
When the girls came weeping to the pipal,
Mahangu Mahila lifted his stick and beat them.
'You are those very girls who went to bathe
When Hirakhan was married.
You brought the cholera to us and destroyed half the kingdom.
Today, you *hagri*, you would go again.
Turn back or I will kill you.'
When Bodrahin heard this she raised her stump straight like a spear.
She rushed at Mahangu Mahila the impotent;
She struck him with her stump and he slid twelve hands away.

Bodrahin hung him over her stump, his backside was nought but blood.
Then Mahangu with great difficulty saved himself.
The girls went to the tank and took off all their clothes.
Bodrahin was playing with them and teasing them.
Into one she'd push her stump, she 'd sit another on it;
She would lift her up with it right into the sky.
So they bathed joking and laughing together.
Now when the girls had bathed, they sat down on the bank
To comb their hair and talk. 'This same impotent Mahangu
Tried to stop the girls when Kamal Hiro was married.
To such antics his organ is accustomed.
May his ashes soon blow through the air, the impotent!'
Then Paniya Dokari, whose breasts swung like country shoes,
Says to Bodrahin, 'Is not this Mahangu your mother's sister's son?
Are you not brother and sister? That is why Mahangu used to have you.'
Bodrahin says, 'Not so, grannie, though it's true he is my brother,
We have only met now after many days,
And I couldn't go to him because of the stump.
That's why he mounted it as if it were a horse.
That's how we met each other, but we couldn't do anything,
So I put it round my shoulder and as we couldn't do it,
I was angry and attacked him. I got onto him
And as I was thrusting my stump into his body,
You came and separated us at Kamal Hiro's wedding.'

45

RAJNENGI PARDHAN

Gopalpur, Mandla District

The Raja of Margarh was Mara Kshattri. One day he took his friends to hunt with his falcon. They went to the great plain Lilarangibata. There was a gotiya tree there. Mara Kshattri said, 'Let the falcons fly in the air'. The birds flew up in a cloud and settled on the tree. There were so many that you could not see the tree for birds.

On Lilarangibata plain there were many quails and partridges. When they saw the falcons they were very frightened and said to one another, 'What is this? What disaster has befallen us?' They went to Kanwa

Lawa the magician and told him what they had seen. He said, 'Why are you afraid when I am here to save you?' For a time he remained silent; then he said, 'Bring me gotiya leaves'. He made a winnowing-fan and a gourd with them, put some spear-grass in the gourd and taking the fan in his hands sat down to find out from the gods what was the matter. He made Ghaghar Lawa sit by him holding the gourd. As Kanwa Lawa shook the rice in his fan, Ghaghar Lawa fell to the ground in trance. He saw the fate of the birds and Kanwa Lawa cried, 'What do you want, O Mother?' Speaking through Ghaghar Lawa, the Mother replied, 'Offer me a white goat and I will save you all'. Kanwa Lawa said, 'Listen, all of you', and the birds answered, 'We are listening'. 'Are you willing to give or not?' and the birds answered, 'We are willing'.

So now when Mara Kshattri and his friends sent their falcons to catch the birds, Kanwa Lawa turned the quails and partridges into stones. The falcons flew up and down, but they could not catch a single bird. Kanwa Lawa turned himself into a great partridge and flew up into the air towards Mara Kshattri's own falcon. The name of this bird was Dhauri Kabri. One of its wings was white and one was speckled. It caught Kanwa Lawa by the wing, but he turned into a stone and fell to the ground. The falcon was frightened, for there were nothing in its beak but wings. 'There is some magic here. My master will think I have eaten the bird and I will be killed'. In fear the falcon flew away.

Mara Kshattri, seeing his bird flying away, decided to follow it. It flew away away away; it looked back and saw Mara Kshattri following on his horse. It came to where a Raja's daughter was sitting. She had many servants and she sent them to catch it. None of them could find it. So she called Bodrahin. This girl tried to catch the bird by throwing a net and then she threw a cloth, but it was no good. At last she unwound her navel stump—it was twelve cubits long. She anointed it with vermilion, tied new ribbons at the tip and lay on the ground on her back. The great stump went straight up into the air. The falcon saw it and tried to catch it with its claws. It scratched the stump and the blood flowed. Bodrahin wept and told the Raja's daughter, 'I cannot catch this bird'. The princess replied, 'If you don't, I will kill you'. So again Bodrahin lay down and this time when the falcon came she caught it with her stump and took it to the princess who placed it in a golden cage.

Just then Mara Kshattri arrived. He went to an old Malin and with her help disguised himself as a girl. He made friends with the princess and played *chaupar* with her. The following day the princess took Bodrahin and the other girls riding on elephants to the lake to bathe. The elephants went with the girls into the water. When they had finished and had mounted their elephants again, Bodrahin's elephant suddenly ran away into the jungle. It went on and on to the Land of Elephants where they lived together in a great palace. The elephants kept Bodrahin there and treated her with honour, offering a pig to her great stump every three years.

But when Mara Kshattri heard that it was Bodrahin who had caught his falcon he mounted his horse and followed her. He came to the palace and took her away. Now Bodrahin was very beautiful. Mara Kshattri tied her long stump round and round her waist. He put her on his horse and they rode away quickly to the lake. When they got there he said, 'Let us bathe', and they went together into the water.

There was a great fish in the lake and seeing the long stump, it thought that somebody's entrails had come out and had been thrown away. It swallowed both the stump and Bodrahin herself. Mara Kshattri was mad with grief and went to the Raja of that place. The Raja sent his Dhimar who caught the fish and cut it open. When the people saw Bodrahin they fell in love with her, for she was so beautiful, and took her to the Raja so that he could marry her himself.

But at the marriage Mara Kshattri was the Dosi. He made the Raja very drunk and carried Bodrahin off. He found his falcon and took his new wife and his bird back to his own country.

46

RAJNENGI PARDHAN

Uphri, Rewa State

In Cheopara Batukatola lived Jhalmaha Dokara and his beautiful young daughter Paniyabillo. This girl was very lovely but she had a stump growing from her navel that was one-and-a-quarter cubits long. She could bring this stump in and out as she willed.

After her marriage when her husband approached her she brought out the stump and it stood upright above her body. When he saw it the boy ran away for fear and her parents-in-law sent her back to Jhalmaha Dokara.

Paniyabillo used to go to many girls with her stump and she made them pregnant. One day the grand-daughter of Paniya Dokara, Dhanidhusari, was getting married. Many boys and girls and men and women escorted the girl to her husband's house. Paniyabillo brought out her stump and tied it up completely with ribbons of every colour so that none could see it.

When the party reached the bridegroom's house the villagers came out to welcome them. They got very drunk and there were people lying about on the ground everywhere. Paniyabillo wandered about sticking her stump into men and women.

At last she came to Mahila Diwan. He too was drunk but kept his senses. When the girl approached him he drew his knife and cut off the stump. He threw it to a mare which was tethered nearby. It ate it and conceived. When the colt was born, they found that it had an organ which it could bring in and out just like the stump of Paniyabillo.

After that Paniyabillo and Mahila Diwan ran away together and lived as husband and wife.

BIBLIOGRAPHY FOR CHAPTER EIGHTEEN

The references in this Bibliography are to specific accounts and discussions of the Vagina Dentata and related legends.

Boas, F. *Indianische Sagen von der Nord-Pacifischen Küste Amerikas* (Berlin, 1895), 24, 30, 66.

The Mythology of the Bella Coola Indians (Publications of the Jesup North Pacific Expedition, i. Leiden, 1898), 76.

'The Eskimo of Baffin Land and Hudson Bay', *Bulletins of the American Museum of Natural History*, xv (1901), 170.

Tsimshian Mythology (Thirty-First Annual Report of the Bureau of American Ethnology, 1909-10, Washington, 1916), 604, 614, 773, 778, 809.

Kwakiutl Tales (Columbia University Contributions to Anthropology, ii. Leiden and New York, 1910), 171, 459.

'Mythology and Folk-Tales of the North American Indians', *Journal of American Folk-Lore*, xxvii (1914).

Boas, F. and Hunt, G. *Kwakiutl Texts: First Series* (Publications of the Jesup North Pacific Expedition, iii. Leiden and New York, 1902 and 1905), 96.

Kwakiutl Texts: Second Series (Publications of the Jesup North Pacific Expedition, x. Leiden and New York, 1906), 238.

Bogoras, W. *The Chuckchee* (Publications of the Jesup North Pacific Expedition, viii. Leiden and New York, 1904-9), 72.

'The Folklore of North-eastern Asia, as compared with that of North-western America', *American Anthropologist*, iv (1902), 667.

'Tales of Eastern Siberia', *Anthropological Papers of the American Museum of Natural History*, xx (1924) 97 ff, 127.

Chamberlain, B. H. 'The Ainu', *Folk-Lore*, 1888, 38.

Dawson, G. M. 'Notes on the Shuswap People of British Columbia', *Transactions of the Royal Society of Canada*, 1891, Sect. ii, 32.

Dixon, R. B. 'Maidu Myths', *Bulletins of the American Museum of Natural History*, xvii (1902), 69.

Dorsey, G. A. *Mythology of the Wichita* (Carnegie Institution of Folk-Lore, xi, 1898), 114.

'Traditions of the Skidi Pawnee', *Memoirs of the American Folk-Lore Society*, viii, 35.

Dorsey, G. A. and Kroeber, A. L. *Traditions of the Arapaho* (Field Columbian Museum, Anthropological Series, v. Chicago, 1905), 260.

Elwin, Verrier *The Baiga* (London, 1939), 423 ff.

The Agaria (Bombay, 1942), 164, 269.

The Muria and their Ghotul (Bombay, 1947), 423 f.

'The Vagina Dentata Legend', *British Journal of Medical Psychology*, xix (1943), 439 ff.

Farrand, L. *Traditions of the Chilcontin Indians* (Publications of the Jesup North Pacific Expedition, ii. New York, 1900), 13.

Goddard, P. E. 'Jicarilla Apache Texts', *Anthropological Papers of the American Museum of Natural History*, viii (1911), 202 f.

'Myths and Tales from the San Carlos Apache', *Anthropological Papers of the American Museum of Natural History*, xxiv (1920), 32 ff.

Jacobs, M. *Coos Myth Texts* (University of Washington Publications in Anthropology, viii. Washington, 1940), 206, 245.

Jochelson, W. *The Koryak, Religion and Myths* (Publications of the Jesup North Pacific Expedition, vi. Leiden and New York, 1908), 116.

Kroeber, A. L. (Editor) 'Walapai Ethnography', *Memoirs of the American Anthropological Association*, No. xlii (1935), 272 ff.

Landtman, G. *Folk-Tales of the Kiwai Papuans* (Helsingfors, 1917), No. 398.

Lincoln, J. S. *The Dream in Primitive Cultures* (London, 1935), 108.

Lowie, R. H. 'The Test-Theme in North American Mythology', *Journal of American Folk-Lore*, xxi (1908), 110.

'The Northern Shoshone', *Anthropological Papers of the American Museum of Natural History*, ii (1909), 237.

'Myths and Traditions of the Crow Indians' *Anthropological Papers of the American Museum of Natural History*, xxv (1918), 167 f.

Money-Kyrle, R. *Superstition and Society* (London, 1939), 41, 87 f.

Phinney, A. *Nez Percé Texts* (Columbia University Contributions to Anthropology, xxv (New York, 1934), 53 f.

Pilsudski, B. *Materials for the Study of the Ainu Language and Folk-Lore* (Cracow, 1912), 85 ff.

Roheim, G. *Animism, Magic and the Divine King* (London, 1930), 4, 25, 48, 53 ff.

Seligman, C. G. 'Anthropological Perspective and Psychological Theory', *Journal of the Royal Anthropological Institute*, lxii (1932), 219.

Steward, J. R. 'Some Western Shoshoni Myths', *Anthropological Papers of the Bureau of American Ethnology* (1943), 349.

Swanton, J. H. *Haida Texts* (Publications of the Jesup North Pacific Expedition, x, Pt. II. Leiden and New York, 1908), 349.

'Myths and Tales of the South-eastern Indians', *Bulletins of the Bureau of American Ethnology* (1929), 179, 231, 270.

Teit, J. *Mythology of the Thompson Indians* (Publications of the Jesup North Pacific Expedition, viii. Leiden, 1912), 221, 339, 366.

Waterman, T. T. 'The Explanatory Element in the Folk-Tales of the North American Indians', *Journal of American Folk-Lore*, xxvii (1914), 49 f.

Wissler, C. and Duvall, D. C. 'Mythology of the Blackfoot Indians', *Anthropological Papers of the American Museum of Natural History*, ii (1908), 16.

CHAPTER NINETEEN

THE COMING OF DEATH

A NUMBER of legends about the origin of death[1] have been recorded by Indian anthropologists. The Birhor, like the Juang and other tribes, have a theory of temporary death. They say that the spirits who take away the souls of men sometimes do so only with the object of taking forced labour from them as landlords take labour from their tenants. Consequently when a Birhor dies in a forest during a storm there is a chance that he may recover, for high wind, lightning and rain are regarded as signs that the spirits are going on a marriage procession. At such a time, if they see a human being out in the jungle they sometimes make his soul join them to act as a torch-bearer. In such cases on their return journey the spirits send back the soul of the man to his body and he revives.[1]

The Birhor also say that in the old days all deaths were a temporary separation of soul and body and death only became permanent as a result of a trick practised on man by the *lindum* centipede. A Birhor who had died revived as usual and having bathed in a stream was returning home when he met a centipede. The crafty creature barred his way and said to him, 'First count my legs and then you can go home'. The man began to count them but before he had finished, the centipede moved a few steps forward and the man had to begin all over again. When he had almost finished counting the second time, the centipede moved a few steps backward and the man had to begin counting once more. The centipede went on repeating the trick with the result that it was impossible for the man ever to finish his task and return home. Since that time, say the Birhor, the dead do not return to life.

Another story from the hill people near Simla was recorded by Mrs Dracott:

> When God first made the world, he took two handsful of ashes and placed them in a corner and hid himself. These became a man and a woman. God then called the man by name, saying; *Manoo*, and the man replied, *Hoo* instead of *Ha Jee* respectfully, as he should have done.
>
> For this reason was everlasting life denied him, and where he stood, there were his ashes when he died. Even to this day, if a man should scratch himself, a line of the white ash of which he was made is seen. If any man addresses another as *Jee* it is accounted to his good.[2]

The Lakher myth likewise attributes the origin of death to the Creator Khazangpa's annoyance with men for their bad behaviour.

[1] Roy, *The Birhors*, 252 f.

[2] Dracott, 5.

After the Great Darkness which nearly obliterated the world, Khazangpa said, 'If I cause another total darkness, the people in the world will be entirely destroyed. I will therefore not cause another such darkness, but if people are wicked and disobey me, one in every family shall die from time to time, and the family in which the death occurs shall suffer in the same way as all men did during the Great Darkness.'[1]

The notion that if nobody died the world would become overcrowded and unable to support the population is widely distributed and has been recorded in Assam.

There is a Rengma Naga legend that describes how 'at the beginning of time day and night were the same, and the dead lived in the same world as the living and worked at the same time.' This led to a situation when God had to divide time into day and night, giving 'the day to the living in which to work, and the night to the dead.

'And he moved the dead to another world, too, for when the dead and the living lived in the same world they were so numerous that there was danger of there not being enough land to *jhum*.'[2]

There is a similar idea in the Golaghat (Assamese) legend which describes how Yama sent two diseases to the world, but they returned ashamed, unable to do anything. The result was that the population increased until the world could scarcely bear the burden of it. At last Yama went riding on a water-buffalo to Brahma and beat him till he promised to create men with some weakness that would cause them to die.[3]

The curious notion of the division of souls appearing in the Pardhan story from Mandla (No. 25) is found also among the Kharia and the Munda. The Kharia describe how after the human race had been destroyed by the rain of fire sent by Ponomosor, he found himself without anyone to offer him sacrificial food. Dakai Rani rebuked him and refused to show him where the human survivors were. Ponomosor promised that he would never destroy mankind again and that Dakai Rani should have seven shares and he the Creator should have only one share of mankind. The seven shares of Dakai Rani are the bodies of men that are subject to every kind of disease and the one share of Ponomosor is the soul of man after death. This is why, so long as a man is alive, Ponomosor has no claim on him.[4]

The Munda legend is similar but the names are different. Here it is Singbonga who discovered that there were two human beings

[1] Parry, 489.
[2] Mills, *The Rengma Nagas*, 271.
[3] Lewison, 353.
[4] Roy, *The Kharias*, 417.

who had survived the great conflagration. These were living with Nage-Era and before she would give them up, he had to promise that he would never destroy mankind again and that Nage-Era would henceforth have a share of the human race. He assigned to her all those people who had leprous sores or marks on their bodies and he himself took the rest. It is said that Nage-Era, in order to swell the number of her people, sometimes sprinkles water on folk who are bathing in tanks and springs in order to affect them with leprosy or leucoderma.[1]

There is an interesting parallel to the Dhoba story on p. 418 in a Warli legend.

A pair of bullocks, hearing that the messengers of Yama were coming for their master, warned him of his danger and told him how to avert it.

'Get a plank of wood,' said the bullocks to their master. 'Carve the figure of a goddess on it. Invite all the people in the village for the festival of this goddess. The messengers of Yama also will come tomorrow and will sit in the courtyard, unseen by anyone, waiting for the opportunity of taking your life. Instal the image in a wooden box. Invite all the people assembled to have a *darshan* of the goddess and bow to her. When all the people have bowed to the goddess, look at the front yard and say, "Why do you sit there? Why don't you come and have the *darshan* of the goddess as others did?" Then Yama's messengers will think, "This fellow sees us; let us approach the goddess." When you think they have come near the box and peeped inside, at once shut the box and lock it from outside.'

The master followed the instructions of the bullocks to the letter. Yama's messengers were thus locked in the box and the man's life saved.

Yama was at a loss to know why his messengers did not return and suspected that some mischief was played on them. He wanted to find out where they were interned. He hit upon an ingenious plan. 'Liquor reveals everything,' thought he. He created liquor. Liquor shops were started everywhere and people began taking liquor immoderately.

The farmer who had locked up the messengers was once quarrelling with another man in a liquor shop. In order to put down the man opposite, he proudly said, 'I would not spare you. I have even locked up Yama's messengers.' This secret was revealed to the other messengers of Yama who were moving there in human form. They made friendship with the farmer and treated him with more liquor, so much so that he lost his senses. The other messengers while accompanying him home expressed a desire to see Yama's messengers in the box. The farmer being under the influence of liquor opened the box. The interned messengers at once flew away and the poor fellow lost his life.[2]

[1] Roy, *J. B. O. R. S.*, ii, 208.

[2] Sawe, 183 f.

Akin to the Bison-horn Maria and Juang tradition that the dead, after being carried out to the burial-place, got up and came home is the legend recorded by Radcliffe Brown in the Andamans. A boy took a knife from where it was tied to the back of his neck to cut up meat and cut himself. Then his mother knew that he was dead. She said to him, 'You are dead now. You had better go away. We do not want you here any more'. She took him up and carried him into the jungle and buried him, returning home. Very soon he returned. His mother exclaimed, 'O, I thought you had gone'. He replied, 'Mother, I did not die. Why did you bury me?' But she knew he was dead, so she took him and buried him again. He came back again. This happened three times. Then she took him into the jungle to a big tree in which there was a big hole. She kicked the tree with her foot and said, 'You go in there.' He went inside. 'Well! Have you gone?' his mother asked. He answered, 'Yes.' 'Tell me how the spirits talk', she asked him, and he replied, '*To kit*'. Then his mother knew that he was with the spirits and said, 'O my child, you are finished now. You will never come back again.' After a few days he came back (as a spirit) to see his brother who was busy building a hut. When he saw him he killed him. Before this there had been no death. But the boy's mother told the people, saying, 'You see what has happened; well, we shall all of us die like this, like these two have done.'[1]

The Juang have a large number of legends to account for the existence of death, a fact that seems to indicate that they have given an unusual amount of thought to its tragedy and deprivation. Their ideas about the future life, so far as I could discover them, are scanty enough; except under Hindu influence, they have no idea of re-birth; some souls are elevated to a sort of godhead—the kind of dignity that a robber chief might acquire, others wander sad and frustrated round their former homes, others go to Mahapurub and enjoy a life of happiness with him in the Upper World. A pathetic tale from Tambur in Pal Lahara suggests a contrast between that world and this.

Each of these stories testifies to what has appealed even to the most advanced nations as the supreme hint of immortality—the energy and power of the human soul. Death is unnatural; man was made to last for ever; only the most drastic means can conquer his strong and vivacious soul. It is no matter for astonishment, therefore, that this energetic soul, once conquered by death, should be essentially dangerous.

[1] Brown, 216 f.

I

AGARIA

Daldal, Mandla District

In Koeli-Kachhar lived a Baiga and a Baigin. When Bihi Mata saw that nobody was dying she was troubled; she made from the dirt of her body a Sahis and his wife and sent them to the Baiga saying, 'Make a drum of earth and go and dance in front of these Baiga'. The Baiga could not help it, he fell in love with the Sahis woman. Now, before that time, man and woman had never been to one another and that was why there was no death in the world. But when the Baiga met the Sahis woman alone in the forest there was an earthquake. Mother Earth trembled and the Baiga died immediately. From that time there has been death in the world.

2

BAIGA

Bohi, Pandaria Zamindari

(From *The Baiga*, 329)

Bhagavan grew tired of the Baiga. He wanted other lives in the world. But he could not kill Nanga Baiga. So he made the sensation of itching and Nanga Baiga began to scratch. All day and all night he scratched till his nails were all worn away and his skin torn to threads. But there was one part of his body that he couldn't reach, the small of his back. He used to pick up sticks and scratch himself there.

One day, when Nanga Baiga picked up a stick to scratch himself, Bhagavan turned it into a cobra. It bit him and he died. We would never have been subjects of death if Bhagavan had not tricked us.

As Nanga Baiga was dying he said to his sons, 'Don't bury my body or throw it away, but cut it up and put it in an earthen pot and boil me and then eat my flesh.' So his sons did this, but Bhagavan seeing what would happen if they ate their father's flesh was frightened, and came to them disguised as a sadhu. 'What is this?' he asked.

'We are cooking Nanga Baiga,' they answered, 'and we are going to eat him when he is ready.'

'But that is a great sin,' said Bhagavan. 'You had better throw the pot into the river.'

They were afraid of the sadhu, so they did as he told them. But a little of the steam escaped from the pot and entered the nostrils of the youngest son, and he became the first Gunia. But all the rest of Nanga Baiga's magic was lost to us through this Hindu god's deceit. Down the river, three women ate Nanga Baiga's flesh and became witches.

3

BHUIYA

Ronta, Bonai State

In the days when there was no death, Mahaprabhu came to the Middle World and said to the people, 'Now you have got to begin dying.' They replied, 'We are willing, but we don't know how to.' Bhagavan therefore died himself to teach men the way of death. Before he died he said, 'Take my body out of the village and throw it away. If you leave me inside the boundary I will turn into a dangerous ghost and will devour you.' Bhagavan died and his seven daughters carried him out of the village and threw him away. After that, whenever anyone died the people took the corpse out of the village and buried it and thus death came to the world.

4

BHUIYA

Champajor, Keonjhar State

Men have always died, but at first it was as if they had been to a bazaar. They came back the next day. There was an old man who lived with his wife and daughter. One day the old man died. Next morning the wife went to the clearing for roots. When the old man came home, he asked his daughter, 'Where has your mother gone ?' 'To the clearing for roots.' 'Go and tell her that I have come home.' The girl went to her mother, but the old woman said, 'Your father's dead ; how could he come back ?' The girl returned home and told her father what her mother had said. When he heard that, the old man was very sorry. He said, 'Well, bring me some ash from the hearth.' He put some of the ash on the threshold and some on his forehead and marked his feet with it, and went away. When his wife came home and saw the ash on the threshold she wept loudly crying, 'Why didn't I come quickly?' Since then, when men have died, they have not returned.

5

BHUIYA

Nagira, Pal Lahara State

Jug Burha and Jug Burhi were born first in the world. So long as they were alive no one died, no one could die. People increased in number so much that there was no room for them to live. Mahaprabhu thought in his mind, 'Everyone is being born and no one is dying; where will there be room for all these people?' So Mahaprabhu thought, 'I must kill Jug Burha.' He found a centipede and sent it to bite Jug Burha and Jug Burhi. The centipede bit them, they died and death entered the world.

6

BISON-HORN MARIA

Dualkarka, Bastar State

In the old days, even when the dead were cremated, they used to come to life again the following night and return home. In this way there began to be too many men and women in the world—for they were always being born and never died. At last Mahapurub cursed mankind so that no one should ever return again from the dead.

7

BONDO

Andrahal, Koraput District

Formerly people did not die and Mahaprabhu thought, 'If nobody dies how will there be room in the world for everybody?' So he went to Goigecko, the lord of death, and said to him, 'These Remo[1] people

[1] The Bondo refer to themselves as Remo.

do not die; you must arrange that they do.' So Goigecko sent his messenger, but the Remo shot and killed him with their arrows. Then Goigecko made a tiger and sent it to kill the Remo, but they killed it also. Then Mahaprabhu himself took a hair from the head of Sitiya-Mahalakshmi and turned it into a snake and sent it to kill the Remo.

When the snake reached the Remo village, a little child was playing in the street and his mother was sitting nearby. The snake bit the child and he fell down. When the mother saw it she picked up a stick and killed the snake. But the child also died. The mother said to the dead snake, 'Because you killed my child I am going to roast and eat you.' She took it into the house and roasted and ate it.

Because of the child death came into the world. Because the mother ate the snake, came witchcraft and magic.

8

DHANWAR

Barbhata, Uprora Zamindari

Formerly men were immortal. Whenever one of the messengers of death came, they would remove their skins and give them instead of their souls, and the messenger would take them to the Under World and hang them up to dry in the store there.

One day as a messenger was going along the road, a skin in his hand, towards the store, he passed a snake's twelve-year-old daughter playing. The messenger fell in love with the girl and took her to his house and married her. Some time after his marriage he said to his snake mother-in-law, 'I must go to fetch some skins.'

There was living nearby the brother of the snake woman. His name was Jaddu. He said to the messenger, 'Take my skin instead.' The messenger took Jaddu's skin and prayed to the King of Death, 'Look, master, I have married the daughter of these people. Let me bring their skins instead, and then they will live and men will die.' The King of Death agreed and since then it has been the snake that has changed its skin and man who has died.

9

DHOBA

Silpuri, Mandla District

There were two friends, the son of a Bania and the son of a Gond carpenter. A chaprasi came from the Under World, the Kingdom of Death, and seized the Bania and was taking him away. The boy cried, 'Friend, this chaprasi of death is going to take me away.' The Gond boy said, 'Don't be afraid. I'll stop him.' He said to the chaprasi, 'Leave my friend alone today, for he has many arrangements to make in his house; you can take him away tomorrow morning.' The chaprasi agreed.

Near the village was a very large hollow cotton tree. In this the Gond had made twenty-one little rooms and had driven an iron nail in each. He took the chaprasi there and climbed up with him to the highest room. He shut him in with a nail so that he could not escape and climbed down again. After some days the chaprasi died for lack of food. In the Under World, the Death Raja said, 'There is no news of my chaprasi; what has happened to him?' He called his Baiga and told him to look for the man with his measuring-sticks. The Baiga saw that he had not returned from the Middle World, but was still somewhere there.

The Death Raja sent a sadhu and some men to find the chaprasi. On the way they passed a hollow mahua tree. Rain had fallen into the hollow which was full of the flowers. A maina and a parrot were sitting in the tree, drinking the liquor and laughing and talking. The maina said, 'Don't talk so much, brother. One day or other everyone must die, just like that Bania.' When the sadhu heard that he sent one of his men to climb the tree and see what was going on. 'There is water here, and mahua,' he said. 'Bring me some,' said the sadhu. They both drank it and soon were very drunk. The sadhu went to the village and camped under a tree.

A Kalarin went by on her way to bathe in the stream. She had her clothes on her head and a pot under her arm. The sadhu called her. 'What caste are you?' 'I am a Kalarin.' 'Have you a husband?' 'Yes.' 'Then send for him.' When the husband came, the sadhu said, 'Have you any work to do?' 'No, we are dying of hunger.' 'Then get four pots and some bamboo tubes.' The Kalar brought them and the sadhu taught him how to make a still.

Presently the Gond and the Bania came that way. The Bania said, 'What is this smell?' The Gond recognized it and said, 'It is liquor.' 'How do you know?' said the Bania. 'Am I not a Gond?' said his friend. The Gond brought a quarter of a bottle of the double-distilled spirit and they both got drunk, drunk like Raja Bijra with his blood-red eyes. He took another rupee's worth and they went drunk as mad dogs to the village and quarrelled with everybody. In the Bania's garden was a well. A woman was getting water. She said, 'Why didn't the chaprasi take this fellow away?' The sadhu heard it, and the people told him what had happened. He climbed the tree and found the corpse. He cut his own finger and put the blood up its nose. It sat up and its life returned. Then they went down and took the Bania away.

10

GADABA

Gelaguda, Koraput District

In the Upper World (Indalok) lived Bhima Mahaprabhu and his young son. When the world was remade and men were born, the gods were born at the same time. Thakurani wandered here and there seeking for food; she saw Bhima's son and desired him. She went to Bhima and said, 'I am hungry; give me your son to eat.' Bhima said, 'The boy has gone to see his grandparents; he'll be back in two or three days; when he comes, I'll give him to you.' Thakurani went away and Bhima and his wife hastily hid the boy in a wooden box and put it behind the house. On the third day Thakurani came and demanded the child. Bhima said, 'He hasn't come home yet; when he does I myself will bring him to your house.' Thakurani was very annoyed and went away cursing Bhima and his son. When Bhima therefore opened the box, he found his son covered with sores, great wounds in his head alive with maggots, his eyes running with pus. When Bhima and his wife saw this, they fell to the ground and wept bitterly. They took five goats and a sack of coconuts to Thakurani and she came and cured the boy. 'But where shall we put this disease?' asked Bhima. 'Let us throw it down to mankind,' said his wife. They threw it down and in this way came disease and death into the world.

II

GOND

Jubbulpore District

In the Under World the sixty-four Jogini were all menstruating. They went down to the sea to bathe. They had with them a carpet made of cowhide. Standing upon it they removed their clothes. As they did so some blood dripped on the cowhide and the shadow of a hawk flying overhead fell on the blood and from it a girl was born. The girl flew up into the air like a hawk and flying flying saw the whole world. She came down and in the form of a girl sat on the shoulder of the eldest Jogini. The Jogini said, ' You were born on cowhide. Therefore, your name is Chamarin '.

The girl asked the Jogini for food and they said, ' There are plenty of men in the world ; go and eat them'. The girl took the form of a hawk again and flew to the world where she pecked off men's heads and ate their bodies. But the men went through her body and passed out in her excreta and so returned to life, for in those days men had the Water of Immortality in a hollow bamboo.

Soon the girl found out that she could never get enough to eat and she went back to the Jogini and said, ' No sooner do I eat than they get out and then I am hungry again'. The sixty-four Jogini went to Mahadeo and asked him what they had better do. Mahadeo went to the Middle World and stole the Water of Immortality and now when the girl ate men they did not come back to life afterwards. She used to eat the bodies and take their souls to Jam Raja. He used to stuff them into a gourd. Many days passed in this manner and at last the hawk-girl said to Jam Raja, ' I am tired of going to and fro carrying the souls of men. After this you must send your own chaprasis for them.' Since then there has been death in the world and Jam Raja has sent his servants to fetch the souls of men.

12

JUANG

Gonasika, Keonjhar State

There was no death at first. Dharam Deota sent Kalpar Rakas to give death to the world. But after men had died and their bodies were thrown out, they used to get up and walk home. So Kalpar Rakas used to catch the bodies and cut off their feet. They could not walk home and they remained dead.

13

JUANG

Balipal, Keonjhar State

At first men did not die. In those days Rusi and Rusain had many children. Mahapurub thought, 'Soon there will be no room in the world. How can so many people live in such a small place?' So he sent Jamudeota to Rusi and Rusain and said, 'I am great, I am great, I am great, I am great'—that was all he said; he said nothing more. When Rusi heard it he was angry and said, 'No, I am great, for it is I who give birth.' Jamudeota said, 'Well, if you are great, if you give birth, prove you are greater still by eating your children.' Rusi devoured all his children. 'Now bring them out again,' said Jamudeota. But they were dead, and that is how death came into the world.

14

JUANG

Kirtanpur, Dhenkanal State

In the days before men began to die, there was a Brahmin who lived by begging. One day he got a little rice and mahua and was very pleased. When he got home he thought, 'How hungry I am! What shall I cook first?' As he was cooking the mahua, a poisonous centipede came by and asked the Brahmin, 'What are you doing?' The Brahmin said, 'Why are you wasting my time by talking when you can see that I am dying of hunger?' The centipede said, 'What, do you know what dying is?' 'No, I have never heard of it. What is it? Teach me, brother, and I will then know how to die.' In front of the Brahmin the centipede fell into pieces. The Brahmin stood up and tried to do the same. While he was trying hard to break into little bits, the centipede came alive and bit him so that he died. Since then all men have died.

15

JUANG

Kirtanpur, Dhenkanal State

At first no one died. An old man was counting grains of oil-seed during the night. There was no sleep in those days. The old man used to spend all night counting oil-seeds. He spent all day counting oil-seeds. He even forgot to eat. Then Mahapurub sent a Rawatin to sell curds. The curds had sleep-medicine in them. The old man bought the curds and mixed them with rice. After he had eaten sleep came to him and he died.

16

JUANG

Tambur, Pal Lahara State

An old man and woman had seven sons and one grandson. In those days no one ever died. Mahapurub thought in his mind, 'None die, what shall I do?' Now everyone in that family loved the little grandson. 'If he was not with us, how wretched we would be.' But Mahapurub called the mother of his mother and said to her, 'The old man and woman have a grandson. Bring him here; I want to play with him.' She said, 'How can a little child come such a long way?' But she dressed in tattered clothes and leaning on a stick hobbled along to the house and said to one of the sons, 'Where has your mother gone? You must certainly give me something.' When she saw the grandson, she felt pity on him for his beauty and because they all loved him. 'I won't take him,' she said, 'or they'll die of weeping.' She returned and told Mahapurub, 'They look on him as their very life; how could I bring him?'

But Mahapurub was angry and drove her away. 'You must bring him,' he said. This time the grandmother took the form of a black cow and she caught the boy as he was playing and killed him with her horns. They wept and threw the body away. Then the grandmother took her own form again and carried the child to Mahapurub who restored him to life. But on earth the family wept and wept and found no comfort. 'I have done a great wrong,' thought the old grandmother. She carried the child back to the place where they had thrown him away. In her own form she went to beg at the house. When she saw them weeping, she asked, 'What is the matter?' When they told her she said, 'Take me to the place and let me see him.' They took her to the place and she made the child alive again.

But the boy had been very happy with Mahapurub. He had as much food as he could eat and there were always games to play. He had no desire to stay on earth. Every day he would say, 'I must go back to Mahapurub.' In the end they had to keep him tied up to stop him going. Then he refused to eat or drink; he only thought of Mahapurub. At last he died and from that day there has been death in the world.

17

JUANG

Korba, Keonjhar State

In the old days men used to die, but they came back to life again. When the people took a man's corpse to bury it, the man would get out of the grave and sit beside it. An old man and woman had no children. When the old man died, the widow could not dig the grave, so she dragged the body to the jungle and threw it away. Mahapurub thought, 'It is those who have relatives who bury their dead; others are only thrown away.' He came to the Middle World and said to the people, 'If you bury the dead they return to life; if you throw them away they become dangerous ghosts and devour you. If you find such a one returning, burn him and he will trouble you no more.' The people were very frightened and collected a great deal of wood. When the old man came back in the usual way, they thought he was a ghost. They caught him and took him to the pyre and burnt him. That is why we burn the corpses of the dead for fear they may return to life and trouble us.

18

JUANG

Andhari, Pal Lahara State

Of old the tongue had growing from it a hair twelve hands long. One day it wearied and cried, 'O if only I could die!' It died and after that death filled the world.

19

KOL

Sanhrwachhapar, Mandla District

There was once a god called Amrit in whose belly was the Water of Immortality. Whenever any human child was born, she used to take a little of this water from her belly and give it to drink, whereupon the child would become immortal.

Bhachka Dano had a child born in his house and went to Amrit Deo to get some of the water for it, but the god refused and there was a quarrel. The Dano turned himself into an old cow and fell into a ditch near the house. Presently Amrit Deo came by. 'Whose poor old cow is this?' He tried to get it out of the ditch but when he had got it on its feet the cow suddenly turned on him and pierced his belly with its sharp horn. The Water of Immortality poured out and fell to the ground. Another god heard Amrit's cries and came running to help him. When he saw what had happened he said, 'Take your belly to a stream and wash it there.' He did so and the other god pushed the entrails back inside him and tied up the wound.

Before this people did not eat because of the Water of Immortality in the belly, nor did they excrete, nor did cattle do any work. But now they had to eat and excrete and they began to die. For its share in bringing death to the world the cow was put to the plough and made to work.

20

KOND

Dussurguda, Koraput District

Raja Atalsingh ruled in Sakrigarh. He had seven daughters, all virgin or at least unmarried. No one came to ask for them. There were few men in the world in those days, but the Raja's Diwan had one son, and the Raja's daughter was in love with him. In spite of the great love between them, the boy had to marry another girl. In despair the Raja's daughter went to Bhim Raja and danced in his court. Bhim Raja was very pleased and told her to ask for anything she desired. The girl said, 'If you want men in the world, send death to make them die and you can send them back to be reborn.'

Bhim Raja gave the girl a bottle of death-water. He said, 'Bury it somewhere, and people will begin to die'. He sent two chaprasis with her. The girl went home. She said to the chaprasis, 'Take the Diwan's daughter-in-law first of all'. On the threshold of the Diwan's house she buried the bottle. The daughter-in-law at once fell ill and died. The girl married the Diwan's son. But death had come to the world, and in the end even the lovers died.

21

LANJHIA SAORA

Munisingi, Ganjam District

Bhimo and Ramo were brothers. When the world sank below the water, these two alone survived. When the world was formed anew, these two brothers made men. Now Bhimo, the elder, lived in the sky and Ramo on the earth. From above Bhimo sprinkled the water of immortality: it fell into lakes and rivers and men drank it and none died. But soon Bhimo wearied of scattering the water drop by drop and he sent a message to Ramo to take it all and distribute it himself. Ramo sent his chaprasi the leech for it, but on its way home it drank it all itself, and told Ramo that Bhimo had refused to give it. When Bhimo heard what had happened, he caught the leech and in rage made a pile of wood and burnt it. But a few drops of the water remained in its belly and kept it alive. But there was none left for men and they now began to die.

22

MURIA

Masora, Bastar State

(From *The Muria and their Ghotul*, 264)

In the old days the Muria did not die, yet could not keep their youth. They sat in the courts of their houses propped up with bits of wood ; they could not use their hands or feet, and their gruel had to be poured into their mouths by their relatives. At last they went to Mahapurub and asked him to give them the gift of death. ' Do you want death for everyone', he asked, ' or only for yourselves ?' ' For everyone ', they replied. From that day both young and old have died.

23

MURIA

Berma, Bastar State

(From *The Muria and their Ghotul*, 264)

In the Middle World no man died, and Mahapurub wondered how he was to get souls for his kingdom. He had a son. He killed him and prepared to carry him out for burial. But when his wife heard of it, she ran weeping to the place and, taking her son from him, sat with the corpse in her lap. Mahapurub said, ' We must bury the child, don't be foolish'. But she cried, ' No, I'll never give him to you'.

Mahapurub then planted a jamun tree behind her. When it fruited, some berries fell to the ground before her. She picked them up and ate them and her mouth was reddened with the juice. Mahapurub came again and said, 'Give me the boy. You are a witch, you are eating his flesh'. He brought a mirror and when she saw her reddened mouth, she thought she really was eating the boy. She wept bitterly, but gave the body to Mahapurub. He buried it and from that day, death has been in the world.

24

MURIA

Palari, Bastar State

(From *The Muria and their Ghotul*, 264f.)

At the beginning of the world men were very small; they ploughed with rats and had to pull down brinjals as if they were getting mangoes. The ground was so soft that you could fall through it down to the Lower World. In those days men could remove the tops of their heads, examine them for lice, and put them back again.[1]

When the first men died, their neighbours took them out to burial, but the corpses got up and came back and sat in front of their houses. When the neighbours came in, they asked, 'Where have you been?' 'We've been out burying you'. 'What sort of folk are you? We were just sleeping and you carried us here and there. When we awoke we returned home'.

When Mahapurub heard of this, he wondered how he was to get lives for his kingdom. He thought, 'I must stick the tops of their heads on; then they will certainly die'. He ground flour, mixed it with water into a paste and hid it. Then he went to see the first man and woman. 'What have you got inside your heads?' he asked. 'Do show me'. They removed the tops of their heads, and Mahapurub quickly smeared the edges with paste, muttering, 'Never come unstuck again'. When the first man and woman put the tops of their heads back, they stuck and soon afterwards people began to die.

And now for fear that the dead might come back again to their houses, the neighbours burnt their bodies and they never returned to life.

[1]There is a Santal tradition that in the old days 'men did not have to pick the lice out of each other's hair; men's skulls grew loose and each man could lift off his own skull and clean it and then replace it.' Thakur Deo was angered by the dirty habits of men and fixed the skulls on. But this is not associated with the coming of death.—Bompas, 401.

25

RAJNENGI PARDHAN

Patangarh, Mandla District

Before Bhagavan was made there was a great Devi. First she called the witches and said, ' If anyone annoys you or abuses you or quarrels with you, you may take him away.' Then she called the gods, Bara Deo, Thakur Deo and the rest, and said, ' If anyone fails to give you offerings and neglects you, you may take him away.' The witches and the gods took many lives, and they themselves killed them, and took them to the Devi. In this way few lives went to Bhagavan.

Then Devi gave power to the witches. ' Take a sparrow, and a castor branch, a cloth soiled with menstrual blood and some water from a shoe and go to a cross-road. Get the liver of a dead man on a bit of broken pottery and offer these things to it and the man will be roused to life and you can offer him to me.' Witches have done this ever since.

But those who died of old age were taken by Bhagavan ; they were killed by him and went to him. Only the young, who died out of time, went to the Devi.

PART FOUR: HUMAN INSTITUTIONS

CHAPTER TWENTY

SOME ASPECTS OF RELIGION

I

AHIR

Uphri, Mandla District

When Mahadeo's marriage was over he took Parvati home and put her in a house with seven rooms. Then he went away to the Kajliban to make a plough. But before he went he said, 'You may use six of the rooms, but never go into the seventh.'

When he had gone, Parvati said to herself, 'Why did he tell me not to go into the seventh room?' She had no interest in the other six rooms, but at once went to the seventh. This was the room where Mahadeo used to piss and some very fine red spinach had sprung up there. When Parvati saw it she was delighted and picked it and cooked it for her supper. As a result of eating the spinach, she conceived.

After seven months she became anxious and lonely without her husband. She broke a hair from her head, turned it into a krait and sent it to Mahadeo. It wriggled along and seeing him hissed loudly at him. Mahadeo threw a chip of wood at it; it became a mongoose and chased the snake back to Parvati. Then Parvati rubbed some dirt from her breast and made a tiger. Mahadeo threw many bits of wood at the tiger and these turned into jungle dogs and chased it back. But now Mahadeo thought, 'Parvati has twice sent for me, I had better go and see what is the matter'.

When Mahadeo met his wife he said, 'If you see the child being born, you will be frightened to death, so put your head in the hole at the bottom of the grain-bin and your children will be born without your seeing them.'

When her pains began Parvati lay down and put her head into the hole of the grain-bin. Many children were born, but Mahadeo was waiting and he killed everyone of them. He put them in pots, and buried them in the hills, in the fields and in tanks. Presently the buried children turned into gods. The first to be born had seven heads and thirteen eyes. He was Bara Deo. The one buried on Lingo Hill became Lingo Deo. The one buried by the river became Samduria Deo. The one buried at the cow's resting-place became Marra Deo.

2

GOND

Bhendi, Dondi-Lohara Zamindari

An old Gond and his wife had a violent quarrel about their food. There were seven chapatis for supper, and the old woman said, 'I have cooked them, so I should have more.' The man said, 'I have paid for them, so I should have more.' They quarrelled till they were exhausted and lay down to sleep, their supper still uneaten. At midnight the old man sat up and said, 'Whoever speaks first will have three of the chapatis; whoever keeps silence longest will have four.'

Then they both lay down and kept silent. Not a word did they speak all night and when dawn came they remained quiet. They stayed lying down all that day and the next and then the neighbours said, 'What has happened?' and went to see. They opened the door of the house and saw the man and wife lying silent on the ground. They called to them, but they said not a word, and the people decided that they were dead and should be taken out to burial.

Seven men came to carry them to the burial-ground, but when they were about to lower them into their graves the old woman said to her husband, 'I will eat three; you can have four.' When the seven men heard the corpse speak, they thought it was referring to them, and ran for their lives. The old man and woman, wondering what was the matter, ran after them. The seven men reached the village crying that ghosts were coming to devour them and the people ran for their lives. They went to the Police Station and reported the matter, but the Sub-Inspector looked out and saw the old man and woman coming and he and his constables too ran for their lives. They went on to the Raja and the Rani, and soon the palace was deserted.

The old man and woman occupied the palace and lived there in great comfort. But after this fear came to the world, and men have been afraid of ghosts.

3

Bara Pen

GOND

Bilhar, Bilaspur District

The Gond used to live in Kachmach Raj, and at that time they had no gods. Five men came together—Uika, Syam, Naitam, Pandro and Marabi—and said, 'How can we live without gods?' They sent their request to Bhagavan and he made Bara Pen[1] for them and appointed Palo as his chaprasi. They worshipped Bara Pen with a white bull and Palo with a black bull.

One day Jhariya Raja came to see the place and said, 'Let me see how much Sat there is in this god of yours. Unless he shows me his Sat I will throw him away.' He made an iron pillar inside a plantain tree and prepared a wooden sword. Bara Pen picked up the wooden sword and with a single blow cut the iron pillar in half. Then the sword came towards the Raja. And the Raja full of fear fell on his face before it and promised Bara Pen a goat in sacrifice.

The Gond were very poor; they prayed Bara Pen to send the sword to the jungle. It went there and cut down the trees of a great clearing, and they followed and burnt the trees and sowed seed there and got a splendid crop.

Since that time we have worshipped Bara Pen.

4

GOND

Pakhri, Mandla District

Kusro and Marabi were *samdhi* and they were celebrating the marriage of Kusro's daughter and Marabi's son. The women had gone to fetch the special earth for plastering the marriage platform, carrying lamps on their heads. The lamps were filled with sesamum oil and the wicks were roots of turmeric. From the flame of the lamp were born Bara Deo and Dulha Deo.[2]

[1] Bara Pen or Bara Deo is the 'great god' of the Gond, whose traditional home is the sacred saja tree (*Terminalia tomentosa*, W. and A).

[2] Dulha Deo, the 'bridegroom deity' of the Gond and several other tribes, must be appeased at weddings.

When the Marabi were going with their marriage-party, they came to a river and suddenly without rain it came down in flood. They could not cross. But with them they had a Baiga—his name was Paniha—who was the Dosi of the ceremony; he looked in his measuring-sticks to see the cause of the flood and in the sticks Bara Deo and Dulha Deo said, 'It is because of us. Give us food-offerings and the water in the river will sink.' The people said, 'Let us go and we will give you your offerings.' At this the water in the river sank and the people finished the work of the marriage and went home. A few days later in the Marabi's house there was born a child. They offered food to Dulha Deo behind the hearth and to Bara Deo outside under a saja tree.

5

GOND

Khairtola, Chhindwara District

In Janjhnagar there lived a Gond called Kurthi and his wife. They were rich in grain and cattle but they had no children. Kurthi went to Jalandar Guru and served him for seven years. At the end of that time the Guru blessed him saying, 'You will have twelve sons and three daughters'. He gave Kurthi some medicine to give his wife secretly in her food on the day she washed her head at the end of her period. Kurthi did as the Guru bade him and after ten months his wife gave birth to twin boys. The name of the elder was Bara Pen, the younger was called Jethu. Each had a separate cord and placenta. When the midwife came, as she was about to cut Bara Pen's cord, one of her eyes went blind. She took the placenta and buried it by the nearest stream.

On the Chhatti day when Bara Pen was supposed to be sleeping on a cot in the courtyard he disappeared. The people searched for him everywhere but could not find him. The Gunia consulted his measuring-sticks and said, 'This child was not a human being. He was a god.' That night Bara Pen gave a dream to Kurthi and said, 'I am Bara Pen. Let all the Gond worship me. I will give you sons and grain and you must give me food, a spotted goat and a bottle of liquor once a year beneath a saja tree. You must never burn saja wood and you must give me food and drink in cups made of saja leaves.'

Kurthi got a goat and a bottle of liquor, but no one knew what a saja tree was. But as he was down by the river he saw a tree growing out of the pit where the child's placenta had been buried and he heard a cry, 'This is a saja tree'. That is why there are knots in the saja tree just as there are knots in the umbilical cord. Formerly all the Gond went to this very tree to sacrifice to Bara Pen, but now saja trees are found throughout the world and sacrifices are made to them in every village.

6

GOND

Jubbulpore District

A Gond Raja had a lakh of sons and one-and-a-quarter lakhs of grandsons. His family grew greatly and he became very rich. Then one day Bara Deo was born from the gum of a saja tree. He made a bow of surteli wood and a fiddle of koeli-khamara wood. He stretched cowhide across it and made the *timme*, *dodha* and *manjha* strings of hair from the cow's tail. With this *bāna* he produced lovely music.

The Gond heard it and gathered to listen. They asked him who he was. "' I am your old Guru'. At that time the Gond were threshing their grain. They went to worship Anna-Kuari and took Bara Deo with them. After worship they got drunk and lay down to sleep.

As they were sleeping the Raja's youngest son stole some of the grain to give to a girl who loved him. Bara Deo saw him and said to the boy, 'The Gond are brave and strong, but they have brought loss to Bhagavan and he is angry. That is why I have come to protect you from him'. Hearing this the Gond were pleased and began to worship Bara Deo.

Then said Bara Deo to the other Gond, 'This boy has taken the grain although it was *paraiya dhān* (another's grain) and so his name will be Pardhan'.

7

GOND

Bamhni, Bindra-Nawagarh Zamindari

Formerly the whole country belonged to the Gond and they were strong because of the help they had from Bara Pen, whom they pleased with many offerings of pig and fowl. The English invaders came but found the Gond too strong for them. But the English have great wisdom ; they thought and thought how to win the kingdom and discovered that the obstacle was Bara Pen. They decided to sacrifice a cow and a human being to Bara Pen. They found a Panka boy and a cow and sacrificed them. Bara Pen was pleased and went over to their side. The English made the god a fine bungalow with seven doors. These were always kept shut and four-and-twenty watchmen, twelve for the day, twelve for the night, guarded them. And the land came under their control.

The Gond wondered how to get the land back. A Gond dressed as an Ahir. He bought a bottle of liquor for Bara Pen; he cut open his thigh, hid the bottle inside and sewed it up. He went to Bara Pen and said, 'I am an Ahir: I will clean the house and worship'. They let him go in and, as he approached, the doors opened of their own accord. The watchmen thus knew he was a Gond, and they killed him. In Bara Pen's hand were two swords: if the Gond had got them he could have saved the land. Now Bara Pen is only a name. We worship him, but he has no power, for he is in the hands of the English.

8

GOND

Koelari, Rewa State

Parteti and Dhurwa were two Gond Rajas living together. They were very great men and their palaces were made of gold. The first-born son of Parteti was Madur Singh. The boy used to go out grazing the cows and buffaloes in the jungle. One day Bara Deo was born in a saja tree and made a mud-house up in the branches and lived there.

One day when Madur Singh was grazing the cattle as usual, Chandi the lord of the buffaloes went near the saja tree and Bara Deo caught it by the tail. The buffalo tried to escape but Bara Deo would not let go. The boy too came and tried to free Chandi but nothing happened. When the boy went home Bara Deo came upon the Durwa Raja and spoke through him, 'I Bara Deo have taken birth in the world. I will bring destruction on the Gond, but if they feed me well I will help them'. The Dhurwa and Parteti Rajas promised goats and fowls and liquor and Bara Deo let the buffalo go. They cut down the saja tree and brought it with the mud-house to the palace, where they planted it in the courtyard and offered goats to it and Bara Deo was pleased. After a time the Parteti Raja wanted to arrange the marriage of his son. Dulha Deo said to Bara Deo, 'They are all honouring you, but nobody takes any notice of me and I have to go hungry'. Bara Deo said, 'Be born in the haldi and in the grindstone'. When the Suasin began to grind haldi for the marriage the stone stuck to her hand. The Parteti Raja sent for the Gunia; he looked in his measuring-sticks and found that it was Dulha Deo who was causing the trouble. They promised to give him a goat at every marriage and he set the girl free.

9

PARDHAN

Batama, Chhindwara District

In former days the Pardhan never paid taxes. One day an Englishman came to their country and told them that they must pay taxes just as the Gond did. Mana Pardhan said to the Englishman that since the Pardhan had no fields and lived by playing on the *bāna* and singing, they would not pay. The Englishman abused Mana and his Bara Pen. When Mana heard this he said, 'Do not abuse me any more, come with me and I will give you your taxes'.

Nearby there was a great lake. Mana went to it and walked on the surface of the water. When he reached the centre of the lake he put his hand into the water and pulled out handfuls of precious stones. He threw them at the Englishman and shouted, 'Here are your taxes. Tie them to your hairs and go away'. But the Englishman, when he saw what Mana was doing, was afraid and fell at his feet and became his disciple. He began to worship Bara Pen and it was by the god's blessing that the Englishman got India under his control.

DULHA DEO

10

PARDHAN

Sukua, Chhindwara District

Norta Raja and his Rani Birar lived and ruled in Garh Gubaoli. So passed twelve years and thirteen ages, but Bhagavan gave them no child.

One day the Rani, when the time came for cleansing her head at the end of her monthly period, took her clothes to the Khongha Ghat in the Kabaoli river. As she was bathing seven hairs fell out of her head. She gathered up the hairs and thinking that it would be dangerous to drop them in the river, threw them away on a little hill. The hairs turned into the snakes called the Seven Sisters. Then as she was rubbing her body some of her pubic hairs came out and she threw these away also and they turned into spear-grass. When she had finished her bath she went home and after a few days found herself pregnant. Ten months went by and a son was born. Though he appeared to be an ordinary child, he was really Dulha Deo.

When the child grew up and did not get the food he wanted he said to himself, 'Whom can I possess in order to force them to give me what I want?' The first person he possessed was his own mother; he gave her pain in her womb and waist. The Raja did his best to cure the pain by giving medicine, but it had no effect. Then he heard that in Karjalpur there lived a Guru called Ladhaita. He sent for him and when the Guru saw the woman and had examined his measuring-sticks, he discovered that the cause of the trouble was Dulha Deo. The Guru told the parents that the boy whom they supposed to be an ordinary human child was Dulha Deo himself. He said they must give him a brown goat and a black fowl. The Raja accordingly made these offerings and the mother's pain ceased.

Near the palace there lived a Gond. Dulha Deo went to his house and began to trouble him. The Gond also sent for the Guru who said to him, 'Arrange the marriage of your son, but before the ceremony send for me and I will tell you what offerings you must make'. The Gond got everything ready for the marriage but forgot to call the Guru. When the bride and bridegroom were going round the pole together Dulha Deo, angry at being neglected, attacked them and they both fell senseless. At that moment the Gond remembered the Guru and sent for him. When the Guru came he discovered that the trouble was again caused by Dulha Deo. He said to the god, 'Whatever you wish I will give you'. Dulha Deo said, 'I want the left testicle of the bridegroom and the clitoris of the bride'. The Guru said, 'I will give you whatever you want'. Hearing his promise, Dulha Deo allowed the bride and bridegroom to recover. They went round the pole and finished the marriage and then the Guru took them into the house. By the hearth he made a little platform of the earth from the marriage-booth. He made the bride and bridegroom strip themselves naked and sit on the platform before the hearth. Then he found that the boy was suffering from hernia on the left side and that the girl's clitoris was a cubit-and-a-half long. He cut off both the things and offered them to Dulha Deo. But the Guru said, 'Dulha Deo, we will always worship you, but do not ask for such sacrifices as these another time or you will not get them'. From that day in fear of what Dulha Deo may ask, people are careful to remember him before a marriage.

BHIMSEN

11

GOND

Koelari, Rewa State

Koliha Dewan the jackal took a fox as its horse and a long tikur leaf as its sword and went out to hunt. All day it rode through the forest and got nothing and in the evening came home disappointed. But outside its village it saw a dead buffalo lying by the road and it dismounted from its horse and began to eat it. Eating eating it got right into the belly of the buffalo and the flesh closed about it and it could not get out. Gradually the skin dried round it. There came a great wind and from the buffalo's nostrils Bhimsen[1] was born.

From inside the belly the jackal cried, 'Who are you?' 'I am Bhimsen; who are you?' 'I am Bhimsen', said the jackal. When Bhimsen heard this, he was very angry and said, 'Very well, let us have a test. Whoever can make the rain fall will be Bhimsen'. The jackal did its best but it could only make a little rain come down *jhirmit-jhirmit*, but Bhimsen picked up twelve hills and made the rain fall in torrents. The body of the buffalo swelled and the jackal escaped. Since then Bhimsen has been the god of rain.

12

PARDHAN

Batama, Chhindwara District

In Deodongri lived a royal vulture. One day it went to the jungle to get something to eat. There was a crow there and it caught hold of the vulture and copulated with it. The vulture became pregnant and

[1] Bhimsen, the Pandava hero, has everywhere caught the imagination of the Indian aboriginal. He is now generally regarded as the god of rain.

gathered a great quantity of thorns and grass and bits of wood and made a nest in a cotton tree. There it laid two eggs. The first was three cubits long and the second two-and-a-half cubits long.

When the vulture saw these enormous eggs it was frightened and flew away to a tamarind tree and sat there. The tamarind tree said to it, 'Look at all the children I have to carry. How many children have you that you should come and add your weight to my burden ?' The vulture told the tree about its two great eggs but the tree laughed and said, 'That is nothing compared to what I have to look after. From those two eggs gods will be born'. When the vulture heard that, it flew back to the cotton tree and sat on its eggs. After some time the two eggs broke and from them two boys were born. The boys said to their mother, 'Here we are two brothers, give us names'. To the boy that came from the egg three cubits long the vulture said, 'Your name will be Bhimsen' and to the younger boy it said, 'Your name will be Lingo Pen'.

When the boys grew up they said to their mother, 'Where are we to live ?' The vulture said to Bhimsen, 'Son, go to Khairagarh and rule over it' and to Lingo Pen, it said, 'Go to Ratanpur and from there to Tundaigarh and catch Juna Bhoi and his wife. When you have done that they will offer you sacrifice and they will always worship you'. Lingo Pen did as his mother has told him and ever since the Gond have worshipped him and his brother Bhimsen.

Sleep and Dreams

13

GOND

Bilhar, Bilaspur District

When men come in weary from their toil in the fields, they rest in all their eighty chambers and seventy-two veins. They sleep and the soul goes out to search for the wealth they have not found in the day. That is why sleep is given to men, for without it they would have no courage. In sleep a man thinks he is wise and rich ; he goes all over the world. Without sleep he could not bear the work he has to do every day.

14

GOND

Baihar, Balaghat District

A Chamar's son and a Raja's son were friends. The Chamar were very generous, but the Raja and his son were mean. In time the Raja died, and the Death Chaprasis came to arrest him. They carried him off beating and kicking him.

The Raja's daughter-in-law had a mirror which was dream. She saw in this mirror-dream what was happening, and said to her husband, the friend of the Chamar's son, 'Your father was very mean and now I have seen his punishment in a dream.'

But when the Chamar died, the Death Chaprasis carried him to Bhagavan in their arms.

Now as the Chaprasis were taking the Raja through the air, and he was struggling and screaming and they were beating and abusing him, they passed over a river where a rich Dhimar was catching fish. He looked up and saw them. 'Why are you beating him?' he called. They said, 'He was very mean.' This Dhimar also was a very mean man, and so was his wife. He ran home and called his wife. 'Come and see the tamasha down by the river.' She too called to them, 'Why are you beating him?' They answered, 'Because he was so mean.'

When she heard that, the wife was frightened and ran home as fast as she could. There she gave a great feast and opened her store to give presents to children and widows and any sadhu that came to beg.

Since the Raja's daughter-in-law looked in her mirror, there have been dreams in the world.

15

MURIA

Berma, Bastar State

(From *The Muria and their Ghotul*, 476)

Long ago men could read the future in their dreams. An owl heard of it and said, 'If men can see the future in dreams, they will never die'. The owl waited till the gods were holding a Darbar and then fell with a bang into the midst of them. The gods said, 'What is the matter?' The owl replied, 'I have had a dream, and in that dream I was marrying a Raja's daughter. We had done eleven rounds of the Lagir; had it been twelve she would have been mine; but I awoke and fell to the ground.

Now I must marry this girl. What am I to do?' The gods were concerned and said to one another, 'How can a red-eyed bird marry a Raja's daughter?' The owl replied, 'But all the world gets what it sees in dreams; how can it be that only my dreams are false?' At that the gods cursed men saying, 'From now on, let all dreams be false'.

The Jawara

16

PARDHAN

Patangarh, Mandla District

In Kajliban the goddess Hinglajin had her shrine and the monkeys used to serve her. Away in Binjhiban there was a Rawat and his wife. The woman worked all day and at night wept because she had no children. When she heard the sound of the weeping, Hinglajin sent one of her monkeys to find out what was the matter. The monkey told the woman to go and serve his mistress for twelve years at her shrine. They did so and when the period was completed, Hinglajin promised the woman a child. But she said, 'Make a garden for me'. The Rawat and his wife sowed seed in baskets and made a beautiful garden of flowers and fruit and grain.

The woman conceived and at the end of eight months the gods assembled to see the child, for in her belly was Dhanu Panda; in eight months all his eight parts were perfect and complete. The gods, knowing that their great servant was coming to the world, were pleased. The Rawat gave them a feast and they went away. In the ninth month Dhanu Panda was born at midnight and as he fell from the womb a great trident came down from the sky.

Hinglajin said, 'Whenever you need help prepare a little garden of grain, sowing it in baskets, and I will come to your aid'. As the child grew up the old couple died but Dhanu Panda sowed the gardens of Jawara [1] and the custom spread through the world. On the eighth day he kept Atwai to celebrate the coming of the gods to see him when he was eight months in the womb and on the ninth day he threw the garden into the river.

[1] The Jawara is a pleasant ceremony, conducted at irregular intervals to promote crop-fertility, wherein little gardens are made in specially-constructed shrines. Worship, singing and dancing continues for eight days and on the ninth the baskets of sprouting grain are carried in procession to the nearest stream, and there immersed.

CHAPTER TWENTY-ONE

WITCHCRAFT AND MAGIC

SEVERAL types of story are current in Middle India about the origin of witchcraft and disease. One traces it to a sinister pilgrimage round the country: wherever the party camps a new form of evil is born. One Muria legend describes how the first witch was a girl who secretly drank the blood of sacrificial animals in disobedience to a command; another describes a trick, whereby Tallur Muttai first deceived Lingo into killing his wife and then persuaded a number of pregnant women to eat her flesh: those that did so became witches.

The Baiga myth is also a tale of trickery and deceit. It is derived from the classic Hindu legend of Dhanwantari, the physician of the gods, who attempted to cure Raja Parikshit who had been deceived and bitten by Takshaka, the king of the snakes. But it was Dhanwantari himself who died, and he asked his sons to cook and eat his body and thus take his magic into themselves. But Takshaka stopped them and they threw the cooking-pots into the Ganges. There the notorious Lona Chamarin found them and ate their contents, and so gained Dhanwantari's magical powers.[1]

The Baiga myth, which is given in *The Baiga* [2], is as follows.

Nanga Baiga was living Nanga Pahar. Bhagavan had given him this boon: 'From your left side will flow black blood, from your right side will flow red. Whoever drinks the black blood will be a witch; whoever drinks the red blood will be a gunia.'

One day Nanga Baiga said to the four brothers, 'Take me beyond the seven seas and the sixteen streams.' So they took him there and Nanga Baiga sat beside the Seven Seas. At night blood began to flow from both his sides. A snake came to drink the black blood. Its name was Ajghar. A mongoose came and drank the red blood.

Nanga Baiga heard that a man was dying in a village nearby, and he sent one of the brothers with a little of the red blood. He touched the dying man with it and he recovered.

Many little animals came and drank of the black blood and they turned into poisonous snakes and scorpions.

Then Bhagavan, being jealous of Nanga Baiga, sent a snake to bite him. Nanga Baiga wanted to scratch his back, and thinking the snake was a stick, picked it up, and it bit him and he died.

As he was dying, Nanga Baiga told his sons and disciples not to bury him, but to divide his body into twelve portions, put them into twelve

[1] Crooke, ii, 285.

[2] *The Baiga*, 340 ff.

pots and cook them for twelve years. At the end of that time, they should eat him, and all his magic would pass to them.

But this was just what Bhagavan was anxious to avoid. So when the twelve years were over, he came disguised as a Brahmin sadhu, smeared with ashes, a gourd in his hand, and told the sons what a great sin it would be to eat their father's flesh. They thought it over and agreed, and at last decided to throw the twelve pots into the river. But as they were doing so, one of the brothers got a whiff of the steam or, according to other versions, one scrap of the flesh, and he became the first gunia.

There is, unfortunately, no real agreement as to who this first guniar was. Some think it was the youngest of the four guru—Danantar; others say that it was the youngest of Nanga Baiga's own sons. But whoever it was, he only got a sadly attenuated portion of Nanga Baiga's magic, a mere whiff of the steam of it in his nostrils.[1]

But the twelve pots floated away down the river. There on the bank Kani Gondin, Sukhi Chamarin and Langri Dhobnin were bathing naked. Some say they were playing in the water with the seven Samduria sisters. They saw the pots floating down and waded out to get them. When they brought them to the bank, they found them full of meat. They tasted it, and it was sweet and good. So they ate it all. The Chamarin ate the head and became the first *tonhi*. The Gondin ate the chest and became the first *sodhe*.

Then they were filled with Nanga Baiga's magic, but it had turned evil. They looked at a fig tree growing on the bank of the river, and with the poison of their gaze it withered away.

A Santal legend of what is obviously the origin of witchcraft appears to be derived from the same source. The chief Guru of the Santal is Kamru : he was the first of the Ojha magicians : he is still invoked in charms. He was married, but his wife was a witch. The two sons of his elder brother lived with him.

When he was old, he was bitten by a snake. He sent his nephews for medicine but his wife followed them and persuaded them to throw it away. Kamru died, but he first told his nephews to pour water over the pyre after his body had been consumed, whereupon they would find two small pieces of flesh. If they ate these, they would acquire his *vidya* (science).

[1] 'In this age of iron incantations have lost much of their power. The reason of this is that Mahadeo was so disgusted with the wickedness of the world that he shut up all the spells which used to be powerful in his box so that they might not minister to the spirit of greed and revenge which prevailed throughout the world. But as he was shutting them up Parvati managed to conceal a few under her feet, and it is these alone which the sorcerers of the present day are able to use ; and as Mahadeo shut up the best of them before Parvati intervened, this accounts for the ill-success of all the magical spells which are used in these evil times.' —Recorded by R. G. Chaube, *N. I. Notes and Queries*, iv, iii.

The two young men did as they were told and found the bits of flesh, but they were afraid to eat them and threw them into a stream. They failed to inherit Kamru's science, but Kamru's wife was watching and she found the meat and ate it. She was already a witch and now had the Guru's power and wisdom. She lived thereafter in Kamru land, where there are only women and where they can turn a man into a dog or any other animal.[1]

Another Santal version of the origin of witchcraft differs considerably, however, from this. Marang Baru decided that he would teach men witchcraft. He fixed a day for it and told them to come dressed in their cleanest clothes.

So the men all went home and told their wives to wash their clothes well against the fixed day, as they were going to Thakur to learn witchcraft. The women, of course, began to discuss this new plan among themselves and the more they talked of it the less they liked it; it seemed to them that if men were to get this new strange power it would make them more inclined to despise and bully women than ever; so they made a plot to get the better of their husbands. They arranged that each woman should brew some rice-beer and offer it to her husband as she was starting to meet Marang Baru and beg him to drink some lest his return should be delayed. They foresaw that the men would not be able to resist the drink; and that having started they would go on till they were dead drunk: it would then be easy for the women to dress themselves like men and go off to Marang Baru and learn witchcraft in place of their husbands. So said, so done—the women duly made their husbands drunk and then put on *pagris* and *dhoties* and stuck goats' beards on their faces and went off to Marang Baru to learn witchcraft. Marang Baru did not detect the imposition and according to his promise taught them all the incantations of witchcraft.

When the men came to their senses they hurried off to Marang Baru and begged him to teach them but he explained that their wives had tricked them and that since the women had reaped the crop the men could only have the gleanings. So he taught them the art of the Ojha and, in order that they might have the advantage of their wives in one respect, he also taught them the craft of the Jan and with that they had to be content.[2]

The Munda say that the first witch was actually one of the two wives of Singbonga, their chief deity. This is in line with the common conception that magic and witchcraft are a perversion of the highest known to man. Singbonga's son fell very ill and when all his heavenly remedies failed, he sent his bird-messengers to earth

[1] Bodding, 123 ff.
[2] Bompas, 422. For another version of this story, see Mukherjea, 176 f.

to call the two great medicine-men, Narangi-Jhuppi and Osagi Deonra.

These two were such powerful sorcerers that they would yoke tigers to their ploughs with snakes for yoke-straps. It did not take them long to find out that Singbonga's younger wife was a witch who had caused the sickness that afflicted the boy. When the sorcerers declared the result of their divination, Singbonga sent down his bird-messengers to call Barnda to him. Barnda soon arrived, and on being told what had happened, sought to dissuade the younger wife of Singbonga from dealing in witchcraft any more. But she was deaf to all persuasion and refused to forego the secret knowledge and the devilish powers which she valued more than anything else.

The two medicine-men then did their best to get rid of the witch. They shut her up in a cave, but it was no use. They tried to marry her to some young Munda but everyone was afraid of her feet with the heels in front. They tried to burn her to death. Then they carried her round the country in a box, trying to get rid of her by saying that they had a beautiful cat to give away, but anyone who opened the box found that the cat was one with flames coming from its mouth. At last the carrying-pole of the box broke, and the woman was left in that place and it is not known where she is now.[1]

I

Witchcraft and Magic

I

DEWAR

Kodua, Raipur District

Jhapa Guru and his wife lived on the Daunagir Mountain in Sumringarh. They had no children. One day Kawal Guru came to their house from Khairagarh. They greeted him with great honour and, standing before him with folded hands, said, 'What is written in our fate that we have no children?' Kawal Guru thought in his mind and said, 'Fast for seven Mondays and take these ashes made by my *mantra* and eat them. On the seventh Monday your wife will conceive.' So it

[1] Roy, *J.B.O.R.S.*, ii, 203.

happened and in the tenth month the woman bore two children, one a boy and one a girl.

On the Chhatti day they invited Kawal Guru to come and give the children their names. To the boy he gave the name of Waichani Kawar and to the girl the name of Beti Rautain. He blessed them saying, 'This boy will be a great Gunia and will have twelve cartloads of Vidya. The girl will be a witch and will have thirteen cartloads of Pap-Vidya.' He made a little pipe from a reed and blew his own Vidya into their ears.

The boy and girl grew up and Waichani Kawar became the first Gunia and Beti Rautain the first witch. This was the first time that Vidya and Pap-Vidya[1] came to the world.

2

DHANWAR

Baira, Matin Zamindari

Dhangar Guru and Jangha Dewar were brothers. They were born in Mutni Andhiyar Kothi, and with them were born twelve cartloads of Vidya and thirteen cartloads of Pap-Vidya. The brothers put the bullock-carts on the road and set out for Garh Lahari. As they reached the boundary of that place they put up their yellow, black and red tent. They spread their bedding inside, covered themselves with their blankets and lay down to sleep. They said to their disciples, 'If anyone comes here, do not laugh or talk with them. For this place is full of witches who will turn you into birds unless you are very careful'.[2]

When the witches of Garh Lahari saw the tent they said, 'Let us go and see who are these people camping by our lake.' So twelve witches went to see. They found the disciples sitting round the tent and were very excited about them. They said to one another, 'These are very handsome men. They are clean and straight as constables. Let us laugh and talk with them and persuade them to come home with us.' The women did their best, but the disciples would not speak a word and sat aloof and silent. At last the witches got very angry; they threw black and yellow rice over the disciples and by their science turned them

[1] Vidya: the science of protection, white magic; Pap-Vidya: the science of destruction, black magic.

[2] This account of the Guru with their disciples recalls Puranic pictures of rishis with their trains of pious *brahmachari* students.

into birds and made them fly half-way up the sky. They seized the thirteen carts full of Pap-Vidya and dragged them back to their own houses. By their science they set fire to the tent. The Guru awoke and saw the tent on fire and no disciples and the thirteen carts missing.

They were very disturbed in mind and looked to and fro and up and down. By their science they put out the fire. Then they looked up and saw the twelve disciples flying round and round in the sky. Dhangar Guru picked up a little dust with the toes of his left foot, took it in his hand and blew it towards the twelve disciples, whereupon they came down to earth and turned into men again.

The Guru called the witches of that place and talked sweetly to them. 'You have done well,' he said. 'But bring back twelve of our carts, for I have to go to many villages, giving a little here and a little there.' The witches agreed and they brought twelve of the carts back but kept the thirteenth. The Guru struck his tent and moved on to Chipligarh.

As they went along the party passed a village on the road. A man had died there and the villagers were burning his corpse outside the village by the road side. The two Guru brothers saw this and said, 'If we can save this man by our science, we must do so.' They walked round the pyre seven times and seven times clapped their hands in the name of their science. Then a man was born from the pyre ; he was a leper, the first leper, with hands and feet decayed. He looked like a man whose whole body has been burnt with fire.

The party moved on and in every village they gave a little of the knowledge of evil to the women and of the knowledge of good to the men, and so made their way to Chipligarh. Here the Guru fell ill. As he was about to die, he said to his disciples, 'I am going to die. When I am dead do not burn or bury my body, but cut my flesh up and cook it and everyone of you should eat a little.' When the Guru died, the disciples cut up his flesh and put it in a pot to boil.

At that time a Sadhu came by and asked them what they were doing. They said, 'Today our Guru has died and we are cooking his flesh.' But the sadhu said, 'This is a great sin. Do not eat your Guru's flesh, but throw it into the river.' The disciples did as the sadhu said and carried the flesh in the pots to the river and threw them in. The pots floated far down the river, to where the Agaria went to wash their clothes and bathe. Here seven Agaria sisters were bathing. They got hold of the pots and took them to the bank. 'Here is good cooked meat,' they said, and the eldest picked out a little piece of flesh and ate it.

It tasted very good and she told the others and they all ate it. That night Pap-Vidya came to them in a dream. They learnt everything in their dreams and became witches. They themselves made disciples. Their names were—Pankin with a giggling flirting thing, Patharin with oil-smooth thing, Sonarin with thing full of flying sparks, Kalarin with hair-covered thing, Chamarin with thing like a sickle, Ahirin with thing smoothed with ghee, Gondin with muddy thing. These were the witches.

3

GOND

Banjar, Mandla District

In Lankagarh lived Daugun Guru and Rana Tonhi. They thought, 'What is the use of living like this? We must have disciples.' From the dirt on the right side of her body Rana made three disciples—Sukri Chamarin, Naita Dhobnin, Lohakat Loharin. Daugun Guru made Nindhan Guru, Murha Kawar, Runha Guru and Ustaj Guru. They each taught their disciples part of their Vidya. Daugun Guru's disciples got rather less than the others. So one day Daugun Guru said, 'Bring a bottle of liquor, each of you, and I will teach you the whole of my science.'

Now Daugun Guru and his disciples were living on the banks of a lake, and one day Rana Tonhi passed by carrying a golden water-pot with a silver support. She drew water and placed the pot on her knee in order to put it on her head. Daugun Guru came out and threw black and yellow rice at her, and the pot stuck to her leg. He sent two of his disciples to take the pot from her. He desired to test them whether they had real power or no. But Rana put the pot on her head and turned the two disciples into a pair of gourds, which she filled with water and carried home. When she got back she hung them up in the roof.

Daugun Guru sent another disciple to search for them. But Rana Tonhi turned him into a cobra and hung him up with the others. Ustaj was left and now Daugun Guru sent him. Rana had a liquor-still. Ustaj went to sit there and smoke his pipe. 'Give me some fire,' he begged. The witch filled his clothes with fire, but it did not burn. Then by his science he broke her still. She began to weep and ran away.

After a time she returned and Ustaj said, 'Why are you crying?' 'Look, my still is ruined.' 'What will you give me if I mend it?' 'I will give you plenty of liquor to drink.' Ustaj mended her still and drank all her liquor. He rescued the other disciples and they returned to their Guru. He urinated a little and gave some to each of them to drink. Their science was then perfect and they married the Rana's disciples. But there was no wife for Murha Kawar and the Guru turned him into a eunuch.

4

GOND

Nodora, Chhindwara District

Guru Gorakhnath had twelve disciples whom he instructed in magic and science. When the time came for him to die he called his disciples and said, 'Do not bury me or burn my body, but take it to the river and cut it up into small pieces and throw them into the water. There I shall change into fish of many different kinds.' So saying the Guru died and his disciples carried his corpse to the river and cut it up.

When they threw the pieces of his body into the water they turned into different kinds of fish. The left arm became the aind eel. The right arm became the long bami fish. His two thighs became the thangana fish. His calves became the padina. The fingers of his hands became the little kotri fish. His organ became the tasty saur. The bones of his waist became the bony katiya fish. His chest became the bod fish. His shoulder became the kadharri fish. His toes became the jimta fish. In this way Guru Gorakhnath's whole body turned into fish which began to swim about in the water.

When the disciples saw what had happened, they felt a great desire to eat fish. They got a net and caught some. They cooked and ate them and thus they gained the magic and science of their Guru.

5

RAJNENGI PARDHAN

Patangarh, Mandla District

There were twelve Gond brothers. They went to learn *gun* (magic spells) from Mahadeo. After they had been learning for six months, Guru Mahadeo said, 'Now you've been learning for six months ; go and fetch a winnowing-fan.' The twelve Gond brothers went to get one. But Naita Dhobnin heard of it and thought in her mind, 'If these twelve brothers become adepts at this art, no one in the world will die.' So she took the form of a fly and went to Mahadeo's house and sat on the wall at the back of the house. But Mahadeo knew that she was there and told his disciples, 'Naita Dhobnin's son is sleeping in the court ; go and wake him up and bring him here.' They went and brought the child to Mahadeo.

Mahadeo said, 'Give this child some food to eat'—as people give food to a goat or fowl before sacrifice. When the child had eaten, Mahadeo sacrificed him, and placed the winnowing-fan over his head and body.

The result of this was that Mahadeo forgot to give the winnowing-fan to his disciples. In the meantime Naita Dhobnin went home. When she could not find her child she came agitated and weeping to Mahadeo and fell at his feet. 'Maharaj, where has my child gone?' Mahadeo said, 'I am a sadhu ; what do I know about people's children?' But the woman took no notice of his protestations and at last he said, 'Very well, lift up that winnowing-fan and see what is under it.' She lifted it up and when she saw her child with his head cut off she broke into wild weeping and beat her head against Mahadeo's feet crying, 'Make my child alive again.' Mahadeo said, 'I am a sadhu; how can I make him alive?' But since she gave so much trouble, he took some ash in his hand and with his charms made the child alive, and Naita Dhobnin took him home.

After some time Mahadeo fell ill and called his twelve Gond disciples and said, 'Now I am sick. If I die, take my body to the banks of the lake, cut up my flesh and cook and eat me. Do not throw my body away.'

A few days afterwards Mahadeo died. The disciples took his body to the lake, cut it up, put the pieces into twelve pots and set them on the fire. But Naita Dhobnin knew what was going on, and thought in her mind, 'If they eat Mahadeo's body they will be true adepts and no one in the world will die', so she took the form of a Brahmin woman old as a ghost and came to the place saying, 'Who are you? From what strange land have you come and what are you doing here?' They told her that their Guru had died and that they were cooking his flesh and were going to eat it.

Naita Dhobnin in the form of the old Brahmin woman said, 'You say you are disciples of a Guru and have learnt his wisdom and yet you are eating his flesh. What a great sin is this!' The disciples said—for they were Gond—'Then what shall we do?' Naita Dhobnin said, 'Throw the flesh into the lake.' At this she went away.

The twelve brothers opened the lids of the pots, and the steam of them went into their nostrils. Then they threw the flesh into the lake. Naita Dhobnin took the form of a crocodile and swallowed the flesh. Thus she became the great witch and that is why witches devour men. The twelve Gond disciples only swallowed the steam of the body and so they are good magicians. They do not devour men and they are less powerful than the witches.

II

Love-Charms

'I don't want a love-charm,' once said a handsome Gond youth. 'Not for me! They make you stay all day without relieving yourself. Then you have to get up at dawn and spend four hours under water in the cold. You have to lie all night on one side. Not for me! Besides, I can get all the girls I want without making such a fuss.' And in fact love-magic is not very commonly employed in the primitive communities of India. Gorer says that the Lepcha have indeed a tradition of love-magic 'in which the hairs of two people meant to love another are plaited and concentrated upon'. But it is said that nobody living has performed this magic and it appears to be only a tradition.[1] Among the wilder Vedda, love-charms 'do not seem to exist', though the Seligmans heard that the more sophisticated Vedda women charmed the waist-strings they gave to their husbands in order to ensure their fidelity.[2] Of the Ao Naga, Mills says that he 'knows nothing of love-potions and never uses them; the necessity for such a commodity has probably never arisen'.[3]

Other tribes, however, are less fortunate and Hindu erotics has from the earliest times recognized the religious and psychological value of these charms. The fourth Brahmana of the *Brihad-Aranyaka Upanishad*, which sets forth an ideal of sexual activity

[1] Gorer, 214. [2] Seligman, 204. [3] Mills, *The Ao Nagas*, 291.

which for majesty and beauty has never been surpassed in the literature of any people, gives various charms for fertilizing and invigorating the act of love. Love-charming will be found throughout the older literature. Guhachandra is given a charm to win the love of his celestial wife, and with the help of a further stratagem he is successful.[1] The King of Vatsa, also in the *Katha Sarit Sagara*, is given charms to win the heart of the lady Vasavadatta.[2]

In aboriginal India today there are charms for winning a lover, charms for making a woman beautiful, charms for improving potency or postponing orgasm. Milne has given a very full account of such charms as used by the Palaungs of the Shan States.[3] The Kaw use the wax of two different kinds of bees which live in the same hollow of a tree. When this has been applied to a girl, she becomes restless until she can go to live with her lover. But the Kaw say that such marriages when consummated are neither happy nor prosperous and if children result from the union they do not live.[4] Some Gond of the Central Provinces have the same idea.

In Assam, love-charms are used by the Lhota Naga, most commonly in the villages near the plains. Sometimes they use the feather of a certain bird, sometimes a root which is given with cooked fish. 'If the suit is hopeless the recipient of the root removes all doubt by being sick on the spot.'[5] Luck-stones have the power of attracting love as well as other treasure. An old bedridden Angami Naga is said to have kept such a stone in his pipe. A woman who touched it could not leave his side till he dismissed her.[6] A number of different charms have been recorded for the Rengma Naga. 'A small glittering object is said to be found in a python's head from which a love-charm is produced by rather a long process. If kept in a jar in the house it will turn into nettles and then into tobacco, and so on, through a series of plants, till one with a leaf like garlic is produced. A man has only to touch a woman with a piece of the last plant and she is his for ever.' The leaf can be rendered ineffective if it is pricked with a pig's bristle. Like all love-charms this is dangerous, for if the loved girl eats the leaf, her stomach will become crammed with leaves and she will die. Another dangerous charm is the feather of a bird which is believed to fight with its mate all day—but they sleep with their heads together at night. 'This

[1] Penzer, ii, 43f.
[2] ibid., i, 138.
[3] L. Milne, *The Home of an Eastern Clan* (Oxford, 1924), 109-15.
[4] *Census of India*, 1931, 169.
[5] Mills, *The Lhota Nagas*, 168.
[6] Mills, *The Ao Nagas*, 289 (note by J. H. Hutton).

charm therefore causes the most violent passion, relieved by equally violent quarrels.' A still more dangerous charm, which is liable to cause the user's clan to die out, can be made if a man finds two snakes of a certain type in the act of copulation and cuts off their heads.[1]

Thurston says that the Paniyan of southern India are believed to have the power of turning into animals in order to fulfil their desires. If a man wants a woman he goes to her house at night with a hollow bamboo and goes round it three times. The woman comes out and the man turns into a bull or dog and does his will. But the woman dies soon afterwards.[2]

I have found love-charms in use among the Baiga, Gond, Pardhan, Muria, Juang, Saora and indeed among every tribe I have had the opportunity of studying intensively. Many of the charms are based on the principles of sympathetic magic and they are usually believed to be successful. One of the most remarkable was when a young and handsome Baiga was enchanted by a hideous and worn-out old leper woman.[3] Juang charms appear to be specially effective in what would usually be regarded as hopeless cases, where there is great disparity of age or fortune. The Saora use 'woman-medicine' or 'man-medicine', and often first test its efficacy on a dog. Like the Baiga, the Saora believe that it is essential to remove the charm once it has done its work.

In Middle India, the love-charm is highly respectable. It is not used in vulgar flirtations : it usually leads to marriage. Indeed the use of the charm is one of the things that finally convinces a girl that her admirer's intentions are serious.

The ritual of the love-magic of this area is described in *The Baiga*, and some charms are given in *Folk-Songs of Chhattisgarh*. I will add a few recipes for creating love which have not been hitherto recorded. A Gond of Lapha Zamindari recommended this : 'When a learned man dies, go to his grave on a Sunday and walk round it five times. Pick up a little earth from the ground above his chest, take it home and put it in front of a lighted lamp. At once a whole crowd of ghosts will come to steal the earth, but don't be afraid of them. Make them touch your feet and let them sit on the earth. If you mix this with oil and sprinkle it on a girl you love, she'll be yours within a week.'

Other Gond love-charms are connected with roots. One root is so powerful that when it has been properly charmed it will put an

[1] Mills, *The Rengma Nagas*, 224. See also 237f.
[2] Thurston, vi, 63.
[3] *The Baiga*, 344-49.

entire household to sleep, and a lover can approach his mistress even when she is sleeping by her mother's side. It is also useful to get a little dust from a footprint left by the girl as she is crossing the threshold of her house. An Agaria witch was said to use the menstrual cloth of a virgin and a leech : by rubbing a girl with the powdered body of the leech mixed with oil and applied with the stained cloth, she could, it was said, make the plainest features beautiful and, with an extra charm muttered over the cloth, inspire the girl with love for anyone she chose.

Semen and oil is also used by the Agaria to make a girl beautiful and to ensure her love for her admirer. A girl may put a little of her husband's semen on her pubic cloth, believing that this will make her desirable to him.

6

BAIGA

Gotai, Mandla District

Raja Mara Kshattri one day saw Bijlokin Kaniya and fell in love with her. He went to her and as he stooped to kiss her thing, his mouth stuck to it. He tried to get away, but he could not.

His soul (*jiv*) left his body and went to Guru Jalindar and served him for twelve years. All this time his body lay lost in love with Bijlokin Kaniya. When the Guru was pleased with him he said, 'Tell me what you desire.' Mara Kshattri said, 'I desire to possess Bijlokin Kaniya properly.'

Guru Jalindar made a jackal and told it to sit in Bijlokin Kaniya's garden. It went to the garden, but when the girl saw it she took no notice.

Then Guru Jalindar made a parrot from the dirt of his body and put black and yellow rice and ash of the saja and a black chick round its neck. This was a strong love-charm. When the girl saw it she at once loosed Mara Kshattri's mouth from her thing. The parrot flew to Mara Kshattri and perched on his hand and they went home together. But the girl followed them, for she was possessed by the charm.

After this Mara Kshattri and the girl lived together very happily and since that day love-charms have been known to men.

But owing to Mara Kshattri's mouth sticking there for twelve years, the girl's thing had become very large and suffered from itch. When Mahadeo saw it, he said, 'Oho' and he took a little mud, rolled it into a ball and threw it down. It stuck on the top of the thing and has stayed there ever since as guard and watchman. And the thing itself grew small.

Presently Bijlokin Kaniya conceived ; when the time came for her to be delivered Mara Kshattri was not there. His elder wife took the child and threw it into a great pile of cowdung and put a stone in its place. The child crawled out and became a tortoise. When the mother thought she had given birth to a stone, she took an axe and cut her belly open. She turned into a kite. She said, 'I will eat nothing till I eat Mara Kshattri.' Mahadeo turned her into a snake ; she bit Mara Kshattri and killed him. Then she became a kite again and devoured his body.

7

PARDHAN

Batama, Chhindwara District

In Latagarh lived the wife of Daugun Guru, Mata Gandian. Daugun Guru himself lived in Saidagarh. For twelve years he stayed there, practising his magic and teaching his disciples. He forgot his wife and never went to see her. One day, during her period, she felt filled with love for the memory of Daugun Guru and thought, 'Now twelve years have passed and never once has he come to see me.'

She went to Banbindra Koeli-Kachhar where Juphru Ahir was grazing the Surahi cow and asked him for butter. She brought it home and burned a little of her blood-stained cloth and an areca-nut. She put her magic into it, mixed the ash with the butter and called on Nakti Pat and Dauragirke Karula Pat. She put the mixture in a mohlain leaf and went to see her Guru in Saidagarh.

The Guru was sitting with his disciples. When he saw his wife, he said, 'What do you want ? Why have you come here ?' She said, 'I have come because I remembered you.' But Daugun Guru spoke no word of love to her. At night she said, 'I have seen you after twelve years. Even though you speak no word of love to me, at least I will massage you.' She brought some oil and mixed her love-charm into it and massaged him.

Next morning she went home. After three days the charm began to work. Daugun Guru remembered his wife and a mighty love came to him. He threw away his fan, his gourd, his measuring-sticks and went to Mata Gandian and began to live happily with her.

One day he said, 'What have you done to me? For I cannot live without you for a moment.' She denied that she had done anything, but when he pressed her she at last told him of the love-charm. The Guru learnt what to do and told his disciples and they taught the other magicians.

8

RAJNENGI PARDHAN

Kanchanpur, Mandla District

In Tingatola there lived a Gond called Malwa. He had one daughter and kept a Lamsena to serve for her. After their marriage, the girl found that she did not love her Lamsena and whenever he approached her, she used to weep. The boy said to himself, 'Here I have worked for this girl for twelve years and she does not let me approach her,' and he too began to weep.

As he was sitting in tears, an old man came by and said to him, 'What you are crying for, boy?' The boy told him. The old man said, 'Listen to me and do exactly what I tell you. In Chandragarh there is a Baiga. Go to him and tell him your trouble.' The boy went to Chandragarh and found the Baiga sitting under a rock in the middle of the jungle. That Baiga's name was Jurha. The boy revealed his trouble and the Baiga said, 'I will give you a love-charm.' The boy said, 'What is that?' The Baiga replied, 'Listen and I will tell you. First go and get me some fowls.' The boy brought a red cock, a black hen and a coconut. The Baiga said, 'Go a little distance away and don't look towards me.' When the boy had departed, the Baiga stripped himself naked and picked up a bit of earth from the ground and blew upon it with his charms, calling upon the gods, and saying, 'Make this girl mad. Go Mohani and with your left elbow nudge her. When she sees other men, let her tie her cloth tightly between her legs, but when she sees her husband, let her undo it. When she goes to another's house to grind or husk, let the grindstone break and the mortar be shattered. When she sees others, let her weep; when she sees her husband, let her laugh. O eight hundred kinds of magic, O nine hundred Chittawar, go and fill this girl with desire.' So saying the Baiga made his gods sit in the bit of earth and called the boy back. He said to him, 'Take this earth and when your wife sits for food, drop a few grains of it secretly on her plate. You will find that she will always laugh and be happy with you. When that happens, come back to me and I will tell you everything about love-charms.'

The boy went to his house and did as the Baiga had instructed him. The girl soon found herself in love with her husband and lived very happily with him. The boy went back to the Baiga who taught him everything about love-charms and since then men have begun to use them.

III

The Land of Women

Traditions about a land of women, a land too given up to magic, are widely distributed in Indian folk-lore. By the Santal this land is associated with their great Guru Kamru and bears his name. 'The country is very rich and fertile, and there are only women living there, or else the women predominate, and no one is able to go there and stay.' The missionary Bodding, who makes this report, says that men are not liked by the Kamru women for 'definite reasons that cannot be recorded'. He gives a story of a Santal who went to Kamru and was kept there by the women for five years, by day covered with a large bamboo basket and instructed in the magic arts at night. When he was initiated, he was turned into a kite and flew back to his own country. A Santal child was carried off to Kamru by a vulture. Here he grew up and ultimately married. But when he tried to get away, he found himself always coming back to the place he started from. At last a woman told him he must leave everything behind and not take anything of that country along with him: then he made his escape.

'The traditional Kamru country is a country of strange people with strange powers; the inhabitants can at will turn a man into a dog or any other animal.... It is a land full of magic and witch-craft, but the stories seem to imply that it is the women who are so dangerous and powerful.'[1]

Bodding suggests that since Santal who go to Assam as labourers in the Tea Gardens pass through the Kamrup District, they have probably associated the two names and this is why they locate the land of magic to the east. The Gond and Baiga of Mandla similarly place their land of women in Bengal.

The Angami Naga have a similar legend. 'There is in a certain place a village of women only, and if a man go there they drive him

[1] Bodding, 126.

away by shooting at him with war bows, and they raise not any males save one only, and when other male babes are born they boil water and put them therein to kill them. These women, moreover, do no hard work, but eat great store of starch and oil to make them strong to battle. Others say that when a man go there, the women that be there be so eager for him that in striving to possess him they tear him to pieces utterly.'[1]

In a similar Naga Story recorded by Hutton in *Folk-Lore*, it is said that the women in this village become pregnant through hornets sucking their breasts.[2]

The legend of a Country or Island of Women is very old. The earliest Indian reference to it appears to be in the story of the fifth adventure of the horse released at the Aswamedha rite in the *Mahabharata*. The horse enters the country inhabited only by women, whose Rani is named Paramita. The women become mothers as a result of chance contacts with visitors : male children are killed the moment they are born. Any man remaining in the country more than a month is put to death. When Arjuna arrived in the country he said to his warriors, 'This is a marvellous country whither the horse has led us. If we conquer these women, we shall gain no credit ; if we are conquered, our disgrace will be inconceivable.' But Arjuna was defeated by the women, though in the end he conquered them, for he married their Rani and took her away to Hastinapura.

In the *Matsya Purana* (Chap. xi) Siva and Parvati enjoy themselves in their Saravana, a pleasure-garden beautiful with every kind of tree. They ordain that any man approaching the garden will be transformed into a woman, a fate that befalls Raja Ila when he enters the enchanted area.

There have been many attempts to locate this country. Hutton says that the Sema Naga place it somewhere east of the Patkoi-Barail range.[3] Hiuen Tsiang speaks of a country Po-lo-hih-mo-pu-lo, the Country of the Eastern Women, where the men manage the wars and sow the land, but the women do everything else[4]—a country identified by Wilson with the Malabar Coast where the Nayar system of mother-right might well be supposed to have impressed a stranger.[5] Hiuen Tsiang also describes a Country of the Western Women, which is in Persia, the abode of demons who by intercourse with a

[1] Hutton, *The Angami Nagas*, 263f. For an account of Hirakhan Kshattri's adventures— he was turned into a goat by day—in Bara Bathi Bengala, see *Folk-Songs of the Maikal Hills*, 389f.

[2] *Folk-Lore*, June 1923.

[3] Hutton, *The Angami Nagas*, 263.

[4] S. Beal, *Buddhist Records of the Western World*, i, 198.

[5] H. H. Wilson, *The Vishnu Purana* (London, 1840), 481.

girl of southern India 'engendered a clan of women children'.[1] This story is repeated by Marco Polo and his editor Yule discusses at length the possible position of the islands.[2] Logan suggests that the Island of Women is Minicoy, an island attached to the Malabar District, politically included in the Laccadive group, but ethnologically in the Maldive Islands. The men, who are Mussalmans, are absent on sea voyages for much of the time and the women go unveiled and manage the island. After marriage the girls remain for a time with their fathers, and leave the paternal home in order of seniority, the houses erected for them becoming their own property.[3] 'It is easy to understand,' says Crooke, 'how mariners visiting the island could find none to receive them but women, and everything was arranged and managed by women. The men who remained in the island would probably keep out of the way until the strangers left, as they were pirates, and it would have fared ill with them if they were discovered.'[4]

[1] Beal, op. cit., ii, 240. Hiuen Tsiang continues, 'In the middle of a great iron city of this Ratnadripa (P'ao-chu) was the dwelling of the Rakshasi women (Lo-t'sa). On the towers of this city they erected two high flagstaffs with lucky or unlucky signals, which they exhibited according to circumstances, when merchants came to the island. Then they changed themselves into beautiful women, holding flowers and scents, and with the sound of music they went forth to meet them, and caressingly invited them to enter the iron city; then having shared with them all sorts of pleasure, they shut them up in an iron prison, and devoured them at their leisure.'

[2] H. Yule, *The Book of Ser Marco Polo* (London, 1871), ii, 337f.

[3] W. Logan, *Malabar* (Madras, 1887), i, 287f.

[4] W. Crooke, 'The Land and Island of Women', *Man in India*, ii, 1ff. A convenient summary of traditions, of the Land of Women, which are connected with the parallel legend of the Amazons, from other parts of the world will be found in *Woman*, i, 468ff. Stories about the Amazons go back to Homer. Herodotus describes their capture by the Greeks and settlements in Scythia. Strabo gives the tradition about their mutilation of the left breast so that they could throw the spear better. Diodorus says that in Libya a people lived under the rule of women, but there were men in the country though of an inferior position. It is not until we come to the Middle Ages, however, that we find traditions of a real Land of Women. The Arab geographers describe a great town in an island of the western ocean, entirely free from the rule of men, where the women are visited by slaves at night, and men children are killed. Adam of Bremen describes an exclusively women's community on the shores of the Baltic. They became pregnant by drinking magic brews or through intercourse with monsters which were frequently born among them. The ancient Chinese also had the tradition and a Chinese chronicle of the seventeenth century is quoted as saying that the women conceived through the south wind, before which they placed themselves when naked. The Amazons of Venezuela and Brazil, about whom so much has been written, do not probably belong to this tradition, but in recent times the missionary Chalmers found tales of a Land of Women current in New Guinea, and there is a Papuan tale of two Ginggala men in the Land of Women. Only women lived there and they cut a child out of the mother's body and buried her. Similar legends are said to be current among the Polynesian Maori and the Mentawei Islanders.

The suggestion in the stories in the text that the Land of Women was also the home of good liquor and powerful magic does not appear in the older traditions.

9

AGARIA

Umaria, Mandla District

(From *The Agaria*, 164)

In Bara Bathi Bengala there was magic. There lived Kani Gondin, Sukhi Chamarin and Dhowan Dhobnin. These were the only three human beings in that country, for they had turned all the other inhabitants into cats.

When Guru Daugun heard about this, he took his twelve disciples and gave each of them a pot full of magic herbs to carry and a piece of iron and set out for Bengal. When they reached Bengal they felt hungry and one of the disciples went to a village to get fire. Dhowan Dhobnin was in that village, and she picked up the fire in her hands and offered it to him. But the boy was frightened and ran away. Then the Guru himself went and brought the fire in his dhoti.

There was a pond. They tried to take their cooking-pots there, but there was so much grass they could not get through. While they were struggling with the grass, the Dhobnin turned the twelve boys into stone and the Guru himself into a cat. She kept the cat with her in her house.

At home, Murra-kawar the Guru's son was playing in the courtyard. By accident he broke an old woman's fire-pot. She lost her temper and cried, 'Your father is so clever that he is Guru of the whole world, but he is not so clever that he can escape being turned into a cat in Bengal.'

The boy was frightened and ran to tell Guru Danantar. This Guru went at once to Bengal. He turned himself into a fly and flew into the Dhobnin's house. There was no one there, but a nice cat was guarding the hearth. Danantar by his magic turned the cat back into a man. Then he went to the pond and threw black and yellow rice at the stone figures of the disciples, and they became alive again. So all the human beings in Bengal were changed back from cats into their own shape.

Presently the Dhobnin came home, and now when Daugun Guru asked her for food, the rice she gave turned into scraps of iron. He and his disciples ate the iron and thus they conquered the three witches and got them into their power.

10

BAIGA

Kenda Zamindari

In the south country is a hill called Ganga on the summit of which is a little village. Below is a great cave where Pelansur Dano lived. This Dano had a very great appetite and he devoured all the men in the village on the hill above his cave. But he did not care for women and left them alone.

One day came Narada Muni wandering across the world in the form of a sadhu. He visited the village at the top of the hill and went begging from house to house. But only widows greeted him and he said, 'I can't take food from widows ; where are the women with husbands ?' One of the widows told him what had happened and the sadhu laughed *mus-mus*. When she saw him smile, sin entered the woman's mind and she tried to draw him into the inner room of her house. Narada Muni was very angry and cursed the village and its women. 'Go, not one of you will ever get a man, and if any of you is pregnant she will bear a daughter.'

Thus the Land of Women came into being. After a time these women took to wearing men's clothes and terrorized the neighbourhood with their swords and spears.

11

BAIGA

Lalpur, Mandla District

Long ago there was a hollow mahua tree which became filled with rain-water. The flowers rotted in the water and presently many birds gathered there and began to drink. Soon they were drunk and began to dance and sing. Bhimsen passed by and wondering what they were doing went to the tree and himself drank some of the water. Soon he too was drunk and enjoyed the feeling so much that in the midst of the seven seas and sixteen streams he made twelve stills.

So good was the spirit that Bhimsen made there that many people gathered and a city grew up, the name of which was Bara Bathi Bengala.

When Daugun Guru heard the fame of this spirit he sent his twelve disciples to get some. Now that country was ruled by women, for the men were deformed and hunchbacked. The women were great witches and when the twelve disciples went to the place the women turned them into cats. All day long the women kept them as cats, but at night they turned them into men and lay with them.

When many days passed and Daugun Guru heard no news of his disciples, he took the form of a bee and went to see what had happened. When he reached Bara Bathi Bengala he turned his disciples back into men and they stole the spirit. Since that day there have been stills throughout the world and the Baiga even to-day call every village-still by the old name Bara Bathi Bengala.

12

BAIGA

Bursipakri, Kawardha State

Beyond the seven seas and the sixteen rivers is a country in which only women live. It is called Triadesh, for none are born there except girls. If any boy is born he becomes a eunuch.

When a woman feels desire, she takes the form of a bird and flies away, away, away, to where men live, and finds a handsome youth. She turns him also into a bird and takes him with her flying to the Land of Women. When she gets him there she turns him into a woman and lets him work in the house. But at night he becomes a man and she lies with him and in due time becomes pregnant. But when the other women see that she is pregnant they get angry and she in fear turns her lover back into a bird and sends him flying home. If he does not get back safely, the ruler of the women, who is an enormous fat woman with a great beard, beats her. It is for fear of her that they cannot keep men openly in their houses.

Sometimes these women make wooden organs out of bija wood and two women use it with each other and their itch is eased. Sometimes from this a child is born. Such a child has no bones and dies after a few days.

13

BAIGA

Bohi, Pandaria Zamindari

Makramal Raja ruled in Lotangarh. He was so strong that even the gods could not conquer him and Bhagavan wondered how he could make him die. He sent his messengers, but the Raja brought thread out of his bottom and making a seven storeyed palace shut them up in it for twelve years. When Bhagavan got no news he grew anxious and called the gods to get him news of his messengers. Mahadeo promised to see to everything.

In Bilaigarh lived Mata Gandain. The smell of her body was so sweet that it spread for twice twelve miles and Marra Deo came to her in a dream. She conceived and bore twelve daughters. When they grew up they desired men and went out to find husbands.

Now Mahadeo searching for the lost messengers thought of these man-hungry women. He brought a great load of mahua flowers and put it down in front of them. 'Make this into liquor,' he said, 'and you'll soon get all the men you want.' Each girl made a separate still for herself. They used crocodiles' heads for the big pots, parrots' heads for the little ones, owls' heads to catch the distillation, tubes of bamboo, fire made of khair wood. Soon there were twelve stills and fully-distilled liquor ready in the owls'-head pots. The gods smelt the liquor from afar and crowded round excited. Makramal Raja came too and found the gods drunk. He too got drunk, and tried to seduce each of the twelve girls in turn. Among the gods was one with only one eye. He was annoyed at Makramal Raja's behaviour and said, 'We'll take mischievous fellows like you to Mahadeo ; he'll know what to do with you.' Makramal Raja laughed and said, 'If I could shut Bhagavan's messengers up in a seven storeyed palace, what can a creature like you do ?' Then Mahadeo knew what had happened to the messengers and was very pleased. He got them released and after ten years they took Makramal Raja to Bhagavan.

Then said Mahadeo to the twelve sisters, 'This is Bara Bathi Bengala. This is the Land of Women. After this no man is to come here. Here fully-distilled liquor will always flow in streams.' And this was so for a long while. There were no men in Bara Bathi Bengala, but now because of the sin in the world men and women live there together.

14

GOND

Batama, Chhindwara District

In Jalmanagar only women lived. There were no men at all. Jwala Rani ruled over the city. She was chaste and holy and kept the virgins of the city in her house to guard their chastity. In her house she made a swing and in front of it was a little pond full of lotus flowers. A god lived in the lotus and she worshipped him and he used to tell her everything. All round her house were women guards with swords and guns. If any man entered the city they arrested him and took him to Jwala Rani. She would turn him into a dog or cat or kill him. Whenever she killed a man she threw the blood into her pond.

Once a very handsome youth came to the city. Jwala Rani was swinging in her swing, but when she saw him she fell in love with him and wanted to marry him. The boy escaped and though the servants did their best to catch him he avoided them. Jwala Rani became pregnant by the strength of her love alone, and in due time gave birth to a daughter, Mayadevi. After this girl was born they changed the name of the city to Mayanagri.

One day Chandrasingh, the Rajkumar of Surajnagar, quarrelled with his brother and left his kingdom. He came to Mayanagri. Chandrasingh's Guru was Goraknath. He gave the boy a necklace that had the power of making the wearer invisible, a bag of ashes which when blown onto anyone compelled him to dance and a sword which would cut off people's heads of its own accord. When Chandrasingh reached Mayanagri the god came out of the lotus and laughed. Jwala Rani asked, 'Why are you laughing?' The god said, 'Because such a man has come that if you can bathe in his blood you will become immortal'. Chandrasingh went to see Jwala Rani. Her servants tried to stop him, but he put his necklace round his neck and he became invisible. He saw Mayadevi and she fell in love with him. But Jwala Rani tried to kill him. The boy kept on making himself invisible and the servants soon wearied of searching for him.

Presently the god again came out of the lotus and said, 'You cannot kill Chandrasingh like this. He is the disciple of Guru Goraknath. You must first steal his necklace, his bag and his sword.' Hearing this Jwala Rani took the form of the Guru. She had a pillar erected in the courtyard and said to her women, 'Tie me to this and heap wood round me as if you were going to burn me to death.' When Chandrasingh came, he saw what he thought was his Guru in danger of death. 'Do not come here', cried the Rani, 'but throw your necklace, bag and sword to me and I will be saved'. The boy, thinking it was his own Guru who asked for these things, threw them to her and she took them and laughed at him. Then she and her servants prepared to kill him, but he ran to Mayadevi.

Mayadevi turned him into a garland of flowers and put it round her neck. Her mother came laughing laughing and asked, 'Is Chandrasingh here?' 'No,' said the girl, 'you may search my house, but he is not here'. Jwala Rani went back to her swing. The god came out of the lotus again and laughed and said, 'Mayadevi has the boy in a garland round her neck'. The Rani went back to her daughter and said, 'Why have you deceived me? Throw that garland on the ground'. She did so and the boy stood before her and the Rani cut off his head. She filled a pot with the blood and sent the head and body to Mayadevi saying, 'Here is your husband. Look at him and work your love upon him'.

Jwala Rani returned to her swing and presently the god came out of the lotus and laughed and said, 'When there is an eclipse of the sun, bathe in this blood and you will become immortal'. But Mayadevi was very sad and wept bitterly. As she wandered through the palace she came to the pond and the god came out of the lotus and laughed and said, 'Why are you so sad?' She was angry with him and abused him saying, 'You have ruined my life's happiness'. But the god said, 'You do not know who I am. I am he who can light a fire and can put it out. I can make your lover alive again'. The girl said, 'How can this be?' The god replied, 'There is a great festival in the palace of Indal Raja. Go and dance before him and please him and ask him to make Chandrasingh alive again'.

The girl took the form of Mohani and adorning herself with her best ornaments went to Indal Raja, and danced before him. He was very pleased and when he asked her what she wanted, she fell at his feet and asked him to restore her lover. Now on that very day there was an eclipse of the sun. Jwala Rani was sitting in the courtyard ready for her bath of blood and her women brought the pot and put it before her. Indal Raja sent his messenger to steal it. He put the head and corpse of Chandrasingh together and filled it again with life. Indal Raja then said, 'Now you must kill Jwala Rani. Her life is in that swing'.

Chandrasingh and Mayadevi returned to the city crying 'Victory to Indal Raja!' When Jwala Rani heard it, she tried to kill them but

Mayadevi stole the necklace, bag and sword and gave them to her lover. He blew the ash over Jwala Rani's army of women and they began to dance. Then he broke the swing and set fire to it and as the flames leapt up the Rani's body caught fire and she died.

Then Mayadevi and Chandrasingh were married and after this men as well as women lived in Mayanagri. In this city every house had its own still and the people there drank the best spirit in the world. Presently the city's name was changed again and now it was called Bara Bathi Bengala.

15

JHORIA

Lamda, Koraput District

Korsai Raja lived in Rachgalli village. He was very rich and very wicked. When the Raja had grown old and more bad tempered than ever, a blind man and his son came to Rachgalli to beg. The boy made his father rest on the bank of a stream while he himself went from house to house through the village. But when the Raja saw him, he fell into a passion and had him killed immediately. Evening fell, and the old man was still waiting for his son. All night he wept, hungry and lonely by the stream, and in the early morning the women who came with their pots for water, brought him the news of his son's death. Then the old man stood up and cursed Korsai Raja and his land. 'May every man in this kingdom be destroyed. Henceforth only women will live here.' As he spoke every man and boy in Rachgalli turned to stone and since that day no male child has ever once been born. Only girls are born and only women live there. This Land of Women is in Maliyakand to the north-east of this country.

16

KAMAR

Tikarapara, Khariar Zamindari

The Kingdom of Tiripatna lies towards the sunrise. This is the kingdom of women, where no man may live. Should any man enter the kingdom by mistake or accident, the women seize him and by their magic change him into a bullock. During the day they use in their fields, but when darkness falls they make him into a man and force him to do their pleasure all night long. If any woman there becomes pregnant and bears a male child, they kill it, but they preserve female children with great affection.

Sometimes a man escapes from that country, though but seldom; if he does he carries on his buttocks the marks of a bullock to the day of his death.

17

TAKALA SAORA

Jirango, Ganjam District

Adarsai Raja ruled in Dodsagarh. He was rough and quarrelsome. He had one daughter, a most beautiful girl, whom he would marry to no one. In Dundagarh was Mandarsing Raja. He had one son, a handsome youth, named Chokusai. One day Chokusai came to Dodsagarh and being thirsty went to drink water from the lake. At this moment Adarsai's daughter came to bathe. When he saw her, Chokusai's head spun round and round and he fell in a swoon. When he recovered he called one of the girl's companions and asked whether the princess was married. He rode home in despair and refused to eat or drink till his father promised to marry him to the girl.

Chokusai's mother was full of magic. She gave the boy an enchanted leaf and sent him to do with the girl as he willed. He rode to the lake and hid the leaf under the stone on which the princess used to bathe. When the girl came she was filled with love and Chokusai put her on his horse and rode away with her. Her companions ran home and told Adarsai Raja. Full of rage he summoned his subjects to invade Dundagarh. In the battle Adarsai Raja killed half Mandarsing Raja's people, and Mandarsing Raja offered him half his kingdom but Adarsai Raja refused. Then Chokusai's mother got very angry and turned Adarsai Raja into a pig and his army into rocks and stones. She made a broad river flow round Dodsagarh so that none could go in or out. There were now only women in Dodsagarh, for all its men were killed. It was the Land of Women and here women lay with women. No male children were born—if there was one it had no bones—there were only girls.

CHAPTER TWENTY-TWO

CUSTOM AND TABOO

I HAVE collected many legends of a 'functional' character, that still vitalize tribal custom and taboo, and these are recorded in their proper setting in the monographs on the tribes whence they came. In this Chapter I give a few additional stories that have not found a home elsewhere.

It is curious that, generally, the fewer clothes a tribe wears the more legends it has about clothing. The naked Bondo of Orissa have a great deal to say about the cloth they do not wear. The Baiga have stories about their scanty attire. The labourers of Chhattisgarh whose only clothing was till recently a narrow strip of cloth over the loins account for the habit (which is really due to the great heat) by a legend that when Mahadeo was distributing food to the peoples of the earth, the Chhattisgarhi folk arrived, as usual, late and he said to them, 'All the cooked food has been given away, you can only have the remains which are cold'; and this is why the people of Chhattisgarh eat stale rice in the morning. 'Similarly when the clothes were distributed, the Chhattisgarhi folk were again behind time, and Mahadeo said, "Late again, I have only remnants left now": so they had to take the strips left over from the cloth, and use these'.[1]

There are one or two interesting stories from other parts of India about marriage customs, which may be compared with the legends in the text.

The Ho tradition of the origin of the custom of paying bride-price is connected with a traditional story about yawning. The Ho are said to have regarded anyone who yawned without covering the mouth as a were-tiger and they used to seize him and carry him off to a tiger's den and there abandon him. Once a Munda's daughter was detected in the act and was taken to a tiger's den. She was made to anoint herself with oil and haldi and the people cooked some rice for her and made her eat it. A herdsman, however, watched what was happening from a distance and in the evening came to the place, shot the tiger and took the girl to his house. They settled down as man and wife, but after some months the girl

[1] A. E. Nelson, *Raipur District Gazetteer* (Bombay, 1909), 115. There is a tradition that not so long ago lotus fibre was used for making garments in Chhattisgarh.

was recognized. The herdsman, frightened of the Munda, promised to give them a he-buffalo and three-score cows if they would consent to the marriage. The Munda at first thought that this was a ridiculous price for a useless girl, but after they had received the cattle they gave permission for the marriage. After this it became the custom for everyone to take a price for his daughter before he gave her as a bride.[1]

The origin of the use of vermilion during marriage rites is traced by the Uraon to the following incident. Four friends went together in search of employment and during the night had to sleep under a mango tree in a thick forest. Each took his turn at keeping guard and each adopted different means of keeping awake. The first man was a wood-carver and he picked up a fallen branch and carved it into the figure of a girl. The next man was a smith and he adorned the figure with ornaments. The third man was a weaver and he dressed the image in a sari. The fourth man was a seller of vermilion and he anointed the forehead of the figure with vermilion and it at once came to life. Each of the four friends claimed the girl as his wife and they began to quarrel. A holy man appeared on the scene and when they referred their dispute to him he said, 'The man who made her was her father, the man who clothed her was her brother, the man who decked her in ornaments was her maternal uncle. It is the man who anointed her forehead with vermilion who is her husband'.[2]

Various tribes are reported to have a taboo on sexual intercourse at night or inside a house. The Kadar of Cochin are reported not only to have avoided intercourse in their huts, but to have 'had sexual connections few and far between'. 'Comparisons are odious', says K. G. Menon, 'but one fears that civilized man does not stand to gain much when he is compared with these primitive people in this respect'.[3] Russell and Hiralal declare that 'a Maria Gond thinks it impious to have sexual intercourse with his wife in his house, as it would be an insult to the goddess of wealth who lives in the house, and the effect would be to drive her away.'[4] Grigson observes that 'whoever gave the authors this information must have been drawing on his imagination. There is no "goddess of wealth" among the Marias. The modern Maria becomes hilarious over the idea that it is in any way wrong to have intercourse with his wife in the house; if any con-

[1] Haldar, 128.
[2] Roy, *Oraon Religion*, 160.
[3] *Census of India*, 1931, i. Part III, 214.
[4] Russell and Hiralal, iii, 131f.

sideration deterred the older generation, it was the close proximity of the Pot of the Departed'. But Grigson admits that, although the old prejudice is fast dying out, the Hill Maria are still doubtful about the propriety of men sleeping in the house and regard the jungle or some place overshadowed by the thick leaves of the *bauhinia vahlii* creeper as the right place for intercourse between man and wife.[1]

S. P. Rice, in a charming, if slightly florid, book about Orissa, makes a similar statement about the Saora who do not copulate (my word : Rice's is 'enjoy the pleasures of the conjugal relation') inside a house. 'It is their custom i' th' afternoon to sleep'. 'They retire into the jungle to rest, and the gate of Paradise is guarded by a flaming sword that turns every way. For across the path which leads into Eden is laid a bough or a bramble to warn the profane intruder. The sign is always respected.'[2] What a local writer can make of these remarkable fantasies may be seen in the words of S. N. Roy.

> There is a curious custom prevalent among these people. They do not copulate after nightfall. The custom might have originated from imitation of the habits of certain birds and animals, but about that one cannot speak with certainty. . . . Near their hamlets, we see clean spots inside the forests. Each married couple go to one of these spots to enjoy themselves. They put a thorn bush across the pathway leading to these spots when they are there, as a warning to others not to come that way. . . They say that God has given the day for work and enjoyment and night for absolute rest. It is a sin against nature to copulate at night.'[3]

How far this is still true, if it ever was true, it is hard to say. But it is always difficult for men and women in tribes which do not have the dormitory system to relieve themselves of the embarrassing presence of their children, to find privacy. Doubtless they often have to retire to the solitude of the forest, and what was actually a mere convenience has been exalted into a tradition.

It is curious that so universal a custom as tattooing should be associated with so little mythology and that its patterns should usually have so little meaning. There is a Brahmin story that Lakshmi, the wife of Vishnu, told her husband that whenever he left

[1] Grigson, 113f.

[2] S. P. Rice, *Occasional Essays on Native South Indian Life* (London, 1901), 105.

[3] S. N. Roy, 'The Savaras of Orissa', *Man in India*, vii (1927), 331f. But, it is curious to note, the ancient Hindu tradition, as expressed in the *Prasna Upanishad* (i, 13) is the opposite of this. 'Verily, they waste their life who join in sexual enjoyment by day; it is chastity that they join in sexual enjoyment by night.'

her alone she became frightened. Vishnu therefore took his weapons and pressed them on her body, saying that the marks of his weapons would guard her against evil.[1]

The Baiga consider that tattooing was instituted in order that mankind should have something to take beyond the grave. Some Baiga believe that one of the tattoo figures is a riddle which is intended to be beyond Bhagavan's capacity to solve. The Muria associate the origin of tattooing with the instructions of a goddess and also believe that the marks go with them after death.

The Paraiyan of South India have a legend that once long ago a Paraiyan woman wished her upper arms and chest to be tattooed in the form of a bodice. The operation was successfully carried out until the region of the heart was reached and then a vulnerable part was punctured by the needles with the result that the woman died. There is now, it is said, a superstitious objection to tattooing of the breasts.[2]

In Kumaun there was a belief that 'when the dead appear before Bhagavan, he finds it very difficult to ascertain whether they are Hindus or Muhammedans, and the only way of making this certain is to be tattooed in the regular style'[3]—a notion that finds an echo in a story in the text.

The Origin of Clothes

I

GOND

Rewa State

Putu Dewar lived with his sister in the Sethban. They were both naked as cows. He had a lathi sixteen cubits long, she had a pot that was twenty span across.

When Banhahu Dano gave birth to the Sun and Moon they looked down and saw the two naked Baiga and felt very embarrassed. They ran to Banhahu Dano and he hid them in his belly. The world became dark and many of the gods went to the Dano to ask what was the matter. He told them about the naked Baiga and how the Sun and Moon could not stay in the sky with such a sight below them.

Mahadeo went to Kapasia Mai and told her what had happened. She opened her mouth and from it came a thread of cotton. Mahadeo

[1] Campbell, *The Indian Antiquary*, xxvi, 126.
[2] Thurston, vi, 113.
[3] *N. I. Notes and Queries*, iii, 106.

took water in his hand and repeated a seed-charm over it. From the water in the charm was born a Panka weaver. He took the cotton and first of all he made a pubic cloth for the Baiga and his sister and after that every kind of cloth for men and women.

2

LANJHIA SAORA

Bhubani, Ganjam District

There was a Pano named Sakuli living on the Kantuli Hill. He did no work but cut the jungle and sowed maize in the clearings. In those days both men and women used to go about naked, but one night Kittung came to a priest in a dream and told him that the Saora were to wear clothes and that they must get them from the Pano. The priest went to Sakuli, but the Pano said, 'I don't know how to make cloth and I have nothing to make it with.' So Kittung told the Pano, 'On the Kasuli Hill there is a cotton tree. Go and collect the pods.' The Pano got the pods and made yarn. He made his wife lie down and tied a stick across her breasts. From this he stretched his yarn. He took out her vagina and used it as a shuttle. The cloth he made was long and narrow, narrow as the distance between a woman's breasts.

3

LANJHIA SAORA

Rajingtalu, Koraput District

The penis used to be very long. Saora boys and girls were dancing together. In those days girls were naked, and boys wound the long penis round their waists as a loin-cloth. One of the boys loved a girl's thing and unwound his penis. The girl said to herself, 'This boy wants to shame me in front of this crowd'. She caught hold of the penis and cut it off with her axe. Then she chopped it into three pieces: two she put in her ears as ornaments, the third she buried in the ground.

A Brahmin woman found the buried piece and, thinking it to be Mahadeo's *linga*, took it home and worshipped it. At night she used to take it to bed with her and use it for her pleasure.

Since then Saora men have worn long flaps of cloth in front and behind so that no one will castrate them further, and women too have begun to wear clothes. When we dance we wave axes and swords in the air and shout to frighten away any who would castrate us.

4

LANJHIA SAORA

Talasingi, Ganjam District

A vine grew on the Karmasi Mountain. Two gourds hung from it. When the earth sank below the water, these gourds floated. In each gourd something was born: in one it was a boy, in the other a girl. One day the gourds broke open and the seeds were scattered on the water. The boy said to the girl, 'Tear your cloth and give me a scrap and I'll use it to make the world.' The girl tore her cloth and gave it, all but two hands-breadth with which she covered her privates. The boy covered the gourd seeds with the cloth and then he and the girl became naked and danced on it until the earth was ready. When the boy saw the girl's body naked, his mind grew small for her and he lay with her and from them all mankind was born. Because this girl wore only two hands-breadth of cloth, the Saora only wear half a cloth on their bodies.

Nudity

5

DORLA-MARIA

Dobatota, Bastar State

Mahapurub and his wife were bathing in a mountain stream and her wet cloth clung to her young body. Some Maria came secretly from the Abujhmar to watch and when they saw her they roared with laughter. Mahapurub was angry and said, 'Because you laughed today, your wives will always be naked. And because you embarrassed us in the day-time, you will always go to your wives in the day-time.

The Mahaprasad Friendship

6

GOND

Pakhri, Mandla District

In Binjhpahar lived a Dewar Baiga and in Koeliban lived an Ahir who used to graze the Surhi cow. The Baiga had a son, the Ahir had a daughter and neither were married.

One day when the Baiga went to dig roots on Koeli Hill, he met the Ahir and they sat down together to talk. The Ahir said, ' Brother, I have got no fire with me or I would give you my pipe to smoke '. The Baiga had his flint with him and he made fire and the two men sat down and smoked contentedly together. In this way they used to meet daily and gradually a strong friendship grew up between them.

Then one day, the Ahir said to the Baiga, ' Brother, there is now great friendship between us ; what shall we do about it ? ' The Ahir made a blanket out of the hairs from the tail of the Surhi cow and the Baiga brought a load of roots and the two men sat down together on the blanket to become Mahaprasad friends. At the end of the ceremony the Ahir gave the blanket to the Baiga and the Baiga gave the Ahir his load of roots. After that, although they were of different castes their children were married. Such is the strength of the Mahaprasad friendship.

The Origin of Marriage

7

GOND

Jubbulpore District

In the old days people did not know how to marry each other nor did they eat grain. A man would give a woman sarai leaves to eat and the woman would put some of the leaves in the man's mouth. In this way they came together.

Aibhuj Raja lived in Baibhuj and his Rani's name was Bassarkor. For many months she passed yellow urine on the same patch of ground and at last a girl was born from the earth there. Her name was Hardawali Kaniya. A little while afterwards from the same place a boy was born.

When the two grew up the girl said, 'I am going to have a marriage with my brother'. When the people heard the word 'marriage', they were frightened and asked, 'What is this thing, marriage?' The Rani called the girl and said, 'We have never heard about marriage before. What are you talking about?' Hardawali Kaniya said, 'Go the place where I was born and where you used to piss on the ground'. The Rani went and found that a haldi root had grown there. She pulled it up and gave it to the girl who exclaimed, 'This is the haldi that will put my life in order'.

Hardawali Kaniya caught a spider and pulled out its thread. She called Bendo and his sister Chando and made them Suasa and Suasin. Then she showed the people how to cut sarai branches for the marriage-booth and wild-fig branches for the roof and saleh for the pillar. She tied the spider's thread seven times round the booth. She said to her brother, 'You and I are brother and sister, but we are now going to marry each other, for the people do not know what marriage is and we have come into the world to teach them. Your name will be Piri Marra Deo and mine will be Piri Marrahi. Go and get some ornaments for me and then I will go round the pole with you.'

The boy mounted his horse Ranbaj and rode away to Nain Sonar and had anklets, ear-rings and armlets made for his bride. The girl put them on and told the mother how to grind haldi and apply it to both of them. When the time came for going round the pole together the boy said, 'I won't marry you only for this once'. The girl said, 'No, our marriage is for seven births.' That is why they went round the pole seven times. From that day people in the world have known how to marry.

The Serving Marriage

8

GOND

Jubbulpore District

Tonha Dewar and his wife lived in Madangarh. They had one daughter. As the girl grew to maturity her parents became old and feeble. They said in their minds, 'How are we to make a living? Let us sell our daughter in marriage to someone and then we will have a little money. The Dewar went out to find someone who would marry his daughter

Like an ant he crawled to Kosamgarh where Mahakasur Deo was living with his only son, whose name was Lamsena. The Dewar went to Mahakasur Deo and told him everything. Mahakasur Deo said, 'Do not sell your daughter, *samdhi*. You may keep my son for twelve years in your house. Then I need not pay you anything and your daughter and my son will live with you. They will marry, but your daughter will not leave your house and the two of them will feed you and look after you.' This is how the custom of keeping a Lamsena boy in the house began. In those days he had to work for twelve years, but now it is only for three.

Sleeping on Beds

9

BHUIYA

Uskuda, Bonai State

We are Matisar, born of earth. At first we made our home on a mountain. We had no food and sat silent and hungry. Boram went to make his clearing. When he saw us he taught us what to do. He got roots and roasted them and we ate them with pleasure. We began to make koman clearings ; we cut and burnt the trees ; our beds were ashes and we covered ourselves with ashes.

We fell from the womb of earth to the ground and so we sleep on the ground always. Once we wore leaves and slept in our koman clearings and made our beds of ashes.

There was a Bhuiya Raja. He was proud and said, 'I am going to sleep on a bed.' He had one made and spent a night on it. The next day he fell ill. His cattle went to the jungle and a tiger killed one of his cows. He himself went hunting and a tiger caught him and devoured him. The Rauria[1] tried to discover the reason, and one day a god came to him in a dream and told him that it was because the Raja, who had fallen from the womb to the ground, had slept proudly above the ground.

[1] Magician expert in divination. A Gunia or Siraha.

Tattooing

10

RAJNENGI PARDHAN

Madhopur, Mandla District

One day Mahadeo invited the gods to a feast. A Gond god went with the others. The goddesses seated themselves on the ground and Parvati was amongst them. The Gond god went there to take his wife away but amongst so many he could not recognize which was his. By mistake he put his hand round Parvati's shoulder to drag her away, and she began to scream. Mahadeo knew that it was only a mistake and laughed, but Parvati was very angry. However, in the end Parvati arranged that to distinguish the women of different castes, they should be tattooed in different ways, and since then the custom of tattooing has come into the world.

CHAPTER TWENTY-THREE

FESTIVAL, DANCE AND SONG

I

The Dance

THROUGHOUT aboriginal India the dance is something much more than mere recreation or even a useful sexual stimulant. In many cases it has a definitely religious or magical significance and is often linked with the mythological past of a tribe. A Santal myth derives the origin of dancing very much as the Baiga story in the text, by suggesting that it arose in imitation of the actions of divine beings.

In the beginning the Santals worshipped no deities, and did not know the use of musical instruments, and could not dance. Two of their number set out on an exploring expedition and penetrated deeply into the heart of the great forest. Towards evening they heard the sound of music and not knowing what it was, they went to see from whence it proceeded. On nearing the place they became afraid, and in order to see over the brushwood they climbed up into a tree, and beheld Moreko, Jaher-era, Marang Buru and Gosae-era dancing. Suddenly one of the dancers stood still and said, 'There are human beings near, I smell them'. Jaher-era said, 'Whether you smell men or beasts, do them no harm, but bring them here'. The two adventurers danced with the bongas all night learning both to play and dance. In the morning they were given two drums and dismissed with the following injunction, 'Go and tell your people all about us. Tell them to venerate and respect us and annually to offer sacrifices to us. You must also instruct them to play music and to dance, and we order you to teach the people of twelve villages every night'. This, it is said, they accomplished, and in this manner the Santals learned the use of musical instruments and the art of dancing.[1]

Another rather charming account of the origin of dancing was also recorded by Campbell from the same tribe. Seven sons and seven daughters were born to the parents of mankind. When their children grew up, the old people used to take great care that they never went together into the jungle; the boys were great hunters and the girls used to go to gather herbs, but they always went out separately.

One day the seven sons went to the Surukue forest to hunt; the girls also came to the same place to gather potherbs. Having collected their

[1] Campbell, 197f.

herbs, the girls were amusing themselves, singing and swinging on the branches of a tree. The young men hearing singing said among themselves, 'There are human beings near'. Attracted by the sound they drew near, and saw the girls under the tree. When the girls became aware of the presence of the young men they left off swinging, and began to dance a Dahar dance, and to sing:

> The ants are swarming, Mother,
> On the branches of the tree,
> They are swarming, Mother.

The young men then drew near to where they were dancing, and the girls invited them to join them. They accepted the invitation, and the two parties uniting began a Lagre dance. They paired according to their ages, the eldest son with the eldest daughter, and so on, down to the youngest. During the dance they sang the following:

> Underneath the tree,
> Mother, see the young deer.[1]

A Chenchu story also attributes the origin of drumming, which is so important for the dance, to imitation, but in this case it was the imitation of monkeys.

In the old times, when men had no drums, a man went hunting in the jungle and saw two monkeys, a male and a female, in the branches of a tree. The male monkey was playing on a drum and both monkeys were very happy and danced among the branches. The man wanted to shoot the male monkey, for in the old days men were not allowed to shoot female animals, but his arrow missed the mark and by mistake wounded the female monkey.

Then the male monkey took the female monkey on his back and carried her to the ground; he put some medicine on the wound and then he began playing on the drum to try and divine whether his wife would live. But in spite of the medicine the female monkey died; the male monkey wept and wailed for a long time. In the end he buried the female monkey and heaped stones on the grave and on top of the stones he put his drum.

Now the man had been watching all the time, and when he saw the male monkey leave his drum on top of the female monkey's grave, he went and picked it up and took it to his village. There, he told the other people how he found it and he tapped it with his hands to show how it was played. Only gradually did men learn to play the drum with sticks.

When the man who had killed the female monkey died, his relatives took the drum, but in the end it got lost. By that time, however, other people had learnt to make drums out of wood and hide, and like the monkeys men and women dance when it is played.[2]

[1] Campbell, 21.

[2] Furer-Haimendorf, 225f.

I

BADI

Rewa State

When Mahadeo was distributing their proper work to every kind of man he gave the task of begging to the Brahmin, fighting to the Kshattri, cultivation to the Gond. But when he had given their duties to everyone he found the Bhima and the Badi were left. He could not think of anything to give them to do, but at last he pulled out his organ and, making it sixteen cubits long, tied it as a turban round his head. He put feathers and flowers into it and began to dance the Saila. On the other side Parvati danced the Rina. The Bhima and Badi watched them dancing and learnt how to dance themselves. Afterwards they taught men and women of other tribes to dance as well.

2

BINJHWAR

Raipur District

Raja Hemanchal's daughter was the Rani Gaura. She had a parrot which she loved greatly. This parrot used to tell the girl everything it saw and heard ; and the girl would tell the parrot her joys and sorrows. After her marriage to Mahadeo, her husband took Gaura to his house, but he went away at once to Banbindra to make a plough and a yoke. Gaura used to send the parrot to see what Mahadeo was doing. The parrot would report how Mahadeo would work for a time, grow weary, drink opium, and bhang and lie down stupid as a pig, and then get up to work again.

Because Gaura loved her parrot, people who worship her make an image of a parrot and put it in a basket sitting on rice and flowers. Women carry it on their heads to the dancing-place ; they put it down and dance round it. Thus the Sua (Parrot) dance began.

3

DHANWAR

Uprora Zamindari

There was a Baiga and his wife ; they lived by cultivating their clearings in the forest. They sowed kang and kutki grain and got a great crop. Bringing the sheaves to the threshing-floor the Baiga and his wife threshed them with their feet. They piled the grain up in long mounds. That night Chermatiya Deo, who gives good crops, came to the threshing-floor and danced among the grain. The Baiga, who was sleeping some distance away, awoke and saw him dancing. He got up and soon he too was dancing, swinging his body to and fro.

Then the Baiga went to sleep and Chermatiya Deo came to him in a dream and said, ' You must dance the Karma and Saila dances. Before you begin, worship me and your crops will always be good.' The next morning the Baiga told his wife about his dream and they went out to find something to offer in worship. The Baigin found some wild urid pulse. She brought it home and put it in the grinding-mill, but she was unable to grind it. The Baiga brought the heavy stone called *teliya pathar* (oil-stone) ; with a bit of iron he prepared it and then he was able to grind the wild urid. He and his wife took it to the threshing-floor and offered it among the long mounds of grain. The neighbours gathered to drink liquor and in the evening began to dance. They had never danced before and did not know what to do, but the Baiga remembered what he had seen the previous night and taught them. That was how dancing came into the world.

4

DHOBA

Silpuri, Mandla District

A woman's husband died. She took the corpse in her lap and wept. At that time Mahadeo and Parvati were walking through the jungle and Parvati heard the noise of weeping. ' Let us go and see what it is,' said Parvati. ' You women are always wanting to interfere,' said Mahadeo. But she pressed him and took him to the house. Mahadeo asked the woman why she was weeping. 'My husband has died,' she said. Mahadeo and Parvati sang a song together and when he heard it the man got up and lived again. The woman wanted to learn the song, but she could not get the words right, though she was able to learn the tune. She used to sing the same tune but with other words. From this came the Kajri songs, which young girls sing during the month of Sawan when there is rain. They make swings in their houses and sing the songs as they swing.

5

GOND

Lalkati, Mandla District

At the beginning there were no dances and no songs. Saonti Baiga had two wives, Jalango and Raimat. He lived with these two wives. One day Mother Earth gave him a dream: she began to tremble and said, 'To make me steady you must take your children and sacrifice them to me.'

He took his seven children towards Surguja where Mother Earth has her home. On the way he met Haran Raja. When Haran heard that the Baiga was going to offer his own children, he said, 'Take my bones instead' and he gave them to him.

Presently the Baiga came to an ant-hill. As he approached, it turned into a pig. The pig bowed with folded hands and said, 'Don't take your children for sacrifice; I will come with you instead.'

That night when the Baiga was asleep, a drum came out of the ground and sat on his head. In the morning the Baiga planted a flag in honour of Karma and he and his two wives, after sacrificing the pig and a fowl to it, began to dance round it beating the drum. They danced every kind of dance and gave names to each; one they called Karma, another Sua, another Saila.

Mother Earth was very pleased. 'If you don't always dance Karma,' she said, 'my nose will split open, and you will have to throw me out of your village. Now my happiness is in your hands.' The Baiga and his two wives went home dancing and singing.

6

GOND

Dhanras, Uprora Zamindari

On the Hill of Peafowls' Eggs was born the Saila dance and song. At first peacocks used to dance the Saila. Men went for wood and leaves and they saw the dance ; they too were pleased ; they joined the birds and all danced together. When the men had learnt how to do it, they went home and taught it in the villages. In the jungle was a tall date palm ; the peacocks used to dance round it. As the peacock has a tuft on its head and a fine tail, men too put tufts in their turbans and decorations on their buttocks. As the peacock dances looking back at its own beauty, so in the Saila men dance looking back at their shadows. The first Saila song was :

Khajrāke tari nāchat nāchat hai manjura
Janamane lethai mor jhaliya manjura.
Under the palm tree the peacock dances
It has taken birth, my long-tailed peacock.

But when men had learnt everything, the peacocks stopped the Saila. For they were frightened, and the long-tailed peacocks said to men, 'Make tufts of our tails and put them in your turbans and your Saila will never go wrong.' They pulled out many feathers from their tails and gave them to the men to use in the Saila.

7

PARDHAN

Balaghat District

Karsanbira was Raja of Hardinagar and his son's name was Ram Darwai. In Bandaduar lived Raja Singhbahani with his three daughters—Nakti Devi, Sarada and Sirseti. Karsanbira arranged that his son should be married to Nakti Devi and when the time for the marriage arrived, Sarada and Sirseti, acting as the bride's Suasin, took her to Hardinagar. There were only three of them, these three young girls in the marriage-party, but Ram Darwai had a great company of attendants. When the girls reached Hardinagar and saw so many people waiting to receive them they felt embarrassed and wanted to escape. They made themselves small and jumped into a great pot of liquor set there for the entertainment of the guests. That evening the people drank the liquor and quickly became intoxicated. Suddenly they found themselves singing Dadaria; they sang of their own accord, using words they had not thought of before. The unmarried girls sat in one row singing, the mature girls in another, the middle-aged in a third and the old women in a fourth, they sat in rows and sang.

When the men heard the beautiful singing they were excited and ran to see what was happening. When the tiger hears the song of the kiddari bird it is roused with desire. In the same way when the men heard the Dadaria they were filled with love and during the night they worked their will on the women. In the morning the three girls came out of the liquor-pot and when they saw what was going on they ran away home. But the people in Hardinagar turned into stone. They became stone for ever just as they were, embracing one another, climbing on one another and they still may be seen in the temple at Hardinagar. Whoever goes to that temple at once begins to sing Dadaria of his own accord.

When Ram Darwai saw the three sisters running away he tried to catch them but they escaped and they too turned into stone. Since that time the city has been called Nakti Gatiya Bandaduar.

8

RAJNENGI PARDHAN

Patangarh, Mandla District

When the earth was first made at the beginning of the world the twelve sisters Sarada and Sirseti were dancing the Rina and the twelve brothers Gomshan were dancing the Saila, in Boramdeo in Kawardha State.

Guru Danatar had two sons, Dekhni and Dhathha. One day the boys went to hunt and as they wandered through the forest they came to Boramdeo and found all the gods and animals watching the dance. The boys stood still, filled with wonder at the sight. Dekhni had his bow in one hand and rested his chin on the tip of his arrow. When the dancers saw him they thought he was going to shoot them and by their magic they sent insects to eat through the bow. When the bow broke Dekhni slipped and his chin fell on the point of the arrow and drove it up through his head and he died. When Dhathha saw what had happened he was frightened and ran away.

Running running through the jungle the boy met Hemar Kalar and his wife. They were distilling liquor by the roadside. The boy drank a lot, and courage and desire came to him. He remembered how beautiful Sarada and Sirseti were and thought in his mind, 'I must marry these girls, I will make the whole company drunk and then I'll carry them away.' He got a great pot of double-distilled liquor and had it carried by twelve pairs of men to the dancing-place. There he made everyone drunk, gods and animals, girls and boys. When they were drunk the boys seized the girls and the gods went to the goddesses as they danced. For shame they turned into stone. Sarada, Sirseti and Gomshan, these three escaped. They ran away to Nanga Pahar where Nanga Baiga and Nanga Baigin were living with their twelve sons and twelve daughters.

Nanga Baiga had cut his clearing in Jhinjhiban and had sown kutki. He cut and gathered the crop, threshed and winnowed it and made a pile of the grain. The three gods came to him as he was working on the threshing-floor and entered into his body and all his eight parts itched to dance. Nanga Baigin brought him gruel in a broken pot and the two of them sprinkled a little of it on the pile of kutki and Nanga Baigin said,

> *Chal re buchi handi* !
> *Sao sao khandhi* !
> Come then broken pot !
> Let there be a hundred measures !

But Nanga Baiga said, 'How am I going to winnow a hundred measures of kutki ? I want to dance. Let there first be one shoulder-load for me and one head-load for my wife. That will be plenty for a Baiga.' So saying husband and wife sat down and drank their gruel and found that there was just so much kutki for them to carry. They took it home and then went off to see the dance. Nanga Baiga led the way, followed by his twelve sons in a line; Nanga Baigin followed him with her twelve daughters in a line.

When they reached the place, what did they see ? All round were stone gods and goddesses embracing and fondling one another and in the midst of the jungle was the tiger beating the *māndar* drum, the panther beating the *timki* and the long-tailed peacocks dancing. The Baiga stood and watched them in the light of the moon and thus men learnt to dance.

II

The Karam Festival

It is the Karam Festival which is most firmly established in the mythology of the tribes that observe it, for the recitation of the story of its origin is an important part of the ceremonial. A Santal account describes how a group of young men and women set out with their drums and flutes to take part in an Umbrella Festival on the far side of a river. They found the river in flood and had to return. To cover their disappointment they planned to inaugurate a festival for themselves. The young men assembled in the village street with their drums but when they began to beat them the drums made no sound. So they decided to institute the Karam Festival and cutting a branch of the karam tree they fixed it upright in the ground and danced round it all night. In the morning they pulled up the branch and carried it down to the river to throw it in. It is not stated, but it may be assumed, that the drums began to sound directly the karam tree was honoured.[1]

In *Folk-Songs of the Maikal Hills* there is a full account of the Karam Festival and two Bhuiya stories about its origin are recorded.[2]

Dalton traces the origin of the Karam to a passage in the Bhavishya Purana which, he considers, is intended to explain how it is that the Hindus observe a festival which is essentially aboriginal.

There was a beautiful city named Baranashi, where a highly respectable Brahmin, named Dev Surma, resided. He had two sons, the elder named Karma, and the younger Dharma. One day Dev Sarma informed his sons that he wished to make over to them his property, and devote the remainder of his life to meditation on a future state, and he accordingly divided between them all that he possessed. In a short time after receiving his share, Karma, by his extravagance, was reduced to such indigence that he was obliged to resort to begging for his subsistence. One day, the wife of Karma Surma said to her husband, 'Oh, my lord ! please go today to your brother who is rich and wealthy.' Her husband, according to her words, went to his brother's house. On that day Dharma Surma was employed in the field with his labourers in transplanting the rice plants. Karma engaged himself in the work with them. When the sun set and fearful night approached, Dharma, after taking his meal in the field, went home. Karma Surma waited as a servant with the labourers at his door, but his rich brother gave him neither

[1] Campbell, 192.

[2] *Folk-Songs of the Maikal Hills*, 3 ff.

rice nor paddy. Much depressed, he was returning home, when, on his way, he saw some males and females of the village worshipping the karam tree, by adorning it with flags and flowers, and presenting it with *naivedya* (oblation), incense and other articles. He asked them what was the object of this *vrata*. They told him that it would avert all kinds of misfortune, and that whoever, after fasting, properly performed it, seldom suffered from distress. Hearing this, he returned home, and told all to his wife, who joyfully received this account of the *vrata*, and made a vow to perform it. Accordingly, on the eleventh lunar day of the increasing moon of Bhadra, just at night-fall, Karma Surma and his wife planted the karam tree and rice plants together in the yard of the house and worshipped it, keeping a lamp burning, and offering sandal, flowers, *naivedya*, and incense, and giving money to the Brahmins. By performing this chief of *vratas*, he obtained enormous wealth. Thus, those who with their wives perform this ceremony, become rich and happy in this world ; and their sons and grandsons become rich and happy too ; and all ultimately go to the heaven of the gods.[1]

Roy recorded another version of the story from the Uraon, which resembles to some extent the story given in the text.

> Seven brothers with their wives lived together. One day they went with their pack-bullocks to trade, leaving their wives and children at home. In their absence the women of the village celebrated the Karam Festival and on that very day the returning brothers reached a point only a few miles distant from their village. But the bullocks were too tired to go further and the brothers halted there for the day. They sent the youngest brother, however, to find out how their people were but when he reached the village he got so excited with the festival that he too began to dance and forgot to return. The brothers grew anxious and sent the next youngest, but he too on reaching the village began to dance. In this way all the brothers except the eldest one went to the village and danced. Finally the eldest brother in a very bad temper went himself to see what was happening and when he saw everyone dancing and singing without any thought of him, he kicked the bowl of milk meant for offering to the Karam Raja and went away to live as a sadhu. The Karam Raja was very angry and was about to leave the place but the wife of the youngest brother took him in her arms and persuaded him to remain.[2]

A Bhuiya version of the legend also connects the institution of the festival with a trading expedition. A rich man had seven sons and daughters. One day he set out on a long journey to trade. He was very successful and returned with his boat laden with precious things and anchored it at the boundary of his village. It was the

[1] Dalton, 259 f.

[2] Roy, *Oraon Religion*, 241.

day of the Karam Festival and his wives and his sons' wives were busy dancing round Karam Raja and failed to come out to greet him. The merchant waited till his patience was exhausted and then went home and broke the karam branches and the drums. Directly he insulted the Karam Raja in this way, his boat with its precious cargo disappeared and his cattle were devoured by tigers. The merchant went to an astrologer who told him that the reason for his disaster was his insult to Karam Raja and that he must go on pilgrimage to beg his pardon. The merchant went on a long journey to the sea where he found Karam Raja who told him that if he would make seven altars with seven karam branches, if he would bring seven drums and make his seven wives and seven sons and their seven wives fast, dance and sing for seven days and seven nights in his honour his lost wealth would be restored.[1]

9

BHUIYA

Raisua, Bonai State

In the old days the seven brothers and the seven sisters used to go in the full moon of Kartik to bathe in the Ganges. But it was a long way to go and one day the river said, 'Why do you come so far? I will give you a tree. Take it home and worship it. This worship will be equal to a bath in my waters.' So saying the Ganges gave the brothers and sisters two trees, one for Karam Raja and one for Karam Rani. Since then we have worshipped the karam trees in the name of Karam Raja and Karam Rani and danced the Karam dance in their honour.

10

GOND

Mopka, Raipur District

There was a great famine: there was no rain for three years; there was no food or water, and many died. There was an old Bharewa woman with a very beautiful daughter. The girl grew pregnant of her own accord and when her time came—it was midnight on a Sunday—Sarada

[1] Roy, *The Hill Bhuiyas*, 267.

and Karam Singh were born from her belly below a karam tree. The girl cut the cord with her own hands.

Then Sarada and Karam Singh, very small, no bigger than new-born babies, went from house to house. Every virgin boy or girl was at once possessed by Karam Deo: one beat a bit of wood, one took a lump of earth, another held a stone; everyone picked up something to beat with, and they danced.

The next morning the neighbours saw the girl's belly was empty, but there was no child. But she had kept the flower (placenta) and she showed it to them. They thought her a witch—'She must have eaten her own child'. They were going to kill her, but Sarada and Karam Singh came in and caught her enemies by their arms and told them what had happened. Then the children hid and when the people tried to find them, all they got was the cord lying under the karam tree. They made a great festival then and there, and at once rain began to fall. Now every year in Bhadon or Magh we plant the karam tree and the boys dance hand in hand round it, in the names of Sarada and Karam Singh.

II

GOND

Pandetarai, Matin Zamindari

In Birhigarh lived Anjhar Gond; he was rich and powerful. He had seven sons and married them all to the daughters of big families. He was not an ordinary Gond; he was a big Gond. When Anjhar died, there was a great famine; the grain was spoilt, even the grass and leaves withered in the forest. No one could get food or water and many died. No one would give money on loan and when visitors came people hid in the woods.

The seven sons of Anjhar Gond lived on what was left in their father's grain-bins; when that was finished, what would there be to eat? They said to one another, 'Come, brothers, and let us go to some country to work for a living.' Then one day they decided to dig up the treasure that their father had buried before he died. Here was gold, silver, diamonds, pearls, jewels of every kind stored in seven boxes. They planned to trade with this. They bought cattle and sacks and trappings and rice and salt. They heard that in Kukribariya bazaar the rate was good.

So they loaded their twenty-four lakhs of bullocks and kept three boxes of gold mohur separate. They appointed servants—one Sardar for every hundred thousand bullocks, one Havaldar for every thousand, one Santri for every hundred, one Driver for every ten. Now the seven brothers and their servants were all very stupid ; not one of them knew the difference between what was valuable and what was not.

When the rains began, they said, ' This is the time for trade ' and they loaded their bullocks and set out. They left the youngest brother, whose name was Sarmaha, in charge of their home and the six wives. Along the road they went till they came to Tunki Ghat Padki Maidan and there they made their camp. That night the rain fell in floods. They had no tents or shelter. The salt was spoilt ; it was all lost.

Next day they went on and came to Kukribariya. They made their camp in the Satkosa Padao. That night thieves came and stole some of their things. In the morning they said, ' Let us buy what we can with what is left and go home before everything is lost.' Those brothers did not know what ' weighing ' and ' measuring ' was. They went into the city. One of the brothers saw a Seth making fire with a flint. He was very pleased and asked the Seth the price of the flint. The Seth said, ' To an old customer like you I do not talk about prices ; give what you like.' The brother said, ' Will you take ten thousand rupees ? ' Very quickly the Seth handed him the flint and took the money.

The boy took the flint back to the camp and showed it proudly to his brothers. He put it in a sack and it rolled into a corner. One of the brothers said, ' Now we've lost ten lakhs worth of salt and the thefts of last night and if it costs ten thousand rupees to fill even one corner of a single sack, all our money won't load even one bullock.' They all felt disappointed and upset.

The brothers' Sardar was Buddhu Kshattri. He was a little less stupid than the others. He said, ' Let us go to the city and get help from someone, so that we can at least buy some kodon and kutki or we'll have nothing at all.' They went to a Seth and he taught them how to trade. ' First you must buy a fine tent. Then get many swords and strong poles. Buy some big dogs. One of you should get spectacles, and at least one should dress in English style, with shirt and trousers. But the others must have dhoti and turban, for there is Gandhi Baba. Then when all is ready you may buy your kodon and kutki and load your twenty-four lakhs of bullocks.'

Now let us leave the brothers at the bazaar for a time and see what is happening to their wives. These wives said in their minds, 'Our husbands have gone away. Who knows if they will ever return? Let us get some land and cultivate it ourselves, and so at least we may keep alive.' They went to the Raja of the village and asked for land. The Raja said, 'How are you going to cultivate? You have only your little brother with you.' The eldest woman said, 'There is nothing difficult. We can do it easily. But we must have a bit of land.' So the Raja gave them land near the Jhingajori River where a burning-ground was. He said, 'Cut the grass and make a field there.' So the seven wives and the boy went to the burning-ground and cut the trees and the grass and cleaned the place. There were many ghosts and spirits and Sakani and Dakani there. They ploughed and when the rains came, they sowed rice.

The six wives, deprived so long of their husbands, began to feel the itch of desire. They were so afflicted with it that they fell fainting to the ground. Then they sat together and spoke to one another. 'Who knows whether our husbands will come or no? This is the time of rains when clouds gather overhead and every soul feels a longing for the storm and rain.' The first wife said, 'Let us find some fresh young boy and let him give pleasure to our wasted youth.' Thus spoke the first wife. But the second said, 'No, let us go home to our mothers' houses and there we will not feel this itch so intolerably.' Thus spoke the second wife. But the third said, 'No, let us worship the gods and beg them to bring our husbands back soon.' Thus spoke the third wife. But the fourth said, 'No, let each go where she feels inclined and spend the day in pleasure.' Thus spoke the fourth wife. But the fifth said, 'No, let us find some sadhu who will give us children, for without children there is no content.' Thus spoke the fifth wife. But the sixth said, 'No, you are all making a mistake. Here is our half-husband Sarmaha. Let him delight us and our honour will be saved.' Thus spoke the sixth wife. They were all pleased with this, all except the seventh wife who was Sarmaha's, and they went to find the boy.

They told him that they were unhappy. 'It is the night who is our enemy. With the help of the moon, desire makes great mischief in our hearts.' They said to him, 'Get a *mandar* drum and a *mridang* drum. Play to us and make us dance, and so we will not be so miserable and the night will pass quickly.'

But Sarmaha could not dance or sing. That was why he was called Sarmaha, the Shy. But when they pressed him, he went to the *karam* tree. He broke off a branch and planted it in the courtyard. He worshipped it and brought out the *mandar* drum and slinging it over his shoulder began to play. He did not know how to do it, but the drum beat of its own accord, and the songs came of themselves. The seven wives put on their ornaments and stood in a row to sing. The eldest sang the first song, in honour of the gods and their dewar. Thus Sarmaha learnt how to drum and sing. In this way the nights passed pleasantly and they worked during the day.

When they sang the Megh-rag Karma, rain fell from the clouds and the wind came to help the crops. When the crop was ready in the burning ground, the ghosts, devils and Mua and Massan came running to devour the reapers. The women sang the Muamassan-rag Karma and when the ghosts heard it they were enchanted with love and desire, and they picked up all the stones in the field and threw them into the river.

Now the husbands returned and approached the village. By the favour of Karam Sen the grains of kodon and kutki were turned into diamonds and pearls and every kind of jewel. The loads became so heavy that the bullocks sat down and could go no further. The brothers sent a messenger to say that they were coming. But it was the end of the seventh day and the wives were so lost in their dancing that they could hear nothing. The messenger returned and said, 'Your wives took no notice of me. Who knows what has happened to them? One is beating a drum, another is dancing, a third is singing songs.' The husbands were very angry; they went into the village and broke the drums. They pulled up the branch of Karam Sen and threw it into the Jhingajori River and beat their wives.

But when they returned to their camp they found nothing in their sacks but chaff and straw. When they saw that, they fell senseless to the ground. They went on to the village and told their wives what had happened. The women explained to them that they had disturbed the worship of Karam Sen. 'Until you bring a branch of the tree and dance for seven days, you will have no wealth.' They went to search for the karam branch all along the river bank, but they could not find it. They went on and came to a great forest.

The wild figs were as big as grindstones and as they passed between the trees they fell down *dam-dam*. The leaves were soft as wax. They went on into a dense bamboo grove; when the wind blew the bamboos clashed together like iron bars clashing *than-than*. But the soft young bamboos sounded *kasmas-kasmas* like a dry drum. The korkot leaves brushed against each other and frightened the old fox that hid beneath them. Tigers leapt to and fro and leopards played like dogs. The tigers thundered, the leopards grunted in their throats, the monkeys mocked, the deer jumped in the air. The long-horned gaur and wild buffaloes with every lustful hair erect stamped to and fro.

At last they came to the seven seas and sixteen streams. There was a lotus leaf and on it was the branch of Karam Sen. The brothers saw it and prayed to Bhagavan, and a wave came from the sea and brought the bough to the bank and all six brothers jumped into the water and swam out to get it. But as they approached the branch retreated from them. The boys were defeated and came back. They begged Sarmaha to get it for them. The boy sang a song of love and the sea was pleased and the waves brought the branch near the bank and the boy jumped into the water. He went right underneath and when he came up he had the branch on his head. The six brothers fell at his feet and carried the branch home.

They set it up again in the village. The women put on their ornaments and danced. When the seven days were complete their wealth returned. On the seventh day they threw the branch into the river to cool it.

Since that day the Karma has been danced, with no distinction of tribe or caste, in every village that desires prosperity.

APPENDIXES

GLOSSARY OF TRIBES AND CASTES

The following list gives a very brief account of the tribes and castes represented in this book, together with references to books and articles where more details may be obtained. Unless otherwise stated, the stories were translated from local dialects of Hindi. The Gondi, Kui and Saora stories were translated with the help of trained interpreters.

AGARIA—A word applied rather loosely to a number of small groups of primitive iron-smelters in Middle India. See *The Agaria* for a detailed account.

AHIR—The great caste of cowherds and milkmen, known also as Guala and Rawat. See Russell and Hiralal, ii, 18-38.

ASUR—A group of primitive blacksmiths, chiefly located on the Neterhat plateau of Chota Nagpur, though a few live in the Bilaspur Zamindaris. See *The Agaria.*

BAIGA—A primitive tribe, whose traditional means of livelihood was axe-cultivation and whose tribal hero is Nanga Baiga, living mainly in the Mandla, Balaghat and Bilaspur Districts of the Central Provinces. For a full account see *The Baiga.*

BHAINA—A small tribe, allied to the Baiga, inhabiting Bilaspur District and neighbouring areas. See Russell and Hiralal, ii, 225-33.

BHARIA—A tribe which is probably a branch of the great Bhar community. It is located mainly in Jubbulpore, but is also found in Chhindwara and Bilaspur, and occasionally in Mandla. See Russell and Hiralal, ii, 242-50.

BHUIYA—A large tribe distributed throughout Chota Nagpur, Orissa and Bengal. The Bhuiya from whom these stories were taken are described by Roy, *The Hill Bhuiyas.*

BINJHWAR—What has been described as a 'comparatively civilized' tribe to be found in the Raipur and Bilaspur Districts. In Mandla and Balaghat there is a Binjhwar sub-division of the Baiga. See Russell and Hiralal, ii, 329-36, and *The Baiga.*

BISON-HORN MARIA—A Gondi-speaking tribe of southern Bastar, so named from a significant head-dress worn by their male dancers. See Grigson, *The Maria Gonds*, and my *Maria Murder and Suicide.* The stories are translated from Gondi and Halbi.

BONDO—A small tribe inhabiting a remote plateau to the west of the Dudma Falls in the Koraput District of Orissa. There is a good brief account by C. von Fürer-Haimendorf: 'Megalithic Ritual among the Gadabas and Bondos of Orissa', *J.R.A.S.B.*, ix. 149-78, and my own monograph on the tribe, *Bondo Highlander*, is in the press. The Bondo have their own Austro-Asiatic language, Remo, but most of the men are bilingual and the stories in the text are translated from the Oriya.

CHOKH AGARIA—A group of blacksmiths allied to the Agaria mainly residing in Chhattisgarh. See *The Agaria*.

DEWAR—A small caste of musicians and beggars mostly located in the Chhattisgarh plain. The word Dewar is given by the Baiga to a class of their own priests. See Russell and Hiralal, ii, 472-7.

DHANWAR—A tribe of Bilaspur. Their name means 'bowman' and their hereditary occupation, now largely abandoned, is hunting. See Russell and Hiralal, ii, 488-501.

DHIMAR—A large caste of fishermen. See Russell and Hiralal, ii, 502-14.

DHOBA—A small caste, which has no connection with the Dhobi washermen, residing in the Baiga areas of Mandla District. See Russell and Hiralal, ii, 515-18.

DHULIA—A caste of workers in bamboo who earn a subsidiary livelihood by serving as musicians at weddings and funerals.

DHURWA—A tribe of southern Bastar, formerly known as Parja. They have a language of their own, but most members of the tribe now speak Halbi.

DORLA-MARIA—A rather sophisticated group of Bison-born Maria in south-eastern Bastar.

GADABA—A tribe inhabiting the Koraput District. For details, see the article by C. von Fürer-Haimendorf already mentioned under the heading BONDO. The Gadaba speak an Austro-Asiatic tongue, but are generally bilingual and their stories were translated from the Oriya.

GOGIA PARDHAN—A branch of the Pardhan tribe of the Central Provinces. See Hivale, *The Pardhans*.

GOND—The most important of the Dravidian-speaking tribes, over three million strong and widely distributed throughout Middle India. Curiously, there is no general account of them except by Russell and Hiralal, ii, 39-143. The Maria Gond, however, have been studied by Grigson and a monograph on the Gond of Hyderabad by C. von Fürer-Haimendorf is in the press. About half the tribe still speak Gondi, but the stories in the text were all recorded from Hindi-speaking Gond.

HALBA—A caste residing in Raipur, Kanker and Bastar. They are probably descendents of the old militia and their language, Halbi, is the lingua franca of Bastar.

JHORIA—A branch of the so-called Poroja of Orissa. This particular group is distinguished by its megalithic culture and admirable dancing; it is to be found in the Koraput District.

JUANG—A very primitive tribe, whose women till recently wore leaves, residing in the Keonjhar, Pal Lahara and Dhenkanal States. See my 'Notes on the Juang', *Man in India*, xxviii.

KAHAR—In the Central Provinces the name Kahar is a synonym for Dhimar. See Russell and Hiralal, iii, 291-6.

KAMAR—A small tribe inhabiting the lonely country in the Bindranawagarh and Khariar Zamindaris. These Kamar are not to be confused with the Kamar iron-workers of Bengal and Orissa. There is a brief account in Russell and Hiralal, iii, 323-30, but a useful monograph on the tribe has been written by S. C. Dube and is now in the press.

KEWAT—A caste of fisherfolk belonging to Chhattisgarh. See Russell and Hiralal, iii, 422-6.

KHUNTIA CHOWK—See CHOKH AGARIA.

KOL—A large and very mixed tribe, over two million strong, centred mainly in Chota Nagpur, but with scattered groups all over Middle India. A monograph on them has been written by Griffiths, *The Kol Tribe of Central India.*

KOND—A tribe, once notorious for its Meriah human sacrifices, located in the Ganjam and Koraput Districts of Orissa. The wildest section of the tribe is known as the Kuttia Kond and there are many other sub-divisions. A tribal heroine, Nirantali, who may be the Earth Mother in human form, figures frequently in the stories. The translations were made from Kui and Oriya. See Thurston, iii, 356-415.

KORKU—A tribe of about 200,000 individuals living in the west of the Satpura plateau. See Russell and Hiralal, iii, 550-70.

KOYA—A Gondi-speaking tribe living in the Godaveri area; in Koraput District they closely resemble the Bison-horn Maria. The stories were translated from the Gondi. See Thurston, iv, 37-74.

KURUK—A tribe of fishermen in Bastar.

LANJHIA SAORA—A branch of the great Saora tribe inhabiting the hills of Koraput and Ganjam Districts in Orissa. They have a complex religious system and in their vast pantheon is a class of deified heroes called Kittung. The word, however, is often used in the singular to denote the Creator. The stories were told in the Saora language. See Thurston, vi, 304-47 and G. V. Sitapati, 'The Soras and their Country', *J. Andhra Hist. Res. Soc.*, xii-xiv.

LOHAR—The Hindu caste of blacksmiths. See Russell and Hiralal, iv, 120-26 and *The Agaria.*

Muria—A tribe of northern Bastar distinguished for its elaborate dormitory (*ghotul*) system. See *The Muria and their Ghotul.*

Ojha—A Gond subtribe of soothsayers and minstrels. See Russell and Hiralal, iv, 296-8.

Panka—A caste of weavers. See Russell and Hiralal, iv, 324-9.

Raja Muria—A rather sophisticated group of mixed Maria and Muria in the Jagdalpur Tahsil of Bastar.

Rajnengi Pardhan—A group of Pardhan living mainly in the Mandla District and its neighbourhood. See Hivale, *The Pardhans.*

Takala Saora—A sub-section of Hill Saora which specializes in weaving and basketry.

Yernga Kol—A group of Kol living in Bonai State.

BOOK-LIST

This is not a list of books dealing with Indian mythology or even of all those quoted in the text. It is simply a reference bibliography for the convenience of readers and includes only those works which recur throughout the book, and which are described in the text either by author's name or by his name and short title. It is independent of the special bibliography at the end of Chapter XVIII, which is confined to works that contain some specific reference to the Vagina Dentata legend.

References to my own books are by title only.

AGARWAL, D. D.—' Ethnographic Notes on the Cheros ', *Man in India* ix (1929).

ANDREWS, F. H.—' The Elephant in Industry and Art ', *The Journal of Indian Art*, x.

BASU, M. N.—*The Bunas of Bengal* (Calcutta, 1939).

BHATTACHARJEE, P. N.—' Folk-Custom and Folklore of the Sylhet District ', *Man in India*, x (1930).

BODDING, P. O.—*Studies in Santal Medicine and Connected Folklore* (Calcutta, 1925).

BOMPAS, C. H.—*Folklore of the Santal Parganas* (London, 1909).

BONNERJEA, B.—' Materials for the Study of Garo Ethnology ', *The Indian Antiquary*, lviii.

BROWN, A. R.—*The Andaman Islanders* (Cambridge, 1922).

CAMPBELL, A.—' The Traditions of the Santals ', *J. B. O. R. S.*, ii.

CAMPBELL, J. M.—' Notes on the Spirit Basis of Belief and Custom *The Indian Antiquary*, xxvi (1897).

CARPENTER, J. E.—*Theism in Medieval India* (London, 1921).

CENSUS OF INDIA, 1901—References under this heading in the text are to *Census of India*, 1901, xiii, Part I (Report on the Central Provinces, by R. V. Russell).

CENSUS OF INDIA, 1931—References under this heading in the text are to *Census of India*, 1931, i, Part III B.

CROOKE, W.—*The Popular Religion and Folk-Lore of Northern India* (Westminister, 1896).

CUNNINGHAM, A.—*The Archeological Survey of India* (Calcutta, 1871-87)

DALTON, E. T.—*Descriptive Ethnology of Bengal* (Calcutta, 1872).

DAS GUPTA, S.—*A History of Indian Philosophy* (Cambridge, 1940).

DEHON, P.—*Religion and Customs of the Uraons* (Calcutta, 1906).

DOWSON, J.—*A Classical Dictionary of Hindu Mythology* (6th edition London, 1928).

DRACOTT, A. E.—*Simla Village Tales* (London, 1906).

DUTT, M. N.—*Vishnupuranam* (Calcutta, 1894).

ELWIN, VERRIER—*The Baiga* (London, 1939).
The Agaria (O.U.P., Bombay, 1942).
Maria Murder and Suicide (O.U.P., Bombay, 1943).
Folk-Tales of Mahakoshal (O.U.P., Bombay, 1944).
Folk-Songs of Chhattisgarh (O.U.P., Bombay, 1946).
The Muria and their Ghotul (O.U.P., Bombay, 1947).

ELWIN, VERRIER and HIVALE, SHAMRAO.—*Folk-Songs of the Maikal Hills* (O.U.P., Bombay, 1944).

EMENEAU, M. B.—*Kota Texts* (California, 1944-46).
'Some Origin Stories of the Todas and Kotas', *J.A.O.S.*, lxii (1943).

ENTHOVEN, R. E.—*The Folklore of Bombay* (Oxford, 1924).

FITZPATRICK, W.—'Folklore of Birds and Beasts of India' *J. Bom. Nat. Hist. Soc.*, xxviii (1921-2), 562-5.

FORSYTH, J.—*The Highlands of Central India* (London, 1871).

FRAZER, J. G.—*Myths of the Origin of Fire* (London, 1930).

FURER-HAIMENDORF, C.von—*The Chenchus* (Hyderabad, 1943).

GARIOLA, T. D.—'Folk-Lore of Garhwal', *The Vishvabharati Quarterly*, iv (1926).

GORER, G.—*Himalayan Village* (London, 1938).

GRIFFITHS, W. G.—'Folklore of the Kols', *Man in India*, xxiv (1944). Dr Griffiths has since included this article in his book, *The Kol Tribe of Central India* (Calcutta, 1946), but the references in the text are to his article.

GRIGSON, W. V.—*The Maria Gonds of Bastar* (Oxford, 1938).

GURDON, P. R. T.—*The Khasis* (London, 1914).

HALDAR, S.—'Ho Folk-Lore', *J.B.O.R.S.*, viii (1922).

HELD, G. J.—*The Mahabharata* (London, 1935).

HISLOP, S.—*Papers Relating to the Aboriginal Tribes of the Central Provinces* (Nagpur, 1866).

HIVALE, SHAMRAO.—*The Pardhans of the Upper Narbada Valley* (Bombay, 1946).

HOFFMANN, J. and van EMELEN, A.—*Encyclopaedia Mundarica* (Patna, 1930-41).

HUME, R. E.—*The Thirteen Principal Upanishads* (Oxford, 1931).

HUTTON, J. H.—*The Angami Nagas* (London, 1921).
The Sema Nagas (London, 1921).

IYER, L. A. KRISHNA.—*The Travancore Tribes and Castes* (Trivandrum, 1937-41).

KOPPERS, W.—'Bhagwan, the supreme deity of the Bhils,' *Anthropos*, Tome xxxv-xxxvi (1940-41).

LEITNER, G. W.—' Manners and Customs of the Dards ', *The Indian Antiquary*, i, 90.
LEWISON, R. G.—' Folk-lore of the Assamese ', *J.R.A.S.B.*, v (1939).

MACDONELL, A. A.—*Hymns from the Rigveda* (Calcutta, N.D.).
Vedic Mythology (Strassburg, 1897).
MARSHALL, J.—*Mohenjo-daro and the Indus Civilization* (London, 1931).
M'CRINDLE, J. W.—*Ancient India* (Westminster, 1901).
MEYER, J. J.—*Sexual Life in Ancient India* (London, 1930).
MILLS, J. P.—*The Lhota Nagas* (London, 1922).
The Ao Nagas (London, 1926).
The Rengma Nagas (London, 1937).
MONIER WILLIAMS.—*Brahmanism and Hinduism* (London, 1891).
MUIR, J.—*Original Sanskrit Texts* (London, 1858-72).
MUKHERJEA, C.—*The Santals* (Calcutta, 1943).

NANJUNDAYYA, H. V. and ANANTHAKRISHNA IYER, L. K.—*The Mysore Tribes and Castes* (Mysore, 1928-35).
NORTH INDIAN NOTES AND QUERIES—(Allahabad, 1891-6).

O'MALLEY, L. S. S.—*Gazetteer of the Ganga District* (Calcutta, 1906).

PARRY, N. E.—*The Lakhers* (London, 1932).
PENZER, N. M.—*The Ocean of Story* (London, 1924-28).
PLAYFAIR, A.—*The Garos* (London, 1909).

RAFY, Mrs.—*Folk-Tales of the Khasis* (London, 1920).
RAGLAN, LORD.—*The Hero* (London, 1936).
RISLEY, H. H.—*The Tribes and Castes of Bengal* (Calcutta, 1891).
RIVERS, W. H. R.—*The Todas* (London, 1906).
ROSE, H. A.—*A Glossary of the Tribes and Castes of the Panjab and North-West Frontier Province* (Lahore, 1919).
ROY, SARAT CHANDRA—*The Mundas and their Country* (Calcutta, 1912).
The Oraons of Chota Nagpur (Ranchi, 1915).
The Birhors (Ranchi, 1925).
Oraon Religion and Customs (Ranchi, 1928).
The Hill Bhuiyas of Orissa (Ranchi, 1936).
' The Divine Myths of the Mundas ', *J.B.O.R.S.*, ii (1916).
ROY, S. C. and R. C.—*The Kharias* (Ranchi, 1937).
RUSSELL, R. V. and HIRALAL—*The Tribes and Castes of the Central Provinces of India* (London, 1916).

SAWE, K. J.—*The Warlis* (Bombay, 1945).
SELIGMAN, C. G. and B. Z.—*The Veddas* (Cambridge, 1911).
SHAW, W.—' Notes on the Thadon Kukis ', *J.A.S.B.*, xxiv (1928).
STOCKS, C.deB.—' Folklore and Customs of the Lepchas of Sikkim ', *J.A.S.B.*,xxi(1925).

TEMPLE, R. C.—*The Legends of the Panjab* (London and Bombay, 1884-1901).

TICKELL, LIEUT.—' Memoir on the Hodesum (improperly called Kolehan) ', *J.A.S.B.*, ix (1840).

THURSTON, E.—*Castes and Tribes of Southern India* (Madras, 1909).

TRENCH, C. G. C.—*Grammar of Gondi* (Madras, 1919).

UPRETI, G. D.—*Proverbs and Folklore of Kumaun and Garhwal* (Lodiana, 1894).

VENKATASWAMI, M. N.—' Eclipse Tales among the Telugus ', *The Indian Antiquary*, xxxiv (1905).

Woman.—By H. H. Ploss, M. Bartels and P. Bartels. Edited by J. Dingwall (London, 1935).

MOTIF-INDEX

MOTIF-INDEX

This Motif-Index is based on Stith Thompson's ***Motif-Index of Folk-Literature*** (Helsinki, 1932-6). To classify the 537 tales, each containing from half a dozen to a score of motifs, in ***Myths of Middle India***, according to Stith Thompson's generous and detailed anyalsis, would require at least two hundred pages. I have, therefore, simplified the cataloguing as far as possible. I have omitted a few sections (P. Society; U. The Nature of Life; V. Religion; W. Traits of Character; X. Humour), which are not important for this book, altogether. I have had to collect many references, which should have been analysed in detail, under single heads; such themes, for example, as those connected with Transformation, Dreams, Curses, Mutilations, might each be broken down into a score of subsidiary motifs. I have omitted all cross-references.

But although the Motif-Index as printed here is only a skeleton, it will be found serviceable enough, for all the main motifs are grouped under the proper headings, and the reader who wishes to investigate any topic in detail can, by the turning of a few pages, analyse it for himself.

Motifs marked with an asterisk are not represented in Stith Thompson's Index and their numbers are not his, but mine. They will have to be revised later to correspond with numbers in other classifications.

In the fifth book of this series, which will contain 1000 tales from Orissa and which probably will have to spread itself over two volumes, I hope to make a complete Motif-Index with references to all the volumes of 'Specimens of the Oral Literature of Middle India', and in this every motif will be examined in detail.

A. MYTHOLOGICAL MOTIFS

A0—A99. CREATOR

A10. **Nature of the Creator.** Chap. I and passim
A15.* Potter as creator. i, 12
A30. **Creator's Companions**
A34. Birds as creator's servants. i, 1 ; i, 4 ; i, 9 ; i, 14 ; i, 15 ; i, 16 ; i, 22 ; i, 25 ; i, 26 ; i, 29 ; xiv, 2
A34.1.* Animals as creator's servants. i,2 ; i, 4 ; i, 8 ; i, 16 ; i, 24 ; i, 25 ; xx, 16

A100—A499. GODS

A100. **Deity**
A101. Supreme god. Chap. I passim
A110. Origin of the gods
A111. Mother of the gods. xx. 1
A112. Birth of gods. i, 1 ; i, 32 ; ii, 7 ; iii, 7 ; iii, 11 ; iii, 13 ; iii, 24 ; v, 14 ; vi, 1 ; ix, 3 ; xi, 6 ; xi, 31 ; xii, 2 ; xii, 41 ; xii, 101 ; xiii, 9 ; xv, 3 ; xvii, 4 ; xix, 10 ; xx, 1 ; xx, 3-6 ; xx, 8 ; xx, 10 ; xx, 11 ; xx, 12 ; xx, 16 ; xxii, 7 ; xxiii, 10
A113. Totemistic gods. viii. 14
A120. **Nature and appearance of the gods**
A123. Monstrous gods
123.6.* Goddess with one-and-a-half buttocks. iv. 11
123.7.* God with seven heads and thirteen eyes. xx. 1
A128.1. Blind God. The Wind-god is blind. iii, 11 ; iii, 13
A132. God in animal form. xvii. 13
A133. Giant god. The typical giant god in tribal opinion is Bhimsen (Bhimul, Bhimo). i, 11 ; i, 38 ; ii, 12 ; iii, 3 ; iii, 4 ; iii, 13 ; iii, 14 ; iii, 25 ; iii, 26 ; iii, 31 ; v, 7 ; vii, 11 ; vii, 23 ; viii, 11 ; xii, 78 ; xiv, 2 ; xv, 9 ; xvi, 1 ; xvi, 8 ; xix, 21 ; xx, 11 ; xx, 12 ; xxi, 11 ;
A200. **God of the Upper World**
A220. Sun-god. i, 20 ; i, 33
A240. Moon-god
240.1. Moon-goddess. i, 33
A282. Wind-god. ii, 12; iii, 7 ; iii, 11 ; iii, 13
A283. Cloud-god. ii, 6 ; iii, 26 : vi, 17
A287. Rain-god. iii, 14 ; iii, 26 ; vii, 11 ; xix, 21 ; xx, 11
A300. **God of the Under World**
A310. God of the world of the dead. iii, 2; xii, 62; xii, 100; xix, 7; xix, 8; xix, 9; xix, 11 ; xix, 13
A400. **God of earth**
A401. Mother Earth. i, 1 ; i, 21 ; i, 22 ; vii, 20 ; x, 14 ; x, 21 ; xi, 31 ; xii, 3 ; xii, 60 ; xii, 61 ; xii, 92 ; xiii, 1 ; xvii, 6 ; xviii, 25 ; xxiii, 5
A430. **God of vegetation**
A433.1. Corn-god (goddess). xx, 6 ; xxiii, 3
433.2.* The Seven Grain Sisters. ii, 4 ; ii, 14
A435.1.* Bamboo goddess. i, 1 ; xi, 31
A460. **Gods of abstractions**
A473.1. Goddess of wealth (Lakshmi). ii, 14
A475.2.* Marriage-god (Dulha Deo). xx, 4 ; xx, 8 ; xx, 10
A493. God of fire. i, 1

A600—A1199. COSMOGONY AND COSMOLOGY

A600—A699. THE UNIVERSE

A600. Creation of the universe
A625. World parents ; Sky-father and earth-mother. iii, 13
625.2. Raising of the sky. ii, 8 ; iii, 5

A700—A799. THE HEAVENS

A700. Creation of the heavenly bodies
A701. Creation of the sky. iii, 2
701.2.* Origin of clouds. iii, 1 ; iii, 2 ; iii, 3 ; iii, 8
701.3.* Nature of clouds (covered with skin). ii, 4
A702. Nature of the sky
702.4.* Why the sky is blue. ii, 4 ; iii, 4
A710. Creation of the Sun. Chap. II, passim
A711.2. Sun as a cannibal i, 20 ; ii, 1
A713.1.* Sun and moon from belly of a fish. ii, 2
A714.4. Sun and moon metal mirrors in sky. ii, 9
714.5.* Sun as grindstone full of fire, iv, 2
714.6.* Sun and moon as spangle which falls from creator's forehead into his own urine. ii, 5
714.7.* Sun and moon as eyes of Rama which he tore out after his brother's death. ii, 10
A715.2.* Sun and moon born from a goddess impregnated by the wind. ii, 4
715.3.* Sun and moon born from an ogre. xxii. 1.
715.4.* Sun and moon from breasts of Mother Earth. i, 17
A717.* Hero makes sun and moon from tree and sends them alternately into sky. ii, 3
717.1.* Hero makes sun and moon from tree and vivifies them with blood of creator's son. ii. 8
717.2.* Sun from head of youth offered in sacrifice. i, 3
A720. Nature and condition of the sun
720.1.* Formerly seven suns. i, 20
720.2.* Formerly great heat of sun causes distress to mankind. ii, 1 ; ii, 3 ; ii, 9
A721.3.* Sun shut up in pit. ii. 7
A722. Sun's night journey
722.6.* Sun and moon to remain half their time in Under World. ii, 11
A724. Chariot of the sun. ii. 6
A728. Sun caught in snare
728.3.* Sun visits earth in form of black bull, caught by man, thus causing night. ii, 3
A729.* Sun as king of sky and earth. ii. 4
A736. Sun and moon as man and woman. ii, 1 ; ii, 7 ; ii, 9
736.2. Sun-brother and moon-sister. ii, 4
736.4. Sun and moon married. ii, 2 ; ii, 5, ii, 9
736.6.* Sun and moon as sisters, daughters of Sky-god. ii, 6
736.7.* Sun and moon as friends. ii, 14
736.8.* Sun cursed by moon, ii, 1
736.9.* Sun's affection for human girl rouses moon's jealousy. ii, 7
736.10.* Creator separates sun and moon to prevent birth of more stars. ii, 9
A737. Causes of eclipses. iii, 11-15 : xxi, 14
A738.* Reason for variations in seasonal heat of sun. ii, 1
A739.* Why the sun is red, ii, 8
A740. Creation of the moon. Chap. II, passim and compare A713.1 ; A 714.4; A714.6 ; A714.7 ; A715.2 ; A715.3 : A715.4 : A717 ; A717.1
740.1.* Chest of sacrificed youth becomes the moon. i, 3
740.2.* Moon as grinder which brings fire out of the sun. iv, 12

A750. Condition and nature of the moon
A751.6.* Mark of her mother's hand to be seen on moon's shoulder. ii, 4
751.7.* Mark of tiger's paw on moon. i, 3
A753.1.* Moon married to son of Sky-god. ii, 4
A754.1.* Moon buried in pit. ii, 9
A755. Causes of moon's phases
755.4.* Result of blessing that moon's beauty should be 'always changing and always new'. ii, 4
755.5.* Sun, jealous, cuts moon's bead into pieces (phases). ii, 6
755.6.* Moon's warning caused by menstrual period. ii, 6 ; xii, 60 ; xii, 73
A759.* Miscellaneous motifs
759.1.* Moon deceives sun. i, 20 ; ii, 1 ; ii, 9
759.2.* Sun and moon as divine hero's wedding presents. ii, 11
759.3.* Why the moon is pale. ii, 4 ; ii, 8
A760. Creation of the stars
A763. Stars from objects thrown into sky. i, 4 ; ii, 16 ; ii, 17 ; iii, 1 ; iii, 3
A764.1. Stars as children of the moon. ii, 2
764.1.1. Stars as children of sun eaten by their father. ii, 1 ; ii, 9
764.2.* Stars as drops of the moon's blood. ii, 6
A790. The heavenly lights
A791. Origin of the rainbow. iii, 29 ; iii, 30 ; iii, 31 ; xviii, 41

A800—A899. THE EARTH

A800. Creation of the earth. Chap. I, passim
A810. Primaeval water. i, 2 ; i, 3 ; i, 4 ; i, 9 ; i, 12 ; i, 16 ; i, 18 ; i, 23 ; i, 30
A811. Earth brought up from bottom of primaeval water. i, 15
A812. Earth Diver. i, 1 ; i, 8 ; i, 16 ; i, 27
A813. Raft in primaeval sea (Creator seated on lotus). i, 16 ; i, 23
A814. Earth from object thrown on primaeval water. i, 1 ; i, 14 ; i, 22 ; i, 25
814.6.* Earth from saliva of primaeval potter spreading on surface of water. i, 12
A818.* Earth from worm scratched by creator's nails. i, 9
818.1.* Earth excreted by worm. i, 29
A819.* Earth made by drying up of primaeval water. i, 14 ; i, 20 ; i, 33
A820.* Earth sets like curds. i, 32
A821.* Earth made of lac. i, 1
A822.* Earth made by mud shaken from back of primaeval boar. i, 4-8
A823.* Earth made by cups of earth placed on spider's web. i, 16
A824.* Earth made by transformation of broken ground. i, 26
A825.* Earth made by first couple dancing on bit of cloth laid on water. xxii, 4
A830. Creation of earth by creator
A831.1. Earth from body of son of deity. i, 2 ; i, 3. Cp. i, 23
831.2. Earth from giant's body. i, 17 ; i, 47
831.3.* By sacrifice of son and daughter of first couple. i, 21 ; i, 22
831.4.* By murder of first brother and sister. i, 23 ; i, 31
A840. Support of the earth
A841.3.* Twelve iron pillars steady the earth. i, 1
A842.2.* Goddess standing on her head supports earth, i, 2
842.3.* Old woman supports earth on her head. i, 11 ; i, 28
844.4.* Earth supported on vast number of birds' legs. i, 10
A850. Changes in the earth
A856. Hardening the earth. i, 12 ; i, 16
856.1.* Steadying the earth. i, 1 ; i, 10 ; i, 11 ; i, 15 ; i, 16 ; i, 18 ; i, 21 ; i, 30 ; i, 32 ; iii, 3.

A900—A999. TOPOGRAPHICAL FEATURES OF THE EARTH

A930. Origin of streams. i, 18 ; i, 25 ; i, 29 ; iii, 22 ; iii, 23 ; iii, 24 ; iii, 25 ; xiv, 1
A933. River from urine of goddess (giantess). iii, 24

A950. **Origin of the land**
A951.1.* Contours of land caused by cult-hero driving harrow. i, 29
A960. **Creation of mountains.** i, 2 ; i, 5 ; i, 19 ; i, 24 ; i, 25 ; iii, 11
A970. **Origin of rocks and stones.** i, 2 ; i, 3 ; i, 17 ; i, 23 ; i, 30 : xviii, 19

A1000—A1099. WORLD CALAMITIES

A1000. **World catastrophe**
A1001. Series of world catastrophes. i, 1
A1005. Preservation of life during world calamity. i, 4-9 ; i, 13 ; i, 14 ; i, 15 ; i, 20 ; i, 21 ; i, 25 ; i, 26 ; i, 27 ; i, 33
A1006. Renewal of world after world calamity. i, 4-9 ; i, 14 ; i, 15 ; i, 20 ; i, 21 ; i, 25 ; i, 26 ; i, 27 ; i, 33
1006.1. New race from single pair after world calamity. i, 4 ; i, 8 ; i, 9 ; i, 13 ; i, 14 ; i, 21 ; i, 25 ; i, 26 ; i, 27 ; i, 33
1006.2. New race from incest after world calamity. i, 3 ; i, 4 ; i, 8 ; i, 9 ; i, 13 ; i, 14 ; i, 21 ; i, 23 ; i, 24 ; i, 26 ; xii, 81 ; xii, 82 ; xii, 83 ; xii, 85
1006.2.4.* New race from union of girl and rat. i, 27
A1010. **Deluge.** i, 4 ; i, 5 ; i, 6 ; i, 8 ; i, 9 ; i, 14 ; i, 15 ; i, 20 ; i, 21 ; i, 24 ; i, 25 ; i, 26 ; i, 27 ; i, 29 ; xxii, 4
A1020. **Escape from deluge.** i, 4 ; i, 5 ; i, 6 ; i, 8 ; i, 9 ; i, 14 ; i, 15 ; i, 20 ; i, 21 ; i, 24 ; i, 25 ; i, 26 ; i, 27 ; i, 29 ; xxii, 4
A1030. **World-fire.** i, 1 ; i, 33
A1038. Men hide from world-fire and renew race. i, 33
A1090. **World calamities : miscellaneous motifs**
A1094.* World devoured by ogre. i, 15
A1095.* World turned topsy-turvy and eaten by an earth-worm, i, 29

A1100—A1199. ESTABLISHMENT OF NATURAL ORDER

A1110. **Establishment of present order : waters.** i, 23 ; i, 29 ; iii, 22-25 ; xiv, 1
A1120. **Establishment of present order : winds.** ii, 7 ; iii, 6-13
A1128.* Wind is blind. iii, 11 ; iii, 13
A1130. **Establishment of present order : weather phenomena**
A1131. Origin of rain. iii, 26 ; iii, 27
A1133.* Origin of mist. ii, 4
A1141. Origin of lightning. i, 17 ; ii, 6 ; ii, 11 ; iii, 14-20
A1142. Origin of thunder. ii, 6 ; iii, 14-21
A1145. Cause of earthquakes. i, 2 ; i, 11 ; i, 28 ; vii, 17 ; xii, 60 ; xix, 1
A1150. **Determination of seasons.** ii, 1 ; iii, 26 ; iii, 28
A1170. **Origin of night and day.** ii, 3 ; ii, 8

A1200—A1699. CREATION AND ORDERING OF HUMAN LIFE

A1200—A1299. CREATION OF MAN

A1211. **Creation of man by creator**
A1211. Man made from creator's body
1211.5.* Man made from dirt rubbed from creator's (hero's) body. i, 3 ; i, 30 ; i, 33 ; v, 10 ; vi, 10 ; ix, 4 ; xii, 66 ; xvi, 6 ; xxi, 3
A1216. Man as offspring of creator. i, 23 ; i, 25 ; i, 29
A1220. **Creation of man through evolution**
A1221. Mankind from unusual primaeval mating. i, 17 ; i, 32
A1224.4.* Mankind born from a cow. i, 13
A1230. **Emergence or descent of first man to earth**
A1234. Mankind emerges from ground. i, 1 ; xii, 82 ; xiii, 2
A1240. **Man made from mineral substance**
A1241. Man made from clay (earth). xii, 73
1241.4.* Man made from earth reddened with blood of human sacrifice. i, 3

A1245.5.* Man born from mountains. i, 19
A1250. **Man made from vegetable substance**
A1251. Creation of man from tree. xviii, 21
A1252.1.* Mankind from vivified wooden image. xiv, 8
A1270. **Primaeval human pair.** Chap. I, passim ; ii, 2 ; xii, 81 ; xii, 82 ; xii, 83 ; xii, 85.

A1300—A1399. ORDERING OF HUMAN LIFE

A1310. **Arrangement of man's bodily attributes**
1310.2.* Assembling the body. xii, 1 ; xii, 2
1310.3.* Why men are clothed in skin. xii, 73
1310.4.* Why women have marks on the belly. xii, 36 ; xii, 96
A1311. Origin of hands and feet. xii, 2
A1313. Origin of sex-organs
1313.1. Origin of male sex-organs. xii, 29-43
1313.2. Origin of female sex-organs. xii, 31 ; xii, 36 ; xii, 44-51
1313.2.1.* Origin of clitoris. xii, 52-57
1313.3. Misplaced genitalia. xii, 31 ; xii, 34 ; xii, 45 ; xii, 46 ; xii, 50 ; xil, 51
1313.4. Origin of women's breasts. xviii, 27
A1315. Origin of hair and beard. xii, 3-13
A1316. Origin of facial features. xii, 2
1316.2.* Why men blink. xii, 23 ; xii, 24
A1317.* Origin of urine and excreta. ii, 5 ; xii, 24 ; xii, 97-101
A1319. Origin of other bodily attributes
1319.3.* Origin of sweat. xii, 14 ; xii, 15 ; xii, 16 ; xii, 17
1319.4.* Origin of sneezing. xii, 22
1319.5.* Origin of itching. xix, 2
1319.6.* Origin of the sensation of tickling. xii, 18 ; xii, 19 ; xii, 20 ; xii, 21
1319.7.* Origin of laughter. xii, 27 ; xii, 28 ; xvi, 3
1319.8.* Origin of sleep. vi, 4 ; xii, 25 ; xix, 15 ; xx, 13
1319.9.* Origin of dreams. xx, 14 ; xx, 15
A1330. **Beginnings of trouble for man**
A1335. Origin of death. Chap. XIX, passim ; ii, 5 ; xii, 62
A1337. Origin of disease. Chap. XVII, passim ; i, 19 ; x, 22 ; xii, 1 ; xii, 27 ; xii, 66 ; xix, 10 ; xxi, 2.
A1344. Origin of tears and sighs. xii, 25 ; xii, 26 ; xii, 28
A1345. Origin of hunger. xii, 98
1345.1.* Origin of thirst. xii, 25
A1350. **Origin of sex functions**
A1351. Origin of childbirth. xii, 64 ; xii, 86-96
A1355. Origin of menstruation. xii, 58-76
1355.3.* Previously men menstruated. xii, 7 ; xii, 59
A1356.* Origin of sexual intercourse. iv, 11 ; xii, 77-85 ; xix, 1
1356.1.* Former intercourse by navel. xii, 70 ; xviii, 25

A1400—A1499. ACQUISITION OF CULTURE

A1410. **Acquisition of livable environment**
A1414. Origin of fire. Chap. IV, passim ; xvi, 6
A1420. **Acquisition of food supply.** ii, 4 ; ii, 14 ; Chap. XIV, passim
A1422. Assignment of edible animals. xi, 35 ; xiv, 10 ; xvi, 11 ; xiv, 12 ; xiv, 13
A1423. Acquisition of vegetables. xii, 92 ; xviii, 4 ; xxii, 7
A1427. Acquisition of sprituous liquors. Chap. XVI, passim
1427.2.* Discovered when birds get drunk. xvi, 1 ; xvi, 8 ; xxi, 11
1427.3.* Discovered by Rain-god (Bhimsen). xxi, 11
A1430. **Acquisition of other necessities**
A1432. Origin of iron. v, 2 ; v, 5 ; v, 10
A1433.2.* Origin of gold and silver. v, 1 ; v, 2 ; v, 3 ; v, 4 ; v, 7 ; v, 8 ; v, 12
1433.3.* Origin of brass. v, 7

1433.4.* Origin of copper. v, 2
1433.5.* Origin of marble, v, 7
A1434.* Origin of salt. v, 6 ; v, 9 ; v, 11 ; v, 13 ; v, 14
A1435. Acquisition of habitations. i, 7
A1440. **Acquisition of crafts**
A1441. Acquisition of agriculture. i, 18 ; i, 24 ; i, 25 ; ii, 4 ; xiv, 6 ; xxii, 9
1441.1.*. Origin of ploughing. iii, 3 ; v, 10 ; x, 20 ; xiii, 3 ; xiii, 8
A1446. Acquisition of tools. i, 2 ; i, 25 ; iv, 1 ; v, 10 ; v, 12 ; x, 20 ; xiii, 1 ; xiii, 2 ; xiii, 8.
1446.2. Origin of the axe, xiii, 10
1446.3.* Origin of the ox-goad. xiii, 8
1446.4.* Origin of the adze. xiii, 8
1446.5.* Acquisition of household implements
1446.5.1.* Origin of the broom. xiii, 5 ; xiii, 10 ; xiii, 14 ; xiii, 15
1446.5.2.* Origin of the pestle. xiii, 1 ; xiii, 7 ; xiii, 9 ; xiii, 12
1446.5.3.* Origin of the grindstone. xiii, 4 ; xiii, 6 ; xiii, 7 ; xiii, 9 ; xiii, 11
1446.5.4.* Origin of the winnowing-fan. xiii, 9 ; xiii, 10 ; xiii, 12 ; xiv, 4
1446.5.5.* Origin of baskets. xiii, 10 ; xiii, 12
1446.6.* Origin of the oil-press. xiii, 4
A1447. Origin of metal-working. xiii, 2
1447.1.* Origin of the bellows. i, 15
A1451. Origin of pottery. iv ; 9
A1453. Origin of cloth-making. xxii, 1 ; xxii, 2
1453.2. Origin of weaving. xxii, 1 ; xxii, 2
1454.3.* Origin of leaf-dress. i, 18
A1455. Origin of cooking. iv, 2 ; iv, 3 ; iv, 8 ; iv, 9 ; iv, 10 ; iv, 13 ; iv, 14
1455.1.* Origin of the domestic hearth. xiii, 13 ; xvi, 4
A1456. Origin of distilling. Chap. XVI, passim ; vii, 27; xv, 8 ; xvi, 4 ; xix, 9 ; xxi, 13 ; xxiii, 8
A1457. Origin of fishing. ix, 4 ; xiii, 11 ; xxi, 4
A1460. **Acquisition of arts**
A1461. Acquisition of music. xiii, 3
1461.1. Origin of violin (fiddle). i, 1 ; xx, 6
A1462.* Origin of dancing. Chap. XXIII, passim ; xvi, 3 ; xvi, 8
A1465. Origin of decorative art
1465.1. Origin of tattooing. xxii, 10
1465.2. Origin of ornaments. v, 4 ; v, 5 ; xii, 101 ; xxii, 3 ; xxiii, 6

A1500—A1599. ORIGIN OF CUSTOMS

A1540. **Origin of religious ceremonials**
A1541. Origin of religious feasts. x ; 22 ; xx, 6 ; xxiii, 9
A1542. Origin of religious dances. Chap. xxiii, passim
A1545. Origin of sacrifices. x, 9 ; x, 21 ; xi, 6 ; xx, 3 ; xx, 4 ; xx, 5 ; xx, 10
1545.2.* Animal substituted for human sacrifice. xxiii, 5
A1550. **Origin of customs of courtship and marriage**
A1552.* Origin of the village dormitory. xiii, 3
A1555. Origin of marriage. xxii, 5 ; xxii, 7
1555.1.* The serving marriage. ii, 6 ; ii, 11 ; iii, 15 ; xii, 40 ; xv, 17 ; xvi, 5 ; xxi, 8 ; xxii, 8
A1590. **Origin of other customs**
A1591. Origin of burial. xix, 3 ; xix, 23
A1592. Origin of cremation. xix, 17 ; xix, 23
A1595.* Origin of covenanted friendships. xxii, 6

A1600—A1699. DISTRIBUTION AND DIFFERENTIATION OF PEOPLES

A1610. **Origin of various tribes**
A1611. Origin of particular tribes

1611.4.* Agaria. i, 1 ; v, 10
1611.5.* Bhuiya. i, 3
1611.6.* Bondo. i, 9
1611.7.* Dhimar. ix, 4
1611.8.* Gadaba. i, 13 ; i, 14
1611.9.* Gond. i, 17 ; i, 32 : xiv, 7
1611.10.* Juang. i, 18
1611.11.* Kamar. i, 15
1611.12.* Panka. ix, 5 ; xxii, 1
1611.13.* Pano. xxii, 2.
1611.14.* Pardhan. i, 32 ; xx, 6
1611.15.* Saora. i, 24 ; i, 25 ; i, 27
1611.16.* Sundi. xvi, 7
1611.17.* Various. i, 17 ; i, 30

A1640. **Origin of tribal subdivisions.** i, 32 ; viii, 13 ; xi, 35
A1650. **Origin of different classes**
A1651.* Attitude to untouchables. xv, 15
A1660. **Characteristics of various peoples**
A1688.1.* Why Bhuiya yoke the cow and the bullock together to the plough. xiii, 3
1688.2.* Why Agaria are not afraid of fire. i, 1
1688.3.* Why the Gond and Baiga are omnivorous. xvi, 13
1688.4.* Why Saora wave axes and swords, and shout while dancing. xxii, 3
1688.5.* Why the Kamar offer liquor to gods and spirits. xvi, 6. Why Kond do so. xvi, 7

A1700—A2199. CREATION OF ANIMAL LIFE

A1800—A1899. CREATION OF MAMMALS

A1800. **Creation of mammals.** Chap. XI, passim
A1811. Creation of cat. xi, 8 ; xi, 9
A1815.* Creation of tiger. i, 2 ; i, 3 ; i, 32 ; xi, 8 ; xi, 34 ; xi, 35 ; xi, 36 ; xi, 37 ; xi, 38 ; xiv, 11 ; xix, 7 ; xx, 1
A1831. Creation of dog. xi, 13 ; xi, 14 ; xi, 15 ; xi, 16 ; xi, 17 ; xx, 1
A1832. Creation of fox. xi, 21
1832.1.* Creation of jackal. xi, 27 ; xi, 28 ; xxi, 6
A1833.1.* Creation of hyena. xi, 25 ; xi, 26 ; xi, 36
A1836. Creation of bear. xi, 2 ; xi, 3 ; xi, 4 ; xi, 36
A1854. Creation of rat. xi, 8
A1859.* Creation of mongoose. xx, 1
A1861. Creation of monkey. xi, 29 ; xi, 30 ; xi, 31
A1871. Creation of hog (pig, boar). i, 25 ; xi, 5 ; xi, 32 ; xvi, 10
A1873. Creation of camel, xi, 7
A1877. Creation of cow. xiii, 6
A1878. Creation of bison (buffalo). i, 25 ; xi, 6
A1881. Creation of horse. xi, 23 ; xi, 24
A1884. Creation of sheep. xi, 33
A1885. Creation of goat. xi, 22
A1887. Creation of elephant. iii, 22 ; xi, 18 ; xi, 19 ; xi, 20
A1888.* Creation of deer. xi, 10 ; xi, 11 ; xi, 12
A1895. Creation of bat. xviii, 26

A1900—A1999. CREATION OF BIRDS

A1900. **Creation of birds.** Chap. X, passim
A1919. Creation of crow. i, 1 ; i, 9 ; i, 15 ; i, 16 ; i, 25 ; iii, 8 ; x, 7 ; x, 8
A1927. Creation of sparrow. v, 1
A1931. Creation of vulture. x, 23 ; x, 24

A1937. Creation of hawk. x, 6
A1938. Creation of kite. i, 26
A1958. Creation of owl. x, 6 ; x, 12 ; x, 13
A1966. Creation of stork. x, 1 ; x, 5 ; x, 6
A1988. Creation of chicken (fowl). i, 25 ; iii, 31 ; x, 9
A1993. Creation of cuckoo (koel). x, 10
A1994. Creation of parrot. x, 15 ; x, 18 ; xxi, 6
A1995.* Creation of starling (maina). i, 14 ; x, 11
A1996.* Creation of peacock. x, 1 ; x, 19 ; x, 22
A1997.* Creation of papiha. x, 14

A2000—A2099. CREATION OF INSECTS

A2000. **Creation of insects.*** iii, 31 ; vii, 7
A2011. Creation of ant. i, 26 ; vii, 1 ; vii, 27
A2012. Creation of bee. vii, 2 ; vii, 3 ; vii, 4 ; xii, 2
A2031. Creation of fly. i, 26 ; xi, 32
A2034. Origin of mosquitoes. vii, 20 ; vii, 21
A2041.* Creation of butterfly. vii, 5 ; vii, 6
A2051. Creation of louse. vii, 16 ; vii, 17
A2053.* Creation of maggots. vii, 17 ; vii, 18
A2061. Creation of cockroach. vii, 8 ; vii, 9 ; vii, 10
A2091. Origin of spider. vii, 25 ; vii, 26 ; xiv, 4
A2092.* Origin of scorpion. vii, 22 ; vii, 23 ; vii, 24
2092.1.* Origin of 'leaf-scorpion'. iii, 17
A2093.* Origin of mantis. vii, 19.

A2100—A2199. CREATION OF FISH AND OTHER ANIMALS

A2100. **Creation of fish.** Chap. IX, passim ; iii, 31 ; viii, 5 ; xvii, 7 ; xxi, 4
A2140. **Creation of reptiles.** Chap. VIII, passim ; ii, 11
A2145. Creation of snake. ii, 11 ; viii, 1-10 ; viii, 15 ; xix, 7 ; xx, 1 ; xx, 10
A2146.* Creation of crocodile. viii, 11 ; viii, 12 ; viii, 13
A2147.* Creation of tortoise. viii, 14 ; viii, 15 ; xxi, 6
A2160. **Origin of amphibia**
A2162. Origin of frog. xix, 6 ; xix, 7 ; xix, 8
A2170. **Origin of miscellaneous animal forms**
A2183.* Origin of crab. vii, 11 ; vii, 12 ; vii, 13 ; vii, 14 ; xiii, 10 ; xviii, 14
A2184.* Origin of leech. ix, 1 ; xii, 48 ; xix, 21
A2185.* Origin of earth-worm. viii, 9

A2200—A2599. ANIMAL CHARACTERISTICS

A2300. **Origin of animal characteristics : body**
A2302. Animal's body made smaller
2302.6.* Lice made smaller. vii, 15
2302.7.* Elephant loses its breasts. xviii, 27
A2320. **Origin of animal characteristics : head**
2320.4.* Why crab has no head. vii, 13.
A2322.4. How goat got its beard. xviii, 4 ; xviii, 8
A2330. **Origin of animal characteristics : face**
2330.3.* Why monkey's face is black. i, 4
A2335.4.3. Why dog has black muzzle. xi, 8
A2343.1.5.* Why starling's beak is split. x, 11
2343.1.6.* Why parrot's beak is black. x, 15
A2344.2.7.* Why crocodile has no tongue. viii, 13
A2345.6.* How elephant got its tusks. xviii, 27
A2350. **Origin of animal characteristics : trunk**
A2351.4.* How crab lost its trunk. vii, 13
A2356.2.11.* Why camel has humped back. xi, 7 ; xii, 1

A2365. Origin and nature of animal's genitals
2365.2.* Why horse's member is long. xi, 33 ; xii, 43 ; xviii, 46
2365.3.* Why elephant's member is large. xii, 32
2365.4.* Why donkey's member is large. xviii, 39
2365.5.* Why goat's and cat's members are as they are. xii, 36
A2370. Animal characteristics : extremities
A2371.3.1. Why snake has no legs. xv, 17
A2376.4* How crab got its claws. vii, 14
A2378.4.5.* Why jackal's tail is short. xi, 28
A2410. Animal characteristics : colour and smell
A2411.1.21.* Colour of monkey. xi, 29 ; xi, 31
2411.2.28. Colour of parrot. x, 17
2411.2.29.* Colour of starling. x, 10
A2412.1.5.* Why elephant has white marks on its body. xi, 20
A2413.4. Stripes of tiger. xi, 8
A2420. Animal characteristics : voice and hearing
A2422. How animal lost voice (or power of speech). xii, 1 ; xi, 40
2422.1. Why dogs do not speak. xviii, 24
2422.10.* Why cock does not speak. xii, 40
A2423.2.2.* Cuckoo's sweet voice. x, 10
A2425. Origin of animal cries. xi, 13-17
A2430. Animal characteristics : dwelling and food
A2432.8.* Bee's hive. vii, 3
A2433.5.6.* Why butterflies haunt urine-impregnated places. vii, 5
2433.6.3. Why crabs live in water (among rocks). xviii, 19
2433.6.5.* Why leeches live in water. vii, 16
A2434.1.1. Why birds are everywhere. x, 3 ; x, 4
A2435.3. Food of various animals (mammals). xi, 37
2435.4. Food of birds. x, 8 ; x, 24
2435.5. Food of insects. vii. 20
A2440. Animal characteristics : carriage
A2441.1.7. Cause of elephant's walking (blowing on ground). vii, 1
A2442.3.* How birds began to fly. x, 1-4
A2470. Animal's habitual bodily movements
A2477.1. Why hog roots in ground. i, 4
A2483.1. Why snake sheds skin. xix, 8
A2494. Why certain animals are enemies
2494.1.4. Enmity between cat and rat. xi, 8
2494.2.1. Enmity between leopard (panther) and goat. xi, 4
2494.5.35.* Enmity between crocodile and elephant. xi, 18
2494.5.36.*, Enmity between crab and spider. vii, 11
2494.5.37.* Enmity between elephant and ant. vii, 1
2494.5.33.* Enmity between parrot and starling (maina). x, 5
A2490. Other habits of animals
A2496.* Sexual intercourse of animals. Why dogs get stuck in sexual intercourse. xviii, 24.

A2600—A2699. ORIGIN OF TREES AND PLANTS

A2650. Origin of flowers. vi, 2 ; vi, 3 ; vi, 4 ; vi, 5 ; vi, 6 ; vi, 19 ; vi, 20 ; viii, 15 ; xv, 9 ; xvii, 7
A2665.* Origin of grass. i, 3 ; i, 17 ; i, 23 ; i, 33 ; vi, 7 ; viii, 15 ; ix, 8 ; xiii, 25 ; xiv, 1 ; xx, 10
A2681. Origin of trees. i, 2 ; i, 3 ; i, 6 ; i, 17 ; i, 33 ; vi, 8-20 ; xv, 9 ; xvii, 7 ; xviii, 18 ; xxiii, 9
A2682.* Origin of creepers. vi, 1
A2685.1. Origin of corn. xiii, 6 ; xiii, 9 ; xiv, 1-9
A2686. Origin of vegetables
2686.1. Origin of mushrooms. xii, 92

2686.4.* Origin of edible roots. xviii, 4
2686.5.* Origin of turmeric. xxii, 7
A2691. Origin of narcotic plants
2691.2. Origin of tobacco. Chap. XV, passim ; xiv, 3
2691.3.* Origin of ganja. xv, 16 ; xv, 17
2691.4.* Origin of opium. xv, 18
A2692.* Origin of poison. viii, 4 ; xv, 3

A2700—A2799. ORIGIN OF PLANT CHARACTERISTICS

A2751.4.2.* Why ebony tree is black. viii, 3
A2752.1.* Why bombax tree has thorns. xviii, 12
A2756.1.* Why the bamboo has nodes. iii, 16
2756.2.* Why there are knots on the saja tree. xx, 5
2756.3.* Why the saja tree has no sap. vi, 14
A2768. Why tamarind leaves are small. vi, 16 ; vi, 17 ; vi, 18
A2794. Miscellaneous characteristics
2794.1.* Why the bija tree is often struck by lightning. iii, 16
2794.2.* Why mushrooms are slimy. xii, 38
2794.3.* Why the roots of the banyan hang down. vi, 8

A2800—A2899. MISCELLANEOUS EXPLANATIONS

A2851. The four characteristics of wine. xvi, 5

B. ANIMALS

B0—B99. MYTHICAL ANIMALS

B10. **Mythical beasts**
B12.2. Basilisk's fatal glance. viii, 1 ; viii, 8
B45. Air-going elephant. xi, 18
B60. **Mythical fish.** iii, 12 ; xii, 90 ; xiii, 11
B62.* Mythical crab (Kakramal Kshattri). i, 1 ; vii, 12 ; xiii, 10
B63.* Mythical spider (Makramal Kshattri). vii, 25

B100—B199. MAGIC ANIMALS

B100. **Treasure-animals.** vi, 3
B107. Treasure-fish. xiii, 11
B108. Treasure-serpent. vi, 5 ; viii, 2 ; xiv, 1 ; xv, 3 ; xv, 16
B120. **Wise animals.** iv, 2 ; xiii, 15
B140. **Prophetic animals.** vii, 9 ; vii, 10 ; vii, 11 ; xi, 6
B147. Animals furnish omens. ii, 15 ; x, 7 ; x, 12 ; x, 13
B191. Animal as magician. xiii, 5
191.3.* Bird as magician. xiv, 6 ; xviii, 45
191.4.* Rat gives magic medicine. xii, 70

B200—B299. ANIMALS WITH HUMAN TRAITS

B210. **Speaking animals.** i, 1 ; i, 3 ; i, 4 ; i, 9 ; i, 16 ; i, 26 ; ii, 29 ; ii, 11 ; iii, 20 ; iv, 2 ; v, 1 ; vi, 3 ; vi, 20 ; viii, 2 ; viii, 3 ; viii, 7 ; viii, 9 ; Chaps. IX, X and XI, passim ; xiii, 11 ; xiii, 15 ; xvi, 5 ; xviii, 38 ; xxiii, 1 ; xxiii, 6
B220. **Animal kingdom.** ix, 5 ; x, 1 ; x, 4 ; xi, 28 ; xi, 31 ; xii, 4 ; xiii, 5 ; xvi, 6.
B250. **Religious animals**
B253.4.* Spider performs penance. xii, 66
B280. **Animal weddings.** iv, 2 ; xi, 24 ; xii, 32 ; xiii, 5 ; xviii, 24
B283. Unusual animal matings. x, 5 ; xx, 12

B290. Other animals with human traits
B291. Animal as messenger. xiii, 15 ; xviii, 38
B292. Animal in service to man. vii, 14 ; xviii, 17
B293. Animals dance. xxiii, 6 ; xxiii, 8

B300—B599. FRIENDLY ANIMALS

B350. Grateful animals. vii, 14 ; xviii, 17
B400. Helpful domestic beasts. i, 5 ; vi, 20
B430. Helpful wild beasts. i, 4 ; v. 9 ; vi, 20 ; xviii, 2 ; xviii, 17
B450. Helpful birds. i, 14 ; i, 16 ; i, 22 ; i, 25 ; i, 26 ; i, 29 ; ii, 11 ; x, 15 ; x, 18 ; xiv, 4 ; xviii, 30 ; xviii, 38 ; xxi, 6 ; xxiii, 1
B470. Helpful fish
B478. Helpful crab. i, 1 ; i, 16 ; i, 24 ; iii, 37 ; vii, 11 ; vii, 14 ; xiii, 10
B480. Helpful insects. iii, 2 ; xiv, 4
B491. Helpful serpent. v, 5 ; viii, 2 ; xv, 18
B530. Animals nourish men. xi, 31 ; xi, 38 ; xviii, 45

B600—B699. MARRIAGE OF PERSON TO ANIMAL

B600. Marriage of person to animal. xviii, 5
B600. Animal paramour. i, 27 ; xi, 4 ; xi, 23 ; xii, 83 ; xv, 16 ; xviii, 8
B630. Offspring of marriage to animal
B636.* Offspring of human and animal intercourse. i, 27

B700—B799. FANCIFUL TRAITS OF ANIMAL

B720. Fanciful bodily members of animals
B722. Magic stone in animal's head. xiii, 11 ; xv, 3 ; Cp. vi, 5
B723.* Tortoise has no liver or teeth. xii, 1
B724.* Spider has no blood in body. xii, 66
B750. Fanciful habits of animals
B754.6.* Peacock pregnant without intercourse. x, 22
754.7.* Crab's offspring born through its chest. viii, 12
B782.* Sheep sleeps if anyone ties shoe to its ear. xi, 33

C. TABOO

C0—C99. TABOO CONNECTED WITH SUPERNATURAL BEINGS

C40. Taboo : offending spirits of water, mountain etc.
C43.*. Taboo : offending tree-spirit (Karam Sen). xxiii, 11

C100—C199. SEX TABOO

C100. Sex taboo
C101.* Sex taboo broken : child born without bones. iii, 22 ; xxi, 12 ; xxi, 17
C117.2.* Taboo : intercourse at night. xxii, 5
117.3.* Taboo : intercourse before worship. xvii, 10
C.140. Taboo connected with menses
C141. Taboo : going forth during menses. ix, 7. Cp. xii, 7
C142. Taboo : sexual intercourse during menses. xii, 70 ; xii, 72
142.1.* Ground defiled by menstrual blood. xiii, 6
C150. Taboo connected with childbirth
C152. Taboo during pregnancy. ii, 15 ; xviii, 18
C180. Taboo confined to one sex

C181.4.* Taboo : women not to climb on roof. vi, 7
181.5.* Taboo : Baiga women not to tie cloth between legs. iii, 6
181.6.* Taboo : Bondo women not to wear clothes. xxii, 5

C200—C299. EATING AND DRINKING TABOO

C220. **Taboo : eating certain things**
C221.1. Taboo : eating flesh of certain animals. xiv, 12 ; xiv, 13
221.1.1. Taboo : eating ox. xvi, 12
C224. Taboo : eating certain vegetable
224.2. Taboo : eating forbidden herbs. i, 32 ; xii, 64 ; xx, 1
C241. Taboo : eating food of gods. xvii, 4
C270. **Taboo : drinking certain things**
C271.* Taboo : drinking milk. i, 9 ; i, 13
C310. **Taboo : looking at certain person or thing**
C312.3.* Taboo : on looking at daughter for twelve years. xviii, 38
C320. **Taboo : looking into certain receptacle**
C321. Taboo : looking into box (Pandora). ii, 6 ; ii, 11 ; iii, 15 ; iii, 16
C460. **Laughing taboo**
C461.* Taboo : laughing or talking with anyone. xxi, 2
C510. **Taboo : touching tree (plant)**
C518. Taboo : burning saja (terminalia tomentosa) wood. xx, 5
C519. Taboo : entering forest. v, 14

C600—C699. UNIQUE PROHIBITIONS AND COMPULSIONS

C610. **The one forbidden place.** xii, 60 ; xii, 86
C620. Taboo : partaking of the one forbidden object. i, 32 ; xii, 64 ; xii, 86 ; xx, 1.

C700—C899. MISCELLANEOUS TABOOS

C720. **Taboo : attending toilet needs**
C725.1.* Taboo : use of water after attending call of nature. x. 14

C900—C999. PUNISHMENT FOR BREAKING TABOO

C920. **Death for breaking taboo.** x, 14 ; xii, 7 ; xiv, 12 ; xxii, 9
C930. **Loss of fortune for breaking taboo.** xxiii, 11
C940. **Sickness or weakness for breaking taboo.** ii, 15 ; xiv, 13
C941.1. Leprosy from breaking taboo. xvii, 4 ; xvii, 10
C960. **Transformation for breaking taboo.** xiv, 12

D. MAGIC

D0—D699. TRANSFORMATION

D100. **Transformation : man to animal.** ix, 3 ; xi, 30 ; xi, 33 ; xix, 11 ; xxi, 2 ; xxi, 3 ; xxi, 6 ; xxi, 9 ; xxi, 11 ; xxi, 12
D200. **Transformation : man to object.** ix, 3 ; xv, 1 ; xxi, 3 ; xxi, 9 ; xxi, 14 ; xxi, 17 ; xxiii, 7 ; xxiii, 8
D300. **Transformation : animal to person.** xvi, 7
D410. **Transformation : one animal to another.** x, 20 ; xi, 10 ; x, 37
D420. **Transformation : animal to object.** v, 2
D440. **Transformation : object to animal.** i, 32 ; vii, 9 ; vii, 10 ; vii, 16 ; vii, 19 ; vii, 21 ; vii, 22 ; vii, 26 ; vii, 27 ; viii, 5 ; viii, 6 ; viii, 12-15 ; ix, 2 ; ix, 7-9 ; x, 8 ; x, 10-13 ; x, 17 ; xi, 3 ; xi, 8 ; xi, 9 ; xi, 20 ; xi, 22 ; xi, 25 ; xi, 35-38 ; xii, 48 ; xvii, 7 ; xviii, 14 ; xix, 2 ; xix, 7 ; xx, 10 ; xxiii, 5

D450. **Transformation : object to another object.** i, 2 ; i, 3 ; i, 17 ; i, 26 ; i, 30 ; ii, 11 ; ii, 16 ; ii, 17 ; iii, 2 ; iii, 3 ; iii, 9 ; iv, 12 ; v, 12 ; vi, 10 ; vi, 20 ; ix, 8 ; x, 19 ; xi, 20 ; xi, 30 ; xiii, 4 ; xv, 14 ; xviii, 18 ; xviii, 19
D470. **Transformation : material of object changed.** i, 5 ; v, 1 ; v, 4-9 ; v, 11 ; vi, 1 ; vi, 7 ; vi, 12 ; viii, 4 ; xii, 30 ; xiii, 6 ; xiv, 1 ; xxi, 9 ; xxiii, 11
D480. **Size of object transformed.** vi, 20 ; xii, 22 ; xiv, 2 ; xviii, 26 ; xxiii, 7.
D610. **Repeated transformation.** xxi, 6
D615. Transformation combat. x, 2 ; xvii, 3 ; xviii, 45 ; xx, 1 ; xxi, 2

D700—D799. DISENCHANTMENT

D700. **Person disenchanted.** vi, 1 ; xxi, 2 ; xxi, 9 ; xxi, 11

D800—D1699. MAGIC OBJECTS

D800. **Magic object**
D905. Magic storm. iii, 9
D915.6.* Magic flood. xx, 4
D931.1.2. Magic ashes. vi, 10 ; vii, 4 ; viii, 4 ; viii, 13 ; xi, 10 ; xii, 63 ; xxi, 1 ; xxi, 5 ; xxi, 6 ; xxi, 7 ; xxi, 14
931.2. Magic dust. xxi,2
D955. Magic leaf. xxi, 17
D973. Magic grains. vi, 12
973.1. Magic rice-grains. xi, 9 ; xii, 61 ; xiii, 5 ; xviii, 30 ; xxi, 2 ; xxi, 3; xxi, 6; xxi, 9
D980. Magic fruit. vii, 21
D983.3.* Magic herbs. i, 32 ; xxi, 9
D991. Magic hair
991.2. Magic pubic hair. i, 17 ; viii, 13 ; xi, 9 ; xii, 101
D1002. Magic excrements. xi, 17 ; xxi, 3
D1003. Magic blood. iii, 15 ; xix, 9 ; xxi, 14
1003.1.* Magic menstrual blood. v, 4 ; vii, 7 ; vii, 9 ; ix, 1 ; xii, 73 ; xii, 101 ; xiii, 5 ; xiii, 6 ; xiv, 3 ; xvii, 12 ; xix, 25
D1050. Magic clothes. xxi, 3
D1051. Magic cloth. xii, 12
D1073. Magic necklace. xxi, 14
D1075. Magic bangle. iv, 3
D1080. Magic weapons. vi, 20
D1081. Magic sword. xx, 3 ; xx, 7 ; xxi, 14
D1132. Magic palace. vi, 20
D1162.1. Magic lamp. xi, 31 ; xiii, 5
D1163. Magic mirror. xx, 14
D1206. Magic axe. xiii, 10
1206.1.* Magic sickle. v, 12
D1209.5.* Magic broom. xiii, 5
D1211. Magic drum. xxiii, 6 ; xxiii, 11
D1223.1. Magic flute. viii, 3
D1233. Magic violin (fiddle). i, 1 ; xx, 6
D1241. Magic medicine (charm, amulet). xv, 12 ; xvii, 2 ; xvii, 5
D1242.1. Magic water. x, 18 ; x, 19
D1243. Magic pill. xii, 74 ; xii, 75
D1252.1.1.* Magic iron. i, 1 ; xxi, 9
1252.1.2.* Magic nails. vii, 12 ; xii, 54
D1273. Magic formula (charm). viii, 13 ; ix, 1 ; ix, 8 ; xi, 10 ; xi, 38 ; xii, 17 ; xii, 23 ; xii, 63 ; xii, 64 ; xxi, 8
D1275. Magic song. xxiii, 7 ; xxiii, 11
D1295.* Magic trident. xx, 16

D1700—D1799. POSSESSION AND MEANS OF EMPLOYMENT OF MAGIC POWERS

D1710. **Possession of magic powers**
D1711. Magician. Chap. XXI, passim ; vi, 11 ; ix, 7 ; ix, 8 ; xi, 12
D1712. Soothsayer
1712.1.* Soothsayer at work by various methods of divination. iii, 17 ; iv, 3 ; vii, 1 ; ix, 8 ; x, 21 ; xi, 6 ; xi, 10 ; xi, 38 ; xii, 6 ; xii, 22 ; xii, 60 ; xii, 66 ; xii, 74 ; xii, 92 ; xiii, 5 ; xv, 2 ; xv, 3 ; xvii, 9 ; xvii, 11 ; xvii, 13 ; xviii, 45 ; xix, 9 ; xx, 4 ; xx, 5 ; xx, 8 ; xx, 10 ; xxii, 9
D1720. **Acquisition of magic powers**
D1721. Magic power from magician
1721.2.* Magic power acquired by eating fish which have eaten dead magician's flesh. xxi, 4
1721.3.* Magician blows magic into disciples' ears. xxiii, 1
1721.4.* Disciples drink magician's urine. xxi, 3
1721.5.* Disciples eat magic iron. xxi, 9
1721.6.* Disciples acquire magic powers by study. xxi, 9

D1800—D2199. MANIFESTATIONS OF MAGIC POWER

D1810. **Magic knowledge**
D1812.5. Future learned through omens. ii, 15 ; xii, 22
1812.5.0.1. Omens from sneezing. xii, 22
D1813. Magic knowledge of events in distant place. i, 32
D1850. **Immortality.** ii, 5 ; Chap. XIX, passim ; xxi, 14
D1880. **Magic rejuvenation.** i, 14 ; ix, 2
D1900. **Love induced by magic.** iii, 9 ; v, 1 ; xii, 85 ; xvii, 1 ; xvii, 2 ; xxi, 7 ; xxi, 8 ; xxi, 17
D1980. **Magic invisibility.** xxi, 14
D2050. **Destructive magic power**
D2060. Death or bodily injury by magic. ii, 16 ; iii, 22 ; vii, 3 ; xiii, 5 ; xiii, 13 ; xvii, 5 ; xvii, 11 ; xx, 5 ; xxiii, 8
D2100. **Magic wealth.** xxiii, 11
D2120. **Magic transportation**
D2125. Magic power to walk on water. xx, 9
D2153. Magic control of fires. xxi, 2 ; xxi, 3 ; xxi, 9
D2161. Magic healing power. vi, 14 ; viii, 9 ; viii, 10 ; xvii, 8
D2171. Magic adhesion
2171.1. Object magically attaches itself to a person. xx, 8 ; xxi, 3
D2174. Magic dancing. xxiii, 7
2174.1. Magic singing. xxiii, 7 ; xxiii, 11

E. THE DEAD

E0—E199. RESUSCITATION

E0. **Resuscitation**
E1. Person comes to life. v, 1 ; vi, 5 ; xvi, 4 ; xix, 9 ; xxi, 2 ; xxi, 5 ; xxi, 14 ; xxiii, 4.
E3.* Dead animal comes to life. vii, 13 ; xi, 35
E80. **Water of life.** vi, 5 ; x, 18 ; x, 19 ; xii, 66 ; xix, 11 ; xix, 19 ; xix, 21.
E83.* Milk of life. xii,82
E84.* Water of death. xix,19

E200—E599. GHOSTS AND OTHER REVENANTS

E200. **Malevolent return from the dead.** vi, 12 ; x, 9
E300. **Friendly return from the dead**
E366. Return from dead to give counsel. iv, 3 ; xii, 84

E374. The Dead as agents in creation. i, 24
E420. Appearance of revenant
E421.1.3.* Ghosts visible to dogs. xi, 14
E423.3.5. Revenant as owl. x, 13
E540. Miscellaneous actions of revenants
E583. Dead persons draw chariot (thus causing thunder). iii, 18
E586. Dead returns soon after burial. xix, 4 ; xix, 6 ; xix, 12 ; xix, 17 ; xix, 24

E600—E699. REINCARNATION

E600. Reincarnation.
E616.2.* Reincarnation as scorpion. vii, 24
E630. Reincarnation in object
E631. Reincarnation in plant (tree) growing from grave. xv, 6 ; xv, 11 ; xvi, 5
631.0.1. Twining branches grow from graves of lovers. Twin narcotic plants grow from pyre where lovers are cremated. xv, 15

E700—E799. THE SOUL

E720. Soul leaves or enters the body
E721. Soul journeys from the body. xxi, 6
721.1. Soul wanders from the body in sleep. xi, 9 ; xx, 13
E722. Soul leaves body at death. x, 23 ; xv, 6 ; xv, 11 ; xx, 14
E760. **Life Index.** xviii, 2
E765. Life dependent on external object. Person's life is in a swing ; when this is burnt, she is also burnt. xxi, 14
E780. Vital bodily members. xii, 31 ; xviii, 33-36
E789. Organs exchanged with those of animal. xii, 4 ; xii, 7 ; xii, 8 ; xii, 11 ; xii, 31 ; xii, 32 ; xii, 36 ; xii, 40 ; xii, 56 ; xviii, 24 ; xviii, 27 ; xviii, 39

F. MARVELS

F0—F199. OTHER WORLD JOURNEYS

F10. **Journey to Upper World.** i, 22 ; iii, 2 ; iii, 22
F30. **Inhabitant of Upper World visits earth.** i, 19 ; ii, 3 ; xii, 66
F34. Child of deity stolen and brought down to earth, ii, 8
F50. Access to Upper World
F51.1.1. Spider-web sky-rope. iii, 2
F60. Transportation to or from Upper World
F62.1. Bird carries person to Upper World. i, 22
F80. **Journey to Lower World.** i, 1 ; i, 14 ; i, 15 ; i, 16 ; i, 28 ; ii, 11 ; iii, 14 ; iii, 22 ; v, 1 ; vi, 5 ; vii, 25 ; x, 15 ; x, 21 ; xiv, 2
F90. Access to Lower World
F92.5.* By making hole in ground. ii, 11
F97.* Path of hero's tongue. i,14
F98.* Riding on a tiger. x, 21
F101. Return from Lower World
101.5.* On horse of lightning. iii, 14
101.6.* On bird. x, 15
101.7.* By spider's thread. vii, 25
F110. Journey to terrestial Other Worlds
F112. Journey to Land of Women. xxi, 9-17
F128.* Journey to Land of Elephants. xviii, 45

F200—F699. MARVELLOUS CREATURES

F400. Spirits and demons (general)
F402.1.1. Spirit leads person astray. xi, 2
F403.2. Spirits help mortal. Familiar spirits. ix, 8 ; xiii, 5

F510. **Monstrous persons**
F529.2.* Enormously fat woman with beard. xxi, 12
F540. **Remarkable physical organs**
F544.2. Remarkable tongue
544.2.3.* Tongue with hair growing from it. xiv, 14; xix, 8
F547. Remarkable sexual organs
547.1.1. Vagina dentata. xi, 19; Chap. XVIII, passim
547.1.2.* Enormous vagina. x, 6; xii, 32; xii, 42; xviii, 21; xxii, 1
547.1.3.* Saw in vagina. xviii, 23
F548.* Extraordinary penis
548.1.* Penis aculeatus. xii, 63; xii, 67; xviii, 1; xviii, 9; xviii, 13; xviii, 17; xviii, 18; xviii, 32; xviii, 37
548.2.* Long penis. xi, 12; xii, 29-34; xii, 37; xii, 38; xii, 42; xii, 43; xviii, 13; xviii, 22; xxii, 1; xxii, 3: xxiii, 1
F549.* Extraordinary clitoris. xii, 33; xxi, 6
F555. Remarkable hair.
555.4.* Hair in vulva which becomes a mantis. vii, 19
555.5.* Hair growing from tongue. xiv, 14; xix, 8
555.6.* Remarkable pubic hairs. xii, 12, xviii, 2
F557. Removable organs. xii, 7; xii, 32; xii, 36; xii, 40
F559.* Umbilicus elongatus. xviii, 38-46
F570. Other extraordinary human beings
F582.1. Serpent damsel. xiii, 4; xviii, 3; xviii, 6; xviii, 28-31

F700—F899. EXTRAORDINARY PLACES AND THINGS

F718.* Extraordinary well (of blood). xii, 60
F782.4.* Extraordinary lock and key (made of bones). x, 18
F786.* Extraordinary bed (woven with spider's webs). v, 13
F810. Extraordinary tree. vi, 2
F811.15.* Talking tree
F812. Extraordinary forest. xxiii, 11
F818.* Extraordinary flowers
818.1.* Talking flowers. vii, 4
818.2.* Flower only to be found at midnight. vi, 2
F823. Extraordinary shoes
823.3.* Shoes of rat-skin. xiii, 1
F827. Extraordinary ornaments
827.3.* Ornaments of snakes, hornets, scorpions, dirt and a toad. vii, 23.
F872. Extraordinary bath
872.3.* Bath of blood. xxi, 14
F876.* Extraordinary mount
876.1.* Hero rides on tiger. v, 13; x, 21; xi, 37
876.2.* Hero rides on animated wax elephant. xi. 12
876.3.* Hero rides on winged elephant. xi, 20
876.4.* Hero rides on peacock. xi, 20
876.5.* Jackal rides on a fox. xx, 11.
F877.* Extraordinary plough (made of snakes and drawn by tigers). xiv, 4
F878.* Extraordinary loom (made of a woman's breasts with the vagina as shuttle). xxii, 2
F879.* Extraordinary still (with the heads of crocodiles, owls and parrots as pots). xxi, 13
879.1.* A woman's body used as still. xvi, 4; xvi, 6
F880.* Extraordinary letter (written on human skin). i, 14
880.1.* Letter shot into sky. vi, 17

F900—F1099. EXTRAORDINARY OCCURRENCES

F910. **Extraordinary swallowings.** viii, 11; xviii, 45; xxii, 1
F1052.1.* Bottle concealed in person's thigh. xx, 7

G. OGRES

G0—G399. KINDS OF OGRES

G10. **Cannibalism**
G11. Kinds of cannibals
11.2. Cannibal giant. iii, 4 ; iv, 10 ; vi, 20 ; xiii, 9 ; xxi, 10
11.3. Cannibal witch. xxi, 2 ; xxi, 5
11.6. Man-eating woman. xiii, 9 ; xxi, 2
G12. Transformation to eat own kind. xxi, 5
G72. Unnatural parents eat own children. ii, 1 ; ii, 9
G92.* Cannibalism causes death. xviii, 3
G100. **Giant ogre.** i, 15 ; i, 30 ; iii, 4 ; iv, 16 ; v, 4 ; v, 11 ; vi, 6 ; vi, 20 ; viii, 7 ; x, 6 ; x, 8 ; x, 9 ; x, 12 ; x, 20 ; xi, 19 ; xi, 27 ; xi, 28 ; xi, 36 ; xii, 9 ; xii, 13 ; xii, 18 ; xii, 19 ; xii, 67 ; xii, 98 ; xviii, 4 ; xviii, 26 ; xviii, 36 ; xix, 19

G200—G299. WITCHES

G200. **Witch.** Chap. XXI, passim ; vi, 18 ; vii, 10 ; vii, 21 ; x, 17 ; xi, 9 ; xi, 31 ; xii, 23 ; xiii, 5 ; xiii, 6 ; xiii, 13 ; xviii, 20 ; xviii, 32 ; xix, 2 ; xix, 25, xxiii, 10

G500—G599. OGRE DEFEATED

G500. **Ogre defeated.** i, v ; i, 30 ; iii, 4 ; iv, 10 ; v, 11 ; x, 8 ; xviii, 36

H. TESTS

H200—H299. TESTS OF TRUTH

H220. **Ordeals**
H221. Ordeal by fire. ii, 11
H252. Act of Truth. vi, 15
H254. Oath on boiling oil as test of chastity. vii, 17

H300—499. MARRIAGE TESTS

H310. **Suitor tests.** ii, 11 ; vi, 16 ; ix, 3 ; xviii, 38
H316.4.* Suitor test : garland thrown indicates girl's choice. v, 3 ; xii, 61
H400. **Chastity test.**
H412.4. Chastity ordeal : passing through fire. ii, 11
412.4.2.* Chastity ordeal : oath on boiling oil. vii, 17

H500—H899. TESTS OF CLEVERNESS

H510. **Tests in guessing**
H511. Princess (girl) offered to correct guesser. vi, 16 ; xiii, 1

H900—H1199. TESTS OF PROWESS : TASKS

H900. **Tasks imposed.** ii, 12 ; ii, 13 ; ii, 14 ; vi, 16 ; xx, 3
H970. **Help in performing task.** ii, 11 ; vi, 16
H1010. **Impossible tasks.** ii, 12 ; ii, 13 ; ii, 14

H1200—H1399. TESTS OF PROWESS : QUESTS

H1322. Quest for marvellous tree. xiii, 11
1322.2.* Quest for silver pillar covered with golden flowers. v, 1
H1385. Quest for lost persons
1385.7.* Quest for lost father. iii, 13 ; xxi, 9

J. THE WISE AND THE FOOLISH

J0—J199. ACQUISITION AND POSSESSION OF WISDOM (KNOWLEDGE)

J80. **Wisdom (knowledge) taught by parable**
J88.1. Relative pleasures of sexes in love taught by parable. xii, 80.
J150. **Other means of acquiring wisdom (knowledge)**
J157. Wisdom (knowledge) from dream. i, 32 ; v, 6 ; v, 12 ; v, 14 ; vi, 8 ; vii, 7 ; ix, 7 ; xii, 3 ; xii, 27 ; xii, 58 ; xii, 66 ; xii, 68 ; xii, 84 ; xii, 95 ; xiii, 1 ; xiii, 6 ; xiii, 7 ; xiii, 9 ; xv, 2 ; xv, 11 ; xvii, 4 ; xviii, 26 ; xviii, 42 ; xx, v ; xxii, 2 ; xxii, 2 ; xxii, 9 ; xxiii, 3
J1190. **Cleverness in the lawcourt**
J1191.1. Reductio ad absurdum : the decision about the colt. xi, 28

J1700—J2799. FOOLS (AND OTHER UNWISE PERSONS)

J1700. **Fools**
J1702. Stupid husband. xii, 84 ; xii, 85 ; xviii, 7 ; xviii, 15
J1758.* Tiger thought to be dog. viii, 9
J1771.2.* Amputated penis thought to be fish. xviii, 8
J1833.1.1.* Boy strikes at a fly on his sister's breast : it turns into nipple and girl thinks it due to brother's caress. xii, 81
J2008. **Foolish** bargains. xxiii, 11
J2130. **Foolish disregard of personal danger**
J2131.3.2.* Numskull burns himself. xi, 21
J2310. **Nature of gullibility**
J2311.9.* Foolish peasants carry couple to burial ; when ' corpses ' speak they flee in terror. xx, 2
J2461.3.* Literal numskull laughs at his child's death. xii, 28
J2511. The silence wager. xx, 2

K. DECEPTIONS

K0—K99. CONTESTS WON BY DECEPTION

K1. **Contest won by magic.** vi, 16

K100—K299. DECEPTIVE BARGAINS

K230. **Deceptions in the payment of debt**
K231.1.1. Mutual agreement to sacrifice family members. Moon deceives sun. i, 20 ; ii, 1 ; ii, 6 ; ii, 9

K300—K499. THEFTS AND CHEATS

K341. Owner's interest distracted while goods are stolen. ix, 8
K356.* Objects stolen by means of magic impersonation. xxi, 14

K500—K699. ESCAPE BY DECEPTION

K510. **Death order evaded.** xix, 9 ; xxi, 13
K515. Child hidden to avoid death. xix, 10
K527.2.* Escape by tricking would-be murderer into position of intended victim. xiv, 10

K800—K999. FATAL DECEPTION

K815. Victim lured by kind words approaches trickster and is killed. viii, 2
K983.* Dupe induced to scratch his back with stick which turns into snake and bites. xix, 2

K1300—K1399. SEDUCTION OR DECEPTIVE MARRIAGES

K1326.* Attempted seduction by transformation. ii, 11
K1335. Seduction by stealing clothes of bathing girl. ix, 3
K1372.* Incestuous marriage arranged by trick. i, 4 ; i, 8 ; i, 9

K1500—K1599. DECEPTIONS CONNECTED WITH ADULTERY

K1510. **Adulteress outwits husband.** x, 18 ; xviii, 8
K1550. **Husband outwits adulteress and paramour.** xviii, 23

K1900—K1999. IMPOSTURES

K1919.* Ogre imposes on widow by assuming form of dead husband. vi, 20

K2100—K2199. FALSE ACCUSATIONS

K2116.1.1. Innocent woman accused of eating her new-born child. xix, 23 ; xxiii, 10

L. REVERSAL OF FORTUNE

L0—L99. VICTORIOUS YOUNGEST CHILD

L10. **Victorious youngest son.** v, 1 ; xviii, 2 ; xviii, 3 ; xviii, 30 ; xx, 6 ; xxiii, 11
L100. **Unpromising hero.** v, 3 ; xii, 61
L160. **Success of the unpromising hero.** v, 3

M. ORDAINING THE FUTURE

M250. **Promises connected with death**
M257. Dying monster's request and promise. vi, 19 ; vi, 20
M257.1. Dying hero's (magician's) request and promise to his disciples. xix, 2 ; xxi, 2 ; xxi, 4 ; xxi, 5

M400—M499. CURSES

M400. **Curses.** 1, 32 ; ii, 1 ; iv, 11 ; v, 14 ; vi, 18 ; vii, 2 ; vii, 11 ; vii, 12 ; vii, 17 ; vii, 18 ; viii, 2 ; viii, 7 ; viii, 13 ; x, 3 ; x, 6 ; xi, 1 ; xi, 2 ; xi, 15 ; xi, 28 ; xi, 33 ; xii, 2 ; xii, 6 ; xii, 10 ; xii, 15 ; xii, 16 ; xii, 42 ; xii, 62 ; xii, 64 ; xii, 67 ; xii, 76 ; xii, 98 ; xiii, 1 ; xiii, 6 ; xv, 1 ; xvii, 2 ; xvii, 4 ; xviii, 18 ; xviii, 26 ; xviii, 31 ; xix, 6 ; xxi, 10 ; xxi, 15 ; xxii, 4

N. CHANCE AND FATE

N0—N99. WAGERS AND GAMBLING

N72. Miscellaneous wagers. x, 3 ; xx, 2 ; xx, 11

N400—N699. LUCKY ACCIDENTS

N450. **Secrets overheard.** xi, 21 ; xviii, 30 ; xix, 9
N456. Enigmatical smile (laugh) reveals secret knowledge. vi, 5 ; xii, 60 ; xxi, 14
N640. Accidental healing. vi, 14

N700—N799. ACCIDENTAL ENCOUNTERS

N711.1. King (prince) finds maiden in woods and marries her. x, 3
711.3. Ogre meets maiden while bathing and marries her. viii, 7
N773.1.* Adventure from following ogre to cave. xvii, 5

N800—N899. HELPERS

N810. **Supernatural helpers**
N812. Giant or ogre as helper. v, 4 ; x, 20
N820. **Human helpers**
N844.1.* Sadhu as helper. iv, 1 ; ix, 9 ; xii, 25 ; xviii, 30 ; xix, 9
N851. Merchant as helper. xxiii, 11.
N886.1.* Hunchback leads blind man. vi, 14

Q. REWARDS AND PUNISHMENTS

Q10—Q199. DEEDS REWARDED

Q20. **Piety rewarded**
Q21.* Reward for service of god, hero or ascetic for a period. vii, 4 ; vii, 21 ; ix, 4 ; ix, 6 ; x, 14 ; xii, 3 ; xii, 25 ; xii, 28 ; xii, 67 ; xii, 87 ; xii, 95 ; xv, 14 ; xvii, 10 ; xx, 5 ; xx, 16 ; xxi, 6
21.1.* Dog serves ascetic. xi, 13
Q190. **Rewards—miscellaneous**
Q191.* Blessings. i, 32 ; ii, 4 ; ii, 5 ; vi, 3 ; vi, 6 ; vi, 11 ; vii, 3 ; vii, 11 ; vii, 21 ; vii, 25 ; vii, 27 ; viii, 14 ; viii, 15 ; ix, 6 ; ix, 9 ; x, 11 ; x, 20 ; xi, 9 ; xi, 13 ; xi, 19 ; xi, 22 ; xi, 23 ; xi, 32 ; xii, 19 ; xii, 28 ; xii, 52 ; xiii, 4 ; xv, 14 ; xvi, 4 ; xx, 5

Q200—Q399. DEEDS PUNISHED

Q210. **Crimes punished**
Q212.3.* Theft punished by origin of sweating. xii, 17
Q220. **Impiety punished.** xxiii, 11
Q240. **Sexual sins punished**
Q241. Adultery punished. vii, 17 ; xviii, 33 ; xix, 1
Q244. Punishment for ravisher. xvii, 1 ; xviii, 30
Q270. **Misdeeds concerning property punished**
Q272. Avarice punished. vi, 12 ; xx, 14
Q330. **Overweening punished**
Q331. Pride punished. vii, 22 ; xi, 5
Q380. **Deeds punished—miscellaneous**
Q386.2.* Drunken dancers punished. xxiii, 7 ; xxiii, 8

R. CAPTIVES AND FUGITIVES

R0. **Captivity**
R4.* Sun captured during visit to earth. ii, 1 ; ii, 7
4.1.* Sun and Moon captured by creditor, thus causing eclipse. ii, 12 ; ii, 13 ; ii, 15
R5.* King imprisons all living creatures. iii, 10

R6.* Messenger of Death imprisoned. xix, 9 ; xxi, 14
R7.* Men held captive in the Land of Women. xxi, 9-17
R8.* God (Bara Pen) held captive by the English. xx. 7
8.1.* Many gods imprisoned in iron bin. xvii, 14

R100—R199. RESCUES

R100. **Rescues.** xviii, 38 ; xxi, 2 ; xxi, 9 ; xxi, 11 ; xxi, 13 ; xxi, 14

R200—R299. ESCAPES AND PURSUITS

R210. **Escapes.** ii, 6 ; ii, 11 ; iii, 15 ; iii, 16 ; iii, 19 ; viii, 11 ; viii, 13 ; xiii, 15 ; xiii, 16 ; xviii, 26 ; xx, 11 ; xxi, 14 ; xxi, 16 ; xxiii, 7
R220. **Flights.** xiv, 3 ; xviii, 45
R231. Obstacle Flight
231.1.* Fugitive creates magic barrier against pursuit. xiii, 5
231.2.* Fugitive cuts tail of camel caught by pursuer and it turns into grass. xiii, 15
R260. **Pursuits.** ii, 6 ; ii, 11 ; iii, 15 ; iv, 10 ; xiii, 15 ; xviii, 45

S. UNNATURAL CRUELTY

S100—S199. REVOLTING MURDERS OR MUTILATIONS

S110. **Murders.** xxi, 14
S112. Burning to death. xviii, 17
S140. **Cruel abandonments and exposures.** i, 32 ; v, 1 ; v, 3 ; v, 8 ; xii, 86 ; xviii, 22 ; xviii, 30
S160. **Mutilations.** Chaps. XII and XVIII, passim
160.2.* Self-mutilation with creative purpose. ii, 5 ; ii, 17 ; iii, 9 ; iii, 27 ; iii, 30 ; v, 6 ; ix, 2 ; xi, 22 ; xi, 37 ; xii, 30 ; xii, 41 ; xiii, 7 ; xiii, 8 ; xvi, 4
S165. Mutilation : putting out eyes. xii, 5

S200—S299. CRUEL SACRIFICES

S210. **Children sold or promised.** xiii, 1
S260. **Sacrifices**
260.1. Human sacrifice. i, 19 ; i, 21 ; i, 22 ; ii, 8 ; xii, 92 ; xiii, 1 ; xx, 7 ; xxi, 5

S300—S399. ABANDONED OR MURDERED CHILDREN

S301. Children abandoned (exposed). i, 32, xi, 38 ; xii, 64 ; xxi, 6

T. SEX

T0—T99. LOVE

T0. **Love.**
T2. The relative pleasures of love. xii, 15 ; xii, 78 ; xii, 80 ; xii, 85 ; xii, 95
T10. **Falling in love.** xxi, 6 ; xxi, 14
T24.2. Swooning for love. xviii, 27 ; xxi, 17 ; xxiii, 11
T50. **Wooing.** i, 26 ; iii, 9 ; vii, 17 ; xi, 15
T55. Girl as wooer. iii, 23 ; iii, 25 ; iv, 11
T91. Unequals in love. ii, 7
T96.* Kissing as expression of love. xviii, 28 ; xxi, 6

T100—T199. MARRIAGE

T110. **Unusual marriage.**
T111. Marriage of mortal and supernatural being. iii, 16 ; vi, 7 ; xii, 61 ; **xv, 17**
T117. Marriage of person and object. ii, 6 ; ii, 11 ; iii, 16
T121. Unequal marriage. v, 8
T126. Unusual marriage : miscellaneous motifs
126.1.* Marriage of Mother Earth and ogre. i, 17
126.2.* Marriage of mountain and cockle-shell. i, 19
126.3.* Marriage of earth and sky. iii, 31 ; xiii, 4 ; xiii, 14
T150. **Happenings at weddings.** iii, 16 ; v, 4 ; v, 8 ; v, 13 ; vi, 17 ; vii, 23 ; xii, 4 ; xii, 7 ; xii, 61 ; xiii, 14 ; xv, 17
T172. Dangers to husband in bridal chamber. Chap. XVIII, passim

T200—T299. MARRIED LIFE

T230. **Faithlessness in marriage.** ii, 16 ; iii, 9 ; vii, 3 ; vii, 17 ; vii, 18 ; viii, 12 ; x, 11 ; x, 18
T250. **Characteristics of wives and husbands**
T255. The obstinate wife or husband. x, 3 ; xx, 2

T300—T399. CHASTITY AND CELIBACY

T302.* Methods of ascetics. iv, 1 ; vi, 2
T331. Man unsuccessfully tempted by woman. xxi, 10
T338.* Ascetic successfully tempted by woman. xii, 15

T400—T499. ILLICIT SEXUAL RELATIONS

T410. **Incest.** i, 14 ; xii, 77 ; xii, 90 ; xxii, 7
T460. **Sexual perversions**
T462. Lesbian love. iii, 22 ; xviii, 38 ; xviii, 39 ; xviii, 46 ; xxi, 12 ; xxi, 17
462.1. Lesbian love : women give birth to monsters as result. iii, 22 ; xxi, 12 ; xxi, 17
T463.* Homosexual love. xviii, 2
T470. **Illicit sexual relations—miscellaneous motifs**
T471. Rape. xvii, 1 ; xviii, 30
T481. Adultery. ii, 16 ; iii, 9 ; xii, 11 ; xii, 13 ; xii, 15 ; xviii, 1 ; xviii, 10

T500—T599. CONCEPTION AND BIRTH

T510. **Miraculous conception.** i, 13 ; i, 32 ; ii, 4 ; iii, 11 ; iii, 16 ; iii, 17 ; iv, 13 ; vii, 21 ; vii, 25 ; x, 9 ; x, 19 ; xi, 4 ; xii, 64 ; xii, 86 ; xii, 87 ; xii, 90 ; xii, 92 ; xii, 96 ; xv, 14 ; xvii, 7 ; xviii, 38 ; xx, 1 ; xx, 16 ; xxi, 1 ; xxi, 14. xii, 91 ;
T540. **Miraculous birth.** i, 1 ; i, 13 ; iii, 2 ; iii, 19 ; iii, 30 ; iii, 31 ; vii, 20 ; vii, 25 ; xii, 77 ; xii, 96 ; xiv, 3 ; xiv, 7 ; xvii, 8 ; xix, 11
T550. **Monstrous birth.** v, 1 ; viii, 8 ; x, 9 ; x, 10 ; xi, 19
T554. Woman gives birth to animal. xi, 4 ; xi, 7 ; xi, 12 ; xi, 23 ; xi, 25 ; xi, 27 ; xv, 14
T570. **Pregnancy.** xii, 86-96
T571. Unreasonable demands of pregnant women. xii, 88 ; xii, 89
T572.2. Abortion. xvii, 7
T580. **Childbirth.** xii, 86-96
T586. Multiple births
586.1. Many children at a birth. i, 4 ; i, 32 ; xii, 93 ; xx, 1
586.1.2. Seven children at a birth. xi, 12
T587. Birth of twins. xii, 25 ; xvii, 5 ; xx, 5
T590. **Conception and birth—miscellaneous motifs**
T591. Barrenness or impotence induced by magic. xvii, 1 ; xviii, 32
591.1. Magic remedies for barrenness or impotence. vi, 1 ; xii, 89 ; xii, 94 xvii, 2 ; xx, 5

Z. MISCELLANEOUS GROUPS OF MOTIFS

Z0—Z99. FORMULAS

Z71. Formulistic numbers

Z71.0.3. Formulistic number : two-and-a-half. i, 1 ; vii, 6 ; xii, 30 ; xii, 61 ; xii, 72 ; xii, 75 ; xii, 76

71.1. Forumulistic number : three. ii, 11 ; ii, 14 ; v, 1 ; vi, 10 ; vii, 7 ; ix, 1 ; x, 12 ; xi, 32 ; xii, 17 ; xii, 60 ; xiii, 6 ; xiv, 3 ; xxiii, 7 ; xxiii, 10

71.3. Formulistic number : five. v, 7 ; v, 8 ; vi, 8 ; vii, 27 ; xii, 41 ; xii, 59 ; xii, 72 ; xiv, 3 ; xvii, 13 ; xviii, 31 ; xx, 3

71.5. Formulistic number : seven. i, 8 ; i, 14 ; i, 20 ; i, 30 ; i, 32 ; ii, 4 ; iii, 10 ; iii, 22 ; iii, 23 ; iv, 3 ; v, 1 ; vi, 19 ; viii, 6 ; ix, 3 ; ix, 5 ; ix, 6 ; x, 12 ; x, 16 ; x, 18 ; xi, 21 ; xi, 37 ; xii, 1 ; xii, 7 ; xii, 25 ; xii, 28 ; xii, 60 ; xii, 63 ; xii, 64 ; xii, 66 ; xii, 68 ; xii, 100 ; xiii, 3 ; xiii, 5 ; xiii, 7 ; xiii, 13 ; xiv, 1 ; xiv, 14 ; xiv, 5 ; xv, 9 ; xvi, 2 ; xvi, 4 ; xvi, 9 ; xviii, 2 ; xviii, 26 ; xviii, 30 ; xviii, 39 ; xviii,40 ; xix, 3 ; xix, 20 ; xx, 1 ; xx, 2 ; xx, 7 ; xx, 10 ; xxi, 2 ; xxi, 11 ; xxi, 12 ; xxi, 13 ; xxii, 7 ; xxiii, 5 ; xxiii, 9 ; xxiii, 11

71.6. Formulistic number : nine. viii, 10 ; x, 11.

71.8. Formulistic number : twelve. i, 4 ; i, 9 ; i, 23 ; i, 28 ; i, 30 ; i, 31 ; ii, 4 ; ii, 6 ; ii, 7 ; ii, 8 ; ii, 11 ; ii, 13 ; ii, 16 ; iii, 13 ; iii, 16 ; iii, 22 ; iii, 28 ; iv, 1 ; v, 5 ; v, 10 ; viii, 15 ; x, 8 ; xi, 8 ; xi, 17 ; xi, 18 ; xi, 35 ; xii, 3 ; xii, 12 ; xii, 63 ; xii, 64 ; xii, 65 ; xii, 97 ; xii, 101 ; xiii, 12 ; xv, 5 ; xv, 14 ; xv, 17 ; xvi, 1 ; xvii, 1 ; xviii, 3 ; xviii, 7 ; xviii, 26 ; xviii, 38 ; xviii, 42 ; xviii, 45 ; xx, 10 ; xxi, 1 ; xxi, 2 ; xxi, 11 ; xxi, 13

71.9. Formulistic number : thirteen. iii, 16 ; v, 5 ; viii, 15 ; x, 8 ; xi, 8 ; xi, 18 ; xii, 63 ; xii, 101 ; xiii, 12 ; xv, 5 ; xx, 1 ; xx, 10 ; xxi, 2

71.9.1. Formulistic number : fourteen. v, 5

71.10. Formulistic number : sixteen. ix, 6 ; xii, 42 ; xii, 60 ; xiv, 1 ; xvii, 11 ; xxi, 11 ; xxi, 12 ; xxiii, 7

71.10.1.* Formulistic number ; twenty-four. xi, 35 ; xiii, 4 ; xx, 7

71.10.2.* Formulistic number : twenty-five. xvi, 1

71.10.3.* Formulistic number : twenty-six. xiii, 4

71.10.4.* Formulistic number : thirty-two. v, 1

71.10.5.* Formulistic number : thirty-six. i, 30

71.16. Formulistic numbers : miscellaneous

71.16.1.* Formulistic number : eighty. xii, 43 ; xiii, 5 ; xviii, 20 ; xviii, 38

71.16.2.* Formulistic number : nine hundred. ix, 8 ; xiii, 5

71.16.3.* Formulistic number : sixteen hundred. ix, 8

71.16.4.* Formulistic number : eighty thousand. ix, 9

71.16.5.* Formulistic number : seven hundred thousand. vii, 2

71.16.6.* Formulistic number : fifty-two lakhs (5,200,000). ix, 8

GENERAL INDEX

Agarwal, D. D., 4, 7, 69, 89, 99, 102, 499
Agni Purana, 21
Aitareya Brahmana, 78
Aitareya Upanishad, 3, 10
Alexander the Great, 163, 363
Andrews, F. H., 204 f., 499
Archer, W. G., 132, 254, 263
Atharva Veda, 9

Beal, S., 459
Bellary, D. G., 400
Bhagavata Purana, 21
Bhattacharjee, P. N., 13, 14, 56, 88, 102, 499
Bhattacharyya, V., 203
Bloomfield, M., 293
Boas, F., 299, 355, 357 f., 407
Bodding, P. O., 90, 324, 335, 445, 458, 499
Bogoras, W., 299, 358, 407
Bompas, C. H., 52 f., 55, 75, 130, 147, 200, 323, 427, 445, 499
Bradley-Birt, P. B., 20
Briffault, R., 358 ff.
Briaad-Aranyaka Upanishad, 3, 9, 282 452 f.
Brown, A. R., 16, 79, 103, 413

Campbell, A., 5, 8, 20, 23, 285, 479, 487
Campbell, J. M., 472
Carpenter, J. F., 9, 10
Census of India, 1901, 54, 79, 99
Census of India, 1931, 14, 52, 53, 68, 75, 90, 103, 453, 470
Chandogya Upanishad, 3
Chaube, R. G., 88, 440
Crooke, W., 13, 51 f., 68, 69, 75, 88, 102, 131, 136, 141, 163, 200, 347, 443, 460, 499

Dalton, E. T., 103, 142, 335, 487 f., 499
Das, T. C., 174
Dasgupta, S., 3, 499
Dehon, P., 13, 25, 200, 285, 499
Dickinson, R. L., 371
D'Penha, G. F., 296
Dorsey, G. A., 357, 407 f
Dowson, J., 52, 99, 499
Dracott, A. E., 410, 499
Dube, S. C., 496
Dunbar Brander, A. A., 336
Dutt, M. N., 337, 499

Edgerton, F., 204
Ellis, H., 95, 245, 253, 266 f., 360 f.
Elwin, Verrier, *The Agaria*, 23, 27 f., 54, 107, 300, 320, 495, 500
The Baiga, xii. 4, 5, 12, 15, 71, 75, 83, 84, 90, 148, 239, 272, 283, 313, 344, 443, 454, 495, 500
Folk-Songs of Chhattisgarh, 174, 205, 237, 311, 454, 500
Folk-Tales of Mahakoshal, 132, 174, 225, 320, 344, 347, 500
The Muria and their Ghotul, 62 f., 66, 102, 103, 129, 285, 289, 426, 427, 498, 500
Maria Murder and Suicide, 237, 500
Elwin, Verrier and Hivale, Shamrao, *Folk-Songs of the Maikal Hills*, 169, 174, 500
Emeneau, M. B., 68, 95, 182, 300, 500
English, the, 435 f., 437
Enthoven, R. E., 88, 102, 200, 500

Fitzpatrick, W., 182, 183, 500
Forbes, A. K., 347
Forsyth, J., 163 f., 500
Frazer, J. G., xii f., 79, 106, 500
Fürer-Haimendorf, C. von, 4, 335, 480, 496

Gandhi, Mahatma, 14
Gariola, M. D., 8,300, 500
Gibbon, E., 202
Goddard, P. E., 357 f., 408
Gorer, G., 174, 237, 255, 270, 452, 500
Grierson, L., 16
Griffiths, W. G., 344, 497, 500
Grigson, W. V., 75, 102, 103, 164, 471, 495 f., 500
Gurdon, P. R. T., 56, 79, 500

Haldar, S., 470, 500
Halliday, xiii f.
Hayavadana Rao, C., 336
Held, G. J., 26, 106, 500
Hiralal, 102, 205
Hislop, S., 16 f., 100, 320, 500
Hiuen Tsiang, 459ff.
Hivale, Shamrao, 66, 173, 496, 498

Hivale, Shamrao and Elwin, Verrier, *Songs of the Forest*, 174
Hoffmann, J. and van Emelan, A., 302, 500
Hooper, D., 293
Hume, R. E., 3, 9, 10, 26, 282, 500
Hutton, J. H., 55, 139, 296, 453, 459

Iyer, L. A. K., 13, 68, 89, 102, 142, 500

Jones, W., 95

Kama Sutra, 361
Kautilya, 203
Koppers, W., 6, 20, 22, 26, 174, 284, 500
Ktesias, 254, 299

Landor, S., 361
Landtman, G., 263, 355, 362, 408
Lang, A., xv
Laubscher, B. J. F., 365
Laufer, B., 293
Leech, R., 293
Leitner, G. W., 207, 500
Lewison, R. G., 14, 79, 411, 501
Lincoln, I. S., 354, 408
Logan, W., 460
Lowie, R. H., 355 f., 394, 408

Macdonell, A. A., 3, 51, 80
Mahabharata, 20, 21, 68, 88, 174, 254, 255, 263, 279, 283
Majumdar, D. N., 70
Malinowski, B., xi, 394
Mann, H. H., 293
Marshall, J., 215
Masani, K., 366 f.
Matsya Purana, 21, 51, 459
M'Crindle, J. W., 254, 299
Mead, M., 254
Menon, K. G., 470
Meyer, J. J., 254, 263, 279, 283
Mills, J. P., 14, 52, 54, 55, 103, 202, 255, 347, 411, 452 f., 454
Milne, L., 453
Minakshi, C., 204
Mitra, S. C., 90, 131, 136, 181, 182
Modi, J. J., 70, 182, 362
Moen, S. M., 83
Monier Williams, 26
Moses, S. T., 174
Muir, J., 78
Mukherjee, C., 445, 501
Mundaka Upanishad, 10
Murray, M. A., 371

Myths, recorded from
  Agaria, 27, 80, 107, 119, 164, 218, 314, 345, 373, 374, 387, 414, 461
  Ahir, 76, 81, 104, 157, 164, 206, 345, 431
  Asur, 375
  Badi, 481
  Baiga, 71, 81, 83, 90, 91, 100, 108, 109, 120, 121, 133, 136, 139, 142, 148, 165, 166, 175, 183, 186, 191, 193, 196, 198, 207, 209, 210, 228, 229, 237, 243, 249, 255, 256, 264, 267, 271, 272, 285, 291, 292, 302, 337, 346, 347, 348, 376 ff. 391, 392, 414, 455, 462 ff.
  Bhaina, 184, 214, 230, 246, 292, 303, 314, 349
  Bharia, 82, 121, 393
  Bhuiya, 28, 29, 56, 72, 96, 170, 256, 303, 380, 415, 416, 477, 489
  Binjhwar, 84, 109, 122, 178, 191, 196, 212, 224, 273, 304, 481
  Bison-horn Maria, 30, 31, 32, 57, 110, 215, 264, 268, 286, 320, 380 f., 416
  Chokh Agaria, 293
  Dewar, 58, 91, 153, 446
  Dhanwar, 34, 84, 93, 111, 123, 134, 151, 153, 166, 213, 218, 257, 274, 316, 338, 417, 447, 482
  Dhimar, 197
  Dhoba, 34, 111, 123, 134, 167, 208, 238, 293, 304, 381, 418, 482
  Dhulia, 132, 137, 144, 150, 155, 162, 175
  Dhurwa, 93
  Dom, 382
  Dorla-Maria, 474
  Gadaba, 35, 36, 37, 73, 252, 257, 268, 317, 324, 419
  Gogia Pardhan, 60, 94, 275, 395
  Gond, 38, 39, 61, 62, 82, 85, 86, 97, 101, 104, 105, 112, 124, 125, 135, 138, 141, 142, 144, 149, 150, 151, 152, 154, 156 ff., 168, 171, 172, 176, 177, 178, 179, 180, 184, 187, 190, 193, 194, 197, 199, 208, 209, 211, 213, 216, 217, 220 ff., 227, 228, 230, 236, 238, 239, 246, 249, 250, 252, 257, 258, 268, 276, 287, 294, 298, 305 ff., 317, 318, 325, 351, 388, 393, 398, 420, 432 ff., 439, 440 f., 449 f., 465 ff., 472, 475 ff., 483 f., 489 ff.
  Halba, 185, 240, 277

Jhoria, 259, 467
Juang, 39, 114, 155, 226, 240, 265, 278, 279, 287, 318, 321, 326, 339, 382 f., 421, 422, 423, 424
Kahar, 169, 235, 241, 243, 250, 307, 351
Kamar, 210, 265, 308, 327, 341, 467
Kewat, 309
Khuntia Chokh, 126, 280, 309, 328
Kol, 86, 113, 127, 152, 241, 352, 424
Kond, 40, 41, 42, 241, 242, 259, 266, 288, 294, 328, 329, 341, 383 f., 425
Korku, 280, 288, 385
Koya, 260, 266
Kuruk, 42, 94, 281
Kuttia Kond, 384, 399
Lanjhia Saora, 43 ff., 160, 244, 247, 260, 281, 189, 298, 310, 329, 330, 342, 343, 385, 386, 394, 425, 473 f.
Lohar, 46, 192, 194, 219, 352, 390
Muria, 46, 68, 94, 114, 269, 289, 330, 386, 426, 427, 441
Ojha, 76, 138, 261, 331
Pangia Kond, 399
Panka, 87, 115, 140, 177, 188, 261, 295, 311, 352
Pardhan, 136, 145, 171, 173, 189, 262, 400, 401, 437 f., 439, 442, 456, 484
Raja Muria, 47, 48, 64
Rajnengi Pardhan, 48, 65, 87, 98, 127, 128, 135, 148, 169, 195, 217, 226, 231, 242, 244, 248, 251, 269, 282, 296, 298, 319, 321, 322, 332, 387, 401, 403, 405, 428, 451, 457, 478, 485
Takala Saora, 311, 468
Yernga Kol, 50

Nanjundayya, H. V. and Iyer, L. K. A., 11, 243, 270, 284, 320, 501
Natesa Sastri, S. M., 323
Nelson, A. E., 469

O'Malley, L. S. S., 139

Palakapya, 204
Parry, N. E., 26, 411, 501
Penzer, N. M., 68, 248, 361 ff., 453, 501
Pilsudski, B., 354, 408
Playfair, A., 181, 501
Prasna Upanishad, 471
Prester John, 364

Raglan, Lord, xi
Rafy, Mrs, 53, 89, 183, 202, 206, 215, 324
Ramayana, 3, 52, 255, 262
Reich, W., 367
Rice, S. P., 471
Rigveda, 9, 51, 80
Rivers, W. H. R., 15, 95, 243
Rivett-Carnac, J. H., 364 f.
Roheim, G., 368 f.
Rose, H. A., 13, 14, 69, 89, 102
Roy, S., 255
Roy, S. C., xi 4, 5, 7, 9, 10 f., 13, 16, 19, 24, 25, 52, 53, 69, 75, 79, 89, 99, 103, 129, 130, 131, 147, 181, 182, 200 ff., 237, 335, 347, 41 ff., 446, 470, 488 f. 495
Roy, S. N., 248, 471
Russell, R. V., 54
Russell, R. V. and Hiralal, 69, 70, 320, 470, 495 ff.

Satapatha Brahmana, 20, 21, 174
Sawe, K. J., 75, 79, 147, 313, 412
Seligman, C. G., and B. Z., 4, 217, 354, 452
Shaw, W., 89
Shrigondekar, G. K., 203
Sitapati, G. V., 497
Stocks, C. de B., 54

Teit, J., 357, 409
Temple, R. C., 18, 83, 501
Theobald, W., 204
Thurston, E., 129, 336, 454, 472, 497, 502
Tickell, Lieut, 18, 25, 285, 501
Trench, C. G. C., 5, 16, 290, 502

Upreti, G. D., 201, 502

Venkatachar, C. S., 174
Venkataswami, M. N., 69, 502

Watt, G., 323
Westermarck, E., 361 ff.
Wilson, H. H., 459
Wissler, C. and Duvall, D. C., 357, 409
Woman, 263, 460, 502

Yule, H., 460